From Sadowa to Sarajevo

FOREIGN POLICIES OF THE GREAT POWERS

Edited by C. J. Lowe

The Reluctant Imperialists   C. J. Lowe

Vol. I British Foreign Policy 1878–1902
Vol. II The Documents

The Mirage of Power   C. J. Lowe and M. L. Dockrill

Vol. I British Foreign Policy 1902–14
Vol. II British Foreign Policy 1914–22
Vol. III The Documents

From Sadowa to Sarajevo

The Foreign Policy of Austria-Hungary, 1866–1914

F. R. Bridge

Department of International History,
London School of Economics

Routledge & Kegan Paul
London and Boston

First published 1972
by Routledge and Kegan Paul Ltd
Broadway House, 68–74 Carter Lane,
London EC4V 5EL and
9 Park Street, Boston, Mass. 02108, U.S.A.
Printed in Great Britain by
Western Printing Services Ltd, Bristol

© *F. R. Bridge 1972*

ISBN 0 7100 7269 4

TO GABRIELE

Contents

Illustrations

(The plates are reproduced by kind permission of the Picture
Archives of the Austrian National Library, Vienna.)

Acknowledgments

I wish to acknowledge the kind permission of the officials of the Public Record Office, London, and of the Haus-, Hof-, und Staatsarchiv, Vienna, to make use of the archives within their care.

I am indebted to Miss Elizabeth Cartwright for permission to use the Cartwright papers; to Count Johann Aehrenthal for permission to use the Aehrenthal papers; to Dr P. Hohenbalken for permission to consult his manuscript edition of the Lützow papers; to Dr H. Rumpler of the Kommission für neuere Geschichte Oesterreichs for permission to use the transcripts and microfilms of the Berchtold papers, and to Dr E. R. von Rutkowski of the same commission for permission to use the Mérey papers.

I should also like to thank my friends and colleagues, Mr M. J. Allison, Dr K. Bourne, Professor D. Dakin, Mr C. H. D. Howard, Professor J. Joll, Professor C. J. Lowe, and Professor W. N. Medlicott, who read some or all of the chapters, and whose advice proved invaluable.

I am above all grateful to Professor Franz August Krieger and his family, whose generous and unfailing hospitality over the past ten years not only alone enabled me to carry out the research at a civilized pace in Vienna, but provided ideal conditions for writing in Styria.

Finally, my thanks are due to Miss Janet R. Astley, of the Drawing Office, Department of Geography, London School of Economics, who so skilfully transformed my primitive sketches into elegant maps; and to my sisters, Margaret and Alison, whose unstinting patience and perseverance at the typewriter likewise produced order out of chaos in the manuscript.

F.R.B.

Vienna

R. Danube

Budapest

AUSTRIAN EMPIRE

R. Save

Transylvania

Bosnia

Belgrade

Serbia

Montenegro

O T T O M A N

ADRIATIC
SEA

RUSSIA

R. Dniester

R. Prut

Moldavia

Jassy

S. Bessarabia

Wallachia

Bucharest

R. Danube

BLACK
SEA

Bulgaria

Constantinople

E M P I R E

Salonica

AEGEAN
SEA

GREECE

Athens

———— Frontiers of independent
states

- - - - Frontiers of autonomous
principalities

| 0 | Miles | 150 |

| 0 | Km | 150 |

Crete

JRA

1   The Balkans in 1866

Frontiers of independent states

Frontier between the Dual Monarchy and the occupied territories

Boundaries inside the Ottoman Empire

Existing railways

Railways proposed by Aehrenthal, 1907

| Miles | 0 | 150 |
| Km | 0 | 150 |

2   The Balkans, 1878–1908

3   The Balkans in 1914

4   The Habsburg Monarchy, 1866–1914

Chapter 1

Introduction[1]

The Congress of Vienna left the Habsburg emperor, Francis I, in possession of an empire more extensive, but at the same time more compact, than any of his predecessors since Charles V. In addition to the central and eastern territories retained throughout the vicissitudes of the Napoleonic wars – Austria, Bohemia, Hungary, and Galicia – Lombardy and Tyrol, lost during the wars, had been recovered; and Salzburg, Venice, Illyria, and Dalmatia, annexed and lost again, had been finally regained. The Austrian Empire was thus firmly established in northern Italy and, by virtue of dynastic links with the central Italian duchies and a treaty with the king of the Two Sicilies, in a good position to fulfil its role as a barrier against a resurgence of French militarism anywhere in the peninsula. In Germany, too, Austria was the acknowledged head of the new Confederation – for all its deficiencies from a liberal or nationalist point of view, an eminently sensible arrangement from the point of view of power-political realities. The *Bund* of 1815 combined a realistic recognition of the existence of the Austrian and Prussian monarchies with the creation of an organization in central Europe strong enough to resist pressure from the 'restless' Powers, France and Russia, and yet not cohesive

[1] The following works are of particular relevance to this chapter: H. Ritter v. Srbik, *Aus Oesterreichs Vergangenheit*, Salzburg, 1949, especially the essays 'Erzherzog Albrecht, Benedek, und der altösterreichische Soldatengeist', 'Franz Joseph I: Charakter und Regierungsgrundsätze', and 'Oesterreichs Schicksal im Spiegel des geflügelten Wortes'; F. Klein (ed.), *Oesterreich-Ungarn in der Weltpolitik, 1900–1914*, Akademie-Verlag, Berlin, 1965; H. Benedikt, *Die wirtschaftliche Entwicklung in der Franz-Joseph-Zeit*, Vienna, 1958; A. v. Musulin, *Das Haus am Ballplatz*, Munich, 1924; F. Engel-Janosi, *Geschichte auf dem Ballhausplatz*, Vienna, 1963, especially the essay 'Der Ballhausplatz, 1848–1918'; G. Drage, *Austria-Hungary*, London, 1909; C. A. Macartney, *The Habsburg Monarchy*, London, 1968; A. v. Wittich, 'Die Rüstungen Oesterreich-Ungarns von 1866 bis 1914', *Berliner Monatshefte*, 1932; F. R. Bridge, *Great Britain and Austria-Hungary 1906–1914. A Diplomatic History*, London, 1972.

enough to form in itself a disturbing source of pressure on its neighbours.

Not that the Austrian position was without weaknesses. Indeed, some of these arose from that very accretion of disparate territories under Habsburg rule that was one of its most imposing features. For instance, the Habsburgs might have done better to abandon Galicia, an exposed plateau lying beyond the Carpathians, the natural defensive frontier of the Monarchy in the north-east. This province, constantly at the mercy of the tsar's armies lately established in the puppet kingdom of Poland, was virtually indefensible unless Austria chose to burden herself with the odium of a preventive northward strike. To that extent Galicia remained something of a pledge of good behaviour to Russia throughout the nineteenth century. The annexation of the turbulent republic of Cracow in 1846 could do nothing to solve this basic problem. Similarly, in the south-west, the long Dalmatian coastal strip relied on tenuous maritime communications for its defence, being cut off from the rest of the Monarchy by the Turkish provinces of Bosnia and the Herzegovina. These provinces were themselves, so long as they remained under Turkish rule, a constant source of disorder, strife, and costly border raids. Yet Vienna was reluctant to seek a remedy by taking control of Bosnia. That would weaken Turkey; and Turkey was despite everything still the most convenient neighbour conceivable from an Austrian point of view. If she collapsed, she might be replaced by something far worse – perhaps a string of Russian satellites, as foreshadowed by Catherine II's Greek Project, encircling the Monarchy from the south.

Even so, these strategic deficiencies were of minor importance, compared to the fact that the apparent strength of the Habsburg state itself was to a great extent a mirage. By 1815 the Monarchy had achieved, by dint of a skilful diplomacy which exploited both the combined efforts and the divergent interests of the allies in the war against Napoleon, an imposing, indeed, grossly inflated position that could hardly be maintained in the long run. Economically, the Monarchy was a weak agrarian Power, unable to compete with France and Britain in terms of resources, and lacking the manpower with which Russia made up for her deficiencies in that respect. The first years of peace, which saw a major financial crisis in Austria and the revival of British industrial and Russian agrarian exports, soon revealed the hollowness of the domestic basis of Austria's Great Power position. There could be no question of the Monarchy's attempting, with a population of thirty millions and an army of a mere 230,000, to maintain that position by sheer force against potential threats in Germany, Italy, and the East. (Even the little expedition to Naples in 1821 threw the finances into virtual bankruptcy and undid much of the work of recovery since the Napoleonic wars.[2]) As far as the Austrian Empire was concerned, the argument of force, the *ultima ratio* that alone could give reality to the claim of any state to be a Great Power, was lacking. The mirage that had been conjured up by diplomatic skill and finesse would have to be preserved by the same means. The first time a Great Power seriously challenged it by force, it would vanish into air.

This was what Metternich realized. For over thirty years he managed to perform a sustained conjuring trick, to convince the Powers of the reality, even of the desirability, of Austria's hegemony in central Europe and Italy; and even – apart from some lamentable incidents concerning Greece and Mehemet Ali, when his bluff was called – of the need to maintain the *status quo* in the Near East. His task was made easier, however, by the fact that the other Powers were usually willing to join in perpetuating the myth. The Czech patriot Palacky's famous dictum of 1848 – 'if Austria did not exist, it would be necessary to invent her'[3] – was echoed throughout the chancelleries of Europe. And unsatisfactory though it might be for a Great Power to base its existence on the fact that other Powers could think of nothing better to put in its place, Austria continued, even after the fall of Metternich, and after the disastrous wars of 1859 and 1866, to draw an illusory strength from this simple fact.

In the Metternich period the Monarchy was particularly fortunate, being blessed with, and managing with some success to perpetuate, a favourable international situation. France, exhausted by the Napoleonic wars, was temporarily weak; and such fretful efforts as she made to break the shackles of the Vienna system only convinced the British of the need to support Austria. This was most apparent in the early years of peace, which saw a British foreign secretary endorsing Austrian intervention against constitutionalism in the German and Italian states. But right down to

[2] C. A. Macartney, p. 204.   [3] H. v. Srbik, p. 252.

1859 the Austrian position in Italy was reinforced, albeit to varying degrees, by British fears of a revival of predatory French militarism. The general fear of the monster Revolution, whether emergent from France or indigenous elsewhere – and to Metternich there was but one, many-headed, hydra – was a useful argument to use with the other Power that seemed to threaten the Austrian position, Russia. In the years after 1815 Russian agents were constantly at work, usually with French assistance, to undermine Austrian influence in Germany, Italy, and the Near East. In proposing the Congress of Troppau in 1820, France and Russia were hoping to establish a liberal regime at Naples which would put an end to Austrian influence there. This presented Metternich with a serious problem. He could not dream of opposing France and Russia by war: British diplomatic, or even military and financial, support, could do little to save Austria in such a conflict. He managed, however, by a supreme feat of diplomatic skill at Troppau, to convince Alexander I that the Revolution was a universal menace; and that intervention in Naples should be purely Austrian and reactionary in character (although he had to accept a formal mandate from 'the Alliance' that temporarily estranged his British friends). An attempt to conjure up the same demon to restrain Russia from helping her Greek co-religionaries against the sultan in the 1820s came to grief in the face of Nicholas I's obstinacy and Canning's desire to thwart and humiliate Metternich. But the revolutions of 1830 coming hard on the heels of the treaty of Adrianople brought a chastened Nicholas to sit at Metternich's feet at Münchengrätz. On the whole, Metternich's *tour de force* had been successful.

Yet it was a *tour de force* all the same. Indeed, it was the recognition that this was so, that the Monarchy's position could not ultimately rest, like that of the other Great Powers, on force, that lies behind that stubborn insistence on legitimism and the sanctity of treaties that characterized Austrian diplomacy in the Metternich period and beyond. True, there had been little evidence of this in the cut-and-thrust diplomacy of the Napoleonic wars; and even Metternich showed scant regard for legality in dealing with weaker states such as Cracow. But on the whole, in the Metternich period, Austria remained true to Talleyrand's description of her – 'the House of Lords of Europe'.[4] Only so long as the other

4 H. v. Srbik, p. 249.

Great Powers recognized, or could be persuaded to accept, the doctrine of the sanctity of treaties could the façade of Austrian power continue. With the tsars of Russia, who became under his influence the staunchest defenders of the *status quo*, Metternich had his greatest success, Világos[5] was just as much his triumph as Troppau and Münchengrätz. By the same token, however, if ever Russia should cease to underwrite the Vienna settlement, and if ever that settlement should be seriously challenged by other Great Powers – the France of Napoleon III or the Prussia of Bismarck – then the power and influence of the Austrian Empire would be reduced to accord with military and political realities.

Even failing a direct military threat of such magnitude, the exalted position of the dynasty in Germany, Italy, and even the traditional Habsburg lands, was constantly endangered. In Italy, the dynasty was faced, from the 1830s, with the threat of a nationalist movement under the leadership of Mazzini; and even the conservative governments of the Papal states and Piedmont chafed under the Austrian yoke. This was all the more serious as British support was sapped by Palmerston's doctrine that Austria would do well to abandon Lombardy and Venetia to Piedmont and concentrate on guarding the Near East against Russia – not an attractive proposition when it is considered that Lombardy and Venetia were the two richest provinces of the Empire, and that if Austria attempted to defend her Near Eastern interests by force of arms, she might only find herself used as a battering ram by a Britain too distant to lend any effective assistance. At the same time, in Germany, the Monarchy's position was undermined by the growth of the customs union under Prussian leadership, and by the failure of Metternich's efforts to secure Austria's admittance on terms that would satisfy the protectionist demands of Austrian industrialists. Meanwhile, the growth of nationalist feeling in the Monarchy itself, especially the conflicts between the Magyars and the Croats, and between the Magyars and the central government, portended a serious weakening of the state itself. The raising of all three problems at once and in an acute form, in 1848, nearly brought about the disruption of the Empire even without the intervention of a hostile Great Power.

[5] At Világos, in August 1849, the Hungarian rebel army capitulated to General Paskievich, whom the tsar had sent with an army to Franz Joseph's assistance.

But the Empire survived. The military power of the dynasty was still adequate to deal with threats that were not backed up by Great Power intervention. The Austrian army defeated the attempt of Piedmont and the Italian states to drive the Habsburgs out of Italy, crushed the revolution at home, and, at Olmütz, forced Prussia to abandon her hopes of dominating a new Germany. The truth of Grillparzer's apostrophization of Radetzky seemed self-evident: 'in deinem Lager ist Oesterreich.'[6] For the next ten years Austria was governed in accordance with the lessons of 1848, as a military autocracy. No regard was paid to Magyar nationalism, which had at last thrown off the mask and stood revealed as the mortal enemy of the dynasty. Indeed, no regard was paid to nationalism of any kind, which had proved itself, with the failure of both liberal and federalist attempts to devise satisfactory constitutions in 1848–9, to be no viable basis for governing the Empire. In the 1850s the Habsburg throne was said to rest on four supports: the army, standing; the priest, kneeling; the bureaucrat, sitting; and the spy, rampant.

The disastrous war with France and Piedmont, in which the Monarchy had to fight with one arm behind its back to beat down a threatened rebellion in Hungary, convinced the emperor that these supports were inadequate. Some elements of the opposition would have to be conciliated. Not the Magyars – they were now regarded as more treasonable than ever; but at least the Liberals, whose money would be needed if the Monarchy were to re-equip itself to recover its position in Italy, and who would only lend money to a constitutional, not to an irresponsible autocratic government. In 1860–1 the first steps were taken towards the introduction of constitutional government; but the system could only function haltingly, because the Magyars steadily boycotted it and held out for the ancient liberties of the Kingdom of Hungary. As the German crisis deepened in 1865 Franz Joseph found himself faced with the prospect of another 1859, and made haste to open negotiations for a settlement with his Hungarian subjects. But before these could be brought to fruition the Monarchy was overwhelmed by the War of 1866.

Yet the roots of these disasters did not lie solely in the domestic policies that Franz Joseph had pursued, or failed to pursue, since 1848. In foreign affairs, too, serious errors had been made. The

[6] H. v. Srbik, p. 251.

lesson of Világos had not been learned. It was Russian military aid that had put a speedy end to the Hungarian revolution; and Russian diplomatic support had been an important factor in the timely restoration of Austria's position in Germany. The value of Russian friendship having been so clearly demonstrated, it is the levity of Schwarzenberg's famous boast – 'Austria shall astonish the world with her ingratitude'[7] – that is really astonishing. Admittedly, Russia's activities on the eve of the Crimean War – notably her occupation of the Danubian principalities, portending the encirclement of the Monarchy in the South – presented a potential threat which could hardly be disregarded. Nevertheless, such security as Austria gained for her Near Eastern interests in the Treaty of Paris was brought at a tremendous cost to her interests in the West. From being the chief guarantor of Austria's position in Europe, Russia now became one of the principal agents in its destruction, endorsing both Napoleon III's onslaught on the 1815 settlement in Italy and Bismarck's attack on the Austrian position in Germany.

If this situation was partly the result of Franz Joseph's failure to learn the lesson of Világos, it was aggravated by his having drawn some false conclusions from Olmütz. Throughout the fifties and early sixties Franz Joseph was obsessed by the threat posed by the Revolution rampant in France and Italy. This threat, he sought to counter by a conservative alliance of the two German Powers; but he was only prepared to offer Prussia a subordinate role in this combination. This was asking the impossible. Although the Prussians might look favourably on the idea of a conservative alliance, they had no relish, especially after the humiliation of Olmütz, to demonstrate yet again their subordination to Austria. Franz Joseph nevertheless pursued the chimera with dogged determination for some ten years. But every time there seemed to be a chance of co-operation, in the Crimean War, and above all in the War of 1859, it came to nothing in the face of Austrian unwillingness to concede to Prussia a position of equality. After 1860 the emperor was even more set on a German alliance to take up the crusade against Napoleon III and the Revolution and to recover Lombardy. He readily co-operated with Prussia in the war against Denmark in 1864, in the hope that

[7] A. Schwarzenberg, *Prince Felix zu Schwarzenberg*, New York, 1946, pp. 203–4, questions the authenticity of this statement.

what was essentially a dynastic conservative alliance to take the lead from the liberal middle states of the German Confederation might develop into something of more general application. Yet even here, there was an element of tension between the two allies, both contenders for the leadership of Germany. Once peace was made with Denmark, it soon became clear that Bismarck had no interest whatever in an alliance on Franz Joseph's terms; or, indeed, even in coexistence on the basis of the Austrian legal supremacy in Germany that had prevailed hitherto. Franz Joseph, however, was unable, or unwilling, to see this until it was too late. As Bismarck himself remarked, 'l'Autriche croira à une feinte de ma part encore la veille de la bataille.'[8] The battle was not long delayed, and by July 1866 the final destruction of Austria's position in Italy had brought as much joy to Napoleon III as the destruction of the 1815 settlement in Germany had to Bismarck.

Yet appalling as these disasters might have seemed. Austria's position had in one respect improved as a result of the War of 1866. Her commitments had at least been brought more into line with the realities of her economic and military capabilities. And in a sense, the shock of defeat had been psychologically healthy: the aimless, despairing conservatism of the early 'sixties gave way to a vigorous determination to hold on to what was left of the Empire. Vigilance was the order of the day. After all, the Monarchy seemed beset with almost as many dangers after the war as before. People in 1866 did not know that the Treaty of Prague marked the end of the Monarchy's defeats. It still seemed urgent to ensure that Bismarck did not advance yet further, absorbing the independent south German states into his North German Confederation. The war had shocked Franz Joseph into giving up all thought of a conservative German alliance – at least for the present. Similarly, Italian irredentists opened their mouths wide; and no one was to know that they were to wait until 1919 before laying hands on the Tyrol and the Adriatic territories of the Monarchy. Finally, although the most serious national issue at home – the Magyar problem – was on its way to settlement, the emergence of national feeling among the emperor's south Slav and Roumanian subjects, coupled with national movements in the sultan's Serbian and Roumanian provinces, gave reason to fear

[8] R. Blaas, 'Il problema veneto e la diplomazia austriaca', *Conferenze e note accademiche nel 1 centenario dell'unione del Veneto all'Italia*, Padua, 1967, p. 11.

that Cavour and Bismarck might yet find imitators in Belgrade and Bucharest.

Now this the Austrians were determined to prevent. Expelled from Germany and robbed of their Italian possessions, they were adamant that no third national movement should deprive them of their southern and eastern provinces. In the view of Vienna, moreover, nationalism, like the Revolution before it, was merely one beast with many heads: Cavour, Bismarck, and their henchmen in Belgrade and Bucharest were all members of an international conspiracy – witness the visionary plans of Slav nationalists for the disposal of the Ottoman and Habsburg Empires. On a less dramatic view, the issue had seemed clear enough to Vienna even before the War of 1866. In justifying Austria's refusal to buy off Italy by ceding Venetia, the foreign minister, Count Mensdorff, had spoken, according to the British ambassador, in terms that combined the strict legitimist doctrines of the Metternich era with that frank appreciation of the nationalist threat that was to characterize the foreign policy of the Monarchy for the next forty years.[9]

> The result of war might be that Austria would be dismembered, perhaps destroyed, but she must defend herself and her rights or fail in the attempt to do so, and was resolved not to acknowledge the principle of nationalities, which was now put forward as an argument to induce her to give up Venetia. What was the Austrian Monarchy? It was an Empire of nationalities. If she gave up Venetia today to please King Victor Emmanuel, because he wanted an addition to his territory, where would his ambition lead him? Where would a new boundary line be drawn? Would he rest satisfied before he wrested all the Austrian possessions in the Adriatic from their rightful owner?
> . . . The Prince of Hohenzollern might some day find out that there was a considerable Roumanian population in Transylvania and therefore it would be right if it should be added to Moldo-Wallachia. The Prince of Servia might also claim the Serbs in Austria and demand that they should be annexed to his Principality; in fact, . . . we are determined to take our position in defence of our principles and our rights, which are based on treaties, and if war should be the consequence we shall do our best to protect the various possessions and interests of which the Empire is composed.

[9] [Public Record Office, London], F[oreign] O[ffice] [series] 7/[Volume] 707, Bloomfield to Stanley, No. 313, 2 June 1866.

In the ensuing war the Austria of the Treaty of Vienna was physically destroyed; but its spirit lived on in the Austria of the Treaty of Prague. Moreover, the Austria of 1866, less over-burdened and over-extended than the Austria of 1815, might well prove more capable of defending the traditional principles of the Habsburg state. At first, however, the state was exhausted and in need of recuperation. There could be no question of war for the time being. Austria's 'various possessions and interests' would have to be defended by diplomacy.

Diplomatic history is essentially the history of decision-making. The problems and dilemmas with which the Monarchy was confronted would not solve themselves; nor, as a rule, were the great forces operating at home and abroad to limit the options available so compelling as to make any particular course of action inevitable. Decisions between alternative courses of action had to be taken in particular circumstances by particular individuals in positions of power.

Chief among these was the Emperor Franz Joseph. In the Habsburg Monarchy foreign policy always remained the prerogative of the Crown. Throughout his reign the emperor always insisted, whether rebuking liberal politicians in the 1870s or calling a belligerent chief of staff to order forty years later, that criticism of the foreign minister and his policy amounted to criticism of the sovereign. The minister for foreign affairs was merely 'Mein Minister' carrying out 'Meine Politik'.[10] In fact, whoever the foreign minister might be, the emperor's guiding hand always remained in the background. If there were in practice few instances where the emperor had to pull on the reins, that was because he chose foreign ministers who were willing to steer in the direction in which he wished to go.

Yet not even the emperor was omnipotent. He had to take into account not only intractable political facts in the international situation but also powerful forces inside the Monarchy – notably the Magyars, on whose support the whole political system as reorganized by the *Ausgleich* of 1867 depended. A foreign minister could not long survive once the Magyars were determined to oust him; and Franz Joseph recognized this when he reluctantly sacrificed Kálnoky in 1895 and Goluchowski in 1906. But failing

[10] F. Conrad v. Hoetzendorf, *Aus meiner Dienstzeit*, Vienna, 1921, Vol. 2, p. 282.

an actual ultimatum from Budapest, the emperor's support was usually enough to maintain a foreign minister in office: Aehrenthal survived to die in harness even after earning the dislike of the Magyars and the fanatical hatred of the heir apparent and the chief of staff.

It is not always easy to pinpoint the emperor's influence in specific decisions of foreign policy, many of which were taken after verbal consultation between the monarch and the minister with no written record being kept as to how a particular decision was reached. But the emperor's marginal comments on foreign ministry papers (which he read daily with prodigious industry till the end of his life) are remarkably consistent and give a fair idea of the general drift of his policy.

For Franz Joseph personally the year 1866 was a turning point in the conduct of both domestic and foreign affairs. Henceforward his aim was simply to preserve what was left of the Monarchy after Sadowa. Not that this was a barren conservative policy devoid of ideals; nor did he regard the state, as some extreme conservatives did, as merely a chattel of the dynasty. He seems sincerely to have believed it to be a last refuge of the minority races of central and south-east Europe who, for all their complaints, would have far more to fear from Germany or Russia if ever the Monarchy should disappear. This state it was his sacred duty to uphold. The *Ausgleich* system of 1867 was after all, for all its faults, probably the least unworkable of the available alternatives, recognizing as it did that any system which failed to conciliate the most powerful nation in the Empire could only lead to a repetition of the disasters of the first fifteen years of the reign. Once this system was established, Franz Joseph showed an increasing distaste for plans for a radical re-structuring of the Monarchy. He was always somewhat lacking in creative imagination. And although he was fertile in ingenious tactical moves, and never tied himself exclusively to any party or faction – hence that notorious ruthlessness in abandoning servants who had served their purpose, which made the 'thanks of the House of Austria' a by-word – all his tactical moves after 1867 were made within the framework of the *Ausgleich* settlement and with a view to preserving it.

Similarly, in foreign affairs, his policy was essentially quietist – although when this could be combined with territorial gain without the risk of war, as in the case of Bosnia and the Herzegovina, he was quick to seize an opportunity. The disasters of his wars with France and Prussia had by 1866 finally shattered his confidence in himself as a military leader. There were strong psychological elements in the persistent shrinking from resort to the arbitrament of war that was the most consistent strain in his foreign policy in the half-century after Sadowa. Time after time he resisted demands for preventive wars, whether against Russia, Italy, or Serbia. True, the honour of the Monarchy still held pride of place in Franz Joseph's *Weltanschauung*. And in a sense his policy was the same after 1866 as before – to defend his position as long as possible, to do his duty, and if that failed, to go down with honour. But it was nevertheless for the emperor to judge when the honour of the Monarchy was being too openly challenged. After 1866 he was simply more long-suffering and more reluctant to go to war than in his earlier years. It was not until 1914 that he despaired of maintaining the honour of the Monarchy by diplomatic means.

In addition to the emperor, those close to him at court took an interest in foreign affairs. It was through its connexions at court that the Church came closest to exercising influence over policy. Franz Joseph was after all Apostolic King of Hungary. And although he was an Erastian in Church affairs, and did not scruple to interfere in a papal election in 1903 to prevent the catastrophe of a pro-French Pope,[11] he was conscious of some religious obligations. His refusal to insult the Pope by visiting the king of Italy at Rome was for thirty years an important if unhappy element in Austro-Italian relations. And the Church used not only the Jesuit element at court, but a vociferous clerical press to keep the government mindful of its obligations to protect the Catholic subjects of the sultan. The other main current at court was a reactionary-conservative one, and this was particularly strong in the highest military circles. In the imperial family itself it found its chief expression in Archduke Albrecht, the emperor's uncle and his close adviser, as Inspector-General of the Army, for nearly thirty years. His view of the Monarchy was narrowly dynastic – the state was no more than a family possession – and he generally exerted his influence in favour of a close alignment with the court of St Petersburg. He also supported the

[11] See p. 266.

idea of a Three Emperors' Alliance, although his attitude toward Germany was never entirely free from that rancour dating back to 1866 which he usually reserved for Italy.

Franz Joseph's wife and son, by inclination both pro-Magyar and pro-German seem to have had little influence; but Archduke Franz Ferdinand, heir-presumptive after 1894, was a very different case. To contemporaries, his particular policies and recommendations seemed remarkably changeable; but they were, in fact, all variations on the two great passionate themes of his life – hatred of the Magyars, whose separatist ambitions he thought were destroying the Monarchy, and a fanatical clericalism. From the latter sprang his hostility to the kingdom of Italy – in 1911 people in the British foreign office found it 'most strange that anyone with common sense could dream of re-establishing the temporal power of the Pope'.[12] Equally, his pro-Russian, pro-Roumanian, and pro-Slav inclinations were merely a reflection of his Magyarophobia. After the Bosnian crisis he lost some of his love for Russia, and drew closer to William II, with whom he soon established a close personal friendship; but he never really lost hope of some day seeing a restoration of the Three Emperors' Alliance. But although Franz Ferdinand held strong views, he was in no position to influence policy – especially when he was faced with an Italophile Aehrenthal, who enjoyed Franz Joseph's full confidence. It was in vain that he stormed and raged – so much so that the emperor was by 1911 considering excluding him from the succession on the grounds of insanity.[13] In 1910, for example, Franz Ferdinand resorted to bombarding ministers with messages, by telephone or through his aide-de-camp; but the only result seemed to be to 'cause much inconvenience to the persons who receive them'.[14] It was only when the more pliable Berchtold was at the Ballhausplatz that the Archduke, who kept up a fairly regular correspondence with the minister, gained a measure of influence over policy. And this was exercised directly, not through the emperor, who remained unimpressed by his nephew's fierce and overbearing personality.

Not that the foreign policy of the Habsburg Monarchy was determined simply by the emperor and the imperial family. Even

[12] Cartwright MSS., Nicolson to Cartwright, private, 18 September 1911.
[13] F.O. 371/1047, Cartwright to Nicolson, private, 25 May 1911.
[14] F.O. 371/825, Cartwright to Grey, No. 9, 21 January 1910.

the emperor's decisions were dependent for their formation on the advice, and for their execution on the skill, of the foreign minister, his advisers, and others in positions of power and influence. The *Ausgleich* system, on which the Dual Monarchy rested, not only implicitly recognized the power of the Magyars in Hungary; it explicitly granted to Hungary a certain amount of control over the foreign policy of the Austro-Hungarian state. The Hungarian Law XII of December 1867, expressly gave the Hungarian prime minister the right to be consulted by the foreign minister on matters of foreign policy. Andrássy declared in 1882 that the Hungarian prime minister was directly responsible for everything that happened in foreign policy.[15] And as the Hungarian government was itself responsible to the parliament at Budapest, the opinions of the magnates and gentry dominating that body carried a weight never gained by their counterparts in Austria. (There, neither ministers nor parliament had any constitutional right whatever to be consulted about foreign affairs.) Both the law and political realities, therefore, obliged the foreign minister to consult the Hungarian prime minister before taking any major decision. In 1914 there was no question of going to war until Tisza's consent had been extracted. This is not to say that the Hungarians could dictate the foreign policy of the Monarchy: The warlike demands of Budapest in the later 1880s were ignored by the Ballhausplatz. Altogether, the degree of mutual dependence established by the *Ausgleich* was probably just one more factor making for a generally passive foreign policy. A policy of action that recommended itself to Budapest was always liable to come up against opposition from the Ballhausplatz, and vice versa. So more often than not, a negative, waiting attitude would be adopted.

The non-Hungarian parts of the Dual Monarchy, loosely known as 'Austria', presented the foreign minister with an easier task. For the domestic situation there was much more fluid. The German elements, whatever their social position, never exercised a political dominance comparable with that of the Magyars in Hungary. They were always challenged, often successfully, by Czechs, Poles, Italians, and south Slavs; and from this plethora of nationalities a foreign minister could always find a substantial

[15] J. Galantai, 'Die Aussenpolitik Oesterreich-Ungarns und die herrschenden Klassen Ungarns', in F. Klein (ed.), p. 266.

body of opinion to support any policy he chose to pursue. And although the Austrian government had no constitutional right to be consulted about foreign affairs, the foreign minister generally kept in touch with the ministers in Vienna – not least because they could often be called on to override the opposition of Budapest.

Moreover, some matters, such as the building of strategic railways, and the adjustment of tariffs by commercial treaties, needed the approval of both the Austrian and the Hungarian governments. Indeed, every foreign minister spent long and wearisome hours in conference with the prime ministers and finance ministers of the two governments about these matters. And many were driven almost to despair by the attempt to reconcile the economic interests of Austria and Hungary. These rarely coincided: the Austrians sought to protect their industries against German competition and favoured the importation of cheap Balkan food; whereas the Magyars sought to protect their agriculture from Balkan, and their industries from Austrian, competition. As a British observer noted in 1910, it was 'as impossible to please Budapest and Vienna as it is to serve God and Mammon'.[16] This fact largely accounts for the Monarchy's failure to establish a satisfactory commercial relationship with either Germany or the Balkan states. And it also lay at the root of the great crises that shook the Monarchy every ten years when the commercial institutions common to both halves of the Monarchy came up for revision. The decennial prospect of deadlock and the subsequent economic separation of Austria and Hungary earned for the Monarchy the reputation of a 'Dual Monarchy on short notice' (*auf Kündigung*).

Now this was a serious matter. For the common institutions of the Dual Monarchy, functioning above and separately from the Austrian and Hungarian governments were absolutely essential to the preservation of its position as a Great Power. It was for this reason that in the settlement of 1867 the emperor, while admitting that the common economic institutions might be subjects of negotiation between the governments of Vienna and Budapest, had jealously reserved his prerogative control over the common political and military institutions: the Common Ministry of Foreign Affairs; the Common Ministry of War, which controlled

[16] F.O. 371/827, Howard to Grey, No. 34, 22 April 1910.

the Imperial Army (as opposed to the home-guard forces administered by the war ministers of Austria and Hungary); and the Common Ministry of Finance, which supervised the revenues of the other two Common Ministries (and after 1878 administered Bosnia and Herzegovina).

In defence of his prerogative rights over these common institutions the emperor was always absolutely unbending. Never would he yield to the demands of Magyar extremists who saw in them an infringement of Hungary's liberties and sought to control them or whittle them away. The crisis of 1903–6 between Franz Joseph and the Magyars over the Common Army was the most serious in the whole history of the Dual Monarchy, and gravely jeopardized its existence as a Great Power. Friction over the Ministry of Foreign Affairs was less serious; although in the crisis of 1903–6 the Magyars included among their grievances the complaint that the principle of equality established in 1867 had never been extended to foreign affairs – the diplomats and the foreign minister resided at Vienna, not at Budapest; and Hungary had not had her fair share of control of the Ballhausplatz. It is true that apart from Andrássy, and perhaps Berchtold (who possessed both Austrian and Hungarian citizenship) all the foreign ministers of the Dual Monarchy down to 1914 were drawn from the 'Austrian' half of the Monarchy. (Kálnoky was a Bohemian German, despite his deceptive Hungarian name.) On the other hand, Magyars were well represented in the diplomatic corps. Nor was there ever the slightest hint of separatist or nationalist feeling among the members of that body. All of them, according to one who served his life in it, early developed a single-minded loyalty to the dynasty regardless of any national susceptibilities they may have felt on entering the service. In any case, the emperor was several times influenced in practice by Magyar views on the incumbents of the Ballhausplatz, particularly in accepting the resignations of Kálnoky and Goluchowski, and in appointing Aehrenthal. But he still insisted as a matter of principle[17] – and this was never seriously challenged – that the appointment of the minister for foreign affairs lay solely within the prerogative of the Crown.

Constitutionally, then, whatever influence the Magyars may have exercised – or more usually failed to exercise – in practice, the foreign minister was responsible to the emperor, by whom he

[17] See p. 212.

stood and fell. In theory, he was also responsible to the Delegations – a common assembly, consisting of sixty members drawn from the Austrian and sixty from the Hungarian parliament, which voted the budget for the Ministry of Foreign Affairs. But this body was in practice no more than a rubber stamp. Its debates were usually retrospective, and could in no way be said to determine policy. True, the foreign minister would very often present to the Delegations a survey of the political horizon; and this would be avidly studied abroad for indications of his intentions. Hence, the Delegations were sometimes used for specially emphatic speeches when the foreign minister wanted to make an impression abroad, for example, when Kálnoky launched a virtual threat of war at Russia in 1886;[18] and when Aehrenthal announced to the world his programme of economic expansion in the Balkans and defended the annexation of Bosnia in 1908.[19] Sometimes, they could prove a useful sounding-board for public opinion – but usually only if it suited the foreign minister to lend a ready ear. In 1908 Aehrenthal reminded Berlin that speeches by members of the Delegations – in this instance by Poles, who were outraged by the expropriation of Polish landowners in Prussian Poland – had a certain 'symptomatic value' which Germany would be unwise to ignore.[20] Vienna was always concerned lest such an important section of opinion as the Poles, staunchly anti-Russian and an invaluable support of successive Austrian governments, be forced into opposition to both the Dual Alliance and the government at home. Similarly, the Delegations could be important indicators of the intensity of Magyar feeling: the rough handling they gave to Goluchowski in 1906 greatly contributed to his fall – but it should be noted that in Kálnoky's case the Hungarian parliament had served the same purpose quite adequately.[21] In practice, the Delegations never really restricted the foreign ministers' conduct of policy. They met irregularly – usually only once or twice a year for a couple of weeks (but not at all, for example, between the end of 1908 and late 1910). They certainly did not provide a channel by which public opinion could influence foreign policy. As the British consul-general at

[18] See p. 162.   [19] See pp. 298, 303.
[20] [Haus, Hof-, and Staatsarchiv, Vienna] P[olitisches] A[rchiv] [Series] I/ [Karton] 484, Aehrenthal to Bülow, private, 11 March 1908.
[21] See pp. 208, 288.

Budapest observed in 1905, they were 'a body which is, from its constitution, out of touch with the general public, and any interest which has been excited almost immediately subsides'.[22] And four years later the British ambassador at Vienna reported that 'in neither of the two halves of the Dual Monarchy has the institution of the Delegations been able to secure any real measure of popular sympathy. Its forty years' existence has not helped to enhance its prestige or increase public confidence.'[23]

More important was the rather informal conference of ministers,[24] which met on an *ad hoc* basis when important business arose. This body had changed little since Metternich's day, and remained the supreme organ of decision-making in the Habsburg Monarchy – if organ it can be called, for its composition tended to vary according to the nature of the business in hand. It always included: the foreign minister, who took the chair when the emperor did not preside in person; the Common Minister of War; the Common Minister of Finance; often the chief of staff; the prime ministers of Austria and Hungary, their ministers of finance, and occasionally, their ministers of war, commerce, and agriculture. Here, various influences could be brought to bear on the foreign minister. But they were usually effective only in a negative sense – for example, a refusal to grant money for an armaments programme. It was exceedingly rare that a foreign minister found himself overruled and forced to accept a particular positive policy. In the spring of 1913 Berchtold was bullied by a conference into recommending an ultimatum to Montenegro; but even here the emperor sided with the foreign minister and ignored the conference.[25]

In fact, the most striking thing about the debates in the conference of ministers is the way in which the foreign minister generally got his own way: Kálnoky's policy of peace prevailed (admittedly with Austrian support) over Magyar belligerence in 1888;[26] and even the indolent Goluchowski could, when he bestirred himself, overrule both the Austrian and Hungarian governments on immensely important Balkan issues in 1906.[27]

[22] F.O. 120/825, Stronge to Plunkett, No. 16, 7 March 1905.

[23] F.O. 371/599, Cartwright to Grey, Annual Report, 1 February 1909.

[24] M. Komjathy, 'Amtsgebarung der österreichisch-ungarischen Monarchie zur Zeit des ersten Weltkrieges', in F. Klein (ed.), pp. 285–90.

[25] See p. 352.   [26] See p. 174.   [27] See pp. 278–9.

Besides, the conference of ministers itself was tending to decline in importance before a more autocratic handling of affairs by the foreign minister. Whereas Andrássy had allowed the occupation of Bosnia to be fully debated in conferences of ministers in 1878–9, Aehrenthal was much more perfunctory in regard to the annexation in 1908; and Berchtold, in 1914, short-circuited the conference altogether in order to circumvent and override the opposition of Tisza.[28] In matters of vital importance, the foreign minister of the Dual Monarchy was really the re-incarnation of the chancellor of the old Austrian Empire. Clad in the mantle of Metternich, even the weak Berchtold could force one of the most able and strong-minded statesmen the Monarchy ever produced to bow to his will.

It should be said, however, that in one respect the foreign minister did not have the power of a chancellor. If he might be remarkably free to take decisions on high policy with little regard for the wishes of the Austrian, and even Hungarian, governments, these bodies were equally free to determine such matters as came within their purview without regard for the views of the foreign ministry, even when these matters had serious implications for foreign policy. This could be particularly embarrassing in regard to commercial questions and tariffs, which could have far-reaching effects on the Monarchy's relations with its neighbours; and successive foreign ministers lamented the deficiencies in matters of defence arising from the parsimony of the Austrian and Hungarian governments, or from their periodic lapses into chaos after 1890 – all of which deficiencies the foreign minister was precluded from alleviating by virtue of the constitution of 1867. He was unrepresented in either parliament; and if the parliaments could never dictate to him, he could rarely influence them. After Beust no minister of foreign affairs enjoyed either the title of chancellor or the power that it carried in domestic affairs. Both Kálnoky (Document 12) and Aehrenthal bewailed the absence in Austria-Hungary of a post of real authority comparable to that of the chancellor in Germany.

If the foreign minister had to take into account the opinions of other high officials in the Monarchy in the formulation of policy, he was also dependent, as far as its execution was concerned, on the diplomats at his disposal and the officials of the Ballhausplatz.

[28] M. Komjathy, 'Amtsgebarung . . .', in F. Klein (ed.), pp. 289–90.

The central office was, it is true, a valuable training ground for diplomats, and a successful career there was often a pointer to later success in the diplomatic service abroad: Aehrenthal's career, for example, was greatly furthered by the reputation he acquired as Kálnoky's *chef de cabinet* from 1883 to 1888. But most of the officials of the Ballhausplatz spent their lives in routine business, and played little part in policy-making. The three departments for western, German, and religious-political affairs produced no men of outstanding character in this period. The fourth, the Eastern Department, was a different case, being concerned with matters of the most vital interest to the Monarchy; and some of its personnel, notably Zwiedenek, who had had considerable experience at Constantinople, came to exercise great influence over the formulation of policy under a minister so easy-going and inexperienced as Goluchowski.

Moreover, even the most lowly departments of the Ballhausplatz were closer to the minister than diplomats in the field, who all too often felt that their advice was being taken too little into account by blinkered officials at the centre. The latter, of course, replied that only the central ministry was in a position to take a broad view and see things in perspective. This sort of conflict became increasingly acute between the St Petersburg embassy and the Ballhausplatz in the years between the formation of the Three Emperors' Alliance and the Bosnian crisis, when the possibility of agreement with Russia formed the main debating point of policy. The embassy pleaded consistently for a conciliatory and trusting attitude towards Russia, whereas the Ballhausplatz emphasized the need for scepticism and caution. By the turn of the century the debate had almost reached the point of a public row.

The amount of control exercised by a minister over his officials varied with the incumbent of the office. Aehrenthal was notoriously authoritarian – so much so that some of his *Sektionschefs* were too timid to utter any opinion whatever, and foreign diplomats refused to attempt to do business with them.[29] Berchtold, by contrast, was more inclined to listen to the advice of his officials; although the story that when confronted with an enquiry he would simply press an electric button, whereupon the relevant official would appear and supply the answer, is probably apoc-

[29] F.O. 371/399, Carnegie to Grey, No. 208, 7 December 1908; F.O. 371/1047, Cartwright to Nicolson, private, 3 March 1911.

ryphal.[30] Some Ballhausplatz officials not directly concerned with diplomacy could on occasion influence policy if they managed to gain a personal hold over the minister. The heads of the press-bureau, who saw the minister daily, provided several examples of this – notably the anti-Russian Baron Doczy (1895–1902) whose personal influence over Goluchowski was the despair of the St Petersburg embassy.[31] His successor, Jettel von Ettenach, intervened on his own initiative to fan the flames of an Austro-Serbian press war even when this was directly contrary to the policy of the minister.[32]

The social composition of the foreign service remained largely aristocratic – especially in the upper echelons. One perhaps needed the income of a Mensdorff-Pouilly-Dietrichstein to make a success of the London embassy, the most expensive post in Europe, on the pittance allowed by the foreign ministry budget. (In 1905 alone Mensdorff entertained some 875 persons at his table; and kept up a social life that it would have been impossible to finance on his official salary).[33] Some junior diplomats of more modest circumstances lived, according to Mensdorff, in absolute penury: the birth of twins to Prince Schönburg, secretary at the London embassy and already the father of four was in the ambassador's view a major catastrophe.[34] Not that wealth counted for everything. Examinations, mainly in languages and diplomatic history, were introduced for aspiring diplomats in 1869. And great importance was attached to experience: the appointment of Mensdorff as ambassador at London in 1904 (as a favour to his cousin Edward VII) before he had served as head of a legation was unprecedented. All in all, considering the narrowness of the circle from which it was drawn, the Habsburg foreign service maintained a fair level of competence. True, few figures of outstanding brilliance emerged from it. This was nothing new: Metternich had been imported from the Rhineland, Beust from Saxony, and Andrássy, although a native was not a diplomat. He was, however, the last non-diplomat to hold the post of foreign minister until the appointment of Burián in 1915. And there were no more Magyars until then; nor foreigners. Andrássy's successors were

[30] H. Kanner, *Kaiserliche Katastrophenpolitik*, Vienna, 1922, p. 89.
[31] See p. 244.   [32] See p. 263.
[33] Mensdorff MSS., Karton 4, Tagebuch, 11 May 1906.
[34] Ibid., 25 March 1906.

21

all Austro-Hungarian diplomats, active or retired, and all were learned in the Eastern Question. Kálnoky, Aehrenthal, and Berchtold had all made their careers at St Petersburg. It is perhaps a comment on the moderate quality of the service that no one better than the humdrum Haymerle could be found to replace Andrássy in 1879; and that in 1895 and in 1912 the emperor could find no suitable candidate inside the service and had to turn to men who had already retired into private life. Kálnoky was an honest, straightforward conservative, but by no means outstanding in technical matters such as the drafting of treaties.[35] Goluchowski often left the embassies completely without information – which hardly made for an efficient and cohesive service or for a speedy and decisive conclusion to the internal debate about policy. Aehrenthal certainly made up for what his predecessors lacked in energy, drive, and determination; but even his reputation as the most successful foreign minister of the Dual Monarchy since Andrássy owed something to a comparison with his predecessors and with the mediocrities in charge of the foreign offices of the other Great Powers during his term of office.

Foreign policy in the Habsburg Monarchy, then, was the concern of a small élite – the emperor, his close advisers, and their officials. The influence of public opinion on policy decisions was usually negligible. Of course, when matters of the greatest moment, such as issues of war and peace, were in question, then the state of public opinion in general was as important an element in the background against which decisions were taken as the will of the emperor or the views of the prime minister of Hungary: it would have been a hazardous undertaking for Beust to take the Monarchy into a war of revenge against Prussia in 1870 in defiance of the well-known inclinations of Austrian-Germans who regarded France as the traditional enemy, or of Hungarians who saw in Bismarck's Prussia the midwife of their new-born freedom. Equally, doubts about the loyalty of the non-Polish Slavs were an important deterrent to war with Russia in the later 1880s. On the other hand, even doubts such as these could not sway the issue in 1914. And the only war that would have met with almost universal endorsement from public opinion – war with Italy – was, when it came in 1915, not of the Austro-Hungarian government's volition.

[35] See pp. 132, 139, 165–6.

Public opinion, therefore, could affect foreign policy in a negative sense, by restricting the options open to the decision-makers. The parliamentary bodies, for example, controlled the military expenditure of the Monarchy; and the eternal parsimony of the Austrian and Hungarian governments and their parliaments was an important cause of the weakness of the military forces, an underlying factor that every foreign minister had to take into account. From the 1890s until 1912 the Monarchy fell steadily behind the other Great Powers in military potential; and in naval construction Italy gained a lead over the Monarchy in the later 'nineties that she was never to lose. By 1903 Franz Joseph's subjects were spending more than three times as much money on beer, wine, and tobacco than on the entire armed forces of the Dual Monarchy.[36] And in the next six years, whereas Russia and Italy spent nearly a quarter of their revenues on armaments, and Britain nearly two-fifths, the Monarchy could hardly manage more than an eighth.[37] In this situation, it was hardly surprising that Austro-Hungarian foreign ministers generally felt they had to do everything possible to avoid an appeal to the arbitrament of war. Indeed at times it seemed doubtful whether the Monarchy could survive even if peace were maintained. The domestic crises that broke out in Austria and Hungary in the 1890s, combined, as public opinion grew increasingly inflamed with nationalist passions, to produce a huge upheaval threatening the very dissolution of the Monarchy after 1903. True, the situation improved after 1906; and especially after the display of vitality in the Bosnian crisis. By 1910 the British press was almost universally agreed that the Monarchy had never appeared stronger, and that the recent troubles which so many had taken for death-throes had in fact been 'a lusty re-birth'.[38] But Czech and south Slav discontent – although never as serious a threat as Magyar discontent had been – continued to cause a certain uneasiness about the Monarchy's capability of withstanding the ultimate test of fire.

Apart from in this general sense, however, public opinion was rarely taken into account by the makers of Austro-Hungarian foreign policy. Goluchowski might point to it in seeking to refute

[36] A. v. Wittich, 'Die Rüstungen Oesterreich-Ungarns . . .', p. 868.
[37] F.O. 371/1296, Russell to Grey, No. 223 draft, 29 December 1911.
[38] *Daily Graphic*, 18 August 1910.

Aehrenthal's arguments in favour of restoring the Three Emperors' Alliance;[39] just as Aehrenthal cited it in evidence when he warned Berlin about the possible effects on the Dual Alliance of Germany's draconic legislation against the Poles.[40] But these were largely arguments for particular occasions. Certainly, public opinion was in no sense able to take the lead and force the hand of a foreign minister, prescribing a particular direction for day to day decisions of policy. In the first place, there was among the political institutions of Austria no constitutional forum for the expression of views on foreign policy. (The Liberals fell for ever from power in the 1870s for attempting to transform the parliament into just such a forum.)[41] In the second place, public opinion in such common institutions as existed for the discussion of foreign policy – the Delegations – was never united; and the foreign minister could generally collect enough support for whatever policy he chose to pursue. It was indeed impossible to devise a policy that would be acceptable to all brands of public opinion – from Kramař and the Czechs who advocated alignment with Russia, to the Poles who abhorred such an idea, and the Germans, who demanded an alignment with Berlin or even longed for the day when German troops would march in to put an end to the Monarchy and annex its German territories. In the Delegations, as the British ambassador observed in 1908,[42] the foreign minister was usually 'accused of neglecting some interests and unduly pushing others . . . heckled about the Triple Alliance; accused of too great subservience to one ally and too much indifference to the other, while the Hungarians invariably bring up their thousand and one grievances and make him responsible for all of them'. Opinions being so diverse, and a consensus so obviously impossible of achievement, it was perhaps as well that the Ballhausplatz took its decisions according to what it considered to be the great interests of state, and did not attempt to devise a policy to suit 'public opinion'. Even on the exceedingly rare occasions when public opinion was more or less united – in hostility to Britain during the Boer War, for example – it was ostentatiously ignored by the government.[43]

In Hungary, public opinion – or rather the opinions of the

[39] See pp. 286–7.   [40] See p. 17   [41] See pp. 40–1.
[42] F.O. 120/853, Goschen to Grey, No. 167 draft, 28 October 1908.
[43] See pp. 247–8.

Magyar ruling élite – carried a certain weight by virtue of the constitution of 1867. And as neither Világos nor Sadowa had been forgotten, Magyar opinion was faithfully pro-German and, until the end of the 1880s at least, violently anti-Russian. But this did not prevent Beust from pursuing a generally anti-Prussian policy in the 1860s, nor Kálnoky from holding loyally to the Three Emperors' Alliance in the 1880s. Moreover, by 1890 the generation that remembered 1849 was dying out, and Hungarian opinion was becoming increasingly absorbed with domestic issues – so much so that by 1905 a British consul-general could say that there were 'few countries in the world where foreign affairs are less discussed and understood' than Hungary.[44] The typical politically aware Hungarian (and the opinions of the masses remained, if they existed, an inscrutable mystery) seemed to be 'indifferent to the international standing of the Monarchy. He has always been the subject of a Great Power and perhaps for that reason he fails to appreciate the advantages of his position.' Hence, his complaints about the expense of the Common Army, and his opposition to any activity in foreign affairs that seemed to be to the advantage of Austria and the dynasty. Few people in Hungary had ever seen the sea, and there was never much enthusiasm there for spending money on the fleet. In short, according to the ambassador, there was little likelihood of political and commercial circles in Hungary being stirred by issues of foreign policy unless events threatened to close the markets of Turkey and the Balkans to Hungarian trade. On this, the Magyars did in fact feel strongly – as they did about commercial treaties with their commercial rivals in the Balkan states, and about questions affecting the balance of races within the Monarchy. Even in 1914 they still vetoed any policy involving the incorporation of more Slavs. And ministers of foreign affairs generally respected, or bowed reluctantly to, these shibboleths. But the consul-general was wrong to attribute to the whole Magyar élite that devil-may-care approach to the Monarchy's standing as a Great Power characteristic of opposition politicians who looked back to 1848. Most Magyar politicians had a very real appreciation of the precarious position of Hungary, surrounded as she was by a sea of Slavs. And they realized that it was only as part of a Dual Monarchy that Hungary could hope to

[44] F.O. 120/825, Stronge to Plunkett, No. 16, 7 March 1905.

survive as a Great Power, or indeed survive at all. They generally supported the foreign minister's policy; and alternatives such as the western orientation demanded by Michael Károlyi stood as little chance of realization as Kramař's demand for Russian orientation.

Nor was public opinion as reflected in the press a factor of much importance in policy-making. Not that the press was, as some people abroad assumed, merely a mouthpiece for trumpeting decisions already reached in the corridors of the Hofburg or the Ballhausplatz. It is true that it served such a function to a limited extent. Since the 1860s there had been officials in the Ballhausplatz with the specific task of influencing the press; and a formal press bureau – the Literary Office – was set up there in 1877.[45] This had its beneficent effects. It was to the foreign ministry's control of the press that one British observer attributed the lack of influence of the military over public opinion and foreign policy.[46] And certainly, in 1911, Aehrenthal scotched an attempt by the Army to set up an office of its own for feeding information to the press.[47] To others in the British foreign office, however, it seemed by 1910, that 'of all press bureaus, those at Vienna and Berlin are the vilest. Those who deliberately work them are responsible for their direct and indirect effects, which . . . constitute not only the most shameful, but also the most dangerous feature of modern politics.'[48]

This lurid picture was more illustrative of the growing British obsession with the wickedness of Germany and her alleged satellites than of the actual state of affairs. In fact, the Austro-Hungarian government had nothing like complete control of the press. In the 1880s and early 1890s the warlike language of the Hungarian press was a constant embarrassment to Kálnoky; just as the raucous hostility of the Austrian press towards Britain in the Boer War and its gloating about Russia's defeats at the hands of Japan aroused the Ballhausplatz to impotent rage in the next decade.[49] The strongly – often hysterically – pro-German tone of

[45] K. Paupié, *Handbuch der Österreichischen Pressegeschichte*, Vol. 2, Vienna, 1966, pp. 105ff.

[46] F.O. 120/853, Goschen to Grey, No. 171, 3 November 1908.

[47] *O[esterreich-] U[ngarns] A[ussenpolitik]*, (ed. L. Bittner and H. Uebersberger, 8 vols, Vienna, 1930), [Vol.] 3, Nos 3057, 3149.

[48] F.O. 120/883, Crowe to Akers-Douglas, private, 6 April 1911.

[49] See pp. 248, 271.

much of the Austrian Press in the last years of peace was less the result of official government inspiration (although in British mythology, Austria-Hungary was by then simply the obedient handmaiden of Germany) than of the simple fact that the Austrian and Hungarian press was largely in the hands of German-Austrian Jews with German nationalist sympathies of a liberal kind. Thus, in reporting on foreign affairs they were generally favourable to Germany and hostile to the anti-semitic Tsarist government (and also to Britain as Anglo-German relations deteriorated in the twentieth century). And this regardless of the wishes of the Ballhausplatz.

For many of the newspaper proprietors were men of considerable means and independent views: from Benedikt and Becker, the 'violent and corrupt' – according to a British embassy survey[50] – editors of the *Neue Freie Presse*, 'the leading journalistic representative of Jewish interests on the continent', with the largest circulation of all the Austrian papers, 'read by everybody', and 'feared by all governments'; to the relatively harmless Singer – 'a Jew, who is nevertheless believed to be disinterested and straight', editor of the *Tageblatt* – 'a low class newspaper read by servants and common people, full of tittle-tattle and sensational items of news, somewhat in the style of the *Daily Mail*'.[51] There were exceptions: the clerical-radical *Reichspost*, which was in touch with Franz Ferdinand; the conservative-aristocratic *Vaterland*; the dry but excellent *Fremdenblatt*, semi-official organ of the Ballhausplatz, and allegedly only surviving with its circulation of 20,000 because the emperor liked to read it; and Adler's *Arbeiterzeitung*, which 'still represents the undiluted catastrophic theory of Marx'. None of these was particularly susceptible to German influence. In Hungary, the German-language *Pester Lloyd*, was a Jewish-liberal paper which enjoyed a certain reputation abroad. The rest of the Hungarian press had little time for foreign affairs once the great crises got under way in the 1890s, and its views rarely went beyond a simple devotion to the Triple Alliance. But it joined heartily in the press campaigns that helped to drive Kálnoky and Goluchowski from office. And in Austria both the *Reichspost* and the Germanophile press on occasion launched

[50] F.O. 371/166, Goschen to Grey, No. 56, 18 May 1906.
[51] Grey MSS., Vol. 2, 'Austria', Cartwright to Grey, private, 24 June 1910.

sustained onslaughts on the incumbent of the Ballhausplatz – notably against Aehrenthal personally in his last years of office, and against Berchtold's pacific policy during the Balkan wars.[52] If this last was a factor in stiffening Berchtold in 1914, it would have been the first time the press had exercised a significant influence on the making of policy. For if the foreign ministers' control of the press was slighter than has often been assumed, the newspapers' influence over the Ballhausplatz was slighter still.

Similarly, pressure groups outside the narrow circle of decision-makers could do little to dictate policy – at least in a positive sense. This is seen even in the commercial field: the Austrian sugar-beet industry, one of the most prosperous in the world, was sacrificed to foreign pressure with the concurrence of the foreign ministry.[53] And Goluchowski considered sacrificing Austrian viticulture if the preservation of the alliance with Italy required it.[54] True, pressure could sometimes be exploited by a foreign minister to hasten hesitant Austrian and Hungarian governments along a path he had already determined to take – as Aehrenthal used the complaints of commercial interests suffering from a Turkish boycott during the Bosnian crisis to bring the two governments to accept a settlement with Turkey.[55] But generally, Austrian and Hungarian commercial interests were sluggish and unadventurous: it was the Ballhausplatz, not the capitalists that in 1913–14 planned an excursion into the colonial field in Asia Minor;[56] and even then commercial interests were exasperatingly slow to respond. When all this is said however, there remain two important instances of economic pressure groups influencing policy, the efforts of Austrian industrialists and Hungarian agriculturalists to secure protection against competition from German industry and Balkan agriculture respectively. But even here, these efforts were mostly of a negative kind: a tariff war with Roumania in the later 1880s exasperated a helpless Kálnoky and gravely damaged the Roumanian alliance;[57] and the Magyars managed to hamstring Aehrenthal's efforts to conciliate Serbia by means of economic concessions between 1906 and 1911.[58] And after all, power political considerations triumphed over protectionist lobbies in both Austria and Hungary in the great series of

---

[52] Aehrenthal MSS., Karton 5, Montlong (head of the literary office 1913–17) to Berchtold, undated.   [53] See p. 254.   [54] See p. 267.
[55] See p. 312.   [56] See pp. 364–5.   [57] See p. 160.   [58] See pp. 292, 321.

commercial treaties of 1892–4.[59] As in other fields, these peripheral factors could sometimes restrict the freedom of manoeuvre of a foreign minister, or limit the effectiveness of his policy. But they could not prescribe a positive policy for the Ballhausplatz.

As in the case of public opinion, economic factors were perhaps of more significance in their broadest and most general sense – as constituting one aspect of the given situation on the basis of which the foreign minister made his decisions. Here the fundamental fact was, of course, that Austria-Hungary was a relatively poor, agrarian country. Nor, as the nineteenth century progressed, did her relative position in the ranks of the Great Powers improve. Indeed, with the general world slump in the 1870s and the race to establish tariff barriers – exacerbated embarrassingly enough by her ally Germany – she was hard put to it even to maintain her mediocre prosperity.[60] Political factors at home only increased her difficulties – for example, the government's conscious discrimination against industrialization as a breeding ground of liberal capitalists and socialist workers in the 1880s;[61] and the generous labour legislation designed to win the workers from socialism which tended to raise the price of Austria-Hungary's light industrial exports to an uncompetitive level even on her Balkan doorstep.[62] Nor did the jealousy with which Austria and Hungary each sought to hamper the industrial development of the other help matters: 'the curses of Austria are launched against every fresh chimney-stack erected on Transleithan ground', a Hungarian newspaper complained in 1900, and reciprocated the sentiment.[63]

This general economic weakness, at a time when more advanced industrial rivals, particularly Germany, were developing their commercial interests in the Near East, contributed a great deal to the deterioration of Austria-Hungary's Balkan position; and also lessened her chances of holding her own by diplomacy. At the same time, her economic weakness made itself even more painfully felt in the field of armaments. She could hardly relish the prospect of war even if diplomacy should prove an inadequate shield for her vital interests. To seek salvation in the military capacity of the Monarchy was still, as in the Metternich era, very much a counsel of despair.

[59] See p. 190.   [60] See pp. 136–7.   [61] See p. 137.   [62] See p. 190.
[63] F.O. 7/1303, Thornton to Plunkett, No. 55, 25 October 1900.

Chapter 2

Beust, 1866–71[1]

> A great artist in diplomacy and policy who enjoys
> moderate excitements and the game of lesser intrigues,
> but who fears violent measures and serious involve-
> ments where one must put up heavy stakes and make
> decisions without hesitation.
>
> *Cazaux to Gramont*, 17 July 1870[2]

'The darkest gloom prevails, from which at present there seems
no escape,' reported the British ambassador from Vienna a fortnight after the preliminary peace of Nikolsburg (26 July). 'There
is no one bright spot to which one can look, that inspires confidence as to the future prospects of this vast country.'[3] The
government's prestige had been shattered: lack of patriotic or
dynastic feeling among the population had practically forced the
government to put a speedy end to an unpopular war – the
Viennese had greeted the disaster of Sadowa with relief and celebrations in the streets; and for the first time in his life the emperor
had felt the need of a cavalry escort to accompany him from his
summer palace at Schönbrunn to the capital.[4]

---

[1] The following works are of particular relevance to this chapter: H.
Potthoff, *Die deutsche Politik Beusts*, Bonn, 1968; K. P. Schoenhals, *The
Russian policy of Count Friedrich Ferdinand von Beust, 1866–71*, University
Microfilm Inc., Ann Arbor, 1964; H. de Worms, *The Austro-Hungarian
Empire and the policy of Count Beust*, London, 1877; W. Wagner, 'Kaiser
Franz Joseph und das deutsche Reich, 1871–1914', Doctoral Dissertation,
Vienna, 1951; E. v. Wertheimer, *Graf Julius Andrássy, sein Leben und seine
Zeit* (3 vols), Stuttgart, 1910; and the works by H. Benedikt, G. Drage, F.
Engel-Janosi, C. A. Macartney, and H. Ritter v. Srbik cited in Chapter 1,
note 1.

[2] *Les origines diplomatiques de la guerre de 1870–71*, Paris, 1910–32, Vol. 29,
p. 61.

[3] F.O. 7/710, Bloomfield to Stanley, No. 80, 14 August 1866.

[4] P. Hohenbalken (ed.), *Heinrich, Graf Lützow. Im diplomatischen Dienst der
k. u. k. Monarchie*, Vienna, 1971, p. 5.

Nor was there any hope of salvation in the military. True, the Austrians had done well in Italy – Archduke Albrecht, victor of Custozza and son of the victor of Aspern, enjoyed great prestige; and the spirit of Lissa was to inspire the small, trim navy for decades. But in the north the needle gun had finally proved its superiority over the bayonet and storm tactics of the Austrian infantry, and despite a superior heavy artillery the Monarchy lay prostrate at the feet of Prussia. Politically, the very nature of the state was completely uncertain, the 1861 constitution having been suspended in 1865 pending negotiations with the Hungarians. Economically the prospect was also bleak: with a national debt that had risen from £82½m. to £291m. since 1815, a war indemnity to pay, an annual deficit in the budget, and harvest failures and floods in Hungary, the government was faced within a year with the prospect of Austrian bonds being excluded altogether from the exchanges of Western Europe. Clearly the immediate need was for a period of peace, strict economy, and reform.

Above all, a system of government had to be devised for the Habsburg Monarchy. For this purpose Friedrich Ferdinand Baron Beust, until 16 August 1866 foreign minister of the King of Saxony, proved ideally suited. Untainted with any past record in Austrian politics, and with a good streak of opportunism inherent in his character, he could cut through the tangled undergrowth of the Austrian political scene. Within a bare two months of taking office under Franz Joseph as foreign minister (30 October) he had reached agreement with the Hungarians on the basic principles of dualism. In February 1867 a responsible ministry under the liberal Andrássy took office in Budapest, where Franz Joseph was at last crowned King of Hungary in June. Beust was rewarded with the title of Chancellor, previously held only by Kaunitz, Metternich, and Schwarzenberg. No minister after him enjoyed either this title or the power it carried in the domestic affairs of the Monarchy. Himself prime minister since January 1867, he granted to the non-Hungarian provinces a slightly modified version of the 1861 constitution, whereupon the federalist clericalist, feudalist and Slav parties went into opposition, and a German-Liberal government was installed with Auersperg as prime minister on 1 January 1868. This suited Beust well enough. In so far as he had any convictions they were liberal. More important, he was anxious to humour the German elements in Austria (on whom he feared Bismarck still had designs) and to raise the prestige and influence of Austria among the liberal governments of the south German states. This might provide some substitute for the legal ties severed in 1866, and reinforce the independence of those states from Prussia as guaranteed by Article IV of the Treaty of Prague (23 August 1866). Indeed for Beust, the restoration of constitutional government in Austria and Hungary was above all a means to restore the international position of the Monarchy.

Much the same may be said of the other reforms of the period – text-book liberal measures all designed to give Austria a more modern image as a potentially valuable ally in the European diplomatic game. The press law, the judicial system, and educational system were liberalized – although the education reform caused a quarrel with the Papacy which was perhaps as much a hindrance to close relations with France as a help in relations with Italy. On the economic front, thanks partly to a series of good harvests after 1867 a period of general prosperity, indeed, 'a perfect orgy of speculation' set in, which was to last until the great crash of 1873. The new prosperity permitted a rapid development of the railway network. And the importance of this was not only strategic – in Galicia, for example – but commercial and political. The Vienna-Constantinople projects of the later 1860s promised much for Austro-Hungarian trade and influence in the Balkans. Even the spate of commercial treaties, with Prussia (1865–8), France (1865), Italy (1867) and Britain (1868), which represented the high water-mark of free trade in Austria, were not without political significance. In the case of the British treaty Beust explicitly stated that the advantages of a possible political *rapprochement* must outweigh the opposition of Austrian industrialists fearing competition.[5] When all this is said, however, the government was unable to tap the new wealth really effectively; finance ministers declared that taxation simply could not be raised any further, and the parliaments kept a jealous control of the purse-strings of military expenditure. So Austria-Hungary could still not always act effectively in a crisis demanding an intimidating show of force or involving a risk of war. The military reforms devised by Archduke Albrecht and Friedrich von Beck, head of

[5] [Haus-, Hof-, und Staatsarchiv, Vienna.] Kab[inettsarchiv, Karton] 17, 1868, Beust memorandum, 7 April 1868.

the Emperor's Military Chancellery, were delayed by the financial and constitutional objections of the parliaments in Vienna and Budapest until the end of 1868. As a result the new Common Army was still in the throes of reorganization and totally unfit for war in the summer of 1870.

Franz Joseph's choice of Beust as foreign minister had much to commend it. With nearly twenty years of experience at the head of affairs in Dresden, Beust had a fair command of the relations between the German states, even though his own plans to build up the middle states as a counterweight to both Prussia and Austria had come to grief on the rock of military realities. He was, moreover, a respected figure on the international stage: it was he whom Franz Joseph had chosen to send to Paris to seek Napoleon III's good offices after Sadowa. There was moreover, simply no one available in Austria with a comparable reputation or with a skill in domestic politics equal to the task of internal consolidation. Considerations of chivalry may also have helped to guide the emperor's choice: Beust had sided with Austria before the war, and as a result of it faced political ruin, the victorious Bismarck having forced the King of Saxony to dismiss him as a condition of peace. Contemporaries, however, found a more sinister explanation for Beust's appointment. Abroad, it was widely interpreted as the signal for a policy of *revanche*. The Prussian press was beside itself with rage, and even British and Russian observers feared trouble. Yet these fears were unfounded. There could be no question of *revanche* in the immediate future: an early war would only give Prussia a chance to get hold of the south German states. Indeed, as Franz Joseph defined his aims to Beust on 1 September, these were: to raise Austria to the position of a Great Power again by means of domestic peace; to strengthen her ties with the south German states and to keep the latter out of Prussia's grasp; and to give up the idea of war 'for a long time' (*auf lange Zeit*).[6]

Even this task seemed formidable enough, for in the autumn of 1866 Austria stood friendless in Europe, partly owing to prevailing doubts as to her vitality, partly owing to the diplomatic situation. A *rapprochement* with Prussia was psychologically impossible for the policy-makers at court, whatever the German population of Austria might think; Russia, whose interests clashed

[6] H. Potthoff, p. 46.

with Austria's throughout the Near East, was in close alignment with Prussia; Italy was in Prussia's debt for Venetia; Britain was isolationist; and Napoleon III, although he had no reason to love Bismarck, still saw himself as the champion of nationalities, and was anxious to co-operate with Russia in defence of the Christians of the Balkans. Only the internal consolidation of Austria, coupled with patient diplomacy, could improve this situation. True, the idea that Austria might in the long run recover, or even improve on, her pre-1866 position in Germany by war was dear to the military party and some aristocrats, and was not ruled out even by the emperor. But for the time being, Austria needed peace, and Beust's task would be to prevent a further worsening of the situation: to prevent, by diplomatic means, the absorption of the four south German states into the North German Confederation. Even here, he had to tread carefully. The adoption of a threatening tone towards the south German states would only further Bismarck's aims. For the moment, therefore, he confined himself to sending more capable diplomats to Bavaria, Württemberg, and Baden (the budget would not run to a separate mission to south Hesse) to impress on them the desirability of maintaining their independence according to Article IV of the Treaty of Prague.

The immediate and most pressing question of the day lay not in Germany, however, but in the Near East. There, the decay of Turkey was apparent to all, not only in the demands of Serbia, to be freed from the last vestiges of Turkish control, but in the full scale rebellion which had broken out in Crete in the summer of 1866. Beust's position was difficult. On the one hand, he did not want to see the Eastern question raised until Austria had recovered her strength; on the other, he could not simply ignore these developments, which seriously affected Austrian interests. A Cretan success, or the union of Crete with Greece as France and Russia were demanding, would increase the ferment among all the Christians of Turkey and might ultimately affect the Slav subjects of Austria. Beust was convinced that the Cretan rising was part of an international revolutionary movement, in which he knew that the Roumanian nationalist leader, Bratianu, was in correspondence with those notorious enemies of the House of Habsburg, Kossuth and Mazzini. Moreover, a diplomatic success for Russia in Crete would also increase Russian prestige throughout the whole

Slav world. At the same time, however, he was reluctant to adopt a policy of absolute opposition to nationalist movements. Mere repression might provoke an enormous explosion in the long run. More immediately, it would drive the Slavs into complete dependence on Russia, whereas skilful handling might bring them to play the role of barriers against Russian imperialism. He decided, therefore, to work for timely measures to satisfy the more immediate grievances of the Christians while leaving the substance of Turkish power intact. His aims were still essentially conservative; but he felt that the old, negative, conservative-legitimist methods would no longer suffice. According to the British chargé d'affaires,[7] he waxed eloquent on this theme:

It has been the lot of Austria to attend 'les pompes funèbres' of all those 'legitimate rights' which she had most sincerely and staunchly supported. It had been so in Italy, and now she had seen the rights of the old German Confederation carried to the grave. He feared that the same destiny might still follow her, were she to advise Turkey to continue to uphold certain, though incontestable, rights midst the difficulties that surround her.

As regards Serbia, his new policy met with some success. He was able to oblige Belgrade by helping to persuade the Turks to give up their rights to maintain token garrisons in the principality. At the same time he maintained a firm opposition to Serbian demands for an increase in territory. He was fully aware of the potential attractive power an enlarged and too successful Serbia might have for the Slavs of Austria: Bosnia and Herzegovina, for example, 'must be either Turkish or Austrian, no third possibility is admissible'.[8] As regards Crete, however, he met with a rebuff. In January 1867 he proposed a conference to compel the Turks to settle the legitimate grievances of the Cretans on condition that other Balkan revolutionary movements ceased. Always willing to sacrifice legalistic rights for the sake of general peace in the Balkans, he even sought to make his proposal attractive to Russia by suggesting that the conference might free her from the Black Sea clauses of the Treaty of Paris. (He might have been hoping also to achieve, under cover of the conference,

[7] F.O. 7/712, Bonar to Stanley, No. 87, 18 December 1866.
[8] Quoted in K. P. Schoenhals, p. 39.

a *rapprochement* with France for use against Prussia.) The Russians, however, did not bite; Britain, fearful of Russia and believing that Turkey would best survive if only left alone, refused to consider his proposal; and a Franco-Russian suggestion of February that Greece should acquire not only Crete, but parts of mainland Turkey, showed that Napoleon III still preferred Russia to a disordered and bankrupt Austria.

It was only in the spring of 1867 that Austria emerged again as a Great Power. Her internal difficulties were by then on the way to settlement; and the sudden quarrel that blew up between France and Prussia over Napoleon III's attempts to purchase Luxemburg presented her with a golden opportunity. Even so, her freedom of action was limited by the fact that the Luxemburg crisis had aroused German national feeling, which was soon in full cry against France. Beust had to be careful to do nothing that might encourage France to start a war on what would be for Prussia so favourable an issue. Not that there was any doubt as to where his sympathies lay. He rebuffed a Bavarian proposal of 13 April for a German Grand Alliance, and for a revived 'Holy Alliance' with Russia (the so-called Tauffkirchen proposal). For both he and Franz Joseph were still smarting under the publication, in March, of Bismarck's defensive military treaties of August 1866 with the south German states. In Beust's view, these treaties had undermined the independence of the south German states even before Bismarck had – with typical cynicism – piously proclaimed it in the Treaty of Prague. Besides, the Tauffkirchen proposal did not seem to offer Austria anything of value in either Germany or the Near East. It might, rather, only serve to embroil her with France. In the Luxemburg crisis, therefore, he confined himself to polite offers of mediation. And although in the end it was Russia who brought about the London conference that settled the affair, Austria could be well satisfied with the result. After all, Prussia had been obliged to withdraw her garrison of some fifty years' standing from the fortress of Luxemburg; and Beust was pleased to see in this a salutary demonstration to the German states of 'what Germany is or can achieve without Austria'.[9] In fact, Austria's uncommitted position, as enhanced by the recent crisis, suited him quite well. France and Austria were henceforth more bold in their diplomatic pressure on the

[9] Quoted in H. Potthoff, p. 115.

south German states; and the latter responded. In May they rejected a Prussian proposal for closer links between north and south Germany.

Nevertheless, despite his bolder line in the German question, Beust was always aware of the risk that too close an alignment with France on this issue might stir up German national feeling against him. He had been unimpressed when, on 23 April, the French ambassador Gramont had proposed an offensive and defensive alliance to secure the Rhine frontier for France and gains in South Germany for Austria (Document 1). This, he felt, was the worst conceivable basis for a Franco-Austrian alliance. Moreover, public opinion even inside the Monarchy would be against it. Franz Joseph could not take his ten million German subjects into a war, the express object of which would be to put German soil under foreign rule. Nor were the Magyars interested in restoring Austria's position in Germany: Vienna might proceed from there to revoke the concessions granted to Budapest in the hour of defeat. In a war against Russia over the Near East, by contrast, both German-Austrians and Magyars would be only too willing to fight. If Prussia intervened in such a war, then France could make her gains in Germany under the cloak of a general settling of accounts.[10]

On this latter basis however, there could be little progress, as was shown by the Salzburg meeting between Franz Joseph and Napoleon III (18–21 August) (Document 2). The French emperor was not willing to sacrifice the Russian connexion for a militarily weak Austria which offered so little. Beust insisted that Austrian policy was based on the maintenance of the Treaty of Prague by peaceful means. If the French stirred up German national feeling, they would paralyse any Austrian government; and in any case, Austria was in no condition to fight. Indeed, even if Prussia advanced south of the river Main, 'closing the Prussian ring from Oderberg to Salzburg and Bregenz', creating a state of perpetual unrest in Austria's German provinces, and causing France to take up arms, Austria could only offer mediatory action at most.[11]

At the same time, Beust's demands on the French were not modest. In his opinion, the chief threat to Austria came from

[10] Kab. 17, Beust to Metternich, 27 April 1867.

[11] Kab. 17, Beust, reports to Franz Joseph, dated '1867', and 19 August 1867.

Napoleon's friends in St Petersburg; and the only possible basis for a Franco-Austrian alliance was that France should abandon those friends and join Austria and Turkey in destroying Russia's prestige among the Christians of the Balkans by defeating her in the Cretan question. To this end, he suggested a combination of Austria, France and Britain to promote an inquiry into Crete on the basis of continuing Turkish rule. He seems to have thought that he had opened Napoleon's eyes to Russia, who was deceiving France and would never abandon the Prussian alliance. He was himself the dupe, however. In October he had to admit that a new and very stiff Franco-Russian note on Crete was 'quite at variance with what had passed at Salzburg and showed that France was again inspired from St Petersburg'.[12] Neither Franz Joseph's visit to Paris in October, nor Beust's proposal of January 1868 for a revived Franco-Austro-British combination to isolate Prussia and Russia in the Near East did anything to alleviate Austria's glaring isolation and helplessness.

Nor was there any immediate hope of escaping from this by improving relations with Prussia and Russia. Austro-Prussian relations were well illustrated by the brief and icily formal meeting between Franz Joseph, en route for Paris, and William I, at Oos railway station at 7.00 a.m. – Beust would have preferred 4.00 a.m. – on 22 October.[13] Relations with Russia were bedevilled not only by mutual suspicion over the Near East – Austria's determination that Russia and her potential satellites should not be the sole heirs of Turkey, and Russia's suspicions of Austrian designs on Bosnia and Herzegovina – but by internal developments. The *Ausgleich* had left the Slavs of the Monarchy, particularly the Czechs, discontented; and this at a time when the Panslav movement was spreading apace. The underground activities of Russian diplomats, the language of the Russian press, the visit of a sizeable Czech delegation to a so-called ethnographic Panslav Congress in Moscow in the summer of 1867 and the consequent flood of Panslav literature into the Monarchy alarmed the Austrian government. Indeed, the formally correct attitude of the Russian government, and its denial of responsibility for the actions of its agents and for the language of its press, only made it all the more difficult to get to grips with the problem and clear it

[12] F.O. 7/726, Bloomfield to Stanley, No. 350, 15 October 1867.
[13] H. Potthoff, p. 153.

up in the interests of better relations between Vienna and St Petersburg. Equally harmful to those relations was the Austrian policy, inaugurated after the *Ausgleich*, of granting virtual home-rule to Galicia in order to conciliate the Poles, the only Slav race of the Monarchy for whom fear of Russia counted for more than Panslav solidarity. As the Austrian ambassador to St Petersburg reported in November 1866, 'the Muscovite colossus is afraid of the ghost of Poland just as a murderer is haunted by the shadow of his victim'.[14] Alexander II and Gorchakov never tired of lecturing the Austrians on the folly of their Polish policy, reminding them of the Poles' ingratitude to Alexander I. Beust, for his part, always refused to discuss what he insisted was a purely internal affair, and countered with complaints about Panslav intrigues among the Ruthenian peasantry of Galicia. On these issues, debate proved futile, and by the summer of 1868 the two courts had withdrawn their ambassadors and were communicating with each other through mere chargés d'affaires.

If the year 1868 saw some improvement in the diplomatic position of Austria-Hungary, as the Habsburg Monarchy was known since the completion of the *Ausgleich* settlement, this was due less to any increase in her inherent strength – the army reform was not even approved by the Austrian and Hungarian parliaments until December 1868 – than to Beust's skill in taking advantage of situations created by others. The Cretan question, for example, became less embarrassing in February, when the Turks took the wind out of the sails of the Greek Cretans by granting an 'Organic statute' to the islanders. Such sporadic fighting as now occurred could only serve, Beust felt, to depress the hopes of the Balkan Christians by showing them what a hard struggle lay ahead. Indeed, by the end of the year the revolt was kept alive only by Greek intervention. At this point a Turkish master-stroke, in the form of an ultimatum to Greece, which terrified the Powers into summoning a conference at Paris (January 1869) to take the matter in hand, gave Beust his chance. He aligned himself with the British in limiting the agenda strictly to the Cretan question, and the conference duly ended with an endorsement of the Turkish position and a condemnation of Greece. Gorchakov, to avoid isolation, made haste to disavow the 'ministry of clowns'[15] in Athens. For one brief moment,

[14] K. P. Schoenhals, p. 19.   [15] K. P. Schoenhals, p. 74.

Beust had achieved his combination of Britain, France and Austria to bring Russia to heel; but its *raison d'être* disappeared together with the crisis.

More striking was Beust's success in dealing with the problem of the Danubian principalities of Moldavia and Wallachia. The auspices were not good. Beust himself always regretted the Austrian withdrawal from the provinces at the end of the Crimean War; now, as autonomous provinces of Turkey enjoying since the summer of 1866 a *de facto* unity under the Hohenzollern Prince Carol, they presented a constant source of friction and disorder on the Hungarian frontier. For example, in the summer of 1867 the 'Roumanian' government (as the government of the principalities was loosely termed) had embarked on a large-scale persecution of Jews, many of whom were expelled or even drowned. Beust had constantly to protest on behalf of Austrian citizens in the principalities (most of whom were Jewish merchants). The princely government, for its part, was not without grievances against Austria-Hungary, whose very existence, containing as she did nearly three million Roumanians, constituted an offence in the eyes of the liberal prime minister Ion Bratianu. Beust despaired of ever achieving tolerable relations with 'the Roumanian Cavour',[16] whose policy was avowedly based on the assumption that Austria's days were numbered. By the summer of 1868 a serious crisis was developing. The Roumanian government was harbouring Bulgarian nationalists who were sending raiding parties into Turkey. In this, the Austrians discerned, as usual, a general conspiracy, with branches in Serbia, Greece and Montenegro, and seeking to promote the dissolution of Turkey (Document 3). Worse still, the Roumanian government was arming to the teeth. Prussia, with the connivance of Russia, was supplying weapons and military instructors; and Austrian officials were struck by the military bearing and strict discipline of large numbers of Prussian 'railway workers' travelling to Roumania via Galicia.[17] All this led Beust to conclude that the intended victim of the conspiracy (which included Prince Carol and his master, Bismarck) was not so much Turkey as Austria-Hungary.

By skilful handling, he was able nevertheless to turn the

[16] Kab. 17, Beust, memorandum, 25 September 1868.
[17] Kab. 17, Beust, résumé of information on political agitation among the states subject to Turkey, February 1870.

situation to his advantage and to score a resounding success. In the autumn, he sounded the alarm about Prussia's 'living arsenal'[18] on the Hungarian frontier. This was an argument that found ready ears; not only in the parliaments, which were still dragging their feet over the army reform, but in Budapest and Paris. Andrássy was impressed: he had just heard that in Prince Carol's drawing room hung a map on which Transylvania already appeared as part of Roumania. Napoleon III was even more impressed, and suggested an attack on Prussia. But Beust drew back. This was not his aim: both he and Franz Joseph felt that for war Austria-Hungary must be able to put up at least 800,000 men, whereas as yet she could muster only 280,000, and those still in the throes of reorganization. What Beust wanted was a success in Roumania and the diplomatic humiliation of Russia and Prussia. This, he thought, would compromise Bismarck in Russian eyes. If Russia and Prussia were so foolish as to launch a war, then at least Prussia would be fighting without the backing of German nationalism, and France and Austria could in the end make their gains in Germany. But Bismarck too was well aware of this, and of the fact that the Magyars, now unfortunately furious with Prussia, would in the last resort always be a more effective means of restraining Vienna than Roumania, however well armed, could ever be. In the end, therefore, Beust got his diplomatic victory. In November, Bismarck sounded a full retreat, persuaded Carol to dismiss Bratianu, and tried to cover his tracks with a press campaign denouncing Beust as a warmonger. Even this last Beust turned to his advantage, citing it as evidence of Prussia's inveterate jealousy of Austria's constitutional advance and internal consolidation.

As Bismarck's undignified retreat showed, a Franco-Austrian combination over the Near East, presenting Prussia with the choice either of deserting Russia or of staking her existence on an unpopular war, was always a more deadly threat to Prussia than any Franco-Austrian alliance based on the German question. This could only highlight Prussia's role as the defender of Germany's integrity. Yet with the ending of the Roumanian and Cretan crises early in 1869 Beust was reduced to making the best of the latter possibility. Already in August 1868 there had been another fruitless Franco-Austrian discussion. Beust had again

[18] F.O. 7/739, Bonar to Granville, No. 164, 3 November 1868.

rejected Napoleon's suggestion of an offensive alliance against Prussia. Even if victorious, Austria would find her position in a new Germany hopelessly compromised *vis-à-vis* German opinion if she owed her restoration to French arms.[19] He was equally unattracted by a French proposal for diplomatic co-operation to tie Prussia's hands by a European guarantee of the *status quo*. Neither isolationist Britain nor revanchist Russia would undertake such a commitment, and the German states would resent an attempt to put them under the tutelage of Europe.[20] His counter-proposal, to embarrass Prussia by suggesting a general disarmament came to nothing. So did his ingenious plan to create a league of Austria, France, Britain, and Italy, in November 1868. Ostensibly this was designed to solve the Spanish succession question raised by the expulsion of Queen Isabella: Spain and Portugal were to be united and the legitimist Carlist line excluded (another example of Beust's willingness to abandon traditional Habsburg ties). In reality, Beust intended to use such a bloc for more general diplomatic purposes.[21]

In November 1868 both Beust and Napoleon III began to move towards the idea of a triple alliance with Italy. The plan was attractive to Vienna, where bitterness against Italy was not nearly so strong as against the other enemy of 1866. Moreover, a link with the kingdom of Italy might make German and anti-clerical opinion at home less suspicious of Napoleon III. Beust's own relations with the Pope had taken a turn for the worse when Pius IX issued an allocution against the liberal education laws in May; and he was even prepared to consider ceding the South Tyrol to Italy if Austria got compensation in Germany. Altogether, he felt that a triple alliance would be safer than an agreement with Napoleon III alone: it would be well 'to put the . . . wild and warlike French elephant between two tame ones'.[22] By careful cultivation of Napoleon III – supporting his designs on the Belgian railways in May 1869, for example, and dismissing the guarantee treaty of 1839 as in the long run impractical (to the dismay of the British) – Beust was able to secure a draft agreement very favourable to Austria-Hungary by the summer. The draft

[19] Kab. 17, Beust memorandum, 2 August 1868.
[20] Ibid.
[21] Kab. 17, Beust memorandum for Franz Joseph, 7 October 1868.
[22] H. Potthoff, p. 269.

treaty committed her only to neutrality in the event of a Franco-Prussian war in which Russia did not intervene. Admittedly this was partly intended for the consumption of the public, which was still not disposed to fight for the German mission of the House of Habsburg. That mission was well catered for in the final settlement envisaged in the alliance however – an Austria restored to her pre-1866 position, a Prussia reduced even beyond her pre-1866 limits, and gains for the middle German states. Here was no simple *revanche*. But the project came to little. The Italians demanded territory on the Isonzo and the immediate evacuation of French troops from Rome, whereupon Napoleon at once broke off negotiations. An exchange of letters between Franz Joseph and Napoleon III promising each other assistance if attacked was all that had resulted by September 1869.

This was not the end of Franco-Austrian diplomatic co-operation. Franz Joseph's visit to Egypt in November for the opening of the Suez canal, in the presence of Napoleon III and in the conspicuous absence of the sultan, was as much a tribute to French achievement and French designs in Egypt as to Austria-Hungary's not inconsiderable commercial interests in the area. In Constantinople Franz Joseph even went so far as to advise the sultan to grant more power to his Egyptian vassal. At the highest military level too co-operation developed. In November 1869 General Lebrun convinced Napoleon III that he must know which allies he could count on in drawing up his plans; and in February 1870 Archduke Albrecht went to Paris. His personal advice to the French, to make an unassisted thrust at Nuremberg and then to await Austrian and Italian help, did not commit the Austrian government; but it served to convince Paris of the war-like intentions of the Austrian military party. In June, Lebrun went to Vienna. His proposal for a simultaneous offensive got nowhere. The Archduke was unwilling to promise more than he could be sure of fulfilling, and the hard fact was that Italy and Austria-Hungary would both need six weeks to mobilize. Even so, his own plan, for a French offensive through south Germany, with Italy and Austria-Hungary joining in the final grand battle in Saxony, was hardly more realistic and betrayed a grave miscalculation as to feeling in south Germany and as to Prussia's striking power. Indeed, Franz Joseph added a warning to the effect that if Napoleon III appeared in south Germany as an invader, instead of as the defender of south German liberties against Prussia, Austria could not march at all in his support. Lebrun seems to have taken this lightly, and left Vienna well pleased; but Napoleon III was anything but satisfied with the result.

Beust, for his part, certainly had no desire to encourage Napoleon's impetuosity. The situation in Germany was developing just as he wished. Austria's internal consolidation as a German liberal state enabled her to speak with more authority in German affairs. Franco-Austrian pressure after the Luxemburg crisis had thwarted the project of a pan-German confederation; and a judicious mixture of warnings and encouragement after the Salzburg meeting stimulated a particularist outcry against the Zollverein treaties in the autumn of 1867 and helped to produce a particularist victory in the Customs-Parliament elections in the following spring. Beust's publication at this time of the first Austro-Hungarian foreign office Red Book was an astute move, designed to show that Austria-Hungary was adopting British parliamentary habits, and that her policy, unlike Prussia's, had no need to shun the light of day. Altogether, the movement for union with Prussia was clearly making little headway in south Germany. True, Beust's plans for a south German confederation to bind the southern states together against Prussia, themselves came to grief on the particularist rock. But the Austrians were beginning to realize that this rock must be the basis of their policy. As they pursued a policy of strict abstention and reserve (leaving it to France to use strong language where necessary), mistrust of Prussia and of Prussian methods – *Steuerzahlen, Soldatwerden und Maulhalten*[23] – was growing apace. True, Vienna lost some prestige at the end of 1869 when attempts to suppress an anti-conscription rebellion in Dalmatia with insufficient troops almost ended in a fiasco for the new army; and in April 1870 the appointment of a Slavophile ministry under Potocki suggested that Austria might not long remain a German state after all. Nevertheless, the collapse of the German settlement of the Treaty of Prague was in no sense a foregone conclusion. Beust's German policy was by no means a proven failure; and in the spring of 1870 Bismarck seemed as far from his goal as ever.

[23] 'Pay your taxes, become a soldier, keep your mouth shut.' Quoted in H. Potthoff, p. 385.

Whereas in the German question a policy of letting well alone served Austria-Hungary's purpose best, the Near East in 1869–70 continued to demand careful attention and busy activity if the Balkan states were to be prevented from drifting into the position of being mere satellites of Russia. Beust felt this question to be urgent, and he was never less disposed to resigning himself to a strictly conservative policy of supporting Turkey at all costs, as was still being recommended by the Austro-Hungarian embassy in Constantinople. Rather, he strove to humour the Balkan states so far as this could be done without jeopardizing Austro-Hungarian interests. His benevolence extended even to Montenegro, the most 'Russian' of the Balkan states, which began to agitate in the spring of 1869 for more territory and a port on the Adriatic. On this, Beust refused to lift a finger: Austria-Hungary had no wish to see a potential Russian naval base in the Adriatic. But he was accommodating in respect to telegraphic concessions and cash payments to the Montenegrins, who in turn made no trouble for the Austrians during the Cattaro rising in the autumn. (He also wisely ignored the assertions of local and military officials that the rising, caused in fact by Vienna's breaking a promise of 1814 not to introduce conscription, was inspired from Russia and Montenegro.) In 1870 he tried to move the Turks to be generous to Montenegro in a frontier dispute. True, he failed to outbid the Russians, but their policy collapsed before a compromise solution arranged by the Concert in the summer, in much the same way as it had collapsed over Crete some eighteen months before. All in all Beust managed to maintain some Austro-Hungarian influence in Montenegro, even if the cost was a corresponding decline in Austro-Hungarian influence at Constantinople.

Towards Serbia, Montenegro's sister state and rival, and at this time the least hostile to Turkey of all the Balkan states, Beust could be even more forthcoming. The assassination of Prince Michael Obrenovich in June 1868 put an end to that ruler's schemes for a Balkan league; and to Vienna the rule of his youthful son Milan, even with a pro-Russian regency, was an infinitely lesser evil than a Serbo-Montenegrin union under Prince Nikita of Montenegro. By 1869, in fact, the Austrians were pleased to discern very little Russian influence in Belgrade, and they successfully used their influence to secure Turkey's assent as suzerain to a new constitution for Serbia. Indeed, Andrássy and his protégé in Belgrade, Benjamin Kállay, were prepared to go even further. Whereas Beust still insisted that territorial acquisitions by Serbia would ultimately whet her appetite for Austro-Hungarian territory, Andrássy and Kállay were by the spring of 1869 thinking in terms of using Serbia as a stalking horse to increase Austro-Hungarian influence in the Balkans. In 1869, and especially in the autumn of 1870, they both hinted to the Serbs that Austria-Hungary would not object if Serbia one day absorbed some Slav districts of Turkey. Beust, for his part still insisted that the risk was too great. Serbia might some day become a stalking horse for Russia, to further the latter's 'great object . . . of extending her power towards the Adriatic'.[24] He preferred to rely on Turkey, at least a certain friend; and on railway construction to spread Austro-Hungarian influence. In the spring of 1870 he at last persuaded the Austrian government to back a project for a railway from Vienna to Salonica, which a Franco-Belgian group had agreed to finance. He told the British ambassador that he washed his hands of Andrássy's 'attempts to meddle in foreign affairs'; but Andrássy was an essential element of the government in Hungary, and Beust 'was obliged to bear much from him'.[25] Andrássy may have done something to raise Austria-Hungary's stock at Belgrade; but again this was matched by a decline in her influence at Constantinople.

With the Danubian principalities relations had improved since the dismissal of Bratianu. The conservative 'boyar' government that succeeded him continued to arm feverishly but eschewed revolutionary propaganda. Nevertheless, persecutions of the Jews continued, despite Austrian protests, to add to the domestic chaos, and the Austro-Hungarian government was constantly debating the question of what to do should law and order collapse completely in the principalities. Although as late as February 1870 Beust was still thinking in terms of reverting to the settlement of 1856, which had separated the two principalities, he became better disposed towards them in the spring. For Russia was already treating them as a virtually independent state, and he thought that Austria-Hungary might do well to make some generous gestures too. The union should be upheld – Wallachia was a

[24] F.O. 7/768, Bloomfield to Granville, No. 119, 27 September 1870.
[25] Ibid., Bloomfield to Granville, No. 149, 13 October 1870.

46

useful restraint on Russophile Moldavia; so should Prince Carol, who had thrown off Prussian leading-strings, and who at least kept Bratianu at bay. Indeed, to strengthen Carol's position, he was even considering recognizing him as 'Prince of Roumania'; and at the outbreak of the Franco-Prussian war, his admonition to Paris checked a French-inspired plot against the Hohenzollern ruler. Still, the Austrians continued to have nightmares about unilateral Russian intervention 'to restore order' in Roumania. This would completely undermine the strategic position of the Monarchy and paralyse it for action elsewhere, say, in Germany. Endless conferences of ministers[26] and military men discussed this threat, which became a veritable obsession during the great international crises of 1870–1. No clear decision was ever reached as to the strategically appropriate counter-measure; but opinions generally, and especially in Budapest, inclined to war with Russia, rather than an invasion of the principalities.

Relations with Russia herself continued as bad as ever. In the summer of 1869, following St Petersburg's retreat in the Cretan question and the failure of the alliance negotiations with France, Beust had made some attempt to improve them. He met Gorchakov at Ouchy in Switzerland in September, assured him that Austria-Hungary was not opposed to a revision of the Black Sea clauses of the Treaty of Paris, and received in return an assurance that Russia did not intend to disturb the *status quo* in the Balkans. But the old rivalry persisted, with respect to Montenegro and Roumania in particular; and the old sources of mistrust remained. True, full diplomatic relations were resumed at the beginning of 1870. But the new Russian ambassador to Vienna, Novikoff, proved to be an ardent Slavophile; and the Panslav Benevolent Societies in Russia, alarmed by Austria-Hungary's Balkan railway projects, began to step up their propaganda among the south Slavs. The Austrians were particularly upset by the publication of a book[27] by General R. A. Fadeyev advocating the forceful liberation of the Austrian Slavs. The Russians for their part took alarm at the appointment of the Pole Potocki as Austrian minister-president in April; and when this was followed by further con-

[26] P.A. XL/285, Ministerratsprotokoll, 15 July, 6 November and 14 November 1870.

[27] *Opinion on the Eastern Question*, 1870, containing the famous sentence, 'the road to Constantinople lies through Vienna.'

cessions to Galicia Alexander II lectured the Austro-Hungarian ambassador yet again: 'you have to admit that Prussia's Germanification of the Poles . . . as well as our forceful Russification, have been crowned by success. Your system, which is based on the opposite point of view, will produce regrettable discord between our two governments.'[28] Since March 1868 Russia had had a defensive military agreement with Prussia; and according to the Austro-Hungarian ambassador, on the German question, 'the Russian tsar purely and simply used the language of the Prussian diplomatists.'[29]

Such language was disconcerting to Austrian ears. For Austria-Hungary's relations with Prussia had hardly improved at all. A speech by Beust in the summer of 1869, accusing Berlin of hindering a reconciliation, had produced yet another Prussian press campaign against him; and although he agreed to visits to Vienna by the Prussian Crown Prince in October and to Berlin by Archduke Charles Ludwig in January 1870 – partly as a sop to German opinion at home – these were mere courtesy calls. He was still determined to make no step towards Prussia that might jeopardize his relations with France.

Yet it was France, ironically enough, and not Prussia or Russia, who was to strike the blow that was to destroy Beust's delicately and patiently constructed edifice of Austro-Hungarian influence in Germany, and ultimately to endanger the Monarchy's interests in the Near East and its whole position as a Great Power. In the early stages of the Hohenzollern candidature dispute Beust had been pleased to see a welcome embarrassment for Prussia: here was a dynastic, non-German issue which might well deepen the rift between Prussia and the south German states. But the speed with which the dispute flared up into a German national issue after Gramont's warlike speech of 6 July took Beust completely by surprise. He simply had no time to attempt to condition the south German states psychologically. A hasty summons to neutrality now would have been widely interpreted as '*undeutsch*', and would have damaged Austria's reputation in Germany beyond repair. He had hoped to assist France to a peaceful diplomatic victory, but in this the French were not interested. Despite his warnings that he could only co-operate if he were properly consulted in good time, the French rushed recklessly

[28] K. P. Schoenhals, p. 129.   [29] Ibid.

1 Franz Joseph I

2 Friedrich Ferdinand Baron (1869, Count) Beust

3 Julius Count Andrássy

4 Heinrich Baron Haymerle

5 Gustav Count Kálnoky

6 Agenor Count Goluchowski

7 Alois Baron (1909, Count) Lexa von Aehrenthal

8 Leopold Count Berchtold

ahead. For Gramont had formed his own optimistic assumptions about Austrian policy during his nine years' embassy at Vienna. On 15 July he coolly informed the Austro-Hungarian ambassador that 'la guerre est décidée: si l'Autriche comprend ses intérêts elle marchera avec nous', and flew into a rage when the ambassador mentioned the word 'congress'.[30] On 19 July France declared war; the south German states all fell into line behind Prussia in defence of the national cause, and the very situation arose that Beust had striven most to avoid.

Already on 18 July a conference of ministers had met in Vienna to discuss the situation.[31] The emperor was in the chair, and the common ministers, the prime ministers of Austria and Hungary, and Archduke Albrecht, Inspector-General of the Army attended. Beust made it clear from the start that Austria-Hungary was under no obligation to France. On the contrary, it was against insistent advice from Vienna that France had gone ahead and transformed the Spanish question into a German national issue. True, the common war minister, the fiery Baron Kuhn, swore that 'the Prussians on the Inn means *Finis Austriae*'. He was for immediate intervention and even a general settling of accounts in a world-wide conflagration. But all the others, hoping for a French victory, and expecting in any case a prolonged struggle, declared for neutrality. It was decided that armed neutrality was too dangerous, and might provoke Prussia to a pre-emptive strike at Austria. Nevertheless, certain preliminary military measures – notably a strengthening of the fortifications in Galicia – were agreed on. These were designed to cope with possible threats from Prussia and Russia, and with disorders followed by Russian intervention in the Danubian principalities. They would, it was hoped, put Austria-Hungary in a position to act effectively later – either to deal Prussia the death-blow, or to restrain whichever Power proved victorious and make good Austria-Hungary's claim to the gratitude of the south German states.

For the time being, all except Kuhn were agreed, the Monarchy

---

[30] H. Potthoff, p. 344.

[31] Memorandum by Kuhn, in E. v. Glaise-Horstenau, *Franz Josephs Weggefährte. Des Leben des Generalstabschefs Grafen Beck*, Vienna, 1930, p. 458; P.A. XL/285, Ministerratsprotokoll, 18 July 1870; H. Ritter v. Srbik, 'Erinnerungen des Generals Freiherrn v. John 1866 und 1870' in *Aus Oesterreichs Vergangenheit*, Salzburg, 1949.

could do no more. In the first place, the state of public opinion was a serious obstacle to intervention against Prussia. The Germans in Austria were opposed, as was the whole of Hungary; and the Prussians had bought the Viennese press. In these circumstances the parliaments simply would not vote the money. In the second place, the Monarchy was not nearly so well prepared militarily as Kuhn made out. Franz Joseph was informed of the true position before the meeting by General v. John and Beck.[32] Indeed, a memorandum by Beck at this time envisaged a retreat into central Hungary in the event of a Prussian attack.[33] Added to all this was the undoubted risk of some Russian counter-action if Austria-Hungary intervened. Although the Austrians were not aware that Russia and Prussia had actually concluded a military convention in March 1868, they knew well enough that St Petersburg was on cordial terms with Berlin; that Austria's strategic railways in the direction of the Carpathians were still far from completion; and that the summer was the best possible season for Russia to go to war.

Yet strangely enough, so far as Austro-Russian relations were concerned, the Franco-Prussian war presented what was to be perhaps one of the great missed opportunities of history.[34] On 23 July Alexander II sent for the Austro-Hungarian ambassador and made some very conciliatory offers. He was in fact seriously alarmed at the possibility of a French victory, bringing in its wake the raising of the Polish question. If Austria-Hungary would help to localize the war, Russia would give her a territorial guarantee, secure for her a protectorate over southern Germany, and keep the Near East calm. If, on the other hand, Austria-Hungary resorted to threatening military measures, particularly in Galicia, Russia would be forced to take counter-measures and there was no knowing where such a process might end. The ambassador, Count Chotek, was impressed by Alexander's evident sincerity, and urged Beust to be conciliatory and to help the tsar and the peace party to retain control of Russian policy. Beust, however, preferred to keep a free hand; and Andrássy was extremely suspicious, being convinced that it was only Russia's own military unpreparedness that had prevented her from attacking Austria-Hungary already. A conference of ministers on 24 July

[32] H. v. Srbik, pp. 85–6.   [33] E. v. Glaise-Horstenau, p. 171.
[34] K. P. Schoenhals, p. 171.

decided, therefore, to go ahead with the Galician fortifications. Beust explained to St Petersburg that, unlike Russia, Austria-Hungary was unfortunately surrounded by enemies, simply by dint of geography; and as for a protectorate over southern Germany, the Treaty of Prague suited her well enough. Undaunted by this rebuff, the tsar persisted. After the first major French defeats of 4 and 6 August new fears alarmed him, namely, an overweening Prussia, the fall of the Bonaparte dynasty, and a red regime in France. Again he urged the Austrians to cease their armaments and to join Britain and Russia in their efforts to mediate.

Vienna was in fact even more displeased by the turn events had taken, and the conference of ministers of 22 August[35] met under the shadow of what Franz Joseph termed the 'frightful catastrophes'[36] in France. It was now at least obvious to all that there could be no question of armed intervention. The conference decided to support the mediation idea – partly as a sop to the tsar – and to try and take the lead in restraining Prussia by diplomatic means. The tsar could also be humoured with an assurance that Austria-Hungary did not intend to stir up the Polish question. On the point of most interest to Russia, however – the Austro-Hungarian military preparations in Galicia – the conference decided to make no concession whatever. Suspicion of Russia's motives was fairly general at the meeting; and Andrássy, while not averse to some conciliatory gestures, was most insistent on the matter of armaments: 'Austria's mission remains, as before, to be a bulwark against Russia, and only so long as she fulfils this mission is her existence a necessity for Europe.'[37] The Austrian reply to Russia, accompanied by a catalogue of hoary complaints about Panslav activities, was not unnaturally considered profoundly unsatisfactory at St Petersburg. As a modern authority observes, Beust had simply buried the tsar's offers in 'an avalanche of worn-out accusations'.[38] After a further rebuff on the same issue in September, Russia gave up and went her own way. The mediation idea was soon scotched: after Sedan no Power would risk bearding Prussia; and the

[35] P.A. XL/285, Ministerratsprotokoll, 22 August 1870.
[36] W. Wagner, p. 53.
[37] P.A. XL/285, Ministerratsprotokoll, 22 August 1870.
[38] K. P. Schoenhals, p. 200.

Austrians decided that it might after all be in their interests if Prussia took Alsace-Lorraine, two indigestible provinces which would ensure her a permanent enemy on her Western frontier. Perhaps they were right too in considering Russia's conciliatory offers to be merely the insubstantial result of her temporary embarrassment. The cost of rejecting them, however, was to be high.

This was soon apparent. By the end of October the Balkans were buzzing with rumours of some impending Russian *coup*. Vienna feared that this would take the form of an occupation of Roumania, and on 6 November a conference of ministers[39] decided to suspend all reductions of armaments for the present. It was with some relief, therefore, that Beust learned on 10 November that Russia had merely denounced the Black Sea clauses of the Treaty of Paris – the revision of which he had himself suggested several times. Public opinion was by no means outraged: although the Hungarians were somewhat bellicose the Germans were conciliatory and the Czechs even pro-Russian. So in the conference of ministers of 14 November[40] Beust emphasized that there could be no question of going to war. He recommended a mild protest, after the manner of the British, both for form's sake and to deter Russia from any further adventures. The chief danger spot was still Roumania, he felt, and any Russian move there would force Austria-Hungary to fight. Andrássy took a stronger line, arguing that Russia was now clearly on the move, and that only a joint protest of the Powers would deter her and sober up the south Slavs. But Beust had the meeting on his side, pointing out that such a protest would end in a fiasco, as France and Prussia, both seeking Russia's favour, would abstain. The emperor too feared that Russia might have a majority of the Powers on her side – hence a conference was to be avoided. In the end Beust sent a legalistic note to Russia which started off a tedious and acrimonious debate with Gorchakov about the validity of treaties.

At this point, Britain and Prussia, who wanted only a speedy end to the affair, proposed a conference in London, and on 2 December the Austrians very reluctantly decided to attend. On 17 December a conference of ministers[41] determined the instruc-

[39] P.A. XL/285, Ministerratsprotokoll, 6 November 1870.
[40] Ibid., Ministerratsprotokoll, 14 November 1870.
[41] Ibid., Ministerratsprotokoll, 17 December 1870.

tions for the Austro-Hungarian delegation. These are chiefly remarkable for their toughness, and betray a complete mis-appraisal of the diplomatic situation. For with France a nullity and Prussia strongly supporting Russia, the Monarchy was prob-ably weaker and more isolated than at any time since 1866. Beust was certainly too sanguine when he told the meeting that Austria-Hungary would have the support of Britain, Italy and Turkey. He had already failed to persuade these Powers to join in separate negotiations as a preliminary to the conference. Nevertheless, the Austro-Hungarian programme at the conference was to include: the admission of a specific number of European vessels into the Black Sea to counterbalance any Russian fleet; the obligation on Turkey to open the Straits to these vessels, and to place a port at their disposal; an increase in the number of ships guarding the mouth of the Danube; the reduction of international restrictions on Austro-Hungarian sovereignty in respect of the Danube (as compensation for Russia's increased sovereignty in the Black Sea); and the public admission by Russia that her original action in denouncing the clauses had been illegal.

The London conference (January–March 1871) revealed the extent of Beust's miscalculations (although it may be said in his defence that he had been under considerable pressure from Andrássy, who was talking even in terms of war). Britain, anxious to avoid both war and extra commitments, would have nothing to do with the idea of a permanent Western presence in the Black Sea. The Turks too were unhelpful: Beust's recent Balkan policy had made them suspicious of him in any case; and they declared their strong opposition to handing over a port to the Powers and to any increase in the number of ships guarding the Danube. In the end, Russia admitted that treaties could not be altered unilaterally, and the convention of 1841 forbidding the entry of warships into the Straits was slightly amended to allow the sultan to summon armed naval assistance if he felt himself endangered. The Hungarian government was given permission to undertake, together with Turkey, some clearance works on the Danube to render the river more easily navigable for trading ships, and to recoup the expenses by levying tolls on the users. (Such tolls had been forbidden by the Treaty of Paris.) With this, Vienna and Budapest had to profess themselves content.

Meanwhile, Beust had made his peace with the new Germany.

The French attack, driving the south German states into Prussia's arms, had itself confounded his German policy: the French defeat had rendered this disaster irreversible. After a couple of months Beust abandoned his hopes of mediation and on 2 November started to reduce the armaments programme. Neither he nor Franz Joseph had any illusions about the probable effect on the German population of Austria of a clash between the Habsburg state and the German national idea, and the emperor now finally buried his yearnings for the past. When the Prussian ambassador informed Beust on 5 December of the new conformation intended for Germany, the chancellor assured him that he would not uphold 'the formal right of the Treaty of Prague' against 'the logic of mighty events through which the leadership of Germany has fallen to the Prussian crown'.[42] An evasive attitude, he feared, might precipitate a Prussian attack on Austria and the loss of her German provinces. On 26 December he sent Franz Joseph's formal assurances to Berlin. Yet even now he characteristically kept an eye open to possible turns of the wheel of fortune: he decided not to send any greetings to the House of Hohenzollern, but only to the German people, and praised their ancient connexion with the House of Habsburg.[43]

By the summer of 1871 the dust stirred up by the Western and Eastern crises had had time to settle, and the Austrians could take stock of the situation. Russia still seemed to stand out glaringly on the horizon as the chief threat, and her supposed designs on Roumania were particularly worrying. She seemed to be trying to stir up Prussia to make a diplomatic row about the pro-French and anti-Hohenzollern riots with which the Roumanians had greeted the news of the Treaty of Frankfort in March. And this manoeuvre might be a prelude, either to getting the Turks to dismember Roumania on the lines of the 1856 settlement, or to a Russian invasion to 'restore order'. From March to July conferences of ministers in Vienna racked their brains over the problem of counter-measures, the plan now being to let Russia occupy Roumania and then to attack her over-extended lines of communication.[44] Yet there was little hope of any help from

[42] P.A. III/102, Beust to Wimpffen, 5 December 1870.

[43] Kab. 17, Beust to Franz Joseph, 25 December 1870; Beust to Wimpffen, 26 December 1870.

[44] P.A. XL/286, Ministerratsprotokoll, No. 107, 31 March 1871.

others. France was still friendly – Beust had hastened to recognize the new regime and to declare that France must keep her place in the European system – but in her weakened condition she could be of no more practical use than isolationist Britain.

It was against this background that Beust undertook a thorough reappraisal of Austro-Hungarian foreign policy in a memorandum he wrote for the emperor on 18 May 1871.[45] After 1866, he argued, agreement between Austria and Prussia had been impossible because Prussia would neither allow Austria back into Germany nor help her against Russia in the Near East. But recently the situation had become simpler, for Austria-Hungary had abandoned all hope of re-entering Germany. The new German Empire, moreover, was a national state, which by its connexions with the Germans in Austria could gravely embarrass the Habsburg government if provoked. The best policy for Austria-Hungary, therefore, would be to cultivate Berlin in the spirit of the dispatch of 26 December. The Russo-Prussian dynastic alliance was an unnatural union, and Bismarck would soon feel irked by it and seek support elsewhere. Not that Beust had any illusions about the possibility of steering the Germans on a positively anti-Russian course. On the contrary, a reconciliation with Berlin might eventually improve relations between Vienna and St Petersburg – especially if some sort of co-operation against 'the Revolution' could be devised. Altogether, therefore, Beust advised the emperor to abandon the illusions of past epochs, and settle for a general understanding with Prussia. This would make the two Central Powers predominant on the continent: no longer organically united, but side by side.

The new policy went into operation at once. It was not forced on Beust by Andrássy, as Wertheimer maintains,[46] let alone deferred until Andrássy replaced him at the Ballhausplatz. In July the British ambassador remarked on the 'vast and rapid improvement' in Austro-German relations,[47] and after six years of communication through chargés d'affaires the two courts at last resumed full diplomatic relations through ambassadors. Italy, too, was loosely drawn into the same orbit. In June, Beust transferred

[45] P.A. XL/54, Beust memorandum for Franz Joseph, 18 May 1871.
[46] E. v. Wertheimer, *Graf Julius Andrássy: Sein Leben und Seine Zeit* (3 vols), Stuttgart, 1910, Vol. 1, pp. 530–1.
[47] F.O. 7/789, Bloomfield to Granville, No. 237, 11 July 1871.

the Austro-Hungarian mission from Florence to Rome, and took advantage of the Pope's assumption of infallibility to declare the Concordat entirely void, on the grounds that one of the contracting parties had changed its nature. His only conciliatory gesture towards Pius IX was the appointment of a promising young diplomat, Count Gustav Kálnoky, to represent Franz Joseph at the Vatican.

The Austro-German reconciliation was completed by Beust's meetings with the German emperor and Bismarck in August. True, the first encounter with William I at Ischl was marred by the emperor's lack of tact[48] in suggesting that the Austrian government ought to side with the German element against the Slavs in the political debate then raging in Vienna. But at Salzburg on 28 August Beust and Bismarck reached a measure of general agreement on the lines of Beust's memorandum of 18 May. Both agreed that there was still, as in the years 1866–71, no basis for an actual alliance: Austria-Hungary did not wish to bind herself to fight France, nor Germany, Russia. But the two chancellors promised to work for better relations based on the recognition that German and Austro-Hungarian interests no longer clashed. The Austrians were not entirely free from their old suspicions. Although Beust was pleased to hear Bismarck renounce all desire to annex the Germans of Austria – 'a nest (*Herd*) of Catholics' – he still felt there was a need 'to keep a sharp eye open'.[49] And Franz Joseph, fearful for Austria's independence, refused a German offer of a post and telegraph agreement and an extended commercial treaty.[50] Nor would Beust help Bismarck to persuade Turkey to chastise the 'nation of thieves'[51] in Bucharest, who were engaged in a dispute with German railway shareholders. On the other hand, they were both agreed that the International, which seemed to them to be pursuing its activities more openly and unashamedly, should be opposed by more definite co-operation between governments. The Commune in Paris was barely three months dead, and in June the Hungarian parliament had taken the lead in urging that governments should co-ordinate their action against the international socialist move-

[48] W. Wagner, p. 83.
[49] Kab. 17, Beust, report to Franz Joseph, 28 August 1871.
[50] W. Wagner, pp. 84–6.
[51] Kab. 17, Beust, report to Franz Joseph, 28 August 1871.

ment. Bismarck was all for repressive legislation, but Beust thought that this should be accompanied by some more positive investigation of the 'worker problem'.[52] His ideas were vague, however, and little was done in practice. A meeting between William I and Franz Joseph in Salzburg in September ended the series on a cordial note. Although only at the price of recognizing Prussia's equality, Franz Joseph's old dream of the two German Powers standing together to form a common conservative front against 'the Revolution' had in a sense been realized.

Beust held fast to the new alignment so long as he continued to direct the foreign affairs of the Monarchy. He had lost much of his influence over domestic affairs in the spring, when Franz Joseph had taken the initiative in appointing the Hohenwart-Schäffle ministry to seek agreement with the Czechs and Poles on constitutional reform. (Since the Germany of 1866 had gone, it was now less important for Austria-Hungary to keep up appearances as a German state.) The approaching conclusion of the negotiations in October, however, threw the German opposition into a frenzy; and Beust now chose to add his weight to the German and Magyar pressure on the emperor to call a halt. His love of the plaudits of the mob drew him into some compromising situations: at a ceremony at the university of Vienna which degenerated into a riot in which two Slavophile ministers were violently expelled, he saw fit to remain on the platform acknowledging the cheers of the German students. This sort of behaviour earned him the strongest disapproval of the emperor – and of Andrássy waiting in the wings.

On 13 October Beust sent the emperor a memorandum, rather tactlessly reminding him of the German emperor's admonitions at Ischl, and stressing the need to humour Berlin at all costs. 'The group Germany-Austria-Italy guarantees us peace and security: if this combination is upset, we drive Russia and Prussia closer together and have then to expect the group Russia-Germany-Italy, and where will the Monarchy find its support then?'[53] These arguments, coupled with the unpalatable fact that ten million hostile Germans and five million hostile Magyars could make more trouble than three million hostile Czechs forced the emperor to retreat. On 25 October he dismissed the Hohenwart-Schäffle ministry.

[52] Ibid.   [53] Kab. 17, Beust, report to Franz Joseph, 13 October 1871.

Beust's triumph was short-lived. The emperor recognized the weight of his arguments: he could not forgive the humiliation. On 1 November he suddenly asked Beust for his resignation. The chancellor spent the rest of his active career as ambassador at London (1871–8) and Paris (1878–82).

Beust fell, a victim of *hubris*. In the end he had succeeded, helped of course by circumstances, in bending even the emperor to his will; but the success was to cost him his career. It was the urgent domestic needs of the Monarchy that had raised him to power in 1866, and it was a domestic question that had brought him down. Perhaps he never really mastered the internal situation. Perhaps indeed, given the complex national structure of the Monarchy, no man could for long succeed in squaring the circle of the national and international problems of the Monarchy. For example, with the *Ausgleich* Beust seemed to have found for a while a stable system of government to serve as a basis for a renewed assertion of Austrian power. Yet no one was to have more trouble from the Magyars than Beust himself, who having hoisted them to power found their views on foreign policy quite the opposite of his own. Other aspects of his domestic policy were less savoury – particularly his handling of the press (although despite his lavish bribes he was in the end himself the dupe, as the attitude of the press in the summer of 1870 showed). Personally vain, and, as his memoirs show, insufferably conceited, his departure was little lamented among those who had to do business with him. According to the British chargé d'affaires[54] it was

certain that he has done more in five years, than any other statesman could have effected in fifty years, to lower the tone of political morality at Vienna. The most interested partisans of the late chancellor do not attempt to deny that he has habitually employed his political information in pecuniary speculations and the secret service money of the state in purchasing panegyrics on himself from the home and foreign press. [During his occupancy the Imperial Chancellery] has been the notorious resort of stockjobbers, journalists known for their venality and other persons whose intimacy would be a discredit to any private, and a disgrace to any public, man.

In foreign affairs, perhaps, Beust cuts a better figure. He had managed to raise Austria from impotence and isolation in 1866 to

[54] F.O. 7/791, Lytton to Granville, No. 62, 18 November 1871.

a fairly strong position by the spring of 1870; and when France collapsed leaving the Monarchy isolated in the storms of 1870–1 he salvaged what he could and then had the resilience to change course and establish a useful link with Germany. His sense of the possible was sometimes at fault, particularly in his sanguine assessment of British Near Eastern policy in 1867–8 and 1871. But he had a good nose for the impossible – for instance, Napoleon III's suggestions of common military action in Germany. The personal rivalry between Beust and Bismarck and the resultant press campaigns certainly deepened the rift between Austria and Prussia. But there was in fact hardly any basis for a reconciliation so long as Austria still hoped to re-enter Germany and Prussia could offer her nothing in Germany beyond what she already had by virtue of the Treaty of Prague, and no support in the Near East against Russia, her chief worry after 1866. This being the case, Beust can be credited with some success in defending Austro-Hungarian interests in the Balkans (even at the cost of a slight estrangement of Turkey); and with achieving the somewhat limited aims he had set himself in Germany, namely, the prevention of any Prussian advance beyond the limits set by the Treaty of Prague (until Napoleon III upset the boat and presented Bismarck with a united Germany).

Perhaps he could have done more to conciliate Prussia and Russia. But this would have involved a fight with the court and army in the first case and with the Magyars in the second. And after all, when Prussia's victory in 1870–1 finally removed the obstacle of Austrian nostalgia and hopes of revenge, he was quick enough to seize the chance to escape from isolation. Perhaps he was hoping thereby to strengthen Austria-Hungary's position against Russia. Certainly alignment with one of her powerful immediate neighbours was potentially a more effective check on the other than an alignment with distant France against both Russia and Prussia combined. Nor did he ever share Andrássy's illusions that Austria-Hungary could force German policy into an anti-Russian course – illusions which were, ironically enough, to render closer co-operation between Vienna and Berlin more difficult to achieve under Andrássy than under Beust. Although the appointment of Andrássy may have helped in the personal sphere, it did not herald a new era in Austro-German relations. This had already been inaugurated under Beust.

Chapter 3

Andrássy, 1871–9[1]

> Andrássy was an out-and-out Hungarian . . . He entered
> the common Austro-Hungarian service not out of a
> hyphenated (i.e. Austro-Hungarian) patriotism, but
> because he believed that he could be useful to the Hun-
> garian half of the Dual Monarchy.
>
> Julius Andrássy the younger,
> *Bismarck, Andrássy, and Their Successors*

The Habsburg Monarchy in which Andrássy took office as
minister for foreign affairs on 13 November 1871 was apparently
in a healthier state than at any time since 1866. On the economic
front, prosperity continued and industry flourished: in the spring
of 1872 Austrian stocks almost reached par, for the first time
since 1848. Liberalism remained the doctrine of the day, and
Austria-Hungary's network of commercial treaties was extended
in 1870–3 to include Sweden, Spain, Portugal, and some of the
South American states. The financial bases of this prosperity
remained unsound, however. Speculation, especially in a host of
dubious mushroom enterprises, reached new heights until in
1873, the year which saw the great festival of economic liberalism
in Austria with the international exhibition in Vienna, the
inevitable crash occurred. This coincided with the start of a
general European depression, and the later 'seventies in Austria-
Hungary saw growing demands from industrialists for protection,
only partly assuaged by a general 15 per cent increase in tariffs in

[1] The following works are particularly relevant to this chapter: T. v. Sosnosky, *Die Balkanpolitik Oesterreich-Ungarns seit 1866* (2 vols), Stuttgart,
1913–14; J. Andrássy, *Bismarck, Andrássy, and Their Successors*, London, 1927;
E. v. Glaise-Horstenau, *Franz Joseph's Weggefährte. Das Leben des Generalstabschefs Grafen Beck*, Vienna, 1930; W. N. Medlicott, *The Congress of Berlin
and After*, London, 1963; the works by H. Benedikt, G. Drage and C. A.
Macartney cited in Chapter 1, note 1; and those by W. Wagner and E. v.
Wertheimer cited in Chapter 2, note 1.

1878–82. For the government, too, 1873 saw the first of a decade of budget deficits; 1879, with the occupation of Bosnia and the Herzegovina to pay for, was the government's most impecunious year. Although a direct connexion is not easy to prove, it would seem that these economic difficulties added a new note of urgency to the government's efforts to develop opportunities for Austro-Hungarian trade by means of commercial treaties with the Balkan states and by improving transport facilities by rail and water to European Turkey.

On the political front, the 1870s were on the whole a period of stability. In Vienna, the German Liberals were in a chastened mood after their narrow escape from political death in 1870–1. Having defeated the Czechs, they were content to obey the emperor and Andrássy and grant some concessions to make sure of the Poles. Although, still centralists at heart, they had reservations about Andrássy, the incarnation of Dualism, they recognized in him a fellow Liberal; and although they sometimes jibbed at expenditure on the armed forces, they managed to avoid a serious clash with the Supreme War Lord until the occupation of Bosnia provoked them too far. Hungary, after an upheaval in Deák's '1867' party, settled down to a new era of stability in 1875 under the masterful Koloman Tisza, newly converted to Dualism by Andrássy. By and large, therefore, Andrássy could count on the backing of both the Austrian and the Hungarian governments until after the Congress of Berlin.

The position of the Monarchy in Europe too had improved markedly since the Franco-Prussian war. By the reconciliation with Germany Beust had done much to rid Austria-Hungary of that hostile combination of her two most powerful neighbours that had proved so disastrous to her in the 1860s; and there was some truth in his parting boast that his successor would find the way ahead not only marked out, but cleared of all rubble. Even so, Andrássy chose at first a path that diverged slightly from that of Beust. On the one hand, whereas the latter seems in 1871 to have envisaged a possible adventure into Bosnia – at least, he approved of some speculative remarks made in this sense by Bismarck at Salzburg – Andrássy declared for a policy of the strictest conservatism, rejecting all notion of territorial expansion. This could only swell the Slav element in the Empire, a prospect that was anathema to the Germans, and even more so to the

Magyars. 'The Hungarian ship is so overloaded,' he told the Russians in 1872 (*à propos* the Poles in fact), 'that any addition whether a hundredweight of gold or a hundredweight of dross (*Schmutz*) would sink it.'[2] On the other hand, although, as he told the German ambassador on 22 November 1871, close co-operation with Germany remained the basis of his whole political system. Andrássy was more ambitious and less realistic then Beust in hoping to steer the Austro-German combination in an anti-Russian direction. He even hoped to enlist Britain and Italy to form a four-Power combination designed, he explained to the British chargé d'affaires on 27 December, to reinforce Austria-Hungary as a bastion of the *status quo* (particularly in the Near East) and to keep the restless Powers, France and Russia, 'on their good behaviour'.[3]

Such a four-Power *entente* would be particularly useful, Andrássy felt, in the Near East, where Austria-Hungary had some difficult neighbours – 'wild Indians who could only be treated like unbroken horses, to whom corn should be offered with one hand while they are threatened with a whip in the other'.[4] If these neighbours would abandon their territorial ambitions and their intrigues among the Slavs and Roumanians of the Monarchy, they might be given corn; but for the present, the whip was needed. True, Roumania was calmer. Russia's attempts to get Berlin to move against Prince Carol were thwarted when the bondholders dispute was settled by diplomacy in December 1871. But Serbia was becoming a source of alarm, especially to Budapest. Andrássy's exaggerated cultivation of Belgrade in 1869–70 had borne bitter fruit: the first state visit of the young Prince Milan in October 1871 had been paid to the tsar, and had conjured up the prospect of a territorially enlarged Serbia under Russian, not under Austro-Hungarian influence. Since then, Panserbian propaganda had been flooding into the Monarchy, causing a great outcry in the Hungarian press; and the impecunious Serbian government had introduced fiscal tariffs to the detriment of Austro-Hungarian trade. As a result Andrássy now professed himself 'entirely converted'.[5] He agreed with the

[2] E. v. Wertheimer, Vol. 2, p. 32.
[3] F.O. 7/791, Lytton to Granville, No. 108, 27 December 1871.
[4] F.O. 7/812, Buchanan to Granville, No. 247, 7 September 1873.
[5] F.O. 7/791, Lytton to Granville, No. 76, 23 November 1871.

Turks that Serbia's ambitions were indeed insatiable, and urged them to join him to watch her closely 'and crush her the moment she moves'.[6] Reforms would never satisfy the Slavs of Turkey, he told the British ambassador, and Britain should help Turkey to hold them down by brute force. By May 1872 he had decided that Turkey was Austria-Hungary's 'strongest and most reliable ally'[7] in the Near East, and that in the event of a Christian revolt, Austria-Hungary should try to assert the doctrine of non-intervention, 'holding the ring' to allow Turkey to suppress it.[8]

Beust's policy of cultivating Austro-Hungarian influence in the Balkan states, even at the risk of offending Turkey, had been swung violently into reverse. Yet this was not to offer a practicable or durable basis for an Eastern policy. It was, rather, a temporary aberration on the part of Andrássy, who was extraordinarily sensitive to any threats, however remote, to the integrity of Hungary, and always inclined to over-react at first until time showed that the danger was perhaps not all that imminent. There was some truth in Disraeli's assessment of him: 'a picturesque-looking person but apparently wanting calm'.[9] Be that as it may, the very fact that he was now so emphatic about Turkey's self-sufficiency was to some extent an admission that by the summer of 1872 his original grand design of a four-Power *entente* actively to maintain the *status quo* had proved unrealizable. Already in January the British had fobbed him off with a completely non-committal answer. The Germans had assured him that the tsar had no designs against Austria-Hungary, and had reminded him that Germany was very much indebted to Russia. Franz Joseph's return visit to William I at Berlin in September merely confirmed Andrássy's failure to enlist German support against Russia. For the tsar, worried about a possible Austro-German alliance ever since Beust's meeting with Bismarck in 1871, secured for himself an invitation to Berlin at the same time, thereby substituting a demonstration of monarchical solidarity for the demonstration of Austro-German solidarity, with anti-Russian overtones, which Andrássy had intended.

Yet ironically enough, so far as relations between the three

[6] Ibid.   [7] P.A. XL/287, Ministerratsprotokoll, 17 May 1872.
[8] F.O. 7/798, Buchanan to Granville, No. 223, 29 August 1872.
[9] Beaconsfield to Queen Victoria, 12 June 1878, in G. E. Buckle, *Life of Benjamin Disraeli, Earl of Beaconsfield*, Vol. 6, London, 1920, p. 316.

courts were concerned, it was only Austro-Russian relations that showed any noticeable improvement as a result of the three emperors' meeting in Berlin (6–12 September). The Russians, of course, had good reason to be conciliatory, fearing an Austro-German alignment and still needing a breathing space for their domestic reforms. But there were also voices raised at Vienna in favour of a *rapprochement*, notably in the anti-Prussian military party, still smarting under the wounds of 1866: a memorandum from Archduke Albrecht warning the emperor to have nothing to do with the devious Bismarck had almost provoked Andrássy's resignation in the summer of 1872. Andrássy himself, once he got to Berlin, found both the tsar and his chancellor surprisingly friendly. Gorchakov was even willing to endorse his doctrine of non-intervention in the event of upheavals in Turkey. But little of positive value emerged from the meeting. A formal declaration of war – the only war that could now be waged in Europe, according to William I – was launched against the International. But there was little sign of any plans to fight, apart from some desultory discussions between the police authorities in Vienna and Berlin. For the rest, Austro-German relations had not progressed one jot beyond the stage where Beust had left them.

Nor did the next three years bring much improvement. An undercurrent of suspicion of Berlin persisted at the Austrian court. Archduke Johann Salvator, who in the spring of 1875 fell into disgrace for publicly advocating war with Germany, was admittedly an extreme case. But even during the three emperors' meeting Franz Joseph had been disconcerted to hear of a Prussian scheme to buy a controlling share in the Austrian Southern Railway, a line of vital strategic importance; and as late as 1874 he vetoed an exchange of information on torpedo development with Berlin. In October of the same year Vienna shrugged off a German request for the nullification of Article V of the Treaty of Prague, which had burdened Prussia with the embarrassing obligation to hold a plebiscite in north Slesvig. Moreover, with the Near East enjoying three years of unusual calm, Austria-Hungary found she could cope well enough without German support; whereas the questions that most exercised Bismarck – the French threat, the *Kulturkampf*, and a combination of the two in a Catholic alliance against the new Germany – provided hardly any scope for co-operation between Vienna and Berlin.

True, Austria-Hungary's relations with the Vatican left much to be desired. Franz Joseph had forbidden the promulgation of the dogma of Infallibility in his dominions; in 1872 he again refused asylum to the Pope; and in 1874 pressed ahead, despite a papal threat of excommunication, with new laws to fill the gap left by the denunciation of the Concordat. Andrássy, for his part, was impressed by Bismarck's intense, almost obsessional, hatred of Pius IX: he had observed, during William I's visit in October 1873, how the blood always flushed to the rims of Bismarck's eyes at the very mention of the Pope.[10] He was, therefore, at some pains to convince the Germans – citing in evidence the king of Italy's visit to Vienna in September 1873 – that Austria-Hungary would never join any Franco-Papal alliance. Such a combination, he fully realized, could only drive Berlin closer to St Petersburg. At the same time, however, it was not for nothing that the emperor bore the title 'Apostolic Majesty'. Franz Joseph assured the Vatican in April 1874 that there would be no *Kulturkampf* in Austria-Hungary; nor could Andrássy consider obliging Berlin by expelling the Jesuits, who were far too well entrenched at court; and they both discountenanced Bismarck's plans for a concerted diplomatic offensive against the Papacy, despite his insistence that the Curia was a far greater enemy of all governments than the Communists were. True, for a brief moment in the summer of 1874, Andrássy managed to persuade Franz Joseph to swallow his monarchical and Catholic feelings, leave the tsar in the lurch, and join Berlin in recognizing the republican regime in Spain – a move promoted by Bismarck as a blow against Carlism and ultramontanism. But it was a struggle, and he had to descend to anti-German arguments to convince the emperor: Bismarck was trying to bring off a *coup* and isolate Austria-Hungary.[11] Moreover, conservative dynasticism soon regained the upper hand at Vienna. Early in 1875 it was Franz Joseph who took the lead in persuading Russia and Germany to recognize the government of Alphonso XII.

The slightly increased emphasis on monarchical solidarity which marked Austro-Hungarian policy since the departure of Beust was equally an obstacle to a close alignment of Austro-Hungarian and German policies regarding France. To Vienna, a monarchist regime in Paris seemed infinitely less dangerous than a

[10] E. v. Wertheimer, Vol. 2, p. 107.   [11] W. Wagner, pp. 98–9.

possible red republic under Gambetta. Moreover, although a French republic might suit Bismarck because it could be more easily isolated in a monarchical Europe, this very reasoning made the prospect doubly unattractive to Vienna. For the sake of the balance of power, Franz Joseph emphasized to the French ambassador in St Petersburg in March 1874, Europe had need of a strong France; and Andrássy told the British ambassador that if Bismarck were really trying to annihilate France as a Great Power, his brain must be disordered. He had no sympathy with Bismarck's efforts to depict France and the Vatican as war-mongers in the spring of 1875: 'within the last six months his good sense seems entirely to have deserted him'; and he even blamed the alarmist German press for the general economic depression (although he defended German purchases of war material in Austria because they provided employment). When things reached the level of an actual war scare in May, however, he was careful to stand aside and allow Britain, Italy and Russia to bell the German cat.[12] The result could not have been better for Vienna: Bismarck had been taught a lesson; France and the peace had been saved; best of all, any danger of an embarrassingly close Russo-German alignment had disappeared with Gorchakov's clumsy démarche in Berlin. 'Bismarck will never forgive him!' exclaimed Andrássy, who then performed three exultant hand-stands on his office table.[13]

Yet relieved though Andrássy was to see St Petersburg at odds with Berlin, he had been careful, in the years following the three emperors' meeting, to improve his own relations with the Russians. True, as a conference of ministers recognized on 8 January 1873,[14] Russia still presented the only serious military threat to Austria-Hungary: her whole military preparations were directed against that Power; and the conference decided to push ahead with the fortification of Přemysl and Cracow in Galicia as bases for launching an offensive into Poland should it ever come to a war. Failing that eventuality, however, and granted that Andrássy had been unable to win German support for an anti-

---

[12] Franz Joseph may in fact have dropped a very discreet hint at Berlin; according to a minute quoted in W. Wagner, p. 102; 'Il l'a fait sans être à Berlin. A[ndrássy].'

[13] E. v. Wertheimer, Vol. 2, p. 243.

[14] P.A. XL/287, Ministerratsprotokoll, 8 January 1873.

Russian policy, there was much to be said for attempting to live on good neighbourly terms with Russia. The latter's Balkan ambitions had abated, and the Polish question, in any case less acute since the disappearance of Napoleon III, chief patron of the Poles, proved to be no insurmountable obstacle after all. Andrássy made it clear that, like Beust, he would never sacrifice the Poles, the only non-Panslav Slav race, or risk driving them into alliance with the Czechs. But the concessions made to Galicia were kept within reasonable bounds; and he gave the Russians categorical assurances that he had no desire to revive the Kingdom of Poland, nor any intention of permitting anti-Russian agitation in Galicia.

A definite step forward was made during Alexander II's visit to the Vienna exhibition in June 1873. The tsar's proposal for a military convention similar to the Russo-German convention of the previous March was too much for Franz Joseph and Andrássy, who were anxious to avoid any ties with Russia or Germany that might commit Austria-Hungary to war against Britain or France. Nevertheless, the Schönbrunn convention (6 June) concluded, to emphasize its permanence, between the monarchs rather than the ministers, was an important achievement (Document 4). It was only an 'agreement to agree' in time of trouble; and its general endorsement of the *status quo* – possibly even against Germany – did not go beyond what Andrássy and Gorchakov had agreed at Berlin the previous autumn. For as regards the Near East, it simply implied that the two Powers could best preserve the *status quo* by hopefully abstaining from meddling. All the same, an Austro-Russian agreement now existed. And when the German emperor acceded to it during his visit to Vienna in October 1873 an imposing Three Emperors' League was created, with the theoretical emphasis strongly on monarchical solidarity against 'the Revolution'. In reality, however, the League remained essentially an Austro-Russian arrangement. This was evident during Franz Joseph's return visit to St Petersburg in February 1874, which set the seal on the reconciliation of tsar and emperor when Franz Joseph did pious homage at the tomb and the deathbed of Nicholas I. There were the usual references to the revolutionary menace; very little talk about the Balkans (although Andrássy assured Gorchakov that Austria-Hungary had no intention of annexing Bosnia); but the latent suspicion of the third partner, characteristic of relations within the Three Emperors' League, had not abated. Andrássy explained to Gorchakov that Austria-Hungary wanted good relations with Russia in case Germany should become expansionist again. A year later the semi-official *Fremdenblatt* was talking in almost approving terms of an inevitable Russo-German war, and of Russia's consequent need to keep Austria-Hungary friendly.

It was of course an essential condition of improved Austro-Russian relations that Austria-Hungary should not feel menaced by Russian and Panslav activities on her southern frontier. In fact, the years 1872–5 saw a considerable relaxation of tension in the Balkans, partly, no doubt, because no major disturbance occurred to force Russia to defend her reputation as the protector of the Slavs; also because the Russian government, fearful of the new German Empire, and above all of an Austro-German alliance, was at some pains to humour Vienna. Indeed, the Russians were even prepared to swallow a few defeats in these years. For example, in 1870 the Turks had granted the Bulgarians their own autocephalic Church, the Exarchate; and when in 1872 this was declared schismatic by the Russian Church, Russian influence among the Bulgarians was very severely reduced. Nor did the Austrians sit with folded arms. Andrássy spent a good deal of secret service money in combating Russian, and promoting Austro-Hungarian, influence in Bosnia by building Catholic churches and schools and encouraging the propaganda activities of the energetic Croatian bishop, Strossmayer. Indeed, his policy towards the Balkan states now became altogether more flexible and less nervously negative. Like Beust, he was now prepared, while remaining opposed to the territorial ambitions of the Balkan states, to consider minor concessions to ease relations with them. The 'wild Indians' were to be plied with corn.

In 1872 Andrássy managed, by exercising pressure on Constantinople, to prevent Russia's gaining all the credit for the recognition at last awarded to Prince Carol as Prince of 'Roumania'. At the same time, he forced the Prince to drop his claim to the title 'Prince of the Roumanians', which would have implied a connexion with the three million Roumanian subjects of Franz Joseph in Hungary. Already Andrássy had his eye on Roumania as a potentially useful barrier against the slavicization of the Balkans. He scored a further success over Russia at Bucharest in July 1875, when Austria-Hungary became the first state to conclude a commercial treaty with Roumania, a state which, as a vassal state of Turkey, had no legal right to conclude treaties at all. It was not only politically astute to flatter the Roumanians, but it also made good sense commercially (especially in view of Austria-Hungary's growing economic difficulties after 1873) to replace the haphazard *ad hoc* tariffs hitherto prevailing by a mutually agreed system. Between 1874 and 1876 the Austrian State Railways duly built the Budapest–Bucharest railway.

In Serbia, too, Austro-Hungarian influence recovered in the summer of 1872 when Belgrade, finding St Petersburg unwilling to back its territorial ambitions, sought a *rapprochement* with Vienna. Although Andrássy remained as firm as ever in advising the Serbs to abandon their hopes of territorial expansion, trade between Serbia and the Monarchy was furthered by the establishment at Vienna of a Serbian diplomatic agency. And in the spring of 1874 Andrássy opened negotiations with the Serbs for the building of the railway to Constantinople via Belgrade. He pressed this project, which offered immediate commercial benefits – especially attractive after the crash of 1873 – against the Turkish plan for a strategic line through the barren mountains of Bosnia (which plan he now felt was less necessary in view of his improved relations with Russia). Serbia, he was so bold as to inform St Petersburg, would always be commercially dependent on her great northern neighbour; and even politically Austro-Serbian relations were further improved when a more conciliatory government appeared in Belgrade in the spring of 1875. As early as November 1873 Andrássy told the British ambassador that he had broken with the 'old' policy of simply supporting Turkey, because this only united the Balkan states in solidarity against Turkey and Austria-Hungary.[15] He was in fact returning to the policy of Beust.

This was perhaps the only realistic policy. Conciliation of the Balkan states involved – although it should be noted that this was as much a cause as a consequence of Andrássy's change of tack – a certain strain on relations with the suzerain Power. Andrássy had in fact soon become disillusioned about the identity of Turkish and Austro-Hungarian interests. In the autumn of 1872 he found the Turks unwilling to co-operate over the projected navigation works to clear the Danube (still Austria-Hungary's most im-

[15] F.O. 7/814, Buchanan to Granville, No. 321, 17 November 1873.

portant economic lifeline in the south-east). The Turks professed to be afraid of causing floods; in reality they were afraid of the effects of competition on the railways they were planning to build in Roumania to please Russia. As regards the railways in which Austria-Hungary was interested – in the Western Balkans – the Turks were dilatory in the extreme, abandoning even the Bosnian project in 1876 and doing very little, naturally enough, in the troubled years that followed. Indeed, until the 1880s, such bits of railway line as the Turks constructed (a few lines into Macedonia from the Aegean) only worsened the commercial position of Austria-Hungary by furthering the penetration of cheap seaborne French and British wares into Macedonia. Even politically, the Turks were proving less than helpful, raising legalistic objections to the Austro-Roumanian commercial treaty, and seeming intent (Andrássy concluded from their heavy-handed behaviour in a minor border incident with Montenegro in the winter of 1874–5) rather on provoking disturbances among the Christians than on preventing them.

The Turks, for their part, were not without grievances against Austria-Hungary. The governor of Bosnia had been complaining since 1873 about her increasing 'cultural' activities there, and her designs on that province seemed to receive new confirmation in the spring of 1875 when Franz Joseph made a spectacular and unusually prolonged tour of the neighbouring Austrian province of Dalmatia. The effect on the Christian populations of Bosnia and the Herzegovina was electric, and delegations were sent to greet the Emperor and to ask for his protection. Andrássy himself sensed that the visit might provoke serious trouble, and seems to have advised the emperor against it. A direct connexion between the visit and the Bosnian revolt of July 1875 is difficult to prove: Prince Milan's triumphal progress through Serbia in June was equally inflammatory and more closely coincident in time. Nevertheless, by June there were 4,000 rebels under arms in the Herzegovina, where trouble had been endemic since the end of 1874, and the Christians of Bosnia rose in July. Andrássy's expectation that the Turks would soon suppress the rebellion proved unfounded. The Turks took no effective military measures until the Bulgarians rose in the following year. In the meantime the question of the future of Bosnia had been posed in a most acute form.

For the past fifty years Bosnia had been a source of constant disorder on the southern frontier of the Monarchy.[16] The Austrian government had shown considerable restraint, however, preferring to hold to its policy of preserving Turkey, even in the face of incessant frontier raids by Moslem bands (which cost the Austrian government some nine million guilders, for example, in the years 1815–30 alone), and resorting only occasionally to military reprisals. This was no solution. Inside Bosnia conditions grew progressively worse, with bloody rebellions of the Islamized landowning beys against attempted reforms from Constantinople or, when Turkish control was relaxed, rebellions of the Christian peasantry against the oppressive regime of the beys. The last major rising, in 1861–2, necessitated the intervention of some 50,000 Turkish troops – partly owing to the meddling of Montenegro. So it is not surprising that as early as the 1850s voices were raised in Austria suggesting intervention and military occupation as the only effective means of bringing peace to the frontier.

By the 1860s these arguments were gaining ground in military and naval circles. Already in 1856 Radetzky had maintained that the possession of part of the Bosnian hinterland was strategically necessary for the defence of the Dalmatian coastal strip, which contained no suitable land route for troop transports and depended for its security on the ability of the small Austrian fleet to control the eastern Adriatic. Besides, Dalmatia could never flourish economically without its hinterland – an argument which lost nothing in force as Austria's Adriatic trade developed and as economic conditions became more difficult in the 1870s. With the loss of Venice in 1866 it became even more important, as Vice-Admiral Tegetthof pointed out, to make absolutely sure of Dalmatia, now the only possible base for the navy. To Franz Joseph himself, who had so far managed only to lose territories, the idea of acquiring a province naturally had certain attractions for prestige reasons; and as the devout heir to a three-hundred-year-old protectorate over the Catholics of the Western Balkans he could not feel completely indifferent to the appeals of his suffering co-religionists across the frontier. Above all, as Beck reminded him in 1869 and again in 1875, Austria-Hungary must make sure that not only Bosnia, but Herzegovina as well, did not fall into the hands of the Slav states, Serbia and Montenegro –

[16] T. v. Sosnosky, Vol. 1, pp. 108ff.

otherwise, both Dalmatia and Croatia would soon be lost. The Sanjak of Novibazar, the strip of the vilayet of Bosnia lying between Serbia and Montenegro, would be, as the gateway to Salonica, a doubly useful acquisition. By the mid-seventies, the military party, who in 1874 managed to get rid of the Liberal parliamentarian war minister, Kuhn, were increasing their influence over policy-making. They saw in Franz Joseph's tour of Dalmatia a chance to spy out the land: Beck noted that the Herzegovina seemed a fertile paradise compared to the Dalmatian Karst. Indeed, during his tour Franz Joseph even told General Mollinary, commander in Dalmatia, that he would be put in charge of the occupying expedition if ever it seemed that the provinces were about to slip from Turkey's grasp.

Andrássy, however, was as loath to see an Austro-Hungarian occupation of Bosnia as the emperor was keen. Personally, perhaps, he still felt some gratitude to the Empire which had sheltered him, an exile under sentence of death for treason, in 1849. As a statesman he realized, like Metternich, that a feeble Turkey, tiresome though she might sometimes be, was still the best possible neighbour for Austria-Hungary, who would be foolish to do anything that might precipitate her collapse. On the other hand, it was obvious that there could be no question of fighting to uphold Turkey: this would merely play into the hands of a Russia seeking to pose as the patron of the Slavs. Indeed, although, as a Magyar, Andrássy had no desire to see more Slavs inside the Monarchy, he felt that this would be a lesser evil than the expansion of potentially hostile south Slav states outside the Monarchy. Thus, he reluctantly came to consider the possibility of an occupation, not, like Beck, as a forward, expansionist move, but rather as a preventive action to stop the Slav states sealing the Monarchy off from areas of trade and influence in the south. Thanks to his energy and force of personality, he managed to impose his views on Franz Joseph, who had learned to value his skill as a diplomat especially his success in establishing tolerable relations with Russia. Andrássy himself defined his policy thus: 'not to push the Turks out of the two provinces, rather to support them as long as possible there by giving advice and recommending reforms; nevertheless, should the occasion arise, to take their place should they lack the strength to defend their position.'[17]

[17] Quoted in E. v. Wertheimer, Vol. 2, pp. 260–1.

The immediate situation in the summer of 1875 was menacing in two respects: the lesser Slav states, Serbia and Montenegro, might intervene in the Bosnian affair; or Russia herself might do so. As regards the first possibility, Andrássy hoped that the Turks would suppress the rebellion before the following spring, i.e. before Serbia and Montenegro were militarily prepared. He was sceptical about the complaints of the Bosnian Christians and decided – especially in view of the stubborn refusal of the rebels to negotiate with the Turks, and the excited language of the Slav press from Zagreb to Prague – that the whole rising had been organized by the international revolutionary committees. Of course, this only made the prospect of Serbian and Montenegrin intervention, and the possibility that those two states might take possession of Bosnia and the Herzegovina, all the more dangerous. On the other hand, unless this latter danger appeared imminent, Andrássy was reluctant to come forward with a veto: that would only draw on Austria-Hungary the wrath of the whole Slav world, and might even provoke a revolutionary outburst in Belgrade and the replacement of the relatively amenable Prince Milan by Prince Nikita of Montenegro. For the time being therefore, he decided it would be safer to do nothing, even if Serbia went to war – provided she did not turn the war into a Slav revolutionary crusade, which might after all not confine itself to liberating the Slavs of Turkey. When the governor of Dalmatia, embarrassed by a growing flood of refugees, suggested a quick military solution, namely, to occupy Bosnia after squaring Serbia and Montenegro, Andrássy persuaded the emperor against any such policy (Document 5). The Monarchy should beware of flattering Montenegro into the role of a Balkan Piedmont; and in any case the Balkan states would never hold themselves to any agreement with Austria-Hungary unless the latter had first squared Russia. The question was one for Europe, and particularly for Russia and Austria-Hungary to settle.[18]

Not that Andrássy was willing to co-operate with Russia on absolutely any terms. He turned down a suggestion of Gorchakov's that the three emperors together should bring Turkey to reason as being too restrictive of Austria-Hungary's freedom of action in an area of vital concern to her. But the danger was ever present that Russia, left to herself, might take advantage of the

[18] Kab. 18, Andrássy to Franz Joseph, 27 August 1875.

rising to increase her prestige among the Balkan Christians. The government in St Petersburg was under great pressure to make some gesture to Panslav opinion, and in August proposed that Bosnia and the Herzegovina might be granted an autonomous regime similar to that of Roumania. At this, all Andrássy's worst suspicions of Russia revived overnight, and for a time he completely lost his balance. In an excited letter to the emperor,[19] he emphasized the need to be wary of Russia. Here was the justification, he declared, for his humouring Bismarck in the Spanish question. The Russians had not changed their spots after all. For any Russian government, even for that of Alexander II and Gorchakov, Russia's historic mission would always count in the last resort for everything, and consideration for Austro-Hungarian interests for nothing. Gorchakov's proposal he described as the 'purest nonsense'. Autonomy might be practicable for an entirely Christian region, such as Bulgaria; but such a weak system of government would never be able to maintain order in Bosnia, with its warring Moslem, Catholic, and Orthodox populations. Worse, the Russian proposal would only provoke similar claims from Bulgaria and declarations of independence by the Turkish vassal states: 'everything that should be kept stable will then really begin to move.'

Luckily for Austro-Russian relations, Gorchakov did not press his plan for the present, and Andrássy eventually recovered his nerve. After all, there was something to be said for working with Russia. Austria-Hungary, without an ally, was in no position to fight; and unless Russia could be seen to be co-operating with Austria-Hungary in the search for a compromise solution, the rebels would never be brought to negotiate with Turkey. Moreover, there was always a risk that if Andrássy and Gorchakov failed to suggest a solution the lead might be taken by Ignatiev the insubordinate and violently Panslav Russian ambassador at Constantinople. Towards the end of the year, therefore, after consular investigation into conditions in Bosnia had proved futile, Andrássy began to prepare, in concert with the Russian ambassador, and despite British warnings about Russia's treachery, a moderate programme of reforms which was put before the Powers in the so-called Andrássy Note of 30 December 1875. His

[19] Kab. 18, Andrássy to Franz Joseph, 30 August 1875.

intention was to preserve Turkey by encouraging her to remove the causes of the upheavals that weakened her; to take the initiative himself and thereby to wrest from Russia the role of protector of the Slavs; and possibly also to stake out a claim to Austria-Hungary's prime interest in the Bosnian question, to facilitate an occupation should this become necessary. Be that as it may, the Note came to nothing. It was clear by the spring of 1876 that Andrássy had been wildly optimistic in thinking that his proposals – essentially a repetition of the still unfulfilled Turkish promises of the Hatti-Hamayun of 1856 – would remotely satisfy the rebels. The latter gave the Note very short shrift; and the crisis assumed a more serious aspect, from the Austro-Hungarian point of view, when Gorchakov began to move again, asking to meet Andrássy during Alexander II's forthcoming visit to Berlin in May.

Austria-Hungary's diplomatic position was by no means strong when Andrássy arrived in Berlin on 9 May. The prospect of any German support was as distant as ever, and Bismarck made it clear from the start that he did not wish to take sides between Vienna and St Petersburg. True, his suggestion that those two governments might settle their differences by annexing Bosnia and southern Bessarabia respectively was not unattractive to Andrássy: Russia's recovery of territory which she had already held until 1856 would bring her little prestige, and Austria-Hungary would at least make sure that Bosnia did not fall to Serbia and Montenegro. On the other hand, Andrássy preferred that there should be no intervention of any kind. He found William I friendly enough, and the tsar particularly keen to go hand in hand with Vienna. Gorchakov, however, arrived with a full dress programme for intervention by the Concert, and presented Andrássy with a memorandum condoning the rebellion and envisaging armed intervention in Bosnia and a congress to discuss further means of coercing Turkey (Document 6).

Andrássy was again seized with a fit of suspicion of Russia. He told Gorchakov that his proposals were quite unacceptable, and went off to make his feelings clear to Bismarck's underling Bülow:[20]

[20] R. Hegedüs, 'The Foreign Policy of Count Julius Andrássy', in the *Hungarian Quarterly*, 1937, Vol. 3, No. 4, pp. 632–3.

This unnatural thing that calls itself the Three Emperors' League comes from Germany. It was you who made the Russians so great and it is no business of ours to take the consequences. When it begins to rain into this miserable shed of a League we shall take our umbrellas and walk out . . . This memorandum is a noose they are pleasantly trying to put round our necks. Do they think we are too stupid to see it or too weak to break it? I tell you, we shall break it.

As in the previous summer, however, his fears proved exaggerated. The tsar was in no mood to risk a clash with Austria-Hungary, and in the face of Andrássy's decided stand Gorchakov modified his original proposals beyond all recognition. The 'miserable shed', or rather, the desire of the Russians to preserve it, provided some protection after all; and Andrássy, by threatening to walk out, had managed to exploit the situation to his advantage. The end result of Gorchakov's initiative was, therefore, that the so-called Berlin Memorandum of 12 May was drafted largely by Andrássy. This document merely urged the Turks to grant an armistice to the rebels and to institute reforms on the lines of the Andrássy Note. A mere hint of stronger measures - probably a naval demonstration - if the Turks refused, was all that Gorchakov could salvage from his original proposals for intervention (Document 7). Not content with this success, Andrássy took advantage a week later of a British refusal to consider any kind of pressure on the Porte to scotch the Memorandum altogether. He seemed to have foiled the Russians completely.

Events beyond the control of Vienna and St Petersburg at this point gave the crisis a new and dangerous turn. A palace revolution followed by chaos at Constantinople in June removed all hope that the Turks would soon master the rebellion. By the beginning of July Serbia and Montenegro had declared war on Turkey, Prince Milan issuing an appeal to all the Balkan peoples to join the fray. (The Bulgarians had already risen, and had been subjected to fearful massacres as a result.) Fortunately for the peace of Europe, however, both Russia and Austria-Hungary were anxious at all costs to avoid being dragged into war with each other by these untoward events. True, Gorchakov was apprehensive about Panslav pressure for action if Serbia were defeated; but this fear made him all the more anxious to square Vienna without delay. Andrássy, for his part, decided that the Three Emperors' League was after all worth preserving. He had in fact little alternative. Working within the League was the only policy that offered Austria-Hungary the slightest hope of support from Berlin; and there was precious little hope of aid from any other quarter. Although the British, Austria's allies of old in the Near East, might still fight for the Straits and Constantinople, they were now chary of supporting in the Balkan peninsula the government responsible for the Bulgarian massacres. Moreover, they were inclined to accuse Andrássy (whom they, perhaps under the influence of his rival Beust, now ambassador in London, tended to dismiss as a vain Magyar) of starting the whole trouble by arranging Franz Joseph's Dalmatian tour. At most, therefore, Britain might be a factor to be held in reserve in Andrássy's calculations. For the present, he had to try to maintain the Three Emperors' League. He welcomed, therefore, the Russian suggestion of a meeting between himself, Gorchakov, and their two imperial masters at the Bohemian castle of Reichstadt in July.

At Reichstadt (8 July 1876) Gorchakov and Andrássy achieved their aim of effectively eliminating the war between Turkey, Serbia and Montenegro as a possible source of conflict between Russia and Austria-Hungary. They agreed that if Turkey were victorious, she was to be prevented from exploiting her victory to change the *status quo*; if she were defeated, however, she was to be virtually expelled from Europe. In the latter case, Russia would recover Bessarabia, and Austria-Hungary would take Bosnia. (According to Andrássy's view – there was no agreed statement in writing – Austria-Hungary was also to occupy the Herzegovina.) Greece was to gain Crete and Thessaly; and Serbia and Montenegro were to expand to a common frontier in the Sanjak of Novibazar. The remaining provinces of European Turkey – Bulgaria, Roumelia, and Albania – were to receive autonomous regimes. On the whole, Andrássy could be well content. Turkey might after all survive; but even if she collapsed (in which event Austria-Hungary could not risk forfeiting the sympathy of the whole Slav world by insisting on her preservation) Austro-Hungarian interests had been fairly well secured. Serbia and Montenegro would not gain possession of Bosnia and Herzegovina. True, by absorbing the Sanjak, they would effectively seal off Austria-Hungary from the rest of the Balkans in a territorial sense; but at this stage Andrássy seems to have thought the

Reichstadt arrangement a sufficient guarantee of Austro-Hungarian predominance in the Western Balkans (which, after all, he had never intended to exert by means of territorial expansion). Even Franz Joseph was satisfied with the agreement, and Tisza promised the support of the Hungarian government. At Salzburg in August the Austrians gave the German emperor the gist of the agreement, but they left the other Powers pretty much in the dark. Indeed, whereas the Andrássy Note and the Berlin Memorandum had been drawn up for presentation to the other Powers, the Reichstadt agreement was a major step towards the withdrawal of Russia and Austria-Hungary from the Concert of Europe.

Not that the latter abandoned its efforts to solve the crisis, which became even more menacing in the autumn. By then, the crushing defeat of the Serbs had made the Turks less willing to consider a compromise with the Christians, and the danger of Russian armed intervention under pressure from Panslav opinion correspondingly increased. It took a Russian ultimatum – ominous sign – to bring the Turks to grant an armistice to Serbia at the end of October. Thereafter the Powers, acting in concert through a conference at Constantinople (December 1876–January 1877) further determined that Turkey should be asked to grant a wide measure of autonomy under European supervision to Bosnia and Bulgaria. Andrássy thought these proposals rather drastic, but he decided to fall into line rather than offend their chief authors, Britain and Russia, who seemed to be drawing uncomfortably close together. After all, if the proposals were accepted the Ottoman Empire would at least suffer no territorial loss. This proved a vain hope. The Turks wriggled, first offering a constitution for the whole Empire, and then, early in January, putting the Powers recommendations to an assembly of Christian and Moslem notables, which unanimously rejected them as amounting in effect to a partition of the fatherland. Faced with this, the Powers were completely nonplussed. Events were playing into the hands of those who, for some months now, had been saying that it was a waste of time to expect the Concert to find a solution by such devices as the Constantinople conference and that the only hope lay in some bilateral Austro-Russian arrangement.

The St Petersburg government had already sounded Vienna to this end. As Panslav excitement mounted, Gorchakov had to consider the possibility of war with Turkey, and to attempt to secure, if not the co-operation, then at least the acquiescence, of Austria-Hungary. Of active Austro-Hungarian co-operation in weakening Turkey there was in fact never the slightest hope, as the ensuing negotiations showed. Indeed, these negotiations amounted not so much to a plot between two accomplices as to yet another attempt by Andrássy – as at Berlin and Reichstadt – to exercise restraint and secure what he considered vital interests in the face of a Russian initiative. In September 1876 Alexander II made the first move with a letter to Franz Joseph suggesting drastic pressure on Turkey in the form of temporary occupations of Bosnia and Bulgaria by Austria-Hungary and Russia respectively. Andrássy gave this 'absurd proposal' very short shrift. The present was certainly no time for armed intervention, Franz Joseph replied to the tsar in October; for Turkey might yet be brought to reason by negotiation. Again he vetoed the idea of an autonomous Bosnia: for the sake of her own domestic peace, Austria-Hungary must at all costs prevent the creation of an autonomous south Slav state between her Dalmatian and Croatian provinces. Neither the Germans nor the Magyars would tolerate it; and if Alexander had his Panslavs, Franz Joseph had his parliaments to consider. It was in Austria-Hungary's interests, the emperor continued, to preserve Turkey as long as possible: the Reichstadt agreements only provided for her collapse, not for her destruction by Russia. In view of these reservations, and of Andrássy's express stipulation as a *sine qua non* of any negotiations that no big Slav state be allowed to form on the southern frontier of the Monarchy, it might seem at first sight surprising that, rather than oppose Russia, the Austrians consented on 23 October to discuss with her the conditions on which they would be prepared to acquiesce in a Russian attack on the Ottoman Empire.

The unpleasant fact was, of course, that Russia could not be effectively opposed unless Austria-Hungary was willing to go to war in defence of Turkey, sacrificing her position *vis-à-vis* the whole Slav world, both outside and inside her frontiers. Her diplomatic position had not improved since the summer. She still had no ally in Europe, and was in the last resort as isolated as in 1866 and 1871. As far as Germany was concerned, Vienna was convinced that so long as the old emperor lived there was not the slightest chance of winning German support for any action

against Russia. True, Bismarck declared in a speech of 1 Decem
ber that Germany could not let Austria-Hungary be attacked an
annihilated by Russia; but two days earlier he had warned th
Austrians that he was not prepared to come forward agains
Russia, and that they should square her at Turkey's expens
France wished only to please St Petersburg. As for Britain, he
commitments were likely to be of an extremely limited natur
hardly going beyond the defence of Constantinople. Salisbury, o
his way to the conference there in December, told Andráss
straight out that British opinion would not permit the goverr
ment to fight for Turkey. Neither did Britain's support for th
idea of an autonomous Bosnia, nor her close collaboration wit
Russia at the conference, augur well for Anglo-Austrian solidarit

The military situation was equally depressing. Moreover, th
persons most qualified to speak on it, Archduke Albrecht an
Beck, were both old-style conservatives, highly suspicious c
Berlin and inclined by temperament towards the court of S
Petersburg. The advice the emperor received from militar
circles was, therefore, to avoid a war with Russia at all costs
provided she did not commit the enormity of erecting a larg
Slav state on Austria-Hungary's frontier – and to work out son
agreement with her. Beck even had visions of the Monarch
expanding as far as Salonica by these means. A war with Russi
he insisted, was far too dangerous: the army was not read
Russia would take a long time to be defeated, as Napoleon I ha
learned; and there was even a serious risk that Germany an
Italy might seize such an opportunity to attack Austria-Hungar
Moreover, according to military thinking at Vienna, as repr
sented in a memorandum[21] presented to Franz Joseph by Arch
duke Albrecht and Beck in November, 'long wars cannot b
borne by a modern (*Kultur-*) industrial state using univers
conscription'. They were too exhausting, as had been proved.
1866 and 1870–1.

> Therein Russia has the advantage over all other Powers. Least of a
> therefore, should Russia's nearest, half-encircled neighbour, Austri
> Hungary, who cannot like the Western Powers withdraw from th
> war when she thinks fit, be among the first to take the field. She mu
> rather preserve her full strength to the end, and then the decisio
> will lie in her hands.

[21] E. v. Glaise-Horstenau, p. 191.

Even Andrássy, although he still felt that the Monarchy should arm as fast as possible so as to be able to take the offensive if its interests were threatened, was by the end of the year reconciled to the prospect of the entry of Russian troops into Roumania. For he, too, firmly believed that a war with Russia was not something to be undertaken lightly: it would last for generations, and end only with the destruction of one or both combatants. It would be wise, therefore, while avoiding helping or encouraging Russia in her designs on Turkey, to see whether Austria-Hungary's more immediately important interests could not be secured by some bilateral agreement.

The ensuing negotiations, culminating in the Austro-Russian Budapest Convention (15 January 1877) defined the military conditions on which Austria-Hungary would acquiesce in a Russo-Turkish war. This was not yet certain – after all the Constantinople conference was still sitting; but anything might happen, and Russia was anxious to proceed with her military preparations in case war should become necessary in the spring. The negotiations were on the whole a success for Andrássy. The Russians, fully conscious of their own weakness and of the need to make sure of Vienna, proved as accommodating as in the previous summer. The Austrians had been very worried lest Russia march into Serbia and transform the war into a revolutionary Slav orthodox crusade which would have grave repercussions among the Slavs of the Monarchy. This point was adequately safeguarded in the convention: Russia promised to confine her military operations to the eastern Balkans. As far as the war was concerned, Austria-Hungary pledged herself to benevolent neutrality and to preventing mediation by the Powers or the application of the Austro-Franco-British guarantee to Turkey of 15 April 1856. The results of the war were apparently to be minimal: Bosnia and the Herzegovina were to receive a measure of autonomy on the lines of the Andrássy Note, and Bulgaria a rather more far-reaching autonomy. At the same time, Andrássy reserved the right to occupy both Bosnia and the Herzegovina, forcing Gorchakov to recognize the Austro-Hungarian version of the Reichstadt agreement, and documenting anew the Monarchy's prime interest in the two provinces. Possible more far-reaching changes were reserved for a later, additional convention.

This additional convention, dated 15 January to correspond

with the original convention, was concluded at Budapest on 18 March. By then the prospect of a Russo-Turkish war had drawn nearer, and with it the danger that the Ottoman Empire might collapse altogether under the strain. The second Budapest convention was designed to deal only with the latter contingency. It was essentially a restatement of the Reichstadt agreement, and awarded Bessarabia to Russia, Bosnia and the Herzegovina to Austria-Hungary, and territorial gains to the Balkan states. The only significant difference was that whereas Andrássy still agreed to the partition of the Sanjak of Novibazar between Serbia and Montenegro, there was now to be a 'later agreement' guaranteeing to Austria-Hungary the use of commercial routes through the strip. By this means Andrássy hoped to safeguard Austro-Hungarian trade and influence in the western Balkans without the burden of annexing yet more territory. On the whole, the Budapest convention and the annex of 18 March bore the stamp of their place of origin. Andrássy made the somewhat sanguine calculation that, if Russia observed it, her territorial gains would be small, and she would by no means have established her influence in the peninsula – especially as her military presence in the eastern Balkans was to cease with the end of the war. And if she broke her word, she would be in the worst conceivable military position – weakened by war, with over-extended lines of communication, and facing a hostile Austria-Hungary (and possibly Britain).

Even so, it should be emphasized that for Andrássy the agreement was very much a *pis aller*. He still hoped that the Ottoman Empire would not in fact collapse, and that the day would never come when it would be necessary to apply the Budapest convention. In a sense, however, the very fact that he had concluded it and sanctioned the possibility of a Russo-Turkish war, only hastened that day. Not that the Russians were actually seeking war; but that particular option was now no longer closed to them. As late as the end of March they still joined readily with the other Powers in a last effort to keep the peace – the innocuous London Protocol of 31 March, which reduced the Powers' January proposals to a mere recommendation to Turkey to adopt reforms. But all hopes failed when the Turks rejected the Protocol on 12 April. On 24 April the tsar declared war.

For the first eight months the Russo-Turkish war gave Andrássy little cause for alarm. He kept his nerve as Russian troops advanced into Roumania, and when the latter, despite his advice, decided to lend Russia her assistance. This 'war between the one-eyed and the blind', as Bismarck termed it, seemed unlikely to precipitate the much-feared collapse of the Ottoman Empire; and by the summer of 1877 the Russians, held up completely before the fortress of Plevna, were using very moderate language at Vienna. On 26 July the tsar assured Franz Joseph[22] that he had no intention of permanently occupying Bulgaria, or of introducing any 'democratic' elements there; that the Powers could assert their interests in the final peace settlement, and that Russia, for her part, would hold scrupulously to the Reichstadt agreement.

This being the case, Franz Joseph and Andrássy were careful to keep the more turbulent spirits in the Monarchy under control. Anti-Russian feeling was particularly strong in Hungary, where a Szekler volunteer force had to be restrained from marching into Roumania when the Russians crossed the Danube. The Turks made an astute move at this time in restoring the treasures of the medieval kings of Hungary to Budapest, where massive demonstrations were held in support of Turkey. But Andrássy felt that, thanks to Tisza's continued support, he could ignore this 'foolish excitement'.[23] The governors of Dalmatia and Croatia, who had come to Vienna in April, hoping to draw up plans for the occupation of Bosnia, were told by Beck to hold their hand. And on 31 July a conference of ministers even rejected Tisza's request for two observation *corps* on the Serbian frontier: these would only be necessary if Serbia launched a 'revolutionary war' in Bosnia.[24] Beck's story[25] that Andrássy was planning to intervene against Russia to stop the war at this time does not seem to be supported by other accounts, or by any archive evidence.

On the contrary, the drift of his diplomacy in the summer of 1877 lay quite in the opposite direction. He might be anxious to draw close to Berlin, even to the extent of hinting to Bismarck at

[22] P.A. I/469, memorandum by Aehrenthal, May–June 1895, on Austro-Russian relations 1872–94, hereafter cited as 'Aehrenthal memorandum, 1895'.

[23] E. v. Wertheimer, Vol. 3, p. 17.

[24] Ibid., pp. 46–8.

[25] E. v. Glaise-Horstenau, p. 196.

Salzburg on 18 September that Austria-Hungary might be accommodating about Article V of the Treaty of Prague. But he was not trying to turn Germany against Russia. The whole emphasis during the Salzburg talks was on maintaining the Three Emperors' League. Of course, the latter might yet prove a broken reed, and it was for this reason that Andrássy did not wish to lose touch entirely with the British. He had put out a tentative feeler to London as early as November 1876; and by May 1877 he was ready to try again. For there seemed a danger that the Russian military on the spot – who had yet to encounter the prolonged delays of Plevna – might carry all before them and spread the war to the whole Balkans in defiance of the Budapest convention. Yet even so, both the emperor and Andrássy felt the need for great circumspection in handling London; and they warned Beust not to lead the British on to the extent of compromising Austria-Hungary. So long as the tsar kept his word, Franz Joseph would not commit himself to Britain. And Andrássy was apprehensive lest Britain might only be trying to use Austria-Hungary in order to frighten Russia into making an agreement – perhaps to secure British interests at the Straits by giving Russia a free hand in the Balkans. Nor was he himself willing to tell the British exactly how closely he was tied to Russia. Anglo-Austrian soundings in the summer of 1877, therefore, never proceeded beyond the most tentative stage. On 20 May Andrássy rejected a British suggestion for an agreement over the Straits (an area of greater importance to Britain than to Austria-Hungary). And he was not, even in the Balkans, quite in line with London, attaching more importance to making sure that Russia did not establish a permanent military presence in Bulgaria than to defining the future territorial limits of that province. Although on 26 July he agreed to keep in touch with the British, he would still undertake no commitments to fight. He was still hoping that Russia would stay loyal to her agreements.

And so it remained until the turn of the year. Andrássy refused to join the British in issuing a warning to St Petersburg even in December, when it appeared that the Russians, having broken the Turkish resistance at Plevna, and advancing on Constantinople, might not keep their word after all. In a letter of 9 December to Franz Joseph, the tsar now talked ominously of ceding parts of

Bosnia to Serbia and Montenegro, and of occupying Bulgaria for two years. Although in fact the Austrians did warn the Russians against such proceedings, they did so independently of the British. On 9 January 1878 Franz Joseph reminded the tsar that Turkey had not fallen to pieces: hence there could be no question yet of applying the Reichstadt agreement. At the same time, he pointed out that Austria-Hungary's right to occupy Bosnia was contingent on Russia's recovery of Bessarabia, not on her establishing a military presence in Bulgaria – to which, moreover, Austria-Hungary would object. And in any case, a definitive peace could only be made by all the Powers together, whose protection Turkey had enjoyed since 1856. These objections made little impression on the tsar. In a threatening reply of 16 January, Alexander dismissed them as based on 'irrelevant assumptions and prejudices'.[26] Although he conceded that Austria-Hungary could take Bosnia in her own good time, he insisted on occupying Bulgaria and on recovering Bessarabia not by virtue of the Reichstadt agreement (which St Petersburg too admitted did not apply to the existing circumstances) but because Russia had only lost it as a result of Austria's treachery in the Crimean war. Franz Joseph was prepared to accept this latter argument, but maintained his objections to the projected Russian occupation of Bulgaria.

Not that this deterred the Russians. In the intoxication of victory, and despite a good deal of muddle caused by Ignatiev (who was apparently ignorant of the terms of the Budapest convention) they managed to force the panic-stricken Turks to a speedy preliminary peace at Adrianople at the end of January. From Ignatiev and his Panslav friends the Austrians could expect little consideration. But even Gorchakov, while conceding on 12 February that Austria-Hungary was still free to occupy Bosnia, nevertheless insisted on occupying Bulgaria; and coolly explained that Austria-Hungary's objections to the creation of a compact Slav state had been overridden by *force majeure*. The final formulation of the Russian terms in the Treaty of San Stefano (3 March) was, therefore, completely unacceptable to Vienna. In a strictly legal sense, the Austrian position was not all that strong: Russia was not herself bound to secure Bosnia for Austria-Hungary; and both Russia and Austria-Hungary were agreed that the conditions had not arisen that would bring the Budapest convention

[26] P.A. I/469, Aehrenthal memorandum, 1895.

into force, namely, the total collapse of Turkey. Nevertheless, Vienna could not unreasonably argue that the Treaty of San Stefano was a flagrant violation of the spirit of the convention, and a serious threat to those very interests which Andrássy had been concerned at Reichstadt and Budapest to safeguard. Russia had chosen to settle single-handed questions which for the past thirty years had been the concern of all the Powers, and particularly of Austria-Hungary. By creating an antonomous Bosnia and a Big Bulgaria which would be occupied by Russia for two years, and, what was worse, by doing this in the face of advance warnings and protests from Vienna, the Treaty of San Stefano portended the annihilation of Austria-Hungary's prestige and influence in the Balkan peninsula.

The Austrians had in fact been racking their brains as to how to stave off such a disaster ever since it became clear at the beginning of the year that Russian policy had definitely changed. The prospects of attempting to reverse the situation by military means remained as bleak as ever. Andrássy shrank from the prospect of a war with Russia which, even if temporarily successful, would leave such a legacy of hatred between the two nations that Austria-Hungary would be burdened for generations with the enormous expense of standing permanently on guard and armed to the teeth against her mighty eastern neighbour. In view of this, and of the all too well-known opinions of the military, he did not even suggest war as a feasible policy to a conference of ministers of 15 January.[27] Nor did the conference show any enthusiasm for his suggestion that Russia might be brought to reason by a military demonstration, such as Austria had undertaken in the Crimean war. The military authorities present could not in any case agree as to where this might best be attempted.

There was, moreover, throughout these months, a strong anti-war current at court. Although Russia's behaviour aroused universal indignation, the idea of a war with the tsar was not attractive to the more conservative aristocrats like Archduke Albrecht; and some like the Court Chamberlain Hohenlohe (who had large estates in Russia) even had a material interest in avoiding it. In military circles too there were many – notably the military attaché at St Petersburg – who still regarded Bismarck as the chief enemy of Austria-Hungary, and who used all their influence with Beck

[27] E. v. Wertheimer, Vol. 3, p. 63.

to make the most of the political and military-technical objections to war. Indeed, Beck is described by his biographer as the chief counter-weight to Andrássy in the crisis.[28] As a German centralist and defender of the Common Army, he was naturally suspicious of any Hungarian influence on policy, and although his own influence on foreign policy was unofficial, it was none the less weighty; as head of the emperor's military chancellery, he saw Franz Joseph every day. On 14 February he told the emperor straight out that the military position was worse than in 1859 or 1866. Any war would have to be fought on four fronts – against Russia, the south Slavs, Germany, and Italy. (He had just worked out a plan of campaign against Italy.) But to what purpose? Public opinion might understand a war to conquer half the Balkans; but a war costing 600m. Gulden just to drive Russia back? – the parliaments would never vote the money. 'The whole thing is a Hungarian policy, a war of revenge for Világos.'[29] Three days later Franz Joseph assured him that the conference of ministers had decided that there could be no question of war. With the offer of only a loan not a subsidy, from Britain, Austria-Hungary was virtually bankrupt (*auf dem Trockenen*).[30] She simply could not afford it.

It remained to be seen, therefore, whether Russia could be brought to reason by diplomatic means. Certainly Andrássy was not prepared just to accept her *fait accompli*, as he had made clear to the ambassador at Berlin as soon as he learned the terms of the preliminary peace on 28 January: 'Russia has played us false. Prince Gorchakov seems to want to settle the whole Eastern question by a *coup* like that of 1871. For us is reserved the endorsement and the humiliation. No minister can survive before the Austrian or Hungarian parliament in such a situation, myself least of all.'[31] He proposed, therefore, that a conference should meet to discuss the settlement. This choice of diplomatic weapon was significant. He still preferred to give Russia the chance of saving face under cover of the Concert, rather than to risk a deadlock and war by openly challenging her, say, by means of an *entente* with Britain. Indeed, although Britain was equally strongly opposed to Russia's proceedings, Andrássy's doubts as to her real value remained as strong as ever. Any Anglo-Russian war would

---

[28] E.v. Glaise-Horstenau, p. 186.   [29] Ibid., p. 200.
[30] Ibid., p. 201.   [31] E. v. Wertheimer, Vol. 3, p. 70.

be an inconclusive fight between the shark and the wolf, he declared, and it would fall to Austria-Hungary to bear the brunt of the fighting. Indeed, the British might only be seeking in Austria-Hungary a battering-ram for use against Russia, to be discarded when convenient. Andrássy's decision to seek a solution by the Concert, instead of by collaboration with Britain was in fact a decision to try, even at this late date, to save the Three Emperors' League; to find a solution in agreement with Russia, if the latter were still amenable to reason.

He was only confirmed in his decision by the attitude of Berlin. Bismarck's famous 'honest broker' speech of 19 February was something of a disappointment to the Austrians, who had hoped for more positive support; and at the end of the month Bismarck again warned Andrássy that although Germany would not obstruct Austria-Hungary's diplomacy, she would lend it no assistance against Russia. Bismarck wanted above all, for the sake of Russo-German relations, to stay clear of the Austro-Russian dispute, and was in fact somewhat embarrassed when Andrássy and Gorchakov eventually agreed on Berlin (rather than Vienna as Andrássy had originally proposed) as the venue of the conference. Nevertheless, Austro-German relations improved a little at this time. Andrássy skilfully offered the bribe of the nullification of Article V of the Treaty of Prague – persuading Franz Joseph that the plebiscite principle embodied in it was full of menace for Austria-Hungary; and that it could only be useful if Berlin were under some debt of gratitude to Vienna at this juncture. (A secret agreement nullifying the objectionable article was at last concluded on 13 April, although when it was published early in 1879 the date was altered to October 1878, lest the public make disparaging remarks about Austrian bribes to Bismarck before the Congress of Berlin.) In March Crown Prince Rudolph received in Berlin the somewhat cold comfort of an assurance that Germany would never let Austria-Hungary perish in a war; and on 25 March the emperor could declare that Austro-German relations were 'of the best' (*das beste*).[32] Nevertheless, the underlying assumption of even this tepid support from Berlin was that Andrássy should seek to square Russia and preserve the Three Emperors' League.

The Russians, for their part, seemed at first willing to co-

[32] W. Wagner, p. 109.

operate. They had, of course, a real interest in dividing their chief opponents, Britain and Austria-Hungary; and to this end sent the tsar's cousin, Prince Alexander of Hesse, and then Ignatiev himself, on explanatory missions to Vienna in March. Andrássy spoke frankly to Ignatiev. Basing himself on the spirit (not, of course on the inapplicable text) of the Reichstadt and Budapest agreements, he again insisted on Austria-Hungary's right to a voice in the settlement. The new Bulgaria, he said, was just such a big Slav state as had been forbidden in the agreements; and Russia could occupy it for at most six months, not two years. Moreover, he now demanded possession not only of Bosnia and the Herzegovina, but of the Sanjak of Novibazar: Russia having proved herself so untrustworthy, Austria-Hungary could only be satisfied with a clear territorial access to the Western Balkans. Only if Russia respected these interests, Andrássy emphasized to Ignatiev, would Austria-Hungary stay inside the Three Emperors' League and refrain from seeking agreement with Britain. No definite agreement was reached, however; and in the ensuing months Russia showed that she was not particularly interested in one. For she managed to come to terms with the British in May, agreeing in principle to reduce the size of Big Bulgaria, and to submit the whole of the San Stefano treaty to the Congress. Her attitude towards Austria-Hungary stiffened in consequence. By 8 May she was talking of giving the whole of the Sanjak to Serbia – a suggestion which even Bismarck termed 'frivolous'.[33] The Three Emperors' League had after all proved a broken reed.

On the eve of the Congress of Berlin, therefore, the diplomatic position of Austria-Hungary was not brilliant. On the one hand, the Three Emperors' League had provided no solution, and little more could now be expected from Germany than the most platonic expressions of goodwill. On the other hand, the Monarchy was still hardly in a position to back up its demands by a threat of military action. As Andrássy complained to the minister-presidents of Austria and Hungary, public opinion was lamentably apathetic; and the most he could extract from the two governments was a special grant of a meagre 60m guilders to lend some credibility to his diplomacy – and that only at the price of a pledge that he did not intend to use it for war. It was only at the last minute, moreover, that the voting of the decennial revision of the

[33] E. v. Wertheimer, Vol. 3, p. 100.

commercial *Ausgleich* removed the danger that Austria-Hungary would have to go to the Congress while herself on the verge of disintegration. Yet the outlook was not completely bleak. Britain had already managed to cut Russia's claws as regards the size of the new Bulgaria; and on 6 June Andrássy managed to patch up an agreement with London securing British support in the Bosnian question. Moreover, the Treaty of San Stefano had so alarmed all the non-Bulgarian races of the Balkan peninsula as to make them potential clients of Austria-Hungary. Andrássy was also hopeful – although here he was making a disastrous mis-calculation – that he would enjoy the support of Turkey at the Congress.

In the event, the Congress of Berlin proved to be the most striking success of Andrássy's diplomatic career. He was ably seconded in the negotiations by Károlyi, Austro-Hungarian ambassador at Berlin, and less so by the nerve-racked Haymerle, ambassador at Rome, who nevertheless was something of an expert in the tangled details of the Eastern question. But the very success of the Congress automatically redounded to the prestige of the man who had done so much to bring it about, and who, with his Magyar panache and colourful uniform, was one of the most striking figures at this, the biggest international gathering since the Congress of Vienna. In the case of the Congress of Berlin, the programme was much less ambitious; and the negotiations, conducted in a brisk and businesslike manner, with special commissions of the most interested Great Powers to sort out the details before the plenary sessions met, were concluded within a month. The decision to tackle the thorny Bulgarian question before dealing with less contentious matters, also made for the expeditious dispatch of business. True, it failed to produce the Anglo-Russian rift that Bismarck desired as a preliminary to reviving the Three Emperors' League. In fact, it strengthened Andrássy's hand to resist Bismarck's plans. He forced his way early into the Anglo-Russian special commission, where he proved his value to the British in holding Russia to her promise to dismember Big Bulgaria; and to the Russians by encouraging Britain to take a more lenient view on certain minor frontier questions. He also agreed in the end to a Russian occupation of Bulgaria lasting nine months – not six, as originally proposed by France. All this perhaps helped to put Russia in a better mood when the time came to deal with the Bosnian question. In any case, Andrássy could be well satisfied with the Bulgarian settlement of the Treaty of Berlin, which reduced the size of the new state by two-thirds, and promised Turkey a defensible frontier in the Balkan mountains.

At the end of June the question of Bosnia and the Herzegovina came up for discussion. By carefully explaining the Austro-Hungarian case to London during the previous three months, Andrássy had already made sure of British support; and Salisbury agreed to put the case for Austro-Hungarian occupation to the Congress. Germany's attitude was less satisfactory. In Berlin there had been a good deal of gloating (no doubt intended for Russian ears) over the fall of Turkey; and the Russophile language of the German ambassador at Constantinople gave the Austrians cause for concern throughout the Congress. Indeed, according to one of Andrássy's *aides*, as late as 28 June Bismarck himself sent his son Herbert to visit Andrássy in a vain attempt to persuade him to drop the Bosnian question for the sake of relations with Russia.[34] Not that Andrássy reported any such incident to Vienna. In all his reports to the emperor from Berlin he carefully avoided saying anything that might feed the monarch's suspicions of Germany or throw an unfavourable light on her policy. He wished to keep the way open for closer relations with Berlin should the chance arise. In the end, no harm was done, and Germany came into line over Bosnia when Russia did. But it was a measure of Andrássy's skill that he managed to hold doggedly to his limited aims while under constant pressure, throughout the Congress, from an imperial master whose views diverged widely from his own.

This divergence was nowhere more apparent than in the Bosnian question itself, where Andrássy was well aware that the emperor wanted to annex the provinces outright in full sovereignty. But he was also aware that public opinion at home was dead set against annexation: this would raise the unanswerable question of the final destination of the provinces within the nicely balanced constitutional structure of the Dual Monarchy. It would also more than likely require the use of force – possibly, Andrássy feared, even a war with Turkey. (Islamic law forbade

[34] A. Novotny, *Quellen und Studien zur Geschichte des Berliner Kongresses, 1878*, Graz, 1957, Vol. I, p. 52.

the outright cession of territory that had not been lost in war.) Public opinion would not stomach such a policy, which would look like complicity with Russia in despoiling the Ottoman Empire. At the same time, for Andrássy, the conclusive argument was that unless Austria-Hungary established herself in the provinces, they would sooner or later be bound to fall from the hands of Turkey – especially of the now weakened and partially dismembered Turkey – to Serbia and Montenegro. He decided for occupation rather than annexation in the hope that this could be peacefully achieved with the consent of the Turks. He sought, moreover, an occupation on the basis of a European mandate (in obtaining which, and in convincing the emperor, British support was to prove invaluable). Such a mandate would represent the public endorsement by Europe of Austria-Hungary's role as a guardian of order in the Near East.

On 28 June Andrássy presented to the Congress the case against a continuance of Turkish rule in Bosnia, which could offer at best the risk of anarchy or, in the event of the establishment of a weak autonomous regime, the near certainty of civil war between the Christian and Moslem populations. Salisbury then proposed the occupation, endorsing Andrássy's arguments, and adding that if Serbia and Montenegro were ever to acquire the provinces this would create a chain of Slav states threatening the other races of the Balkan peninsula. By now, all the other European Powers were prepared to agree to the occupation. Only the Turkish representatives, under fierce pressure from the Sheik-ul-Islam and conservative circles in Constantinople, at the last minute refused their consent. Their opposition apparently took the other diplomats – particularly Andrássy – completely by surprise. In vain did Andrássy point out the advantages to Turkey of giving Austria-Hungary a territorial base from which she could help Turkey to preserve what remained to her in Europe; in vain did the other diplomats, anxious to conclude the business, profess their indignation – Bismarck, as this was a matter on which Russia and Austria-Hungary were for once in agreement, came forward with particular energy to belabour the hapless Turks. The latter could only be brought to drop their opposition when Andrássy made them a formal (albeit secret) declaration on 13 July, stating that the occupation would only be temporary, and expressly reserving legal sovereignty over the provinces to the sultan. The settlement of the final details was reserved for a separate Austro-Turkish agreement. It seems that Andrássy, no doubt exasperated by the unexpected delay, felt himself entitled to treat the Turks with something less than honesty. At any rate, he never intended the occupation to be anything but permanent; and although he assured the Turks that, as far as the Sanjak was concerned, he was interested only in securing military and commercial routes, not in occupation, he took care to extract from Russia a promise not to oppose an eventual occupation of the enclave.

With most of the remaining decisions of the Congress Andrássy had reason to be pleased, in that they documented an increase in Austro-Hungarian political and economic influence in the Balkan peninsula. Ironically enough, it was perhaps Russia herself who had done most to bring this about. The Big Bulgaria she had created at San Stefano had proved in the end a most effective bogeyman to drive all the other Balkan states to seek the protection of Austria-Hungary (or, in the case of Greece, of Britain and France). Only Montenegro, the state least threatened by San Stefano, remained on reasonably good terms with Russia. Andrássy made the most of the opportunity, willingly sanctioning the independence of Serbia, Montenegro, and Roumania – although the last-named principality was in future to be accountable to the Powers for the treatment of its unfortunate Jews. He earned the gratitude of the Serbs by helping them to acquire Nish – thereby at the same time directing their gaze southwards, away from Bosnia and from the south Slav provinces of the Monarchy. Roumania had, in view of her services to Russia during the war, most reason to be displeased with that Power, who now deprived her of the comparatively fertile province of Southern Bessarabia. She too ended up indebted to France and Austria-Hungary, who managed to secure for her slightly more compensation than had originally been intended (albeit only in the barren Dobrudja).

More than this, Austria-Hungary's economic interests were well safeguarded. The projected railway from Vienna to Constantinople moved a step nearer realization when Turkey, Bulgaria and Serbia assumed under the Treaty of Berlin the obligation to complete their railways in the direction of the Austro-Hungarian frontier. True, railway construction in the Balkans was a slow business: the final negotiations with Serbia and Bulgaria were not completed until the early 'eighties, and it was not until 12 August 1888 that the first train left Vienna for Constantinople. Nevertheless, Andrássy could fairly claim to have consolidated at the Congress at least the foundations for the spread of Austro-Hungarian trade and influence into European Turkey. As regards the Danube, which still remained, until the railways were built, the Monarchy's most important commercial route to the Near East, he managed to check the increased influence of Russia (now re-established on the delta) by strengthening and giving more permanence to the international commission. He even managed to free Austria-Hungary from the millstone of Turkish 'co-operation' in clearing the river of obstacles to traffic, and to secure for her the right to undertake the work single-handed. On the whole, therefore, the results of the Congress could be regarded in the Monarchy as highly satisfactory. Nevertheless, the emperor still had regrets about the secret declaration of 13 July limiting his rights in Bosnia; and, above all, it yet remained to be seen whether Austria-Hungary's paper claims to that province could be made a reality without too great an expenditure of blood and money.

In the event, the actual occupation was little short of a disaster. It was undertaken both too late, and with insufficient forces to ensure a quick success; and for these shortcomings Andrássy himself must bear much of the blame. Even after the difficulties he had had with the Turks at Berlin, he persisted in the erroneous belief that they would eventually be brought to see the ultimately pro-Turkish intention of his policy. He had little justification for this. As early as 5 July great demonstrations in Bosnia had made it clear that since the pro-Austrian demonstrations of 1875 Serbian propaganda had done its work, and that – apart from among some of the Catholic Croatian inhabitants – there was no longer any desire in the provinces for an Austro-Hungarian occupation. Moreover, the Constantinople embassy had warned Andrássy time and again not to believe the rosy accounts coming from Austro-Hungarian consular officials in Bosnia. Yet, as the ferment daily grew, Andrássy still delayed action, hoping against hope that the Turks could be brought to conclude the agreement embodying their final consent. (Tisza had warned him on 30 June that he doubted whether he could defend a violent conquest before public opinion.) The Turks, of course, had no intention of smoothing the way, being rather less impressed by the deeper conservative motives of Andrássy's policy than by the fact that they were about to lose two provinces. They made endless delays, hoping that public opinion in the Monarchy might force the government to abandon its intention. Even when the Austro-Hungarian troops were ready to move, on 27 July, Andrássy still held back. But on 27–29 July there were great riots in Sarajevo, both the Austro-Hungarian consul and the Turkish authorities were expelled from the town, and Vienna decided that it could wait no longer.

Despite the weeks of delay, the way had not been well prepared for the Austro-Hungarian expedition which advanced into Bosnia on 29 July. The Austrians had not spent nearly enough in bribes among the local population, who were anything but impressed by Franz Joseph's proclamation asserting that the sultan had 'entrusted Bosnia and the Herzegovina to the protection of his mighty friend, the Emperor and King', and merely adjuring them to 'obey the authorities'. Nor was the occupying force of four divisions totalling 160,000 men anything like adequate to prevent bloodshed by an overwhelming display of power. Here again, Andrássy must bear much of the responsibility. As late as mid-July he had been talking gaily of carrying out the occupation by a division of infantry and a military band; and in the conferences of ministers he urged the emperor, despite the advice of the military, to keep the size of the expedition to an absolute minimum. He was above all anxious to avoid the appearance of a war against Turkey (which he suspected the military of planning) and to avoid spending more than the special credit of 60m. Gulden, which would necessitate further recourse to the parliamentary bodies, who were likely to be in a difficult mood. Andrássy's political arguments convinced the emperor.

The upshot was that an inadequate occupying force had to conduct a regular campaign in extraordinarily difficult country. It advanced in three columns along river valleys, but contact between them was virtually impossible owing to the mountainous, rugged terrain. Moreover, in view of the poverty of the area, the force was burdened with enormous baggage trains; and had beyond that to cope with hostile natives ensconced in numerous fortresses abandoned by the Turks. In Herzegovina, Jovanović, who knew the country well, was able by 6 August to make a

triumphal entry into Mostar; but in Bosnia one column was overwhelmed by a guerilla concentration and thrown back; and
although Sarajevo fell on 18 August, it was not until 20 October
that the last of the fortresses had been mopped up. This was the
second near-defeat for the reorganized Austro-Hungarian army
within a decade. The lesson of the Cattaro rising, where again
insufficient forces had been employed at the outset, had not been
learned – at least, not in the foreign office. Even so, given the
conditions and the army's minimal superiority over the guerilla
forces the occupation was, militarily speaking, perhaps no mean
achievement. Politically, however, the repercussions were most
embarrassing: not only abroad, where the Turks issued a circular
on 8 October alleging brutalities by the occupying forces and
found sympathetic ears in Rome and St Petersburg, but on the
domestic front as well.

In the first place, Andrássy had to fend off a renewed demand
for outright annexation from military circles round the emperor,
who now argued that Bosnia was Austria-Hungary's by right of
conquest; and to reach some agreement with the Turks, who were
reluctant to recognize even an occupation. Against the annexa-
tionists he stood firm, although he admitted resignedly to the
Empress Elizabeth that 'the emperor does not understand the
Eastern question and will never understand it.'[35] In a conference
of ministers on 14 August he insisted that Austria-Hungary must
stick strictly to the Treaty of Berlin, and not give Russia any
pretext to evade her obligations with respect to Bulgaria.[36] Besides, annexation would raise intolerable constitutional difficulties. As he emphasized to the ministers on 12 September: 'we
shall occupy and govern that province, no more, no less'.[37] At the
same time, he had no intention of ever evacuating Bosnia: Europe
had put Austria-Hungary there as a check on Serbia and Montenegro, to prevent the forcible slavicization of the Balkans.
Equally, his views on the Sanjak were unadventurous, but firm.
'The possible occupation of the Sanjak of Novibazar', he told a
conference of ministers on 16 February 1879, 'is by no means
intended as a stage in the march on Salonica as public opinion
wrongly conceives it. Its only object is to protect our position in

[35] R. Hegedüs, *Hungarian Quarterly*, 1937, p. 639.
[36] P.A. XL/290, Ministerratsprotokoll, 24 August 1878.
[37] Ibid., Ministerratsprotokoll, 12 September 1878.

Bosnia and it can only be carried out in complete agreement with Turkey and in the sense of the Treaty of Berlin.'[38] Some Austro-Hungarian presence there, he held to be essential. For the Sanjak was to Bosnia and the Herzegovina what the Straits were to the Black Sea: a gateway to the East which must be kept open. If Serbia and Montenegro held it, Bosnia would become a cul-de-sac, not a base for Austro-Hungarian influence in the Near East; and a Turkey completely cut off from Austro-Hungarian support could not long survive. Worse still, if Serbia and Montenegro took the Sanjak, they might then unite to form one big Slav state, which would naturally proceed to expand towards Bosnia and Dalmatia.

Yet limited though Andrássy's aims might be, a final settlement with the Turks was not easy to achieve. For the sultan was not only genuinely fearful of popular uprisings if he signed away any Moslem territory, but hopeful that public opinion in the Monarchy particularly in Hungary, might come to his rescue. It was not until the spring of 1879 that he could be persuaded to accept a draft convention that omitted all reference to the provisional character of Austria-Hungary's occupation rights in Bosnia and the Herzegovina. Andrássy, for his part, was prepared to be con-ciliatory. He was content with garrison, not occupation, rights in the Sanjak of Novibazar – and those only in the western half of the Sanjak. And even those rights he was too cautious to exercise until the Russians were safely out of Bulgaria in August 1879. Not that all this won him much credit at the Porte. Even after the signature of the final Austro-Turkish Convention of 21 April 1879 the sultan's resentment against his Austrian despoilers was one factor in his decision to rescind the secret article envisaging Austro-Turkish military co-operation in the Sanjak should any of the garrisons there be attacked. For the rest of 1879 the sultan continued in this sullen mood and Austro-Turkish relations showed no sign of improvement.[39]

This was all the more remarkable in view of the fact that not only Andrássy, but also the British, were throughout these months assiduous in urging the sultan to improve his relations with Vienna, and to keep a watchful eye on his chief enemy,

[38] P.A. XL/291, Ministerratsprotokoll, 16 February 1879.
[39] W. N. Medlicott, *The Congress of Berlin and After*, London, 1963, pp. 262ff.

Russia. The latter might yet try to break the fetters imposed on her by the Treaty of Berlin. And although British hopes of an Austro-Hungarian guarantee of Turkey in Europe to balance the British pledge to guard her Asian possessions proved illusory in the light of the sultan's new hostility to Austria-Hungary, the supposed Russian menace was at least a fruitful source of Anglo-Austrian co-operation. Until the summer of 1879 the two Powers worked together against Russia on the boundary commissions that defined the frontiers of the new Bulgaria and Eastern Roumelia. And in May Andrássy took advantage of rumours that Russia was about to refuse to evacuate Bulgaria to make a gentlemen's agreement with the British: henceforth, London and Vienna were to take no steps in the Near East without consulting each other. Andrássy seemed to be making progress towards establishing that great defensive bloc against Russia that he had sketched out in 1871. All the more so as 'the chancellors' war' between Bismarck and Gorchakov was fast blighting any hopes there may have been in Berlin for a restoration of the Three Emperors' League. Not that Andrássy would have considered reviving the League for one moment when he was doing so well in London.

Yet his triumph was limited. Whatever hopes it may have held out for the future, even the Anglo-Austrian *rapprochement* was proving of little practical effect in assuaging the sultan's wrath and improving Austro-Turkish relations. This was a disappointment to Andrássy. And it was all the more galling that this – indeed, the whole question of the occupation of Bosnia – should be adding to the steady growth of criticism of his policy at home.

The murmurings of the annexationist party at court were as nothing compared to the storm the occupation unleashed among the public. Such qualified approval as Andrássy's policy earned came from the Slavs and from military-aristocratic circles, who mistook an essentially negative preventive move for a first step on the road to expansion and a great role in the Slav world. Otherwise, there was no trace of patriotic feeling among the inhabitants of the Monarchy: Andrássy's return from the Congress stood in the most glaring contrast to the reception accorded to Beaconsfield in London. Both Germans and Magyars saw only the potential threat to their predominance within the Dualist structure. Moreover, to the Magyars, who since 1848 looked askance at anything connected with the Imperial Army, and to German Liberals, who regarded the Army as the very incarnation of reaction, the military character the occupation assumed gave only further cause for offence. The Magyars felt that, if there were any fighting to be done, it should be to resist Russia, not to despoil Turkey, Hungary's friend. The German Liberals' grievance was – in form at least – constitutional: that Andrássy had carried out the occupation without consulting the parliaments. Indeed, worse, he had deceived them. Had he not, as late as 9 March, when asking the delegations for the 60m. Gulden credit, declared that he had absolutely no thought of occupying Bosnia provided that Austro-Hungarian interests were not threatened? – a proviso that had perhaps not carried its full weight in the context of a speech intended to reassure. Now, with the occupation an accomplished fact, the fury of the German Liberals knew no bounds. Sensing the impossibility of reversing the Treaty of Berlin, however, they were reduced to the expedient of approving it, while at the same time trying to get a vote against the policy that had led to it, in the hope that this might bring Andrássy down.

Constitutionally, they were on extremely thin ice in attempting any kind of discussion of the Treaty of Berlin, which was not one of those lesser commercial treaties over which the Austrian parliament had the final word. As far as Austria-Hungary was concerned, Andrássy was undoubtedly constitutionally correct in stating unequivocally that 'foreign policy in the monarchical-constitutional state is the sphere in which the Crown has the right to act without the previous assent of the legislature.'[40] The emperor too, was jealously on guard against any attempt to usurp his prerogatives, and even suspected that the Liberals were trying to make him look foolish in the eyes of Europe by rejecting a treaty which he had already ratified. In fact, there was no question of this. Even some of the opposition abated when Andrássy to the discomfiture of the German Liberals, lost no time in presenting a cogent defence of his policy to the delegations at the end of the year. In January 1879 the Austrian parliament approved the Treaty; in February the delegations voted all the extraordinary expenses of the occupation; and in March, thanks largely to Tisza's efforts, the Hungarian parliament assented to the Treaty of Berlin.

[40] E. v. Wertheimer, Vol. 3, pp. 195–6.

Apart from encouraging the Turks to delay the final settlement of the occupation in the hope that it might be abandoned, the storm had serious repercussions in domestic politics. Neither Andrássy nor his German Liberal opponents long survived it. For the latter, of whom the emperor had at last had more than enough, ruin was sure and swift. For in contrast to Hungary, where perhaps nothing could be done, in Austria an alternative government stood ready to hand in the feudal, clerical, and Slav fractions. The emperor had perhaps in his inmost heart never finally written them off, even in 1871; they had remained well represented at court throughout the 1870s, particularly in military circles; and in view of their patriotic reception of the occupation they now stood higher in favour than ever. In August Franz Joseph dismissed the German Liberal government and appointed as minister-president his boyhood friend, Count Eduard Taaffe, a conservative Tyrolean nobleman of Irish extraction (and still a viscount in his own right in the peerage of Ireland). Taaffe, as 'the Emperor's Minister' duly set to work to form a government of clerical, conservative landowners, with a view to winning Slav support in general, and to conciliating the Czechs in particular.

This, of course, was hardly to the liking of Andrássy, who had opposed just such a policy as a threat to Dualism in 1871. His victory in the parliamentary struggle had proved after all to be a pyrrhic one. His own position *vis-à-vis* the parliaments had been gravely weakened; and although the parliaments had of course no direct control over foreign policy, no foreign minister could ignore with impunity the bodies which in time of crisis supplied the extraordinary credits. Now, Andrássy found that those on whom he had always counted for his support, particularly in the Austrian parliament, had become his bitterest foes. His reputation among the public generally had also suffered, and he now had some of the most influential newspapers against him, notably the German *Neue Freie Presse* and the Magyar *Pester Lloyd*. Disputes over the blame for the shortcomings of the Bosnian campaign had embittered further his relations with the military, already tense enough since the war crisis of 1877–8. Nor could he – even had he wished to – rely on the continued support of Slavs and federalist nobles. In this situation, the support of the emperor would in the long run not be enough. Andrássy decided that perhaps the time had come for him to go. Domestic politics were not the only motive for his resignation. He had, in fact, for some time, even during the Congress of Berlin, been attracted to the idea of leaving office while his prestige was high; and in December 1878 had told the emperor for the first time of his intention. A marked deterioration in his health was no doubt also an important factor – indeed, according to Beck, who had no reason to flatter Andrássy, the only one. Andrássy was now, it is true, only fifty-six, but thirteen years of high political office had undoubtedly taken their toll of him. In May 1879 he offered his resignation to the emperor, who refused to accept it; in June, he was seriously ill with pneumonia. When at last, on 6 August, by which time the political scene had cleared and the Berlin settlement was in a fair way to becoming reality, he again asked to be relieved of the burdens of office, the emperor gave way. It seems that Franz Joseph did not mention Andrássy's impending resignation to the German emperor at Gastein because he still hoped to persuade him to change his mind; and he told the German ambassador that Andrássy would certainly come back again. Clearly, despite the emperor's slight disappointment at the results of the Congress of Berlin, Andrássy enjoyed the support of his imperial master to the end.

Even at this stage in his career Andrássy's achievements were worthy of some admiration. Already with a considerable reputation behind him in Hungarian politics, he had proved himself as able a statesman on the European stage as any of his contemporaries. True, his first years in the foreign office had brought him some disappointments. His original grandiose concept of a quadruple *entente* against Russia had soon proved impossible to realize, thanks to the lack of interest on the part of the other governments concerned. This being the case, he had set to work to make the best of the situation; and although he did not succeed in establishing really close relations with Germany or Britain, he worked with some success in the years 1872–5 to establish tolerable relations with Russia. When the eastern crisis burst upon him in 1875 he strove patiently to maintain the Three Emperors' League, partly out of a desire to humour Berlin; chiefly because he realized the necessity, given the military weakness of the Monarchy, of trying at all costs to defend Austro-Hungarian (and particularly Hungarian) interests without recourse to war. With the Panslav triumph in the spring of 1878 the Three Emperors'

League was unable to cope – although it cost Andrássy some wasted months of effort before he was convinced of this. But he made a good recovery at the Congress of Berlin, and the final settlement undoubtedly strengthened the position of Austria-Hungary. Even the occupation of Bosnia can fairly be described as a creditable defensive success. Although relations with London and Berlin were perhaps slightly closer after the Congress, Andrássy's original idea of a defensive bloc consisting of the Central Powers and Britain still seemed an idle dream. Yet already great changes were occurring on the European diplomatic scene. Even now, after his resignation had been accepted, it was to be vouchsafed to Andrássy to realize, at least in part, the project which for the past eight years had eluded him.

Chapter 4

The Making of the Alliances, 1879–85[1]

> The developments of the past twenty years pushed
> Austria-Hungary back from her old historic position . . .
> We have only the East . . . We cannot allow the com-
> pletion of the Russian ring from Silesia to Dalmatia. A
> Slav conformation of the Balkan peninsula under
> Russian material or moral protection would cut our
> vital arteries.
>
> *Austro-Hungarian Foreign Office memorandum*,
> August 1884[2]

The news of Andrássy's impending resignation caused the greatest consternation in Berlin. Bismarck's neurotic fear of anti-
German coalitions reached a new intensity as the prospect
presented itself to him that the Taaffe government in Austria,
once freed from Andrássy's influence, might complement its

[1] The following works are of particular relevance to this chapter: W. N.
Medlicott, *Bismarck, Gladstone and the Concert of Europe*, London, 1956; W. N.
Medlicott, 'British Foreign Policy in the Near East, from the Congress of
Berlin to the accession of Ferdinand of Coburg', M.A. thesis, London, 1926;
Agatha Ramm, European Alliances and Ententes 1879–85, a study of con-
temporary 'British information', M.A. thesis, London; E. R. v. Rutkowski,
'Gustav Graf Kálnoky von Köröspatak, Oesterreich-Ungarns Aussen-
politik von 1881–1885', Doctoral dissertation, Vienna, 1952; A. F. Pribram,
The Secret Treaties of Austria-Hungary (2 vols), Cambridge, Mass., 1921; L.
Salvatorelli, *La triplice alleanza, storia diplomatica, 1877–1912*, Milan, 1939;
E. R. v. Rutkowski, 'Oesterreich-Ungarn und Rumänien 1880–83, die
Proklamierung des Königreiches und die rumänischen Irredenta', *Südost-
Forschungen*, Vol. 25, 1966, pp. 150–284; E. R. v. Rutkowski, 'General
Skobelev, die Krise des Jahres 1882 und die Anfänge der militärischen
Vereinbarungen zwischen Oesterreich-Ungarn und Deutschland', *Ost-
deutsche Wissenschaft*, Vol. 10, 1963, pp. 81–151; A. F. Pribram, 'Milan IV von
Serbien und die Geheimverträge Oesterreich-Ungarns mit Serbien 1881–9',
Historische Blätter, 1921, pp. 464–94; the works by H. Benedikt, G. Drage,
F. Klein (ed.), and C. A. Macartney cited in Chapter 1, note 1; W. Wagner,
Chapter 2, note 1; and E. v. Glaise-Horstenau, Chapter 3, note 1.

[2] E. R. v. Rutkowski, 'Kálnoky . . .', pp. 645–6.

pro-Slav domestic policy by persuading the emperor to make an alliance with the tsar. Worse still, the clericals might bring in Catholic France as well, to create that combination most deadly to Prussia, a 'Kaunitz' coalition. This was all the more worrying to Bismarck because he was, for the first time, by the summer of 1879, beginning to feel unsure of Russia, even threatened by her. Her constant complaints about relatively trivial incidents arising from the enforcement of the Berlin settlement, her endless armaments, and the hostile language of the Russian press, which since January 1879 had been blaming Germany for all Russia's humiliations, had combined to produce (for a few gloomy months in the summer of 1879 at least) a radical change in Bismarck's attitude towards Russia. Andrássy's idea of an Austro-German alliance, which Bismarck had for years rejected as likely to cause hostility between Russia and Germany, now appeared to him as a possible remedy for a hostility that seemed already to have developed. When, on 15 August, the tsar sent a further list of grievances to his imperial uncle in Berlin, Bismarck took the opportunity to declare that Russia could no longer be relied on; and to familiarize the emperor with the idea of an alliance with Austria-Hungary (both as a source of assistance in the event of war with Russia, and as a means of ensuring that the Dual Monarchy would not join the ranks of Germany's enemies). Already, on 13 August, he had asked Andrássy to meet him at Gastein.

Although at Gastein, on 28 August, Andrássy was not above playing on Bismarck's fears with an astute reference to Austria-Hungary's ties with Britain and France in the Eastern question, Bismarck soon saw that his apprehensions as to a pro-Slav orientation of Austro-Hungarian policy following Andrássy's departure were groundless. Nevertheless, he still wanted some firm guarantee for the future. So he came straight to the point and proposed an Austro-German alliance. What Andrássy had for so long sought in vain was now being offered for the taking; and he was quick to make the most of the psychological advantage he enjoyed over the anxious Bismarck. On the one hand, he welcomed the idea of an alliance: there was now nobody in the Monarchy, he declared, with any desire for revenge for 1866. Even Archduke Albrecht was now no exception – the eyes of the military party had been opened to the danger from Russia in 1878.

Perhaps this was an exaggeration. Of the sincerity of Andrássy's desire for an alliance, however, there can be no doubt. Russia's truculence with regard to the practical application of the Treaty of Berlin, and the news that in February 1879 she had sounded Italy as to her attitude in the event of an Austro-Russian war, showed clearly enough where the chief external threat to the Monarchy lay. On the other hand, Andrássy was determined that any alliance must be on his own terms: it must be directed solely against Russia, and should not in the slightest jeopardize or restrict Austria-Hungary's relations with the Western Powers. Indeed he hoped, as in 1871, that Britain would eventually join the combination. He made it clear to Bismarck, therefore, that the alliance must not be a general one: any suspicion that Austria-Hungary was abetting Germany against France would offend France's friends in London. Bismarck was slightly disappointed at this, but the two statesmen agreed to pursue further the idea of an alliance after consulting their respective sovereigns. Andrássy promised to defer his resignation until the negotiations were completed, and left Gastein 'very contented'[3] to report to the emperor at the Bruck manoeuvres.

He found Franz Joseph entirely in agreement with the idea of an alliance against Russia; and the emperor congratulated him and authorized him to pursue the negotiations further with Bismarck in Vienna. The Emperor William, however, was of a very different frame of mind, his faith in Russia having been but little shaken by Bismarck's gloomy talk. He went off to meet his Russian nephew at Alexandrovo (3 September) and forbade Bismarck to go to Vienna at all. It needed a threat of resignation from Bismarck to get him to change his mind; and even then he refused to consider anything so offensive to Russia as an alliance directed solely and explicitly against her. He authorized Bismarck to conclude an alliance only in general terms.

This was in fact the central point of the Vienna discussions between Bismarck and Andrássy (23–24 September). Andrássy would still not hear of a general alliance: the existing Waddington government in Paris was eminently peaceful, conservative, and Anglophile; but it might not survive the shock of an Austro-German alliance directed apparently against France. The danger might then arise of a revolutionary alliance between France,

[3] E. v. Wertheimer, Vol. 3, p. 244.

Italy, and a Russia already thoroughly riddled with Panslav revolutionary ideas. Nor, he warned, would he have anything to do with an agreement *à trois* with Russia. Again, such a monarchical league would appear to be directed against France. Austria-Hungary, he emphasized, must be free to say to Britain that she had no commitments whatever against France, provided the latter did not join a coalition against the Central Powers. The alliance, therefore, must be clearly directed against Russia. Apart from this reservation, the two sides were already in broad agreement. The Austrians particularly liked the idea of a strictly defensive alliance, considering that the Monarchy had nothing whatever to gain from an aggressive war against Russia, and might only risk being used as a battering ram by the Western Powers. They raised no objections either when Bismarck suggested a declaration to the Powers (and to Russia in particular) emphasizing the conciliatory spirit of the alliance and making its defensive purpose perfectly clear. In the end, Bismarck gave way. 'Accept my draft,' he said to Andrássy, rising from his seat and drawing himself to his full height, '. . . or I shall have to accept yours.'[4] On 24 September the draft was duly agreed, and after a further tussle Bismarck managed to extract the consent of the German emperor.

The alliance was signed at Vienna on 7 October (Document 8), and Andrássy resigned on the following day. He could be well content with his work. The alliance pledged the two Powers to mutual support if either were attacked by Russia; if either were attacked by another Power, the other was obliged to observe benevolent neutrality only; but if the attacker were supported by Russia, the *casus foederis* again arose. These terms suited the Austrians exactly. Yet this was – for both parties – no *ad hoc* war alliance, like the alliances of the 1850s and 1860s. However strictly limited its terms, it might always have broader implications for the general policy of the contracting parties. Such implications had been in Andrássy's mind throughout the 1870s; and perhaps in Bismarck's in the summer of 1879. Franz Joseph too was aware of them, and was pleased at last to have realized his ideal of a conservative alliance of the two German Powers, which he had vainly sought from a hostile Bismarck in the early 'sixties and from an indifferent Bismarck in the early 'seventies. The question remained, however – what were these broader implications?

[4] E. v. Wertheimer, Vol. 3, p. 284.

Despite the unanimity over the terms of the alliance, there was a wide divergence of view between Vienna and Berlin as to its ultimate purpose. True, for the immediate present, both parties could feel more secure against Russia; and Bismarck had dispelled the threat of a 'Kaunitz' coalition – if that threat had ever existed outside his own mind. On the long-term purpose of the alliance, however, there was no agreement. Indeed, even before the alliance was actually signed, Bismarck had begun to think that a conflict with Russia was perhaps not too likely after all. He had been encouraged in this not only by the Emperor William, who refused to contemplate such a possibility, but by the Russians themselves, who, at the news of the impending alliance, had at once become more amenable. The prospect of a war with both German Powers at once confirmed the tsar in his fundamentally pacific intentions. He decided that he would do well to seek a *rapprochement* with his German neighbours – possibly in the hope of dividing them; and hinted to Bismarck that he would welcome a restoration of the Three Emperors' League. This, of course, had always remained Bismarck's ideal. It was also the implication of his boast to the Russian ambassador that in concluding the alliance he had succeeded in digging a ditch between Austria-Hungary and the Western Powers.

Nothing could have been further from the truth. Andrássy had been scrupulously careful in the negotiations to avoid anything that might cast a cloud over his relations with London and Paris; and Salisbury, in particular, had welcomed press reports of the alliance as 'glad tidings of great joy'.[5] For Andrássy, the alliance was to be a step towards the realization of his old ideal of a grand alliance against Russia. For him, in contrast to Bismarck, suspicion of Russia was no passing mood. 'A warmed-up Three Emperors' League', he declared, would meet with great opposition from public opinion; Russia was 'full of perfidy';[6] and after his recent experiences he would hesitate 'not only as a minister but as a gentleman' to recommend an agreement with her on the Eastern question.[7] Whereas the Dual Alliance was for Bismarck a stepping-stone towards a new Three Emperors' League, it was for Andrássy the tombstone of the Three Emperors' League.

[5] *The Times*, p. 10, 18 October 1879.
[6] E. v. Wertheimer, Vol. 3, p. 297.
[7] P.A. I/469, Aehrenthal memorandum, 1895.

Franz Joseph, for whom the construction of a conservative bloc in Central Europe was the essential idea, was more flexible as to whether this could best be reinforced from the west or from the east. It remained an open question, therefore, whether those who came after Andrássy would realize his great objective, or whether they would accept Bismarck's.

There could be no doubt about the personal inclinations of Andrássy's successor, Heinrich, Baron Haymerle. This cautious, unadventurous career diplomat, who had served at Constantinople, Athens, and Rome, and as Andrássy's aide at the Congress of Berlin, was well versed in the details of the Eastern question. The British were hopeful that 'his intimate knowledge of Turkish affairs'[8] would prove a serious obstacle to Russia's supposed designs. 'This,' Beaconsfield confidently declared, 'is an anti-Russian appointment.'[9] By the same token, St Petersburg, where most of Russia's recent humiliations were ascribed to 'expressions insidiously inserted into the Treaty [of Berlin] by Baron Haymerle', was 'very little pleased'.[10] And it was not so much Haymerle's woebegone appearance or nervous manner as his unwillingness to venture into any agreement with Russia that lay behind Bismarck's deprecatory comments on him: 'he is timid, he is not accustomed to high politics, he fears responsibilities'; and behind the notorious jibe attributed to Bismarck, that Haymerle always 'uttered an emphatic "No" three times on waking up in the morning for fear of having undertaken some commitment in his sleep'.[11] From the start, he was determined to continue Andrássy's anti-Russian policy: to stand firm by the Treaty of Berlin, and if possible to enlist British support in forcing Russia to observe it.

The treaty of Berlin had provided Austria-Hungary with a good basis for a strong Balkan policy. Of course, this policy would not be one of territorial expansion – the annexation of more Slav areas could fatally upset the balance of races within the Monarchy – but one of exercising a preponderant influence over the Balkan states. The prospects were inviting. Even in Bulgaria, where Russia temporarily enjoyed by virtue of the Treaty of Berlin a measure of political control over the government and

---

[8] Agatha Ramm, p. 61.   [9] Ibid., p. 86.   [10] Ibid., p. 85.

[11] L. Ritter v. Przibram, *Erinnerungen eines alten Oesterreichers*, Stuttgart, 1912, Vol. 2, p. 114.

army that the Austrians felt it wise not to challenge, Austria-Hungary had preserved a strong foothold in the fields of commerce and communications. By Article VIII of the Treaty of Berlin the Great Powers had subjected Bulgaria to the 'unequal' trade treaties of 1860–2, which were designed to hold Turkey down as a ready market and source of cheap raw materials. Customs duties, for example, were fixed at 10 per cent, and according to the Capitulations could not be increased without the consent of the Powers. Even without these measures, of course, the sheer weight of economic imperialism would in any case have served to hold the Balkan economy in fee to the Great Powers.

Austria-Hungary was the chief beneficiary of this system. Over the Western Powers she had enormous geographical advantages. Proximity and the Danube – which provided cheap transport – meant that Austro-Hungarian exports (chiefly light industrial goods) could easily command the Bulgarian market by virtue of their cheapness; and this despite British competition and the efforts of the Bulgarians to develop their own light industries. Links with Vienna were also fostered by the Austrophile inclinations of the Bulgarian bourgeoisie (whose nationalist susceptibilities were in any case offended by Russian bullying), and by the dominant role of Austro-Hungarian capital in Bulgarian railway construction. In 1879 the Orient Railway Company, which controlled the Bulgarian section of the line to Constantinople, had passed from French to Austro-Hungarian control, and had transferred its headquarters to Vienna. In this situation, Russia found herself completely outmanoeuvred. Such capital as her own very primitive economy could spare generally went to easier markets in Asia; and Russian government intervention in Sofia to compel the Bulgarians to accept loans only roused opposition and undermined Russia's political position in the principality. Both Vienna and St Petersburg recognized the great importance of commercial channels as the conductors of political influence; and although it is true that Bulgaria only accounted for about 6 per cent of the total trade of the Monarchy, this 6 per cent was a huge amount for a state the size of Bulgaria. In fact the Monarchy was able to impose successive renewals of the 'unequal' trade treaty, and to maintain its position as Bulgaria's chief trading partner right down to 1914.

In the other Balkan states the Monarchy was in an even stronger position, in that it did not have a Russian-controlled government to contend with – although it should be said that sometimes, by virtue of its political predominance, it came up against the hostility of that very nationalism that in Bulgaria worked in its favour. The coldly-calculating governments, however, in Turkey, Serbia, Roumania and Greece were still very much haunted by the shadow of the Big Bulgaria created by Russia at San Stefano. They had no doubts as to where their chief enemy lay. Turkey, for example, was already looking to the Central Powers to supply the financial and military-technical aid no longer forthcoming from Britain. Even in Serbia, the government of the Liberal Ristić, pro-Russian by instinct, was now faced with the task of bringing to fulfilment that *rapprochement* with Austria-Hungary over commercial and communications questions on which Serbia, deserted by Russia, had been forced to embark at the Congress of Berlin. In the event, Ristić dragged his feet. He well knew that Serbian opinion had not forgiven the Monarchy for the occupation of Bosnia and the Herzegovina; and that the taxes required to pay for the projected railway links would be deeply resented by his peasant supporters. His resistance was encouraged by Russian agents, and, to some extent, by Britain, who still provided Serbia with one-third of her imports, and who strengthened her negotiating position with a commercial treaty in January 1880. By the summer, however, the Monarchy had forced Serbia to agree to construct the railway line to Hungary before that to Salonica (which would only have furthered British trade). In June Prince Milan, fanatically Austrophile by temperament, paid a visit of homage to Franz Joseph in Vienna; and when Ristić, greatly incensed by this, at last resigned in October, Serbia seemed to be moving completely into Austria-Hungary's orbit.

Roumania presented a similar picture, with fairly strong Austro-Hungarian political influence and nationalist and irre-dentist counter-currents. On the one hand, Austria-Hungary had been the first Great Power to recognize the independence of Roumania in 1878 (while Germany and the Western Powers were still haggling over the treatment of German bondholders and Roumanian Jews). Both Vienna and Bucharest recognized a common interest in ensuring that Roumania, situated 'entre les deux Russies' as Bratianu remarked,[12] should not become a mere

[12] E. R. v. Rutkowski, 'Oesterreich-Ungarn und Rumänien', p. 151.

highway from Russia to Bulgaria. A visit by Archduke Albrecht to Bucharest in the autumn of 1879 had produced a general understanding about mutual military assistance in the event of a Russian attack; and Haymerle agreed with Andrássy and Prince Carol that the two states, which together formed a major barrier to the Slavicization of south-east Europe, might some day even make a formal alliance. On the other hand, Haymerle was as resolutely opposed as Andrássy had been to Roumania's hopes of elevation to the rank of kingdom. Such a grandiose gesture could only foster irredentist designs on Transylvania and Bukovina, and encourage similar ambitions in Serbia. More serious, the two governments themselves became estranged over the question of the control of shipping on the lower Danube, which the Congress of Berlin had entrusted to a commission to be established by the Great Powers. For Austria-Hungary, the Danube was still the main commercial route to the Balkans; the Austrian Danube Steamship Company held a virtual monopoly of Danubian shipping; and Haymerle was determined not to permit the subjection of these important interests to control by any Balkan state. In January 1880, therefore, with German and Italian support, he began to seek for Austria-Hungary a controlling influence on the new commission. The Roumanians, with Russian support, were equally determined to prevent this, and by the summer relations between Vienna and Bucharest were seriously strained.

Austria-Hungary's Balkan position in 1879–80 was, therefore, strong but not unchallenged. And behind the threats to it, Vienna discerned everywhere the hand of Russia. Indeed, while Austro-Hungarian policy might be seen objectively, and especially by Russia, as aiming at predominance, it was regarded in Vienna as defensive, as an attempt to prevent Russia from establishing her own predominance. True, Kálnoky reported from St Petersburg, the Russian government, confronted with the Dual Alliance, might well have decided to abandon its blatant opposition to the Treaty of Berlin. This, however, by lulling the other Powers into a false sense of security, only made it all the more difficult for the Monarchy to thwart the now more underhand designs of Russia, which were still being busily furthered by Russian agents and the Russian press. It was to be Haymerle's task to sound the alarm.

With Bismarck, Haymerle made no headway at all. His suggestions in the autumn of 1879 that the Central Powers enlist the support of Britain, as Andrássy had desired, only drew the crushing retort that the alliance was strictly for defence purposes, and was not designed to support any particular policy in the Balkans whatever. In January 1880, following an irredentist demonstration in Italy,[13] Haymerle tried another approach. It seems, according to a memorandum of Beck's of March 1880,[14] that the Austro-Hungarian government was at this time seriously worried about the possibility of a 'revolutionary' alliance between Italy, France, and a potentially nihilist Russia. At any rate, on 7 February, Haymerle sent Kálnoky to see Bismarck and to convince him of the need to treat Italy kindly.[15] The Monarchy could gain nothing by war with Italy – indeed, this might only present Russia with the opportunity to resume an adventurous policy. Perhaps Britain could be persuaded to restrain Italy, Haymerle suggested, and even to join the Central Powers in a bloc so formidable that Russia would never dare to challenge it. A Roumanian alliance would also be useful. Bismarck would have none of this. True, he wished to maintain the alliance with Austria-Hungary; but at the same time he was immensely concerned to hold on to Russia. The latter, he told Vienna, was now suffering from a nightmare of coalitions, and should be comforted and reassured. Ramshackle Italy could be kept in order by threatening language; and as for Britain, who was gratuitously provoking Russia, her isolation was the price to be paid for Russian friendship.

The Austrians, for their part, were unmoved by Bismarck's arguments. They might be prepared to discuss the occasional specific issue, such as Bulgaria, with Russia; but there was no basis for any habitual *tête-à-tête* or general agreement. This would be tantamount to a revival of the Three Emperors' League, which, Haymerle maintained, nobody in the Monarchy desired, and which Hungarian opinion would never permit. The emperor agreed. When the military attaché at St Petersburg reported on 21 April that the Russian press was full of talk of Russia's Slav mission; that official assurances were worthless in the face of such mighty currents of opinion; and that 'the sooner people admit this and stop deceiving themselves' about Russia the better, Franz Joseph minuted 'very sound assessment' (*Sehr richtige Auffas-*

[13] See below, p. 130–1.
[14] E. v. Glaise-Horstenau, p. 247.
[15] Kab. 18, Haymerle, report to Franz Joseph, 7 February 1880.

sung).[16] Besides, Bismarck's startling change of front with regard to Russia since the summer was in itself enough to make Vienna mistrustful. Haymerle decided, therefore, that 'so long as our interests in the Near East are so closely parallel with those of the English, we should be unwise to abandon England.'[17]

Nor did Haymerle allow personal factors to weaken his determination to follow the path dictated by Austro-Hungarian state interests. For example, Gladstone's return to office in Britain in April 1880 might have been a serious obstacle. In January, Franz Joseph had remarked to the British ambassador that 'it would be difficult to feel confidence in the maintenance of the present relations if he returned to power';[18] and during the British election campaign a similar remark was attributed to the emperor by the Viennese press. Gladstone retorted on 17 March with a public denunciation of Austrian interference in British internal affairs, took the opportunity of demanding an end to Beaconsfield's 'Austrian foreign policy', and went on to make a very famous statement: 'there is not an instance, there is not a spot upon the whole map where you can lay your finger and say, "There Austria did good".'[19] At this the Austro-Hungarian ambassador in London, Károlyi, talked of resigning if Gladstone came to power. In the event, however, tactful handling of the incident by diplomats in Vienna and London smoothed matters over, and even created what Haymerle was pleased to call 'an entirely satisfactory starting point for our new relations'.[20] He turned a deaf ear to Bismarck who, secretly afraid that Gladstone's anti-Turkish views might tempt Russia and weaken her desire to restore the Three Emperors' League, tried naïvely to convince Vienna that Gladstone was a dangerous revolutionary. Indeed, in April, he rejected yet another German proposal for an agreement with Russia precisely because – by enforcing the closure of the Straits to protect Russia from the British fleet, for example – it would alienate Britain. Haymerle remained determined to co-operate with Gladstone in executing the Treaty of Berlin.

[16] W. Wagner, p. 123.
[17] W. N. Medlicott, *Bismarck, Gladstone and the Concert of Europe*, p. 52.
[18] Agatha Ramm, p. 145.
[19] W. E. Gladstone, *Political Speeches in Scotland (1880)*, Vol. 2, p. 41.
[20] W. N. Medlicott, *Bismarck, Gladstone . . .*, p. 62.

He was to be disappointed. The settlement of the outstanding issues inherited from the Congress of Berlin – the delimitation of the Greek and Montenegrin frontiers – was in itself a tedious and exasperating problem which was to put the solidarity of the Great Powers to a severe test. For on both questions the Powers were faced with stubborn Turkish opposition; and in the Montenegrin case with local Albanian armed resistance. Not only this, Haymerle soon began to doubt whether Austro-Hungarian interests were best served by abetting Britain in what was tending to become an increasingly anti-Turkish policy, and one which Russian backing made even more suspect. For example, on a practical level, he disliked the readiness of the other Powers to subject still more Albanians to Montenegrin rule. Already in 1878 the Austrians had seen in the spirited Albanian protests to the Congress evidence of a potentially useful barrier against the complete slavicization of the Balkans. At the same time, they wondered whether the pro-Christian Gladstone would show an equal devotion to international law if it came to maintaining the sultan's rights in Bulgaria and Eastern Roumelia against a Russian attempt to unite the principality and the province. More generally, and more serious, Haymerle had grave misgivings about the whole policy of coercion, to which the Powers, having exhausted their repertoire of paper condemnations of Turkey, were being steered by Britain and Russia in the summer of 1880. Not only might naval and military action bring British, and even Russian, forces to the shores of the Adriatic (which Vienna regarded as an Austro-Hungarian preserve); it might well provoke serious disturbances in Turkey, even her total collapse, with all the attendant risks of war. This the Austro-Hungarian press was not slow to point out; and by October Haymerle was wondering whether the moment had not come 'to administer a clear and effective diplomatic rebuff (*Schlappe*) to Mr Gladstone'[21] by coming out openly in opposition to further coercion. Since the late summer he had been coming to the conclusion that his pro-British policy had been a dangerous mistake; and that there was perhaps something to be said for a cautious approach to Russia.

It was in this frame of mind that Haymerle sought out Bismarck at Friedrichsruh (4–5 September). Of course, he still wished to base his policy on the maintenance of the Treaty of

[21] Kab. 18, Haymerle, report to Franz Joseph, 4 October 1880.

Berlin; but at the same time he recognized that certain developments – for example the union of Bulgaria and Eastern Roumelia – might occur of their own momentum, and Austria-Hungary would be powerless to prevent them. To this extent, therefore, he recognized 'the advantages of standing well with Russia, particularly since England is so actively trying to undermine Turkey and can no longer be counted on'.[22] From St Petersburg, Kálnoky gave him strong support: Russia had probably already squared Britain on the Bulgarian question; Austria-Hungary, therefore, might do well to come to some agreement with St Petersburg to secure her own interests, especially her supremacy in Serbia, so necessary for the security of Bosnia and Herzegovina. The latter, Kálnoky thought, might well be formally annexed. At Friedrichsruh Haymerle found Bismarck enthusiastic: indeed, he had already sounded the Russians, and he now suggested to Haymerle immediate tripartite negotiations with the Russian ambassador Saburov, for an agreement to give Russia security at the Straits (by maintaining their closure against Britain) and, in return for the union of the two Bulgarias, offering the Monarchy a free hand to annex Bosnia and the Herzegovina.

Haymerle thought such a definite proposal premature, and fobbed Bismarck off with the excuse that he would first have to seek Franz Joseph's instructions. Nevertheless, the Friedrichsruh meeting marked a decisive development in Austro-Hungarian policy in so far as Haymerle now agreed in principle to look into the possibilities of agreement with Russia. As he explained to the emperor,[23] it was a question of safeguarding Austro-Hungarian interests in view of Britain's unreliability and the Monarchy's consequent inability to prevent the union of the two Bulgarias. He did not wish to make an approach to Russia himself at this stage: the Delegations were about to meet in Hungary, and he wished to say that he had his hands free. Perhaps rather naïvely, therefore, he entrusted Bismarck with the task of sounding the terrain at St Petersburg and preparing a draft agreement. At the same time, however, he was careful to spell out to Bismarck the

[22] W. N. Medlicott, *Bismarck, Gladstone* . . ., p. 180.

[23] Kab. 18, Haymerle, report to Franz Joseph, 9 September 1880. The full text of Haymerle's reports to Franz Joseph on the Friedrichsruh meeting is in W. N. Medlicott, 'Bismarck und Haymerle: Ein Gespräch über Russland', *Berliner Monatshefte*, November 1940, pp. 719–29.

particular Austro-Hungarian interests which any agreement must safeguard. The union of the two Bulgarias must come about naturally, and not at Russia's instigation or behest; nor must it lead to further Bulgarian expansion into Macedonia, where the Monarchy had interests of its own; nor must it be seen as a condition of Austria-Hungary's annexing Bosnia and the Herzegovina – Russia had already agreed to that in 1877. The Dual Alliance must be in no sense weakened. Indeed, it should be strengthened – there should be some guarantee of Roumania's security against a Russian attack. Finally, Russia must cease to oppose Austro-Hungarian influence in Serbia. What Haymerle was in fact demanding – and his elaboration of Austro-Hungarian interests in his letters to Kálnoky in December make this clear[24] – was the predominance of Austro-Hungarian influence in Roumania and the Western Balkans (by forcing Russia to recognize the intangible advantages gained by the Monarchy at the Congress of Berlin) and also a fair measure of influence in Bulgaria. For example, a union of the two Bulgarias was not to impinge on Austria-Hungary's interests in railways and commerce there: these were to be guaranteed. It was indeed sanguine of Haymerle to suppose that Bismarck would seriously press this policy at St Petersburg.

Of course Bismarck, for whom the negotiations were primarily a means of making sure of Russia, did no such thing – as the Austrians were dismayed to discover when they received the Russo-German draft treaty on 23 January 1881. True, William I tried to sugar the pill, pointing to the desirability of cultivating the conservative elements in St Petersburg; and Franz Joseph was in fact impressed by his argument that a treaty would demonstrate to anarchical elements in Europe that monarchical solidarity could survive political differences. Nevertheless, the Russo-German draft caused the gravest misgivings in Vienna. First, it provided for the mediation of the third contracting party in the event of a dispute between the other two. This the Austrians feared might some day be used by Bismarck to escape from his obligations under the Dual Alliance – if, for example, Austria-Hungary felt obliged to reject the decision of mediators in Berlin. Worse still, on the point of Bosnia, Russia promised merely to accept the *status quo* as defined in the Austro-Turkish convention of 1879, i.e. considerably less than the eventual annexation she had agreed

[24] W. N. Medlicott, *Bismarck, Gladstone* . . ., pp. 254–7.

to in 1877. Franz Joseph and Haymerle were quick to object to this; and they again emphasized that the Dual Alliance must in no circumstances be weakened or watered down by the admission of a third party (as the mediation clause implied). They even went on to demand (and Beck was most emphatic on this point) that Austria-Hungary should have an absolute veto on the entry of Russian troops into Roumania, a state of vital strategic importance to the Monarchy; and that the Dual Alliance be extended to cover the case of a threat not only to Austria-Hungary's territory, but to her military capacity (*Kriegsmacht*) – such as would arise from a Russian occupation of Roumania. Bismarck, however, would not consider extending the *casus foederis* to Roumania; and his counter-proposal of a blanket clause making the military occupation of any Balkan state dependent on the consent of the other two partners in the alliance was rejected out of hand by Haymerle: Austria-Hungary could never sign such a clause, which would completely bind her hands in her dealings with her south Slav neighbours. Throughout February the deadlock continued.

The Austro-Hungarian counter-draft of 3 March omitted both the mediation clause and a clause on the closure of the Straits; and demanded a free hand in Bosnia, the Herzegovina, and also in the Sanjak. At the same time, the Roumanian point was now abandoned, and on the whole the reply went a considerable way towards meeting the Russo-German draft. The Austrians were certainly beginning to retreat from their extreme position of December. In the first place, the diplomatic situation had shown no sign of any change in their favour: the deadlock between Greece and Turkey, with its attendant risks that Britain might drag Russia along the path of violent coercion, was not resolved until the Turks suddenly surrendered in March. Second, Bismarck, while with one hand offering Vienna the sop of a formal statement that the Dual Alliance retained its full force, wielded the big stick with the other: on 1 March he informed Vienna that if the negotiations failed, it would be his painful duty to tell St Petersburg who was to blame. Third, the role of Kálnoky, since January promoted to permanent ambassador at St Petersburg, must be emphasized. According to a later account of Aehrenthal, who knew Kálnoky intimately, this was of the greatest importance, and undoubtedly influenced Haymerle's decisions.[25]

[25] P.A. I/469, Aehrenthal memorandum, 1895.

The emperor too was a great admirer of the ambassador's dispatches. The case for co-existence with Russia was strongly urged in a dispatch from Kálnoky on 18 February:[26] the Monarchy was simply too weak to implement the only feasible alternative policy of hurling Russia back into Asia for ever; and perhaps the present moment was the least unfavourable and should not be allowed to slip. For Russia was temporarily reasonable (having been weakened by a disastrous harvest in 1880); and whereas negotiations *à deux* would be dangerous for Austria-Hungary as the weaker party, she might do well to negotiate at a time when she could count on the backing of Germany by virtue of the Dual Alliance (Document 9).

If the Austrians really set any store by this latter consideration, they were greatly in error. The subsequent negotiations saw one Austro-Hungarian retreat after another, and all accomplished under brutal pressure from Bismarck himself. The Russians were determined to secure a formal reaffirmation of the principle of the closure of the Straits, but at the same time refused to give Austria-Hungary a free hand in the Sanjak (after all they had in 1878 consented only to its eventual occupation, not annexation). They played their cards well. The assassination of Alexander II on 13 March presented them with an admirable opportunity to delay the negotiations; and they kept the Central Powers on tenterhooks for three silent weeks. They rightly calculated that Bismarck would lose his nerve and put pressure on Vienna. True, the new tsar professed his devotion to his father's policy; but this also included a filial devotion to the original Russo-German draft. Moreover, the situation in St Petersburg was genuinely uncertain: the appointment of Ignatiev as minister of the interior was an ominous sign; and Kálnoky began to wonder how long the conservative Giers would retain any influence at the foreign office. In this situation, Bismarck bullied the Austrians mercilessly, threatening in April to conclude a treaty with Russia without them. During May Haymerle gradually gave way on all points except the right to annex Bosnia, the Herzegovina, and the Sanjak. This should not only be recognized, but recognized in the body of the treaty, as a *quid pro quo* for the Straits clause. Bismarck, surprised at the extent of Haymerle's concessions, promised his support; but when the Russians still held out, he again

[26] Ibid.

abandoned Austria-Hungary. After another appeal from Kálnoky, pointing to the uncertainty of the situation in Russia – the relatively well-disposed Alexander III might at any moment suffer the fate of his father – and another formal summons to surrender from Bismarck, the exasperated Haymerle again gave way. The eventual annexation of Bosnia and the Herzegovina ended up in an annexe, and as for the Sanjak, Russia merely reaffirmed her promise of 13 July 1878 to countenance an Austro-Hungarian occupation.

Nevertheless, considering the diplomatic isolation of Austria-Hungary, and the extent to which her expectations of German support had even turned against her, the Three Emperors' Alliance, signed in Vienna on 18 June (Document 10), was by no means an unmitigated defeat. The reinforcement of monarchical solidarity and of peace between the three empires expressed in the preamble was more than mere phrases. True, Austro-Hungarian and German support for a Russian circular of 31 March proposing an international conference on revolutionary plots, made little headway against the opposition of Britain, France, and Italy. But if the treaty gave the Russian government a breathing space to re-establish itself after the assassination of the tsar, it was also designed to give the new order of things in Bosnia and the Herzegovina time to consolidate itself. Indeed, it may well have been a contributory factor to the firm stand taken by the Austro-Hungarian government against anti-monarchical elements generally in the early 1880s. For example, a spate of assassinations of officials between 1882 and 1884 was met with great severity: anarchists in the Monarchy saw their newspapers suppressed and their societies dissolved; and they lost their right to trial by jury.

Even from a purely diplomatic point of view, the Austrians had not done too badly. The Dual Alliance had been formally declared to have survived unimpaired (18 May); and the obnoxious mediation clause had disappeared without trace. The main clauses of the treaty actually brought some positive advantages. True, Article III, endorsing the principle of the closure of the Straits was a pure gain for Russia; but the sense of Article I at least gave Austria-Hungary rear cover against Italy in exchange for her promise of benevolent neutrality in the event of Franco-German or Anglo-Russian wars. Article II, concerning the principles of action in the Balkans (spelt out in more concrete terms in an annexed protocol) really only dealt with developments that were in any case regarded as inevitable. And if the Austrians had had to rest content with a mere reaffirmation of existing Russian pledges regarding Bosnia, the Herzegovina, and the Sanjak, they had at least brought Russia to recognize Austro-Hungarian interests in Bulgaria: the union was not to be hastened, nor was it to be extended into Macedonia. Haymerle had been careful to exclude the slightest hint of a division of the Balkans into Austro-Hungarian and Russian spheres of interest, such as would have abandoned Bulgaria to Russia (not that the latter would have been prepared to hand over Serbia and Montenegro to exclusive Austro-Hungarian control either). Thus, if the Austrians had perhaps achieved little in the way of positive gains, they had also given virtually nothing away.

Indeed, the very fact that the treaty said in effect so little, and placed no restriction whatever on the development of Austro-Hungarian influence, particularly economic influence, was a major advantage in Austro-Hungarian eyes; and one which the Monarchy intended to exploit. More than this, though Russia might not have pledged herself not to invade Roumania, Austria-Hungary had retained an equally free hand to coerce Serbia or Montenegro. Further, whereas the renunciation by the three contracting parties of their freedom of military action against Turkey (and Bulgaria was technically still part of Turkey) was an important sacrifice for Russia to make, it cost Austria-Hungary, who had no designs on Turkey or Bulgaria anyway, very little. The Monarchy's Balkan position was therefore at least no weaker after the Three Emperors' Alliance Treaty than before. Indeed, by the joint instructions to Russian and Austro-Hungarian representatives in the Balkans, drawn up supplementary to the treaty in the course of the summer, and ordering them to co-operate and refrain from intriguing against each other, impecunious Russia had renounced what was perhaps her only effective weapon to counter the extension of Austro-Hungarian influence by means of trade. How far Russian diplomats on the spot would in fact obey the joint instructions and abstain from fanning the flames of local nationalism against Austria-Hungary, particularly in Serbia and Roumania, was of course a moot point which no treaty could settle. Nevertheless, in some respects, the prospects for Austria-Hungary had undoubtedly improved.

So confident were the Austrians in fact that they even connived at a slight increase in Russia's political influence in Bulgaria in the summer of 1881. True, they hoped to see even Bulgaria in the Austro-Hungarian camp in the long run, and took good care to cultivate the Prince, Alexander of Battenberg. But for the present they busied themselves with their railway projects and did not attempt to challenge Russia's political supremacy at Sofia. This, they tended to regard as something of a necessary evil, if Alexander were to survive in the turbulent domestic politics of the principality. In July, therefore, Austria-Hungary became the spokesman of the Three Emperors' Alliance in bringing a reluctant Gladstone to accept a Russian-inspired authoritarian constitution to replace the unworkable liberal one granted to Bulgaria in 1879. True, the Austrians here formally abandoned the policy pursued since 1878 of co-operation with Britain to check Russian influence in Bulgaria. Yet Haymerle was perhaps only renouncing a policy inherited from Beaconsfield and Andrássy, which Gladstone was highly unlikely to enforce. (Much the same may be said of Haymerle's conversion to the principle of the closure of the Straits.) Indeed, the one thing on which all members of the Three Emperors' Alliance were agreed was the exclusion of Gladstone's influence from the Near East. This applied not only to the sultan's Christian dominions in Europe, where all three sought only to preserve peace, if not quiet; and to Egypt, where, in the face of British and French meddling in 1881 and 1882, all three paraded their scrupulous regard for the sultan's rights in an effort to ingratiate themselves at Constantinople; but also to Bulgaria and Serbia, where Austria-Hungary in particular was irritated by British commercial competition. In the latter principality, Haymerle had just brought off something of a *coup*.

The replacement of Ristić and the Liberals by the Progressives – the party of Prince Milan – in October 1880, had provided no immediate solution to the issues pending between Serbia and the Monarchy – the construction of the railway links agreed with Andrássy at the Congress of Berlin, and the negotiation of a commercial treaty. The first was delayed partly by the Austrian government, which until the autumn of 1880 refused to pay anything towards the cost of a line which would be built entirely in Hungary; and partly by the Serbs, who in the spring of 1881 were still toying with the idea of entrusting their section of the line to Constantinople to a British firm. As for the commercial treaty, when negotiations began in November 1880, even the Progressive government jibbed at what the British minister – admittedly an interested observer – described as Austria-Hungary's 'monstrous pretensions'.[27] By the early summer, however, these issues had been settled: the Serbian government placed the railway contract with the Union Générale, a French Catholic-monarchist bank with Austro-Hungarian affiliations; and further agreed to standardize Serbian railway rates with those of the Monarchy (to prevent under-selling by British and French wares coming through Turkey from Salonica). The Austrians for their part had already agreed not to ask Serbia for any money towards the clearance works they were undertaking on the Danube. Finally, on 6 June 1881 a commercial treaty was signed admitting Serbian livestock and agricultural produce into the Monarchy on favourable terms and securing the Serbian market for Austrian light industry.

The commercial treaty was followed by a secret political treaty, negotiated by Prince Milan in person during a visit to Vienna in June (Document 11). As Milan saw the situation, Serbia, deserted by Russia at San Stefano, and estranged from her fellow Balkan states by the vexed question of the eventual partition of Macedonia, needed the support of Austria-Hungary; just as Milan needed it to free himself from the pro-Russian Liberal and Radical parties. The treaty of 28 June 1881 provided for Austro-Hungarian diplomatic support, should Serbia declare herself a kingdom, and should she seek territory in the south in the event of the collapse of Turkish rule in Macedonia. Serbia, for her part, was to abandon hope of gaining the Sanjak or the occupied provinces. Indeed, she was obliged not to tolerate on Serbian soil any intrigues against the Monarchy, Bosnia, or the Herzegovina. More than this, by Article IV – which Haymerle regarded as 'our greatest achievement'[28] – Milan bound himself to conclude no further treaties whatever without prior agreement with Vienna. This last was too much even for the Progressive government in Belgrade, who foretold their own ruin and the return of the Russophiles to power if ever the treaty leaked out. In the end, the

27 Agatha Ramm, p. 371.
28 A. F. Pribram, 'Milan IV von Serbien . . .', p. 471.

article was watered down; but Milan gave the Austrians a personal assurance which in effect maintained it in its original vigour.

The difficulty was that the treaty, and indeed the whole position of Austria-Hungary in Serbia, stood and fell with Prince Milan. The treaty had no roots in the wishes of the Serbian population; and Austro-Hungarian propaganda could never hope seriously to compete with that of Russia, which could harp on the enslavement of Bosnia and the Herzegovina. The best hope for the Austrians was to emphasize mutually beneficial commercial links (if agrarian Hungary could be persuaded to take a benevolent view of Serbian competition in the internal markets of the Monarchy), and to keep the population of Bosnia and the Herzegovina happy. Even this – admittedly a forlorn hope against such an inherently irrational phenomenon as nationalism – was in the long run to prove beyond the capacity of Vienna and Budapest. For the present, however, given that Milan was still in control in Belgrade, the Austrians had managed to reinforce their Balkan position with a guarantee that Serbia would neither go over to Russia, nor revive the plans of Prince Michael for a Balkan League.

Only in Roumania did the Austrians make no progress. When, in February 1881, the Roumanians sounded the Central Powers about the possibility of declaring the principality a kingdom, Haymerle maintained his opposition. But he could see that no other Power would help to restrain Bucharest; and so he prepared to make Austro-Hungarian recognition dependent on Roumania's giving way in the Danube question and binding herself in general terms to the Monarchy. The Roumanians, however, got wind of his plans and decided – especially in view of rumours of an impending Three Emperors' Alliance which might freeze the Balkan situation – to rush the proclamation through in March. (It had originally been planned for May.) Haymerle had been made to look rather silly; and in the end he had to join the Russians and Germans in recognizing the new kingdom unconditionally. Worse still, as he and Andrássy had feared, the proclamation did indeed give a boost to Roumanian irredentism. A wave of demonstrations and spectacular excursions to and from Transylvania resulted by August in a veritable press war between Hungary and Roumania. To complete Haymerle's discomfiture, the other Powers had rejected his project for the Danube Commission, and it was left to the French to prepare another.

Yet despite this setback in Roumania, Haymerle had managed to build fairly successfully on the foundations laid by Andrássy at Berlin. And he had surpassed Andrássy by establishing tolerable relations with Russia at the same time. The German ambassador had reported on 14 June that the negotiations over the Three Emperors' Alliance had 'not increased Austria's love for Russia. I am speaking not only of Haymerle, but also of the emperor and Andrássy, who will not easily forget that the Russians would have preferred to leave Bosnia and the Herzegovina out of the treaty altogether' (*herauseskamotiert*).[29] But in fact, for the rest of 1881 the new Alliance enjoyed a honeymoon. Personal relations between the emperors improved. Franz Joseph saw William I every summer after this; and he warmly approved of the Russo-German Danzig meeting, where the socialist menace was discussed. In an affectionate exchange of telegrams with Alexander III he spoke of his unity with the tsar in the struggle 'contre les dangers qui menacent l'ordre social et qui sapent la civilisation chrétienne'.[30]

Changes of personnel in Vienna reinforced this conservative trinity. On 11 June Beck was appointed chief of the Austro-Hungarian general staff. This was partly because he had found favour with the emperor in fourteen years of personal service as head of the military chancellery; also because it was hoped that he would carry out effectively the reforms of army organization he had so often recommended – and this in fact he did, reorganizing the general staff along more efficient Prussian lines. It was also a political appointment, however, for Beck had long urged that the chief of the general staff be responsible, not to the war minister and the Delegations, but directly to the emperor – another Prussian idea. His wish was now granted, and the lamentations of the liberal press about the 'reactionary' nature of the appointment, and the whittling away of parliamentary control over a major element in the state, were loud. They were not without foundation. For Beck was certainly a staunch conserva-

---

[29] W. Windelband, *Bismarck und die europäischen Grossmächte 1879–85*, Essen, 2nd edn, 1942, p. 277.

[30] P.A. I/469, Aehrenthal memorandum, 1895.

tive – he got on very well with the Inspector General, Archduke Albrecht – and in foreign affairs too he was an appropriate herald of the signature of the Three Emperors' Alliance on 18 June. True, he was anxious that the Monarchy should be fully prepared for war; but he was equally anxious to prevent such a catastrophe for the conservative order by finding a *modus vivendi* with Russia. Five months later the drift to strict conservatism was further emphasized by a change at the Ballhausplatz. Haymerle died of a heart attack in the foreign office on 2 October, the second anniversary of his appointment. In the haste to find a successor, Andrássy was considered, but he could not bring himself, as a liberal, to work with Taaffe and Beck, whom Franz Joseph was determined to keep. The range of talent available was limited: Károlyi had no wish to move from the London embassy to the Ballhausplatz; Kállay, Haymerle's under-secretary and a brilliant expert in Bosnian affairs, had had too little experience as a diplomat; so the emperor's choice finally fell on the ambassador at St Petersburg.

Gustav, Count Kálnoky was born in 1832 of a German Moravian family which had emigrated from Transylvania in the eighteenth century – hence the deceptively Hungarian name. Having spent his early years as a cavalry officer, he always retained a stiff, military manner and, like Bismarck, preferred to wear uniform for portraits and photographs.[31] According to Lützow,[32] most people, especially younger diplomats, dreaded having this dry, reserved man as a neighbour at table; and as his brother reminded Aehrenthal, he was always a severe judge of a diplomat's wife.[33] Entering the foreign service in 1854 he served in Munich and Berlin; and from 1860 to 1870 in London where, confronted with Palmerston's flounderings and Stanley's hesitations, he acquired a deep and lasting mistrust of parliamentary foreign policy. In 1870 he was appointed to the Vatican; but, as a devout clerical he soon quarrelled with Andrássy, who would do nothing to help the Pope, and he left the service for two years in 1872. After a spell in Copenhagen, he was appointed temporary ambassador to relieve the sick Langenau at St Petersburg in 1879. But although he was a success – particularly, as a military man with Alexander II – Andrássy would not hear of making

[31] H. Kanner, p. 4.   [32] P. Hohenbalken (ed.), *Lützow*, p. 75.
[33] Aehrenthal MSS., Karton 2, Hugo Kálnoky to Aehrenthal, July 1902.

him permanent ambassador. Kálnoky, for his part, was not ambitious. When the emperor offered him the foreign office he twice refused. For he felt the post demanded someone with parliamentary connexions – it was impossible for a mere diplomat to cope with the politics of Austria, let alone those of Hungary, which so often impinged on foreign policy (Document 12). The Monarchy really needed a chancellor on the German model, he said. But in the end he accepted the appointment, on 20 November, and took over the foreign office from Kállay on 10 December.

The new appointment did not portend any drastic changes in policy. Kálnoky had worked well enough with Haymerle, and shared his concept of the Three Emperors' Alliance as a means of securing Austro-Hungarian interests by agreement with St Petersburg. His experience in Russia had strengthened his conviction that war with that Power could never bring gains sufficient to compensate for the destruction and misery it would cause – indeed, so much so that perhaps under Kálnoky a slight change of emphasis can be discerned in Austro-Hungarian foreign policy. Whereas Andrássy and Haymerle had both had an instinctively 'western' orientation – although diplomatic facts had worked against them in the end – with Kálnoky there was to be more emphasis on the need for the three eastern empires to stand together against the revolution, and of course against the midwife of revolution, war. Kálnoky was sometimes prepared to pursue this policy at a cost to Austria-Hungary's freedom of action, and even state interests, that horrified Andrássy. But with the full support of Taaffe and his aristocratic, clerical and Slav satellites, Kálnoky was not usually unduly perturbed by Magyar opposition. The British ambassador's assessment of him was fair enough: 'he clings to the alliance with Bismarck and to the Dreikaiserbund'.[34]

The Three Emperors' Alliance proved well worth clinging to in the first crisis with which Kálnoky was confronted – the Bosnian revolt of 1881–2. This arose from the government's decision to impose conscription in the occupied provinces – technically an encroachment beyond the powers accorded to it by the Treaty of Berlin – and to enforce the existing conscription law for south Dalmatia (suspended since the rebellion of 1869). The government had so far done nothing to win over the Christians of Bosnia

[34] Agatha Ramm, p. 250.

and the Herzegovina, who had hoped that the occupation would at least be followed by some land reform; nor had its inactivity on this point conciliated the Moslem landowners, who chafed under the loss of the political freedom they had enjoyed under Turkish rule. In November 1881 the discontent exploded into armed rebellion, to which the government's initial response, as in 1869, was inadequate – although it should be said that fighting conditions in the severe winter of 1881–2 were exceptionally unfavourable. Only in March 1882, after prolonged and difficult operations – some of them in snow chest-deep – was order restored. In the meantime, the revolt had raised acute problems.

On the domestic front, the argument was heard again that so long as Turkey was sovereign over the provinces, they would never settle down – an argument which Kálnoky himself had formerly urged on the cautious Haymerle. Against this, Károlyi reported from London that Gladstone, who had only swallowed the conscription laws with some difficulty, would certainly make a fuss if the Monarchy proceeded to annex the provinces. A Vienna foreign office memorandum of April 1882 added the objection that the annexation would be costly; and repeated Andrássy's argument that Turkey was the best possible neighbour for Austria-Hungary, who would have time enough to annex the provinces if Turkey should ever disappear.[35] Kálnoky, however, decided to look into the possibility of annexation, and was supported by Kállay, an ardent proponent of annexation as a preliminary to a thoroughgoing reform of Bosnian law. A conference of ministers of 3 June[36] made no progress on the thorny problem of the ultimate destination of the provinces within the Dual Monarchy; but Kálnoky and Kállay went ahead and in October drew up a draft annexation law, putting the provinces directly under the emperor. In the face of violent Hungarian objections to anything smacking of Trialism this project had come to nothing by January 1883.

There were also weighty external obstacles to it. Kálnoky had been unable to get much sense out of Constantinople, where chaos reigned in high places at the end of 1882; the Russian government might be bound hand and foot by the Three Emperors' Alliance, but Russian public opinion was a very different matter – it would certainly become enraged, and might even force the government

[35] E. R. v. Rutkowski, 'Kálnoky . . .', pp. 203–9. [36] Ibid., pp. 210–18.

to precipitate a union of the two Bulgarias to recoup Russian prestige; Britain, and probably France, would be hostile; and Prince Milan had told Kálnoky straight out that although he personally would be well disposed, the annexation of the provinces would rouse Serbian feeling to a frenzy and certainly cost him his throne. In view of the difficulties, Kálnoky retreated. Perhaps an opportunity had been missed: Russia's binding commitment was valuable and should perhaps have been exploited while it still held. On the other hand, it was hardly unreasonable in 1882 to hope that the future might produce a rather more favourable situation.

Externally, the Bosnian revolt raised the problems of preventing foreign intervention and of maintaining good relations with Russia, both of which were fairly satisfactorily solved thanks to the forbearance and co-operation of St Petersburg. The revolt naturally caused a stir in the Balkan states. In Bulgaria the Russian minister, Hitrovo, was known to be supplying money and passports to volunteers who sought to help the rebels; and Montenegro had to be bought off by Vienna at the cost of some 100,000 Gulden. (This was still cheaper, Kálnoky reminded the indignant military, than the suppression of a revolt prolonged by Montenegrin assistance.) Prince Milan, of course, was loud in his encouragement of the Austrians, although this only whipped up more anti-Austrian feeling in Serbia and further weakened the throne. Turkey too, wished for a speedy suppression of a revolt which might spread to Albania, and even offered Vienna her assistance in the form of an alliance in February 1882. This, Kálnoky rejected: Turkey was too unstable – Calice, the ambassador at Constantinople, even described her as a dying Power at this time. But Kálnoky let the Turks down lightly – they were commercially important; and they might some day be of use in the big game against Russia. He was careful to humour them over Egypt at this time, telling them that such co-operation showed that an alliance was superfluous. Most important of all, the attitude of the Russian government was scrupulously friendly and correct. In that respect at least, the Bosnian revolt showed the value of the Three Emperors' Alliance. At the same time, however, the virulence of the reaction of 'unofficial' Russia made the Austrians suddenly and painfully aware of its limitations.

For four long months the Russian press raged against the Dual

Monarchy; and the minister of the interior, Ignatiev, whether personally approving or merely welcoming a diversion from the government's unpopular domestic policies, seemed to do nothing to restrain it. Feeling ran particularly high in the army; and in January 1882 the popular General Skobelev made a much publicized speech in a St Petersburg restaurant, drawing attention to the fight for faith and fatherland that was going on in Bosnia. He then went off to Paris, where he made a speech about the inevitable conflict between Teuton and Slav. This alarmed many people in Germany, but Bismarck carefully refrained from any diplomatic reaction; and Kálnoky, too, assured visiting diplomats that he trusted in the tsar, not in Skobelev. Nevertheless, his faith in Alexander III had been shaken; especially when his secret, but increasingly urgent, appeals to the Russian government to come out in the open and calm public opinion by disavowing Skobelev produced no result. By March, the Austro-Hungarian ambassador was reporting from St Petersburg that a curious situation had arisen: officially, Russia was on the best of terms with her neighbours; yet public opinion feverishly expected war – there was undoubtedly a great conflict of political forces going on inside Russia, 'and no one can say whether the dam of the state's authority might not one day be swept away'.[37]

True, with the end of the Bosnian revolt, the Russian press at last calmed down – especially after a very energetic protest by Kálnoky (17 March), whose military sensitivities had been touched by a *Novoye Vremya* article alleging Austro-Hungarian 'atrocities' in Bosnia; and the appointment of Giers as minister for foreign affairs on 23 March was certainly a reassuring sign. In July Kálnoky was further gratified to hear of the sudden death, in a Moscow brothel, of Skobelev himself – 'the one man in Russia who might have prevailed against sensible people'.[38] But his confidence had, nevertheless, been severely shaken. And this not so much on account of Skobelev's speeches as on account of the government's, and especially the tsar's, timid reaction to them. Henceforth, Kálnoky had serious misgivings about the efficacy of the Three Emperors' Alliance. The very crisis that had demonstrated its tactical usefulness had shown equally clearly that it could provide no lasting security.

[37] E. R. v. Rutkowski, 'General Skobelev . . .', p. 127.
[38] Ibid., p. 151.

The Skobelev crisis was in fact the starting point for a general reinforcement of Austria-Hungary's diplomatic and military defences against the day when the Three Emperors' Alliance should fail her. 'From now on,' Beck declared in February, 'war against this Power [Russia] must be constantly kept in mind';[39] and he recommended approaches to Rome and Bucharest. In the next two years the Dual Alliance was strengthened by a military understanding; an alliance was concluded with Roumania, and a fairly successful effort made to get a firmer grip on the Balkan states. More immediately, the Skobelev crisis precipitated the formation of the Triple Alliance.

Austro-Italian relations had not been happy in the later 1870s. In Italy the government had been in the hands of the Left, traditionally associated with irredentism, since 1876; and Austria-Hungary's Balkan activities in 1877–8 had aroused jealousy across the Adriatic. Andrássy had never concealed his views on Italy's irredentist ambitions, and had warned Rome that 'at the first sign of an Italian annexationist policy, Austria-Hungary would attack'.[40] Nor, indeed, would the Monarchy permit Italy to gain territory anywhere on the Adriatic. In 1878 the decision was taken to fortify the Tyrolean frontier. Yet despite all this the Austrians appreciated the desirability of good relations with Italy. Andrássy hoped that even irredentism might provide common ground for co-operation between the two governments. For it was an object of loathing to both. At least, whatever his ministers thought, the conservative, military-minded King Humbert regarded it as a mere cloak for republican propaganda and detested it as heartily as Andrássy did.

Haymerle – he had not been ambassador at Rome for nothing – was equally anxious to improve Austro-Italian relations. The Austro-Hungarian government was much concerned to play down the repercussions which followed irredentist demonstrations at the funeral of General Avezzana in January 1880, and confined itself to a modest strengthening of the frontier defences. This proved to be just enough to bring a panicky Italian government to proffer its apologies without causing any lasting estrangement. Austro-Hungarian public opinion was more exercised, however, and according to the British ambassador, aggression by Italy would have been met with 'a unanimous alacrity that would be wanting' in the case of any other war.[41] Bismarck did his best to fan the flames. An Austria-Hungary on bad terms with Italy would be more amenable to his plans for a Three Emperors' Alliance. Haymerle's efforts in February 1880 to make sure of Italy as a preliminary to taking a firm stand against Russia, therefore, came to nothing. Yet he did not despair. Indeed, by February 1881, in response to Italian feelers following on Rome's decision of the previous summer to seek a *rapprochement* with the Central Powers, he was prepared to support Italian designs in Tunis, and even to offer Crete, provided Italy renounced her Balkan ambitions. True, he was now engaged in seeking agreement with Russia, but an agreement with Italy would strengthen his position to drive a hard bargain with St Petersburg. For this very reason, however, Bismarck, who preferred a weak and malleable Austria-Hungary, poured cold water on the whole idea; the Italians were indecisive; and the negotiations faded away.

The French occupation of Tunis in May 1881 spurred the Italians to make a more serious effort to escape from their painful isolation. But what was for them a cogent incentive was for the Central Powers a serious obstacle to an agreement. For neither of them had the slightest desire to be dragged into a quarrel with France. Added to this, a violent anti-papal demonstration in Rome on 12 July made Italy an even more questionable ally for the Apostolic King of Hungary. King Humbert's visit to Vienna (27–31 October), therefore, falling in the interlude between the death of Haymerle and the appointment of Kálnoky, signified little more than a *détente* and a willingness to forget past quarrels. It achieved nothing positive, as Kállay rather tactlessly announced in the Delegations. The Italians were disappointed; and were even more dismayed by Bismarck's flattery of the Pope in a Reichstag speech of 29 November. Indeed, some people in Rome seem to have panicked. At any rate, on 23 December Blanc (the secretary-general of the Consulta) formally appealed to the Austro-Hungarian ambassador for an alliance to save Italy from her disastrous isolation, and to give a much-needed boost to the prestige of the monarchy. In the new year, as a token of goodwill, Italy ostentatiously brought her Egyptian policy into line with that of the Three Emperors' Alliance, and ceased to press her grievances about Tunis.

[41] Agatha Ramm, p. 165.

Despite, or rather because of his fears about the strength of irredentist forces undermining the monarchy in Italy, Kálnoky was anxious to do something to strengthen the forces of order there. As the Italian ambassador pointed out, the Central Powers themselves had an interest in preventing the contagion of republicanism spreading from France to the whole Latin world. Kálnoky, therefore, commended the Italians to a hesitant Bismarck, and managed to persuade him that it would be asking too much to demand that the Italian government first come to terms with the Pope. Not that he had any intention of committing Franz Joseph, the leading Catholic monarch, to anything like an acceptance of the Italian view in the quarrel between Quirinal and Vatican. Indeed, it was chiefly for this reason that in February 1882 he rejected a far-reaching Italian proposal for a treaty of territorial guarantee. His own suggestion of a simple neutrality treaty, on the other hand, offered Italy too little – in fact no more than she already had in practice. So Bismarck, impressed by Skobelev's visit to Paris and the spectre of a France in league with Russia, persuaded Kálnoky to offer Italy some support against France. It was on the basis of an Italian draft along these lines that Kálnoky drew up the terms of the Triple Alliance of 20 May 1882 (Document 13).

Despite some unfortunate ambiguities in the text – Kálnoky was no expert in drafting, and he received no help from Bismarck – the treaty suited Austro-Hungarian interests well enough. Austria-Hungary was committed to help Italy only in the extremely unlikely event of an unprovoked French attack; and she maintained her freedom from any obligation to help Germany in the event of a Franco-German war. Although Kálnoky had told the German ambassador that the Monarchy would in fact fight in such a case, Hungarian opinion was still too averse to involvement in Franco-German disputes to permit of any treaty commitment. And even Kálnoky himself, while agreeing to the so-called Mancini declaration which stated that the alliance could not be construed as directed against Britain, would not consider admitting Britain into the alliance – precisely because he was afraid that Gladstone would not keep secret an alliance which would be offensive to France. It is true that Italy had gained security against both her potential enemies, and had offered Austria-Hungary nothing beyond neutrality in return. The

Austrians, however, were not in the least interested in securing positive help from Italy: this would be of little value, and might entail greater commitments against France, or an Italian demand for a voice in Near Eastern affairs. Kálnoky's main aim in concluding the alliance had been to make absolutely certain of Italy's neutrality, and thus to free all the resources of the Monarchy for a possible war in the east. As he explained to the Austro-Hungarian ambassador at Rome on 1 April, the chief justification for the alliance from his point of view lay in 'the dreadful confusion (*Zerrüttung*) prevailing in Russia'.[42]

To that extent, the alliance suited Kálnoky's purposes. It was also a useful reinforcement for the conservative bastion in central Europe: one of the Latin monarchies at least had been strengthened. Kálnoky emphasized this aspect of the alliance in his efforts to dispel the indignation the alliance had aroused in the Vatican. Against the two great revolutionary threats of the day – the Orthodox Church in league with Panslavism, and revolutionary socialism emanating from France – all conservative elements, including, he reminded the Pope, the Italian monarchy, must stand together in defence of the principle of authority, 'qui en dernière analyse est la base de tous les états'.[43]

Otherwise, the alliance had serious weaknesses. Like the Serbian Alliance and the Three Emperors' Alliance, it had no roots in popular feeling on either side. For example, in December 1882 after the execution of Oberdank (a deserter from the Ausrian army who had planned to assassinate Franz Joseph during his visit to Trieste) vast demonstrations were held in Italy, where every town of any significance soon had its 'Piazza Oberdan'. The Italian government was scrupulously correct, and publicly disavowed the irredentists; and an unemployed tailor who threw a stone at the coach of the Austro-Hungarian ambassador to the Vatican got three years – more than he would have got in Austria, Franz Joseph observed.[44] Even between the two governments, however, difficulties arose. No solution could be found to the vexed question of Franz Joseph's return visit to King Humbert: whereas the emperor could not offend the Pope by visiting the king at Rome, the Italian government said it could not vouch for

[42] P.A. I/457, Kálnoky to Wimpffen, private, 1 April 1882.
[43] P.A. XI/226, Kálnoky to Paar, private, 7 December 1883.
[44] E. R. v. Rutkowski, 'Kálnoky . . .', p. 161.

his security from hostile demonstrators if he returned the ᵥ
anywhere else. The Austrians now had cause to regret their ᶜ
shortsightedness in receiving Humbert in Vienna. All the same
long as the simple soldier-king reigned at Rome, the allia
would be safe; and there was a lull in irredentist activity a
1883. Indeed, by April 1884 Kálnoky was hopefully predict
that it would only be a matter of time before the alliance came
earn that popular approval in the member states which
regarded as 'the final cement' (*den letzten festen Kitt*).[45]

In fact, only one of Austria-Hungary's alliances ever recei
this 'final cement': The Dual Alliance. And after the Skobe
crisis this alliance was further strengthened by a military unᶜ
standing. Since 1871 the German military had regarded it
certain that France and Russia would fight together, sho
Germany become involved in a war with either. Originally, t
planned to eliminate France first in such an eventuality; bu
1879 they changed their plans and decided to concentrate
Russia first. Now the Dual Alliance had brought no co-ordinat
of military planning between the Central Powers. It was only
nationalist ferment in Russia in the spring of 1882 that convin
the German military – and even Bismarck for a short time –
the need at least to find out something about Austria-Hunga
plans. Franz Joseph and Kálnoky agreed to consultations with
Germans, although they put in a caveat against drifting into ᵗ
of preventive war; and in April, Beck drew up a long memor
dum[46] on the military position. A war with Russia, with
widespread Panslav ramifications, would be like a return to
Völkerwanderungen, and the Monarchy would need all the helᵖ
could get. The impending Italian alliance would be a great gᵃ
but the Balkan states would still need watching – perhaps Tur
would help here; and there was an urgent need for more fortif
tions in Galicia, and for more strategic railways to reduce
Austro-Hungarian mobilization time of 44–33 days. Equᵃ
urgent, however, was the need to discover Germany's intentiᶜ
In a memorandum he wrote in preparation for his talks ᵥ
Moltke's aide, Waldersee, at Strobl,[47] Beck was far less cautiᶜ
than the emperor and Kálnoky on the question of preventive ᵥ

[45] P.A. I/457, Kálnoky to Ludolf, 15 April 1884.
[46] E. R. v. Rutkowski, 'General Skobelev . . .', pp. 140–2.
[47] Ibid., pp. 142–3.

'The great idea must be the offensive,' he declared, and went on to sketch out an ambitious plan for an Austro-German pincer movement deep into Russian Poland, to encircle and destroy the main Russian army there at the first sign that Russia was making serious preparations for war. Nothing so specific was agreed at Strobl on 3 August, or in Beck's meeting with Moltke at the Breslau manoeuvres in September. But the two general staffs were agreed on a strong joint offensive into Poland – Waldersee even promised that more than half of Germany's forces would be put in the east – and Beck could henceforth be confident of strong German support.

Thus heartened, he proceeded in November 1882 to draw up an important memorandum[48] embodying what was to remain the basis of Austro-Hungarian military thinking down to 1914. The immediate military need, however, was to re-group the Cracow army further east, round Lemberg, and to do everything possible to speed up Austria-Hungary's mobilization plans. For there were, after all, limits to the trust one could put in even the best of allies: if Austria-Hungary wanted to secure a worthwhile share of the spoils, she should not allow the Germans to win the early victories unaided, herself appearing late in the day with a sort of reserve army. Speedy Austro-Hungarian victories would also be of vital importance in holding the Balkan states to an awed neutrality. Kálnoky gave Beck his full support, and persuaded the conference of ministers in February 1883 to pay for more strategic railways in Galicia. By 1885 the Austrians had succeeded in reducing the time needed for mobilization from 40 to 21 days. This suited Bismarck, who was constantly telling the Austrians to trust in their defensive fortifications in Galicia, rather than in desperate tactical offensives. Although the military talks had imposed no binding commitments on the governments of Vienna and Berlin, the understanding reached in 1882 was in practice an important addition to the effectiveness of the Dual Alliance against Russia.

In most other respects, Austro-German relations remained much the same. The Dual Alliance was renewed in the spring of 1883, this time to run on automatically unless denounced. Kálnoky was firm in resisting Bismarck's attempts to extend it to cover the case of a Franco-German war. For the Magyars were insistent that Hungary could not conceivably have any quarrel

[48] P.A. I/466, Beck, memorandum, secret, 11 November 1881.

with France; and besides, Kálnoky said, in the event of a Franco-German war, the Monarchy would have to put all its forces in the east to keep Russia quiet.

In one respect – economic relations – the two allies even drifted apart in the 1880s. For in 1878 Germany decided to adopt a policy of protection, and refused to renew the Austro-Prussian commercial treaty of 1868. Restrictive measures reduced German cattle imports from the Monarchy from 1,254,000 in 1878 to 458,000 in 1880; and in 1881 the Germans imposed a total ban, on the pretext of an outbreak of cattle plague. This drove the Hungarian government in turn – despite the risk to the Monarchy's influence in the Balkans – to close the frontier to livestock from the Balkan states. Although the commercial treaty with Germany was prolonged from year to year pending negotiations, it was finally dropped in 1881, when the Monarchy was also subjected to the full German tariff on cereals. Not unnaturally, this situation alarmed Haymerle who, with the support of Hungarians anxious to save at least their grain exports, had striven manfully (but in vain) to persuade the Austrian government that even an unfavourable treaty would be valuable for political reasons.[49] Kálnoky was even haunted by the spectre of a tariff war, which would have a most baleful effect on the popularity of the alliance in both countries.[50] But Bismarck's perspective was narrowly diplomatic. Economic questions (like colonial questions) he felt could be kept on an entirely different plane from diplomatic relations; and in any case, he said that German agriculture could not possibly face the competition of Hungarian and Roumanian cereals since the railway network had been extended in south-east Europe. The deadlock continued, therefore, and in the end Austria-Hungary had no alternative but to follow her best and most powerful trading partner and adopt protection likewise. To continue a free trade policy would certainly have entailed the utter ruin of Austrian and Hungarian industry in the face of German competition. Even the Hungarians eventually came to see this. So between 1878 and 1882 Austro-Hungarian tariffs were generally increased by 15 per cent; and in 1887 further increased to correspond with German rates.

[49] P.A. XL/291, Ministerratsprotokoll, 10 December 1879; P.A. XL/292, Ministerratsprotokoll, 11 April 1881.

[50] P.A. XL/294, Ministerratsprotokoll, 7 April 1885.

The results were not an unmitigated disaster either for Austria-Hungary or for the alliance. Despite the duties, total trade with Germany increased during the 1880s. And the Great Powers, unlike the Balkan states, did not usually allow commercial considerations to determine their diplomatic and military alignments. Indeed, the Monarchy's internal market enjoyed a measure of prosperity under the shelter of the new tariff policy – there was a steady increase in domestic consumption, and, as a result of railway development in Hungary and the Balkans, quite a boom in the iron industry. Moreover, Austria-Hungary was still far more advanced economically than the Balkan states; and her commercial treaties with them did something to make good her losses. Nevertheless, her exports stagnated on the whole; and there was certainly no perceptible strengthening of her hold over foreign markets against competition that would soon grow increasingly fierce from the stronger industrial states of western Europe. Even in the Balkan states, the Monarchy was to a great extent living on the capital of a past pre-eminence. Nor was the Taaffe government doing anything to equip the Monarchy with a sound industrial basis to maintain that pre-eminence. On the contrary, it consciously fostered agriculture and the crafts at the expense of Austrian industry. The latter was now officially frowned on as a hotbed of liberal capitalists and socialist workers; and after 1885 it found its competitive capacity seriously reduced by the very advanced social legislation with which the government sought to combat the spread of socialism. The Monarchy, in fact, enjoyed only a mediocre prosperity in the 1880s; and this, coupled with an ineffective taxation system and, from 1879 to 1885, an annual budget deficit, at least partly accounts for its relatively feeble performance in the field of military expenditure. Diplomacy, however, could still do something to redress the balance.

In Roumania, for example, Kálnoky in the end managed to salvage a good deal from the wreck of Haymerle's policy. But at first, relations got still worse before they got better. Indeed, when King Carol, in a speech from the throne at the end of 1881, spoke scathingly about Austria-Hungary's behaviour in the Danube question, Kálnoky even determined to break off diplomatic relations with Bucharest. For he worked on the principle that small states like Roumania 'lick the hand that beats them, or that they fear will beat them'.[51] It was only under pressure from Franz Joseph that he contented himself with an apology instead. The year 1882 saw no improvement. Although Kálnoky managed to insert most of Haymerle's desiderata into the French compromise proposal on the Danube question Roumania steadily vetoed it in the European Danube Commission (in which decisions required unanimity). In 1883 the Great Powers, exasperated by Roumania's obstruction, settled the matter by summoning a special conference in London of the signatories of the Treaty of Berlin (at which Roumania, of course, was not represented). There, Kálnoky managed to secure the main objective to Haymerle's policy: Austro-Hungarian interests were not to be placed at the mercy of the small riparian states. But Roumania obstinately refused to accept the decision of the London conference. And her rage against Austria-Hungary, heightened at this time by a bout of irredentist fever, now knew no bounds.

Matters came to a head in June 1883 at a state banquet held in the presence of the king and queen of Roumania in Jassy, capital of Moldavia and a stronghold of Russophile feeling. Speeches were made expressing regrets for 'the pearls still missing from the crown of St. Stephen the Great'; and the royal guests accepted a toast to 'the king and queen of the Roumanians'.[52] This Kálnoky decided, was too much for a Great Power to tolerate, and he decided to call a sharp halt. On 1 July he sent what was virtually an ultimatum (Document 14): Roumania's explanations were unsatisfactory, and 'we must now insist on an explicit and clear declaration that the government condemns this unlawful agitation against the peace of our border territories, and, as is its duty, will not tolerate them. . . We are completely in the right and will pursue this matter, if necessary, to the point of war (*bis in den letzten Konsequenzen*).'[53] The Bucharest government at last saw into the abyss that yawned before it, and immediately presented an apology virtually dictated by Kálnoky. The success of the firm, if not overbearing, approach, was amply demonstrated: in July, the Roumanian foreign minister Stourdza made the pilgrimage to Vienna to assure Kálnoky that Roumania considered

[51] E. R. v. Rutkowski, 'Kálnoky . . .', p. 54.
[52] E. R. v. Rutkowski, 'Oesterreich-Ungarn und Rumänien . . .', p. 228.
[53] Ibid., pp. 242–3.

herself Austria-Hungary's 'born ally';[54] and the emperor congratulated Kálnoky on having brought Roumania so smartly to heel. Kálnoky's 'ultimatum' had set a precedent that was to be imitated several times, and sometimes with less happy results for the Monarchy in the next thirty years.

Kálnoky received Stourdza's assurances coldly; and it was only after seeing Bismarck at Kissingen on 18 August that he began to consider a more positive response. For Bismarck was again temporarily worried about Russia's armaments, and suggested that it might be well to extend the 'league of peace' eastwards by bringing in Roumania. Kálnoky agreed in principle with this idea (and also took the opportunity to inform Bismarck of Haymerle's Serbian alliance). At the same time, however, he insisted that King Carol was weak; that Stourdza had no influence in the country; and that the alliance, if it were to have any value, must be negotiated with the prime minister Bratianu. Even now, as in the case of the Dual and the Triple Alliances, a catalyst was needed in the form of a temporary scare about Russia. On this occasion, it was provided by a serious row in Bulgaria between the tsar and Alexander of Battenberg. Now Bratianu, who saw Roumania's chief enemy in the Panslav threat, was even more alarmed than the Austrians at the prospect of a Russian invasion of Bulgaria. Roumania's fear of Russia, and Kálnoky's unrelenting attitude towards irredentism (a demonstrative tour of Transylvania by Beck at this time had a most sobering effect in Bucharest) combined to hasten the Roumanians along the path to Canossa. King Carol, after a headwashing in Berlin, agreed to the negotiations, which were conducted between Kálnoky and Bratianu at Vienna and Gastein in September.

Kálnoky was never at his best in the hard bargaining involved in negotiating alliances. In this case too, he allowed Bratianu to jockey him out of including a clause similar to that in the Serbian treaty which explicitly forbade the toleration of irredentist activities. Nor did he manage to bring Roumania to modify by one jot her stubborn attitude on the Danube question. Indeed, Bucharest remained absolutely unyielding on this even after the alliance was made; and Kálnoky in turn was only wearied by Bismarck's advice to humour Roumania: 'no one outside Austria can have any idea what patience is needed when one is surrounded by a collection of

[54] Ibid., p. 246.

half-barbarian states whose arrogant interpretation of their newly-acquired independence gives rise to perpetual friction.'[55] Despite these setbacks, however, he had achieved a good deal: the Russian minister at Bucharest, who was on his track, was at any rate highly disgruntled, and soundly berated the Roumanians for having gone over to Austria-Hungary, 'who is the enemy of Russia'.[56] True, the alliance depended entirely on the king and Bratianu – not even the whole Roumanian cabinet knew about it and it had no roots in public opinion. On the other hand, while it lasted, the alliance of 30 October 1883 (Document 15) gave the Monarchy valuable military cover in the south-east in the event of a Russian attack. More important still, Germany's immediate accession to the alliance constituted in practical terms that very extension of the Dual Alliance to cover Roumania that Haymerle had sought in vain from Bismarck in the spring of 1881.

At the same time, the Austrians consolidated their position in the rest of the Balkans. In Serbia, this was mainly a question of maintaining Prince Milan on his shaky throne. In January 1882 the collapse of the Union Générale bank, involving the Serbian government in considerable losses, dealt a severe blow to Milan's prestige and almost brought the Russophile Liberals and Radicals to power. But Vienna stepped in with timely financial aid; and when, in March, in a move to strengthen the dynasty Milan proclaimed himself king, and altered the constitution in his own favour, Franz Joseph made haste to recognize the new kingdom (as of course he was in any case obliged to do by the treaty of 1881). Kálnoky accepted all this. But he had misgivings lest Milan's proclamation, coming at the time of the Bosnian rising, should encourage Panserbian ambitions; and he took care to warn the king that 'we are in those provinces and we shall stay there'. The energetic Khevenhüller, Austro-Hungarian minister at Belgrade, was assiduous in giving advice to Milan, and did much to strengthen Austro-Hungarian influence in his counsels.

In the country, however, Milan's pro-Austrian orientation continued extremely unpopular, associated as it was with high taxation resulting from the government's railway projects and disastrous financial ventures; and even more with the negation

---

[55] E. R. v. Rutkowski, 'Kálnoky . . .', pp. 488–9.
[56] P.A. I/460, Liasse XIII, Mayr to Kálnoky, 2 April 1884.
[57] E. R. v. Rutkowski, 'Kálnoky . . .', p. 256.

cherished national ambitions in Bosnia and the Herzegovina. The Austrians, for their part, preferred to adopt a conspiracy theory, and blame Russian agents for fomenting all the opposition to King Milan. Kálnoky, certainly, seems to have been sincerely convinced that this was the root of the trouble. In January 1883, he lectured Giers, who was passing through Vienna, on the need for co-operation between the great monarchies in support of the minor dynasties in the Balkans. None of these dynasties had any roots in its adopted country, and all of them were confronted with the same international revolutionary movement – which only adopted different guises (socialist, nationalist, or liberal) according to varying circumstances.[58] Given the narrowly monarchical nature of most of Austria-Hungary's alliances, there was no doubt a touch of *Realpolitik* in Kálnoky's emphatic insistence that blows to monarchies abroad were indirectly blows to the Habsburg Monarchy; and that it was a 'vital necessity' (*Lebensnotwendigkeit*) for Austria-Hungary to oppose challenges to the monarchical principle wherever they arose.[59] But the argument was a good one to use with the eminently conservative Giers, who promptly promised to support the Obrenović dynasty in Serbia despite Milan's shortcomings.

Not that Kálnoky for his part was in the least interested in stirring up the Serbian government to a positively anti-Russian policy. This could only weaken the Three Emperors' Alliance, his chief means of keeping Russia in order. Indeed, in the summer of 1883 he was urging a very recalcitrant Milan to try to improve his relations with St Petersburg. Nevertheless, he issued another warning to Giers at the same time: Austria-Hungary did not wish to interfere in the Balkan states; but she could not, for reasons of her own security, tolerate openly hostile governments on her frontier in Montenegro or, especially, in Serbia 'which lies so completely within our sphere of influence'.[60] 'We must insist on a friendly government in Belgrade.' If a revolution there produced chaos or a hostile government, the need to preserve the tranquillity of the south Slav frontier districts of the Monarchy would compel Vienna to intervene by force of arms. Hence, Kálnoky told Giers, it would be in Russia's interests not to encourage such revolutions. But he had strung the bow too tight.

[58] P.A. I/469, Liasse XXIII/a, Kálnoky, memorandum, 20 May 1883.
[59] E. R. v. Rutkowski, 'Kálnoky . . .', p. 274.   [60] Ibid., pp. 303–4.

Giers took great alarm at these veiled threats, and protested tha
the spirit of the treaty of 1881 (which, of course, technicall
applied only to Turkey and Bulgaria) forbade Austria-Hungar
to intervene in Serbia without the consent of her treaty partners
And his protest was effective. Indeed, Kálnoky made an astonish
ing retreat. For, perhaps only to pacify Giers, perhaps concludin
that after all salvation lay only in close co-operation with 'officia
Russia, he now made the extraordinary and gratuitous concessio
of accepting this Russian interpretation of the Three Emperors
Alliance.[61] This involved a serious potential restriction on th
Monarchy's freedom of action against Serbia – and one whic
Haymerle had resolutely resisted. And to this extent there
some justification in Andrássy's complaint that 'whereas th
Congress of Berlin led Russia out of the Balkans, my successo
brought her back in again.'[62] For the present, however, the que
tion was academic. By the end of 1883 Milan had rounded u
large numbers of his opponents, and had engineered a politic
stability in Serbia that was to last until 1885.

In Bulgaria the Austrians could feel equally sure of themselve
By the end of 1882 the Russians had managed to unite the Prin
and all the political parties in opposition to their dominatio
Kálnoky was, therefore, even more determined to hold to t
policy of abstention from open opposition to Russia (whi
might only provoke a great crisis and the fall of Alexander).
was well content to let Russia go on making herself more u
popular. Indeed, by January 1883 he was coming to the view th
a strong united Bulgaria would not be a Russian satellite (as
had feared in 1881) but perhaps the best means of driving Russ
out of the Balkans altogether – an extremely dangerous ambitio
even if only a long-term one; and one which illustrates well h
the originally defensive concept of safeguarding Austro-Hu
garian interests against an overweening Russia could be pervert
into something extremely offensive against a Russia already
retreat. After all, Austria-Hungary's interests were flourishi
well enough despite, or rather because of Russia's fumbli
attempts to establish her political control in Bulgaria. In
spring, Kálnoky had had quite a triumph when agreement was
last reached with Turkey and Bulgaria for the construction of

[61] Ibid., p. 308.
[62] Kab. 19, Andrássy to Franz Joseph, 24 November 1885.

railway links with the Serbian network (which were to be given priority over the strategic lines desired by Russia). During the August crisis, therefore, he stayed calm, and advised Alexander to avoid provoking an actual showdown with the tsar. If Russia were so foolish as to embark on anything so drastic as an invasion, he calculated, this would only compromise her further. It would also – as was observable in Roumania – drive all the other Balkan states into the arms of Austria-Hungary. Besides, if the worst came to the worst, other Powers, notably Britain, might be persuaded to pull the chestnuts out of the fire. At any rate, he himself was careful not to respond when the British very tentatively suggested joint opposition to Russia's designs in Bulgaria. Indeed, in December 1883 he coolly informed London that that was a British, not an Austro-Hungarian interest. The Monarchy could afford to sit and wait.

Kálnoky's growing hopes of Bulgaria largely explain his rebuff to the king of the Hellenes, who in September 1883 approached him about an alliance to support Greek territorial ambitions in Turkey and Greek cultural interests threatened by Bulgarian propaganda in Macedonia. Kálnoky hereby broke with Andrássy's policy of supporting the Greeks against the Slavs; but this policy was now outdated. Greece was not worth much militarily; and alliance with her would only estrange the Slavs, particularly Bulgaria; and in any case her impatient greed for Turkish territory was anathema to Kálnoky. Towards the Turks, he successfully continued his policy of friendship without any definite pledges of support. Like his partners in the Three Emperors' Alliance he found in the Egyptian question a cheap means of humouring the sultan; though he was also concerned – or so he told the British in August 1882 – lest Britain contrive by misusing the Concert to give Turkey the impression that all the Christian Powers were in league against her. In May 1883 he refused to support Gladstone's attempt to bring the Turks to implement their promises of reform in Armenia.

By the beginning of 1884, therefore, Vienna was in a fairly confident mood. In February, Beck surveyed the horizon: relations with Italy had become increasingly stable, the only threat to them being a revolution in Rome and a consequent realignment of the Latin races under the republican banner in a battle against the monarchical principle. With Roumania, relations had been greatly improved and clarified by the alliance (though that state might still hesitate to lend positive assistance in a war). Bulgaria was no longer a problem; but it would be well to keep in favour with Turkey, who could be useful in preventing trouble from Montenegro or in the occupied provinces. Russia, therefore, was in a fairly isolated position – particularly now that her friend France was so busy overseas. Of course much still needed to be done to improve the Monarchy's defences and to reduce the time needed for mobilization. But all in all, Beck decided, 'the year 1883 has brought a real change for the better'.[63]

It was in this contented mood that the Austrians proceeded to the renewal of the Three Emperors' Alliance. They still kept a wary eye on Russia. For example, at Salzburg in August 188 Kálnoky rejected out of hand a Russian proposal which Bismarck put to him that the alliance be modified in the sense of the Reichstadt Agreement of 1876, to take account of the eventual collapse of Turkey, and even of Russia's designs on Constantinople. The emperor and the Hungarians would never agree to this, he said. Besides, the alliance was strictly defensive; and the Monarchy had no interest whatever in anything remotely offensive to Turkey, who might still prove useful in a war. Nor had he any time for Bismarck's favourite idea of spheres of influence in the Balkans. Russia would not observe the principle in Serbia and Montenegro, and hence it would just be pure loss for the Monarchy to abandon Bulgaria.

During the negotiations for the renewal of the treaty he made only one concession to Russia. That was an important one: the text was amended to extend the prohibition of military action without prior consultation from Turkey proper and Bulgaria to the whole of the Balkan peninsula. Admittedly, he had sold the particular pass to Giers in the summer of 1883; but this formal amendment was to give the Austrians a good deal of trouble in the Serbo-Bulgarian war of 1885. Otherwise, there were no significant changes. Kálnoky rejected Bismarck's suggestion that Italy might be brought in: this would overthrow the whole basis of existing treaties, he said, in which Italy's role was only as part of the wall he had built against the danger of Russian attack if the Three Emperors' Alliance failed. (By the same token, he later refused another suggestion of Bismarck

[63] P.A. I/466, Beck, memorandum, dated '1884'.

144

to admit Russia to the Triple Alliance, and told Bismarck to confine himself to informing Russia of its conservative monarchical content.) Besides, Kálnoky said, the Near East was no business of Italy's: she would only complicate matters. When Giers seemed to be prevaricating about Bosnia and the Herzegovina, Kálnoky firmly reminded him that their annexation was not to be regarded as a change in the *status quo*; and that it would not authorize Russia to precipitate a union of the two Bulgarias – all of which Giers accepted. On this basis, the treaty was renewed for three years at Berlin on 27 March 1884.

Now during the negotiations Kálnoky had agreed to a Russian suggestion for a meeting between Franz Joseph and Alexander III at the tsar's hunting lodge at Skiernewice in Poland, to take place in the summer. But hardly was the ink dry on the renewed treaty than he began to find Russia's behaviour exasperating. In the spring, there were difficulties over Eastern Roumelia, where in view of the impending expiry of the term of office of the Turkish governor general, Aleko Pasha, a nationalist movement was growing up in favour of union with Bulgaria; and this spread to the principality. The tsar, meanwhile, was pressing strongly for the appointment of a pro-Russian successor to Aleko Pasha – no friend of St Petersburg. All this alarmed Kálnoky: for with a pro-Russian governor general in Eastern Roumelia, the Russians might expel Alexander from Bulgaria, and recover their prestige by bringing about a union under Russian auspices. To make matters worse, Bismarck seemed to be lending the Russians every assistance. For example, in June, he gratified the tsar by delivering a crushing humiliation to Alexander of Battenberg, preventing the prince's marriage to the half-English Princess Victoria of Prussia.

To a certain extent, Kálnoky felt constrained to keep in step with his partners in the Three Emperors' Alliance – at least to the extent of not actually opposing the Russian nominee for Eastern Roumelia. And he co-operated with them in sorting out a Serbo-Bulgarian frontier dispute despite Franz Joseph's indignation at Russia's stiff opposition to Serbia's 'just claims'. On the other hand, a bland suggestion from Bismarck that he should accept that Bulgaria lay in Russia's sphere provoked him too far. Again he declaimed against the doctrine of spheres of influence, which, as he rightly observed, Russia herself did not accept.

Austria-Hungary could never give Russia a free hand in Bulgaria: to do so would be to create that same big Slav kingdom under Russian control that Andrássy had so tenaciously opposed. Such a state would dominate the whole Balkans. Besides, Austria-Hungary had a great material stake in Bulgaria.

On top of all this came an exasperating suggestion from Bismarck that the German emperor should also participate in the Skiernewice meeting. This filled the Austrians with alarm: the participation of Germany in her present frame of mind could only benefit Russia; and it might even look like a downgrading of the Dual Alliance in favour of the Three Emperors' Alliance. Besides, such a spectacular meeting could only cause general wonder and disquiet: 'You can imagine what a noise it will make'[64] Kálnoky complained to the ambassador at London. Yet at the same time, it could do no good to snub the Germans, especially at a time when the Russians were so alarmingly assiduous at Berlin. To make the best of an embarrassing situation, therefore, the Austrians decided to comply with Bismarck's plan, but to make sure that the Skiernewice meeting was preceded by meetings between Franz Joseph and William I, and between Kálnoky and Bismarck, at Ischl and Varzin. This would put the Dual Alliance in the foreground, and give the public the impression that Skiernewice was merely a subsidiary reinforcement of Austro-German solidarity. Franz Joseph was most anxious that Germany should be squared in advance of any tripartite talks. Not that he was expecting much of lasting value to emerge from Skiernewice anyway: 'my distrust of conditions in Russia is so deep-rooted.'[65]

An Austro-Hungarian foreign office memorandum[66] reviewing the situation in August took an extraordinarily gloomy view: the Balkan situation had recently become extremely precarious. Austria-Hungary might well prefer to humour Giers and the conservatives in Russia, but she might nevertheless soon have to call on that Power to halt – for she herself could not retreat in the Balkans without sacrificing the hard-won gains of recent years. Faced with this problem she was virtually isolated: the feeble Gladstone government seemed to have withdrawn from the Near East; and although the Dual Alliance remained the basis of

[64] P.A. I/460, Liasse XIIa, Kálnoky to Károlyi, private, 28 July 1884.
[65] P.A. I/460, Liasse XIIa, Franz Joseph to Kálnoky, 26 July 1884.
[66] E. R. v. Rutkowski, 'Kálnoky . . .', pp. 636–45.

Austro-Hungarian policy, Bismarck, with his talk of spheres of interest was giving the Monarchy virtually no backing. It would be essential at Varzin, therefore, to find out just what Bismarck had in mind. This was also Kálnoky's view, and in the weeks before he went to Varzin, he did his best to humour the Germans. He supported their opposition to an Anglo-Portuguese treaty about the Congo basin, and impressed strongly on Károlyi in London that it was vitally important in the London conference then meeting on Egypt, to lend Bismarck wholehearted support against Gladstone. The latter's policy was in any case 'a disaster' (*höchst unheilvoll*) for Austria-Hungary who had no interest whatever in seeing him continue in office.[67]

In the event, William I showered Franz Joseph with fulsome expressions of loyalty at Ischl; and at Varzin Bismarck, while not having any significant suggestions to make, at least did not return to his obnoxious advice of the summer. The talks at Skiernewice too (15–17 September) were also academic; but they were very remarkable for their cordiality. Indeed, in this respect they surpassed all expectation, and provided a good illustration of summit diplomacy at its most successful. This first personal contact brought a real improvement in the relations between Franz Joseph and the tsar; and from this moment Kálnoky too began to take a markedly more hopeful view of the possibility of lasting co-existence with Russia. Sosnosky's assessment of Skiernewice[68] – 'the electrifying of a corpse, which . . . could deceive only the shortsighted' – certainly underrates the importance of the meeting. The Italians, for example, were not shortsighted in discerning a significant down-grading of the Triple Alliance, the *raison d'être* of which was of course the possible collapse of the Three Emperors' Alliance. They felt resentful at not being invited to join in the junketings of their allies – 'siamo noi servitori?'[69] – and tried in vain to find out what had transpired. The Three Emperors' Alliance had in fact made a real recovery.

Kálnoky had no doubts about this. Indeed, when, in October, Tisza allowed the Hungarian parliament to express its suspicion of Russia in a formal vote, his rage knew no bounds. He even went so far as to tender his resignation.[70] Not only was it

[67] P.A. I/460, Liasse XXIIa, Kálnoky to Károlyi, private, 28 July 1884.
[68] T. v. Sosnosky, Vol. 2, p. 68.   [69] Quoted in Salvatorelli, p. 89.
[70] P.A. I/467, Kálnoky to Franz Joseph, 13 October 1884.

intolerable, he complained to the emperor, that Tisza should allow any debate at all in the Hungarian parliament, rather than in the Delegations, where the minister for foreign affairs would at least have a chance to defend his policy. The content of the Hungarian declaration was even more serious: 'for Austria-Hungary today it is a question of life and death to avoid war with Russia.' At Skiernewice he had managed to secure peace and friendship with Russia, without even a written agreement, 'with a handshake, so to speak'; and here were the Hungarians giving the impression that the Monarchy was now drawing back.[71] In the end, Franz Joseph refused to accept Kálnoky's resignation; and Tisza promised to behave more correctly in future. But the incident is as eloquent of Kálnoky's renewed faith in Russia as of the continuing mistrust of that Power in Hungary.

The Hungarians were at the same time raising obstacles in the way of Kálnoky's Balkan policy. Agrarian Hungary gained little from the Monarchy's commercial treaties with the Balkan states; but so long as she could send 75 per cent of her own exports to Austria and the rest to Germany and Western Europe, she was prepared to admit cheaper Balkan livestock for home consumption. Now in October 1884 foot and mouth disease broke out in Serbia; and when Serbia persisted in sending infected animals into Hungary, the Hungarians reacted drastically and closed the frontier to all livestock from Serbia, Roumania, and Bulgaria. The Serbian government, backed up by Khevenhüller, protested at this; and Franz Joseph and Kálnoky eventually prevailed on the Magyars to relent and reopen the frontier (December). The affair had of course done nothing to raise the popularity of Hungary among the ordinary peasants, who made up the bulk of the population in Serbia. Worse still, in February 1885, infected cattle from Roumania passed through Hungary to Germany, and a major disruption of the international cattle trade resulted. Britain forbade the entry of German cattle, Germany thereupon closed the frontier to Hungary; and Hungary to Roumania. (The Hungarian government wanted to extend the ban to Serbia too; but Kálnoky and the emperor insisted that the Monarchy could not ignore its treaty obligations towards Serbia just because a third party had made difficulties.) Relations with Roumania, of course, became seriously strained. Irredentism was as rife as ever

[71] Ibid., 22 October 1884.

but Kálnoky had resignedly concluded that no Roumanian government, however well-intentioned, would ever have the power to check it effectively. Now, however, Bucharest decided not to renew the Austro-Roumanian commercial treaty, due to expire in 1886; and the Hungarians, to Kálnoky's dismay, did not seem to care. The Russophile press in Roumania of course had a field day; but Kálnoky's appeals to Budapest went unheeded. He was again feeling the shackles of the 1867 constitution, which allowed the foreign minister only an advisory function in internal and economic questions. He had no legal means of enforcing his views about a commercial policy which was made by others, but which had none the less important consequences in foreign policy for all that.

On top of these difficulties came a political crisis in Serbia, where the king's political embarrassments were now complicated by the fact that his licentious life had alienated his Russian-born queen. The royal pair quarrelled openly in the cafés of Belgrade. Milan now began to despair, and yearned for a life of pleasure in Paris or Vienna. But he had no money. In the summer of 1885, therefore, he hit on the idea of amending the Austro-Serbian treaty. The Austrians could provide him with a pension if he ever abdicated; and they could also educate his son in Vienna, away from the influence of the queen. In return, Milan would allow them to annex Serbia if they saw fit. He concocted a draft with the help of Khevenhüller, who sent it to Vienna.

Kálnoky would have nothing to do with it. He rebuked Khevenhüller, and in June took Milan himself to task in Vienna; monarchs had duties as well as privileges, he told the abject king, and it was Milan's duty to remain in Serbia and govern his people. Unless an openly hostile regime appeared in Belgrade to threaten the tranquillity of Austria-Hungary's southern Slavs, no one in the Monarchy had the faintest desire to intervene in Serbia. 'A flourishing and independent Serbia on friendly terms with us suits our . . . intentions best – in any case, better than the possession of an unruly province.'[72] At the same time, Kálnoky had no illusions about the vital importance of Serbia. That state, he told Taaffe in September 1885, was 'the key to the Monarchy's position in the Near East'.[73] True, he was at the time trying to persuade

[72] P.A. I/456, memorandum by Kálnoky, 9 June 1885.
[73] P.A. I/456, memorandum drawn up by Kálnoky for Taaffe, September 1885.

Taaffe to give Milan some secret service money. Nevertheless h
was sincerely convinced that if Austria-Hungary did not contro
Serbia, Russia would; and 'that moral encirclement by the leadin,
Slav Power, which will always remain the chief danger fo
Austria-Hungary, would then extend from Montenegro to th
banks of the Vistula; Austria-Hungary would be cut off from th
Near East.' Worse still, the south Slav idea would then hav
found a material basis for its political activity and would soo
penetrate deep into the Monarchy – which would then fin
foreign problems turning into domestic problems. This prophec
of doom was remarkably percipient; and even in the immediat
future Kálnoky can have drawn but little comfort from th
thought that the personality of King Milan was the 'surest an
almost the only guarantee against these dangers'.[74]

In this situation it seemed vital to preserve the good relation
with Russia achieved at Skiernewice. Certainly, there seemed n
hope of salvation from any other quarter, from the Wester
Powers, for example. On the contrary, Kálnoky found Italy'
expedition to Massawa in February 1885 profoundly unsatisfac
tory, and would have liked Bismarck to tell Italy plainly that sh
could expect no help from the Triple Alliance if she embroile
herself with France in the Red Sea. By the summer, both Bis
marck and Kálnoky had a very poor opinion altogether of Italy
and at Varzin in August 1885 they agreed that although the Tripl
Alliance was probably still worth renewing, Italy should be give
no further concessions whatever. The behaviour of Britain, wh
in the spring became involved in a dispute with Russia ove
Afghanistan was equally unsatisfactory. The idea that Britai
might choose to fight out this remote quarrel in the Black Se
filled Kálnoky with alarm. For if Turkey allowed a British flee
through the Straits, Russia would take this as an act of war; an
the conflagration would spread to the whole Balkans. To avoi
this catastrophe, therefore, and in accordance with her obliga
tions under the Three Emperors' Alliance, Austria-Hungary los
no time in joining the other continental Powers in reminding the
Turks that they must in no circumstances open the Straits. No
that the Austrians were ready to render Russia any active assis
tance if Britain actually forced the Straits. They had no desire t
see British influence disappear altogether from the Near East.

[74] Ibid.

where it might one day prove a useful counter to Russia's. Nor did they share in the least Bismarck's relish for an Anglo-Russian war. Any gains that might accrue to Austria-Hungary from the weakening of her commercial rival, Britain, would be more than outweighed by the danger of an increase in Russia's prestige or, if Russia were defeated, by the danger of a revolution in Russia which might produce an adventurous, Panslav policy.[75]

Nor was France regarded at this time in Vienna as a potential source of support. Indeed, as Kálnoky came to rely more on the Three Emperors' Alliance, considerations of monarchical principle assumed increased importance; and in this respect he saw in France, perhaps not an enemy as Bismarck did (and after all, Austria-Hungary still had no quarrel of her own with France) but a potential menace to the Monarchy's alliance system and hence to its security. His attitude was therefore less narrowly diplomatic than Bismarck's – Germany was simply confronted with a hostile neighbour who had to be isolated. And at Varzin in August 1885 he impressed on Bismarck that 'the long continued existence of a French Republic, recognized as a fully equal Power, is a dangerous matter for the monarchical principle.'[76] There was more than sentiment to this: the greatest menace was the extension of the republican principle to France's Latin neighbours – 'the realization of the well-known idea of the *confédération des races latines*'.[77] It would be very serious if some eighty million people from Cadiz to Lake Constance, from Syracuse to the North Sea, came to live under a republican system of government. Belgium, with its numerous revolutionary elements would not hold out for long. One dream of the revolution would be realized; and this would threaten the three eastern empires, for the Confederation of Slav States and the United States of Germany were inscribed on the same programme. Clearly, it was more than ever important that the three empires stand together. A few days later (25–26 August) a very cordial return visit by Alexander III to Franz Joseph at Kremsier proclaimed again the Austrians' new-found faith in the Three Emperors' Alliance.

[75] P.A. I/469, Liasse XXIII, Teschenberg memorandum on the possibility of an Anglo-Russian war, April 1885.

[76] P.A. I/460, Kálnoky, notes on a conversation with Bismarck at Varzin, August 1885.

[77] Ibid.

In the summer of 1885 Austria-Hungary seemed to enjoy a reasonable measure of security. This was in great part due to the alliances she had built up in the past six years. True, Andrássy's original simple idea of a grand alliance including Germany, Britain, and Italy to resist Russia had proved unrealizable owing to the vagaries of British policy and Germany's obsessive concern for good relations with Russia. It had been transformed by his successors into a more complex, but basically dualistic, system of alliances. On the one hand, undoubtedly in the ascendant since Skiernewice, was the Three Emperors' Alliance, embodying the desire to co-operate with 'official' Russia and by the exercise of mutual self-restraint to avoid a clash over the Balkans that could only prove disastrous to all three great monarchies. On the other hand, and temporarily of less urgent importance as the Three Emperors' Alliance seemed to be working and the risk of war receded, was the Dual Alliance and its ramifications, which would strengthen the Monarchy in war if the Three Emperors' Alliance should fail to keep the peace. Of these alliances, the Dual Alliance was clearly the most important, with its promise of German military assistance. The Roumanian alliance promised a support that would hardly materialize, and the Triple Alliance no support at all. Moreover, the alliances with Serbia, Italy and Roumania were all plagued with irredentism. Nevertheless, all these alliances were important if the Monarchy needed rear-cover to concentrate its resources on the Russian front. And even in peacetime they were useful, like the Three Emperors' Alliance, in bolstering up the monarchical principle and conservative interests generally. Apart from this, the Monarchy had managed to establish good relations with Turkey, and had a firm foothold in Bulgaria – both of which states might prove useful, even without an alliance, in the event of war. Finally, with Salisbury's return to power in London (June 24) there even seemed a chance of some British support.

Yet even the most elaborate alliance system can hardly provide for every case. The alliance system of 1879–83 offered Austria-Hungary a fair chance of peaceful co-existence with Russia, provided the pacific tsar continued to direct Russian policy; and as strong a military position as she was ever likely to attain in the event of a final armed confrontation with Russia. There always remained the problems of day-to-day diplomacy, however; perhaps of less obvious urgency than the risks of actual war and annihilation, but, none the less, of vital importance when taken together over a number of years. The perpetual struggle for influence in the Balkan states had immense implications for the whole Great Power position of the parties concerned. At least, this was the conviction of those directing policy in Vienna and St Petersburg. It might happen that a diplomatic crisis would prove severe enough to estrange even 'official' Russia from the Monarchy and to destroy the Three Emperors' Alliance, but would yet stop short of that war which would bring the other alliances into operation. Such a crisis would not only intensify the contradictions in the Balkan alliance system, given the conflicting ambitions of the Monarchy's friends and allies in the peninsula; it would also reveal the inadequacy in diplomacy of alliances designed for use in war.

Chapter 5

The Decline of the Alliances, 1885–95[1]

> The Triple Alliance is in a somewhat parlous condition,
> which I truly deplore. It is mutually suspicious, which
> is the worst of signs.
>
> *Rosebery to Mallet*, 3 January 1894[2]

By the summer of 1885 the Three Emperors' Alliance had established a *modus vivendi* amongst the Great Powers concerned; yet, by virtue of its very nature as a negative, self-denying agreement, it could never exercise much positive direction over events in the small Balkan states. On 18 September a nationalist *coup* in Philippopolis, capital of Eastern Roumelia, proclaimed the union of the two Bulgarias, which Prince Alexander perforce accepted. To this blow to the Balkan balance as established at the Congress of Berlin the kings of Serbia and Greece (in Vienna at the time) immediately reacted by claiming compensation. The Great Powers, taken completely by surprise, were nonplussed; and their mutual suspicions revived overnight. Whereas Russia suspected a plot between Britain and Prince Alexander to deprive her of the privilege of bestowing unity on the Bulgarians, it was Russia herself who came under suspicion at Vienna. It was essential to prevent the revival of the Big Bulgaria of San Stefano, the emperor and Kálnoky decided; on no account therefore must the movement be allowed to spread to Macedonia. Franz Joseph also stressed the need to bear in mind the 'justified claims' of Serbia

[1] The following works are of particular relevance to this chapter: Margaret M. Jefferson, 'The Place of Constantinople and the Straits in British Foreign Policy, 1890–1902', M.A. thesis, London, 1959; G. Ritter, 'Die Zusammenarbeit der Generalstäbe Deutschlands und Oesterreich-Ungarn vor dem ersten Weltkrieg' in *Zur Geschichte und Problematik der Demokratie* Berlin, 1958; and the works by H. Benedikt, G. Drage, F. Klein, and C. A. Macartney cited in Chapter 1, note 1; by W. Wagner, Chapter 2, note 1; b E. v. Glaise-Horstenau, Chapter 3, note 1; and by W. N. Medlicott and I Salvatorelli, Chapter 4, note 1.

[2] Quoted in Margaret M. Jefferson, p. 98.

and Roumania, two states which 'we must at all costs keep within our sphere of influence and on good terms with us'.[3] At the same time, it might be possible to support Alexander and encourage the Bulgarian nationalist movement to take a direction independent of Russia. To this end, the Austrians were initially inclined to the British policy of supporting the prince, while granting Eastern Roumelia only a personal union, not unification, with Bulgaria.

On 4 October, however, Russia came out strongly with a radically different policy, firmly condemning Alexander and demanding the restoration of the *status quo ante*. It was now perfectly clear that the Philippopolis revolution had not been engineered in St Petersburg; and, as innocent Russia also enjoyed the loyal support of Berlin, it was hardly surprising that by 8 October Kálnoky decided to bring Austro-Hungarian policy into line. He was above all concerned to co-operate with St Petersburg and to preserve the Three Emperors' Alliance: but a policy of upholding the Treaty of Berlin would also have the advantage of relieving the Powers of the task of devising compensations for Bulgaria's neighbours. On the other hand, it was not without risks from the point of view of Austro-Hungarian interests. As Andrássy pointed out, the Philippopolis *coup* was designed to create a Bulgaria independent of Russia; whereas a restoration of the *status quo ante* would also restore to Russia the chance of bringing about a union under Russian auspices.[4] The most serious objection to the policy of the Three Emperors' Alliance, however, was its impracticality. As the ensuing conference at Constantinople showed, the Turks were by no means anxious to undertake the reconquest of Eastern Roumelia; and the British for once had the relatively easy task of obstructing action by the Concert. By mid-November, the Constantinople conference had achieved virtually nothing.

In this situation it became increasingly difficult for Kálnoky to restrain the Serbs. In September, he had advised Milan to trust to Austro-Hungarian diplomacy to secure compensation for Serbia, and to do no more than strengthen his frontier defences. In October, when Milan, despite Kálnoky's advice, mobilized the whole army, whipping up feeling in Serbia to a dangerous degree, Kálnoky told him to trust to the Constantinople conference

---

[3] P.A. XL/55, Franz Joseph to Kálnoky, 20 September 1885.
[4] Kab. 19, Andrássy to Franz Joseph, 24 November 1885.

to restore the *status quo*. When it became clear that the conference would not be able to offer even this sop, the Serbs decided to seek their own salvation. On 14 November Milan's army suddenly invaded Bulgaria. Now the fact that Austria-Hungary's protégé, Serbia, had attacked Russia's – albeit erring – protégé, Bulgaria, caused acute embarrassment in Vienna. Kálnoky decided that Britain, by frustrating the efforts of the Constantinople conference, was chiefly to blame. She seemed to be trying to break up the Three Emperors' Alliance and set Russia and Austria-Hungary by the ears. But she would not succeed.[5] These sentiments were echoed in the Austro-Hungarian embassy at St Petersburg, a notable shrine of the Three Emperors' Alliance. Britain, the ambassador Wolkenstein declared, was a greater enemy of the Monarchy in the Near East than Russia was: 'she is striving for our commercial annihilation.'[6] And the military attaché had little sympathy for the Serbs: 'it is a great pity these nationalist pigs think they have a right to boast of our protection.'[7] The embassy was relieved, therefore, when Kálnoky agreed without much ado to a Russian proposal of 19 November for joint diplomatic intervention by the Powers to stop the Serbian invasion of Bulgaria.

Ironically enough, by 19 November Kálnoky had compelling reasons of his own to agree. For on that day Prince Alexander defeated the invaders at Slivnitsa and in turn invaded Serbia. Kálnoky was now faced with a desperate appeal for help from a panic-stricken Milan; and with the prospect that a continued Bulgarian advance might increase the ferment among the south Slavs of the Monarchy – already alarming enough – to such a pitch that the Monarchy might have to mobilize troops in the frontier districts. To prevent this, Kálnoky determined that the war must be stopped at all costs; and when a joint note from the Powers was accepted by Milan but not by Alexander, he resorted to the famous Khevenhüller mission. The Austro-Hungarian minister at Belgrade (telegraphic communication with Sofia had been cut) was instructed to go to Alexander's headquarters and, using such arguments as he felt necessary, persuade the Prince to

[5] P.A. XV/98, Kálnoky to Károlyi, Tel. 117, 24 November 1885.
[6] Aehrenthal MSS., Karton 4, Wolkenstein to Aehrenthal, 27 October 1885.
[7] Aehrenthal MSS., Karton 2, Klepsch to Aehrenthal, 15 October 1885.

call a halt. In accordance with the spirit of the Three Emperors' Alliance, Kálnoky showed these instructions to the Russian ambassador, who in turn reported his government's approval.

Unfortunately, such general instructions were dangerous in the hands of one so ebullient as Khevenhüller, who in the event went so far as to warn Alexander that if the Bulgarian invasion caused a revolution in Serbia, Austria-Hungary would occupy the country, whereupon Russia would occupy Bulgaria and depose Alexander. The arguments were efficacious; but caused a nasty contretemps with St Petersburg. Austro-Hungarian diplomats there were anything but pleased: 'Khevenhüller's *coup* was a great surprise for us here at the embassy. No wonder Russia didn't like the threat of a Russian occupation of Bulgaria (which nobody here is thinking of).'[8] But Kálnoky did not take the matter too seriously: Khevenhüller had gone farther than his instructions warranted; and Russia was probably only piqued at seeing Austro-Hungarian prestige increased (Document 16). He assured St Petersburg that no one in Vienna had talked of occupying Serbia; and irritably reminded the complaining Bismarck that Austria-Hungary had acted in order to forestall, not to precipitate, a situation in which she might have had to take measures which would cause strife within the Three Emperors' Alliance.[9]

In the event, the Three Emperors' Alliance survived the incident. True, Andrássy still thought the whole policy of co-operation with Russia misguided, and in a long memorandum to the emperor (24 November)[10] urged that the Monarchy take the initiative and work for the complete independence of a united Bulgaria. On the other hand, the St Petersburg embassy was equally assiduous in extolling the virtues of peace, the Monarchy's only really vital interest. According to Wolkenstein, there was in Europe 'a great revolutionary subversive party just waiting for the crash and for the great conservative Powers to weaken and exhaust each other in the conflict, and then the radical reform can begin'.[11] The Bulgarian victory had in fact helped matters, both by bringing even Russia to recognize that the *status quo ante* was

[8] Aehrenthal MSS., Karton 4, Wacken to Aehrenthal, 13 December 1885.
[9] P.A. XV/85, Kálnoky to Széchenyi, 14 December 1885.
[10] Kab. 19, Andrássy to Franz Joseph, 24 November 1885.
[11] Aehrenthal MSS., Karton 4, Wolkenstein to Aehrenthal, 16 December 1885.

an unrealistic aim, and by disposing of any Serbian hopes of compensation. Nevertheless, Kálnoky seemed for a moment to waver, and at the turn of the year considered seizing the initiative and asking Russia to show her colours. But Bismarck, who hoped that Britain and Russia might come to blows if only left alone, was strongly opposed to any such step. Kálnoky, once more in a minority within the Three Emperors' Alliance, again came into line.

Bismarck was wrong; and in the event Britain and Russia came together to determine the Turco-Bulgarian settlement of February 1886. Kálnoky was content for the most part to stay in the background and hold to the Three Emperors' Alliance. The personal union proposed for Bulgaria and Eastern Roumelia suited Austro-Hungarian interests well enough; and he even supported a Russian-inspired clause limiting Alexander's tenure of office in Philippopolis. The Monarchy played a similarly self-effacing role in the naval demonstration by which in the spring the Powers brought Greece to abandon her strident claims to compensation. In the Serbo-Bulgarian peace negotiations at Bucharest, however, the Austrians assumed the role of honest broker with some success. The settlement – confined to a simple restoration of peace – was realistic. The Austrians secured their main point: Serbia was not burdened with a war indemnity. Although they had some trouble from King Milan, who threatened to abandon the alliance and appoint a Radical ministry if Austria-Hungary permitted any aggrandizement of Bulgaria, Kálnoky sharply reminded him that Serbia's sad predicament was only the result of her having ignored Vienna's advice in the autumn; and he found the Serbian foreign minister, Mijatović, sensible enough. At the same time, he managed to avoid offending Bulgarian susceptibilities. Altogether, he could be well content with the negotiations at Bucharest.

The Three Emperors' Alliance continued in good health until the summer. In August Archduke Karl Ludwig paid a highly successful visit to St Petersburg; and Kálnoky prepared to dispel any doubts among the public by announcing that 'Austria-Hungary has no intention of weakening the relationship that was sealed at Skiernewice and Kremsier, and which came into practical operation in the last Bulgarian crisis.'[12] In this situation, reinsurance in the west against the collapse of the Three Emperors'

[12] P.A. I/469, Aehrenthal memorandum, 1895.

Alliance seemed, of course, less necessary. In July Kálnoky humoured St Petersburg by refusing to join Britain in denouncing Russia's unilateral abrogation of the Batum clause of the Treaty of Berlin. And the Triple Alliance was certainly at a discount. Italy's attempts to initiate an active Balkan policy – albeit in support of the Three Emperors' Alliance – in the Bulgarian crisis, and her hints that the Balkans should be brought within the purview of the Triple Alliance, were coldly received in Vienna. At Kissingen and Gastein in the summer of 1886 Bismarck and Kálnoky remained firmly of the opinion that if the Triple Alliance were renewed, there could be no question of amendments or concessions to Italy.

The state of the Monarchy's Balkan alliances inspired less confidence. By November 1885 King Milan – whom Kálnoky had been describing in September as the only support of Austro-Hungarian influence in Serbia – had shown himself to be devoid of military virtues (a failing that counted for much with Franz Joseph and Kálnoky); and his continued misgovernment and threats to tear up the alliance convinced Vienna that his political sense was of an equally low order. Yet Kálnoky, perhaps lulled by the apparent success of the Three Emperors' Alliance, perhaps at a loss for an alternative policy, viewed these developments with remarkable aplomb. In November 1885 he told Franz Joseph that he 'had always thought it would be wrong to base our position in Serbia' too exclusively on Milan.[13] If the latter fell as a result of Serbia's defeat, Kálnoky advised co-operation with a regency under the queen, the essential point being to maintain the Obrenović dynasty and keep the Russophile Nikita of Montenegro off the Serbian throne. The dynasty, plus what he optimistically termed a hard political fact, namely Serbia's inevitable dependence on her powerful northern neighbour, provided a better basis for influence than any amount of chasing after Milan or ephemeral public opinion. Such arguments were perhaps only an attempt to make the best of an obviously bad job. At any rate, Kálnoky's Serbian policy henceforth became increasingly passive, and steered clear of the maelstrom of Serbian domestic politics.

The Roumanian alliance was beset by still greater difficulties. During the Serbo-Bulgarian war Bucharest was in a very anti-Serbian mood; and it even looked as though Russia was counting

[13] P.A. I/456, Kálnoky to Franz Joseph, 22 November 1885.

on irredentist designs on Transylvania to turn Roumania actively against the Monarchy in the event of a great war. The political alarm subsided in the spring of 1886. Not so the Austro-Roumanian commercial quarrel. Kálnoky's efforts to persuade the Hungarians to make some concession, such as re-opening the frontier to Roumanian livestock, came to nothing – even though in a conference of ministers in January 1886 he emphasized the evil political consequences of allowing the commercial treaty to expire, and pointed out that in economic terms too the Monarchy would be the chief loser.[14] The treaty duly expired in June 1886, and the resultant tariff war lasted for seven years. It brought some benefits to Hungarian agriculture, now sheltered from Roumanian competition; but Austrian industry suffered heavily, and lost most of the Roumanian market to Germany, Britain, and Belgium. The Monarchy's imports from and exports to Roumania fell by 90 per cent and 40 per cent respectively between 1885 and 1887. Such a state of affairs could only bode ill for the alliance.

The only bright spot on the Balkan horizon was Bulgaria. True, public opinion there had tended to associate Austria-Hungary with the marauding Serbs in the crisis of 1885–6; and Kálnoky was always somewhat sceptical of Alexander's more effusive protestations of loyalty. But he nevertheless recognized in the prince 'a convinced and sincere enemy of Russian influence',[15] whom it was in Austria-Hungary's interests to support. For Kálnoky was still not prepared to tolerate Russian control of Bulgaria and the encirclement of the Monarchy that he feared would follow. Yet far from seeing in his defence of Bulgaria from enslavement by Russia a source of danger to the Three Emperors' Alliance, he relied on the Alliance to restrain Russia from pressing Bulgaria too hard. And for this greater end, even Alexander was expendable. When the prince was kidnapped by Russian officers on 19 August and released from Russia into Austria a week later, Kálnoky advised him not to return to Bulgaria without the blessing of the tsar; and when this was crushingly refused and Alexander abdicated, Kálnoky obligingly agreed with Giers on 11 September that the simplest solution would be the speedy election of a new prince.

A few days later, however, when Alexander's supporters had

[14] P.A. XL/294, Ministerratsprotokoll, 7 January 1886.
[15] P.A. XV/99, Kálnoky to Károlyi, 11 February 1886.

recovered control in Bulgaria and were clearly preparing to elect a like-minded successor, St Petersburg decided that the election should be delayed, and an effort made to influence Bulgarian opinion in Russia's favour. Suddenly, and without prior consultation with his partners in the Three Emperors' Alliance, the tsar sent General Kaulbars to Sofia. To Vienna this looked suspiciously like a bid for the political control of Bulgaria; and this Kálnoky was not prepared to tolerate. Bismarck's bland suggestion that Bulgaria was after all in Russia's sphere of influence, he rejected out of hand: if Russia occupied Bulgaria, the Monarchy might not fight immediately; but the prospect of a prolonged Russian occupation was 'unthinkable for Austria-Hungary. The question of what would happen to Roumania is automatic and unanswerable.'[16] But he found no support whatever in Berlin. Nor had he enough confidence in the British to abandon the Three Emperors' Alliance and cast in his lot with Salisbury.[17] He may have been hoping that Britain would come forward alone and oppose Russia, allowing Austria-Hungary to preserve her good relations with St Petersburg. At any rate, for about two weeks London and Vienna circled each other in a strange diplomatic quadrille, each waiting for the other to take up a firm position. Even when the British did so, on 30 September, suggesting Anglo-Austro-Italian co-operation at Sofia and Constantinople to support the Bulgarians against Kaulbars, Kálnoky in the end decided that that would involve too great a risk of war with Russia. That being the case, he had left himself with little alternative but to try unaided to bring the Russians to reason within the framework of the Three Emperors' Alliance.

The Alliance availed him little. The Russians offered Vienna only the vaguest explanations as to their intentions, which only made Kálnoky fear the worst. His own views – stated openly by Tisza in the Hungarian parliament in October – that no European treaty gave any Great Power a special position in the Balkan states, which should be left to settle their own affairs without interference, caused immense irritation in St Petersburg, where memories of 1877 were still fresh. The Russians claimed to be seeking to liberate Bulgaria from 'a regime of terror and violence' and accused the Austrians of collaborating with 'cosmopolitan

[16] P.A. I/469, Aehrenthal memorandum, 1895.
[17] W. N. Medlicott, *British Foreign Policy in the Near East* . . ., pp. 320ff.

radicalism to transform Bulgaria into a hotbed of anarchy and hostility to Russia'[18] – a neat variation on Kálnoky's favourite theme; but the Austrians discerned in all this a bid for political control. There was no room for compromise. Indeed, Kálnoky was not even prepared to allow Russia the position she had enjoyed before the Philippopolis revolution: this had no basis in treaties, he decided. A new note of acrimony was added when the whole debate was given a public airing in the Delegations at Budapest in November. True, the Vienna foreign office strove hard against Hungarian pressure for war, and attributed Andrássy's fulminations in the debates to injured vanity.[19] Nevertheless, Kálnoky felt bound to reaffirm that the Bulgarian question could be settled only by Europe, not by General Kaulbars; and threatened Russia pretty clearly with war if she proceeded to use force against Bulgaria. Kálnoky's speech of 13 November, and a similar one by Salisbury, stiffened Bulgarian resistance immeasurably. The tsar's policy collapsed in ruins, and on 20 November the Kaulbars mission was withdrawn, an utter failure.

Kálnoky's victory had only been bought at a price. True, the Russians were thankful that they had to deal with him rather than the warlike Andrássy; but they were none the less bitter. By mid-December they were hinting that the days of the Three Emperors' Alliance were numbered; and the Austro-Hungarian embassy at St Petersburg, which had had no business to transact for some weeks, gloomily concluded that diplomatic relations between Russia and Austria-Hungary had to all practical purposes been broken off.[20] Such conciliatory gestures as Kálnoky felt at liberty to make – and he was very much restricted by his determination to preserve the autonomy of Bulgaria – were largely ineffective. He promised not to oppose the Russian candidates for the Bulgarian throne – two relatives of the tsar, and the Prince of Mingrelia (son of a Georgian prince who had sold his crown to the tsar), whose drunken and licentious wife the Austrians wryly observed seemed an appropriate counterpart to Kaulbars.[21] But the Bulgarian regents would not consider these candidates; and Kálnoky warned the Russians against resorting to coercion, and

[18] P.A. I/469, Aehrenthal memorandum, 1895.
[19] Aehrenthal MSS., Karton 4, Pasetti to Aehrenthal, 17 November 1886.
[20] Aehrenthal MSS., Karton 4, Wacken to Aehrenthal, 23 December 1886.
[21] Aehrenthal MSS., Karton 5, Tavera to Aehrenthal, 20 November 1886.

lent them no support in their efforts (ably countered by Britain) to persuade the Turks to replace the council of regents by a care-taker government more amenable to St Petersburg. By the sum-mer of 1887 Russia had still made no progress whatever in Bulgaria; and Kálnoky's repeated advice to allow the regents to proceed with an early election was received with very bad grace at St Petersburg.

If the obvious bankruptcy of the Three Emperors' Alliance were not depressing enough, it was becoming increasingly clear that the other alliances which were kept in reserve to meet just such a contingency were all well below par. The Dual Alliance had been worse than useless in the crisis. Only a very categoric statement from Vienna in October had brought Bismarck to cease his irritating incantations about spheres of influence; and Kálnoky never succeeded in winning Germany's moral support in Bulgaria, even when he warned Berlin that the attitude of the German press, which defended Russia's machinations, was des-troying the faith of the populations of the Monarchy in the Alliance.[22] Bismarck's famous 'Hecuba' speech of 11 January 1887, proclaiming to the Reichstag and the world that 'it is a matter of complete indifference to us who rules in Bulgaria and what becomes of her',[23] finally convinced Kálnoky of Germany's diplomatic uselessness. And this was matched by doubts as to her military reliability. In a memorandum of 7 March Archduke Albrecht wondered whether Germany would still be prepared to co-operate in the east, where thirty-six Austro-Hungarian divisions were likely to face sixty-two Russian divisions in the event of war. He went on to suggest that if Austria-Hungary could not extract a definite promise that eighteen German divisions would appear in the east, she should declare herself freed from all obli-gations to her ally.[24]

Kálnoky still thought the Dual Alliance worth clinging to, for all its defects, and tried to calm the Archduke down. He pointed out that with the revival of French military power since 1885,[25]

[22] P.A. I/464, Liasse XVI, Kálnoky memorandum on a conversation with the German Ambassador, 6 October 1886.

[23] Bismarck, *Die gesammelten Werke*, Vol. 13, p. 213.

[24] P.A. I/466, memorandum by Archduke Albrecht on military co-opera-tion between Germany and Austria-Hungary, 7 March 1887, with comments (*Gegenbemerkungen*) by Kálnoky.

[25] Ibid.

Germany was simply no longer in a position to put as many men in the east as she had planned to do in 1882. Moreover, in his view France was quite as dangerous as Russia, and quite as much in need of watching. For if she ever defeated Germany 'the republican and socialist menace would sweep through Europe like a flood when a dam has been broken.' In any case, Austria-Hungary would do well to avoid being too specific in her own military promises: if the Italian monarchy fell, Montenegro provoked a rising in the occupied provinces, and Roumania proved disloyal, the Monarchy would certainly not be able to put up anything like thirty-six divisions against Russia. Nor could one declare oneself freed from obligations to an ally because that ally refused to comply with demands made subsequently. The Monarchy had after all done something to strengthen its own defences; and the Delegations had just accepted a large military budget with a heartening unanimity unusual in that heterogeneous body. Kálnoky was right not to panic. By the early summer the situation looked much brighter. He rejoiced that Bismarck had been able to give France 'a real fright' in 'the ridiculous Schnaebele affair', and calculated that once Boulanger was out of office Russia too would begin to behave with more circumspection.[26] Nevertheless, as he confided in a secret and private letter to Széchenyi, the ambassador at Berlin,[27] grave doubts had taken root among the public about the value of the Dual Alliance. And this, he said, was no wonder, considering the ostentatious indifference towards Near Eastern questions shown in official speeches and the semi-official press in Germany; and Germany's continued 'harshly negative' attitude in commercial questions.

Meanwhile the Triple Alliance, plagued from the start with the problem of mistrust between the populations of Austria and Italy, had had to undergo the ordeal of a formal renewal which considerably increased mistrust between the governments of Vienna and Rome. In October 1886 Bismarck, alarmed at developments in France and, above all, anxious to make sure of Italy's assistance, was willing both to extend Germany's obligations and to bully the Austrians into extending theirs. Kálnoky, on the other hand, had no relish for the amendments proposed by Rome: that the

[26] P.A. I/460, Kálnoky to Wolkenstein, private and confidential, 7 May 1887.
[27] P.A. I/464, Liasse XVII, Kálnoky to Széchenyi, private and secret, 12 May 1887.

allies should support Italy if she got into war with France over the Tripoli question; and that in the event of changes in the *status quo* in the Balkans, Italy should be granted compensation. He was as anxious as ever not to increase Austria-Hungary's commitments against France, and almost as unwilling to bind the Monarchy's hands *vis-à-vis* Italy in the Near East or to recognize an Italian sphere of influence there. Besides, the cloven hoof of irredentism was all too evident in the compensations proposal. Nevertheless, under strong pressure from Berlin, and enticed by Italian hints of possible military assistance against Russia, he seemed ready by mid-December to give way.

In January 1887, however, he suddenly withdrew all his concessions and declared for the simple renewal of the alliance unchanged. The decisive factor, he explained to Széchenyi,[28] was Bismarck's 'Hecuba' speech, which had disheartened Austria-Hungary's friends and supporters everywhere, and clearly showed that she would have to rely on her own strength to defend her Near Eastern interests. She could not afford to dissipate that strength, therefore, by assuming increased commitments in the west: the more Germany concentrated on France, the more the Monarchy would have to concentrate on the east. This produced further German pressure and a stern reminder from Bismarck that although Italy might not be able to give Austria-Hungary much help, she could do her a good deal of harm by going over to France and Russia. This argument was unanswerable. There was no denying that the eastern crisis had completely transformed Italy's bargaining position since the summer of 1886. Kálnoky, consoling himself with bitter reflections on Italy's '*Trinkgeldpolitik*',[29] at last gave way. On 2 February he agreed to an additional Austro-Italian treaty covering the Balkans (similar in form to a German-Italian additional treaty on Tripoli) (Document 19, n. 2). Franz Joseph was most emphatic that the annexation of Bosnia should not be held to constitute a change in the *status quo* warranting compensation under the new treaty; and that whatever compensation Italy might receive should not come from Austro-Hungarian territory. The Italian ambassador in Berlin stated that this was 'obvious'.[30] It was nevertheless remarkably ingenuous – or

[28] P.A. I/462, Kálnoky to Széchenyi, secret, 20 January 1887.
[29] P.A. I/461, Széchenyi to Kálnoky, private and secret, 1 April 1887.
[30] L. Salvatorelli, p. 117.

slipshod – of Kálnoky to content himself with the ambassador's verbal declaration as a sufficient guarantee. It was certainly not binding on any Italian government – as the Austrians were to find to their cost in 1915.

The Triple Alliance had survived. Indeed, its existence was at last published to the world in March 1887. But it had gained nothing in internal strength, nor, from the Austro-Hungarian point of view, in usefulness. The Italian hints of military aid were eventually explained away as a misunderstanding. Not that Kálnoky, who had 'never attached much weight'[31] to Italian assistance, was worried or surprised. Indeed, he doubted whether Italy would observe even neutrality if the Monarchy were involved in war in the east. Széchenyi agreed: 'but what can one expect from a country where the mob rules the sceptre?'[32]

Even so, the Mediterranean scene had its brighter spots. The British, after the failure of their soundings at Vienna in September 1886, had managed to establish a link with Italy – the agreement of 12 February 1887 for diplomatic co-operation to maintain the *status quo* in the Mediterranean and neighbouring seas. And this they saw as a chance to resume contact with Austria-Hungary. On 8 February the British ambassador, Paget, had suggested to Kálnoky that Britain might be able to help Austria-Hungary in a war with Russia; and Kálnoky had enthusiastically agreed. The recent crisis had cured him of his illusions about the Three Emperors' Alliance: and if it really came to a war Britain and Austria-Hungary might not be able to destroy Russia, but they could at least secure a lengthy breathing space by co-operating to bleed her white.[33] He was already assuming, he told Paget, that Britain's own interests would bring her into any Austro-Russian war, whether a prior agreement existed or not. On 19 February the British took a further step: Paget informed Kálnoky of the Anglo-Italian agreement; and Kálnoky enquired in London as to the possibility of a similar Anglo-Austrian agreement. Károlyi reported back that Salisbury personally would stake his political existence on coming to the aid of the Monarchy in a war with Russia, a promise which the ambassador said was as good as an

[31] P.A. I/462, Kálnoky to Bruck, private and secret, 15 February 1887.
[32] P.A. I/462, Széchenyi to Kálnoky, secret, 12 February 1887.
[33] P.A. I/461, Kálnoky, memorandum on a conversation with Paget, 8 February 1887.

alliance in principle. Kálnoky, certainly, was content with a mere 'agreement to agree' should trouble arise. It entailed no onerous commitments for Austria-Hungary in the western Mediterranean (although she now broke with the Three Emperors' Alliance in Egypt, and promised her diplomatic support to Britain); and yet it ensured that British policy would not 'wander away again' (as it had done in 1885). On 24 March the Monarchy acceded to the Anglo-Italian agreement; and in May, this group was further reinforced by the addition of Spain. Neither Kálnoky nor Bismarck would consider Italy's idea of bringing Spain into the Triple Alliance – geographical factors prevented the Central Powers ever rendering Spain any effective assistance. But Vienna welcomed the Italo-Spanish exchange of notes on general lines of policy (4 May) because it strengthened conservative and monarchical ideas in Spain against 'the dangerous idea of a republican brotherhood of Latin races'.[34] Austria-Hungary formally acceded on 22 May.

The Monarchy's eastern alliances, on the other hand, continued to decay. In Serbia the feud between the king and queen was reducing political life to utter confusion; and Milan's mental state, his threats to abdicate, to change his foreign policy, and to bring Ristić and the Liberals to power dismayed Vienna. By August 1887 the legation at Belgrade remarked on the advancing decay of Austria-Hungary's connexions there: the ministry of foreign affairs, formerly very co-operative, was now always difficult to handle. Yet Kálnoky still held to the bland assumption that Serbia, 'despite all her dislike of us, does not want to become Russian, and in the long run will not be able . . . to escape from our influence'.[35] Perhaps a more active policy would only have hastened the collapse of the alliance. Still, it must be admitted that Kálnoky's passivity brought few returns. Perhaps he himself saw this and was secretly galled by it. At any rate, when Baron Hengelmüller, minister at Belgrade, lectured him at length on the futility of a passive policy, Kálnoky rewarded him with a decoration and the Washington legation, where he spent the next twenty years bewailing Kálnoky's obtuseness and his own ruined career.[36]

[34] P.A. I/461, Kálnoky to Bruck, private and very secret, 19 March 1887.
[35] P.A. I/460, Kálnoky to Wolkenstein, private and confidential, 7 May 1887.
[36] Aehrenthal MSS., Karton 1, Hengelmüller to Aehrenthal, 6 October 1900.

Relations with Roumania were still bedevilled by the tariff war, described by the Austro-Hungarian legation at Bucharest as 'a disaster' for the Monarchy.[37] Stourdza's government, weak, and faced with a feud between the king and Bratianu, simply could not afford to make any concessions. But Kálnoky condemned its openly anti-Austro-Hungarian attitude[38] and toyed with the idea of establishing contacts with the traditionally pro-Russian Conservative party. Bismarck lent Vienna no help at all; and even Count Agenor Goluchowski, appointed to Bucharest in February 1887 and, thanks to his geniality and his august connexions (his wife was a princess Murat) a great personal success there, 'could not move mountains' in the commercial question, which for Roumania was 'more important than all others'.[39] This being the case, it was small consolation that the overthrow of Alexander of Battenberg had given the Roumanians a healthy fright, bringing Stourdza to Vienna with assurances of loyalty; or that in October 1887 Kálnoky and King Carol agreed to regard the alliance as prolonged for another three years. The very crisis that inspired these gestures of loyalty had shown their limitations: in February 1887 Archduke Albrecht had told the Roumanians that the Monarchy would need all its forces for the crucial offensive in Galicia, and would have none to spare to assist Roumania directly.

The Three Emperors' Alliance, of course, was in full dissolution. In the spring of 1887 the news of its existence – leaked to the press by Saburov – had called forth a Panslav outcry which had almost driven Giers from office. By 7 May Kálnoky was admitting to Wolkenstein:[40] 'I cannot boast that my years of effort to establish stable and friendly relations with Russia have been successful; but I don't regret them, and can say with good conscience that I have done what I could' – there had never been any spirit of reciprocity in St Petersburg. He nevertheless told Wolkenstein to raise the question of the renewal of the treaty; but he thought the chances slim, and was not surprised by the tsar's refusal. Bismarck's attempt to repeat the tactics of 1879 – he persuaded

[37] Aehrenthal MSS., Karton 1, Heidler to Aehrenthal, 3 October 1886.
[38] Ibid., Heidler to Aehrenthal, 25 August, 6 September 1886.
[39] Ibid., Heidler to Aehrenthal, 16 February 1887.
[40] P.A. I/460, Kálnoky to Wolkenstein, private and confidential, 7 May 1887.

Kálnoky to agree to the communication of the actual terms of the Dual Alliance to Russia, in the hope that such a display of solidarity would bring her into line – failed completely. For the tsar, already mortally offended by the Monarchy's opposition to the Kaulbars mission – his own brainchild – had been deeply impressed by the public outcry against the alliance. The Three Emperors' Alliance expired on 18 June 1887.

Kálnoky was not unduly worried. Indeed, it was Russia who seemed to have lost most from the disappearance of the Alliance. For the Monarchy was now freed of even a moral obligation to humour St Petersburg; and when in June Russia proposed, with German support, that the three empires take the lead in replacing the recalcitrant council of regents in Bulgaria by a single provisional regent – such as the Russian General Ehrenroth – she was frustrated by Kálnoky's refusal to co-operate. Her clumsy tactics in Bulgaria (for example, she gave open *post factum* approval to an abortive military *coup* in March) only precipitated a further and more spectacular Russian defeat. The Bulgarians now made haste to secure themselves against Russian influence once and for all; and on 7 July a special sobranje unanimously elected Prince Ferdinand of Saxe-Coburg-Koháry to the Bulgarian throne. As an Austrian army officer, a member of the Hungarian branch of the Saxe-Coburg family, a relative of the British ruling house, and especially as a Roman Catholic, Ferdinand was from the point of view of St Petersburg the most obnoxious candidate conceivable. A Russian circular of 13 July declared the election to be illegal, 'an unworthy comedy staged by the most wretched rabble'.[41] Yet even the Austrians were not entirely happy about such a spectacularly anti-Russian choice. Franz Joseph thought it politic to refrain from receiving Ferdinand at Ischl; and on 7 July Kálnoky reminded Ferdinand that before he could be legally installed in Bulgaria he would need the approval of the signatory Powers, which was not likely to be forthcoming. Not that the Austrians, for their part, intended to stand in his way, for they considered the election perfectly legal and correct. But when Turkey also raised objections, Kálnoky again warned Ferdinand that he could expect no positive support from Austria-Hungary.

Ferdinand set out for Sofia none the less; and once he had arrived in Bulgaria, the Austrians swallowed their irritation and

[41] P.A. I/469, Aehrenthal memorandum, 1895.

decided that they had better support him. For he was clearly popular there: Russia's suggestion that the Turks expel him would inevitably have entailed the shedding of a good deal of Christian Bulgarian blood, and was regarded in Vienna as a particularly shameless example of her cynical ruthlessness. The Russians, with Bismarck's support, were still angling at Constantinople for the appointment of a provisional regent – the Ehrenroth plan – and this Franz Joseph told the Germans he could never accept. He had no designs on Bulgaria himself: but he could not allow Bulgaria to become a Russian province – Roumania, Serbia, and Montenegro would soon follow. Besides, he felt obliged to consider his partners in the Mediterranean agreements. The latter were indeed proving of sterling worth. Throughout the autumn the three Powers waged a masterly campaign of passive resistance in the face of attempts by Russia and her French and German suitors to move the Turks to action. This gave Ferdinand time to consolidate his position in Bulgaria. By November Russia was ready to call off the diplomatic campaign at Constantinople, and to try the less exhausting tactics of fomenting plots at Sofia. Her fury had by no means abated; and expressed itself in massive troop concentrations in Poland which were to cause a serious crisis at the turn of the year. But her defeat in Bulgaria was none the less complete for that.

Throughout the wearisome diplomatic struggle over the fate of Bulgaria, the Mediterranean *entente* had been of more use to Austria-Hungary than all her alliances put together. And from the late summer of 1887 negotiations were in progress to extend the *entente* to guard specifically against Russian machinations at Sofia, Constantinople, and the Straits (Document 17). For France and Russia still carried great weight at Constantinople, Russia ruling the sultan according to Calice, 'by intimidation'.[42] In the summer, for example, they had bullied the sultan into rejecting the Drummond-Wolff Convention (by which the British had sought to extricate themselves from Egypt while keeping the door open for a re-occupation should the need arise). And this despite the fact that Britain had Germany as well as the Mediterranean *entente* behind her. By August, Germany had suddenly gone back to supporting Russia – in Bulgaria. This, Kálnoky said, completely confused the sultan's view of Great Power alignments, and was

[42] P.A. I/458, Liasse VIIIb, Calice to Kálnoky, private, 24 September 1887.

'the most harmful element in the present situation'.[43] The Austrians were not hopeful, therefore, of the chances of drawing Turkey any closer to what they liked to refer to as 'our group' at Constantinople. Nevertheless, on 19 September Kálnoky approved the academic discussions that Calice was holding with his British and Italian colleagues about possible ways of restraining Turkey, by threats or even by force, from throwing in her lot with France and Russia. He still felt the need to tread cautiously. For example, when Calice drew up a draft agreement of eight points, some of the suspicions of 1886 revived. On 25 September, Kálnoky reminded the ambassador that it would be well to emphasize Constantinople and the Straits – a pre-eminently British interest – rather than the Balkans, lest Britain try to push Austria-Hungary forward and shelter behind her (*zu sehr hinter uns verkrieche*).[44]

Nevertheless, when he saw in Bismarck's reception of Crispi at Friedrichsruh on 2 October a sign that Germany might be willing to lend her moral support, Kálnoky decided to take the initiative. The Germans had in fact been irritated by Russia's flirtations with France for some time now. At Gastein in August Franz Joseph had been pleased to note that even the old emperor's faith in Russia had been much shaken: 'after no other meeting with the Emperor William have I had such a favourable impression.'[45] Moreover, despite, or perhaps because of, the secret Reinsurance Treaty of 18 June, by which Germany had pledged her support to Russia at Sofia and Constantinople, Bismarck could only welcome it if another group of Powers would assume the task of deterring Russia from actually precipitating a crisis. On 9 October, therefore, Kálnoky told Calice that his draft would do as a basis; and that he would approach London and Rome. The essential point, he said, was to get an agreement *à trois*, for without Britain, Italy was not worth much. And he was still suspicious of Italy and her attempts to tie the Monarchy's hands in the Near East. It was partly for this reason that he turned down an Italian suggestion that the agreements should be extended to deal with the final break-up of Turkey. The spirit of Reichstadt had long been banished from the Ballhausplatz.

[43] Ibid., Kálnoky to Calice, 18 August 1887.
[44] Ibid., Kálnoky to Calice, secret telegram, 25 September 1887.
[45] W. Wagner, p. 157.

After a pause to make sure of Bismarck's co-operation, Kál-noky sent the draft agreement to London on 25 October, together with a warning: Austria-Hungary would never be able effectively to defend the Straits and Constantinople, even with Italian support. Here Britain was in the first line, and the Monarchy only in a supporting role. The suggested agreement would still give Vienna enough confidence to hold to the policy of keeping Russia out of Constantinople, but if Britain withdrew, Austria-Hungary would also have to retreat and concentrate on guarding her narrower and more vital interests in the Balkan peninsula. For she could more easily tolerate Russia in Constantinople than in Macedonia and Bulgaria.[46] This argument, and a letter of com-mendation from Bismarck, impressed Salisbury; and by 12 De-cember – Kálnoky insisting on keeping the lead in the final formalities 'as the matter has been furthered so much by our ini-tiative'[47] – the agreement was completed (Document 17). All in all it was a felicitous conclusion to the Bulgarian triumphs of 'our group'.

Even so, according to a gloomy Austro-Hungarian estimate of October 1887, Russia's sullen response to her Bulgarian defeat (a formidable concentration of troops in her western provinces) had cancelled out all the advantages the Monarchy had gained from speeding up its mobilization programme in the last four years. It had also caused disquiet in Berlin; and the Germans, who always thought the Austrians took too casual a view of their military obligations, advised Vienna to look to the defences of Galicia. For Bismarck, this advice was merely the military counterpart of his blessing the Mediterranean *entente*: a militarily prepared Austria-Hungary could more effectively deter the Russians from blundering into some *coup* which might make war inevitable. The military in Berlin went further, of course: on 12 December Moltke actually proposed to Vienna a joint preventive attack on Russia, drawing the response from Beck that the Monarchy would be ready to fight by 15 January 1888. But the civilian authorities in the Monarchy would have none of this. Neither Franz Joseph nor Kálnoky believed that Russia was seriously preparing to attack; and in any case, midwinter was the worst conceivable time for major troop movements to Galicia. They contented themselves

[46] P.A. I/458, Liasse VIIIb, Kálnoky to Biegeleben, private, 25 October 1887.   [47] Ibid., Kálnoky to Bruck, Tel. 92, secret, 3 December 1887.

with a few precautionary measures there; but not on such a scale as to provoke Russia to greater efforts, or to necessitate a sensational summoning of the Delegations.

This proved sufficient. The Russians were impressed, if somewhat put out, and made haste to assure Vienna on 23 December that they were not contemplating war or the shedding of a single drop of blood for Bulgaria. Kálnoky countered with assurances of Franz Joseph's peaceful and defensive intentions, but he still remained decidedly sceptical about Russia. In a memorandum of 1 January 1888[48] he analysed the nature of her grievances, concluding that they originated with the rise of Germany to Great Power status, and the formation of the Dual Alliance. These developments had ousted Russia from the artificially inflated position she had enjoyed in Europe since the Napoleonic wars. Hence, as both the German Empire and the Dual Alliance were there to stay, there could be no real prospect of an end to Russia's hostility. Indeed, unless Russia came into line with the Central Powers (and the state of Russian opinion made this unlikely) or unless France deserted her (and opinion in France was in fact becoming more pacific), it would be the sword which would ultimately have to decide 'whether Slavic Russia will dominate Europe or not'. On the next day he told Lobanov, the Russian ambassador, that the time was not appropriate to discuss the restoration of lasting good relations; and at the end of the month he was still telling the Germans that 'Russia desires war'.[49] Bismarck, by contrast, was completely satisfied with Russia's chastened attitude, and on 11 January proclaimed in the Reichstag that all danger of war had disappeared.

Unfortunately for Bismarck, however, the original German advice to arm had roused some powerful demons in the Monarchy; and a conference of ministers on 18 December[50] was much exercised with the question of a preventive war. Kálnoky, after justifying the limited nature of the preparations in Galicia, went on to describe the idea of preventive war as 'madness'. The Monarchy was neither militarily, nor, above all, diplomatically prepared. The Dual Alliance was strictly defensive (and Germany, preoccupied in the west, would in any case be unable to render much

[48] P.A. I/469, Kálnoky, memorandum, 1 January 1888.
[49] E. v. Glaise-Horstenau, p. 316.
[50] P.A. XL/294, Ministerratsprotokoll, 18 December 1887.

assistance); relations with Britain and Italy were on a purely defensive basis; and, as the Monarchy relied on an army of conscripts, public opinion would also have to be considered. He threw out a sop to the warmongers with a reference to the ultimately inevitable settling of accounts between Germanism and Slavdom; but his main point was that the Monarchy could only proceed in complete accord with Germany. This, even Tisza had to admit, although he still thought that the Monarchy could only lose by delay, for the Slavs were at that moment still loyal – they might not be so after a few more years of Russian propaganda. Opinions differed on this point – in a conference of 5 January Kálnoky[51] argued that the Central Powers stood to gain by delay, as both Germany's armaments and Russia's financial embarrassments would grow. And even on this occasion, when he had no illusions about Russia's apparent change of heart, and described the situation as 'bad, because the basic causes of the evil have not disappeared', he still advised that 'at present there is nothing we can do but put up with it'. That being the case, the conference of 5 January decided against any further armaments increases – unless Bismarck should change his mind and decide on war.

Nevertheless, the debate had not been completely barren. Kálnoky had decided to seize the opportunity to clear up a contentious aspect of the Dual Alliance. When, in the conference of 18 December the war minister pointed out that Galicia could not be defended except by an offensive thrust into Poland, Kálnoky explained that he was about to ask Berlin whether in fact the terms of the Alliance would permit of such a measure. (After all, as Franz Joseph remarked in a conference of 19 December,[52] the military in Vienna and Berlin had always planned to take the offensive if war with Russia became inevitable.) Bismarck, however, insisted that the Alliance was strictly defensive, and refused to consider the possibility of taking the offensive in any circumstances. Undeterred, Kálnoky pressed the reluctant Széchenyi to pursue the matter. As he explained at some length (Document 18), it was not a question of changing the defensive character of the Alliance, or of waging a preventive war. The military simply needed to know in advance – for there would be no time to start planning in a crisis – whether it would be at all permissible to

[51] Ibid., Ministerratsprotokoll, 5 January 1888.
[52] Ibid., 19 December 1887.

take the offensive. The extremely unfavourable geographical conformation of Galicia rendered the Austro-Hungarian line of
march hazardous in any case; but the allies would give up enormous advantages and severely compromise the whole issue of the
war if they waited for the Russians to attack. The only guarantee
of success lay in an immediate offensive and a simultaneous thrust
from Germany. Russia's growing armaments were making war
increasingly likely, and the question should be cleared up without
delay. If Austria-Hungary knew definitely that she would have
to give up the 'huge military advantages' of an offensive and let
the Russians into the country, she would have to think hard
about whether it would be at all possible to go to war with
Russia.[53]

This last threat, intended as a hint that Austria-Hungary might
abandon Germany for Russia, misfired completely. When
Széchenyi put it to Herbert Bismarck, the latter expressed his
approval – thinking that Kálnoky was considering abandoning
Bulgaria.[54] The Germans stubbornly refused to discuss even the
possibility of an offensive: according to Széchenyi, the old
emperor was the chief obstacle; but Bismarck agreed with him
entirely. True, in practical military terms nothing much had
changed: the soldiers went on making plans regardless of the
political situation. A memorandum by Moltke of February 1888
still talked of a common offensive in Poland; and although the
Germans could not put up so many men as in 1882, the improvements in the Austro-Hungarian army since then ensured to the
allied armies a superiority of some 178,000 over Russia. On the
other hand, the political atmosphere within the Dual Alliance had
undoubtedly worsened. Kálnoky's initiative had ended in a complete fiasco. Franz Joseph was resigned, but bitter, for he felt the
Germans suspected him of trying to misuse the alliance. There
had never been any question of a preventive war, or of the military's controlling policy, he complained. But the Monarchy ought
to be told in what circumstances it could count on Germany –
otherwise it would be impossible to make any serious military
plans at all. Nor did he agree that the *casus foederis* only arose when
Russian troops were actually on Austro-Hungarian soil: it was

[53] P.A. I/464, Liasse XIXd, Kálnoky to Széchenyi, No. 2, secret, 12
January 1888.
[54] Ibid., Széchenyi to Kálnoky, No. 7, secret, 21 January 1888.

time Berlin realized 'that "politically defensive" and "militarily offensive" are not contradictory terms'.[55]

In this situation, such gestures of solidarity as the publication of the terms of the Dual Alliance in February 1888 provided small consolation. Indeed, this was also a gesture designed to reassure Russia and to emphasize the purely defensive character of the Alliance for the better information of the chauvinist Hungarian press. And Kálnoky, for his part, soon proved himself Bismarck's equal in the strict interpreting of treaties. In the military discussions between the Triple Alliance Powers in Berlin in January he scrupulously reserved the Monarchy's treaty rights to observe neutrality in certain wars against France; and agreed to permit the passage of Italian troops through Austrian territory to the Rhine only if Austria-Hungary were herself already at war with France. Yet even so, the Monarchy's alliances and *ententes* were still worth something, as Kálnoky recognized in a memorandum of March 1888.[56] Germany and Austria-Hungary were doing fairly well in their policy of preserving peace by building up such an imposing assemblage of states that France and Russia would not dare risk starting a war. True, not everything was perfect: Germany's dubious attitude at Constantinople was still confusing the Turks and disheartening Britain and Italy; nor could Britain and Austria-Hungary ever accept Bismarck's view that Russia had a claim to permanent predominance in Bulgaria by virtue of the Treaty of Berlin. Yet even Bismarck had his uses: the personal hold he had established over Crispi by dint of judicious flattery was of great value, for in Kálnoky's view the Italian connexion was Austria-Hungary's chief means of holding on to Britain.

In one respect – the creation of a link between Italy and Roumania – the year 1888 even saw a strengthening of the interconnexions of the Austro-German alliance system. Of course, the Austrians had no use themselves for Italian help; and when this was mooted in the military talks at Berlin Kálnoky turned it down, suspecting in it a Trojan horse for irredentist claims. On the other hand, the idea that Italy might send a contingent to assist Roumania found more favour in Vienna. True, Kálnoky thought Italy so ramshackle that she would probably not be able

[55] W. Wagner, p. 162.

[56] P.A. I/469, memorandum by Kálnoky for the use of Archduke Rudolph during his visit to Berlin, 14 March 1888.

to spare a man from the French front in the event; the logistic difficulties were enormous; and Crispi was obviously only trying to strengthen Italy's foothold in the Balkans. Indeed, Archduke Albrecht thought it positively dangerous to foster any links between two irredentist states with claims on the Monarchy. Nevertheless, Kálnoky decided that closer co-operation between the two Latin races against the Slav flood could only help to weld the alliances together. From the spring of 1888 he worked hard at Rome and Bucharest and managed by August to secure the accession of Italy to the Austro-Roumanian alliance. This was pure gain from the Monarchy's point of view, in that, like Germany's accession in 1883 it bound an ally (albeit in this case a feeble one) to help Austria-Hungary out in the event (albeit an unlikely one by this time) of a Russian invasion of Roumania.

Yet although the alliances would clearly be militarily invaluable in the event of actual war, that was a contingency which Austro-Hungarian policy was very much concerned to avoid. Indeed the outbreak of war would in itself indicate a failure of the very important deterrent function of the alliances, at this period still operating with a fairly comfortable preponderance of strength against the 'restless' Powers, France and Russia. Moreover – and this was to assume greater importance in Austrian minds in the decade after 1888, when there were no major confrontations between the continental Powers – the Monarchy also looked to the alliances to serve its interests in the humdrum but hardly less essential diplomacy of peace, and to ensure good relations with its neighbours. In this respect, the alliances were proving sadly deficient. Strange behaviour on the part of the unstable governments in Belgrade and Bucharest was by now coming to be accepted in Vienna as a fact of life; but in the summer of 1888 even the Dual and Triple Alliances were severely plagued with mistrust. Indeed, Germany and Italy seemed almost to be conspiring together against the Monarchy. For example, when William II succeeded to the German throne in June, he not only chose demonstratively to honour St Petersburg with his first state visit, but followed this up with a visit to the king of Italy at Rome. If the papal protests he provoked were not embarrassing enough for his allies in Vienna, William spent much of his time discussing the internal affairs of Austria with Crispi, who joined him in condemning the pro-Slav and clerical policies of the Taaffe government.

On the whole Kálnoky had come to the conclusion that the papal and irredentist questions were insoluble, and that Vienna and Rome would do best to resign themselves quietly to living with this unfortunate fact. For example, in the autumn of 1887 he refused to adopt an anti-papal policy at Italy's request, but justified himself with the remarkably frank argument that it would be like asking Crispi 'to state publicly in the Chamber that Italy finally and for ever renounced Trentino and Trieste'.[57] But he drew the line at Germany's supporting Italian claims to Austrian territory, even if only in minor frontier disputes; and in July 1888 he asked bitterly whether Germany would consider ceding Lorraine to France 'in the interests of general European peace'.[58] Irredentism was at this time threatening to become quite a serious problem in Austro-Italian relations. In January 1889 Kálnoky took the gravest umbrage at an Italian law enfranchising Italian-speakers outside the kingdom. In November it was only under pressure from Rome and Berlin – and with perhaps understandable bad grace – that Franz Joseph intervened to stop the trial for sedition of the editor of the Trieste *Independente*; and in July 1890 the closing down of *Pro Patria*, the leading national association for Italian Austrians, was interpreted in Italy as another wicked plot by Taaffe and the clericals to undermine the Triple Alliance. Italy still needed the Alliance of course, and it was under this banner that in the autumn of 1890 Crispi at last launched a great onslaught on the irredentists after closing down all the societies dedicated to Oberdank. Kálnoky was much gratified; but the ensuing Italian elections showed that the irredentists were still as numerous as ever.

The Dual Alliance too was at something of a discount in 1888. When William II, returning from Rome, at last appeared in Vienna in October, his visit was a disaster in every respect. He quarrelled with Crown Prince Rudolph, and infuriated the emperor with gestures that were nothing less than blatant intrusions into the domestic affairs of the Monarchy. For example, he presented Tisza with the Black Eagle – the highest German order – but

[57] A. Sandonà, *L' irredentismo nelle lotte politiche e nelle contese diplomatiche italo-austriache*, Vol. 3, p. 146.
[58] Ibid., p. 151.

ostentatiously refrained from giving Taaffe any decoration at all.
Franz Joseph and Kálnoky thought this behaviour monstrous.
Nor were they impressed when Herbert Bismarck took the opportunity to preach the doctrine of spheres of influence in the
Balkans. 'I know this is your father's idea,' Franz Joseph told him;
'but I could never accept it in the past; and I must also reject it
today.'[59]

The strange behaviour of the Germans – particularly their
attempts to ingratiate themselves at St Petersburg, alarmed Vienna.
For Austro-Russian relations had not improved at all. 'How we
are supposed to get out of this without a war is not clear to me,'
Franz Joseph told Waldersee in June 1888.[60] It was just as well,
therefore, that the Monarchy should look to its own defences. In
the summer, the troop concentrations in Galicia were strengthened; and the Delegations voted 100m. Gulden without a mur-
mur. In April 1889 an Army Bill, envisaging the eventual doub-
ling in size of the Common Army was voted by both parliaments.
True, this was not achieved without a struggle. There were
people in Budapest who thought even the *Ausgleich* of 1867 a
needless sacrifice of Hungary's liberty; and who regarded the
creeping growth of the Common institutions as an even graver
menace than the power of Russia. Thanks partly to the support
of the German ambassador, Tisza eventually prevailed in parliament against what Kálnoky termed the 'radical rabble';[61] but he
had to buy them off. To Beck's dismay the title of the Imperial
General Staff was altered to 'Imperial and Royal' – a minor
change but another ominous sign of things to come. For the
struggle over the Army Bill in Hungary marked the beginning of
an instability in Hungarian politics that was seriously to weaken
the Monarchy as a Great Power in the next decade. And it was to
be the last Army Bill the government could extract from Budapest
until 1912. For the present, however, the new law offered proof
enough that the Monarchy was firmly determined, as the German
military attaché rather patronizingly put it 'to become a real
Great Power' (*ebenbürtig zu werden*).[62]

Thus strengthened, the Monarchy was in fact about to embark

[59] W. Wagner, p. 166.
[60] E. v. Glaise-Horstenau, p. 324.
[61] Aehrenthal MSS., Karton 6, Kálnoky to Aehrenthal, 4 June 1888.
[62] E. v. Glaise-Horstenau, p. 330.

on a period of relative security which lasted for about four years. The year 1889 saw a remarkable improvement in the international situation and the Monarchy, perhaps for the last time in its history, was able to maintain successfully a firm posture against Russia with a fair amount of support from its friends and allies. On the one hand, William II, whose effusive gestures had been rebuffed by the dour tsar, now fell into an anti-Russian mood. He also became increasingly unwilling to listen to Bismarck. On the other hand, with France paralysed by the aftermath of the Boulanger affair, and with the Balkans relatively calm, it was Russia's military efforts in Poland that now began to absorb the German military mind. By the summer of 1889 the Austrians felt they had good reason to hope that Germany would after all be prepared to pay as much attention to the eastern front as to the western. And with William I dead and Bismarck's influence in decline, Kálnoky thought it might be time to raise certain thorny questions at Berlin. Franz Joseph's forthcoming return visit to William II would provide a good opportunity. It might be possible, he speculated in July,[63] to persuade Germany to become at least neutral in the Bulgarian question – her continued support of Russia at Constantinople was still paralysing Austrian efforts to reconcile the sultan and Prince Ferdinand. And reverting to his ideas of 1887–8, he determined to make yet another effort to settle the question of the compatibility of a military offensive with a defensive alliance.

Franz Joseph's visit to Berlin in July 1889 was a tremendous success, surpassing even the Austrians' wildest hopes. True, Bismarck was not particularly forthcoming, refusing to lift the ban on pig imports from the Monarchy, and making tactless remarks about the growth of Slav influence in Austrian politics. But the Austrians could afford to ignore Bismarck, for the military conversations could not have gone better. Waldersee declared that Russia was definitely the chief enemy of Germany, who would evacuate Lorraine if necessary to finish the war in the east with all speed. Beck was so pleased at this that he at once abandoned a plan he had been working on for a defensive mobilization behind the Carpathians. More important still, the Germans now suddenly and enthusiastically adopted the Austrian view on the Alliance. The words of the war minister, Verdy du Vernois, to

[63] P.A. I/469, Kálnoky, memorandum, secret, July 1889.

Beck – 'Your mobilization will be for us the signal to come in with all we have got' (*mit Allem einzusetzen*)[64] – were perhaps nothing unusual from a military quarter. But now the Emperor William himself declared: 'whatever reason you may have for mobilizing, whether Bulgaria or anything else, the day of your mobilization will be the day of mobilization for my army, whatever the chancellors (*die Kanzler*) may say.'[65]

The Austrians could hardly have wished for a more explicit assurance. Their only doubt was to its real value, coming from one so volatile as William II and at a time of growing political instability in Berlin. (Within a matter of months, for example, Verdy had been removed from the war ministry.) These misgivings account for the mixed feelings with which the news of the fall of the Bismarcks, in March 1890, was received at Vienna. The military, of course, were jubilant: 'Thank God we are rid of the whole family,' Archduke Albrecht wrote to Beck.[66] Franz Joseph hoped that Austria-Hungary might now be able to speak with more weight in the Alliance; and he lost no time in reminding William II that the two German Powers must stand up to Russia, 'because then she always retreats'[67] – a dangerous lesson to have drawn from the recent Balkan crisis. Even he, however, in some ways preferred Bismarck's firmness to the emperor's wobbling; and Bismarck was certainly more sound on the socialist question. Kálnoky, too, might henceforth feel able to speak with more authority in the counsels of Europe. He had always been discouraged by the thought that the Bismarcks were really more Russian than Austrian in sympathy: now there was nobody with 'Russian feelings' in office at Berlin.[68] Yet even he had doubts about William II's stability, and hoped he might be kept fully occupied with domestic affairs.

For a time William II continued on an Austrophile course. At the Rohnstock manoeuvres in September 1890 the Austrian visitors received his strong backing – but again only verbal – in the Near East. He agreed that a solution of the Straits question along the lines desired by Russia (i.e. that Russia alone should gain a right of passage to and from the Mediterranean) was 'impossible'; and he endorsed the Austrian view that the question was one for

[64] E. v. Glaise-Horstenau, p. 337. [65] Ibid., p. 338.
[66] Ibid., p. 342. [67] W. Wagner, p. 175.
[68] Aehrenthal MSS., Karton 2, Kálnoky to Aehrenthal, 12 April 1890.

Europe to handle. The Austrians for their part seem to have accepted William's story that, until Bismarck's fall, he had been entirely ignorant of the Reinsurance Treaty (which he revealed to them on this occasion, with a display of feigned indignation at Bismarck's perfidy).[69] In the new year William seemed to wobble again: his sudden and brutal dismissal of their old friend Waldersee was a great blow to the Austrians; and Archduke Albrecht had qualms about the new chief-of-staff, the taciturn Schlieffen: 'I fear he is a slippery eel.'[70] At Moltke's funeral in April, however, Schlieffen himself assured Beck that he was not thinking of departing from Waldersee's plans, and that Russia remained Germany's chief enemy. Altogether, therefore, although the whims of William II were hardly the best guarantee, the Dual Alliance seemed to have gained considerably in effectiveness and importance.

The Triple Alliance experienced no such revival. True, Kálnoky recognized that for Germany the alliance had acquired increased importance since the revival of France in the middle 'eighties. Bismarck's 'gross flattery'[71] of Crispi was paying dividends, and King Humbert's visit to Berlin in May 1889 was a spectacular demonstration of German-Italian solidarity. Austria-Hungary, however, was very much a third partner in this alliance. The papal question still ensured that there would be no Austro-Hungarian state visits to Rome. And after all, Italy could only be of positive value to the Monarchy by giving diplomatic support at Constantinople in accordance with the Mediterranean agreements. The Balkan clause in the Triple Alliance was only a nuisance from the Austro-Hungarian point of view. Indeed, in a memorandum of July 1889 Kálnoky admitted that all Vienna asked of the Italian ally was that she should refrain from harassing the Monarchy in a war with Russia. Indeed, whereas Germany, seeking effective military aid from Italy, wished to see an end to the internal chaos that prevailed in the kingdom, the Austrians decided that 'the more uncomfortable Italy's domestic position is . . . the more secure we can feel.'[72] Above all, Kálnoky was determined not to

---

[69] P.A. I/476, Liasse XXXIIIg, Szögyény to Goluchowski, very secret, 31 October 1896.

[70] E. v. Glaise-Horstenau, p. 342.

[71] P.A. I/469, Kálnoky, memorandum, secret, July 1889.

[72] Ibid.

be drawn by Italy into a war with France. In the spring and summer of 1889, therefore, he rejected an Italian proposal (which enjoyed the support of Berlin) to reinforce the Triple Alliance by military and naval agreements. As regards the former, he thought neither Italy nor Austria-Hungary would have a man to spare from the French and Russian fronts respectively. A naval agreement he feared might increase the chances of the Monarchy's coming to blows with France. In any case the naval interests of Italy and Austria-Hungary lay in quite different parts of the Mediterranean; and the Austro-Hungarian fleet, though trim, was really only designed for coastal defence in the Adriatic.

Fortunately, the Balkan situation did not seem to call for any drastic remedies in these years. As Zwiedenek, head of the Eastern Department at the Ballhausplatz, observed in March 1889, Kálnoky's policy of supporting the independent development of the Balkan states against Russia's attempts to establish her tutelage was meeting with success. The completion of the railway network to Constantinople in 1888 had strengthened Austria-Hungary's connexions with the Balkan states and her influence was growing. Altogether, the 'advancing development of the Balkan states forms an important obstacle to Russia's power-drive towards the west, and that is decidedly a success for our recent policy'.[73] This success was hardly attributable to Austria-Hungary's Balkan alliances, which remained precarious. Indeed, as Serbia slipped into chaos, the Austrians gradually shifted the basis of their Balkan position from the Serbian and Roumanian alliances to a Bulgarian-Roumanian axis. As Kálnoky observed in February 1891,[74] Roumania and Bulgaria were destined to be the most important elements in the Balkan situation – provided they realized their interest in staying on the side of western civilization and the Central Powers. If they were agreed on maintaining the *status quo*, they could form a most effective territorial barrier to the spread of Russian influence in Serbia, and the internal disorders there need then give no cause for concern.

The strange and desperate behaviour of King Milan was now quite beyond the control of Vienna. His feud with the queen raged unabated; and in 1888, without consulting the Austrians at

[73] Aehrenthal MSS., Karton 4, Zwiedenek to Aehrenthal, 28 March 1889.
[74] P.A. I/471, Liasse XXXa, Kálnoky to Goluchowski, secret, 9 February 1891.

all, he embarked on a short-lived experiment with a Radical ministry, and then arbitrarily altered the constitution. By November he had had enough of Serbia, and suddenly informed Vienna that he had decided to abdicate. This was serious news; for Kálnoky was determined that the dynasty must at all costs be maintained. If it disappeared, leaving the way clear for a government openly hostile to the Monarchy, the latter would have to intervene in Serbia by force. All the same, the general Balkan situation was reassuring – particularly in view of the growing independence of Bulgaria – and when Franz Joseph and William II failed to move Milan to a sense of his monarchical duties, the Austrians decided that they would be satisfied if the regency that would rule for Milan's thirteen-year-old son, Alexander, were well-disposed towards Austria-Hungary and strong enough to prevent Serbia from falling into complete anarchy. This they managed to secure. The abdication went off calmly enough in March 1889 (although Kálnoky complained of the indignant ravings of some Hungarian newspapers). Ristić himself was one of the regents, and the influence of the queen-mother added a slightly Russian flavour to the government; but the Austrians soon established tolerable relations with it. Ristić had his work cut out to produce any kind of order out of the economic and political chaos bequeathed to him by Milan, and had no desire to burden Serbia with a quarrel with her powerful northern neighbour. He had agreed, as part of the abdication arrangements to accept the prolongation of the Austro-Serbian treaty to 1895; and the Austrians in turn were content to forget about the domestic chaos of the ramshackle Serbian state.

One worrying aspect of the Serbian constitutional crisis had been the possibility of repercussions in Roumania, where King Carol was under attack from the Russophile Conservative party. In the event, however, the abdication of Milan, and especially the gloating of the Russian press, had a salutary effect in reviving Roumanian fears of Russia. And when the Conservatives came to power briefly in the spring of 1889, Kálnoky's fears that they might look to St Petersburg proved unfounded. The chief difficulty was that the king was too frightened to initiate the Conservative government – or even the short-lived Liberal government of General Mano that followed it – into the Austro-Roumanian alliance, which now existed only by grace of the king, and had no foothold at all in the government. Throughout 1891 Kálnoky desperately urged Carol to make the alliance known to the leaders of both political parties, and to make the general drift of his policy clear to his people. He also pressed the king hard to renew the alliance. For the Monarchy, of course, its chief value lay not so much in the prospect of any military aid, as in binding Germany to defend Roumania. The present moment was a good one, he urged on Bucharest in the spring; for even Britain and Italy were collaborating with Austria-Hungary. Besides, if Germany once escaped, the allies might never get her back. Moreover, if Roumania aligned herself with Russia, this would bring down the anti-Russian government of Stamboulov in Bulgaria; and with Bulgaria in Russian hands, Roumania herself would not long survive.[75] The return to power of the Conservatives in 1892 caused further delays before the king could screw up his courage to initiate the government into the alliance. It was not renewed until July. (Germany and Italy acceded in November.) In one respect there was some improvement, for Kálnoky had had enough of battling with the timid king, and the alliance was this time renewed for four years, after which it would renew itself automatically for a further three unless actually denounced.

In the following year it was strengthened by an Austro-Roumanian commercial treaty, which at last put an end to the long tariff war. The Monarchy gradually recovered its commercial position in Roumania after this, although Germany, who had meanwhile established her position there, always remained a strong rival. On the irredentist front there was no improvement. On the contrary, a '*Liga Culturale*', founded in 1891, was organizing hatred of Hungary; and was helped in its task by a sensational trial of Roumanian nationalists in Transylvania in 1894. Kálnoky did his best to keep the temperature low, refusing to countenance Roumanian complaints about Magyarization, and equally ignoring Hungarian demands to bring Bucharest to book for tolerating irredentist activities within the kingdom. He only succeeded in displeasing both parties.

Austria-Hungary's chief Balkan success in these years was achieved in Bulgaria, a state with which she had no alliance at all. It was still 'of the greatest importance', Zwiedenek declared in

[75] P.A. I/471, Liasse XXXa, Kálnoky to Goluchowski, private and secret, 6 March, 12 April 1891.

August 1889, to thwart Russian attempts to hinder Bulgaria's autonomous development; for a Bulgaria independent of Russia was 'the best guarantee against the success of Panslav and Great-Serbian designs'.[76] Not that the Monarchy was completely successful in advancing Bulgaria's interests: Russia, with German backing, had managed to convince the sultan that Ferdinand was an enemy, who even coveted Turkish territory. In 1890, however, the diplomatic situation changed. Although the Mediterranean *Entente* Powers were still not strong enough to bring the sultan to grant Ferdinand formal recognition, they at last secured German support on minor Bulgarian questions; and in July together persuaded the sultan to give Ferdinand some satisfaction by appointing more Bulgarian bishops in Macedonia, to fortify the Bulgarian inhabitants against Greek propaganda. Of course, the association of the Mediterranean *Entente* with Ferdinand's cause played into Russia's hands at Constantinople to some extent, for the Turks were haunted by rumours of an international conspiracy based on Bulgaria to drive them out of Europe altogether. But in fact, Kálnoky was as content as anybody to see the territorial *status quo* in the Balkans maintained; and Russia's frantic opposition to anything that smacked of Bulgarian expansion into Macedonia suited him quite well.

Similarly, Russia's persistent, and futile, efforts to embarrass the Bulgarian government internally – her fomenting of plots, her refusal in February 1892 to extradite the assassins of Ferdinand's representative at Constantinople – were only grist to the Austro-Hungarian mill. In 1891 Franz Joseph graciously received the Bulgarian ruler in Vienna; and Kálnoky blandly explained to the complaining Russians that 'little Ferdinand'[77] had been since his childhood a personal friend of the emperor. By the end of 1892 Stamboulov felt strong enough to abolish the stipulation in the constitution imposing the Orthodox religion on all rulers of Bulgaria after the first; and in January 1893 Ferdinand married the Catholic Marie Louise of Parma, who had Habsburg blood in her veins. By this time the Russians were ready to wash their hands of Bulgaria. On the other hand, Kálnoky's assumption

[76] Aehrenthal MSS., Karton 4, Zwiedenek to Aehrenthal, 15 August 1889.

[77] Aehrenthal MSS., Karton 2, Kálnoky to Aehrenthal, 15 July 1891.

that, saving some catastrophe such as the assassination of Stamboulov, Russia would never be able to recover her influence in Bulgaria, was perhaps unduly sanguine. True, Austria-Hungary retained her commercial predominance, but her ruthless exploitation of what the Bulgarians regarded as an unequal treaty was resented at Sofia. Politically she had certainly succeeded in saving Bulgaria from Russian domination; but she had been unable to secure what her protégé Ferdinand most craved – international recognition. That, only a change of heart in St Petersburg could secure. This fact was the Achilles' heel of the Austro-Hungarian position in Bulgaria.

That was a problem for the future. In 1891 the Monarchy still enjoyed the security of its alliances and *ententes*. In the spring the Triple Alliance was renewed without too much trouble. True, Kálnoky had been alarmed when Crispi suggested amalgamating the three treaties of 1887, as he still had no intention of giving Italy anything more than diplomatic support in the western Mediterranean; and for the same reason he refused to consider bringing Spain into the Alliance. But he rightly calculated that Crispi would not be able to devise a formula to accommodate the diverse geographical interests of Austria-Hungary and Italy in the Mediterranean; and when Crispi's successor, Rudiní, in a weak position at home, and gaining no laurels from an abortive attempt to improve commercial relations with France, declared himself ready to renew the Alliance practically unchanged, Kálnoky seized the opportunity. On 6 May the Alliance was renewed and the three treaties were inserted into one document (Document 19). But they still remained separate, and the Monarchy had thereby assumed only the most tenuous moral connexion (being technically a signatory) with the Italo-German clauses concerning North Africa. It was to avoid assuming any further real commitments against France that in the summer Kálnoky again turned down an Italian suggestion for naval and military talks. It was to Britain that Italy should look for support in the Mediterranean, he said. He was therefore delighted when in June the British parliamentary under-secretary, Fergusson, acknowledged in the Commons that Britain had a common interest with Italy in maintaining the *status quo* in the Mediterranean. And he was even more encouraged by the resultant chorus of approval in the British press, regarding this open support from British public opinion as being worth far more than the secret declarations of a prime minister.[78]

In fact, the summer of 1891 saw something of a festival of the Triple Alliance and the Mediterranean *Entente*. Following on Fergusson's declaration came a flamboyant speech by Rudiní (29 June) proclaiming the renewal of the Triple Alliance and boasting of Italy's ties with Britain. Kálnoky thought this unduly sensational; but Franz Joseph himself had already caused a stir by going to Fiume to welcome a British squadron visiting the Adriatic; and King Humbert followed his example at Venice on 3 July. On the next day – two days after the conclusion of the Anglo-German Heligoland-Zanzibar Treaty – William II left for a ten-day visit to England. Nor was the western Mediterranean forgotten. The same month saw the settlement of an Anglo-Portuguese east African dispute, which Kálnoky, exercising his good offices at Salisbury's request, had been trying to smooth over. True, he had refused to enter into the merits of the question; and there was little he felt he could do about the Portuguese government, which he considered deplorably lenient towards the noisy republican opposition. In fact, his good offices had consisted largely of urging the British to let Portugal down lightly. For if she were humiliated and the monarchy fell, the monarchies of Spain and Italy would soon follow, and the international revolutionary parties (*Umsturzparteien*)[79] would be correspondingly heartened to proceed against the great Germanic and Slav monarchies. In April Italy and Spain had extended the agreement of 1887 to include diplomatic co-operation to maintain the *status quo* against France in Morocco; and to this Kálnoky, ever keen to reinforce the influence of the Triple Alliance at Madrid, made haste to accede.

Not unnaturally France and Russia, where the press had been predicting the approaching end of the Triple Alliance, were greatly disconcerted by its spectacular renewal, and the prospect of Britain's joining it. Within a month they had made a secret military agreement. But their public counter-demonstration of solidarity (the visit of a French squadron to Cronstadt at the end of July) was not nearly enough to shake Kálnoky's confidence;

[78] P.A. I/461, Liasse XXIV/2, Kálnoky to Bruck, No. 1, secret, 22 June 1891.
[79] P.A. VIII/172, Kálnoky to Deym, private, 21 March 1891.

and he calculated that when the smoke from the Cronstadt 'fire-work' had cleared, things would remain much the same.[80] After all, Russia had no reason to tie her hands *vis-à-vis* a France which could always be had for the asking; and the approaching famine in Russia should at least give food for thought to any warmongers in St Petersburg. Indeed, Kálnoky advised a council of ministers at this time that it would be safe to reduce armaments expenditure to help balance the budget.[81] And he was at some pains to calm the nervous anxiety that any gesture of Franco-Russian collaboration always aroused in Berlin. He rejected a German suggestion that the sultan be initiated into the Mediterranean agreements: the Turks would only leak the agreements to France and Russia, who would then be spurred to even greater efforts at Constantinople. And they had influence enough there already. Russia's new Black Sea fleet impressed the Turks; and despite Anglo-Austrian diplomatic opposition, she was making pretty free with the rule of the Straits, sending armed ships in and out more or less at will. (It was now the British who were anxious to maintain the closure of the Straits.) Kálnoky was quite content with the Mediterranean agreements as they stood – 'certain fundamental and general theoretical promises' – and he did not wish to enquire too closely into their binding character.[82] (This might move the British to reduce it to a minimum.) Although Rosebery, who succeeded Salisbury in March 1892, refused to read the agreements or put them to the Cabinet, the Austrians were still sanguine enough about their general diplomatic position to be satisfied with his rather less definite statement that 'Anglo-Austrian relations must rest exclusively on reciprocal confidence'.[83]

Kálnoky's confidence was further increased when it at last proved possible in these years to bring the commercial policies of the allied Powers into line with their diplomatic commitments. This was, of course, only attainable once Bismarck with his narrow diplomatic view of the alliances was out of the way; and when Germany, Austria-Hungary's most important and most powerful trading partner, and still virtually the arbiter of her commercial policy, had a change of heart. Caprivi's policy was designed partly to win the masses from socialism at home – by

[80] Aehrenthal MSS., Karton 2, Kálnoky to Aehrenthal, 28 July 1891.
[81] Ibid., Kálnoky to Aehrenthal, 19 October 1891.
[82] Margaret M. Jefferson, p. 87.   [83] Ibid., p. 88.

importing cheap foreign food to lower the cost of living; and partly to reinforce the alliances by economic ties, with the ultimate objective of a central European customs union under German leadership. In a sense it was also a counterblast directed at France and Russia, who since 1887 had been engaged in tariff wars with Italy and Germany respectively. Caprivi lost no time in ending the commercial estrangement of Austria-Hungary, and between August 1890 and May 1891 negotiated a commercial treaty which from 1892 gave Austro-Hungarian agrarian exports increased access to the German market in return for a lowering of Austro-Hungarian tariffs on German industrial exports. The Monarchy then concluded treaties with Italy, Switzerland, Serbia, and Belgium (1892); Roumania (1894); and Japan (1896); and in 1897 forced Bulgaria to renew the 'unequal treaty' yet again. This plethora of treaties did not really mean a return to an era of free trade – many duties still remained high. But it was an improvement on the protectionist chaos of the autonomous tariff policy of the 1880s, and marked the start of a commercial armistice which lasted for the next ten years. Of course, for Austria-Hungary, political considerations were an important motive. The Roumanian and Italian treaties were notable examples of sacrificing economic interests in order to strengthen the alliances. In the first case, Hungarian agriculture was subjected to severe competition, and in the second, the Austrian wine industry. (Imports of Italian wine soared from 20,000 to 150,000 quintals per annum.) Nor was that all, France, unable to secure the Italian tariff for her own wines, retaliated with higher tariffs on Austro-Hungarian exports.

For the political advantages of the treaties, therefore, the Monarchy had to pay a certain economic price. Although trade – particularly with Germany – increased, there was no spectacular boom in Austria-Hungary in the 1890s. Indeed, Austrian industry, already struggling to be competitive under the burden of what the founder of the Social Democratic party described in 1891 as 'the best industrial worker legislation in the world'[84] (a burden from which the rival Hungarian industry was almost entirely free), now had to face German competition as well. Hungarian agriculture, too, suffered from increased Serbian and Roumanian competition – especially from the latter when Hungary at last completed the navigation works on the Danube (1888–96). On

[84] H. Benedikt, p. 131.

the other hand, the completion of the railway network to Constantinople in 1888 furthered the Monarchy's Balkan trade, which managed to maintain its proportionate share – still only about 6 per cent – of the Monarchy's increased total trade. The building of the Arlberg railway in 1896 gave a boost to Hungarian corn exports to Switzerland and, until the dispute with Paris over the wine tariff, to France. Some industries enjoyed great prosperity – the Bohemian beet sugar industry, for example, was by the 1890s producing one fifth of the world supply, and attained a particularly strong hold over the Roumanian market. Even years of crisis and tension, such as 1887 and 1888, were not without consolations for the iron and armaments industries. Besides, as general prosperity increased, government finance could be stabilized. The year 1888 saw the last of the long series of budget deficits; and after 1892 the government undertook a much-needed currency reform and started buying up the remaining privately owned railways. In the 1890s Austrian government stock gradually became one of the most stable – though indeed hardly the most lucrative – commodities on the European exchange.

The Monarchy was thus in a relatively strong position in the years 1888–92; and it is hardly surprising that these years saw no attempt to catch a rather questionable bird in the bush in the form of a *rapprochement* with Russia. True, there might have been a chance of success. Russia was becoming noticeably less menacing: the tsar and Giers certainly desired peace; and Russia's economic weakness (especially the great famine of 1891–2) left her with little enough to spare to buy influence or undertake adventures in the Balkans. Even Russian public opinion, tiring of perpetual humiliations in Bulgaria, was beginning to concern itself with Russia's narrower national interests: Panrussianism was replacing Panslavism. Better still, many of these Russian interests lay in Asia, whither the Trans-Siberian railway, started in 1891, began to divert Russian attention.

Kálnoky was cautious. Russia's apparent retreat might not be permanent, he observed in June 1888. For developments might arise – for example, a military dictatorship in France, the fall of the dynasties in Serbia and Roumania, or even of Stamboulov's regime in Bulgaria – which might tempt Russia to try her luck in war, especially if she could revolutionize the Serbs against the Monarchy. Hence, Austria-Hungary must look to her armaments.

Kálnoky's former private secretary, Aehrenthal, isolated and alarmed in the remote outpost of Bucharest, urged him to seek a *rapprochement* with Russia, and to beware of German intrigues to foment ill will between Vienna and St Petersburg. But Aehrenthal's views were not those of the Ballhausplatz, and he was sternly informed that there was simply no basis for a *rapprochement* with Russia, the ultimate aims of that Power in Bulgaria being completely opposed to those of Austria-Hungary. This was also the emperor's view. When, in September 1890 a Russian diplomat was reported as saying that Russia would await an Austrian approach benevolently but 'with proud reserve', he commented, 'then they can wait a long time'.[85] The official visit of the tsarevich to Vienna in October, and Archduke Franz Ferdinand's return visit to St Petersburg in February 1891 perhaps improved personal relations between the two courts. But when the Russian press professed to discern signs that Austro-Hungarian policy was becoming more conciliatory towards Russia the emperor was emphatic: 'I know absolutely nothing about a change in our policy.'[86] The general brandishing of diplomatic instruments in the summer of 1891 actually deepened the Austro-Russian estrangement; but Kálnoky trusted to the impending famine – 'may God continue to help!'[87] – to keep Russia in order.

God did not help for much longer. The year 1893 was a bad one for Austria-Hungary, and was marked by a severe deterioration in the political situation in both halves of the Monarchy. In Hungary, where calm had never been really re-established since the crisis over the Army Bill, the government was facing increasing opposition from magnates, clericals and a motley collection of radical elements, over such contentious issues as a civil marriage law. And this was personally embarrassing for Kálnoky himself, a notable clerical and already in some ill favour at Budapest on account of his allegedly pro-Roumanian attitude. In Austria, the Taaffe government made a disastrous attempt to abolish the curial voting system, which protected the bourgeois national parties who would find themselves swamped by Christian Social and Social Democrat votes under any system of general suffrage. But Taaffe's conservative and clerical supporters took

[85] W. Wagner, p. 186.
[86] Ibid.
[87] Aehrenthal MSS., Karton 2, Kálnoky to Aehrenthal, 15 July 1891.

fright. Kálnoky too was firmly opposed to anything that would strengthen Social Democracy; and his intervention – in the form of a complaint to Franz Joseph – was very probably a major factor in bringing Taaffe down. Nevertheless, Kálnoky was sorry to see Taaffe go – his government had represented 'an unusual stability': 'they were capable experts with whom one could work well. If Taaffe had only kept to his old system and muddled on, he would still be prime minister today.'[88] As it was, Taaffe was followed by a succession of weak governments which for the rest of the 'nineties strove in vain to compose the increasingly violent quarrels of German, Czech, and south Slav. This internal weakening of the Monarchy was accompanied by serious deterioration of its international position after the end of 1892. The previous four years had been nothing more than an Indian summer.

It was in the military field that the Austrians felt the first tremors of the instability prevailing in Berlin. They had never found either Caprivi or Schlieffen particularly communicative – the Waldersee era was well and truly over. The chancellor kept an almost Bismarckian control over the military; and Schlieffen, who had little faith in the military capacity of Austria-Hungary, did not wish German planning to depend too closely on that Power. In August 1892 he began to shift the centre of gravity of German planning towards the western front. He had decided, as Russia steadily built up her armaments, that it would be impossible to defeat her in a quick war. Therefore, the only hope of salvation lay in a lightning strike against France. Consequently the war in the east would become for Germany – at least in the opening stages – very much a side-show; and the Austrians would have to cope as best they could. This bombshell burst in Vienna at the end of 1892. But Beck kept his nerve, and decided not to change his plans, but to make the best of the situation. After all, the Germans were still planning to launch some kind of offensive into northern Poland; and this would still be useful, even if now only as a diversion. The Galician railways had been extended by 50 per cent in the past few years; and Beck still hoped by the 21st day of mobilization to have two armies ready near Lemberg for an offensive towards the east.[89]

[88] Aehrenthal MSS., Karton 2, Kálnoky to his brother, 7 November 1893.
[89] E. v. Glaise-Horstenau, pp. 343ff.; G. Ritter, p. 530.

Kálnoky did his best to help, reminding a conference of ministers on 2 February 1893[90] that although the political situation might be calmer and all governments pacific, the military situation was becoming very threatening. For the Western Powers, who needed time to mobilize their civilian conscript armies, lived daily under the menace of Russia's huge professional army standing ready to strike at any moment. Moreover, with Germany so heavily involved on the Rhine, Austria-Hungary would now have to do more in the east. Beck's figures showed that, despite the Army Bill, the Monarchy was not in fact keeping pace with the other Powers. More should be done; and not only for the Common Army: the Austrian *Landwehr* was in a dreadful state; and the Hungarian Honvéds existed only on paper. In these circumstances, there was nothing to spare for the navy, which would have to continue to confine itself to coastal defence. But even these modest demands were ill received by the cheese-paring Austrian and – particularly – Hungarian governments.

In the summer of 1893 came another surprise from Berlin. Schlieffen now declared that the river Narev was an impassable obstacle to any German thrust eastwards in north Poland; and that the Germans would therefore march south to meet the Austro-Hungarian army. The Austrians did not like this idea. Co-operation with the Germans in south or west Poland might well reduce the chances of an effective break-through towards the east (the Austrians were still hoping to carry out their part of the original Austro-German pincer movement). And it was not as if the Germans would agree to put their forces – depleted though they would now be – under Austro-Hungarian command. Worst of all, the German plan would draw the whole weight of Russia's forces southwards on to Austria-Hungary. But Beck accepted even this; and he and Kálnoky took comfort from the fine performance of the Common Army at the Güns manoeuvres in September. In the spring of 1895, however, Schlieffen changed his plans for a third time. Deciding that East Prussia could not just be left undefended, he discovered that the river Narev was not impassable after all. In May 1895 he informed the bewildered Beck that the Germans would not now move south, but would make a small eastward thrust into north Poland; and he suggested that the Austrians take on virtually the whole Russian army by means of a three-pronged offensive which would extend their left flank as far as Prussian Silesia. Beck was aghast, and insisted that such a hazardous dividing of the Monarchy's forces just did not bear contemplation. He pleaded with Schlieffen to stand at least by the plan of 1893; but he made no impression.[91]

These highly unsatisfactory developments were accompanied by a sudden deterioration in the diplomatic situation, which caused a crisis of confidence in both the Triple Alliance and the Mediterranean *Entente*. In October 1893 Franco-Russian solidarity was startlingly demonstrated to the world in a spectacular visit by the Russian fleet to Toulon; and this was followed by the news that Russia intended to establish a permanent squadron in the Mediterranean under Admiral Avellan. The sultan was tremendously impressed; and by November Calice was reporting that France and Russia had once more gained the upper hand at Constantinople. To make matters worse Germany, dismayed by the growing solidarity of France and Russia and anxious not to provoke them, had for some time been more lukewarm in support of the Mediterranean *Entente* at Constantinople. Kálnoky now began to fear that Russia might be tempted to establish her supremacy there once and for all, either by forcing the Straits, or by means of a bilateral agreement with the sultan to give her control. In Kálnoky's view the whole balance of power in the Mediterranean was now at stake. For Britain, confronted with such an imposing display of French and Russian power, might abandon the Mediterranean. This would be all the more disastrous for Austria-Hungary, in that the Italians had been in a state of 'collapse' ever since the Toulon visit.[92] A huge economic crisis in Italy (caused largely by her inordinately swollen armaments budget and exacerbated by French economic pressure) had combined with a rising in Sicily in December to cause Kálnoky grave concern. For he knew France and Russia to be busy also at Lisbon and Madrid. He decided that there was a serious danger that Italy might despair and submit to the threats and blandishments of France – who could after all help her a good deal towards an economic recovery. With Britain and Italy gone, and Germany lukewarm, Austria-Hungary would be virtually isolated in the Near East.

[91] E. v. Glaise-Horstenau, pp. 347–50, 377–9; G. Ritter, pp. 531–4.
[92] P.A. VIII/174, Kálnoky to Szögyény, private and secret, 10 December 1893.

In January 1894, therefore, Kálnoky instructed Deym[93] in London to find out whether Britain would stand firm against Russia in the Mediterranean (Document 20). Of recent years, he explained, Russia had shifted her pressure from Bulgaria to the Straits; and now it was Britain who was in the first line. Referring to his letter of 25 October 1887, he repeated that although Austria-Hungary would still prefer to join Britain and Italy in resisting Russia, yet if Britain were to allow Russia to have the Straits, Austria-Hungary would be forced to retreat and secure her own immediate interests in the Balkan peninsula. Rosebery was not unforthcoming and said that if Constantinople were at stake, Britain would certainly not shrink from war with Russia. However, she could not cope alone with both Russia and France, and he therefore asked for an assurance that the Triple Alliance would keep France neutral. For this, Kálnoky had to appeal to Berlin – which he did with some apprehension. His misgivings were justified. The Germans were not only anxious to humour Russia, but almost obsessed with the fear that Britain, once the war started against France and Russia, would retreat to her island, leaving the Triple Alliance in the lurch. They therefore refused to give the required assurance: Britain must first show her seriousness of purpose by striking the first blow. They talked of allowing Russia to have Constantinople, and advised Kálnoky to secure compensation in the Balkans by means of a deal with St Petersburg. This, of course, Kálnoky was only prepared to consider as a last ditch contingency if Britain actually defaulted, and he angrily rejected the German advice. As he told Szögyény on 21 March,[94] he was bound in loyalty to Rosebery not to settle the Straits question without Britain: it was a European question. And the Monarchy was not interested in compensation or material gains: it was a question of preventing a general displacement of the European balance of power. It was only in this context after all that issues such as the Straits – and Alsace-Lorraine, and Bosnia and Herzegovina as well – acquired any importance.

Worse was to come. In June the Germans tried to humour France too, and joined her in forcing the British to abandon a Congo treaty they had just concluded with King Leopold. This moved Rosebery to utter a chilling warning to Deym: 'If Germany

[93] P.A. VIII/174, Kálnoky to Deym, No. 1, secret, 25 January 1894.
[94] Ibid., Kálnoky to Szögyény, very confidential, 21 March 1894.

continues to show herself so hostile to the Cabinet of St. James, I shall feel obliged to take back the assurances which I have given on the subject of Constantinople.'[95] In the event, he did not take them back; and all in all Kálnoky's soundings had evoked at least a promise of armed resistance to Russia, and of diplomatic support if France and Russia attempted to raise the Straits question with the sultan. After all, as Rosebery told Deym on 12 July, Britain could hardly make any concessions to Russia at the Straits without hurting her own interests. Kálnoky's policy remained the same: diplomatic co-operation with Britain. And at Constantinople Anglo-Austrian co-operation was in fact becoming more effective since the appointment of the energetic Currie to the British embassy there. In the Armenian question, which Britain was trying to settle in harness with suspicious France and Russia (the two other Powers most interested by tradition and geography in the unfortunate Christians of that part of Asia), Currie always kept Calice well informed, and in turn found him sympathetic and helpful. The crisis of 1893–4 had shown that the *entente* with Britain, despite its limitations, could still serve Austro-Hungarian interests well enough. It had also shown, that as far as Austro-Hungarian interests in the Near East were concerned, the alliances with Germany and Italy were, at the most favourable estimate, useless.

Since the end of 1893 Kálnoky had been seriously worried about Germany's Near Eastern policy. Her single-minded pursuit of commercial concessions in Turkey had brought her no political influence there at all; and now she seemed to be going back to Bismarck's policy of leaving the defence of Constantinople and the Straits to others. On 29 December he lamented[96] the general aimlessness (*Zerfahrenheit*) that prevailed in the Wilhelmstrasse: Caprivi had no understanding of foreign affairs, and Marschall no experience; and as a result 'the *Neue Kurs* has no policy at all', especially not in the Eastern Question. Yet at the same time people in Berlin would become nervous – out of timidity or jealousy – when Austria-Hungary tried to take the lead and suggest a clear policy for the Triple Alliance. In February 1894 the

[95] H. W. V. Temperley and Lillian M. Penson, *Foundations of British Foreign Policy 1792–1902*, London, 1938, p. 492.

[96] P.A. VIII/174, Kálnoky to Szögyény, private and secret, 29 December 1893.

failure of his approach to Berlin produced another round of complaints, and he described Germany's attitude as 'the worst feature' of the whole situation.[97] With the *Neue Kurs*, Vienna had managed to interest Germany in the Eastern question; but now, he feared, she had gone back to Bismarck's policy. Of course, he understood Germany's great fear of a war with France and Russia; but if Russia were allowed to establish herself in the Mediterranean, that could only make matters even worse. Reports that Schlieffen, and William II himself, had said that Germany would not object if Russia seized Constantinople filled him with dismay; and he bitterly observed that this was in flagrant contradiction to the promises the Germans had made at the Rohnstock manoeuvres in 1890.[98]

Indeed, Kálnoky lamented, German policy was now even more disastrous than it had been under Bismarck.[99] Although Bismarck had given Austria-Hungary no support in Bulgaria, he had at least helped her to win British support; and he had had too much sense actually to promote the preponderance of Russia in the Mediterranean. Now, the Germans seemed to be trying to frustrate Austria-Hungary's efforts at London. This was dangerous: whereas Austria-Hungary had been compelled by her own vital interests to stand guard in the Balkans, whatever Germany did, Britain was by no means compelled to stay in the Mediterranean (and there were enough radicals in Britain urging a *rapprochement* with Russia and peace at any price). Moreover, if Britain abandoned the Mediterranean, it would not be long before Italy would be forced to come into line with France. The emperor's interview with William II at Abbazia in March, therefore, when Franz Joseph emphasized the threat to the balance of power without any success whatever, was completely unsatisfactory. William II's vague and effusive professions of loyalty as a 'true ally' only exasperated Kálnoky: 'such general phrases do not really have any place in a serious discussion of great political questions.'[100] Italy was equally useless. Crispi, who had returned to power in December 1893 was becoming increasingly absorbed in a search for prestige in east Africa, and was seeking German support. He

[97] Ibid., Kálnoky to Deym, No. 3, secret, 19 February 1894.
[98] P.A. I/468, Kálnoky to Szögyény, No. 3, secret, 27 February 1894.
[99] Ibid.
[100] P.A. VIII/174, Kálnoky to Szögyény, No. 1, 20 April 1894.

even joined the Germans against Britain in the disastrous campaign against the Congo treaty.

Relations between Vienna and Berlin were also plagued with suspicion on the point of relations with Russia generally. Although the Germans might seek temporary relief from the Mediterranean dilemma by recommending Austria-Hungary to reach agreement with Russia, they had no desire to see those two Powers on such good terms that Germany would be their mere appendage, or even left out in the cold. Indeed, in December 1893 the German ambassador made so bold as to warn the Austrians not to make any agreements with Russia without informing Germany, drawing from Kálnoky the crushing retort – albeit delivered 'in a joking tone' – that Austria-Hungary certainly had no intention of signing any Reinsurance treaty behind the back of her ally.[101] Kálnoky, for his part, was fully alive to the danger of a Russo-German *rapprochement* that might injure Austro-Hungarian interests – a danger that seemed to become more real when Germany and Russia at last reached agreement on a commercial treaty in the unhappy winter of 1893-4. His alarm can be seen in his handling of the commercial negotiations which had been progressing, or, rather, failing to progress, between Russia and Austro-Hungary.

At the end of 1893, these had still not got beyond the stage of the rejection by the Austrian and Hungarian governments – especially by the latter – of Russia's demands for a reduction in the rye duty, and for Russia's admission to the favourable Serbian tariff, or failing that, at least a general freezing of tariffs. True, Austrian industry stood to gain something from a commercial treaty; but Hungary clung desperately to the heavy rye duty – it was only since its imposition in 1887 that her trade deficit had disappeared. At last, in March 1894, Kálnoky intervened in the negotiations and summoned a special conference of the Austrian and Hungarian ministers to impress on them the need for agreement with Russia. Not only would it be generally desirable in the interests of peace, he argued,[102] to establish reasonable commercial relations with Russia for a decade or so; the developing Russo-German *rapprochement* meant that there was actual danger in delay. For Germany now had no quarrel with Russia; whereas

[101] Ibid., Kálnoky to Szögyény, private and secret, 29 December 1893.
[102] P.A. XL/296, Ministerratsprotokoll, 4 March 1894.

the conflicting interests of Russia and Austria-Hungary could lend serious dimensions to any incident that might crop up – say in Bulgaria. 'Without expressing any lack of confidence in Germany's loyalty as an ally,' he wryly observed, 'a state of cordiality between Germany and Russia on the one hand, and a state of bitterness resulting from a tariff war between Russia and ourselves on the other would put us in a very unfavourable, if not dangerous position.' A failure to conclude a treaty would therefore be very bad for 'the most vital interests of Austria-Hungary'. He reminded the obstinate Hungarians that the Monarchy was now facing Russia's final terms, and could not afford to prevaricate for a tariff war would be a far greater disaster than a reduction of the rye duty. He insisted on a more flexible attitude; and thanks partly to the personal intervention of Alexander III,[103] for once in a benign frame of mind, the treaty was finally concluded by 9 March. Kálnoky could congratulate himself on having staved off the danger of isolation in the face of threatening Russo-German alignment; and he calculated that, good commercial relations having been established for ten years, tension would be reduced and a generally more friendly atmosphere created. But, as he observed on 21 March, he did not expect this to lead to any real change in Russia's policy. In other words, a *détente*, not an *entente*, had occurred.

Even a *détente* was welcome enough, in view of the open desertion of the Monarchy by Germany, and the limited nature of Britain's support. In fact, relations with Russia continued to improve throughout 1894. In the first place, the Mediterranean crisis faded away during the summer, and Russia continued to display an almost ostentatious restraint in the Balkans. Dynastic relations had begun to improve as early as the end of 1892, when the tsarevich paid a successful visit to Vienna – which even the *Pester Lloyd*, to Kálnoky's pleasant surprise,[104] reported with unusual decorum. The betrothal of the tsarevich to a grand-daughter of Queen Victoria in the summer of 1894 was taken in Vienna as a sign that Russia still valued her ties with Britain and Germany as much as those with France.[105] More important, one of the greatest

[103] P.A. I/469, Aehrenthal memorandum, 1895.
[104] Aehrenthal MSS., Karton 2, Kálnoky to Aehrenthal, 14 November 1892.
[105] P.A. VIII/174, Kálnoky to Szögyény, No. 1, 8 June 1894.

obstacles to any *rapprochement* with Russia, Hungarian public opinion, was undergoing a change in the early 1890s.[106] Not only were the Magyars becoming increasingly and passionately pre-occupied with domestic politics, but the generation that remembered 1849 was passing away (Andrássy had died in 1890). True, Hungarian opinion was still very much on the defensive; but Russia seemed to have stopped inciting the Balkan states against the Monarchy – and even Andrássy had held that the Slavs could only be a serious threat if Russia supported them. By the summer of 1894, therefore, there was generally more willingness in Vienna and Budapest to consider at least an accommodation with Russia.

It was at this time that Russia made a positive step towards a *rapprochement*. At the beginning of 1894 a major crisis had occurred in Serbia, where, faced with a total collapse of the economy, the regents had suspended the constitution. Kálnoky had been careful to abstain from all intervention or advice, lest the Monarchy be blamed for disasters which appeared to him inevitable. Giers nevertheless seems to have feared that Vienna might be tempted to intervene; and on 5 May he appealed to Kálnoky to co-operate with Russia in localizing the deepening chaos in Serbia. Austria-Hungary and Russia, he proposed, should agree on a policy of non-intervention; and should not let the Serbian crisis trouble their 'relations de confiance et d'amitié'.[107] In return, Russia would abstain from interfering in Bulgaria. This suited Kálnoky well enough – after all, he was being asked to say nothing that he had not said before. He assured Giers,[108] therefore, that he would certainly not depart from the principle of non-intervention (with the usual rider, 'sans y être forcés dans l' interêt de notre securité'); and he too expressed the hope that Austro-Russian relations would continue to improve. The Austrians were in fact much gratified, and decided that Russia had at last accepted their own principles of non-intervention and the maintenance of the *status quo*. Summing up a year later, Aehrenthal stated that it was at this point that Russia and Austria-Hungary had 'found their way back to an agreement in principle

[106] I. Dioszegi, 'Einige Bemerkungen zur Frage der Österreichisch-ungarischen Aussenpolitik' in F. Klein (ed.), pp. 240ff.
[107] P.A. I/469, Aehrenthal memorandum, 1895.
[108] Ibid.

to treat the maintenance of peace, a vital interest, as more important than their own rivalries or the teething-troubles (*Kinderkrankheiten*) of the Balkan peoples'.[109] It should nevertheless be noted that all that had been achieved so far was a statement of intent: no formal agreement had been made; and the bare principle of non-intervention was strictly negative. There had been no return to Reichstadt, or even to the Three Emperors' Alliance, which had envisaged certain changes in the *status quo*. Nevertheless, the Austro-Russian *entente* which is usually associated with the name of Goluchowski could already be discerned on the horizon – at least as a possibility – in Kálnoky's last year of office.

The *détente* had nevertheless not developed so far that the Austrians could feel completely secure. Indeed, even the death, in November, of their old opponent Alexander III was not an unmixed blessing: the new tsar was an unknown quantity, and for Kálnoky, 'what is incalculable is always most unwelcome to a foreign minister'.[110] The military, with a duty of course to prepare for the worst, were always inclined to look on the dark side, as Beck's memorandum of 18 December 1894[111] bears witness: Italy had recently grown weaker; Bulgaria, freed from Russian bullying, was now less reliable; and there was uncertainty in St Petersburg. Although the forces of the Central Powers were superior in quality to those of Russia, the latter had a superiority of numbers. In war, therefore, it would be a question of somehow dividing Russia's forces without dividing those of the Monarchy. Other Powers, such as Britain, Turkey, Bulgaria, and Sweden, might be of some assistance here. (It is notable that none of the Monarchy's allies figured in Beck's calculations.) Russia must at all costs be prevented from taking Constantinople and the Straits – the realization of the dream of Catherine II would have a tremendous and disastrous effect among the Balkan states. For the same reason, it was imperative that Austria-Hungary should not suffer an early humiliation in Bosnia. Serbia was too weak and disordered to make much trouble there, and in any case, Bulgaria might keep her in check. Against Montenegro, the Albanians might be enlisted; but the Monarchy could cope with that state

---

[109] Ibid.

[110] Aehrenthal MSS., Karton 2, Kálnoky to Aehrenthal, 31 August 1894.

[111] P.A. I/466, Beck, memorandum on the general military situation, 18 December 1894.

provided the Adriatic fleet could maintain supplies of troops to the coastal provinces (there was no adequate railway communication with the interior of the Monarchy). The German Baltic fleet might create a diversion, and Sweden and Turkey might be roused to turn the Russian flank; but Britain would have to help Turkey out in the Black Sea. For Roumania could not be relied on – according to Beck's information, the Russians even expected Roumanian support. As for German and Italian rear cover, Beck was resigned to the prospect that this 'will become less and less effective'. Indeed, the whole memorandum is a remarkable comment on the insignificant role of the Monarchy's allies, Germany, Italy, Roumania, and Serbia, in Austro-Hungarian military plans. Of course, Beck was trying to convince the Austrian and Hungarian governments that the only sure guarantee was the Monarchy's own strength, and that there was a need for a new Army Bill. But in view of the increasingly difficult parliamentary situation in both halves of the Monarchy there was virtually no hope of this.

The civilian authorities took an equally sceptical view of the value of the alliances in the autumn of 1894. On 30 November[112] Kálnoky emphasized to the German ambassador that although a new era had dawned in which peaceful rivalry would be the keynote of international relations, it would be no less important for success to keep alliances and friendships in good repair. Germany's policy, therefore, was disturbing: there seemed to be no guiding hand in Berlin; and junior officials could not make high policy, no matter how clever they might be. Caprivi had fallen at the end of October: 'the latest surprise from Berlin is regrettable', the emperor had commented, wondering what was coming next.[113] Worse, thanks to Germany's display of hostility to Britain in colonial questions, the Monarchy's relations with the latter Power were in jeopardy; and this, given Italy's dependence on Britain, weakened the whole Triple Alliance. Kálnoky had therefore decided to speak plainly to Eulenburg:[114] Germany should not underestimate the danger of estranging Britain – some people in the Liberal party there wanted peace at any price, and would even

[112] P.A. VIII/174, Kálnoky to Szögyény, No. 1, 30 November 1894.
[113] W. Wagner, p. 188.
[114] P.A. VIII/174, Kálnoky to Szögyény, Nos 1 and 2, 30 November 1894.

come to terms with France and Russia to get it. He went on to complain of the spiteful tone of the German press towards Britain – making fun of her abortive efforts to mediate in the Sino-Japanese War, for example – and pointed out with some acuity that the worst aspect of all this was the disastrous and long-lasting effect it must have on British public opinion. Kálnoky's arguments may of course have been devised for German ears; but he was nevertheless more percipient than those who, like Szögyény in Berlin and Aehrenthal in Bucharest,[115] shared the German view that Britain's differences with France and Russia were too vast ever to admit of a settlement. There were already signs of an Anglo-Russian *rapprochement* in the liquidation of the Pamirs affair; and as Kálnoky shrewdly observed, it was highly dangerous for Germany to think that she could isolate Britain 'and force her to recognize Germany as a colonial equal'.[116]

The winter passed off without incident, and Kálnoky gradually came to take a calmer view. But this was due less to any renewal of confidence in the alliances than to an improvement in the general situation and the continuance of the *détente* with Russia. In April 1895 the appointment of Lobanov, the long-standing Russian ambassador at Vienna, to succeed Giers at the foreign office, was a blessing the Austrians had hardly dared to hope for.[117] On 17 April Kálnoky went so far as to tell a conference of ministers[118] that the foreign situation was now so satisfactory that he would even recommend a reduction in the armaments budget. Tension had been reduced by several factors, he explained: the determination of all monarchs to avoid war and the shocks it would bring to the social order; the inexperience of the new tsar (which he now decided – turning the worrying signs of the previous autumn to suit a different argument – would cause Russia to shrink from adventures); and the preoccupation of the other European Powers with Asian and African questions. (He even suggested that Austria-Hungary might increase its navy, in view of the growing importance of colonial questions; and that some

[115] Aehrenthal MSS., Karton 4, Szögyény to Aehrenthal, 8 December 1894.
[116] P.A. VIII/174, Kálnoky to Szögyény, No. 4, 30 November 1894.
[117] Aehrenthal MSS., Karton 3, Liechtenstein to Aehrenthal, 14 February 1895.
[118] P.A. XL/297, Ministerratsprotokoll, 17 April 1895.

bigger ships might be sent to show the flag in the Far East. But it seems that this was just speculative musing: at any rate it did not lead to much. It was difficult enough to get money for the army, let alone for the navy in a country most of the inhabitants of which had never seen the sea.) True, Russia was steadily increasing her armaments; but the Monarchy should try to counteract this by improving the quality rather than the quantity of its forces.

He took an equally assured view of the foreign political scene. The Balkan situation, he told the conference of ministers,[119] had much improved. Serbia was completely rotten, but she was isolated and hardly able to harm the Monarchy (the *détente* with Russia helped here). Roumania too was a harmless neighbour, even if, owing to irredentism, an uncomfortable one. But after all, he explained (probably for the benefit of his Hungarian listeners) no Roumanian government could do much about a nationalist current like that: the Monarchy should be thankful that the Bucharest government was at least outwardly correct. After all, the *Liga Culturale* was now short of funds and a prey to corruption and faction. So he still thought it best to go on smoothing over any incidents that might crop up. Nor did the domestic troubles of Turkey present any major problems: the Great Powers were determined not to be misled by Christian propaganda into interfering in Macedonia; and the Monarchy could be well content to leave the Armenian question to the three Powers most concerned. True, the Italian ally was in exceedingly poor shape – commercially and financially ruined, and politically shattered – but this need not disturb Austro-Italian relations. And the Monarchy enjoyed excellent relations with Germany, Britain, Russia, and even – despite the continuing dispute about the wine tariff – with France.

The state of the alliances was in fact a good deal less happy than Kálnoky was prepared to admit openly. In the first place, the informal agreement of 1887 between the Triple Alliance Powers and Spain, renewed in 1891, was on the verge of collapse; and this was having a generally bad effect on the Mediterranean *Entente*. Since the end of 1894 Italy had been trying to bully the Spaniards, on pain of non-renewal, into openly declaring their position by publishing the agreement. In this she was supported by Germany, who was seeking to bring Spain to heel in a commercial dispute.

[119] Ibid.

Kálnoky disapproved entirely.[120] Spain was not like Roumania, he pointed out. The Triple Alliance could be of no material assistance to her; and hence she simply could not come out openly against her powerful French neighbour. Whereas the Triple Alliance should be trying to make friends in Spain, and to strengthen the hand of the monarchists and the Habsburg queen regent, all this bullying could only play into the hands of the French ambassador at Madrid. He urged Rome and Berlin to be satisfied with the secret agreement as it stood: it was quite enough to have secured Spain's diplomatic support in north African questions, and to have bolstered up the Spanish monarchy. No wonder, he complained on 23 March 1895, that Britain was becoming reserved when she saw Germany and Italy treating Spain in this way. He was exasperated to see that the allies – between whom he said there was nothing to choose – had only succeeded in bringing a less conciliatory government to power in Madrid. But his warnings made scant impression in either Rome or Berlin; and this was a problem he bequeathed to his successor.

The atmosphere within the Triple Alliance was altogether deplorable. In the spring of 1895 Italy, embarrassed in east Africa where France and Russia were supporting the Emperor Menelik against her, tried to extend the Alliance to bind her allies to more positive support of her designs in Tripoli. This the Central Powers turned down flat. The Alliance was an insurance company Berlin declared, not a joint stock venture.[121] Indeed, for Kálnoky above all anxious lest Italy's ambitions drag the Monarchy into war with France, it was hardly even that. He was intensely irritated[122] by a whining list of complaints from the Italian foreign minister Blanc, according to which all the Powers of Europe were abetting France against Italy; and when the Germans tried to put in a word for Italy he finally lost patience. In an indignant private letter to Szögyény in Berlin,[123] he now rejected even the German argument that the Alliance was valuable to the Monarchy as a guarantee against the irredentist threat. True, the rear cover Ital-

[120] P.A. I/463, Liasse XXVI, Kálnoky to Bruck, secret, 11 January 1895 to Szögyény, No. 57, secret, 23 March 1895; to Dubsky, No. 62, secret, 2 March 1895.

[121] A. F. Pribram, *Secret Treaties*, Vol. 2, p. 104, n. 228.

[122] P.A. I/470, Kálnoky to Szögyény, No. 55, secret, 23 March 1895.

[123] Ibid., Kálnoky to Szögyény, No. 70, private and very confidential 4 April 1895.

offered was of some use; and the Alliance had a certain moral value. But Italy could present no serious threat to the Monarchy. She was far too weak, and would herself be lost without the Alliance. One had only to look at her – her internal collapse and her total lack of able statesmen. Indeed, he concluded, Italy's defection would not be all that much of a disaster for the Monarchy.

Nor had the Roumanian alliance much to offer. The Germans had decided that it would never be of much practical value in war unless it were supplemented in advance by a military convention. People in the Ballhausplatz were inclined to agree, but had to admit in December 1894 that feeling in Roumania was now running so high against Hungary that there was for the present not the slightest hope of persuading Bucharest to strengthen the alliance in this way. The Austro-Hungarian legation there was by the spring of 1895 seriously alarmed at the ill-feeling aroused by the Magyarization of Transylvania: unless Vienna intervened to restrain the Hungarian nationalists – who, with their separatist demands directed against the very heart of the constitutional structure of the Monarchy, were a far greater menace than a few Roumanian irredentists – 'there will be a serious row here sooner or later'.[124] Hungarian nationalists, however, insisted that irredentism spreading from Roumania was the cause, not the symptom of the disease, and that the remedy lay in Kálnoky's taking a stern line with the government of Bucharest. Already in 1893 this attitude had driven Goluchowski to resign his post in despair; and it was to be a contributory factor in Kálnoky's sudden fall from power.

Roumanian irredentism had been the subject of a guerilla campaign against Kálnoky in the Hungarian press since 1894. But already for some years he had been increasingly disheartened by the deepening domestic confusion in the Monarchy. It was the old problem, and the one which had at first made him shrink from taking office in 1881, namely, that it was intolerable for a foreign minister to see his policies obstructed by domestic problems over which the constitution of 1867 denied him any control. Since the early 'nineties he had been dismayed by the growth of more intransigent varieties of Hungarian and Czech nationalism. The

[124] Aehrenthal MSS., Karton 5, Welsersheimb to Aehrenthal, 28 February 1895.

meetings of the Delegations tended to drag on endlessly while these parties ranted and raged about matters which, in Kálnoky's view, were not the fault of the Common Ministers at all.[125] (It should however be noted that he was himself a staunch defender of the Dualism which was in a sense the root cause of the nationalist fury – in so far as it ratified the supremacy of the Magyars in Hungary and of the cosmopolitan aristocracy and (socially at least) the Germans, in Austria.) In 1895, however, Kálnoky came under attack from even the relatively moderate governing faction in Hungary, when a quarrel blew up between Budapest and the contumacious papal nuncio, Agliardi, who had launched a campaign against the Hungarian government's civil marriage bill. A few tactless remarks soon served to bring Kálnoky, a notorious clerical, into deep disgrace at Budapest; and when the prime minister, Banffy attacked him openly he suddenly resigned (15 May).

As he wrote later, it would have been possible for him to defend himself in the Delegations; but, a strict conservative to the last, he felt that the sight of the minister for foreign affairs standing up and contradicting the Hungarian prime minister in open debate would have been nothing less than a scandal. He thought it especially unfortunate that there was no strong government in Austria to keep the Hungarian politicians in order: 'the gang needs watching.'[126] And perhaps in a sense, as Lobanov in St Petersburg feared, he had fallen victim to a Hungarian bid for greater influence over foreign policy – not that the Magyars, increasingly preoccupied with domestic wrangles, made much of an effort to exercise such influence after his departure. Certainly, he had fallen victim to the growing intensity of national feeling in Hungary – even the government had to play to the gallery. And after all, as was to be demonstrated again eleven years later Hungary's position under the dual constitution was so strong that no foreign minister could long survive once Budapest was really determined to get rid of him.

Kálnoky, for his part, was glad to be out of the fray; and he retired to live as a country squire on his estate at Prodlitz in Bohemia. 'There is such a *fin de siècle* air about politics, I can hardly bear to watch,' he wrote to his friend Aehrenthal in Ma-

125 Aehrenthal MSS., Karton 2, Kálnoky to his brother, 21 May 1893.
126 Aehrenthal MSS., Karton 2, Kálnoky to Aehrenthal, 11 June 1895.

1896.[127] And although Franz Joseph appointed him to the house of peers in 1897, he thought this a bore, and said he would attend as little as possible.[128] Still, after years of hard work at the Ballhausplatz (unlike Andrássy, he wrote most of his own dispatches, in a painstaking, cramped hand) he found it difficult to adjust to life at Prodlitz, and his last years were spent in melancholy loneliness. The great ones he had served for so long soon forgot about him – his sister was extremely bitter about this, and asked Aehrenthal to put on record 'the shameful way in which he was treated after his retirement . . . The thanks of the House of Austria should go down as a fearful warning for future generations.'[129] On 11 February 1898, although suffering from a chill, he went out to saw wood – almost his only pastime; but this brought on some sharp pains in the heart. Two days later he was dead.[130]

The House of Austria certainly owed something of a debt to Kálnoky even if, as usual in the case of servants it had once discarded, it did not pay it. He had steered the Monarchy through fourteen anxious years and seemed in the end to have dispelled the most dangerous of the threats to it – encirclement from the south by a ring of Russian satellites. And this result was due, at least in part, to his own determination, hard work and patient diplomacy. On assuming office he had been prepared to work through the alliance system he had inherited, in which – in matters of day-to-day diplomacy at least, and failing the catastrophe of a general war – the Dual Alliance was subordinated to the Three Emperors' Alliance. When, at the time of the Skobelev affair, the latter seemed to be failing, he had strengthened the Monarchy's position by securing rear cover from Italy, through the Triple Alliance, and from Roumania; and had reinforced the Dual Alliance with a military understanding. But he still preferred to seek a diplomatic solution to the problem of encirclement by working within the Three Emperors' Alliance – as was proved at Skiernewice and in the Bulgarian crises of 1885 and 1886. By 1887 this policy had failed. The Three Emperors' Alliance lay in ruins;

[127] Aehrenthal MSS., Karton 2, Kálnoky to Aehrenthal, 3 May 1896.
[128] Ibid., Kálnoky to Aehrenthal, 27 May 1897.
[129] Ibid., Karton 4, Christina Thun to Aehrenthal, 28 December 1898.
[130] Ibid., Karton 2, Duchess of Sabran-Pontevécs to Aehrenthal, February 1898.

and the glaring inadequacy in diplomacy of the other alliances, designed for use in war, seemed to leave the Monarchy in a position of some danger. This was hardly Kálnoky's fault. The Dual Alliance could never be of much service in defending the Monarchy's Near Eastern interests by diplomacy so long as Bismarck held to his narrow interpretation of it and preached the facile and unrealistic doctrine of spheres of influence in the Balkans. And the decline of the Monarchy's Balkan alliances was perhaps inevitable, given the underlying economic and political conflict between Magyar chauvinism and Serbian and Roumanian irredentism. In the event, Kálnoky was resourceful enough to devise other means of safeguarding the Monarchy's position. The Mediterranean *Entente* of 1887 served Austria-Hungary well, and with the menace of a Russian-controlled Bulgaria apparently dispelled, she could face the future with more assurance after 1888 – all the more so as it at last proved possible to reinvigorate the Dual Alliance and to reinforce it with economic and military agreements. But the year 1893 showed that the Monarchy was not Atlas, but Sisyphus. Germany slipped away again, and a worsening international situation was complemented by the start of a long period of political instability inside the Monarchy. Again, Kálnoky was resilient enough to meet the situation. He struck the right note of informal co-operation in cultivating Britain (although he found his partners in the Triple Alliance an obstacle rather than a help in this); and at the same time he made an important contribution, by his handling of commercial and Balkan questions, to establishing a *modus vivendi* with Russia. For more than ten years after his fall the continental Powers were not confronted with any great crisis threatening an actual outbreak of war such as might have resuscitated the Monarchy's alliances; and the latter continued their decline. However, Kálnoky had bequeathed to his successor two other diplomatic instruments, rudimentary as yet, it is true, and ultimately incompatible, but either of which might be developed into an effective means of safeguarding the Monarchy's interests – the *entente* with Britain and the *détente* with Russia. It remained to be seen, to which of the two his successor would turn.

Chapter 6

The Austro-Russian *Entente*, 1895–1908[1]

> A situation in which we were solely concerned to avoid clashing anywhere, and adopted the role of a passive spectator, while Russia systematically pursued her policy of advance unhindered would be quite unacceptable, as it would put us in a worse position than that that existed before 1897.
>
> *Goluchowski to Aehrenthal*, 29 December 1901[2]

The end of the *Mediterranean* Entente, *1895–7*

As Kálnoky's successor, Franz Joseph chose Agenor Count Goluchowski the younger, a rich Polish aristocrat and son of the author of the shortlived conservative-federalist constitution of October 1860. After serving for some seven years as a popular Austro-Hungarian minister at Bucharest, but finding his admonitions about the handling of Roumania ignored at Budapest, Goluchowski had retired from the diplomatic service in 1893 to live the life of a great provincial nobleman on his Galician estates. He was always sensitive where his vanity was concerned. No pushing career diplomat he: indeed, he was if anything nonchalant to a fault, as his methods of work, or rather, lack of them, at the Ballhausplatz were to show. Nevertheless, some of his colleagues[3] found his *bonhomie*, tact, sincerity, and charm a pleasing contrast to the 'frosty aristocratic manner' of his predecessor, and to the 'dry bureaucratic tone' of his successor. His geniality

---

[1] The following works are of particular relevance to this chapter: W. M. Carlgren, *Iswolsky und Aehrenthal vor der bosnischen Annexionskrise*, Uppsala, 1955; D. Dakin, *The Greek Struggle in Macedonia*, Salonica, 1969; H. Hantsch, *Leopold Graf Berchtold* (2 vols), Graz, 1963; and the works by H. Benedikt, G. Drage, F. Klein, C. A. Macartney, and F. R. Bridge cited in Chapter 1, note 1; W. Wagner, Chapter 2, note 1; E. v. Glaise-Horstenau, Chapter 3, note 1; and Margaret M. Jefferson, Chapter 5, note 1.

[2] P.A. I/475, Liasse XXXII/h.   [3] P. Hohenbalken (ed.), *Lützow*, p. 76.

in handling the prickly Delegations was especially felicitous; and despite his Roumanian sympathies he managed to remain in favour at Budapest for ten years. The Magyar onslaught on Kálnoky proved, in fact, to have been a spontaneous outburst rather than a move in a sustained campaign to seize control of foreign policy. It was never followed up – all the more so as Franz Joseph issued a stern reminder to Budapest that the appointment of the minister for foreign affairs rested entirely within the prerogative of the crown. And with Goluchowski, whom he came to call his *Minister vom angenehmen Aeusseren*[4] the emperor remained long content.

The new appointment was by no means universally popular abroad. True, Goluchowski was *persona gratissima* in France, whither he was wont to retire for most of the summer to the family estates of his wife, a Princess Murat – to the great annoyance of Ballhausplatz officials who had then to refer all important business by telegraph to Vittel. But as a notable ultramontane he was suspect at Rome; and as a Pole, at Berlin and St Petersburg. Lobanov was particularly dismayed to see such a man replace the of late more amenable Kálnoky, and as the result of a Hungarian intrigue to boot.

Nor were Goluchowski's views on foreign policy heartening to St Petersburg. True, they were conservative enough. Goluchowski was acutely aware of the domestic weaknesses of the Monarchy and always regarded a quietist policy as the best palliative for its ills (in contrast to the vigorous exercise later prescribed by Aehrenthal and Conrad). Like Kálnoky, he abjured all thought of territorial expansion, or even any strong diplomatic initiative, such as an attempt to secure a more positive, ambitious *entente* with Russia. This might be achieved by finally carving up the Balkans into spheres of influence. But in Goluchowski's view, a Russia established in Constantinople would exercise a fatal influence over the Slavs of the Monarchy; and this must be prevented at all costs. Indeed, the transition from Kálnoky to Goluchowski was initially marked by a more negative attitude towards Russia. To Kálnoky, watching anxiously from the wings, it seemed by the autumn of 1895 that 'we could very easily get back into the

---

[4] Ibid., p. 90. This is a play on the words '*Minister der Aeusseren Angelegenheiten*', 'Minister for External Affairs', and '*Minister vom angenehmen Aeusseren*', 'of pleasant external appearance'.

track of hostility to Russia'.[5] During a visit to Vienna he had learned that Beck and the military were pressing for further troop concentrations in Galicia as a counterweight to Russia's growing armaments – a futile gesture that could only anger St Petersburg to no purpose. To allow the military a voice in matters of policy would be 'to make the goat the gardener', and he tried to stiffen Goluchowski to resist.[6] But he found the minister himself strongly of the view that Russia was planning for war within two years. In such circumstances it seemed that, of the two embryonic policies inherited from Kálnoky, it would not be the Austro-Russian *détente* that would be developed.

In the summer of 1895 Near Eastern affairs had been dominated by alarming signs of the advancing decay of Turkey, where to the Armenian embroglio was now added a sudden crisis in Macedonia. The lot of the Christians in European Turkey had long been hard; but since 1893 a Bulgarian-controlled terrorist and propaganda organization had been preparing a rebellion in Macedonia. The aim was to provoke the Turks into committing atrocities there. The Great Powers might then intervene and constitute Macedonia as an autonomous province which might later be added to Bulgaria, after the fashion of Eastern Roumelia. When a rising occurred in July 1895, however, it was a complete fiasco. Not even the Bulgarian government dared move in its support, so strong was the united disapproval of the Great Powers. The raising of the whole Eastern question – and this would certainly have been the consequence of Bulgarian intervention, bringing Greek and Serbian counter-claims in its wake – was the last thing the Great Powers desired.

A more delicate if less dramatic problem was posed for Vienna by the gradual ending of the Russo-Bulgarian estrangement. The Austrians had done nothing to prevent the fall of Stamboulov, Russophobe but too independent-minded for Kálnoky's liking, in May 1894; and now in July 1895 a Bulgarian delegation found its way to St Petersburg, laid a wreath on the tomb of Bulgaria's old enemy Alexander III, and was very cordially received by the young tsar. Russian diplomatic agents at long last returned to Bulgaria; and Vienna was convinced that Russia would make full use of her new opportunities to meddle there. Indeed, Goluchowski

---

[5] Aehrenthal MSS., Karton 2, Kálnoky to Aehrenthal, 27 October 1895.
[6] Ibid.

sternly reminded the Russian ambassador that although the Monarchy sought no special position for itself in Bulgaria, it would concede none to any other Power. Not that the Ballhausplatz approved of the alarmist tone of the German and Austrian press, which raised a great outcry about a supposed threat to the Monarchy's position in the Near East. At any rate, Zwiedenek, head of the Eastern Department, and now a man of some influence, given Goluchowski's inexperience, took the sanguine view that so long as Russia respected Bulgaria's independence, the Monarchy could only welcome the ending of the tiresome Russo-Bulgarian quarrel. And after all, Vienna still stood by Kálnoky's doctrine of the independence of the Balkan states. Moreover, the Russo-Bulgarian *rapprochement* had given the Roumanians a healthy fright: in August King Carol came to Ischl in a very chastened mood, swearing that all political parties in Roumania now favoured an alignment with the Triple Alliance; and that the *Liga Culturale* was in full dissolution.

But a policy of restricting the spread of Russian influence could never be based on the Balkan states alone. It usually necessitated some form of co-operation with Britain. In the summer of 1895 Vienna debated the feasibility of maintaining the British connexion and the Mediterranean agreements. Salisbury's public criticism of the sultan's government, and exaggerated reports from Berlin of his casual remarks about a possible partition of Turkey had caused a stir in Austrian diplomatic circles. Aehrenthal gladly seized the chance to point to the hazards of relying on a Britain who would throw Austria-Hungary over at any moment if she could thereby come to terms with the increasingly awesome Franco-Russian bloc. He urged that Austria-Hungary should herself make haste to square Russia – perhaps only on the basis of the *status quo* for the present; but ultimately, should Turkey fall to pieces, by partitioning the Balkans into Russian and Austro-Hungarian spheres. The Monarchy might absorb Serbia and establish a strong Albania at the expense of the Slavs.[7] Beck, whose influence had increased since he had taken over some of the functions of Inspector-General of the Army after the death of the Archduke Albrecht in February, was of similar mind, and used his position to send memoranda in this vein to the emperor

[7] P.A. I/461, Liasse XXV, Aehrenthal, memorandum, September 1895.

behind Goluchowski's back.[8] Even Calice at Constantinople questioned the value of a mere renewal of the Mediterranean agreements.[9] These had been designed, after all, chiefly to cope with a Russian threat to Bulgaria. Now, Franco-Russian pressure was concentrated on Constantinople and the Straits; and without a definite British promise to fight, Austria-Hungary ought hardly to commit herself to onerous obligations in a question which was clearly of greater importance to British policy.

Nevertheless at the Ballhausplatz, traditional views prevailed. Zwiedenek sternly insisted that a lasting agreement with Russia was out of the question. That Power was ultimately bent on world-rule (*Weltherrschaft*).[10] She already exerted enormous pressure on the Monarchy; and if she advanced any further she would not only establish a disastrous influence over the Slavs of the Monarchy but also strangle Austria-Hungary's commercial development. With Russia established in Constantinople, Bulgaria, and then Roumania and Serbia, would soon be lost. A binding agreement with Britain would be ideal; but failing that, the vaguer agreements of 1887 would do well enough. At any rate, Goluchowski declared himself satisfied with them when Salisbury assured him in November that London regarded them as still in force.

Of the limitations of these agreements, however, Goluchowski was fully aware. As the crisis worsened with further Armenian massacres in August, he was by no means anxious to put the Mediterranean agreements to the test in a showdown with France and Russia. On the contrary, he decided that a united Concert would provide the best safeguard for the essentially conservative interests of the Monarchy. All the more so as the friendly governments of London and Rome, under strong pressure from public opinion, were embarrassingly demanding drastic measures of coercion to bring the sultan to heel. Such demands, Goluchowski realized, could only divide the Powers – for Turcophile France and Russia would never consent – and increase the risk of a general war, a war which would after all bring far more death and destruction than any number of Armenian massacres. He therefore

[8] E. v. Glaise-Horstenau, p. 380.
[9] P.A. I/462, Liasse XXVb, Calice to Goluchowski, private and secret, 12 September 1895.
[10] Ibid., Zwiedenek to Calice, private, 25 September 1895.

strove to restrain his own *entente* partners, while making use of the bogeyman of a separate Anglo-Italian initiative to keep St Petersburg in line. In October, for example, he successfully took the lead in persuading the Powers to agree that the Armenian question was a matter for the Concert; and in December he brought the Russians to join with the other Powers in a mild naval demonstration at Constantinople – although the Germans, ever anxious to humour the sultan, abstained in the end. The outcome of all this, at least from the Armenian point of view, was exceedingly meagre: some vague promises of reform from the sultan, with no guarantees as to their realization. Nevertheless, Goluchowski claimed in a conference of ministers in April 1896[11] that his main aim had been achieved, in that the unity of the Powers had been preserved. Not that his efforts earned him much thanks abroad. The Russians accused him of collaborating with Britain; and in Berlin, where hopes of an Anglo-Russian war prevailed, the Kaiser angrily observed that Goluchowski 'ought to go to school again'.[12]

The attitude of the Monarchy's allies was certainly a major obstacle in the way of any more positive policy, such as a return to the *Neue Kurs* grouping of the Mediterranean *Entente* strongly backed by Germany. Indeed, the Germans were now showing an almost obsessive concern to stand well with their increasingly powerful French and Russian neighbours. True, in November, the Kaiser declared somewhat patronizingly that Germany would come to the rescue of Austria-Hungary if she were ever in mortal peril; and even that it would be for Franz Joseph alone to decide when such a peril existed, in which event a German army would appear on the scene without any further debate about the existence of the *casus foederis*. Goluchowski and Franz Joseph, who felt that 'war with Russia must come sooner or later',[13] decided that this was the 'most important declaration as to the scope of the alliance since its foundation'.[14] But they soon found that the Kaiser's grandiose words meant little in terms of practical politics in the Near East: the Germans still insisted that Constantinople was not worth a war, and were conspicuously absent – to Golu-

---

[11] P.A. XL/297, Ministerratsprotokoll, 13 April 1896.
[12] J. Andrássy, *Bismarck, Andrássy . . .*, p. 244.
[13] W. Wagner, p. 203.
[14] Ibid., pp. 201–2.

chowski's great annoyance – from the international naval demonstration in December.

Nor was the alliance any more closely knit in practical military terms. On the contrary, by the end of the year Schlieffen had decided to concentrate almost everything in the west, and advised the Austrians to look to their own salvation. In April 1896 Beck resignedly asked the Germans to bind as many Russian forces as they could on the Narev. For the next thirteen years there was no further correspondence between the Austro-Hungarian and German general staffs and each went ahead with its own plans without consulting the other. By 1908 they were completely out of touch, a plan of Conrad's of that summer blithely assuming that Germany intended to concentrate her initial attack in the east.[15]

Similarly, the Germans were of no help in reinforcing the general diplomatic position of Austria-Hungary. Goluchowski found them as exasperatingly useless as Kálnoky had done in his efforts to persuade Italy to preserve the Mediterranean agreement with Spain; and by November Spain and Italy had decided to content themselves with 'relations de confiance'. This Vienna regarded as worthless.[16] Worse still, the Germans positively seemed to hinder Goluchowski's attempts to bind Britain more securely to the Mediterranean *Entente*.

In November the Germans had reverted to warning Vienna against co-operation with Britain, who they alleged had now abandoned the defence of the *status quo* and was plotting with Russia to partition Turkey. At the same time, an Italian sounding in London for a formal renewal of the Mediterranean agreements drew a disconcertingly evasive response from Salisbury. By late December the German chancellor, Hohenlohe, was urging Goluchowski to square St Petersburg; Constantinople must after all fall to Russia in the long run, and the Monarchy would do well to make sure of some compensation for itself in the western Balkans. This idea was still anathema to Goluchowski. Any policy of compensations could only be fatal for the Monarchy: for once Russia was established in Constantinople, she would inevitably dominate the whole Balkans sooner or later. Nevertheless, Goluchowski had himself begun to have serious doubts

[15] G. Ritter, pp. 537–8.
[16] P.A. I/463, Liasse XXVI, Bruck to Goluchowski, 67D, secret, 4 November 1895; Goluchowski to Dubsky, Tel. 5, secret, 19 April 1896.

about Britain's devotion to the *status quo* – her drastic Armenian policy seemed to him cavalier to say the least. Besides, 'in political action one must base one's position on certainties', not on vague agreements such as those of 1887, which might draw Austria-Hungary into a posture of hostility to Russia while yet providing her with no active assistance.[17] In January 1896, therefore, he decided to ask London for an assurance that Britain was still devoted to the *status quo* and to resisting the aggression of Russia. This assurance must be given not in the form of a mere renewal of the 1887 'agreement to agree', but in the form of what would in fact be a new and far-reaching treaty containing definite pledges to fight.[18]

His fears as to British intentions were in fact unfounded. Salisbury was not thinking of abandoning Turkey, let alone of making a deal with Russia. As he reminded the cabinet in February, he was still 'strongly against any policy that would cut Austria adrift. It would reconstitute the *Dreikaiserbund* – a state of things which must be injurious to Great Britain.'[19] Nevertheless, the awkward fact was that, given the sultan's unpopularity in Britain as a result of the Armenian massacres, he simply could not promise that Britain would fight in the sultan's defence on absolutely any occasion: that possibility would depend on the mood of parliament at the time – a mood which, as he consolingly told Deym on 4 February might still change in Turkey's favour if Russia actually moved against her. For the present, however, he could consider nothing more than a simple renewal of the 1887 agreements, although – indeed, precisely because – the latter did not commit him to much. This did not satisfy the Austrians. They decided that it would be dangerous to undertake an anti-Russian commitment to Britain on such an uncertain basis – after all, it was Austria-Hungary, not distant Britain, who would have to bear the brunt of any war over the Near East. Goluchowski at least knew where he stood: although for the present there could be no closer alignment with Britain, and although he had no wish, for his part, to renew the agreement of 1887, yet he could console

[17] P.A. I/461, Liasse XXV, Goluchowski to Deym, private and very secret, 9 December 1895.
[18] J. A. S. Grenville, 'Goluchowski, Salisbury, and the Mediterranean Agreements, 1895–1897', *The Slavonic and East European Review*, Vol. 36, 1958, pp. 340–69. [19] Quoted in Margaret M. Jefferson, p. 197.

himself with the thought that there still existed in England 'the inclination to go hand in hand with the Triple Alliance'.[20] This being the case, there was as yet no need for him to change the pro-British and ultimately anti-Russian orientation of his policy.

Vienna's suspicions of St Petersburg had in fact intensified in the spring of 1896 as Russia began to strengthen her position in Bulgaria. When Crown Prince Boris was baptized into the Ortho-dox Church in February, Franz Joseph and Goluchowski were beside themselves with rage, resolving that the ungrateful 'ape' Ferdinand should never again be received at court.[21] Zwiedenek and others in the Ballhausplatz did their best to convince them that it would be wise not to condemn the Bulgarian people along with the erring prince. For the continuing sensitivity of the Bulgarians on issues of national and religious independence might yet es-trange them from Russia again and draw them back into the Austrian fold. But Goluchowski decided to try to construct a counterweight to the Russo-Bulgarian bloc by furthering a *rapprochement* between Serbia, Roumania, and Greece. The pros-pects were hardly inviting. Greece was worth little; and Serbia, in a state of complete chaos economically, even less. (It had mattered little to Vienna that she had allowed the alliance to expire in 1895; and Goluchowski was content to note that she had become perfectly harmless as a neighbour.) Roumania's re-newed enthusiasm for the alliance was more positively encourag-ing; and although the Roumanians' request for cover should the menace of the Russo-Bulgarian *rapprochement* provoke them to attack Bulgaria could not be granted, both Franz Joseph and Goluchowski were determined to establish really cordial relations with Bucharest. And Magyar opinion would have to come into line. In April they arranged a spectacular state visit to Bucharest, to follow on King Carol's visit to Hungary for the celebrations of the completion of the Danube navigation works in the autumn. Thus, although certain circles – and Beck and the St Petersburg embassy were now joined, if somewhat cautiously, by Zwiedenek and Calice – seized on the failure of Goluchowski's feeler to London and the developing Russo-German *rapprochement* to recommend an accommodation with Russia, the Ballhausplatz

[20] P.A. XL/297, Ministerratsprotokoll, 13 April 1896.
[21] Aehrenthal MSS., Karton 1, Goluchowski to Aehrenthal, 24 March 1896.

remained set on an anti-Russian course. When, in February, the German ambassador Eulenburg made so bold as to recommend a *rapprochement* with Russia, *Sektionschef* Welsersheimb sharply reminded him that the Russian menace constituted the only *raison d'être* of the Triple Alliance: after all, Austria-Hungary did not care who held Alsace-Lorraine.

The acerbity of this retort was a measure of the exasperation with which the Austrians viewed the failure of their efforts to build up a really effective anti-Russian front. The failure was certainly glaring. It was partly attributable, no doubt, to factors beyond the control of the Ballhausplatz – the spectacle of domestic weakness which the Monarchy now presented to the world. Strife between Czech and German still paralysed parliamentary life in Austria; and this was particularly embarrassing as the negotiations for the renewal of the commercial *Ausgleich* loomed up at a time when Hungarian chauvinism had been fired to fever heat by a Millennial Exhibition and other celebrations of the entry of the Magyars into Europe in 896. There were disasters abroad too. The Triple Alliance suffered a severe loss of prestige with the humiliating defeat of Italy at the hands of Abyssinian hordes in March. But it was Germany's behaviour that really infuriated the Austrians. On 3 March Goluchowski took Eulenburg severely to task:[22] Germany's whole policy of coquetting with Russia and fobbing the Monarchy off with fair words was intolerable. For example, Germany had just quashed an Austro-Hungarian suggestion for settling the revolt that had recently broken out in Crete, and had then ostentatiously supported an almost identical proposal of Russia's. The Germans had also been 'very stupid' in refusing to press Italy to come to terms with Spain. It was not as if the Triple Alliance Powers were doing Spain a favour: France, being richer than Italy, could offer Spain far more. With the ending of the Italo-Spanish link, the Triple Alliance was 'facing a grave diplomatic defeat'. Altogether, Germany's behaviour was destroying the authority of the Triple Alliance. Friendly Powers were becoming estranged from it. This last lament was taken up by Welsersheimb, who told Eulenburg that it was William II's 'Kruger telegram' of 3 January that had caused the failure of the Austro-Hungarian approach to London: 'now England will not

[22] P.A. I/476, Goluchowski, memorandum on a conversation with Eulenburg, 3 March 1896.

make agreements with Germany's allies.'[23] Franz Joseph, too, had considered the Kruger telegram 'frivolous and irresponsible'.[24] He approved heartily of all that Goluchowski had said to Eulenburg and expressly authorized him to reiterate his complaints during his forthcoming visit to Berlin.

In the event, Goluchowski's visit to Berlin went off very well, and certainly did much to dispel German suspicions of his Polish origins and of his allegedly meddlesome policy in the Armenian question.[25] He was able to explain his aims frankly and at some length.[26] Like the Germans, he too sought good relations with Russia; but he must make it absolutely clear that the Monarchy would not tolerate a Russian preponderance in the Balkans – hence Russia must never be allowed to acquire Constantinople or special privileges at the Straits. Although it was just as well to know that the Monarchy could not count definitely on Britain, Goluchowski would still seek to co-operate with that Power, and he hoped that Berlin would help by humouring Britain and by restraining the German press. Italy was in need of comfort and consolation from her allies, for should the House of Savoy be sacrificed as a scapegoat for her recent disasters, the way would then be clear for a confederation of republics as planned by the Pope and the Francophile Cardinal Rampolla. Spain might yet be brought back into the fold of the Mediterranean *Entente*; and as for the Balkans, Austria-Hungary was for the present chiefly concerned to bring about a Greco-Roumanian *rapprochement* to balance Russia's growing influence in Bulgaria. Germany should help in this. Goluchowski found the Germans effusive in expressions of sympathy, and they assured him that their humouring of Russia was not symptomatic of a desire to restore the Three Emperors' Alliance: so long as the Franco-Russian alliance continued, that would be quite impossible. But they promised nothing very specific.

The ensuing months only partially fulfilled Goluchowski's hopes of reinvigorating the old system of a Mediterranean *Entente* with strong German backing. In May the Triple Alliance was renewed virtually without a hitch, Goluchowski raising no

---

[23] P.A. I/461, Szögyény to Goluchowski, Tel. 40, secret, 4 March 1896.
[24] W. Wagner, p. 215.
[25] Aehrenthal MSS., Karton 2, Jettel to Aehrenthal, 24 March 1896.
[26] P.A. I/476, Goluchowski, memorandum, March 1896.

objections when Berlin refused to revive the Mancini declaration on the grounds that it would have given the alliance a too narrowly anti-Russian emphasis. In London Salisbury again reaffirmed his desire to lean on the Triple Alliance without belonging to it; and the old connexion between Britain and the Central Powers in Egypt was reactivated – for the last time in fact – in April when, in the face of frantic opposition from France and Russia, the Mediterranean *Entente* Powers and Germany granted money from Egyptian revenues to cover the cost of a British military expedition to Dongola in the Sudan. Yet even here, Goluchowski's assumption that the more Britain was 'nailed down' in Egypt, the more she would feel constrained to defend her own (and Austria-Hungary's) interests in the eastern Mediterranean,[27] was to prove mistaken. Indeed, it was precisely Britain's strong position in Egypt that was to render Constantinople less vital to the defence of the Mediterranean route to India. Spain proved an even greater disappointment, raising her price to include a guarantee of her possession of Cuba. This was too much even for Goluchowski, and the Spanish link with the Mediterranean *Entente* was finally dropped. Roumania was more amenable. In July King Carol talked of prolonging the alliance so as to bind the new Liberal government; and during the very successful state visit of Franz Joseph, Goluchowski and Beck to Roumania in September, the alliance was duly extended, by the Goluchowski-Stourdza Protocol, to run to 1903. But even here, the Germans, ever-fearful of Russia, dragged their feet, and only acceded to the Protocol after several reminders in 1899. The unlimited German support of the early years of the *Neue Kurs* was clearly not forthcoming.

Nor could Goluchowski have complete confidence in Britain. Although in April he was congratulating himself on her return to the posture she had maintained before her drastic Armenian policies had isolated her, he still had some doubts about her devotion to the *status quo*. She did not seem fully to realize the need to handle the sultan with circumspection, and to avoid provoking him to some lunatic act of desperation such as would throw the whole Ottoman Empire into turmoil. The old system of the Mediterranean *Entente* – even without German backing – might still be desirable from the point of view of the Monarchy's long-term objectives. But in the short-term, as regards the practical

[27] Aehrenthal MSS., Karton 1, Goluchowski to Aehrenthal, 7 April 1896.

issues of the day, it was becoming increasingly clear that Goluchowski's policy of maintaining the *status quo* at all costs could be more easily reconciled with the policy of Germany – or even of Russia – than with that of Britain.

The Cretan question was a case in point. In 1889 the Turks had revoked certain constitutional concessions granted to the Christians of Crete in 1869, after which tension in the island had increased until the spring of 1896 when Christian and Moslem came to blows. The crisis was potentially dangerous, in that it might spread to Macedonia and raise the whole Eastern question. Indeed, so alarmed was Goluchowski that he seized the initiative – with Russian support – and urged the sultan to restore and extend the constitutional rights of the Christians. But nothing was done, and the situation worsened as the Moslems in Crete remained obdurate against all concessions and as supplies of arms for the Christians began to arrive from Greece. In July Goluchowski suddenly proposed a collective note of warning to Athens and a blockade of Crete – a panicky and ill-prepared move which earned the surprised disapproval of Calice; and which came to nothing when the British government, under strong pressure from a Grecophile public opinion, refused to co-operate. In the end, Goluchowski set to work with the French to examine the demands of the rebels, and temporary relief arrived in September when the sultan promised some concessions. But Goluchowski's notorious vanity had been mortally wounded by the rejection of his blockade proposal – which still rankled a year later; and this added a note of personal bitterness to the failure of the Mediterranean *Entente* to come up to his expectations.

Not that he had the slightest intention of abandoning it. In a conference of ministers on 13 April,[28] while admitting that relations with Russia were tolerably good, he emphasized the dangers that still threatened the Monarchy from that quarter. There was still plenty of inflammable material in the Near East; Russia's perpetual armaments must give food for thought. Her involvement in the Far East had produced no reduction at all in the troops she maintained on the Austro-Hungarian frontier; and she was now more interested than ever in the Mediterranean route to the Far East through the Straits and the Suez canal – witness her renewed activity in Egyptian affairs. There was every need to

[28] P.A. XL/297, Ministerratsprotokoll, 13 April 1896.

keep a sharp eye open. With this argument, however, not all his countrymen agreed. Wolkenstein, now ambassador at Paris but still an ardent champion of an Austro-Russian *entente*, was in despair: 'why are they always talking about a Russian attack on Constantinople?' he complained to Aehrenthal.[29] Kálnoky too thought that a chance was being missed to establish that co-existence with Russia for which he had always striven. The emperor's speech to the Delegations of 1 June, extolling the Triple Alliance, he thought deplorable: for what had the Triple Alliance ever done in the Near East? Did it even have a policy there? Goluchowski talked far too much.[30]

In this situation, the state visit to Vienna in August of Nicholas II, who was accompanied by Lobanov, resulted in nothing more than a fairly good personal relationship between Franz Joseph and the tsar. Goluchowski was sceptical of Russia's professed devotion to the *status quo*, especially when Lobanov turned down his suggestion that an international control of the Ottoman finances might put Turkey on her feet again. In Goluchowski's view, this proved only too well that Lobanov was not interested in a real cure for Turkey's ills, but only in letting her stagger on for another two or three years until the Trans-Siberian railway was completed.[31] Then – and this was a constant refrain in the Ballhausplatz in these months – Russia would suddenly raise a whole complex of 'questions' – Constantinople, the Straits, and Suez. Even the less pessimistic Kálnoky admitted that a constructive agreement was hardly possible with one so notoriously convinced as Lobanov of the Monarchy's irremediable decrepitude.[32] At all events the whole affair soon became academic: Lobanov dropped dead – fortunately not on Austro-Hungarian territory – in the homeward-bound imperial train.

Goluchowski continued to pursue his plans for a Greco-Roumanian *rapprochement*. He reminded the visiting king of the Hellenes in November[33] that the fate of a few Greeks in Rou-

[29] Aehrenthal MSS., Karton 4, Wolkenstein to Aehrenthal, 31 May 1896.
[30] Ibid., Karton 2, Kálnoky to Aehrenthal, 1 June 1896.
[31] P.A. I/476, Goluchowski, memorandum on a conversation with Lobanov, August 1896.
[32] Aehrenthal MSS., Karton 2, Kálnoky to Aehrenthal, 20 September 1896.
[33] P.A. I/476, Goluchowski, memorandum on a conversation with the king of the Hellenes, November 1896.

mania, and of the Roumanian 'Koutzo-Vlachs' harassed by Greek nationalists in Macedonia, was a mere triviality which should not be allowed to obscure the vital need for Greece and Roumania to stand together against the Slav menace as exemplified in the Russo-Bulgarian *rapprochement*. He agreed with the king that Greece and Austria-Hungary had a common interest in furthering the national consciousness of the Albanians to counter-act Slav and Italian ambitions in the western Balkans. But his efforts to bring Greece and Roumania together made painfully slow progress; and by the spring of 1897 Serbia and Bulgaria had signed a secret treaty to co-operate against Greek and Austro-Hungarian influence in Macedonia – the Balkan kaleidoscope was always such that a displacement of power in one area usually produced a countervailing realignment in another.

The Monarchy's diplomatic position was still unsatisfactory therefore, when as a result of a further round of Armenian massacres at the end of August 1896 – this time in the Turkish capital itself – the Ottoman Empire was again plunged into a major crisis. Like the other ambassadors on the spot, Calice was appalled by the bloodshed, and even warned the sultan that the Powers would depose him if he proved unable to provide better govern-ment. But most statesmen in the distant European capitals were above all anxious to maintain the *status quo* and to play down the crisis. All the Concert could agree upon was virtual inaction. Austria-Hungary, certainly, was in far too weak a position both at home and abroad to take any bold initiative at this juncture. As Kálnoky pointed out,[34] she had recently moved away from Britain without moving any closer to Russia. Her German allies were strictly abstentionist, the Italians, weak. And a major domestic crisis loomed up over the decennial renewal of the com-mercial *Ausgleich*. Goluchowski gave a mildly favourable recep-tion to a new batch of reform proposals from London in October. But he was only too relieved when early in 1897 the Powers, alarmed by rumours of Russian plans to seize the Straits, and by a revival of the Cretan crisis, decided that matters were becoming too hot to handle, and that at least the Armenian question could be shelved.

The wearisome Armenian crisis had nevertheless raised grave

[34] Aehrenthal MSS., Karton 2, Kálnoky to Aehrenthal, 20 September 1896.

and urgent problems, notably the possibility of the early collapse of the Ottoman Empire. The dreaded issue of the repartition of Turkey-in-Europe in fact occupied the minds of statesmen in Vienna for the next eight months. As early as 26 August Golu-chowski informed a conference of ministers[35] that the decay of Turkey, no longer capable of saving herself by reform, was pro-ceeding apace. The Monarchy must be ready to act in the event of her final disintegration. For although Austria-Hungary had no further claims to make on Turkish territory, she had great inter-ests at stake: Bosnia and the Herzegovina would have to be finally incorporated. This in itself posed an awkward constitutional problem: it would be impractical to divide the provinces between the two halves of the Monarchy; and impossible to bring either half to renounce them in favour of the other. In the end, Goluch-owski suggested that they be incorporated into the Monarchy as a *Reichsland*, and governed as a colony common to both halves. (This the Magyars were prepared to accept, with the proviso that nothing be done which would weaken the principle of Dualism.) A further meeting on the same day settled the draft of the procla-mation incorporating this decision, to be held in readiness should annexation become an urgent necessity.

A series of conferences of experts from the Ballhausplatz and the Common Finance Ministry (which was responsible for the occupied provinces) at the end of 1896 discussed the fate of the rest of Turkey-in-Europe. In Goluchowski's view,[36] the general picture was fairly clear: the Monarchy had little interest in pre-dominantly Serbian or Bulgarian areas; but in Albania it had vital interests to guard. That area must under no circumstances come under the influence of another Power – such as Italy (who would then control both coasts of the narrow Straits of Otranto and be in a position to close the Adriatic). Nor must Serbia or Bulgaria be permitted to expand to the Adriatic: this would mean the com-pletion of Russia's 'iron ring' encircling the Monarchy. Serbia would have to be allowed to expand somewhere – perhaps into northern Macedonia or the eastern Sanjak: but the Monarchy would have to retain the western Sanjak, if only to prevent a future union of Serbia and Montenegro into that big Slav state,

[35] P.A. XL/297, Ministerratsprotokoll, 26 August 1896.
[36] P.A. I/473, Liasse XXXI/a, protocols of confidential discussions of 17 November, 18, 23 December 1896.

anathema to the Monarchy since the days of Andrássy. The Monarchy's concrete aim would therefore be, granted that a direct occupation of Albania was not desirable, the creation of an independent Albania under the moral protection of Austria-Hungary. Like Bosnia, Albania called for immediate and practical policy decisions. As yet the Albanians were mere tribes who had never formed a state. They would need help if they were to survive amongst their greedy neighbours.

The conferences of experts decided to bolster up Austria-Hungary's position in the area by developing the consular service, spending more on subsidies, and making more of the Monarchy's rights – dating back to an Austro-Turkish treaty of 1612 – as protector of the Catholic tribes in northern Albania. Goluchowski was not indisposed to enlisting Greece in the cause and rewarding her with a slice of southern Albania. But the main emphasis was to be on encouraging a sense of Albanian national consciousness and independence among all Albanians, rather than simply among the northern Catholics – especially as some 77 per cent of the inhabitants of central Albania were Moslem. Even so the going would be difficult. As Calice saw, a new, active policy might revive at Constantinople a mistrust of Austro-Hungarian intentions which it had taken some twenty years of hard work to dispel. Indeed, almost immediately, when the Cretan question developed into a Greco-Turkish war and several Albanian chieftains seized the opportunity to raise a rebellion, Vienna thought it better to defer the implementation of the new policy and advise the consuls in Albania to lie low.

The cautious attitude of Vienna in the Near Eastern crisis of 1896–7 was no doubt partly attributable to the Monarchy's continuing military and diplomatic weakness. As Goluchowski reminded a conference of ministers on 29 August 1896[37] the Monarchy's own defences left much to be desired: the strategic railways of Galicia and Hungary were still mostly single-track. Moreover, in the event of a serious crisis, even one involving the *casus foederis*, the Monarchy should not hope for too much from its allies. Certainly Germany, squeezed between France and Russia, would have little to spare. Beck was equally gloomy:[38] war with Russia might arise not from a direct clash, but from events in the

[37] P.A. XL/297, Ministerratsprotokoll, 29 August 1896.
[38] Ibid., memorandum of 14 August 1896.

south east; in which case Germany might refuse to recognize the *casus foederis*. If the Monarchy, already engaged in the south east, had to turn and cope alone with Russia, it would be in mortal peril indeed. An agreement with Russia would have the great advantage of securing the Monarchy's rear for local military operations in defence of its Balkan interests. But in any case more money should be spent in building up the army. The function of diplomacy was in Beck's view merely to be on the alert and, if war became inevitable, to prevent wearisome negotiations which would give the enemy time to organize and deprive the Monarchy of the advantages of the offensive.

Goluchowski's view of the function of diplomacy was expressed in yet another attempt to clarify the relationship with Britain. He had heard that Salisbury had been hinting that it was Austria-Hungary, not Britain, who stood in the first line in defence of the Straits. In January 1897 he reminded the British ambassador, citing Kálnoky's letter of 25 October 1887,[39] that Britain was in the first line on that question. If Britain would give a clear promise to fight, Austria-Hungary was in turn ready to agree how best to support her. But the Monarchy could not even consider fighting Russia over that issue unless it was absolutely clear beforehand that Britain would fight. The risk would be far too great – especially as Germany could no longer be counted on. In reply Salisbury, who still regarded Austria-Hungary as Britain's 'only friend in Europe',[40] repeated his assurances of 1896. But he could still give no clear pledge to fight. Public opinion was for the present, he bitterly confessed, most unlikely to fight in defence of the slayer of the Armenians. There were, moreover, practical reasons to doubt – since the Turks had fortified the Dardanelles against Britain but not the Bosporus against Russia – whether Britain could do much to save Constantinople from a Russia already assured of French naval backing in the Mediterranean.

In these arguments Deym rightly perceived a change in the situation since the previous winter: Salisbury's personal policy might be the same, but he was several degrees less confident of being able to carry it out. As for Goluchowski, he declared that he would 'be forced to forget' the earlier understanding with Britain and henceforth keep a completely free hand.[41] His wis-

[39] See p. 172.   [40] Margaret M. Jefferson, p. 229.   [41] Ibid., p. 232.

dom has been questioned. By insisting on a clear all-or-nothing commitment he had abandoned a basis of co-operation which, for all its vagueness, might yet have been developed into something more definite: even a mere renewal of the 1887 agreements would have been a more positive achievement than anything France was to extract from Britain in 1904 or Russia in 1907.[42] On the other hand, although Goluchowski was perhaps unrealistic to aim for a formal treaty commitment, even Kálnoky in 1887 had insisted that the defence of the Straits was primarily a British interest. The situation which he had then characterized as unacceptable to Austria-Hungary had now presented itself: Salisbury had undoubtedly moved, under pressure from public opinion, the cabinet, and strategic realities, from confidence in 1887, to mere hope by 1896, and by 1897 to almost hopeless gloom.

Even so, Goluchowski did not panic. He merely hoped that Russia would not come to hear of the change in Britain's position; and that if Russia actually moved, 'the British guns might yet go off by themselves.'[43] Moreover, he still hoped to work with Britain in practical questions: in January and February he co-operated with London in bringing the other Powers to agree on some measures of coercion to be adopted if the sultan rejected their proposals for Armenian reform. But with the shelving of this question, one issue which might possibly have strengthened Vienna's hopes of a policy based on informal day-to-day co-operation with Britain disappeared from the diplomatic arena. It soon became clear that Crete, which now replaced Armenia as the centre of attention, could by no means provide an adequate substitute.

By February 1897 the failure of the Turkish authorities in Crete to introduce any serious reforms, coupled with a drastic reduction of the Turkish military presence in the island at the bidding of the Great Powers, had resulted in a serious rebellion. This time the Greek government lent its support officially to the rebels; and an incident on the Greco-Macedonian frontier, ominously symptomatic of the interconnexion between Cretan and Balkan affairs and the whole Eastern question, sparked off a Greco-Turkish war. Within weeks, and to the surprise of the Powers, the Greek aggressors were soundly defeated.

[42] J. A. S. Grenville, 'Goluchowski, Salisbury, and the Mediterranean Agreements, 1895–1897', *Slavonic Review*, Vol. 36, pp. 367–8.

[43] Margaret M. Jefferson, p. 238.

Now Goluchowski's policy in this affair was threefold. First, to prevent the escalation of the conflict into a general Balkan war. Here he found Russia, who co-operated in restraining the Balkan states from intervention, surprisingly helpful (the first notable example of Austro-Russian co-operation since the Serbian crisis of 1894). Second, to preserve peace between the Great Powers by maintaining the unity of the Concert. Third, to ensure that Greece did not profit in any way from her reckless adventure. That would set a deplorable precedent for the other Balkan states and would be tantamount to the moral bankruptcy of the Concert. Hence, both Vienna and Berlin were insistent from the start that if Crete were eventually granted autonomy, this should not be instituted under the auspices of a member of the Greek ruling house. Goluchowski, still smarting under the rebuff of the previous summer, was reluctant to take the initiative. But he worked to promote harmony within the Concert, joining in when the Powers sent 'fire-brigade' detachments of troops to Crete in February, and rebuking the Germans for their unnecessarily harsh opposition to some of Salisbury's suggestions.

But maintaining the unity of the Concert was a soul-destroying business; all the more so as the British government, under strong pressure from a Grecophile public opinion, was proving strangely unco-operative. Indeed, in May, Salisbury, anxious to avoid obstruction from a Turcophile Germany, suggested that Britain, France, and Russia, as the protecting Powers of Greece, should alone attempt to mediate peace between Greece and Turkey. In the end, Greece and Turkey came to terms before the disunity of the Concert could be fully revealed (July), leaving the fate of Crete to be decided by the Powers. But Salisbury's proposal had given Goluchowski a nasty shock: Russia's loyalty to the *status quo* was by no means above suspicion, and could only be further weakened by association with such Grecophile Powers as France and Britain. Franz Joseph, visiting St Petersburg at the time, expressed his disappointment to the British ambassador, and insisted that the matter was one for the Concert to deal with. Both the content and the timing of Salisbury's proposal had only served to drive Goluchowski to seek closer relations with Russia. Indeed, throughout the early summer of 1897, on the practical issues of the day, Austria-Hungary found herself more in line with the two northern empires than with her erstwhile friends in London.

The failure of Goluchowski's hopes of *ad hoc* co-operation with Britain on issues of the day was the last of a series of disappointments. By the summer of 1897 he was at last forced reluctantly to recognize the inadequacy of a policy based on the Mediterranean *Entente*, unsupported, even disapproved of, by Berlin, and relying in the Balkans on a rickety Greco-Roumanian *entente*. It was force of circumstances, notably the disturbing behaviour of London and Athens, not doctrinaire considerations, that led him to consider a re-orientation of policy. At the same time, the British were bowing to realities and withdrawing from the Balkans and Constantinople to defend the Mediterranean route to India on the Nile. But for Austria-Hungary, forced by geography to remain in the arena, a substitute would have to be found for the Mediterranean *Entente*. This could only be some kind of agreement with Russia. And perhaps circumstances were conspiring to render even this no longer the impossibility it had hitherto seemed to Goluchowski. True, if, as in 1896, Turkey seemed to be on the point of collapse, and the maintenance of the *status quo* an impossibility, then it might be desirable to build up a bloc of anti-Russian forces for use when the general scramble occurred. But Turkey's success in the war with Greece had shown that she was by no means on the point of collapse, and that the *status quo* might indeed be a viable basis for a policy. This Goluchowski was certainly prepared to consider.

Austro-Russian coexistence, 1897–1902

The period immediately preceding Franz Joseph's visit to St Petersburg of 27–9 April had not seemed to offer much hope of any significant improvement in Austro-Russian relations. In the opening months of 1897 the constant threat of the collapse of Turkey kept the apparent irreconcilability of Russian and Austro-Hungarian interests in the forefront of Austrian minds. Beck could make no headway with his suggestions that the partition of Turkey might provide a fruitful basis for co-operation; that the Monarchy would do well to reconcile itself to Russia's acquisition of Constantinople and to her domination of the eastern Balkans; and that Austria-Hungary should rest content with the occupied provinces and control of Serbia, Montenegro, and Albania, leaving Macedonia as an autonomous province.[44] Franz Joseph and

[44] E. v. Glaise-Horstenau, pp. 38off.

Goluchowski would have none of this. They had no intention of abandoning Bulgaria and Roumania to Russia; and they feared that an autonomous Macedonia might in the end serve only to swell Bulgaria to a dangerous size. Temperamentally too, as Kálnoky observed, Goluchowski was totally lacking in self-confidence in dealing with Russia;[45] certainly, as late as April he was determined not to take any initiatives.[46] Even en route to St Petersburg he told Beck that he doubted whether Russia would be interested in negotiations, drawing the exasperated retort that in that case it would have been better not to have undertaken the journey at all.[47]

In the event, Franz Joseph's visit to St Petersburg proved to be a surprising success and a real turning point in Austro-Russian relations. Admittedly, it coincided with a favourable turn in the international situation, with Salisbury's unfortunate attempt to settle the Greco-Turkish war to the exclusion of the Central Powers, and with Turkey's military resilience pointing to the feasibility of co-operation to prolong the existence of the Ottoman empire rather than to grapple with the thorny question of its dissolution. But the visit itself was an important catalyst. Personal factors, notably the remarkably cordial welcome extended to the Austrian visitors, undoubtedly helped; as did the notorious pliability of Nicholas II. The tsar accepted Goluchowski's entire catalogue of Austro-Hungarian interests which Russia must respect as 'self-evident' (*selbstverständlich*)[48] – although as there was no written protocol agreed by both sides, the tsar's goodwill was perhaps a factor of limited value.

At any rate, as Goluchowski explained to a conference of ministers[49] six months later, broad agreement was reached on four principles: first, the maintenance of the *status quo* in the Near East for as long as possible; second, the strict observance of the principle of non-interference with the independent development of the Balkan states (merely a reaffirmation of Kálnoky's doctrine); third, co-operation between the representatives of the two powers in the Balkans, to show the Balkan states that they could

[45] Aehrenthal MSS., Karton 2, Kálnoky to Aehrenthal, 23 February 1897.
[46] Ibid., Karton 4, Zwiedenek to Aehrenthal, 24 April 1897.
[47] E. v. Glaise-Horstenau, p. 385.
[48] P.A. I/475, memorandum by Count v. Rhemen . . ., 1903.
[49] P.A. XL/298, Ministerratsprotokoll, 5 October 1897.

gain nothing by attempting to play off the two Great Powers against each other; fourth, if the maintenance of the *status quo* should prove impossible, the two Powers, while expressly renouncing all designs of conquest for themselves, would come to a direct agreement as to the future territorial configuration of the Balkans – and would, moreover, impose this agreement on the other Powers. For Goluchowski, always inclined to treat the Balkan states (except perhaps Roumania) with a high hand, the third principle, which effectively destroyed their capacity to set the Great Powers by the ears as Bulgaria had done in the 1880s, always remained one of the most valuable aspects of the agreement with Russia. And it helps to explain the concessions he made. The fourth point certainly gave the measure of the distance Austria-Hungary had travelled from her former partners in the Mediterranean *Entente*. The Italians were informed only in the vaguest terms of the self-denying aspects of the agreement – to which Rudiní not unnaturally acceded; the British were not informed at all.

The implications of these principles, as elaborated in the Winter Palace discussions, were summarized by Goluchowski on his return.[50] The Straits question had been excluded from the discussions, as it was, in the Austro-Hungarian view, a matter for Europe to settle; and as Russia professed herself content with the *status quo* for the present. If the Balkan *status quo* could no longer be preserved, Austria-Hungary must insist on the possession of Bosnia, the Herzegovina and the Sanjak (for Serbia and Montenegro must at all costs be kept apart); a large Albania must be created; and Russia and Austria-Hungary must later come to some agreement, to ensure that no Balkan state grew so big as to upset the Balkan balance. These points he later emphasized in a dispatch of 8 May to St Petersburg, stressing particularly that the occupied provinces could not form the subject of any debate, and that the Monarchy reserved the right to annex them whenever it saw fit.

The Russians were of a different mind, and their reply of 17 May made important reservations: Russia recognized only the position of 1878 as regards Bosnia and the Herzegovina – their annexation would raise wider European issues and would require special examination; the territorial extent of the Sanjak was as yet

[50] P.A. I/474, Goluchowski to Pasetti, Tel. 74, secret, 4 May 1897; to Szögyény, No. 731, secret, 5 May 1897.

undefined; and as for the future configuration of the Balkans, Russia would take her decisions when the situation arose. The Austrians were undaunted: the Russian ambassador himself, Kapnist, admitted that his government's view of the eventual annexation of Bosnia was wrong; the tsar himself had endorsed the Austro-Hungarian view as 'self-evident'; and in any case, to pursue the argument might seem to suggest that a further Russian declaration would be needed to legitimize the annexation.[51] No reply was sent, therefore, to the Russian counter-note. From the start, the Austro-Russian *entente* rested on an equivocation (Document 24).

Nor, initially at least, was it all that effective in safeguarding the immediate and practical interests of the Monarchy, for example in the tedious Cretan affair. At the end of 1897 Russia, jealous of Germany's growing influence at Constantinople, suddenly sought to demonstrate her own power by putting forward the candidature of Prince George of the Hellenes for the governorship of Crete, now to be granted autonomy under the supervision of the Great Powers. This apparent concession to aggressive Pan-Hellenism was as much resented in Berlin as in Vienna, and in January 1898 Germany ostentatiously withdrew her contingent of troops from Crete and washed her hands of the question. Goluchowski was faced with a dilemma.[52] On the one hand, he wished to avoid openly opposing Russia: any weakening of the credibility of the new *entente*, or any open split in the Concert, could only tempt troublemakers in the Balkans to further attacks on the *status quo*. On the other hand, the *status quo* was equally endangered by Prince George's candidature, which seemed to be a step towards the union of Crete with Greece, an event which would certainly whet the appetites of the other Balkan states. Indeed, he regarded Russia's action as a violation of the spirit of the 1897 agreements. Certainly, he would not go along with her in coercing Turkey to accept the candidature. In the end, he withdrew the Austro-Hungarian contingent from Crete (an ill-timed gesture which cast the Monarchy in the role of a satellite of Berlin), but issued a circular announcing his continuing interest in Crete and his intention of participating with the other members of the Concert

[51] P.A. I/475, memorandum by Count von Rhemen . . ., 1903.
[52] Aehrenthal MSS., Karton 4, Zwiedenek to Aehrenthal, 29 January 1898; P.A. XL/298, Ministerratsprotokoll, 3 April 1898.

in any final settlement of the question. The eventual election of Prince George, in November 1898, did not affect the constitutional position of Crete, and so Goluchowski was able to escape the humiliation of formally participating in it. But it nevertheless marked another defeat for Austria-Hungary.

Altogether, the year 1898 showed the difficulties of putting the *entente* of 1897 into operation. In August the visiting Russian foreign minister, Mouraviev, was taken to task by Franz Joseph himself, and Goluchowski berated Kapnist about Russia's allegedly disloyal behaviour.[53] The tsar had recently given a large present of arms to Nikita of Montenegro, notoriously the most anti-Austrian of all the Balkan princes; the Russian press was for ever engaged in a 'mad campaign' against the Austro-Hungarian administration in Bosnia and the Herzegovina, and was accusing Austria-Hungary of meddling in Serbia, whither ex-King Milan had just returned from his Austrian exile. This last charge, Goluchowski vehemently denied, although he refused to exert any pressure on Belgrade to expel Milan: that would be interference in the internal affairs of a Balkan state as expressly forbidden by the 1897 agreement. In fact, Kapnist worked hard to convince his government of Goluchowski's sincerity; but he was unable to shake the tsar's conviction that Milan was merely 'l'homme gagné de l'Autriche-Hongrie'.[54] Finally, far from being co-operative, the Russian diplomats recently transferred from the rough and tumble of Asian posts to the Balkans – particularly Bachmatiev at Sofia – were guilty, Goluchowski claimed, of 'quite incredible' intrigues against Austria-Hungary.[55] Indeed, he was finding it increasingly difficult to justify the *entente* to public opinion; and was beginning to think it might be simpler if the two Powers reverted to their old methods, safeguarding their own interests and checkmating each other at every turn.

This outburst at least cleared the air, and drew promises of better behaviour from St Petersburg. And all in all, despite these teething troubles, the Austro-Russian agreements of 1897 marked a notable development in both the internal and the external

[53] P.A. I/476, Goluchowski, memorandum on a conversation with Kapnist, August 1898.

[54] P.A. I/474, Liasse XXXII/c, Széchenyi to Goluchowski, Tel. 79, 26 August 1898.

[55] P.A. I/476, Goluchowski, memorandum, August 1898.

position of the Monarchy. The renewed emphasis on Habsburg-Romanov solidarity was especially valuable to Vienna at a time when strife between Czech and German had been augmented by a quarrel with the Hungarians over the renewal of the commercial *Ausgleich* to produce a crisis which in Goluchowski's opinion was the worst for forty years and apparently insoluble.[56] Externally, the *entente* of 1897 – like the renewal of the Three Emperors' Alliance in 1884 – marked a devaluation of the Triple Alliance in Austro-Hungarian eyes. True, Goluchowski told a council of ministers on 5 October,[57] that Alliance still remained the basis of his policy; but he had been as cavalier about initiating the Italians into the 1897 agreements as Kálnoky had been about Skiernewice; and Beck had been working on contingency plans for war with Italy since the end of 1896, the Tauern railway being extended to the river Isonzo. The fact that the 1897 agreements were made over the head of Germany too, and that this was rather resented in Berlin, was another symptom of the decline in importance of the Monarchy's defensive alliance system. Most striking of all was the complete abandonment of the link with Britain, a Power not even mentioned by Goluchowski in his survey of the international situation. Indeed, according to Aehrenthal and his friends, the shedding of all 'illusory proclivities'[58] as regards Britain – a power which, as they saw it, would never be able to give Austria-Hungary any effective help – was one of the most cheering features of the 1897 *entente*, even if it as yet stopped disappointingly short at the mere maintenance of the *status quo*.

While those who thought like Aehrenthal and Wolkenstein wanted something much more positive in the long run, Goluchowski, for his part, was well satisfied with the agreements as they stood: the St Petersburg visit had shown that there was really no basic reason why Russia and Austria-Hungary could not agree; Goluchowski had even been able to dispel Russian suspicions about Austria-Hungary's legendary plans of expansion as far as Salonica; and it now seemed that the Monarchy had nothing to fear from Russia in the near future – especially as she was so deeply engaged in the Far East. On 5 October, he assured the council of ministers that he had reason to hope that 'we can avoid

[56] Aehrenthal MSS., Karton 1, Goluchowski to Aehrenthal, 30 June 1897.
[57] P.A. XL/298, Ministerratsprotokoll, 5 October 1897.
[58] Aehrenthal MSS., Karton 1, Hengelmüller to Aehrenthal, 26 May 1897.

conflict with Russia without giving up any of our vital interests'.[59] This, even Aehrenthal and the partisans of a more positive *entente* would have endorsed. The difference between the two groups was that whereas Goluchowski and the officials of the Ballhausplatz took a generally negative view of the *entente*, as an instrument for safeguarding the particular Balkan interests of Austria-Hungary from the encroachments of Russia, for Aehrenthal and his friends the *entente* was the foundation stone of a positive, far-reaching understanding with Russia, extending eventually to close co-operation in Great Power politics generally. For the sake of this ambitious long-term aim, the exponents of a positive *entente* were prepared to sacrifice some of the Monarchy's narrower particular interests. Thus, whereas Goluchowski tended to put the emphasis on 'without giving up any . . . vital interests', they stressed the need to 'avoid conflict with Russia'. Which view of the *entente* would eventually prevail would depend not only on general domestic and foreign considerations, but on developments in the area with which the *entente* was specifically concerned.

Montenegro, for instance, the chief outpost of Russian influence in the Balkans, remained a thorn in the side of the Monarchy despite the *entente*. Indeed, since the pliable Nicholas II had replaced Alexander III, Nikita had become increasingly bold in his efforts to influence Russian policy through two of his daughters who were married to Russian grand dukes. Minor frontier incidents and commercial disputes continually supplemented the bitterness felt at Cetinje towards the Dual Monarchy, by tradition the tiresome watchdog, the eternal creditor, and the destroyer of the treaty of San Stefano.[60] Vienna in turn maintained a stiff, cold attitude towards the wayward Nikita: Franz Joseph absolutely refused to receive him at court. In the Austrian view, the Monarchy would always have enough influence at Cetinje simply by virtue of its geographical position, however bad relations might be.[61] The Ballhausplatz put its trust in this and in the new *entente* with Russia to prevent Montenegro from becoming too troublesome. Indeed, it seemed for a time in 1901 that this policy was succeeding. The Russian minister at Cetinje, Vlassov, was an ardent supporter of the *entente*, and determined that Nikita should

[59] P.A. XL/298, Ministerratsprotokoll, 5 October 1897.
[60] Aehrenthal MSS., Karton 3, Macchio to Aehrenthal, 2 May 1901.
[61] Ibid.

not lead Russia by the nose.[62] But by the autumn of 1902 Nikita and Panslav elements at St Petersburg had secured Vlassov's recall. Within six months his successor, a man of the Ignatiev school who, according to the Austro-Hungarian minister, treated the *entente* 'as a social game' and shunned all discussions, had re-established a virtual Russian protectorate over Montenegro.[63]

Serbia, Montenegro's sister-state and rival in the struggle for leadership of the south Slav world, continued for a time under Austro-Hungarian influence. Between 1897 and 1900 an Austrophile government under Georgević managed to restore a measure of political and financial stability. True, the young King Alexander was as unstable as his father; and his wild boasts of Austro-Hungarian support were something of an embarrassment to Vienna, as in 1899 when he publicly declared that 'the enemies of Serbia are the enemies of Austria-Hungary.'[64] Nevertheless, Goluchowski supported him, coaxing the common ministers to underwrite a loan to Serbia in 1898. But he was at the same time prolific with advice.[65] Serbia must keep the peace, and refrain from provoking Turkey, or Bulgaria (in Macedonia); and Alexander should give the government more stability by winning over the more sensible elements of the Radical party. This advice, while perhaps constituting an interference in Serbia's domestic affairs, was of course entirely in conformity with the conservative spirit of the 1897 agreements. Not that Vienna was responsible for the return to Serbia early in 1898 of ex-King Milan, whom Alexander appointed to the command of the army. True, the Austrians viewed Milan's return with satisfaction as strengthening Austrophile influences in Serbia, but they soon discovered that this was by no means the same thing as strengthening Austro-Hungarian influence there. For example, on the occasion of a spectacular treason trial of Russophile Radicals at the end of 1899, Vienna's urgent pleas for clemency went unheard, and severe sentences were imposed at the instigation of ex-King Milan. The Russians were furious, and withdrew their diplomatic representatives from Belgrade; and they felt that Austria-Hungary could

[62] Ibid., Macchio to Aehrenthal, 2 September 1901.
[63] Ibid., Macchio to Aehrenthal, 9 October 1902; 27 April 1903.
[64] Aehrenthal MSS., Karton 2, Jettel to Aehrenthal, 18 August 1899.
[65] P.A. I/476, Goluchowski, memorandum on a conversation with King Alexander of Serbia, August 1898.

have done more to check Milan's influence, or even to get rid of it altogether. But this Goluchowski refused to do: such pressure would contravene the 1897 agreement on non-intervention. It would be politically suicidal for the Monarchy to do anything to help Russia to establish her predominance in Serbia; and to cast the Monarchy in the role of a mere tool of Russia in this way would gravely compromise Austro-Hungarian prestige throughout the whole Balkans.[66]

Unfortunately for Goluchowski, Austria-Hungary's prestige in Serbia and the Balkans did not depend solely on the diplomacy of Vienna. Events quite beyond his control were soon to destroy the Monarchy's position in Serbia. On 5 August 1900 King Alexander married the courtesan, Draga Masin, a match which provoked the fall of the Georgević ministry and the voluntary exile of the enraged ex-King Milan. Vienna was not unnaturally dismayed. But Goluchowski proved his loyalty to the non-interventionist principles of 1897 in bad times as in good. (This loyalty was perhaps ultimately to cost the Monarchy dear; as was the inadequacy of the Austro-Hungarian minister at Belgrade, Heidler, a devotee – more out of lethargy than conviction – of Kálnoky's policy of passivity.) At any rate, Goluchowski decided that if Alexander was so lacking in decency as to marry his mistress, that was Serbia's affair. Of course, the fall of the able Georgević ministry was regrettable; but Vienna was prepared to co-operate with any Serbian government that was loyal to Austria-Hungary in turn. It was the king's constant *coups de tête* that worried him most, for Serbia's condition was already chaotic enough; and the marriage had seriously damaged the prestige of the dynasty. If the dynasty should fall, Panslav elements might then attempt to bring about a union of Serbia and Montenegro – a step towards that big Slav state which would cut off Austria-Hungary from the southeastern Balkans. This, Goluchowski declared, Austria-Hungary would never tolerate; indeed, she would prevent it by force if necessary, 'because when the vital nerve of the Monarchy is in question, we cannot yield'.[67] For the time being, however, he was

[66] P.A. I/475, Liasse XXXII, Goluchowski to Aehrenthal, No. 21, 10 January 1900; Liasse XXXII/h, Goluchowski to Aehrenthal, private and very confidential, 29 December 1901.

[67] P.A. I/475, Liasse XXXII, Goluchowski to Aehrenthal, No. 242, 19 August 1900.

content to endorse the bland assumptions of the Kálnoky era: if Serbia became troublesome she could always be brought to heel, 'as by virtue of geography she is so dependent on us financially and economically'.[68]

This soon proved to be a sanguine view. After the withdrawal of ex-King Milan – and Kapnist admitted rather shamefacedly to Goluchowski that St Petersburg had exercised great pressure on Belgrade in the matter[69] – Russia made haste to restore diplomatic relations with Serbia. By the end of 1900 she was moving into the position of Serbia's chief protector, protesting in Vienna about a rumoured extension of the Bosnian railway network into the Sanjak of Novibazar, and speaking sympathetically about Serbia's long-term designs on western Macedonia. In 1901 the death, in Vienna, of ex-King Milan removed the last restraint on the unstable king, who in his efforts to curry favour at St Petersburg went so far as to describe the Monarchy, in speaking to a journalist in 1902, as 'the arch-enemy of Serbia'.[70] According to a Ballhausplatz assessment of July 1901[71] the energetic Russian minister, Charykov, ruled, in fact, both King Alexander and his kingdom, thanks to his contacts with the powerful Radical party. Not that there was any immediate cause for alarm: Charykov was said to have given the *mot d'ordre* to wait for two or three years, till the sons of Petar Karageorgević, head of the rival Serbian dynasty, had grown up. 'Then everything will be decided.' Alexander, apparently, was grateful to Charykov for this respite – he would otherwise already have lost his throne; and Charykov in turn was content to bide his time, advising the Serbian government for the time being to be conciliatory towards Austria-Hungary, and professing his respect for the *entente* of 1897.

Meanwhile, developments in Bulgaria did nothing to redress the Balkan balance in favour of the Monarchy. The later 'nineties in fact saw a continuous decline in Austro-Hungarian influence at Sofia. In the commercial field, the Monarchy maintained, even slightly increased, its trade with Bulgaria; but the greater part of the growth in Bulgaria's total trade was absorbed by Austria-Hungary's increasingly powerful competitors, Britain and Germany. Politically, the Austrians proceeded to commit the very error the Russians had committed in the 1880s. When, in July

---

[68] Ibid.   [69] Ibid.   [70] E. v. Glaise-Horstenau, p. 391.
[71] Aehrenthal MSS., Karton 5, Musulin to Aehrenthal, 12 July 1901.

1897, the Bulgarian prime minister, Stoilov, spoke disparagingly and publicly of Austro-Hungarian policy, Goluchowski summarily withdrew all Austro-Hungarian consuls and diplomatic agents from Bulgaria. Needless to say, this only left the field clear for Russia. By the end of the year the Russophile officers exiled by Stamboulov had been repatriated; and the assiduous Bachmatiev was soon boasting that he occupied at Sofia a position comparable to that of Cromer at Cairo. Franz Joseph and Goluchowski continued to ostracize the Bulgarian ruler, despite the recommendations of Aehrenthal and others in favour of less stiff Spanish etiquette and more flattery after the manner of William II.[72] In the spring of 1900 Bulgaria quarrelled with Roumania about the sufferings of the Macedonian Koutzo-Vlachs at the hands of Bulgarian terrorists; and Austria-Hungary's warm support of her ally naturally did her no good at Sofia.

At the same time, the influence of Russia in Bulgaria was made painfully clear to Vienna. Rumours were circulating in the spring of 1900 of some impending Bulgarian *coup* – either an incursion into Macedonia or a declaration of independence. The latter, Goluchowski might have been prepared to accept as ultimately inevitable; but it must not occur under solely Russian auspices.[73] Consequently, despite the warnings of his advisers against raising hypothetical questions which might only endanger the *entente* to no purpose, he determined to ask the Russians to show their cards.[74] The reply he received from St Petersburg was mildly disconcerting: Bulgaria was not planning any kind of *coup*; and Russia could vouch for her future good conduct. This made him suspect the existence of some secret Russo-Bulgarian agreement; but he consoled himself with the thought that as Russia refused to enter into a discussion, Austria-Hungary for her part had complete freedom of action. Moreover, as Russia boasted so blatantly of her control of Bulgaria, so the Monarchy need be less restrained elsewhere.[75] Yet even as regards Bulgaria, there was a faint chance by the end of 1901, as the conflict in

[72] Aehrenthal MSS., Karton 2, Jettel to Aehrenthal, 21 April 1900; Karton 4, Aehrenthal to Szögyény, 27 September 1901.

[73] P.A. I/475, Liasse XXXII, Goluchowski to Aehrenthal, No. 66, 7 March 1900.

[74] Aehrenthal MSS., Karton 2, Kinsky to Aehrenthal, 4 March 1900; Karton 4, Szécsen to Aehrenthal, 15 March 1900.

[75] Ibid., Goluchowski to Aehrenthal, 26 March 1900.

Macedonia sharpened and Serbo-Bulgarian rivalry intensified, that Russia's new links with Belgrade might some day provide an opening for Austro-Hungarian influence at Sofia.

With Serbia drifting away, and with Bulgaria still beyond his grasp, Goluchowski attempted to make Roumania the pivot of his Balkan policy. The news of the Austro-Russian *entente* had been ill-received at Bucharest, and not without reason. Aehrenthal, for example, had heaved a sigh of relief when Franz Joseph's speech to the Delegations in 1897 dwelt on the new *entente* and contained hardly a word about Roumania. He hoped that Goluchowski's 'Roumanian heart' would not be in evidence again for a long time.[76] Yet Goluchowski, after his experiences of Russian Balkan policy in the succeeding three years, was by no means willing to stake everything on the Russian *entente*. The Roumanian alliance, now almost the only remaining element of the Monarchy's barrier against the spread of Russian influence throughout the Balkans, was far too valuable to be lightly discarded.

In the autumn of 1900, therefore, he spoke reassuringly to King Carol:[77] the 1897 agreements were by no means contrary to Roumania's interests; indeed, they constituted a guarantee of the future free development of Roumania. Nor could they in the least hinder Austria-Hungary's standing up for Roumanian interests in the event of changes in the *status quo*. Thereafter, he continued to press Bucharest to come to terms with Athens;[78] but he no longer advised as in 1897, a *rapprochement* with Belgrade as well. Indeed, he warned the Roumanians against listening to Serbia's enticements: even a *rapprochement* with Bulgaria would be less dangerous. Not that there was much risk even of this. In January, and again in July 1901, the Roumanians were talking rather of attacking Bulgaria, should she attempt to expand into Macedonia; and they embarrassingly asked the Austrians to extend the alliance to give Roumania rear-cover in this contingency. This, Goluchowski could not consider;[79] for it would mean giving Roumania the power to open up the whole Eastern question whenever she saw fit. Roumania should build up her defences and trust to Austria-

[76] Mérey MSS., Aehrenthal to Mérey, 19 November 1897.

[77] P.A. I/472, Liasse XX/e, Goluchowski to Pallavicini, No. 290, secret, 9 October 1900.

[78] Ibid., Goluchowski to Pallavicini, No. 374, secret, 12 December 1900.

[79] Ibid., Goluchowski to Pallavicini, No. 51, secret, 29 January 1901.

Hungary to safeguard her interests in the event of a general redrawing of the Balkan map. In practical terms, Vienna agreed to supply military instructors and equipment to encourage the Roumanians in this policy. And even if Goluchowski's doctrine that the irredentist question, being merely a matter for negotiation between Bucharest and Budapest, had 'nothing to do with the alliance',[80] had something of an unrealistically legalistic air about it, the alliance itself was in a fair state of health. In April 1902 it was renewed, to run for five years, and then automatically for a further three.

Meanwhile, Goluchowski's dogged insistence that the *entente* with Russia was no more than a means of safeguarding Austria-Hungary's interests against a supposed threat from the *entente* partner itself exasperated the partisans of a more positive approach. The stronghold of the latter remained, as usual, the embassy at St Petersburg. At the end of 1898 Prince Liechtenstein had gone so far as to resign his post of ambassador when Goluchowski had rejected a scheme of his whereby Russia would guarantee the integrity of Turkey in return for Austro-Hungarian support in the Cretan question.[81] His successor, Baron Aehrenthal, was even more assiduous; and he could count on the support of a small but influential group of people at home, including such notable Slav politicians as Kramař,[82] and, in the Ballhausplatz itself, Jettel von Ettenach, head of the Literary Office, and a man who strove untiringly to influence public opinion in favour of the *entente* by a judicious placing of articles in the press.[83] Among the diplomats Szögyény, ambassador at Berlin (who may in fact have had an eye on Goluchowski's position for himself)[84] bombarded the emperor with advice in support of Aehrenthal's views. And the Russian ambassador, Kapnist, worked as hard as Aehrenthal to promote mutual understanding and sympathy between Vienna and St Petersburg. Perhaps not surprisingly, his government came

[80] P.A. I/479, Liasse XXXIV/a, Goluchowski to Szögyény, No. 515, secret, 4 December 1901.
[81] Aehrenthal MSS., Karton 3, Liechtenstein to Aehrenthal, 28 December 1898.
[82] Ibid., Karton 2, Kramař to Aehrenthal, 6 February 1899, 2 February 1900.
[83] Ibid., Jettel to Aehrenthal, 28 June 1899.
[84] Ibid., Karton 2, Jettel to Aehrenthal, 21 November 1899.

to regard him as 'a slave of Austrian policy';[85] just as Franz
Joseph observed in 1899 that Aehrenthal was '*ganz russisch*'.[86] In
the Ballhausplatz Russia remained an object of deep suspicion; not
only for Goluchowski, but for his very powerful confidant, Baron
Doczy, who, according to a lament of Jettel's of May 1900, was
closer to the minister than anyone else, and whose word was
law.[87] (As a Jew, Doczy naturally had little love for Tsarism.) The
emperor too found Russia's behaviour intensely irritating and
often complained of her 'unreliability'.[88] He tended to dismiss
Aehrenthal's criticisms of Goluchowski's policy as the expression of some personal animus against the minister.[89]

Matters came to a head in June 1901, when Szögyény went in
person to the emperor to complain about Goluchowski's 'impossible' ways.[90] Even in his technical organizing of the service
and his choice of personnel, Goluchowski was gravely at fault: in
Szögyény's view almost all the Austro-Hungarian representatives
at the Balkan capitals were worthless; and Heidler at Belgrade
was positively harmful. The minister's notorious indolence was
equally exasperating: diplomats were constantly left without instructions, and had to glean what they could of their government's policy from the newspapers – a complaint which was by
no means without foundation, to judge by the private correspondence of Austro-Hungarian diplomats in these years. Franz
Joseph listened graciously to the ambassador's tirade: but
nothing was changed. On the contrary, in August, the Russophile party were further enraged by the publication in *Pester
Lloyd* of an alarmist article inspired by the Ballhausplatz (where
even Jettel was beginning to discern in Russia's activities in
Serbia and Bulgaria a portent of some impending *coup*). The concluding paragraph of the article, written apparently by Goluchowski himself after consultation with the emperor, was a harsh
summons to Russia to explain her recent behaviour, and to state
whether she wished to continue the *entente* or not.[91]

[85] Ibid., Karton 5, Aehrenthal to Goluchowski, No. 11C, 19 February 1901.
[86] Ibid., Karton 6, Jettel to Aehrenthal, 5 January 1900.
[87] Ibid., Jettel to Aehrenthal, 23 May 1900.
[88] Ibid., Karton 6, Szögyény to Aehrenthal, 12 May 1899.
[89] Ibid., Karton 2, Jettel to Aehrenthal, 26 April 1900.
[90] Ibid., Karton 4, Szögyény to Aehrenthal, 10 July, 6 October 1901.
[91] Ibid., Karton 2, Jettel to Aehrenthal, 23 August, 6 September 1901.

At this, Aehrenthal himself went to see the emperor.[92] He complained at length about Goluchowski's 'aimless' and suspicious attitude towards Russia, and pleaded strongly for a more positive approach to the *entente*. The Monarchy should cultivate St Petersburg, both as a means of gaining more independence from Berlin within the Dual Alliance, and – as the days of the Triple Alliance might well be numbered – in order to avoid finding itself some day in the grip of a Russo-Italian vice. But he got the impression that his arguments were only wearying the old emperor; and so, in November, he repeated them in a long letter to Goluchowski.[93] Again he emphasized that minor questions and the particular interests of the Monarchy must be strictly subordinated to the need to preserve cordial relations with Russia at all costs. Goluchowski was not completely convinced, and in a long reply of 29 December,[94] defended his attitude on specific issues such as Crete and Serbia on the grounds of practical necessity (Document 22). After all, co-operation with Russia was worthwhile only in a spirit of reciprocity. It would be quite wrong for the Monarchy to acquiesce in every Russian advance and do nothing just for the sake of avoiding a clash. That, would place the Monarchy in a worse situation than that which had prevailed before 1897, when at least it had had the freedom to take appropriate counter-measures to defend its own interests.

Goluchowski was nevertheless prepared to go some way to meet Aehrenthal's demands.[95] The darkening Balkan horizon was giving him food for thought. The bloodshed in Macedonia, where terrorist atrocities alternated with Turkish reprisals, was growing daily worse. To this, the Monarchy would have to pay some attention, if only for the sake of its prestige (*Vormachtstellung*) in the Balkans. If Russia refused to co-operate, he would return to his pre-1897 policy of opposing her at every turn. St Petersburg must be left in no doubt whatever about this. But he would try first to reach agreement with Russia, as to some means of mitigating the chaos in Macedonia. This need not entail any

[92] Ibid., Karton 4, Aehrenthal to Szögyény, 27 September 1901.

[93] P.A. I/475, Liasse XXXII/k, Aehrenthal to Goluchowski, private and secret, 15 November 1901.

[94] Ibid., Liasse XXXII/h, Goluchowski to Aehrenthal, private and very confidential, 29 December 1901.

[95] Ibid., and Liasse XXXII/k, Goluchowski to Aehrenthal, No. 556, 29 December 1901.

departure from the conservative principles of 1897: it would be quite in order to interfere in Turkey to the extent of forcing the sultan to modify the political and administrative *status quo* in Macedonia for the greater end of preserving the territorial *status quo*. Beyond this, Russia and Austria-Hungary might also exchange views about Crete and Serbia: it must be made quite clear to Russia that the Monarchy could not tolerate a Serbo-Montenegrin union in the not unlikely event of King Alexander's disappearance.

He therefore authorized Aehrenthal to approach the Russian foreign minister, Lamsdorff. His timing at least was auspicious. Aehrenthal had managed to arrange a visit to St Petersburg by Archduke Franz Ferdinand, which went off very well in February 1902.[96] By the spring, Russia and Austria-Hungary were working amicably together to lower the tension in Macedonia – mainly by warning Bulgaria to refrain from all intervention. It seemed that the Austro-Russian *entente* might well be about to develop in a more positive direction.

One factor that was practically forcing Goluchowski to rely more on the Russian *entente* was the apparent lack of any feasible alternative. The old system based on the Mediterranean *Entente* now seemed lost beyond recall – partly because international affairs in the later 'nineties were dominated by extra-European or worldwide issues which hardly provided much common ground between the British world empire and the Monarchy with its narrow interests in south-east Europe. For example, when the United States cast its eyes on Cuba in 1898, Goluchowski was at first disposed to assist the Habsburg queen-regent of Spain by offering to mediate in the dispute – a late echo of Kálnoky's policy of supporting the Iberian monarchies.[97] But he had in the end to content himself with organizing, through the diplomatic corps at Washington, a fruitless appeal to President McKinley's humanity. For Germany frowned on his efforts; and Britain, according to the Austro-Hungarian minister at Washington (a staunch supporter of Aehrenthal), was worse than useless, being solely concerned to appease the United States – a power which ultimately represented a greater threat to Europe than even the

[96] Aehrenthal MSS., Karton 4, Szögyény to Aehrenthal, 22 February 1903.
[97] P.A. XX/68, Goluchowski to Wolkenstein, Tel. 8, 13 March 1898.

so-called Yellow Peril: 'we shall all be ruined commercially and brutalized politically.'[98]

In other cases, the Austrians considered it politic to keep in the background as much as possible. The delicate issue of the Hague Peace Conference, for example, summoned in 1899 at the wish of the tsar, was a source of acute embarrassment to Vienna.[99] The idea of an armaments freeze was not attractive to a power which already had so much leeway to make up; and compulsory arbitration might well deprive the Monarchy of its only military advantage over Russia, that of speed of mobilization. On the other hand, the tsar would naturally be offended if the conference produced nothing at all. In the event Goluchowski managed to appear conciliatory on unimportant issues – he helped to persuade the Germans to accept the idea of voluntary arbitration and a permanent court; and in the armaments question he skilfully kept in the background, allowing the Germans to incur the odium of leading the opposition. He was certainly well satisfied with the results of the conference: public opinion would see in the anodyne declaration on armaments and in the court of arbitration great guarantees of peace; yet none of this would in practice impose the slightest restriction on the Great Powers.[100]

The other major 'world issue' of these years, the Boer War, showed that traces of pro-British sentiment still lingered in high circles in Vienna. The emperor, for example, went so far as to tell the British ambassador, at a ball and in the presence of several people, that 'dans cette guerre je suis complètement Anglais.'[101] In this, there was more than sentiment: the war might lead to invigorating military reforms in Britain, and possibly a revival of British influence in the Mediterranean. An Austro-Hungarian squadron paid a demonstrative courtesy visit to Malta, and Admiral Fisher returned the compliment at Trieste. These gestures were not insignificant at a time when public opinion in the Monarchy, as throughout Europe (except perhaps for certain Magyar and Italian patriots who remembered 1849 and 1860) was

[98] Aehrenthal MSS., Karton 1, Hengelmüller to Aehrenthal, 12 May 1898.
[99] P.A. X/144, Edler v. Krieghammer to Goluchowski, No. 2002, 21 April 1899; protocol of a meeting held on 28 April 1899 to determine Austria-Hungary's attitude at the Hague Conference.
[100] P.A. X/145, Goluchowski to Szögyény, Tel. 37, 14 June 1899.
[101] F.O. 7/1297, Rumbold to Salisbury, No. 11, confidential, 10 January 1900.

so violently anti-British. Despite a considerable uproar in the press, and especially in the Austrian parliament, the governments of Vienna and Budapest steadily ignored this opinion; and the Hungarian government – partly no doubt as a sound economic proposition at a time of depression – pressed ahead with the sale of large numbers of horses for use by the British in South Africa.

Yet nothing positive came of all this. True, when the Boxer rising broke out in China in 1900 the emperor, more prestige-minded and more in tune with public opinion than the Ballhaus-platz,[102] insisted on sending a couple of ships and a detachment of troops, who according to Austrian reports fought better than the Italians;[103] and Vienna welcomed the Anglo-German Yangtse Agreement of October 1900. But Goluchowski, much as he approved of anything that would bind Britain closer to the Triple Alliance, could do nothing to influence the course of the more general Anglo-German alliance negotiations of 1901. Certainly Deym, to whom he gave *carte blanche* to support his German colleagues, rightly took a sceptical view of the situation and kept in the background; yet even he remained blissfully unaware that Britain's reluctance to underwrite the tottering Dual Monarchy was one of the greatest obstacles to an agreement. At any rate, the Germans would be satisfied with nothing less than Britain's joining the Triple Alliance, and by the end of 1901 had rejected what was virtually a British offer to revive the Mediterranean agreements with the pivot in Berlin rather than in Vienna. These very tentative contacts, even failures, could give Goluchowski no reason to contemplate dropping the Russian for a British connection.

The other major components of Kálnoky's defensive bloc, the Dual and Triple Alliances, hardly offered more hope of salvation. The Dual Alliance was seriously undermined in these years by the intensification of national feeling in both Germany and Austria. Even temporary successes of the Slavs on the whirligig of Austrian politics after 1897 were liable to cause friction between the increasingly anti-Slav Germany and its polyglot ally. When in 1899 the Prussian government arbitrarily expelled some Czech and Polish seasonal workers, the Austrian prime minister, Count Franz Thun, a Bohemian nobleman of Czech sympathies, hinted

---

[102] Mérey MSS., Szécsen to Mérey, 12, 22, 27 July 1900.
[103] E. v. Glaise-Horstenau, p. 389.

sharply in parliament at the possibility of retaliatory measures. At this, indignant complaints flowed in from the German embassy, and even from William II himself; but Franz Joseph gave them short shrift and supported Thun. The German unofficial, and even semi-official, press in turn bewailed the Slav tendencies allegedly prevailing in Austria as a threat to the Alliance. But all this only exasperated Goluchowski, who pointed out that no Austro-Hungarian government could afford to ignore such important sections of opinion as the Czechs and the Poles, whatever Berlin might say.

Not that the Austrians were without grievances of their own against Germany (Document 23), whence nationalism of a virulent Pan-German variety was spreading its tentacles across the frontier, linking up with the protestant-nationalist '*Los von Rom*' movement, denouncing catholicism and the House of Habsburg, and demanding the speedy completion of Bismarck's great work. In November 1898 a German nationalist deputy proclaimed in the Reichsrat itself and amidst cheers from like-minded colleagues, that his loyalty lay with the emperor at Berlin. Such demonstrations, which became commonplace in the following years[104] could do the reputation of Germany and the Alliance no good in clerical and monarchist circles; and commercial circles were appalled when Germany reverted to a highly protectionist policy in 1902. In Jettel's opinion, 'Germany has injured us far more commercially than Russia has done politically.'[105] Personal factors deepened the estrangement. Goluchowski, as a Pole, was never really *persona grata* at Berlin; and 1900 saw the elevation to the German chancellorship of Bülow, a man whom Goluchowski had always tended to regard as something of a personal rival since the days when they had both served as head of mission at Bucharest.[106] The emperor too was finding the flamboyant William II increasingly tiresome: 'if only the German Emperor could keep silent! He talks far too much. It is better that we should keep quiet and let our ministers do the talking.'[107] After 1900 he paid no more visits to Berlin.

[104] E. Walters, 'Franco-Russian discussions on the partition of Austria-Hungary, 1899', *Slavonic Review*, Vol. 28, 1949.

[105] Aehrenthal MSS., Karton 2, Jettel to Aehrenthal, 5 January 1900.

[106] Ibid., Karton 4, Thurn to Aehrenthal, 7 March 1899.

[107] Quoted in J. Andrássy, *Bismarck, Andrássy and their Successors*, p. 291.

Yet such considerations alone could hardly account for the lamentable state of Austro-German relations at the turn of the century. There were serious differences between the allies on great issues of foreign policy. The Austro-Russian *entente*, itself very much a product of Austrian irritation at Germany's unreliability and pro-Russian proclivities, aroused in turn much jealousy at Berlin. Franz Ferdinand's visit to St Petersburg provoked only carping comments in the Wilhelmstrasse. For although the Germans, true to Bismarck, had no stomach for the prospect of an Austro-Russian war and all the burdens and dilemmas that it would entail, they had no desire to see their imperial neighbours on such close terms that Germany's services as broker could be dispensed with. Not that Goluchowski was frightened by Bülow's blustering speech in the Reichstag in January 1902 hinting that Germany too could make a deal with Russia, the Triple Alliance being after all less necessary for her than for her allies. He rightly calculated that so long as the Franco-Russian Alliance continued, the continental alliance system was too rigid to permit of a Russo-German alliance or even of a restored Three Emperors' Alliance. But he was nevertheless immensely irritated by Bülow's speech, particularly by its gratuitous downgrading of the Triple Alliance. He was equally appalled by Germany's treatment of Britain, and thought that 'friend Bülow richly deserved' the verbal drubbing he received from Chamberlain in an exchange of parliamentary polemics over the South African war.[108] Worst of all, the Germans were proving highly unco-operative in the Near East. In their efforts to curry favour at Constantinople they ostentatiously took the sultan's part against all the other Powers in a dispute over the maladministration of foreign post offices in Turkey. Goluchowski, who felt that the dignity of the Great Powers was at stake, was greatly exercised about this. Even more serious, the Germans stubbornly refused to join in pressing the sultan to make life tolerable for his Macedonian subjects; and, anxious as ever to stand well with Russia too, they refused to lift a diplomatic finger to support Austria-Hungary's tentative plans to extend the Bosnian railway network into the Sanjak, which at the end of 1902 again came to nothing in the face of Russian opposition and Turkish lethargy.

[108] P.A. I/480, Liasse XXXIV/b, Goluchowski to Szögyény, private, 17 January 1902.

The Triple Alliance was hardly in any better shape. The year 1902 saw the usual crisis over its renewal, with the Italians demanding clearer commitments against France and Russia in the Mediterranean, and the incorporation into the alliance of the Austro-Italian self-denying agreement of 1897. (This had been formalized in an exchange of notes in 1900, by which the two Powers pledged themselves, in the event of Turkey's disappearance, to eschew all desire of conquest and to work for the creation of a large, independent Albania (Document 21).) Goluchowski, for his part, refused to consider any changes at all, insisting that the Alliance was concerned solely with the *status quo*, not with possible future developments. Nor would he commit himself to continue the favourable tariff accorded to Italian wine imports, due to expire in 1903. He had reason to fear a tariff war with France, who was threatening retaliatory duties against the Monarchy if the wine clause were renewed. And in any case the question was one for the Austrian and Hungarian parliaments, and beyond his competence to decide. In the end, all Goluchowski gave the Italians was a declaration (similar to those just made by France and Britain) stating that as far as Austria-Hungary was concerned, Italy could have a free hand in Tripoli if the Ottoman Empire collapsed. Otherwise, he skilfully allowed the Germans to take the lead in rejecting Italy's requests, and the final treaty represented a victory for the views of Vienna and Berlin.

It was a victory that hardly enhanced the value of the Alliance in Italian eyes. Already in 1900 the assassination of the soldier-king Humbert had dealt a severe blow to Austro-Italian relations. Official contact between the Austro-Hungarian and Italian general staffs now virtually came to an end. The fact that the new king, Victor Emmanuel III, was married to a daughter of Nikita of Montenegro augured ill for Goluchowski's hopes of restricting Italy's interest and influence in the Balkans. And the elections of 1902 brought to power an anti-clerical and pro-French government under Zanardelli. Not that the Austrians resented the Francophile inclinations of this government or even the Franco-Italian agreements of 30 June 1902: anything that lessened the risk of a Franco-Italian war which might entail unpleasant duties for Austria-Hungary was welcome to Vienna. But certain delicate questions which had troubled the Alliance in the past had undoubtedly become more difficult to handle. Although the new king soon paid a state visit to Berlin, and even St Petersburg, he and Franz Joseph were still complete strangers to each other – a state of affairs which was, as Goluchowski pointed out, hardly normal between allied monarchs. Yet a *modus vivendi* between Quirinal and Vatican, still the essential precondition of an Austro-Hungarian state visit to Italy, was under the new anti-clerical government further off than ever; and, as the Italian ambassador at Vienna lamented, Zanardelli was assiduous in stiffening Victor Emmanuel against a second Italian state visit to Vienna.[109] Such issues undoubtedly weakened the hold of the Alliance over public opinion at a time when irredentism was still rife in Italy, and when the sharpening of national conflicts inside the Monarchy was awakening the hostility of the south Slavs of the Austrian and Hungarian coastlands towards both their Italian fellow-subjects and the Italians of the kingdom. In terms of practical diplomacy the Triple Alliance meant very little, for all Goluchowski might wish to keep it in reserve and resent Bülow's public depreciation of it. In Albania, rivalry between Austrian and Italian propagandists, consular and religious, raged unabated; and Goluchowski was adamant in his refusal to initiate Rome into such plans as he was considering with St Petersburg to deal with the unrest in Macedonia.

Underlining the crumbling of Kálnoky's system of diplomatic defences against Russia was the deepening confusion which prevailed in the domestic affairs of the Monarchy in the decade around the turn of the century. By the end of 1897 increasingly violent rioting over linguistic and national issues by Czechs and Germans, in the Austrian parliament, the Bohemian Diet, and the streets of Vienna and Prague had brought parliamentary government in Austria to a complete standstill. No government could be found which could command a sufficiently stable majority to carry through the negotiations for the renewal of the commercial *Ausgleich* with Hungary; and after 1897 the old *Ausgleich* was provisionally extended from year to year by a variety of constitutional expedients, Hungary attaining, in theory at least, actual independence as a commercial unit (although in practice the same external tariffs were maintained in both halves of the Monarchy). It was in these years that Austria-Hungary earned the name of 'Dual

[109] P.A. I/476, Goluchowski, memorandum on a conversation with Count Nigra, 15 September 1902.

Monarchy on short notice' (*auf Kündigung*). A deep pessimism gripped those who were called on to find a way out: to some it seemed that 'an archangel could not solve our domestic problems', and that the Monarchy had now sunk to the position of a second-class power like Japan.[110] Naturally, this state of affairs did not go unnoticed abroad. The Monarchy's potential enemies, France and Russia, took its possible disintegration on the death of Franz Joseph into account when they amended their alliance in 1899 to include co-operation 'to maintain the balance of power' – that is, to prevent Germany's acquiring too large a slice of the Habsburg dominions. In 1900 André Chéradame's sensational book, *L'Autriche au seuil du vingtième siècle* propounded the view that the Monarchy had succeeded Turkey as the sick man of Europe and now bode fair to be an easy prey for Pan-German expansionism. As the British refusal to join the Triple Alliance in 1901 showed, even Austria-Hungary's friends were impressed by her apparently inexorably advancing decrepitude.

This decrepitude was reflected in the weakening of the economic position of the Monarchy in the later 'nineties. By 1897 the budget surplus, which had stood at 120m. in 1893 and 57m. in 1896 had fallen to a mere 13m. A depression now set in, intensified by the collapse of parliamentary government in Austria and by a two-month coal strike in 1900, which lasted for four years. There was a slight improvement after the turn of the century, thanks largely to an extensive programme of public works initiated by the government in an effort to divert public opinion from nationalist strife. But it was becoming increasingly clear – and this had serious implications for the political prestige of the Monarchy in the Near East – that Austria-Hungary was finding it difficult even to maintain, let alone strengthen, her position against her Great Power competitors.

This was to some extent due to the proverbial inefficiency of the commercial departments of the government, still very much poor relations in a system essentially military and aristocratic in spirit. In 1903 the go-ahead Austrian journalist, Baernreither, drew a very unfavourable comparison between the Prussian Ministry of Trade (the head of which had just visited the United States) and its counterparts in Austria-Hungary, where most of

[110] Aehrenthal MSS., Karton 1, Biegeleben to Aehrenthal, 26 February 1899.

the *Sektionschefs* never in their lives ventured further than a lunch-time stroll in the Ringstrasse.[111] The commercial department of the foreign office exhibited some of the worst features of Austrian bureaucracy – although it should be said that the chaos affecting the whole government was hardly conducive to a speedy dis-patch of business anyway. The British embassy was kept waiting for some ten months in 1903 for a reply to a simple enquiry about the duty on Canadian whisky;[112] and the chargé d'affaires learned from several of his colleagues 'that unexampled delay now occurs in extracting answers from this government in which ministries other than the ministry for foreign affairs are involved' – particu-larly when reference to Budapest was necessary. 'The dilatoriness of this country, if continued in progressive ratio, will soon rival that of Turkey.'[113]

But the real problem lay much deeper, and was hardly one which could be remedied by administrative tinkerings. In the face of the inexorable intensification of competition from richer and more advanced industrial states whose economies were develop-ing at a rate with which the largely agrarian Monarchy could not hope to compete, the governments of Vienna and Budapest were often helpless. The thriving Austrian sugar-beet industry was virtually ruined when, at the turn of the century, Britain and the United States imposed draconic punitive duties on sugar which was produced with the help of government subsidies, and se-cured international endorsement for this in the Brussels Sugar Convention of 1902. Even more disastrous was the behaviour of Germany, who was still far and away the Monarchy's most im-portant trading partner, absorbing some 52 per cent of its exports (with Britain coming a very poor second with 10 per cent). In 1902 Germany reverted to a fairly stiff protectionist tariff, which hit Austrian and Hungarian cattle and grain exports directly and very hard. At the same time she was steadily securing markets in the Balkans for her own light industrial goods at Austria-Hungary's expense. In Bulgaria, for example, the Austrians barely held their own, with about 30 per cent of Bulgarian trade, in these years, while Germany and Britain increased their share from 27·1

[111] Ibid., Baernreither to Aehrenthal, 27 June 1903.
[112] F.O. 7/1355, Johnstone to Lansdowne, No. 2, commercial, 10 January 1904.
[113] Ibid., Johnstone to Lansdowne, No. 3, commercial, 11 January 1904.

per cent in 1891–5 to 50·2 per cent in 1904–8.[114] In Roumania, too, German competition was severe. True, the Austrians were holding their own as yet in Serbia; but if Serbia ever gained direct contact with the West by acquiring a port on the Adriatic, this market too might be lost. For the time being, if the Monarchy was pushed out of some of its traditional Balkan markets, it could still find others further afield in even more primitive areas in Asia Minor (where more cotton goods were sold than in Hungary in 1906) and Macedonia. The position was by no means desperate. A number of profitable factories were soon operating in Turkey, where by 1908 the Monarchy was running second only to Britain as a trading power. But the prospects were by no means brilliant.

Political confusion and economic weakness combined during these years to reduce the military potential of the Dual Monarchy. The Common Army could only be increased if a new Army Law were passed by both parliaments to increase the size of the contingents recruited annually in Austria and Hungary beyond the level fixed by the Army Law of 1889. Now with Austria in political chaos and much of Magyar opinion traditionally suspicious of the Common Army as a threat to the liberties of Hungary, this simply could not be done. Indeed, the two parliaments provided precious little money even for technical improvements to the existing army. This deficiency was however, as Beck's biographer points out, perhaps a blessing in disguise; for when the money was eventually forthcoming in the last years of peace, the Austro-Hungarian Army at least got some of the best and most modern equipment.[115] But for the time being, army reform plans were a pure waste of time. 'In building up the Army, unfortunately no progress': this was the monotonous refrain of Beck's annual reports.[116] The 1890s, when all the other Great Powers were arming fast, saw the balance of military power shift steadily against the Dual Monarchy. Indeed, in a conference of ministers in June 1899 the emperor stated quite bluntly that if the Monarchy had to fight in existing circumstances it would not have a hope of success.[117]

---

[114] V. Paskaleva, 'Über den wirtschaftlichen Einfluss Österreich-Ungarns in Bulgarien, 1878–1918', in F. Klein (ed.), pp. 187–9.

[115] E. v. Glaise-Horstenau, p. 408.

[116] Ibid.

[117] P.A. XL/299, Ministerratsprotokoll, 29 June 1899.

The emperor's efforts to secure a new army law came to nothing. The prime ministers of Austria and Hungary shrank from the task of finding the money. Nor was anything done for the navy, despite Goluchowski's warnings that it might be needed in a Near Eastern crisis, and despite Franz Joseph's pointing to its general importance for purposes of trade and prestige in peacetime.[118] Admittedly, at the end of 1900, when events in Serbia had clouded the uncertain Balkan sky, an effort was made to strengthen the strategic position of the Monarchy in the southeast by developing the Bosnian railway network. But even here two months of conferences were necessary before the Austrian and Hungarian governments could be brought to agree which railways were to be built, and by which companies. For Goluchowski, the issue was one of the highest policy.[119] He admitted that the Bosnians themselves would hardly benefit from the new strategic railways; but Bosnia had a duty to make sacrifices for the benefit of the Monarchy as a whole. It was after all militarily of the greatest importance that the Monarchy should be in a position to send troops speedily to the frontiers of the Sanjak. It would, moreover, be useful to have a railway connexion with Turkey independent of the Balkan states – the existing line to Constantinople ran through Serbia – if only to strengthen the hand of the Monarchy in any commercial negotiations with the Balkan states.

As the Bosnian network itself was not completed until 1905, it is hardly surprising that nothing much was done at this stage about a further extension into the Sanjak of Novibazar. Yet a mere rumour of such a project drew from the Russian embassy in November 1900 an anxious enquiry, which elicited a careless assurance from *Sektionschef* Szécsen to the effect that the Monarchy could not build railways in foreign territory.[120] Goluchowski was much put out at what he saw as a Russian attempt to whittle away Austria-Hungary's rights, and lost no time in correcting Szécsen's statement. The Bosnian railways, he angrily reminded the Russian ambassador,[121] were a purely internal affair, and would have been built twenty years earlier if the money had been available. Even in the Sanjak, the Monarchy had a clear

[118] Ibid.   [119] Ibid., Ministerratsprotokoll, 21 September 1900.

[120] Aehrenthal MSS., Karton 5, Notiz, 6 November 1900.

[121] P.A. I/476, Liasse XXXIII/39, Goluchowski, memorandum on a conversation with Count Kapnist, November 1900.

right to build railways by virtue of the Treaty of Berlin. Such railways had nothing whatever to do with the *entente* of 1897, which was concerned only with the political *status quo*. Further discussions about a possible Sanjak railway at the end of 1902 again came to nothing in the face of Russia's frowns and Germany's ostentatious refusal of support.

Meanwhile, during the year 1901 the Monarchy had failed to strengthen its military capacity, despite the increasingly threatening Balkan situation. On 29 November[122] Beck had warned a conference of ministers that Austria-Hungary might well be compelled to take action, in defence of her interests, in a way not envisaged by her alliances; and Franz Joseph had remarked that as far as its Balkan interests were concerned, the Monarchy could not count on its allies anyway. It was essential, therefore, to strengthen the army. As Beck pointed out, a continuation of the standstill (*Stillstand*) amounted in effect to a relative decline. Goluchowski expatiated on the serious diplomatic consequences of this situation: indeed, it was the military weakness of Austria-Hungary which lay at the root of her diplomatic weakness – Germany and Italy might soon seek stronger friends elsewhere – and which made Russia so difficult to handle. But none of these arguments made much impression on the parsimonious governments of Austria and Hungary. They agreed to vote some money for the artillery, but beyond that they refused to go. It was quite impossible, the Austrian finance minister declared, to find large sums of money for the army, let alone the navy, in such a time of depression. There was thus still no immediate prospect of the Monarchy's acquiring a military potential that would permit of a strong policy involving a risk of war with Russia. And, it would require consummate skill on Goluchowski's part to achieve from such a position of weakness a really satisfactory and lasting *modus vivendi* with Russia by solely diplomatic means.

Austro-Russian co-operation, 1902–6

The first indication that the Austro-Russian *entente* might be about to develop in a more positive direction came in the summer of 1902, when Kapnist suggested that Russia and Austria-Hungary might establish a kind of joint supervision of Macedonian

[122] P.A. XL/301, Ministerratsprotokoll, 29 November 1901.

affairs. The Russian foreign minister, Lamsdorff, and Goluchow-ski both liked the idea: it would obviate the meddling of the six Powers under Article XXIII of the Treaty of Berlin, or through the even more cumbersome device of a congress.[123] Neither Russia nor Austria-Hungary had any desire to see others inter-fering in what they had come to regard since 1897 as their own particular sphere of interest. The Austrians especially welcomed the idea as an effective means of preventing the creation of a large autonomous Macedonia extending to Albania and the Adriatic which might some day join Bulgaria to create that big Slav state that had been a nightmare of the Ballhausplatz since the 1870s. Nevertheless, the first practical attempts to establish a dual control – a series of Austro-Russian warnings to Sofia and Con-stantinople about the deepening chaos in Macedonia – brought little improvement. At the end of the year a general rising still seemed likely in Macedonia once the snows had melted in the spring.

A major step forward was taken when Lamsdorff visited Vienna in December 1902, after calling at Sofia and Belgrade and warning those governments that Russia was determined to maintain the *status quo*. Goluchowski was much impressed by Lamsdorff's evident sincerity,[124] and the upshot of the visit was the so-called Vienna Memorandum of 17 February 1903. This document was modest enough. Whatever the sultan might think, the two Powers were not in fact seeking to undermine or encroach on his author-ity, but rather to preserve it, and to bolster up the territorial *status quo* by creating tolerable living conditions for the inhabi-tants of Macedonia. The Memorandum urged the sultan to strengthen the hand of his newly-created Inspector-General of Macedonia by making him irremovable without the consent of Russia and Austria-Hungary; and to accept some foreign advisers to help improve the Macedonian *gendarmerie* – who should also be assisted by regular troops in combating Albanian robbers and Bulgarian terrorist bands. On an international level the Vienna Memorandum virtually served notice on the other Powers (who were nevertheless asked to support it at Constantinople) that the affairs of Macedonia were to remain the prime concern of Russia and Austria-Hungary.

[123] Aehrenthal MSS., Karton 2, Kinsky to Aehrenthal, 17 May 1902.
[124] P.A. I/476, Liasse XXXIII/39, Goluchowski, memorandum on a con-versation with Lamsdorff, 2 December 1902.

This development of the *entente* policy found support in Austro-Hungarian diplomatic circles. Szögyény at Berlin saw in it the beginning of a general *rapprochement* between the three Empires, now all set to embark on 'a really conservative policy'[125] – all the more welcome in view of the political turmoil prevailing inside the Monarchy. In Russia, the ultra-conservative minister of the interior, Plehve, talked to Aehrenthal of a possible restoration of the Three Emperors' Alliance, an idea that Aehrenthal had been toying with for some time as a weapon against the rising forces of democracy.[126] But the *entente* in its new aspect still had something of an exclusively Austro-Russian air about it, and resembled more the Three Emperors' League of the 1870s than the Russo-German dominated Three Emperors' Alliance of the 1880s. Even for Aehrenthal, one of the chief advantages of a good understanding with Russia was that the Monarchy could thereby avoid falling too much under the domination of Berlin; and Plehve used the argument that if Vienna would keep the Magyars in order, Russia would readily co-operate in checking the growth of German influence in the Balkans.[127]

Certainly, the news of Lamsdorff's visit to Vienna had been very ill received at Berlin, where fears were rife for Germany's position at Constantinople if her ally were to embark on a policy of bullying the sultan. Indeed, Zwiedenek was from the start anxious that the Monarchy should not damage its relations with friends or allies in London and Berlin by its cultivation of St Petersburg. He suspected that behind Lamsdorff's amiability lay a desire to drive a wedge between Germany and Austria-Hungary, and ultimately to destroy Germany's influence and paralyse Britain at Constantinople.[128] His fears were not unfounded. The new emphasis on exclusive co-operation with Russia necessarily implied yet a further devaluation of the Dual Alliance and of the Monarchy's former partners in the Mediterranean *Entente*. Not that the behaviour of the latter did anything to impede the process. In the German press, the Vienna Memorandum came in for some carping criticism; and there were ominous hints from Britain and Italy

---

[125] Aehrenthal MSS., Karton 4, Szögyény to Aehrenthal, 7 March 1903.
[126] Ibid., Karton 5, Aehrenthal to Goluchowski, private, 16 January 1903, copy.
[127] Ibid., Aehrenthal to Goluchowski, private, 16 July 1903, copy.
[128] Ibid., Karton 4, Zwiedenek to Aehrenthal, 23 January 1903.

that they too would have to be consulted about Macedonian affairs. To Italy, particularly, Goluchowski delivered a very sharp rebuff, refusing point blank to enter into talks with her about the future of Albania. Now that the Monarchy had sacrificed its freedom of manoeuvre in Macedonia by embarking on a joint policy with Russia, it was all the more essential to keep a completely free hand elsewhere.

Meanwhile, as Austria-Hungary drew closer to Russia the remaining tenuous links that bound her to Britain were weakened yet further. Although, as late as the summer of 1902, the Austrians had hoped that with the end of the Boer war Britain would devote more attention to the Mediterranean, and that the old co-operation might be resumed, this hope proved illusory. It was the old story. In the autumn Lansdowne asked the Austrians for support in protesting to Turkey about Russia's declared intention to send four torpedo-boat destroyers – admittedly as yet unarmed – through the Straits into the Black Sea. Goluchowski gave a favourable answer, and even hinted at a possible revival of the old Mediterranean agreements. But when the actual passage of the Russian vessels coincided with Lamsdorff's visit to Vienna, Goluchowski made no bones about deserting the British, arguing that this particular infringement was only a trivial one, and that the Straits question was chiefly Britain's concern in any case. Lansdowne was furious, and washed his hands of Goluchowski and the Mediterranean agreements; and in February 1903 a state paper of the Committee of Imperial Defence declared that so long as Britain held Egypt, the Mediterranean balance could not be all that disastrously affected, even if Russia got control of the Straits. No more was heard of the Mediterranean agreements. Between Russia and Britain Goluchowski had made a clear, and in the long term perhaps a fateful, choice. But in the circumstances it was perhaps the only intelligible choice. At the end of 1902 the explosive situation in Macedonia, which could only be defused with the co-operation of Russia, constituted a far greater threat to Austro-Hungarian interests than what was, after all, a relatively trivial violation of the rule of the Straits.

If the Austro-Russian *entente* in its more positive and exclusive guise meant a weakening of Austria-Hungary's links with her old partners, it was by no means certain that it would adequately protect even her narrower Balkan interests. True, St Petersburg's strict adherence to the *status quo* could only undermine Russia's position with the ambitious government of Sofia; and the whole reform programme, in so far as it protected and preserved the Christian element in Macedonia as the eventual heirs of the Ottoman Empire, was a step in the direction of a Balkan peninsula consisting of free and independent states – perhaps the most effective obstacle to Russian preponderance in the area.[129] Nevertheless, as some Austro-Hungarian observers were quick to point out,[130] the Monarchy had by the same token renounced a chance to strengthen its own influence at Sofia as a patron of Bulgaria's ambitions. If Russia should ever revert to an active policy – and this was always the great risk implicit in the *entente* – the Monarchy might well discover that it had wasted valuable opportunities.

More immediately, in Macedonia itself, the Austrians were jeopardizing their prospects of building up an Albanian barrier against Slavdom. Admittedly, these prospects were slender. Austria-Hungary's efforts since 1896 to encourage the development of Albanian nationalism by an astute use of the *Kultusprotektorat* had already aroused the suspicions of the Turks, who countered by fostering mistrust between Christian and Moslem Albanians and by draconic laws against the teaching of the Albanian language. Now, it seemed, Vienna was wavering in its support of the Albanians. The February Memorandum specifically required the sultan to check their depredations – which to many Albanians meant that Austria-Hungary was throwing in her lot with Serbia against them. The murder, in April 1903, by Albanian soldiers, of the Russian consul at Mitrovitsa produced the spectacle of Austria-Hungary joining with Russia – notoriously the arch-enemy of the Albanians – to demand the condign punishment of the guilty. This cost the Austrians a good deal of credit in the Albanian camp. Indeed, some in Vienna began to fear that the new *entente* policy would eventually drive the Albanians entirely into the arms of Italy.[131]

The collapse of the Austro-Hungarian position in Serbia represented, it might be argued, an even more spectacular sacrifice on the altar of the Austro-Russian *entente*. But this view involves a

[129] Ibid., Zwiedenek to Aehrenthal, 20 February 1903.
[130] Ibid., Karton 3, Macchio to Aehrenthal, 27 April 1903.
[131] Ibid., Karton 2, Jettel to Aehrenthal, 3, 11 April, 1903.

good deal of hindsight. In fact, the murder of King Alexander and his wife by military conspirators on 11 June 1903 hardly bore at the time the crucial significance for Austro-Serbian relations that it was to acquire in the light of Serbia's behaviour under the Karageorgević dynasty. Even in the last months of Obrenović rule Austro-Serbian relations had been far from cordial. Although King Alexander, disappointed by St Petersburg's ostentatious devotion to the *status quo*, had sought early in 1903 to return to the Austro-Hungarian fold, Franz Joseph had had enough of his shiftiness and refused to receive him either at court or at manoeuvres; and Goluchowski, who had long regarded Alexander's regime as irretrievably lost, sharply rebuffed a Serbian request for help in promoting a league of Serbia, Roumania, and Turkey against Bulgaria. Russia and Austria-Hungary, he declared, wanted peace and quiet. Although the murder of the king, exceptional in its brutality even by Balkan standards, was personally shocking to the emperor, it caused no political misgivings in the Ballhausplatz. Nor did it seem in the least to threaten the Austro-Russian *entente*. Indeed, the Russians even hinted that Austria-Hungary might march into Serbia and restore order there.

In the event, the Austrians took no action. In the first place, they were satisfied, on the basis of their own police reports, that 'we have every reason to believe in (*mit Vertrauen entgegenzukommen*) the Austrophile sentiments' of Petar Karageorgević, to whom the conspirators offered the Serbian throne.[132] Despite his Parisian education and Montenegrin marriage, Petar had been born in Hungary, a son of the outspokenly Austrophile Alexander Karageorgević, and had always expressed great sympathy for the land of his birth. Moreover, intervention would have been difficult to justify on the pretext of restoring order, for the country was calm. Indeed, preparations for intervention, which would have taken up some two weeks, might have been the very thing to cause disorder; and might have deterred Petar Karageorgević from accepting the throne. That would have raised the thorny question of an alternative head of state – probably Nikita of Montenegro or a republican president. In these circumstances,[133] therefore, the Austro-Hungarian government tolerated, even

---

[132] P.A. XL/316, memorandum by Zwiedenek on the Karageorgević family, 14 June 1903 (based on a memorandum dated '1901').

[133] Aehrenthal MSS., Karton 1, Dumba to Aehrenthal, 20 July 1903.

welcomed, the enthronement of King Petar, and was the first government to give its recognition and blessing to the new Serbian regime.

It was only after the new regime was firmly established that things began to go badly wrong for Vienna. King Petar, old, and above all anxious to avoid the fate of his predecessor, was determined to leave politics to the military conspirators and their allies in the Radical party. By November 1903 Austrians could see that 'the king is a nullity . . . the whole show is run by the people of the eleventh of June.'[134] As early as 27 September Dumba, Austro-Hungarian minister at Belgrade, had described Austro-Serbian relations as 'as bad as possible . . . All our work and good-will (as regards the *coup*) are now wasted.'[135] He attributed much of the blame to the press, both in Serbia and in the Monarchy, which had been hurling abuse back and forth across the frontier since shortly after the *coup*; and he blamed the Austrian press particularly for starting the campaign. The newspapers ought to have been kept more in hand. (In fact, the Austrian press had at first adopted Goluchowski's cool approach to the murders; and it was Jettel in the Literary Office of the Ballhausplatz who had taken it upon himself to inject what he termed a more 'humanitarian' view of the situation into the newspapers.)[136] The Russians, for their part, were not slow to exploit the situation, reminding the Serbs, according to Dumba, that their future lay in the West and on the Adriatic; and even advising them not to make a commercial treaty with Austria-Hungary, but to export their livestock to Germany instead.

The Austro-Hungarian reaction to all this was unimaginative. The boycott of the Serbian court was resumed: this was one thing on which the emperor, Goluchowski, and even Aehrenthal were all agreed. It was in vain that *Sektionschef* Mérey pointed out[137] that moral indignation expressed some six months after the event was hardly convincing; and that the Monarchy could not after all wish to see King Petar fall, if only because any alternative – a Russian regency, a Montenegrin, or a republic – would be infinitely worse. So Austro-Serbian relations continued bad.

[134] Aehrenthal MSS., Karton 3, Mérey to Aehrenthal, 27 November 1903.
[135] Ibid., Karton 1, Dumba to Aehrenthal, 27 September 1903.
[136] Ibid., Karton 2, Jettel to Aehrenthal, 24 June 1903.
[137] Ibid., Karton 3, Mérey to Aehrenthal, 27 November 1903.

Not that this misfortune could with justice be laid at the door of the Austro-Russian *entente*. On the contrary, the *entente* while it lasted offered some assurance that a Russian-controlled government at Belgrade would not assume an attitude so hostile to the Monarchy as to necessitate intervention. Whether, even so, the Austrians would not have been wiser to intervene and bring Serbia to heel once and for all, is a question that can hardly be answered in the light of the situation at the time. Certainly they would have had the greatest difficulty in reconciling the adoption of a forceful, let alone violent, policy towards the Russophile regime established in Belgrade with their overriding desire to preserve and cultivate the Austro-Russian *entente*.

Not that the Austrians would forgo everything for the sake of the *entente*. When William II visited Vienna in September 1903 he found both Franz Joseph and Goluchowski as resolutely opposed as ever to the Bismarckian doctrine of spheres of interest in the Balkans, and to the suggestion that the Central Powers might make sure of Russia by presenting her with Constantinople. Nevertheless, in less momentous questions, there was much to be said for continuing and developing the *entente*, especially in Macedonia, where the all too tentative February Memorandum had clearly proved inadequate. The summer had seen a good deal of marching and counter-marching in Bulgaria and Turkey; and in August the Bulgarian propaganda organization in Macedonia at last managed to stage its long-planned rising. This was a miserable failure, owing to poor organization and the lack of effective support from anybody but adherents of the Bulgarian Exarchate. (The other Christians of Macedonia – largely Greek or Serbian Orthodox – had been antagonized by years of Exarchist terrorism.) And although it was serious enough to provoke bloody reprisals by the Turks, and, indeed, the hoped-for European intervention, this last was by no means in the sense desired by the Exarchists. Although a visit to Vienna by the tsar at the end of September provided Russia and Austria-Hungary with a convenient opportunity to devise new remedies for the ills of Macedonia, their ultimate purpose was still very definitely the maintenance of the *status quo*.

The two monarchs, accompanied by Goluchowski and Lamsdorff (and also Aehrenthal, who by threatening resignation forced his presence on the reluctant Goluchowski at the last minute) spent a few very enjoyable days at Franz Joseph's hunting lodge of Mürzsteg in Styria. The upshot was the Mürzsteg Punctation of 2 October 1903, essentially an elaboration of the February Memorandum. The idea of dual control was again well to the fore – some British suggestions tending in the direction of autonomy for Macedonia were simply ignored – and the aim was still, as in February, the preservation of the territorial *status quo*, at least for the time being, by establishing tolerable living conditions for the Christians of Macedonia. As regards the means to achieve this end, the Mürzsteg Punctation envisaged a far more stringent control of the Ottoman authorities than the February Memorandum had done. The Ottoman Inspector-General of Macedonia was to be accompanied by an Austro-Hungarian and a Russian 'Civil Agent', who would assist him in his efforts to check the disorders. The *gendarmerie* was to be reorganized under the supervision of a European commander (the Italian General Di Giorgis was eventually appointed) with the assistance of officers from the Great Powers. Financial and judicial reforms were also envisaged. For the time being, Macedonia was to be divided into zones, in each of which a Great Power was to be entrusted with the task of seeing that the reforms were carried out; but ultimately, according to Article III of the Mürzsteg Punctation,[138] Macedonia was to be reorganized into administrative districts more in accordance with ethnic realities.

Although the effects of Article III were later universally recognized to be disastrous (in that the Macedonian Christians were tempted to adjust 'ethnic realities' by means of mutual massacres, against the day of its implementation) it seemed at the time quite a triumph for Goluchowski. True, it implied that Albanian minorities in largely Serbian areas would be lost; but it guaranteed the consolidation of predominantly Albanian areas. As Goluchowski reminded a conference of ministers in November 1903 'the Albanian nation after all forms a dam against the flooding of the Porte's possessions in the Balkans by the Slav

---

[138] The wording of this article was vague and ambiguous: 'aussitôt qu'un apaisement du pays sera constaté, demander au Gouvernement ottoman une modification dans la délimitation territoriale des unités administratives en vue d'un groupement plus régulier des différentes nationalités.' (B[ritish] D[ocuments on the Origins of the War], ed. G. P. Gooch and H. W. V. Temperley, London, 1928, Vol. 5, p. 66.

deluge'.[139] He had now brought the Russians a step further than they had been prepared to go in 1897, when they had refused to commit themselves about the future territorial configuration of the Balkans. He was pleased to have scotched the idea of an autonomous Macedonia which, whether under Slav or Orthodox auspices, or possibly even linked to Bulgaria, could never be in Austria-Hungary's interests. With Mürzsteg, therefore, Goluchowski could be well content.

By the beginning of 1904 the first steps had been taken to implement the Mürzsteg programme. The Great Powers managed to remain fairly united, although the Germans constantly complained that the Powers were encroaching too far on the sultan's sovereign rights, and the British complained that the Mürzsteg Punctation did not go far enough. But there was a good deal of jobbery over the question of zones. Vienna would not hear of Di Giorgis setting up his headquarters in the Italian zone, Monastir, for that would have made Italian influence all too preponderant there; so the General went to Salonica. The Turks still tried, with tacit German encouragement, to obstruct the *gendarmerie* reform for some months, but in the end gave way. And the summer even saw a *détente* on the Turkish-Bulgarian frontier. The immediate crisis, it seemed, had been safely overcome.

This success of the *entente* was accompanied, as usual, by a further decline of the Monarchy's alliances. True, in some respects, relations with Italy had shown signs of improving in 1903, when the elections had brought the conciliatory Giolitti to power, with Tittoni at the Consulta. The new government was not only ever mindful of German financial aid (on which the economic development of Italy had been heavily dependent since the rift with France in the 1890s), but also sincerely desirous of reconciling the Liberals and the Church in a struggle against Socialism. This augured well for relations with Catholic Austria. Franz Joseph, for his part managed, by exercising the ancient *ius exclusivae* (for the last time, incidentally: in 1904 Pius X forbade the practice on pain of excommunication) to veto the election to the papal throne of the arch-enemy of the Triple Alliance, Cardinal Rampolla. Tittoni, whom Goluchowski met at Abbazia in April 1904, seemed to Vienna a great improvement on his predecessor, professing his love of the Triple Alliance, his hatred of

[139] P.A. XL/302, Ministerratsprotokoll, 19 November 1903.

irredentism, and his ready acceptance of Goluchowski's very firmly stated view that an eventual annexation of Bosnia would not constitute a change in the *status quo* such as would entitle Italy or any other Power to compensation.[140]

Nevertheless, such meetings could not cover up the tension that arose from the Austrians' determination to resist Italy's growing Balkan aspirations. Even at Abbazia Goluchowski had had to lecture Tittoni about Italy's misdeeds in Albania: whereas Austria-Hungary's activities there were of a purely religious and educational character, altruistically designed to build up the national consciousness of the Albanians, Italy's propaganda activities were of an essentially 'Italianizing' nature.[141] In fact, in 1902 the Italians had been trying to persuade the Porte to abolish the Monarchy's *Kultusprotektorat*; and they made great play with an Albanian National Congress which was held at Naples in 1903. And if the Italians were in turn greatly irritated by the second-rank role assigned to them in Macedonia by the Mürzsteg Powers, the Austrians were concerned at Italy's determined efforts to set foot across the Adriatic and her increasingly close links with Montenegro, demonstrated in 1904 by the opening of Montenegro's first telegraphic station (built by Marconi at Antivari). On the economic front, the renewal of the Austro-Italian commercial treaty was by no means a certainty. Its lapse, Goluchowski felt, would indeed be 'a veritable catastrophe',[142] for the Monarchy had a positive trade balance with Italy; and Goluchowski would have been quite prepared to sacrifice the Austrian wine industry out of hand. But the matter was one for the cumbersome governments of Vienna and Budapest to settle, and he could only await their commands.

The military was another complicating factor in relations with Italy. From 1903 onwards Beck began to think seriously of transferring troops from Galicia to Tyrol; and in the summer of 1904 Goluchowski had to ask him to desist, for the sake of the alliance, from tours of inspection on the Italian frontier.[143] The autumn saw a fairly serious war scare in Austrian military circles, and some

---

[140] P.A. I/476, Liasse XXXIII/39 Goluchowski, memorandum on a conversation with Tittoni at Abbazia, April 1904.

[141] Ibid.

[142] P.A. XL/302, Ministerratsprotokoll, 19 November 1903.

[143] E. v. Glaise-Horstenau, pp. 394ff.

reserves were called up in the south-west. As the war minister explained to a council of ministers in November,[144] it was in a sense only a question of restoring that balance of forces which had been distorted by a single-minded concentration on the Russian frontier since the 1880s; but recent outbreaks of irredentism in Italy were disturbing, and her latest frontier fortifications – of a temporary nature – indicated 'a definitely hostile intention'. Even Goluchowski supported the war minister. Although relations with Italy had recently 'much improved', there was no telling when Rome might revert to the attitudes of the Zanardelli ministry, 'when one had to be prepared for a *coup* at any moment'. This danger, coupled with the growing obstreperousness of Serbia and Montenegro, who were steadily intensifying their propaganda campaign against the Monarchy's position in Bosnia and the Herzegovina both at Constantinople and in the provinces themselves, meant that the Monarchy would have to keep a sharp eye open in the south.

The Monarchy's relations with its northern ally, meanwhile, were anything but cordial. In Macedonia, Goluchowski's efforts to convince the sultan that the Powers were all united and determined to march in step were even more seriously undermined by Germany's dragging her feet than by Anglo-Italian attempts to force a faster pace. In the economic field the Austrians were having the greatest difficulty in extracting a satisfactory commercial treaty from Germany since she had raised her tariffs on agricultural imports in 1902. True, as Szögyény observed, the proverbial inefficiency of the commercial department of the Ballhausplatz, and the political chaos inside the Monarchy, where industrial Austria and agrarian Hungary were hopelessly at odds, were partly to blame. But there was some truth in Jettel's despairing cry of December 1904: 'Germany is strangling us!'[145] Already in October Dumba had warned the German minister at Belgrade that a failure to conclude a commercial treaty, together with Berlin's continuing persecution of the Poles, would seriously endanger the Dual Alliance, remarks which Goluchowski endorsed when asked by the German ambassador for a disavowal.[146] A commer-

[144] P.A. XL/303, Ministerratsprotokoll, 28 November 1904.
[145] Aehrenthal MSS., Karton 2, Jettel to Aehrenthal, 3 December 1904.
[146] P.A. I/476, Goluchowski, memorandum on a conversation with Count Wedel, 5 October 1904.

cial treaty was eventually concluded in 1906, but the higher tariffs involved did nothing for Germany's popularity in the Monarchy. And the Austrians continued to take umbrage at Germany's commercial activities in the Balkans. Perhaps Dumba went too far when he told the Serbs that if they made a commercial treaty with Berlin before concluding one with Vienna and Budapest, Austria-Hungary would block the transit traffic between Serbia and Germany. As Goluchowski blandly explained to the complaining German ambassador, the Monarchy had no legal right to take such action.[147] But Dumba had been quite right, he insisted, to remind Belgrade that it was customary for Serbia to make her commercial treaties with Austria-Hungary first of all; nor would Vienna be browbeaten in negotiating with Belgrade by any Serbo-German *fait accompli*.

In fact, Austria-Hungary's economic embarrassments were bound to increase as Germany and Britain made ever greater inroads into her Balkan trade, and as tariff barriers were raised all over the continent. And given the economic backwardness of the Monarchy, it was perhaps hardly to be expected that the problem could be solved in terms of the commercial policy of the Austro-Hungarian government. (It was a significant indication of the Monarchy's relatively weak position that emigration, which had been rising steadily since the 1880s, reached the level of 220,000 in 1903; and that by 1907 the Monarchy had attained the leading position among the European states supplying emigrants to the New World.) Yet in fact, the government's economic policies increased the difficulties. The trade treaties which were eventually concluded in 1906 with Germany, Italy, Russia, and Belgium all embodied higher tariffs; and the most important consequence of this was to keep grain prices high inside the Monarchy. Admittedly this permitted a rise in peasant consumption of Austrian industrial products in the internal market. But high food prices at home made Austrian industrial products increasingly uncompetitive abroad. And the protectionist demands of Hungarian agricultural interests great and small remained a formidable obstacle to the re-negotiation of the Monarchy's trade treaties with the Balkan states. The year 1906 was the last in which the Monarchy enjoyed a favourable trade balance.

To add to – indeed, partly to cause – these difficulties, the

[147] Ibid.

domestic crises had taken a grave turn for the worse in 1903. The next three years saw a conflict between the Crown and the Hungarian nation before which the mere paralysis of parliamentary government in Austria paled into insignificance. When the Crown suggested to Budapest that the annual contingent of recruits supplied to the Common Army should be increased in size, a motley coalition of malcontented magnates and separatist politicians, who looked back beyond 1867 to 1848, launched a campaign for concessions aiming ultimately at carving a separate Hungarian army out of the Common Army. Franz Joseph would have none of this: 'common and united, as it is, My army shall remain', ran the famous Chlopy order of 16 September 1903. Deadlock resulted and gradually degenerated into chaos by 1905, when Tisza's government was defeated at the elections by the Coalition Party, following which the Hungarian parliament refused to supply even the normal contingent of recruits to the army. The king and his advisers stood firm and subjected Hungary to virtual martial law; Beck began to work on '*Kriegsfall U*', a plan for the actual invasion of Hungary; and in September Goluchowski showed himself not one whit backward where the unity of the Monarchy as a Great Power was at stake: when an imposing delegation of Hungarian politicians arrived from Budapest seeking a possible compromise, he unceremoniously turned them out after a perfunctory audience lasting only five minutes. This incident destroyed his reputation in Hungary at a blow.

The crisis threatened to destroy the Monarchy itself. In April 1905 the German government considered it timely to put out a feeler to St Petersburg for an *entente* to cover the case of the sudden dissolution of the Habsburg Monarchy. A year later Franz Joseph remarked to the visiting ex-Empress Eugénie that the Empire would not survive him. Certainly, the Monarchy suffered a great deal in these years in terms of its prestige as a Great Power. This was most obvious in the military field: the very existence of the army was in jeopardy; and as the crisis affected all organs of the body politic, even routine measures of strategic defence were held up – as late as November 1905 Admiral Montecuccoli was still urging the need for a railway link between Pola and Dalmatia (as yet, troops would still have to rely on very exposed and hazardous sea-transport). It was all very well, therefore, for patriotic Austrians to lament: 'what a fine figure we could now cut in the

Near East, were it not for our domestic troubles' (*Misère*).[148] The political, military, economic, and hence also diplomatic, weakness of Austria-Hungary was glaring. She enjoyed neither the strength at home nor the respect abroad to take advantage of Russia's growing involvement in the Far East to re-establish her own influence in the Balkans.

It was hardly surprising, therefore, that the years 1903–6 saw the high-water mark of the Austro-Russian *entente*. The statesmen of the Monarchy, confronted with appalling difficulties at home and mistrustful of their allies abroad, were more than ever inclined to cultivate St Petersburg. The Russians, for their part, were in a mood to respond, especially after the outbreak of war with Japan in February 1904. On the 28th the tsar remarked to the Austro-Hungarian military attaché – perhaps somewhat hopefully – that his faith in Franz Joseph was so complete that he would not hesitate to move troops from Russia's western frontier to the Far East should the need arise. As might have been expected, the Austro-Hungarian embassy at St Petersburg made the most of this, and Aehrenthal began to press Goluchowski to broaden the *entente*. Austria-Hungary, he said, was in a similar predicament, and might well have had to move troops from Galicia to Tyrol if the Italian menace continued to grow. He went on to recommend a simple Austro-Russian neutrality agreement; and knowing Goluchowski's sensitivities, explained that this need not touch on Balkan matters – though he incautiously justified this restriction on the grounds that Russia might ask for concessions at the Straits in return for her consent to the eventual annexation of Bosnia.[149] Meanwhile, Jettel backed him up in Vienna with vigorous, if largely ineffective, attempts to restrain the gloating of the Jewish-controlled press at Russia's embarrassments.[150] Goluchowski, for his part, certainly had no wish to bind Austria-Hungary's hands further as regards the future of the Balkans. He felt that the 1897 agreement was quite sufficient for the present; and he was most emphatic – though he failed to convince Aehrenthal – that on no account could the eventual annexation of Bosnia give Russia any claim to compensation. Nevertheless, provided it did not restrict

[148] Aehrenthal MSS., Karton 3, Mérey to Aehrenthal, 15 July 1905.
[149] P.A. I/475, Liasse XXXII/k, Aehrenthal to Goluchowski, Tel. 42, 29 February, private, 24 March 1904.
[150] Aehrenthal MSS., Karton 5, Jettel to Aehrenthal, 29 April 1904.

the Monarchy further in the Balkans, he was fairly well disposed towards the idea of a simple neutrality agreement.[151]

Thus encouraged, Aehrenthal took the initiative at St Petersburg in May. He convinced Lamsdorff that a neutrality agreement would be in the interests of both parties: the only war the Monarchy could expect to fight would be against an irredentist Italy striving to dominate the Adriatic; whereas Russia might have to fight Britain. Not that the Ballhausplatz was particularly anti-British. The Anglo-French agreements of 8 April, and the financial and administrative changes which Britain had proceeded to introduce in Egypt had been accepted in Vienna with a complaisance quite lacking in Berlin. True, Goluchowski refused Lansdowne's request for co-operation in a protest to Turkey about the passage through the Straits of the Russian Volunteer Fleet on its way to the Far East. But equally, he would not go so far as to bind himself in writing to join Russia in opposing British or Italian intervention in Balkan affairs, much as the Russians would have liked this.[152] By the autumn, he had brought Kapnist, and then Lamsdorff, to agree to a simple neutrality treaty (Document 25) to cover the case of a threat to the *status quo* outside the Balkans. Even though, as regards the Balkans, there had been no advance beyond the strictly conservative principles of 1897, the Austro-Russian neutrality treaty (15 October 1904) constituted, as Lamsdorff rightly observed, an important new development of the Austro-Russian *entente*, which was now very definitely extended into the field of general Great Power politics.[153]

It was nevertheless something of a disappointment to Aehrenthal, who pressed Goluchowski to communicate the treaty to Germany and to announce simultaneously that the Three Emperors' Alliance had been restored.[154] Goluchowski would have none of this.[155] A Three Emperors' Alliance would restrict the Monarchy's freedom of manoeuvre; and it would give to Germany, as

[151] P.A. I/475, Liasse XXXII/k, Goluchowski to Aehrenthal, private and secret, 13 April 1904.

[152] Ibid., Aehrenthal to Goluchowski, private and secret, 14 May, 15 July; Goluchowski to Aehrenthal, private and secret, 28 May, 1 September 1904.

[153] Ibid., Aehrenthal to Goluchowski, private and secret, 24 September 1904.

[154] Ibid., Aehrenthal to Goluchowski, Tel. 167, secret, 31 October; private and secret, 3 November 1904.

[155] Aehrenthal MSS., Karton 4, Zwiedenek to Aehrenthal, 14 November 1904.

the strongest of the three parties (and no longer as she had been in the 1880s a disinterested party), a golden opportunity to push ahead against Austro-Hungarian interests in the Balkans. Indeed, he was coming to regard Germany, with her commercial ruthlessness, and her stealthy encouragement of the sultan's resistance to the Mürzsteg reforms, as altogether a nuisance; and he was determined to do nothing to increase her influence in the Near East. Faced with these arguments, Aehrenthal retreated in some dejection. But Goluchowski was satisfied enough, both with the neutrality agreement, and above all with Russia's increasingly obvious military weakness. As he told a council of ministers on 28 November: 'without wanting to prophesy . . . there is no threatening danger from the northern frontier of the Monarchy, and . . . we should have peace and quiet from Russia for a long time.'[156]

Not that peace and quiet implied absolute concord. On the contrary, even the *entente* could not altogether conjure away certain basic differences of view between Vienna and St Petersburg. By the end of 1904 Goluchowski was beginning to have second thoughts about the ultimate disposition of Turkey's possessions in Europe.[157] For a year now, Bulgaria, chastened by the wrath of the Turks and the Great Powers, had been behaving with studied correctness, whereas Serbia's intrigues and propaganda activities in Bosnia were proving increasingly tiresome. He decided that in the event of the collapse of Turkey the Monarchy must strive to restrict the growth of Serbia and Montenegro as much as possible, despite, or rather, especially because of, Russia's inclination to count on those states as her obedient servants. A Big Bulgaria, on the other hand, would be quite in accordance with Austro-Hungarian interests. But he was prepared to sacrifice this on the altar of the *entente* if Russia proved amenable about Serbia. It would be more important to secure a big, autonomous Albania, a 'strong wall' against the advance of Serbia; compensations for Roumania (from north-east Bulgaria) and for Greece; and only modest increases of territory for the Slav states. His apparently sincere hopes of attaining complete agreement with Russia along these lines were to say the least, sanguine.

[156] P.A. XL/303, Ministerratsprotokoll, 28 November 1904.
[157] P.A. I/477, Liasse XXXIII/35, Goluchowski to Calice, private and confidential, 31 December 1904.

Indeed, if 1904 had witnessed the apogee of the *entente*, 1905 saw the beginning of its decline. Its successes in Macedonia in 1904 had given it some strength and vitality. But the sudden and premature death of Kapnist, one of its most ardent supporters, in December 1904 was almost symbolic. Whereas in 1904 Russia's weakness and preoccupation with the Far East had been just sufficient to give Vienna a modicum of relief and security, the New Year saw Russia staggering towards revolution and catastrophic defeat. The very factors that in 1904 had made for harmony assumed in 1905 such proportions that they became a source of embarrassment and tension. The reform and control of the Macedonian finances, to which the Mürzsteg Powers now turned their attention, brought frustration and endless haggling. All the more so as Turkey was emboldened by Russia's glaring weakness, and by the chaos in Hungary, to defy the Mürzsteg Powers and obstruct their every move.

Nor was this all. The Russians, only too painfully conscious of their military and diplomatic collapse, began to doubt the wisdom of working exclusively with Austria-Hungary in Macedonia. For might not the dual control now amount in practice to Austro-Hungarian control? They decided that some counterweight to Austria-Hungary must be found; and that it would be wise to vest control of the reforms – at least as regards the executive aspects – in all six Powers. To this the Austrians were not opposed in principle; they felt, in view of their own domestic troubles, that other Powers might indeed bear a greater share of the burden. They still insisted that the Mürzsteg Powers keep the lead in their own hands as regards the formulation of the reform policy; but in practice they allowed the others a fair amount of influence over this too. Even so, as the negotiations over the financial reform proved, it was infinitely more difficult to work out a programme between six Powers than between two. Indeed, it was something of a wonder that any scheme at all emerged from the interminable conferences of ambassadors at Constantinople. Whereas the Germans raised obstacles and encouraged the sultan to resist, the British pressed enthusiastically for such a stringent control of the Ottoman finances as might well have provoked Abdul Hamid into revolt against the whole Mürzsteg scheme. In the end, the Powers had to stage a joint naval demonstration – from which Germany was ostentatiously absent – before the sultan would accept even the moderate demands of the financial *règlement* which they eventually hammered out (December). This *règlement*, which accorded to the delegates of the other Powers a position of absolute equality with the Civil Agents in dealing with the financial affairs of Macedonia, marked the first serious breach in the Mürzsteg principle of dual control.

Yet it might be doubted whether the Mürzsteg programme, even with the full backing of six Powers rather than two, could still offer an effective remedy for the ills of Macedonia. By the end of 1904 the Macedonian problem was no longer the same as it had been when the Mürzsteg programme had been drawn up. It was no longer so much a question of protecting the Christians from Turkish misrule, the evil effects of which had in fact been greatly mitigated by the reforms. It was rather one of restraining the Christians from slaughtering each other. Since 1904 bands of Greek terrorists, both native and imported, had been taking the field against the Exarchists (who since the disaster of the 1903 rising had been very much on the defensive) and against the Roumanian Koutzo-Vlachs. This evil could be cured only by massive troop formations, which would pursue the terrorists to their lairs in the hills; not by the local *gendarmerie*, nor by the administrative measures envisaged at Mürzsteg. Indeed, Article III of the Mürzsteg programme acted only as an incentive to the warring Christians to secure to themselves as much of the promised land as possible against the day when administrative boundaries would be re-drawn along ethnic lines. The violence grew daily worse.

The Powers, nevertheless, continued haltingly along the path laid down at Mürzsteg. But progress was slow. Discussion of the next item on the agenda – control of the administration of justice – was to occupy the better part of two years. For it became mixed up in a wrangle over the Turks' request for a 3 per cent increase in the customs duties of the Empire (for which the consent of the Powers was necessary under the terms of the Capitulations). The Turks declared that without this additional revenue they would be unable to finance even the existing reforms for much longer, let alone any new ones. They found the Mürzsteg Powers, filled with alarm at the prospect of the collapse of the whole reform scheme, amenable enough. But the British, who stood to lose most by the proposed customs increase, demanded in return a yet more far-reaching control of the Ottoman finances, regardless of the sultan's sovereign rights – if only to ensure that the new revenue really was spent on Macedonia, and not on the Ottoman army or the Baghdad railway project. Endless delays ensued as one British proposal after another came up against the determined opposition of the Turks, encouraged from Berlin. The Mürzsteg Powers were exasperated and refused for their part to proceed with any new reforms – which the British were none the less demanding – until the 3 per cent customs increase had been granted.

As Goluchowski's disappointment and frustration grew, so did his exasperation at the waywardness of the allies in Rome and Berlin. His meeting with Tittoni at Venice in May 1905 was a markedly less friendly affair than the Abbazia meeting of the previous year.[158] He complained bitterly about the busy efforts of Imperiali, the Italian ambassador at Constantinople, to whittle away the leading role of the Civil Agents in Macedonia, and to undermine that special position of Russia and Austria-Hungary which was the essential basis of Mürzsteg. If the Powers now wanted to abandon that basis for a European one, Austria-Hungary would not object. Indeed, she could then resume a completely free hand; and the Powers need not think they could achieve much in the Balkans without her co-operation. Albania, too, still rankled. According to a Ballhausplatz estimate of 1905 Italy had made very serious inroads into Austro-Hungarian influence in the coastal areas of Albania, and had become the leading Power in Albania as regards trade and shipping.[159] At the end of the year Beck, in what was to be his last annual *tour d'horizon*, bleakly concluded that war with Italy had moved noticeably nearer in 1905.

Germany, too, persisted in her tiresome behaviour. Despite dire warnings from Vienna that the failure of the Mürzsteg programme might damage Russian and Austro-Hungarian prestige irreparably and throw the Balkans into a dangerous state of chaos, she continued to obstruct the reforms in Macedonia. Equally, her treatment of her Austro-Hungarian allies in the opening stages of the Moroccan crisis was insensitive to a degree.

[158] P.A. I/476, Goluchowski, memorandum on a conversation with Tittoni at Venice, May 1905.

[159] P.A. I/473, Liasse XXXI/b, Consul Kral, memorandum on Albania, 1901–5, April 1905.

Here, Goluchowski had supported the German demand for a conference on Moroccan affairs, both as a loyal ally and as a party interested in maintaining the open door to trade in Morocco (where he ranked Austria-Hungary, by some strange calculation, third among the Great Powers).[160] As regards Morocco itself, his interest was primarily economic: although he was strongly opposed to the idea of an exclusive Franco-German deal, he would have no objections if the conference conferred a political mandate on one Power – say, France – provided the commercial interests of the Monarchy were safeguarded. But he was well aware of the broader political implications of the crisis and above all anxious lest the defeat of the conference proposal increase the risk of a Franco-German war, in which the Monarchy had no interest whatever. It was with this in mind, in fact, that he interrupted his holiday at Vittel to visit the French prime minister, Rouvier, on 6 July, and according to his own account, managed to persuade Rouvier to accept the idea of a conference.[161] Great was his rage, therefore, when both Vienna and Vittel learned from the newspapers and without a shred of prior communication from Berlin, of the final Franco-German agreement to hold a conference. He now refused to help Germany any further or to press France to accept Tangier as the meeting place of the conference; and the Germans had to compromise on Algeciras.[162] At the same time, Germany had embarked on another round of expulsions of Austrian and Hungarian seasonal workers, despite the remonstrations of Vienna; and she concluded a commercial treaty with Bulgaria, leaving her Austro-Hungarian ally with such scraps as most favoured nation treatment could provide.

This was especially embarrassing at a time when the Monarchy's own commercial relations with the Balkan states were running into grave difficulties. At the end of 1905 Vienna was completely surprised by the news that Serbia and Bulgaria had concluded a secret customs union. In Goluchowski's view this was particularly obnoxious,[163] both as an attempt by Serbia and

[160] P.A. XXXII/14, Goluchowski, memorandum on a conversation with Rouvier, 6 July 1905.

[161] Ibid., and Goluchowski to Franz Joseph (enclosing Goluchowski to Welsersheimb), 5 December 1905.

[162] Ibid., Goluchowski to Mérey, Tel. 2, 17 July; to Szögyény, Tel. 3, 17 July 1905.

[163] P.A. XL/305, Ministerratsprotokoll, 10 January 1906.

Bulgaria to strengthen their bargaining positions for the forth-coming commercial negotiations with Austria-Hungary, and as a pointer to an approaching Balkan League which would check-mate the Monarchy's timeworn policy of maintaining a state of balance between its south Slav neighbours. All the same, Golu-chowski was not at first unduly perturbed. The Monarchy had a good case in international law – Bulgaria's granting special terms to Serbia was a flagrant contravention of Article VIII of the Treaty of Berlin. Indeed, the Serbian minister at Vienna said his government was prepared to drop the new treaty. Goluchowski decided that this showed that a healthy mistrust still persisted be-tween Belgrade and Sofia, and that the 'phantom' of a Balkan League would soon be dispelled. A conference of ministers of 10 January 1906 simply decided, therefore, that as a *sine qua non* of Austro-Serbian negotiations Serbia must state her intention to drop the treaty clearly and in writing. As regards Bulgaria, it was hoped that all the Powers would refrain from attempts to curry favour at Sofia, and stand united by the Treaty of Berlin.

Within a week, these hopes were shattered: both Serbia and Bulgaria showed themselves remarkably stubborn, the former even demanding commercial concessions from Austria-Hungary as a condition of dropping the treaty. For the next two months the problem continued to worry the conference of ministers.[164] Opinions were divided: whereas the Austrian and Hungarian governments were both for settling with Serbia and taking a stiff line with Bulgaria, Goluchowski was set on exactly the opposite policy. One thing was agreed: the Monarchy must not take an equally tough line with both states, for that would only drive them together and promote a Balkan league. Certainly, both states were blameworthy; but as Goluchowski blandly observed when someone pointed to the inconsistency of differential treat-ment, 'in politics, the laws of logic do not always prevail'. In the first place, he felt that Serbia was more guilty than Bulgaria, for there was evidence to suggest that the treaty had originated in Belgrade. But there was also the practical consideration that the Monarchy could bring far more effective pressure to bear on Serbia than on Bulgaria. The Serbs sold far more to Austria-Hungary than they bought from her, whereas in Bulgaria's case the situation was the reverse, and the Monarchy would be the

[164] P.A. XL/305, Ministerratsprotokolle, 16 January, 2 February 1906.

chief loser if things should come to a tariff war. Besides, it was now pretty clear that the other Powers would not help in chastising Bulgaria for her violation of the Treaty of Berlin. Indeed, if the Monarchy cut off its sales of armaments to Bulgaria, Russia would most likely supply them. Finally, from a general political point of view, Goluchowski had decided that Bulgaria was the most viable of all the Balkan states – the military attaché at Sofia even thought she might some day take on Turkey with a hope of success. It would be wise, therefore, to draw this rising star into Austria-Hungary's orbit – especially as Bulgaria, unlike Serbia or Roumania, had no racial brothers inside the Monarchy to give rise to an irredentist problem. Hence, he concluded, 'a good relationship with Bulgaria would always be preferable to one with Serbia, who has been intriguing incessantly against the Monarchy for a few years now, stirring up the Serbo-Croat population and agitating (*wühlen*) against Austria-Hungary in Bosnia and the Herzegovina'.

Goluchowski forced his policy through. Negotiations were started with Bulgaria and Roumania. By March the Serbs, threatened with the full rigour of the Austro-Hungarian veterinary regulations, had begun to climb down, dropping the Bulgarian customs treaty and opening negotiations with Vienna. At this juncture, however, a new dispute arose, when Serbia insisted on placing a large order for weapons with the French firm of Schneider-Creusot, instead of with Skoda of Bohemia as had been usual in the past. Negotiations were again broken off, and the Austrians resorted to economic sanctions, closing the frontier to imports of Serbian livestock. The so-called 'Pig War' lasted for four years, and from the Austro-Hungarian point of view was a disaster in every respect. The Serbs at last began to build slaughter-houses on a large scale – perhaps after all the only long-term solution to their commercial dependence on the neighbouring Monarchy; and they soon found markets overseas, in Turkey, Egypt, Russia, and Western Europe – and above all in Germany, who was only too quick to move in and take over the lion's share of the trade which her ally had lost. All this only gave the Serbs an increased confidence and toughness in their negotiations with Austria-Hungary; and even Goluchowski's more conciliatory successor could not bring the Serbs to agree terms until July 1910. By then, Serbia had largely freed herself from her old commercial dependence, exporting only 30 per cent of her produce to the Monarchy, as opposed to some 80–90 per cent before 1906. Goluchowski's efforts to bring Serbia to heel by isolating her in the diplomatic field were equally abortive. Since the middle of 1905 he had again been working hard to reconcile Greece and Roumania under Austro-Hungarian auspices (warning the Roumanians, incidentally, that Germany was a self-seeking friend and not to be trusted).[165] But by June 1906 Greco-Roumanian hostility arising out of the conflicts between Greeks and Koutzo-Vlachs in Macedonia had led Athens finally to break off diplomatic relations with Bucharest.

All in all, the affair cost Austria-Hungary dear. Her bullying of Serbia won her no sympathy from any of the Western Powers, most of whom were only too glad of the chance to develop their own trade with Serbia. Worse still, it seriously weakened the *entente* with Russia, where not only public opinion, but the government itself adopted a censorious attitude that was 'very worrying'[166] to Vienna. Finally, the obvious failure of Goluchowski's policy (which, as Serbia's growing independence increased her temerity, became increasingly difficult to reverse without yet a further loss of face) dealt a heavy blow to the Monarchy's prestige throughout the Balkans.

These failures in the Near East not unnaturally obscured from the public eye what was in fact a very creditable performance by Goluchowski in Morocco,[167] a field where Austro-Hungarian interests were only marginally concerned. And William II's notorious 'brilliant second' telegram, depicting Austria-Hungary as following meekly in the wake of Germany at the Algeciras conference, tended further to conceal, from contemporaries and historians alike, Goluchowski's tenacious and on the whole successful pursuit of a policy based on Austro-Hungarian interests independently of, and sometimes even in opposition to, Berlin.

At Algeciras, the Germans were as much concerned to achieve

[165] P.A. I/476, Liasse XXXIII/39, Goluchowski, memoranda on conversations with General Mano, 30 July 1905, and with the king of the Hellenes, December 1905.

[166] Aehrenthal MSS., Karton 4, Zwiedenek to Aehrenthal, 20 February 1906.

[167] F. Fellner, 'Die Haltung Oesterreich-Ungarns während der Konferenz von Algeciras 1906', *Mitteilungen des Instituts für Oesterreichische Geschichtsforschung*, 1963, Vol. 71, pp. 462–77.

a diplomatic triumph over France – by thwarting her efforts to secure a large measure of control over the Moroccan police – as to obtain favourable conditions for German trade. The Austrians, too, were fully alive to the wider diplomatic implications – but in the opposite sense to Berlin. Goluchowski and Franz Joseph were above all anxious that the conference should not see a serious clash between the Powers. This would poison the international atmosphere for years, and might even lead to a re-grouping of the Powers to the disadvantage of Germany and Austria-Hungary. As regards Morocco itself, Goluchowski was much more concerned to secure the open door for Austro-Hungarian commercial interests, and a fair share in the control of the Moroccan Bank, than a voice in the control of the police – in which he was not prepared to accept any share at all if it would involve the Monarchy in any expense. It was only within this framework, therefore, that he was initially prepared to support Germany's proposal that the control of the police should lie with the sultan of Morocco and an internationally constituted body of officers.

Moreover, when at the start of the conference, in January 1906, the French declared that the control of the Moroccan police must be vested in French and Spanish officers only (subject, perhaps, to some kind of international supervisory organ in the last instance), Goluchowski accepted the view of the Austro-Hungarian delegate, Welsersheimb, that Germany's demand for complete internationalization was unrealistic, and refused to support it any further. In February the Austrians made great efforts – as Franz Joseph assured the French ambassador – 'to bring the Emperor William to reason'.[168] They pointed out that if the Central Powers gave way on the police question, they would be able to take a firmer stand on the more important financial and commercial questions; and they warned Berlin that the failure of the conference would be an absolute disaster.

By March, they had brought the Germans to accept a compromise proposal of Welsersheimb's for a Franco-Spanish control of the police, subject to an ultimate international authority established at Casablanca and supervised by the diplomatic corps. Goluchowski still had to work hard to bring the French to accept any effective international control at all, and had to agree to the control body's sitting not at Casablanca (where the French feared

---

[168] *Documents diplomatiques français*, 2nd series, Vol. 9/1, No. 315.

it would too greatly restrict their political predominance in Morocco) but at the less important town of Tangier. In the end, however, it was the Welsersheimb proposal that became the basis for the settlement of the police question – the most explosive issue in the crisis. To that extent, Goluchowski could congratulate himself on having saved the conference from failure – the gravest of the dangers he had feared. The French delegate's compliment to Welsersheimb – 'c'est vous qui avez jeté le pont sur le précipice'[169] – was not undeserved. But more than fair words Goluchowski did not secure for his pains, either from France or from Germany, neither of whom paid the slightest attention to Austro-Hungarian requests – for a share in the control of the Moroccan Bank, for example – in settling such minor issues as remained. True, the open door was maintained by common consent. But any laurels Goluchowski had won during the conference were finally blighted by the publication – by the German embassy at Vienna, and despite Goluchowski's strenuous efforts to prevent it – of the 'brilliant second' telegram.

This was the least of Goluchowski's worries, given the serious deterioration in the international situation as a result of the Moroccan crisis. For Germany's reaction to her humiliation at Algeciras seemed almost calculated to intensify her isolation, and to conjure up that very diplomatic revolution that Goluchowski had feared might result from the humiliation of France. The German Emperor's condescending snub to Vienna paled into insignificance before his outbursts against the other participants at the conference – Britain, her 'satellite' Spain, and Russia.[170] The last named Power, he declared, would receive no more money from Germany to repair her shattered finances (whereupon the Franco-Russian alliance was promptly strengthened by a huge French loan). Most alarming of all to Vienna was William II's rage against Italy: at a dinner party at the Austro-Hungarian embassy, he even talked in terms of war against the 'useless' ally.[171]

[169] P.A. XXXII/16, Welsersheimb to Goluchowski, Tel. 64, 31 March 1906.

[170] P.A. I/477, Liasse XXXIII/38, Szögyény to Goluchowski, Tel. 79, 8 April 1906.

[171] P.A. I/481, Liasse XXXIV/b, Lützow to Goluchowski, Tel. 82, secret, 24 May 1906.

Goluchowski was anxious that Austro-Italian relations should not get any worse – certainly not as a result of questions as remote as Morocco. If Germany chose to be angry with Italy, that was her affair, and she need expect no encouragement or sympathy from Vienna.[172] Indeed, when William II visited Vienna in May Franz Joseph insisted that he should join him in sending telegraphic greetings to Victor Emmanuel as 'notre troisième et fidèle allié'.[173] Admittedly, Austro-Italian relations were not growing much closer: in June, the Austrians again evaded an Italian request for naval talks, pleading that the Adriatic fleet was designed only for coastal defence, not for use against France in the Mediterranean. And Vienna was worried by the efforts of Barrère, the assiduous French ambassador at Rome, to weaken and divide the Triple Alliance. As Franz Joseph emphasized to his German guests, 'we two must hold on to (*festhalten*) the Italians; because otherwise those people could become a great nuisance, at least for us here'.[174] In Goluchowski's eyes too, the Triple Alliance was still a valuable factor in the maintenance of peace, if only in a somewhat negative sense: 'Austria-Hungary and Italy must either be full allies or latent enemies, sooner or later at war.'[175]

Such considerations were still in the forefront of Goluchowski's mind when he was drawn into a debate with Aehrenthal about the threatening international situation. The danger of a rigidification into two armed camps, with the Central Powers isolated and in a minority, had undoubtedly been increased by the deterioration of Germany's relations with the Western Powers and with Russia during the Moroccan crisis. Indeed, some people in Vienna seemed resigned to this fact, concluding from Russia's unsatisfactory attitude towards the Austro-Serbian dispute that the Austro-Russian *entente* was after all not worth much if it could not safeguard such vital Austro-Hungarian interests.[176] But these views were anathema to Aehrenthal. He insisted that there was still a good chance of keeping Russia out of the Anglo-French

[172] P.A. XXXII/16, Goluchowski to Lützow, Tel. 23, 2 April 1906.

[173] W. Wagner, p. 227; *Die grosse Politik der europäischen Kabinette, 1871–1914* (hereafter G.P.), Vol. 21/2, No. 7155.   [174] Ibid.

[175] P.A. I/475, Liasse XXXII/c, Goluchowski to Aehrenthal, private and secret, 15 September 1906.

[176] Aehrenthal MSS., Karton 4, Zwiedenek to Aehrenthal, 20 February 1906.

camp. True, the new Russian foreign minister, Izvolsky, was very much an unknown quantity; and there were signs that he would like to wind up Russia's disastrous Far Eastern policy and come to terms with Britain and Japan.[177] Yet the risk that he might then seek to recoup Russia's shattered prestige by reverting to an active policy in the Balkans only rendered it all the more essential, in Aehrenthal's view,[178] that the Monarchy should continue to co-operate with and restrain Russia – all the more so as some of Britain's recent activities had the air of a calculated diplomatic offensive against Germany.[179] Thus, Campbell-Bannerman's declared intention of raising the disarmament issue at the forthcoming Hague Peace Conference concealed not only an obnoxious attempt by the international parliamentary movement to seize the reins of power from monarchical governments, but a sly manoeuvre to isolate and humiliate Germany. The merits of the disarmament issue were not so important to Aehrenthal: after all, smaller, professional armies would probably prove more useful than conscripted masses in suppressing proletarian rebellions. What was important was that the three Eastern Empires should agree on some common programme and prevent yet another diplomatic defeat of Germany at the hands of the Western Powers; and in view of the Russo-German estrangement, it must fall to Austria-Hungary to bring about this *rapprochement*.

This was only a part of the ambitious plan which Aehrenthal pressed on Goluchowski in long private letters at the end of July.[180] First of all, Vienna should seek to strengthen the conservative forces in Russia generally. Perhaps Franz Joseph might send a message of encouragement to Nicholas II to stiffen him in the struggle that was just beginning between tsar and Duma. If the tsardom succumbed – and the French were ominously backing the Liberals in the Duma – then a series of republics with a strongly communistic flavour would appear in its place; and the movement would hardly stop at the frontiers of Russia. The situation was similar to that of 1849: domestic considerations made it

[177] Ibid., Zwiedenek to Aehrenthal, 8 June 1906.

[178] Ibid., Aehrenthal to Goluchowski, No. 1, private and secret, 20 July 1906.

[179] P.A. I/475, Liasse XXXII/c, Aehrenthal to Goluchowski, private and secret, 23 August 1906.

[180] Ibid., Aehrenthal to Goluchowski, No. 1, private and secret, 20 July; No. 2, private and secret, 25 July 1906.

imperative for the two empires to stand together. But the only real solution – and Aehrenthal's ultimate aim – was the restoration of the Three Emperors' Alliance. Admittedly, this would necessitate a major diplomatic upheaval: Russia would first have to abandon her alliance with France. But the advantages would be great: Germany would subscribe to the Austro-Russian treaty of October 1904; and she would be compelled to support the Mürzsteg Powers, not Turkey, in Macedonia. The risk that such a far-reaching agreement with Russia would tie the Monarchy's hands too firmly in the Balkans was not great. After all, Russia would be too weak to undertake anything there for at least ten years.

Goluchowski's reaction was distinctly sceptical. Although he took Aehrenthal's proposals seriously enough to write to the emperor at Ischl about them,[181] the long reply he sent to Aehrenthal in September was essentially negative.[182] He was prepared to consider a friendly message to the tsar – a message which might well be timed to coincide with the opening of the Hague Peace Conference in June 1907 – so as to pave the way for co-operation with Russia against the designs of Britain. But on the point of reviving the Three Emperors' Alliance he was cautious in the extreme. In the first place, it was hardly likely that Izvolsky, with his western proclivities, and his inordinate sensitivity to the criticisms of Liberal politicians of the Duma, would for a moment consider dropping the alliance with France; and even if he did, the restoration of the Three Emperors' Alliance would almost certainly entail the dissolution of the Triple Alliance and the desertion of Italy to the Anglo-French camp. This would have disastrous consequences for Austro-Italian relations. In short, Goluchowski preferred to work within the existing diplomatic framework, unsatisfactory though it might be.

That he gave himself no illusions about the diplomatic position of the Monarchy was clear from his language to a conference of ministers on 29 September.[183] Relations with Italy left much to be desired: she was arming with speed and determination; and was busy with her propaganda not only in Albania, Montenegro, and

[181] Ibid., Goluchowski, report to Franz Joseph, 16 August 1906.
[182] Ibid., Goluchowski to Aehrenthal, private and secret, 15 September 1906.
[183] P.A. XL/305, Ministerratsprotokoll, 29 September 1906.

Serbia, but even in Austro-Hungarian territory. 'And also in the Balkans a net of many meshes is being spun which could prove equally dangerous to us.' Indeed, Goluchowski hinted that he might resign if more was not done to build up the navy. As for the continuing cool relations with Germany, it was significant that he thought it worthwhile to point out that no danger threatened the Monarchy from that quarter. Yet the position was not hopeless, above all because the threat from Russia had 'rather disappeared for the foreseeable future' – albeit thanks rather to her weakness than to her good intentions. He could therefore see no urgent need to jettison the Triple Alliance in favour of a Three Emperors' Alliance – especially as the latter might only prove an obstacle to an independent policy in the Balkans. This, the Monarchy could never renounce for all time.[184] For Goluchowski, the Austro-Russian *entente* was only one means of safeguarding Austria-Hungary's interests, never in itself the end or everlasting basis of Austro-Hungarian policy.

Nor was he moved by Aehrenthal's non-diplomatic arguments, by the appeal to the timeworn doctrine of monarchical solidarity against the Revolution. In the first place, he professed to despair of the Russian monarchy – even a show of force by the tsardom could at most only defer the revolution, which would then be all the more violent when it came.[185] It would hardly be wise, therefore, to bind the Monarchy in an alliance with so unstable a power. Indeed, he managed to turn Aehrenthal's own arguments neatly against him. Russia's troubles might well be the result of the machinations of the international revolutionary party; but by the same token a revived Three Emperors' Alliance, which would be widely regarded as a reactionary league for restoring tsarist autocracy, would be an extremely dangerous undertaking for the Central Powers, in that it would draw on to them in turn the wrath of the international revolutionary movement. Germany might be strong enough to face this without trepidation; but hardly Austria-Hungary, who was still in the throes of a serious domestic crisis of her own. Besides, who in the Monarchy would support a restoration of the Three Emperors' Alliance? Clerical circles hostile to Italy perhaps, some Czechs, and a few conserva-

[184] Aehrenthal MSS., Karton 3, Mérey to Aehrenthal, 3 September 1906.
[185] P.A. I/475, Liasse XXXII/c, Goluchowski to Aehrenthal, private and secret, 15 September 1906.

tives who yearned for the days of the Holy Alliance; but not the Poles, the German Liberals, or the Radicals – even Czech Radicals; and certainly nobody at all in Hungary. With such a weight of public opinion opposed to the idea, it must be ruled out as a feasible policy for a Dual Monarchy already embarking on a new age of democracy. Perhaps Goluchowski on this occasion let slip a chance to develop Austro-Hungarian foreign policy in a direction which might have averted the catastrophe of 1914. On the other hand, it may be said that his negative arguments made up in realism for what they lacked in imagination. Aehrenthal, for his part, was not moved by them to abandon his ideas. Indeed, within a month he was in a position to make these ideas the basis of Austro-Hungarian foreign policy, for on 23 October Goluchowski fell from power.

It was, to say the least, somewhat specious on Goluchowski's part to lecture Aehrenthal on the imperatives imposed on foreign policy by public opinion. For if he recognized the growing importance of democratic forces in the Monarchy, he certainly did not approve of them. Indeed, he was coming to feel increasingly ill at ease in the service of an emperor who was embarking on courses in domestic affairs which seemed to him highly dangerous. In 1906 Franz Joseph had managed at last to solve the Hungarian crisis – by threatening to introduce universal suffrage into Hungary (which would have shattered the carefully contrived electoral supremacy of the Magyars, 1867 Party and Coalition Party alike). The Coalition Party had then agreed to take office on Franz Joseph's terms: the unity of the Common Army had been assured. In return for this, the dynasty abandoned the Slavs and Roumanians of Hungary and no more was heard of universal suffrage in any meaningful sense. For Goluchowski, the situation had become difficult now that Franz Joseph had a Hungarian government which offered, if well handled, a serious chance of calm and co-operation. Since his brush with the Hungarian politicians in September 1905 it had been generally assumed that Goluchowski's head would be the first to be sacrificed to seal any reconciliation between the Magyars and the king.

Political developments in Austria were hardly any more to Goluchowski's liking. Talk of introducing universal suffrage into Hungary had greatly increased the demand for it in Austria; and the emperor himself had begun to look back to Taaffe's project of

1893 – the bourgeois nationalist parties, which flourished under the five-class voting system, would under a system of universal suffrage be swamped by the great mass parties, Christian Socials and Social Democrats, as yet virtually uninfected with nationalism. Big public demonstrations at the end of 1905 – largely repercussions of the Russian revolution – had given the final impetus for the Austrian government to prepare a new suffrage law with all speed. This had dismayed Goluchowski, by temperament an ultra-conservative, and one who had seen France at close quarters and disapproved of what he saw.[186] But matters had not come to a head until the summer of 1906, when the Magyars gave him a very rough handling in the Delegations and launched a sustained campaign against him in the press. By October, Goluchowski had decided that he had had enough of their 'ceaseless baiting'.[187] He had threatened to resign unless the Hungarian government would restrain his attackers, but he had got no satisfaction. The government had merely declared that it would be quite unable to survive in the face of parliament or press if it intervened in his favour; and this despite the fact that Franz Joseph had impressed on Budapest his express will that Goluchowski should continue in office.[188] At this, Goluchowski resigned.

The end of the Austro-Russian Entente, *1906–8*

The autumn of 1906 saw a serious attempt to master the domestic situation by men of imagination. Max Vladimir von Beck, Austrian prime minister since February, and a close associate of Archduke Franz Ferdinand, was determined both to carry through the electoral reform in Austria and to take a firm stand against Magyar separatism in working out the details of the commercial *Ausgleich* already agreed in principle with the new Hungarian government. He was strongly supported by other nominees of the heir apparent: General von Schönaich, Common War Minister since October, and Conrad von Hoetzendorf, appointed Chief of the General Staff in November. For Aehrenthal, now summoned to succeed Goluchowski at the Ballhausplatz,

[186] P.A. XL/304, Ministerratsprotokoll, August 1905.

[187] Mensdorff MSS., Karton 9, Goluchowski to Mensdorff, 4 November 1906.

[188] T. M. Islamov, 'Oesterreichisch-ungarische Beziehungen am Anfang des XX Jahrhunderts', in F. Klein (ed.), pp. 113–14.

a strong constructive foreign policy and a stable, healthy, domestic situation were merely two sides of the same coin. Although precluded by his office from a determining voice in domestic affairs, he was by no means without ideas. In a memorandum of February 1907 he put forward his own suggestions for mobilizing a strong foreign policy in the cause of domestic unity and peace: Bosnia and Herzegovina might one day be formally annexed, and joined to the south Slav lands of Austria and of Hungary, the whole new bloc being granted a genuine autonomy under the suzerainty of the Crown of St Stephen. The accretion of territory would flatter the Magyars (and perhaps develop their all too rudimentary consciousness of the Monarchy's interests as Adriatic Power); the prospect of a common national development in a trialist direction would satisfy the south Slavs and break the point of Panserbian propaganda. But these were as yet mere suggestions for the future. More immediately, the year 1907 saw the introduction of universal and direct suffrage into Austria, the electoral annihilation of the bourgeois nationalist parties by the clerical and socialist mass parties, and the virtual collapse of Magyar pretensions with the conclusion of the commercial *Ausgleich* in October. For the last time in its history the Monarchy was about to enjoy a respite of some three years of relative domestic calm. This at least provided something of a basis for a more effective foreign policy; and the new foreign minister certainly seemed to possess the necessary energy, drive, and sense of direction.

Alois, Baron von Aehrenthal, although born in 1854 a member of the lesser German nobility of Bohemia,[189] had excellent connexions through his mother (a Thun) and his wife (a Széchenyi) with the higher Bohemian and Hungarian aristocracy. Nevertheless, he owed his position largely to his own ability and industry, as evidenced by his career as Kálnoky's private secretary, minister at Bucharest, and latterly as a most successful ambassador at St Petersburg. The brisk and businesslike tone he introduced into the Ballhausplatz was immediately remarked on by diplomats at home and abroad. The new minister was 'quite a different cup of tea' (*ganz ein anderes Café*) from the somewhat lackadaisical Goluchowski: 'the reins are in firm hands.'[190] According to a British

[189] The myth of his Jewish ancestry is without foundation.
[190] Berchtold MSS., Hohenlohe to Berchtold, 19 May 1907.

ambassador, Aehrenthal would not permit his underlings at the Ballhausplatz even to express an opinion on foreign policy.[191] But this personal and centralized approach had disadvantages of its own. Aehrenthal tended sometimes to become too wrapped up in his own grand designs, and even his friend and colleague at St Petersburg, Berchtold, complained of 'Aehrenthal's frightful characteristic of overlooking facts (*Informationen*) that do not fit into his complicated political house of cards'.[192] Mensdorff in London deemed him too much a statesman of the eighteenth century, one who thought only in terms of governments and ignored the great currents of public opinion. It could thus happen on occasion that Aehrenthal's very virtues, his masterful energy and ruthless drive, would only work to compound his difficulties when his plans, which might look fine enough on the diplomatic drawing board, started in practice to go awry.

The general drift of his plans was fairly clear; and the instruments of Austro-Hungarian foreign policy – the alliance system and the entente with Russia – remained the same. But there were differences of emphasis from the Goluchowski era. Goluchowski had pursued an essentially negative, *status quo* policy, coping with problems as they arose on an *ad hoc* basis, viewing the Russian *entente* with a caution bordering on suspicion and alternating between fatalism and helpless irritation as the Dual and Triple Alliances continued their steady decline. In his eyes, the domestic ills of the Monarchy were so grave that, failing an actual threat to its vital interests, the best chance of recovery lay in absolute calm and rest. Aehrenthal, however, prescribed a vigorous foreign policy, to sharpen the patient's self-confidence and interest in staying alive. Although he intended to use the same diplomatic instruments as his predecessor, he had a rather more purposeful and ambitious end in view – the positive strengthening of the prestige and independence of the Dual Monarchy.

For Aehrenthal, as for every Austro-Hungarian foreign minister since 1879, the ultimate safeguard of the Monarchy's security remained the Dual Alliance. His hypersensitive reaction to what he regarded as British attempts to isolate and encircle Germany in the summer of 1906 showed that he was acutely aware of the need to maintain the pre-eminence of the Central

[191] Cartwright MSS., Cartwright to Chauncey, 6 July 1910, copy.
[192] H. Hantsch, *Leopold, Graf Berchtold*, Vol. 1, Graz, 1963, p. 136.

European bloc. At the same time, however, he was determined to secure for Austria-Hungary a greater measure of independence within the Alliance – even to take the lead in it. He was in fact seeking for Austria-Hungary a position similar to that which Germany had enjoyed in the Dual Alliance in the 1880s and 1890s, when the dominant Power had regarded the alliance as something to be kept in reserve against an actual catastrophe, while retaining for itself considerable freedom of manoeuvre in day-to-day diplomacy. To this end, it would be essential – as he had been urging on Goluchowski for some six years – to reduce the Monarchy's dependence on Berlin by improving its relations with its potential enemies.

He lost no time in holding out an olive branch to Italy, in an ostentatiously friendly speech to the Delegations in November 1906. And he was quite undeterred by the clamour of Conrad, Franz Ferdinand, and the clericals, who declared that war with Italy was inevitable, and that the sooner it came the better. By the spring of 1907 the Italians were beginning to reciprocate his friendly sentiments. After a tour of Italy, Prince Liechtenstein reported that Austrophile feeling there was surprisingly strong, particularly – and this was a new if somewhat doubtful compliment – among left-wing circles who were now afraid that if the Dual Monarchy fell to pieces Germany would expand as far as the Adriatic. Aehrenthal's visit to Tittoni at Desio in July 1907 – significantly enough an object of suspicion and anxiety to the German press – marked a further stage in the steady improvement of Austro-Italian relations.[193] Indeed, even world recognition was attained when Aehrenthal and Tittoni were asked if they would accept the Nobel Peace Prize for 1907. But in Vienna it was felt that it would be quite improper for the emperor's foreign minister to accept a large sum of money from a foreign body merely for doing his duty. Besides, if war later broke out *mauvais plaisants* might then well ask whether the money should not be paid back.[194] So the offer of what was still considered a rather curious distinction was declined with much thanks.

With the Monarchy's other potential enemy, Russia, Aehrenthal was even more concerned to improve relations, and this not merely as a means to greater independence from Germany, but as

[193] Mérey MSS., Aehrenthal to Mérey, 25 July 1907.
[194] Aehrenthal MSS., Karton 3, Lützow to Aehrenthal, 24 December 1907.

an end in itself. He was still hoping ultimately for nothing less than the restoration of the Three Emperors' Alliance. He had never approved of Goluchowski's somewhat ambivalent attitude towards the *entente*, which had restricted the Monarchy's freedom of action while not providing the security that would come from a really cordial relationship with Russia. How far his hopes of far-reaching co-operation with St Petersburg could be reconciled with his determination to increase the prestige of Austria-Hungary in the Near East, only the future would show. Potential sources of rivalry were not far to seek. Even Aehrenthal continued Goluchowski's policy in the commercial field, striving to align Bulgaria and Roumania with Austria-Hungary, and vainly urging the Austrian and Hungarian governments to make haste with the commercial treaties; and although he was less averse than Goluchowski to granting commercial concessions to Serbia, this would only be done when that state came to heel and showed to Austria-Hungary 'the respect due to our Monarchy' as a Great Power.[195] Such language could hardly be music to Russian ears. Perhaps Goluchowski's deep scepticism as to the long-term prospects of the *entente* had been justified after all.

The new policy got off to a good start in November 1906 when Aehrenthal returned to St Petersburg to take his leave as ambassador. He was able to sound the tocsin to some effect against Britain's alleged designs to isolate and humiliate Germany by raising the armaments issue at the forthcoming Hague Peace Conference, and against her attempts to push her way in on the dual control of the Macedonian reforms. The tsar and tsaritsa responded warmly to his suggestion that the selfish designs of Britain might best be thwarted by restoring the Three Emperors' Alliance. Izvolsky was rather more difficult to handle. His vanity was always sensitive to criticism in the press and in the Duma from Liberal opinion, which was on the whole hostile to co-operation with Austria-Hungary, and demanded an alignment with the Western Powers and the furtherance of Russian national interests in the Near East. But even Izvolsky promised to continue co-operation with Austria-Hungary in Macedonia, and to implement the projected judicial reform faithfully in the spirit of Mürzsteg. Thus heartened, Aehrenthal returned to Vienna, calling at Berlin en route to admonish the Germans to support the efforts

[195] P.A. XL/305, Ministerratsprotokoll, 6 January 1907.

of the Mürzsteg Powers – for their failure could only pave the way for even more drastic proposals from London.

Yet the practical results of his endeavours were disappointing. In the first place, the drafting of the judicial reform project was a matter for the Austro-Hungarian and Russian ambassadors at Constantinople, Pallavicini and Zinoviev, and for personal reasons the two did not work well together. Second, the whole concept of the Mürzsteg programme was facing a serious challenge from the British. The Austro-Russian view still remained that the Mürzsteg Powers should keep the lead by drafting any reform proposals *à deux*, only then inviting the other Powers to join in carrying them out; and that no further reforms could be taken up in any case until the 3 per cent customs increase had been granted. But the British, despite repeated Austro-Russian remonstrations, doggedly refused their consent to the customs increase until the sultan accepted all their conditions regarding customs house reforms and an effective control of the spending of the money. It was not until April 1907 that the sultan finally gave way. Not that this delay had deterred the British in the meantime from demanding the speedy introduction of judicial reform and offering importunate suggestions as to its content in defiance of the Mürzsteg principle of dual control. To these suggestions, Pallavicini was dismayed to note, Zinoviev seemed all too ready to listen.

The British were proving tiresome in other respects too in the spring of 1907. Edward VII's visits to the kings of Spain and Italy at Cartagena and Gaeta were rightly interpreted in Vienna as portending a new grouping in the western Mediterranean; and agreements to safeguard the *status quo* there – obviously against Germany – followed in May. Campbell-Bannerman's determined pursuit of his disarmament plans provoked Aehrenthal to renew his appeals to St Petersburg: it was essential that Russia should stand together with the Central Powers to prevent all discussion of the issue at the conference, or at least to siphon it off into a harmless sub-committee on which the three Eastern Empires need not be represented. In doing this, he was seeking not merely to counter a supposed British offensive, but to use this very threat as a means of drawing Russia closer to the Central Powers. In May, he went a step further in this direction, hinting tentatively to France and Russia that they might co-operate with the Central

Powers in imposing a moderate tempo in Macedonian affairs and confining the obstreperous British in a strait-jacket, as it were, inside the Concert.

This plan misfired completely. News of it reached British ears and, owing to misrepresentations wilful or otherwise on the part of French politicians and British diplomats, in a very garbled form. Aehrenthal, it was said, had been seeking to exclude Britain from Macedonian affairs altogether, or even, according to the British ambassador at Vienna, to construct 'a Quadruple Alliance to the exclusion of Britain and Italy'.[196] He had of course been seeking nothing of the kind[197] (Document 26); but he now abandoned the project and concluded at the same time that with a waverer such as Izvolsky in charge at St Petersburg, little could be done about closer co-operation with Russia for the time being. It was a measure of his versatility that he did not wait for long to find an alternative policy. Careless of Berchtold's warnings against supping with the devil – or against damaging Germany's position at Constantinople – he determined that if the Russians would not go through thick and thin with Austria-Hungary in Macedonia and flirted with Britain, then he had better forestall them ('*so gehe ich lieber zuerst zu den Engländern*')[198] (Document 27).

Aehrenthal's desire for a *rapprochement* with Britain was sharpened by the more than usually tiresome behaviour of the Germans at this time. In June, he sent off another round of complaints to Berlin: Germany's encouragement of the violently anti-Catholic *Los von Rom* movement in Austria, and the projected Prussian law for the expropriation of Polish landowners in the Ostmark posed serious threats to the popularity of the Dual Alliance inside the Monarchy. In the international field, Germany was adopting at the Hague Peace Conference an attitude of such inflexibility as seemed almost deliberately designed to contrive her isolation. Indeed, once it became clear that on the contentious issue of armaments the conference would produce nothing more binding than the anodyne recommendations of 1899, his chief preoccupation was to prevent Germany from pushing the Monarchy forward as the intransigent Power. He accepted the

[196] Hardinge MSS., Vol. 10, Goschen to Hardinge, 23 May 1907.
[197] Cf. E. Walters, 'Unpublished documents. Aehrenthal's attempt in 1907 to re-group the European Powers', *Slavonic Review*, Vol. 30, 1951, pp. 213–51.
[198] Berchtold MSS., Fürstenberg to Berchtold, 14 July 1907.

British compromise proposals on armaments therefore, and kept well in the background. Altogether, he decided, Germany's policy was 'rhapsodic', whereas Britain's was cool and farsighted. It would be well to bring the Monarchy into line with the cleverer party.[199]

Consequently he was careful to receive the notification of the recent Mediterranean agreements between Britain, France, and Spain in good part, even though he regarded them as undoubtedly directed at Germany, and was scarcely taken in by Grey's naïve explanation that they embodied the same principles as the Mediterranean agreements of 1887. The British, for their part, showed themselves only too ready to forget the recent contretemps when Aehrenthal proceeded to sound out the terrain for a positive *rapprochement*. This could only be in Macedonia; but a highly successful visit by Edward VII to Franz Joseph at Ischl in August produced a verbal agreement in principle between Aehrenthal and the British permanent under-secretary Hardinge, even on this delicate subject. Aehrenthal promised to speed up the Austro-Russian proposals for judicial reform – although both parties recognized that this would be no panacea for the ills of Macedonia, which arose less from Turkish misrule than from the internecine quarrels of the Christians, and from the depredations of terrorists entering Macedonia from Bulgaria, Serbia, and Greece. As a result of the Ischl meeting, the Mürzsteg Powers made an effort to check this particular evil by solemnly warning the Balkan states concerned that Article III of the Mürzsteg programme would take no account of ethnic changes wrought by violence. Altogether, Aehrenthal could be well pleased with the summer's work – all the more so as Izvolsky, passing through Vienna in September, again promised to go hand in hand with Austria-Hungary in Macedonian affairs. The Russian nationalist press raged in vain. The Mürzsteg *entente* seemed secure – even strengthened by the support of Britain. In this situation, Aehrenthal could afford to take a benevolent view of the Anglo-Russian Convention of 31 August as being essentially an Asian affair, certainly of no ominous portent for the Balkans.

In the subsequent negotiations over judicial reform, however, the Anglo-Austrian *rapprochement* came to grief. This was due less to any basic disagreement than to the cumulative effect of a series

[199] Ibid., Aehrenthal to Berchtold, 7 July 1907.

of misunderstandings resulting largely from the cumbersome diplomatic machinery of the Mürzsteg system, namely, conferences of ambassadors at Constantinople. Instructions from governments to ambassadors were often delayed; and when they arrived, they had usually been overtaken by events. More serious, the ambassadors, being susceptible to pressure from the Porte, and confident that they knew better than their distant masters, constantly flouted their instructions and sent back drastically modified proposals for the approval – or more often, disapproval – of their governments. There were thus twelve, rather than six, parties to the negotiations; and with Germany threatening to sabotage the whole project as too offensive to the sultan, and Britain demanding yet more radical measures, it was hardly surprising that it was not until January 1908 that ambassadors and governments finally reached agreement on a draft project. Personal factors increased the friction: Pallavicini was constantly complaining of the efforts of the British ambassador, O'Conor, to tempt Zinoviev from the straight and narrow path laid down at Mürzsteg. Aehrenthal, too, was undoubtedly worried by Britain's growing influence over Russia. But he remained determined to co-operate, both to restrain the British, and to preserve at least the form of the Mürzsteg system of Austro-Russian control.

His hopes brightened in December 1907, when the British clumsily tried to seize the initiative with a proposal that the internationally-controlled *gendarmerie* in Macedonia be greatly strengthened and sent into action against the terrorists. In opposing this, Aehrenthal found himself at one with Izvolsky. As he saw it, only the Turkish regular army could cope with the guerillas. Besides, the Mürzsteg programme had been designed to protect the Christians from the Turks, not from each other: it would be disastrous to involve the *gendarmerie*, and thereby the dignity of the Great Powers, in the maelstrom of Balkan rivalries. The British initiative had in fact produced a consolidation of the Mürzsteg front; and Grey, faced with identical replies from Vienna and St Petersburg, could only abandon his proposal. But this was to be the last triumph of the Mürzsteg *entente*. Already it was ominous that disappointed Slavophile opinion in Britain, and even Russophiles in high places in the Foreign Office, had singled out Austria-Hungary for blame, pointedly leaving the door open for further co-operation with Russia. It was at this juncture that the Sanjak Railway affair occurred, which was finally to destroy the Mürzsteg *entente*.

Already for some thirty years the Monarchy had enjoyed, by virtue of Article XXV of the Treaty of Berlin, the undoubted right to build railways in the Sanjak of Novibazar. But there had so far been no urgency to exercise this right. The Turkish line to Mitrovitsa, at the southern end of the Sanjak, was completed only at the turn of the century, and the Austro-Hungarian line to Uvać, on the Bosnian frontier of the Sanjak, only in 1905. Now in the spring of 1907 Aehrenthal drew up a memorandum,[200] envisaging the construction of a whole series of Balkan railways with a view to developing Austro-Hungarian commercial (and by implication political) influence in the peninsula. These included: a link between the existing Greek and Turkish networks; a coastal railway for Montenegro; and, more important, a line to join the Serbian network on to the Bosnian line to the Adriatic. To Aehrenthal it seemed that Serbia's desire to reach the sea ('*Drang nach Westen*') was a natural tendency which could not be halted in the long run. The Monarchy would do well to accept this fact, and to try to canalize the movement through Austro-Hungarian territory in Bosnia and Dalmatia. By this means, if the terms offered to Serbia were attractive enough, the counter-attraction of a Russian or Italian Danube–Adriatic railway skirting Austro-Hungarian territory and rendering Serbia even more independent of the Monarchy might be overcome. The Sanjak railway was even more important: without it, the recently completed Bosnian lines would remain a mere cul-de-sac; and in terms of commerce and general political influence in Macedonia the Monarchy stood to gain a great deal from a direct railway link with Turkey. (The existing line to Constantinople via Belgrade was after all at the mercy of the Serbs.)

At the end of 1907 Aehrenthal decided that there was no more time to lose. Given Izvolsky's British proclivities, the days of the Austro-Russian *entente* were all too clearly numbered. It was imperative, therefore, to secure Austro-Hungarian interests in the Near East – making full use of such Russian goodwill as the failing *entente* might still offer – against the day when the *entente* should end. That to press the railway project at this moment might actually precipitate the collapse of the *entente* does not seem

[200] P.A. XII/344, résumé of a conference of 6 February 1907.

to have occurred to him. Confident in Austria-Hungary's treaty rights, he decided that the matter was primarily an Austro-Turkish affair and showed what seemed, to the tremulous Berchtold in St Petersburg at least, a somewhat cavalier disregard for the probable reactions of third parties. At any rate, he was undeterred by a mild hint of disapproval from St Petersburg – where the project was not unnaturally seen as an attempt to increase Austria-Hungary's influence in the Balkans at Russia's expense. He merely reiterated Goluchowski's argument that the Sanjak railway was a purely economic project and hence outside the purview of the *entente* of 1897, which was concerned to safeguard only the political *status quo*. On 27 January he announced his railway projects to the world in a speech to the Hungarian delegations.

The speech had an effect on Russian policy and on Great Power alignments in general that Aehrenthal had hardly bargained for. In St Petersburg, the resultant gale of nationalist wrath swept Izvolsky completely off his feet. All this was duly noted in London: 'the struggle between Austria and Russia in the Balkans is evidently now beginning' minuted Hardinge, 'and we shall not be bothered by Russia in Asia. . . . The action of Austria will make Russia lean on us more and more in the future. In my opinion this will not be a bad thing.'[201] The British were all the more inclined to support Russia in that they suspected – and this was particularly galling to Aehrenthal – that the Monarchy was acting as the catspaw of Berlin, either to further German influence in Macedonia, or even (by analogy with the Moroccan affair in 1905) to test the strength of the Anglo-Russian *entente*. To make matters worse, a most unfortunate coincidence now occurred which drove Britain and Russia still closer together in common indignation against Aehrenthal. On 5 February – the day following the issue of the Turkish *iradé* approving the Sanjak railway project – the ambassadors at Constantinople again disobeyed their instructions and refused to present the judicial reform scheme to the Porte because they thought the Turks were not yet in a mood to accept it. In their reports, each ambassador took care to blame his colleagues for this decision; but whereas Pallavicini blamed O'Conor, both O'Conor and Zinoviev blamed Pallavicini. The British and the Russians now nursed the additional grievance (which was in fact without foundation (Documents 28–30)) that to secure the ob-

[201] F.O. 371/581, Nicolson to Grey, No. 63, 4 February 1908, minute.

noxious railway project the Austrians had 'played the mean game'[202] of sabotaging Macedonian reform.

The upshot was that both the Russians and the British decided that Austria-Hungary could no longer be trusted in Macedonian affairs. Izvolsky went so far as to tell the British ambassador on 17 February that he wished 'to get out of a dual action with Austria to rally himself to . . . those Powers who are sincerely desirous of reforms'.[203] After this, Macedonian reform became largely the concern of Britain and Russia. It was to St Petersburg that Grey sent in the first instance his new proposals for dealing with the terrorists by means of mobile columns of Turkish troops. Aehrenthal, who was by no means opposed to this idea, tried to preserve some semblance of the Mürzsteg front by keeping in step with Izvolsky's various counter-proposals. (He even tried to clear his name by urging the immediate presentation of the judicial reform note; but Grey and Izvolsky were no longer interested in that.) He met with no response in London or St Petersburg. Izvolsky was abandoning the Mürzsteg system with alacrity and suggested, on 13 March, that the financial reform delegates of the other Powers should be given a position of complete equality with the Civil Agents – in fact, as he admitted, 'an abandonment of the dual co-operation and the merging of Russia in the general European concert'.[204] He sent his replies to London without any prior consultation of Vienna. By early April Hardinge could observe with satisfaction that 'the Mürzsteg programme is as dead as a doornail'.[205]

Aehrenthal did not mourn it for long. He decided that it was after all a relief to be rid of the burden of civilizing Macedonia. This task he was content to leave to Britain and Russia, particularly as Izvolsky seemed to be exercising a salutary restraining influence on his British friends. The Russians forced the British to drop the idea of a Christian governor-general for Macedonia appointed by the Powers – which the Turks would in no circumstances have accepted. Consequently, Aehrenthal was not in the least put out by Edward VII's meeting with the tsar at Reval in June, when the Anglo-Russian proposals were finally agreed.

[202] B.D., 5, No. 180.
[203] F.O. 371/581, Nicolson to Grey, private tel., 17 February 1908.
[204] F.O. 371/582, Nicolson to Grey, private, 13 March 1908.
[205] Hardinge MSS., Vol. 13, Hardinge to Goschen, 7 April 1908, copy.

Unlike the Germans and the Turks, who took great alarm at this ominous Anglo-Russian constellation, he professed himself ready to accept any Anglo-Russian proposals that were compatible with the sovereign rights of the sultan. Indeed, he angrily warned the Germans, who had been telling St Petersburg that Austria-Hungary took Germany's view in the matter, that he would not hesitate to issue a *démenti* if Germany ever again presumed to speak for Austria-Hungary. And he tartly reminded Berlin that Germany would have done well to lend more loyal support to the much milder Austro-Russian proposals in February. In fact, he was secretly quite pleased to see that the Reval meeting had given the Germans a fright: this could only increase their dependence on Vienna. For similar reasons he was undismayed by the Young Turk Revolution of 22-5 July, which overthrew the sultan's camarilla and caused great despondency in Berlin. To the Austrians it seemed that Turkey, exasperated beyond endurance by the prospect of yet more drastic Great Power intervention after Reval, was at last making a serious effort to put her house in order. At least, the warring Christians of Macedonia seemed to think so, and laid down their arms to greet the new era of fraternity. This in itself rendered superfluous that reform programme which had been one of the chief props of the Anglo-Russian *entente*.

Heartened by these events, Aehrenthal was even prepared to bury the hatchet with the British, and the meeting between Edward VII and Franz Joseph at Ischl in August 1908 was as cordial as that of the previous year. True, Aehrenthal refused to interfere at Berlin to restrain Germany's enthusiasm for the naval race, taking the somewhat ostrich-like view that this was no concern of Austria-Hungary's. But he told the British not to worry, as Germany's finances were not all that sound (*nicht brillant*).[206] The hoary legend that on this occasion Edward VII tried to seduce Franz Joseph from the German alliance and received a sharp rebuff is not supported by any evidence in British or Austrian archives. Nevertheless, Aehrenthal was well content to let the Germans believe the story, which would serve as a salutary reminder to them of their precarious situation and of the value of their alliance with Austria-Hungary.

Throughout the spring and summer of 1908 Aehrenthal's con-

[206] Mensdorff MSS., Karton 4, Tagebuch, 15 August 1908.

fidence had been growing. At the same time that the centre of gravity of the Dual Alliance was moving to Vienna, the Austrians found themselves in the happy position of being able to exploit Izvolsky's continuing desire to maintain a foot in both camps. Although the Mürzsteg *entente* might be 'as dead as a doornail', the *entente* of 1897 was still very much alive. Indeed, by May, Vienna and St Petersburg had embarked on a discussion to clarify the exact nature and purpose of the *entente* – a discussion which was to lead to its further extension in a very bold and positive sense. It was in fact Izvolsky who, despite his experiences with Aehrenthal in the Sanjak railway crisis (indeed, perhaps because that very crisis had increased his craving for prestige) now took the initiative in suggesting on 2 July something in the nature of an Austro-Russian deal. If Austria-Hungary would promise her benevolent support to Russia in altering the rule of the Straits in Russia's favour (to allow Russian warships, but no others, freedom of passage through the Straits), then Russia would assume a similarly benevolent attitude in the event of Austria-Hungary's annexing not only Bosnia and the Herzegovina, but the Sanjak of Novibazar. This was a proposal that went well beyond anything envisaged by Goluchowski or even – except for vague speculations about the future – by Aehrenthal. The *entente* of 1897 seemed about to enter on a golden age.

While these negotiations were going on, the revival of Ottoman nationalism after the Young Turk Revolution was pushing the Austrians in the direction of speedy action to secure their position in the occupied provinces. The new rulers at Constantinople, encouraged by a vociferous nationalist press, were clearly set on reasserting Turkish influence there. They were planning to summon representatives from Bosnia and the Herzegovina to the new Ottoman parliament, and there was a chance that they might give the provinces a degree of autonomy under Ottoman rule. Besides, even if this danger did not materialize, there was no denying the uncomfortable fact that Bosnia and the Herzegovina were now the only provinces in Europe which did not enjoy the benefits of constitutional government. For this deficiency, the only remedy acceptable to Austria-Hungary would be for Franz Joseph to grant a constitution. And this he could do only if he assumed full sovereign powers in the provinces by an act of annexation.

If these considerations alone were not cogent enough, military and prestige factors combined to clinch the arguments in favour of annexation. Within a month of the Young Turk Revolution the Austrians had decided to renounce their rights to keep garrisons in the Sanjak of Novibazar. According to military opinion, the Sanjak, hemmed in between Serbia and Montenegro, was a useless, even potentially dangerous, cul-de-sac. After all, if it came to a showdown with Serbia the Austro-Hungarian army would march directly on Belgrade. And to Aehrenthal it seemed that a military presence on Turkish soil burdened the Monarchy unnecessarily with the risk of immediate and unwelcome involvement in a morass of troubles should the Young Turkish Revolution merely prove the harbinger of perpetual chaos. (The Monarchy's economic interests in Turkey, however, were not to be abandoned. The Sanjak railway was still being discussed in the Ballhausplatz as late as 1912.) But to renounce rights in the Sanjak would incur a loss of prestige, and this could perhaps best be offset by some move such as the annexation of Bosnia. What is more, the retreat from the Sanjak could be made to appear as a sort of compensation to Turkey for the loss of her sovereign rights in Bosnia. Thus, the assertion of Austro-Hungarian interests by the annexation of Bosnia was essentially a conservative move, and anything but a forward thrust into the Balkans. The annexation would put an end to an ambiguous situation which had appeared increasingly untenable since the Young Turkish Revolution; and, by drawing a clear and final line between what was Austro-Hungarian and what was Turkish, the Monarchy would in fact be voluntarily setting a limit to its own frontiers.

The view that the annexation was an attempt on the part of Aehrenthal to cut a fine figure on the international stage out of sheer desperation is a myth. To him the international position of the Monarchy seemed healthier by the summer of 1908 than it had been for some years. He had prestige enough: over-confidence, not desperation, would better account for the bold and independent manner in which he decided to carry through the annexation – presenting Turkey with a *fait accompli*, and hardly taking the other Powers (except Russia) much more into his confidence. When he informed a conference of ministers of his plans on 19 August, he casually observed that Germany, being still in great terror of isolation, would not dare to make difficulties; and that Italy had no right whatever to claim compensation. France, busy in Morocco, and Britain, who 'desires good relations with us', he did not propose to consult at all.[207] Only with Russia would there have to be negotiations, and these were progressing very well. On 27 August he wrote to St Petersburg expressing his general agreement with Izvolsky's plans.

And sure enough, in his conversations of September with the Italian and German foreign ministers, Tittoni and Schoen, he showed an almost Bismarckian disregard for the moral implications of alliances, speaking only in the most general terms about the forthcoming annexation, and giving no inkling of its imminence. (October 7 was the provisional date, the eve of the meeting of the delegations.) Even the final negotiations with Izvolsky, at Berchtold's castle, Buchlau, in Moravia left some points unclear, and the two foreign ministers made no agreed written record of their conversations. According to Austro-Hungarian and recently published Russian documents,[208] it was agreed that Izvolsky should observe a benevolent attitude towards the annexation of Bosnia and the Herzegovina in return for a sympathetic attitude on the part of Austria-Hungary towards Russia's desires in the Straits question; that there could be no question of compensation for Serbia and Montenegro (especially as Austria-Hungary far from annexing the Sanjak, as Izvolsky had suggested, was about to renounce her rights there); and that there should be some sort of conference. Whether this last was only to ratify the annexation, as Aehrenthal said in his summary of the conversations[209] or actually to authorize it, as Izvolsky was later to claim, is not clear. At any rate, Aehrenthal did not inform his Russian visitor of the imminence of the annexation, and Izvolsky left Buchlau for a leisurely tour of the capitals of Western Europe.

Meanwhile, events in the Balkans came into play. In the last two weeks of September a quarrel arose between Turkey and Bulgaria which Aehrenthal used to put a final finishing touch to his plans. When the Young Turks, who had been talking ominously for some time of summoning Bulgarian representatives to the new parliament, began to emphasize Bulgaria's vassal status

---

[207] F. Conrad v. Moetzendorf, *Aus meiner Dienstzeit*, Vol. 1, Vienna, 1921, p. 104.

[208] *Istoricheskii Archiv.*, 1962, Vol. 5, pp. 113–47.

[209] O[esterreich]-U[ngarns] A[ussenpolitik], Vol. 1, No. 79.

in trivial matters of protocol, the government at Sofia eventually lost patience and withdrew its diplomatic representative from Constantinople. On 24 September, it proceeded to seize the Eastern Roumelian branch of the Orient Railway; and rumours began to spread of an impending declaration of independence. Of the seizure of the Railway (the headquarters of the Orient Railway Company were in Vienna, and most of its shareholders were Austrian or German), Aehrenthal disapproved. Indeed, he was even prepared to join the British (who ever since the Young Turk revolution had been anxious to befriend the new, Anglophile, regime) in reprimanding Bulgaria. On the other hand, it had been Austro-Hungarian policy for the past four years to cultivate Bulgaria as a potentially strong card to play against Serbia in the final scramble for Turkey. It was in line with this policy that, just before the Bulgarians seized the Railway, Franz Joseph had received Prince Ferdinand with full royal honours at Budapest. Here Aehrenthal had given him a broad hint that Austria-Hungary might annex Bosnia in the near future, in which case Bulgaria might take the opportunity to declare her independence. He was hoping thereby both to tie Bulgaria closer to the Monarchy, and to arrange a useful diversion of international attention from the annexation. But he did not initiate Ferdinand into the details of his plans, let alone arrange for simultaneous action;[210] and he certainly did not expect Ferdinand to anticipate him.

At any rate, when the British asked him to use his influence at Sofia to deter the Bulgarians from declaring their independence, he fobbed them off, on 4 October, with a pious assurance that he was not aware of any impending Bulgarian *coup*. Unfortunately for him, however – and the coincidence was to be as disastrous as that between the Sanjak railway *iradé* and the postponement of judicial reform nine months earlier – Prince Ferdinand, returning from Budapest, met his ministers at the ancient town of Rustchuk on that very day, and determined to proclaim himself independent tsar on 5 October. That very Bulgarian move which Aehrenthal had hoped might serve as a useful diversion was to prove ironically enough the ruin of his hopes of a favourable reception of the annexation, at least in London. The British were indeed far more worried about Bulgaria than about Bosnia. When, on 4 October, Mensdorff had informed them of the impending annexa-

[210] H. Hantsch, *Berchtold*, Vol. 1, p. 127.

tion, Hardinge was chiefly concerned about the repercussions in Sofia: as for the annexation, he would merely have preferred it to have been 'postponed for a couple of months'.[211] But when the news of the Bulgarian declaration of independence followed hot foot on that of Aehrenthal's refusal to act at Sofia, the British were furious at the perfidy of Vienna and lost no time in denouncing this Austro-Bulgarian plot against the Young Turkish regime 'which is really pure and honest'.[212] By 6 October Hardinge had decided that the annexation of Bosnia was 'a bombshell'.[213]

Elsewhere, it was the annexation itself that caused the greatest stir. Both Rome and Berlin were most unpleasantly surprised; and the German emperor, who first learned of the annexation from the newspapers, angrily declared that twenty years of German hard work in Turkey had been swept away. The Austro-Hungarian ambassador at Berlin had a difficult time (Document 31). Izvolsky arrived in Paris on Sunday 4 October to find awaiting him a letter from Aehrenthal informing him that the annexation would take place on the following Wednesday. He was flabbergasted – all the more so as the Austro-Hungarian ambassador, Khevenhüller, apparently inadequately briefed by Aehrenthal but never at a loss for words, had already announced the impending annexation to President Fallières, adding that Russia and Italy concurred in it. He had also indulged in some loose speculations as to the likelihood of Bulgaria's anticipating Austria-Hungary, which naturally added fuel to the flames in London (Document 32).

Izvolsky's rage defies description. He was indeed in an appalling position. He had not yet secured the approval of either the tsar or the Russian government for the Buchlau agreement; and Aehrenthal had given him no time to prepare Russian public opinion, which soon showed itself to care a great deal about the enslavement of Slav brothers in Bosnia and the Herzegovina but nothing at all for the legalistic and strategic advantages which he was hoping to gain for Russia at the Straits. Worse still, Izvolsky was in danger of losing his meagre pound of flesh, for although he had found Tittoni and Schoen accommodating enough, he

[211] B.D., Vol. 5, No. 287.
[212] Grey MSS., Vol. 61, Grey to Asquith, private, 5 October 1908, draft.
[213] Hardinge MSS., Vol. 13, Hardinge to Buchanan, 6 October 1908, copy.

soon discovered in Paris, and in London, where he arrived on 9 October, that the Western Powers were by no means anxious to harass Turkey, let alone in a cause that ill accorded with their own strategic interests. In utter desperation, he sought to blame the whole fiasco on Aehrenthal: there must be a conference, to call perfidious Austria-Hungary to account before Europe, and to force her to pay compensation to Serbia and Montenegro. Thus, owing to a combination of circumstances – haste, ill-conceived or ill-considered measures, and unfortunate coincidences – the great plan of Aehrenthal and Izvolsky to breathe new and more vigorous life into the Austro-Russian *entente*, had ended by destroying it.

The *entente* had always been a fragile instrument, only effective when it was not subjected to too great a strain or used for ambitious purposes for which it had not been designed. Like the Three Emperors' League and the Three Emperors' Alliance before it, it was essentially conservative, the product of the realization by St Petersburg and Vienna, that so long as Turkey-in-Europe existed, the Balkan situation was unlikely to become intolerable for either Russia or Austria-Hungary. Moreover, the *entente* of 1897, like the earlier Austro-Russian agreements, not only arose from, but materially reinforced this appreciation of the situation. The desire to preserve it disposed Austria-Hungary and Russia to move with circumspection, and even to modify their policies on concrete issues that might precipitate a major crisis. Indeed, in so far as it mitigated the rivalry between Vienna and St Petersburg, the *entente* of 1897 undoubtedly made a major contribution to the maintenance of peace.

Yet it could provide no permanent security. For the diplomatic situation on which it rested was impermanent. The expulsion of the Turks from Europe was generally recognized to be but a matter of time: sooner or later the map of the Balkans would have to be radically revised. And this being the case, Russian and Austro-Hungarian interests were ultimately incompatible. When the Ottoman Empire in Europe finally collapsed, there simply could be no agreement between St Petersburg and Vienna as to what should replace it. The Russian government could never be reconciled to any settlement whereby the land route to the Straits would be exposed to control by an Austria-Hungary exercising a predominating influence at Sofia and Belgrade; nor would Russian public opinion ever accept the subjection of the Slavs of the western Balkans to Austro-Hungarian control. To stave off these dangers, Russia would be forced to seek to establish her own influence from the Black Sea to the Adriatic. Yet by the same token, the prospect of Russia's establishing control of Bulgaria – or possibly Roumania – Serbia and Montenegro was anathema to Austria-Hungary. It would immensely increase the strategic threat from Russia, and would establish a link between a potentially hostile Great Power and irredentist states whose ambitions could only be realized through the destruction of the Dual Monarchy. Vienna, therefore, was determined to restrict the growth of Serbia and dominate her; and to seek additional reinsurance by ousting Russian influence from Bulgaria. The fact was that, as regards the future territorial configuration of the Balkans and the diplomatic alignments of the heirs of the Ottoman Empire, it would be impossible to devise a solution that would satisfy both Russia and Austria-Hungary. Obviously neither Power could be expected to renounce its interests in favour of the other, or even to withdraw in the hope that the other would do so and establish a power vacuum. That would have demanded of each a degree of trust in the future intentions of the other party unprecedented in nineteenth-century diplomacy. The agreement of 1897 might gloss over the ultimate incompatibility of Russian and Austro-Hungarian interests, and even hint hopefully at an amicable solution of the underlying conflict; but it could never conjure it away altogether.

Of this, as the history of the *entente* of 1897 shows, both governments were well aware. Goluchowski never had any illusions about the limitations of the *rapprochement*. He had only embarked on it after two years of fruitlessly striving to resuscitate the Mediterranean agreements and make them the basis of a policy of opposing Russia and all her works. True, both for Russia with her Far Eastern preoccupations and for Austria-Hungary with her internal crisis and her wayward allies, the *entente* had its uses. Nevertheless, friction over its practical operation remained a constant reminder of the ultimate incompatibility of Russian and Austro-Hungarian interests. Rivalry for influence at Sofia and Belgrade continued to cause ill will between Vienna and St Petersburg; no significant progress was made towards an agreement regarding the future disposition of the sultan's territories in Europe;

nor was Goluchowski ever tempted – even by the glittering prospect of a general diplomatic alignment with Russia – to do anything that might help Russia to establish her ascendancy in the Balkans (as Aehrenthal seemed to him to be recommending): that would be to sacrifice those very interests which the *entente* was designed to safeguard. (And even Aehrenthal's suggestion of 1906 that the Three Emperors' Alliance might be restored, was based on the assumption that Austria-Hungary would not sacrifice any of her interests in the Balkans, and that Russia would be incapable of action there 'for the next ten years'.)[214] The successes of the *entente* were either negative – even Austro-Russian co-operation in Macedonia after 1903 was only designed to preserve the *status quo* by rendering it palatable to the sultan's Christian subjects – or irrelevant to the basic issue – the neutrality treaty of 1904 was made with an eye to possible wars in the Far East or the Tyrol, and expressly abstained from pronouncing on possible changes in the *status quo* in the Balkans.

Yet even so, despite their limitations, these various agreements all served to maintain an illustration of co-operation and to conceal the reality of the underlying conflict of interests. They helped to produce a situation tolerable for both parties and rendered valuable service as a practical basis for policy for the best part of a decade. And given that for all their future ambitions and apprehensions the governments of Vienna and St Petersburg felt for the present an urgent need to keep the peace and maintain the *status quo*, they were perhaps wise to base their policies on a useful illusion rather than on a reality that lay, after all, in a distant and uncertain future.

By 1905, even the negative *entente* was beginning to fail. The element of mutual trust on which it rested was undermined as Russia, weakened by war and revolution, and fearful of Austria-Hungary's predominance within an *entente à deux*, sought to bring the other Powers – notably Britain and Italy – into the Balkan arena. This in turn caused the Austrians to doubt the sincerity of Russia's devotion to the *status quo*, and to seek to secure their own interests. The Sanjak railway crisis marked the first significant rift in the Austro-Russian *entente*. Yet even after this Izvolsky and Aehrenthal were still prepared to co-operate. Their aims were limited, in the tradition of the Austro-Russian *entente*: security at

[214] P.A. I/475, Aehrenthal to Goluchowski, No. 2, secret, 25 July 1906.

the Straits, and a formal change in the legal status of Bosnia-Herzegovina; and neither statesman approached the delicate ultimate issue of who should be master in the Balkans. Their pains were ill-rewarded. Both statesmen had badly miscalculated the effect the annexation of Bosnia would have on the mighty current of Slav feeling, which in Russia surged as far as the steps of the throne itself. Even if Britain and France had not deprived Izvolsky of his share of the Buchlau bargain, it is doubtful whether any Russian government would ever have been able to reconcile itself to the annexation of Bosnia.

As it was, the Bosnian issue exposed the underlying incompatibility of Austro-Hungarian and Russian interests to the glaring light of day. From this confrontation with reality Austro-Russian relations never recovered. Russia and Austria-Hungary had gazed upon the Gorgon's head. After this, there could be no question of their continuing to delude themselves with policies designed to conceal what was now known and felt to be a painful reality. Henceforth, both Powers based their policies on an assumption of frank hostility: whatever the one proposed was viewed by the other as part of some devious or openly hostile design. The years 1908–14 were the years of Austro-Russian confrontation – years which at first promised to be all the more difficult for Austria-Hungary in that the annexation of Bosnia had not only brought the conflict with Russia into the open, but threatened to estrange her remaining friends and allies.

Chapter 7

Austro-Russian Confrontation 1908–14[1]

> Unwillkürlich kommt mir hiebei im Moment, wo der
> Zug aus dem Bahnhof rollt und die zur zweiten Heimat
> gewordenen Newagelände allmählich den Blicken
> entschwinden, das schöne Heinesche Lied in Erinner-
> ung von den Herzen, die sich schlecht vertragen und
> dennoch brechen, wenn sie scheiden.
>
> *Berchtold, Diary*, April 1911[2]

If the immediate consequence of the annexation of Bosnia was the
disgrace and isolation of Austria-Hungary, the situation soon
changed in her favour. This was due in no small measure to the
blunders of her opponents. In the first place, Britain, France, and
Russia undoubtedly overreached themselves in demanding that
issues of such vital importance to the Monarchy as the validity of
the annexation, or the kind of compensation (possibly even territorial and at Austria-Hungary's expense) to be paid to Serbia and
Montenegro, should be left to the decision of a conference. They
went on to compound their error by putting forward their conference programme, on 15 October, as a joint proposal from all
three Triple *Entente* Powers. This display of solidarity immediately

[1] The following works are of particular relevance to this chapter: N.
Stone, 'Moltke-Conrad: Relations between the Austro-Hungarian and German General Staffs 1909–14', *Historical Journal*, 1966; F. Fellner (ed.) *Das
politische Tagebuch Josef Redlichs*, Kommission für neuere Geschichte Oesterreichs, No. 39; E. C. Helmreich, *The Diplomacy of the Balkan Wars*, Harvard,
1938; R. J. Crampton, 'The diplomatic relations between Great Britain and
Germany in the Balkans and the Eastern Mediterranean from the Agadir
Crisis to the murder at Sarajevo', London Ph.D. thesis, 1971; and the works
by H. Benedikt, G. Drage, F. Klein, C. A. Macartney, and F. R. Bridge, cited
in Chapter 1, note 1; by W. Wagner in Chapter 2, note 1; and by H. Hantsch,
Chapter 6, note 1.

[2] 'As the train draws out of the station, and the banks of the Neva which
have become a second home to me gradually disappear from sight, I cannot
help recalling Heine's beautiful poem about the hearts which, while unhappy
together, yet break if they part.' H. Hantsch, *Berchtold*, Vol. I, p. 236.

brought the Germans, still haunted by memories of Algeciras, to forget their original anger with Aehrenthal and promise him their full support. And this in turn only confirmed Aehrenthal in his determination that any conference must only be allowed to ratify, not authorize, or even discuss, the annexation; and that there could be no question of territorial compensation for Serbia and Montenegro – whose disappointed hopes of some day acquiring Bosnia and the Herzegovina by no means gave them a *locus standi* in the dispute.

In the negotiations about the conference proposal, Aehrenthal's task was made easier by the crumbling of the Triple *Entente* front. The French soon made it clear that they did not wish to make a big issue of the annexation. They were anxious at this time to secure the good offices of Austria-Hungary in a dispute with Berlin about the behaviour of the German consul at Casablanca; and it was in fact in appreciation of what he regarded as France's 'very correct' attitude towards the annexation that in November Franz Joseph persuaded William II to submit the Casablanca affair to arbitration.[3] Even with the British, Aehrenthal had reached a compromise agreement in principle by early December: the annexation might be put down for discussion at the conference, but preliminary agreements between the Powers would ensure that any discussion would be a mere formality. Only Russia seemed hopelessly stubborn. In his desperation, Izvolsky issued a circular appeal to the Powers on 19 December, insisting that the Powers must go to the conference with their hands completely free, and citing the precedent of the London Conference of 1871. Aehrenthal countered by circulating extracts from the Austro-Russian confidential negotiations of the summer, some of which contained highly embarrassing allusions to Russia's earlier commitments, dating back to the 1880s, to accept the annexation. Faced with this, Izvolsky collapsed, and nothing more was heard of the conference proposal for some months. But Aehrenthal's victory had been bought at a price: Austro-Russian relations were now worse than ever. Indeed, Izvolsky proceeded to declare normal relations with Austria-Hungary suspended: as it was clearly impossible to hold confidential discussions with the Austrians, he would henceforth receive only formal written communications from the Austro-Hungarian embassy.

[3] W. Wagner, p. 250.

Not that Russia was the only Power at odds with the Monarchy by the end of 1908. The Turks were by no means ready to accept the renunciation of Austro-Hungarian rights in the Sanjak as sufficient compensation for their loss of their sovereign rights in Bosnia and the Herzegovina. They rejected out of hand Aehrenthal's suggestion that they recognize the annexation without further ado, and proceeded to institute a boycott of Austro-Hungarian merchandise in the hope of forcing the Monarchy to pay considerable financial compensation, or even to rescind the annexation altogether. Aehrenthal, for his part, at first refused to negotiate with Constantinople so long as the boycott continued; and even when he abandoned this stiff attitude, in December, he was unable to offer the Turks anything substantial. The impecunious governments of Austria and Hungary were reluctant to pay the Turks anything at all, despite his cajolery (all the Monarchy's embarrassments would disappear once agreement was reached with Constantinople) and threats (the alternative would be a very expensive war to bring Turkey to heel).

Indeed, the risk of an Austro-Turkish war seemed so real at the end of 1908 that Tittoni even sounded the British as to what they would do in such an event. The Italians were well aware that in Vienna Conrad was talking wildly of attacking Italy herself; and in Rome anti-Austrian street demonstrations continued well into the winter as evidence that two years of effort on Aehrenthal's part to improve Austro-Italian relations had made little impact on public opinion. In the event the British refused to be drawn by Tittoni. But their own relations with the Monarchy were bad enough. The diplomatic support which Grey had pledged to Serbian and Montenegrin claims for compensation rendered Britain morally responsible, in Austrian and Hungarian eyes, for the clamorous hostility displayed towards the Monarchy by those two states in demonstrations, the founding of propaganda societies (such as the *Narodna Odbrana*, founded as a direct result of the annexation) and even military preparations. The Austro-Hungarian press was not slow to voice Aehrenthal's view that Britain was perhaps indeed the chief troublemaker; and that she was perhaps even seeking to unleash a general war in order to settle accounts with Germany.

The new year brought some improvement, when Aehrenthal was at last able to persuade the Austrian and Hungarian governments to pay financial compensation to Turkey. By 11 January Vienna and Constantinople were agreed that Turkey should recognize the annexation in return for a payment of 2,500,000 Turkish pounds (disguised for prestige purposes as a payment for Ottoman property in the annexed provinces). The final settlement, embodied in the Austro-Turkish Protocol of 26 February, marked a considerable improvement in Austro-Turkish relations generally. Already in the same month the Anglophile Kiamil Pasha had been replaced as grand vizier by an old friend of Austria-Hungary, Hilmi Pasha, formerly Inspector-General of Macedonia. But the Austro-Turkish Protocol could not settle the European crisis; for Britain and Russia still insisted that the annexation infringed not only Turkey's rights under the Austro-Turkish Treaty of April 1879, but the rights of all the signatories of the Treaty of Berlin.

The other offender against the Treaty of Berlin, Bulgaria, had at first been painfully isolated – being in disgrace at the Triple *Entente* capitals, and finding her erstwhile accomplice, Austria-Hungary, suddenly and tiresomely grasping in defence of the claims of the Orient Railway Company shareholders. Certainly the Germans, anxious to recover lost ground at Constantinople, were pressing the Austrians to take a strong line in the matter. By December, however, Bulgaria was surrounded by suitors. Stolypin and the tsar, never much enamoured of Izvolsky's policy of compensations, had decided that the best defence of Slav interests against the supposed ambitions of Austria-Hungary was to be found in a league of Balkan states including Turkey.[4] When this aim proved unrealistic – the Balkan states being too jealous of each other, and more concerned to partition Turkey than to ally with her – the Russians and their British friends determined instead to try to reconcile at least Turkey and her wayward Bulgarian vassal under the auspices of the Triple *Entente*. At this, Berlin took great alarm; and Aehrenthal, although always sceptical of talk about Balkan leagues, tried to soothe the Germans with some gestures designed to keep Bulgaria out of the clutches of the *Entente*. After all, she might still prove a useful pawn to play against Serbia. At the turn of the year, he offered Sofia a military convention. But the Triple *Entente* Powers could outbid the

[4] E. C. Thaden, *Russia and the Balkan Alliance of 1912* (Pennsylvania State University, 1965), pp. 19–22.

Central Powers in the economic field; and in so far as the Bulgarian-Turkish settlement of 2 February 1909 was based on a Russo-Bulgarian-Turkish financial arrangement, it was a triumph for the Triple *Entente* and a defeat for the Central Powers. On the other hand, in so far as it cleared away yet one more complicating factor from the diplomatic scene, it strengthened Aehrenthal's hand in dealing with the one remaining contentious issue, the grievances of Serbia and Montenegro.

Here, Aehrenthal's victory was a foregone conclusion. That it was delayed for some two months was solely the consequence of his desire to bring Serbia and her Russian and British protectors to heel by diplomatic means alone. In fact, his reluctance to go to war was the only strong card in his opponents' hand. Otherwise, Izvolsky's position was little short of hopeless. In the first place, he had himself, at Buchlau, abandoned Serbia's claim to compensation, and lived in daily terror lest Aehrenthal now reveal the fact. Diplomacy offered no salvation: he could no longer safely resort to a conference, being unsure of the French, who were all too anxious 'to give Austria a lift' in the hope of smoothing the course of their Moroccan negotiations with Germany.[5] Nor was Russia in any condition to fight, even if Austria-Hungary invaded Serbia – as Izvolsky himself admitted to Berchtold on 17 February; and Britain's support was strictly diplomatic. In this situation, Britain and Russia never had a serious chance of dictating to Austria-Hungary the line she should take towards Serbia – especially now that Aehrenthal was not only spurred on by his humiliation in the Bulgarian question, and fully aware of Russia's weakness, but also confident of the full support and encouragement of Germany.

In the course of a correspondence between the German and Austro-Hungarian chiefs of staff authorized and supervised by the monarchs and governments of the two allied Powers, Moltke had assured Conrad on 21 January 1909 that if Austria-Hungary attacked Serbia, and Russia mobilized, then Germany would come to the Monarchy's assistance. This was, on the face of it at least, a most important extension of the defensive Dual Alliance.

How much even such a sweeping political promise was worth in practical military terms was another question. In fact, its very generosity was consciously designed to cloak a serious military

[5] F.O. 371/748, Nicolson to Grey, Tel. 23, 20 January 1909, minute.

deficiency.[6] For Moltke's letter was only one item in a three-month correspondence in which Conrad was trying – after a decade of virtually complete lack of communication between the two allied general staffs – to tie the Germans down to specific military commitments. Moltke, by contrast, was concerned to keep Germany's military planning free from dependence on an ally so fragile as Austria-Hungary, and was as evasive as possible on specific military issues. But he was nevertheless hoping, by means of sweeping political promises, to keep the Monarchy from losing hope altogether and retiring on to the defensive behind the Carpathians. This latter danger was by no means imaginary. As the likelihood increased that the Monarchy might find itself involved in war on either its northern or its southern frontier, or both, Conrad had devised two alternative plans to meet all contingencies. Minimal defensive forces were assigned to the south (*Minimal-Gruppe Balkan*, of 12 divisions) and to Galicia (*A-Staffel*, of 30 divisions); and either of these could be brought up to offensive strength by the addition of a third bloc, *B-Staffel* of some 12 divisions. In the event of war with Russia, *A-Staffel* would be brought up to strength for an offensive in Galicia, and *Minimal-Gruppe Balkan* would stand on the defensive. This was *Fall-R* (Russia). A war with Serbia would see the strengthening of *Minimal-Gruppe Balkan*, while *A-Staffel* would stay on the defensive against Russia. This was *Fall-B* (Balkan); and this was naturally anathema to Moltke, who wanted a strong Austrian thrust into Poland to distract the Russians while Germany dealt with France.

A compromise was reached. Conrad showed himself willing to undertake an offensive even with the unstrengthened *A-Staffel* – but only on condition that the Germans would themselves launch a simultaneous offensive from East Prussia to take some of the weight off the Austrians. He at first asked for 20 German divisions in the East by the 35th day of mobilization, whereas Moltke could not promise more than 13 until France had been beaten. (For the French campaign he was thinking in terms of only 3–4 weeks – though he extended this to 4–5 weeks in November 1912 and to 'about 6 weeks' in May 1914.) Nevertheless, in a letter of

---

[6] N. Stone, 'Moltke-Conrad: Relations between the Austro-Hungarian and German General Staffs, 1909–1914', *Historical Journal*, Vol. 9, 1966, pp. 201–28.

19 March 1909, which remained decisive for Austro-Hungarian military planning until 1914, Moltke promised to launch an immediate offensive from East Prussia to coincide with and support an Austro-Hungarian offensive. But he added an important escape clause: 'should the implementation of the plans of one of the allies be rendered impossible by the enemy' the other was to be informed immediately. In view of this clause – which in 1914 was to give rise to serious recriminations – Conrad had perhaps not obtained all that much. But he seemed satisfied enough, and throughout March remained an ardent advocate of a military solution to the Serbian crisis.

The emperor, although at times exasperated by Serbia's behaviour into sympathizing with Conrad and the war party, took an altogether sceptical view of Germany's promises. He comforted Conrad in his disappointment at the peaceful outcome of the crisis with a reminder that after all, there was Germany to be considered, and 'one must not presume too much of her' (*man dürfe ihm nicht zu viel zumuten*).[7] Besides, the state of the Monarchy's own military forces was far from brilliant, with the memory of the army crisis in Hungary still fresh, and with the Austrian and Hungarian parliaments still resolutely refusing to increase the recruiting contingents beyond the levels fixed in 1889. A little more money was voted for war material and fortifications; but not much could be done without manpower. All the Monarchy could do to meet the rumours of war emanating from Serbia was to transport a few extra battalions to Bosnia and to call up some reservists there. And even this put a tremendous strain on the government's financial resources. That this was no time to launch a lighthearted and costly war Aehrenthal, ably seconded by the Common War Minister, von Schönaich, was absolutely convinced. He was determined to do all he could to settle the crisis by diplomatic means.

One thing was clear, the crisis must be settled soon. The tension and the prolonged military preparations were exerting a strain on the economic life of the Monarchy that could not be allowed to go on indefinitely. In mid-February, Aehrenthal told the Germans that he intended to clear up the Serbian situation by the middle of March. He would ask Serbia to abandon her pretensions, to accept the annexation, and to live at peace with Austria-

[7] W. Wagner, p. 252.

Hungary. In return, he was prepared to grant her some economic concessions. Only if Serbia rejected his proposals would he resort to force to compel her obedience. At the same time, he was quite adamant in his refusal to admit Russia's 'mad claim' to act as protectress of Serbia, insisting that no 'Serbian question' concerning the Powers had arisen from the annexation.[8] Nor would there be any negotiations even with Serbia until she had abandoned her claim to territorial compensation. In the face of this, Izvolsky and his British supporters could only beat an undignified retreat. On 28 February Izvolsky told the Serbs to give up all hope of territorial compensation; and on 8 March, with a good deal of grumbling about the injustice of negotiations between 'géant et souris',[9] Britain and Russia at last admitted that even the commercial concessions that Austria-Hungary might make to Serbia were not a matter for the six Powers to determine, but one for Vienna and Belgrade alone.

In considering what commercial concessions he might grant to Serbia, Aehrenthal was prepared to be generous. And not without reason: he was playing for the highest stakes and aiming ultimately at nothing less than the economic, and eventually political, subjection of Serbia to the Monarchy. Now this, he impressed on the Austrian and Hungarian prime ministers on 3 March, could only be achieved by a wise and far-sighted economic policy. Indeed, even if force had to be used against Serbia – and this would only be in the nature of a punitive expedition, for there could be no question of incorporating Serbia into a Monarchy already overburdened with Slavs – the defeated kingdom would have to be treated with generosity. Serbia's drive towards the sea was a natural phenomenon, and it was for Austria-Hungary to come to terms with and canalize this energy. He proposed, therefore, to grant Serbia the use of a free port on the Dalmatian coast, a railway convention to cover the transport of all her products through Bosnia to the Adriatic, and a commercial treaty to last until 1917.

If he hoped by such means alone to bring Belgrade to reason, he was to be disappointed. On 15 March the Serbs, in a note that was considered insolent and unacceptable even in London and St Petersburg, flatly rejected his offer of commercial negotiations.

[8] B.D., Vol. 5, No. 657.
[9] B.D., Vol. 5, No. 627; O.-U.A., Vol. 2, No. 1083.

Aehrenthal now resolved to deliver a very stiff note to Belgrade. It seemed as though the military chastisement of Serbia, with all its implications for Russian and British prestige, was about to begin.

It was to forestall such a disaster that Grey came forward on 16 March with a suggestion that the Powers might persuade Serbia to make submission in a note previously approved by Vienna. Aehrenthal was prepared to accept this way out; but he thought that the text suggested by Grey for Serbia's note was not explicit enough. At this point, the British ambassador at Vienna, Sir Fairfax Cartwright, a man who enjoyed Aehrenthal's confidence, and who was fertile in ingenious suggestions, intervened.[10] Acting entirely on his own initiative, and without any instructions from London, he persuaded Aehrenthal to draft a text of his own as an alternative to Grey's. But Aehrenthal's text, according to which the Powers would ask Serbia to apologize for her past behaviour and accept the annexation (even before the Powers themselves had done so) was considered unacceptable in London. On 22 March Cartwright, again on his own initiative and without informing London, suggested that Aehrenthal amend his text to oblige Serbia to accept not the annexation, but rather any decision the Powers might arrive at; and this on condition that the powers would promise beforehand in writing that they would in fact recognize the annexation at a conference. Aehrenthal readily agreed to this. Cartwright had given him the opportunity of exploiting the awkward predicament of Britain and Russia in the Serbian affair to extract from them their formal recognition of the annexation. Unfortunately, the British rejected also the revised Austro-Hungarian text out of hand. For they were determined to make no promise whatever about the annexation until the Serbian crisis had been peacefully settled. This, they felt, was their only lever over Aehrenthal.

The deadlock was resolved by the diplomatic collapse of Russia. As the invasion of Serbia inexorably approached, Izvolsky lost his nerve and appealed desperately to Berlin to build a golden bridge out of the impasse. Now the energetic Kiderlen, temporarily in charge of the Wilhelmstrasse, was only too pleased to take the initiative, feeling that Vienna had called the tune in the Dual Alliance for long enough. Aehrenthal suspected as much; but he

[10] F. R. Bridge, *Great Britain and Austria Hungary* . . ., pp. 131–2.

could hardly refuse the proffered German help, which came – in typical Kiderlen style – in the form of a rather peremptory request to St Petersburg to recognize the annexation without further ado; otherwise Germany would not restrain Austria-Hungary from attacking Serbia. Izvolsky was only too pleased to comply – all the more so as he could now assume in London and Paris the role of victim of a German 'ultimatum'. He also accepted Aehrenthal's revised text for the Serbian note.

At this, the British, reluctant to seem more Russian than the Russians, also resigned themselves to accepting Aehrenthal's text. But, being totally unaware of Cartwright's activities, they still refused to give that promise to recognize the annexation on which the revised text depended, and without which, as Aehrenthal pointed out, a Serbian promise merely to accept the decision of the Powers would be worthless. Deadlock had again been reached. The Ballhausplatz buzzed with rumours of war. But at the last minute Grey again retreated, giving a verbal promise to recognize the annexation – but only on condition that Aehrenthal gave the Powers time to settle the Serbian crisis peacefully. (If Serbia refused to obey the Powers and present Aehrenthal's note, he would in any case recognize the annexation.) Now as the peaceful settlement of the Serbian crisis was to be, in fact, on Aehrenthal's terms, the condition imposed by Grey was, as Aehrenthal himself observed, hardly an onerous one. Britain and Russia had undoubtedly suffered a resounding diplomatic defeat; and the fact that this was in no small measure due to their own refusal for so long to recognize the harsh realities of the diplomatic situation did not make it any the less painful.

The crisis, at any rate, was over. On the advice of the Powers Serbia delivered at Vienna the formal promise desired by Aehrenthal (Document 33) 'to live in future on terms of friendly and neighbourly relations' with the Monarchy (31 March). Aehrenthal had got all he wanted; and that without the expense of a punitive expedition. The remaining issues were soon cleared up. Montenegro recognized the annexation in a note drafted in Rome and somewhat less draconic than Serbia's; and she was fortunate enough to receive 'compensation' in the form of the abolition of certain restrictions imposed on her frontier fortifications by the Treaty of Berlin. The discomfiture of Izvolsky, who found himself excluded from this Italo-Austro-Montenegrin arrangement, was complete. By mid-April all the Great Powers had taken note of an amendment to Article XXV of the Treaty of Berlin, thereby formally recognizing the annexation of Bosnia.

Yet if Aehrenthal had won the diplomatic battle, the long-term results of the annexation were disappointing. On the domestic front, he was unable to realize his hopes of using the annexation to remodel the Dual Monarchy on a more viable basis. The Magyars were adamant in their opposition to anything smacking of Trialism; and neither Vienna nor Budapest would consider renouncing its share in the government of the newly annexed provinces. So they continued under the ultimate control of the Common Ministry of Finance – 'floating like Mahomet's coffin in the air', as the younger Kossuth put it[11] – even after a constitution had been granted in 1910. Altogether, the annexation had probably sharpened the differences between the two halves of the Monarchy. The relative calm that had followed the settlement of the Hungarian crisis was ending. Even in February 1909, when the Serbian crisis had created something of a national emergency, the Reichsrat had been totally preoccupied with the Czech-German language dispute, and one session, 'made hideous by a concert of foghorns and other instruments' ended in a mêlée reminiscent of the boisterous 'nineties, and had to be closed by imperial decree.[12] By 1911 nationalism had begun to infect even the great mass parties, and Czech and German Social Democrats determined to go their separate ways. Lastly, the crisis left an embarrassing legacy of political trials, starting with the indictment at Agram – apparently as part of the government's attempts to orchestrate anti-Serbian opinion during the Bosnian crisis – of some Croatian deputies on a charge of high treason. The verdict of guilty had to be reversed when the charges were found to have been based on forgeries. Worse still, the historian, Friedjung, who at the height of the Serbian crisis had written an article accusing some south Slav politicians of treasonable ties with Belgrade, was sued for libel; and the documents on which the article had been based, which had been supplied by the Ballhausplatz itself, also appeared to be forgeries. Aehrenthal's reputation recovered somewhat at the end of 1910, with the unmasking of the culprit, one Vasić, who had supplied the documents to the unwitting foreign

[11] F.O. 371/829, Howard to Grey, No. 83, 18 November 1910.
[12] F.O. 371/599, Cartwright to Grey, No. 20, 6 February 1909.

ministry. But the whole affair – although contemporary expressions of indignation came oddly from the France of Dreyfus, the Russia of Beyliss, the Germany of Harden and Eulenburg, and even, perhaps, the England of Parnell – had served to bring discredit on the government, particularly in south Slav circles.

Nor had the south Slav problem been solved in its external aspect. Under pressure of the annexation crisis Serbia had even patched up the dynastic quarrel with Montenegro; and the two states together now proceeded to strengthen their military and political links with Russia. Serbia's formal submission and her promise to live on good neighbourly terms with Austria-Hungary proved an empty gesture. Anti-Austrian propaganda continued to flood into the south Slav territories of the Monarchy from the neighbouring kingdom, the *Narodna Odbrana* pursued its activities unabated, and more extreme organizations continued their campaign of terrorism on Austro-Hungarian soil. From here the road led straight to Sarajevo. Not that the Austro-Hungarian government could have done much to control the sporadic activities of terrorist organizations beyond the frontier. Indeed, such conciliatory gestures as Vienna made towards the south Slav population – and they were few enough – only served to increase the determination of nationalist hotheads in Serbia to wrest the south Slav provinces from the Monarchy, by violent means if necessary, before they could become reconciled to Habsburg rule. (Franz Ferdinand's notorious sympathies for south Slavs oppressed by the Magyar yoke were to constitute, in the eyes of Serbian nationalists, a convincing argument for eliminating him.) But apart from this, even the ordinary peasant population of Serbia was now hopelessly embittered against the Monarchy – all the more so as the customs war dragged on into its fourth year. Not that there was any desire – at least in Budapest – to end it. It was in vain that Aehrenthal pleaded for a far-sighted policy of economic conciliation: the old Magyar fears of Serbian agrarian competition were too strong. By the time an Austro-Serbian commercial treaty could be concluded in July 1910 Serbia had freed herself from her economic dependence on the Monarchy. Meanwhile, the Austrians had lost important armaments contracts to Schneider-Creusot, and most of their remaining Serbian trade to their German allies.

The Monarchy could ill afford such setbacks. One direct consequence of the annexation, the Turkish boycott, had already had disastrous effects which were to prove permanent. Whereas to a contemporary British observer of Austria-Hungary's Turkish trade, 'it seemed in the spring of 1908 as if it only remained for Austria-Hungary to enter her kingdom',[13] the Monarchy now found itself ousted from many of its best markets – to the advantage, as usual, of the German ally; and the Austrian textile industry consequently embarked on a period of stagnation. In the Balkan states, too, German competition grew daily more severe, particularly in Bulgaria, where Germany now replaced Britain as the Monarchy's chief rival. And even the fact that the Monarchy managed to retain its lead at Sofia down to 1914 was not worth all that much politically: for the time being, at least, Bulgaria remained set on a Russian course. Elsewhere in the Balkans, politics and trade were more closely linked: the fact that the commercial treaty which was now at last concluded with Roumania pleased Budapest rather than Bucharest, and that Roumania was granted virtually no reduction at all in the duties on grain, augured ill for the alliance. (This was a serious matter at a time when the intensifying Magyar-Roumanian struggle in Transylvania was subjecting the alliance to strain; and when Aehrenthal, set on a pacific policy of maintaining the *status quo*, would offer Roumania no help or encouragement against the alleged expansionist designs of Bulgaria.) True, the world depression of 1910 affected Austria-Hungary – a state still producing largely for the home market, after all – less severely than the more advanced industrial states of the West. But by the same token, she stood to gain less from any general improvement in world trade. The prospects were not bright. The year 1907 saw the last budget surplus in the history of the Monarchy; and 1909, with the cost of military preparations incurred in the crisis added to such civil burdens as the re-nationalization of the railways, saw a deficit of 42m. Kronen. By 1910 the government was actually planning for a deficit, and resorted to loans; but the two that were raised were emitted at 90, the lowest rate since 1892. In this situation, there could be little scope for costly adventures.

Not that the diplomatic position of the Monarchy was in any case such as to tempt Aehrenthal in that direction. The Bosnian

[13] G. Drage, p. 210.

crisis had produced a hardening of fronts. True, the Dual Alliance had proved its value, perhaps for the first time, as a diplomatic instrument; and its triumph was duly celebrated by a very successful visit of William II to Vienna in May. For Aehrenthal, however, with his almost obsessive anxiety to preserve the independence of the Monarchy, this was a mixed blessing. The appointment of the strong-minded Kiderlen as German foreign minister in June 1910 brought with it a serious prospect that the Dual Alliance would be directed from Berlin, and not from Vienna. And William II's patronizing boasting about 'shining armour' during his visit to Vienna in September 1910 was as embarrassing to Aehrenthal as his 'brilliant second' telegram had been to Goluchowski – and perhaps intentionally so. All the same, there was no denying the fact that the deterioration of Austria-Hungary's relations with Russia, Britain, and Italy had made her more dependent on Berlin – at least if she ever wished to embark on a policy of action. In these circumstances, only a policy of self-sufficient inaction could offer the Monarchy a fair measure of independence.

It remained to be seen whether even this would be feasible in the suspicious and nervously watchful Europe that emerged from the Bosnian crisis. The Triple *Entente* Powers had reached the conclusion that only absolute diplomatic solidarity backed up by massive armaments could restrain the ambitions of the Central Powers. The naval arms race began to dominate Anglo-German relations; and as regards Austria-Hungary, the immediate concern of the *Entente* Powers was now to counter her supposed further ambitions by means of a defensive bloc of Balkan states, and particularly to encourage Serbia to resist any siren-songs from Vienna. Admittedly, the Triple *Entente* did not remain united on this programme for long; and even Anglo-German rivalry abated after 1912. But one factor henceforth remained a constant in European diplomacy until the outbreak of war in 1914: Austro-Russian hostility. The myth that the annexation of Bosnia was merely a harbinger of the legendary march on Salonica – or at least that, given a chance, the Monarchy would lose no opportunity to extend its influence, or even its frontiers – now acquired in St Petersburg the force of an immutable political law. And although Russia's plan to forestall the danger by means of a league of Balkan states was essentially defensive, it became in turn, in so far as its realization would inevitably imply the absorption of the whole area into a Russian sphere of influence, the chief nightmare of Vienna. For the Austrians, at least, the international problem had been simplified. No longer did they have to weigh the advantages of alternative alignments, German, British, or Russian, as in the days of the Three Emperors' Alliance or the Austro-Russian *Entente*. They might still, by judicious diplomacy, attempt to weaken the hold of Russia over Britain and France; but only their alliances offered any serious hope of salvation. The question was, how much support, or at least, freedom of action, would these alliances allow the Monarchy in defending its interests against Russia?

The first major task confronting Aehrenthal after the Bosnian crisis was to dispel the general suspicion with which Austria-Hungary was regarded in almost every European capital except Berlin: to convince the Powers that the annexation of Bosnia had not been the first step in the march to Salonica, but the final rounding off of the Monarchy's southern frontiers; and that Vienna was now genuinely desirous of maintaining the *status quo*.

With Turkey, the Power most directly affected, he had a fair measure of success. The Young Turks, whose relations with Britain and Russia were deteriorating sharply as a result of Turkish interference in Persia and Egypt and Anglo-Russian criticism of the militarism and the brutal Ottomanization policies emanating from Constantinople, were in any case anxious to lean on Vienna. Indeed, on several occasions in 1909 and 1910 they even sought an alliance with Austria-Hungary. But Aehrenthal would not consider an alliance with a Power so unstable as Turkey. Nor, unlike that loud and ardent supporter of the Young Turk regime, William II, would he involve himself in the political maelstrom at Constantinople. Not that he had any particular grievances against the Young Turks: he only hoped that they might succeed in giving the Ottoman Empire a measure of political stability. Above all, he was anxious to avoid a revival of international intervention in Macedonia, such as he suspected Britain and Russia of planning. This, he told Kiderlen, in August 1910, he would prevent simply by refusing to co-operate. And if he had no difficulty in convincing Constantinople of his goodwill and sincere devotion to the *status quo*, his attitude towards the three Turkish 'questions' that arose in 1909 and 1910 – Crete,

Albania, and Macedonia – went a good way towards convincing at least some of the other Powers.

Since 1898 Crete had enjoyed a fair measure of autonomy under the four protecting Powers, whose garrisons in the island upheld the sultan's sovereign rights against an increasingly obstreperous local movement for union with Greece. Although the Central Powers had withdrawn their forces in 1898, Goluchowski had continued to show interest in Cretan affairs. In February 1905 he reminded the protecting Powers that they must not raise the Cretan customs duties without consulting Austria-Hungary, Crete's chief trading partner. Indeed, they must consult Vienna about all fundamental issues in Crete; for once the garrisons were withdrawn (as was due to happen in 1909) all six Powers would once more be equally responsible for Crete. But he evinced no desire to share the Cretan burden for the time being. And no wonder, for the lot of the protecting Powers, chained to the island by their garrisons, was indeed an unenviable one: if they made concessions to the union movement, they drew upon themselves the complaints of Constantinople; whereas resistance brought disorders in Crete and even, in 1905, the task of governing the island by martial law.

Aehrenthal, for his part, lost no time in renouncing even the cautious interest taken in the question by Goluchowski. While professing to stand by his predecessor's pronouncements, he simply refused in practice to recognize any issue as coming within their purview. In May 1908 he told the complaining Turks that the projected withdrawal of the garrisons did not concern Austria-Hungary. And after the Bosnian crisis (when the Greek Cretans had seized the chance to proclaim the union with Greece, and had only been thwarted by Britain's sympathy for Turkey and for the Moslems of Crete) he became even more strictly abstentionist. For the Turks had become more sensitive than ever on the issue. Not that this in itself worried him; as he observed, the Monarchy had nothing to lose if the Cretan question estranged Turkey from the protecting Powers. Yet the protecting Powers were, by the same token, anxious to burden Austria-Hungary with a share of the odium. When the garrisons were withdrawn in July 1909 and the Greek Cretans hoisted a Greek flag, provoking the Turks to take the matter up with Greece herself, and to complain about the revival of Greek propagandist activity in Macedonia,

Grey tried to argue that the matter was one for all six Powers to settle. But Aehrenthal retorted that the dispute was about Crete, which was a matter for the four protecting Powers, and that this was certainly no time to re-open the Macedonian question. In December, Izvolsky tried his hand, suggesting that all six Powers finally settle the status of Crete; but Aehrenthal simply abandoned Goluchowski's theoretical position altogether, declaring that even such a fundamental issue was no concern of Austria-Hungary. Nor would he move in the very serious crisis of the summer of 1910, when an attempt by the Greek Cretans to impose an oath of loyalty to the King of the Hellenes on Moslem deputies in the Cretan assembly was used by Turkey as a pretext to launch a boycott aiming ultimately at the annihilation of Greek trading interests throughout the Ottoman Empire. He merely reminded the protecting Powers that nobody had helped Austria-Hungary when she was faced with a Turkish boycott in 1908, and tendered the unpalatable advice to reoccupy the island. After this, the protecting Powers did not bother him again about Crete. They were wistfully envious of his 'comfortable inertia';[14] but at least he did not seem to be actively fishing in troubled waters.

Comfortable inertia was not an attitude that could be assumed towards developments in northern Albania at this time. There the centralizing and Ottomanizing policies of the Young Turk regime had by the spring of 1910 produced a major rebellion among the Catholic Mirdites tribesmen; and Constantinople's clumsy efforts to suppress it in a welter of blood confronted the Austrians with a major dilemma. On the one hand, observance of the principle of non-intervention had borne fruit – Austro-Turkish relations were better than they had been for years. On the other, the Catholic press of Vienna, notably the *Reichspost* (behind which stood Franz Ferdinand and a powerful circle of clericals and aristocrats), was loud in its denunciations of Turkish 'atrocities' and in its demands that Aehrenthal take action in the name of the three-hundred-year-old *Kultusprotektorat*. There were other important considerations pointing in this direction: if Austria-Hungary did nothing, the Albanians might turn in their despair to Rome; and in any case, indiscriminate massacres of Albanians could only leave the Serbian inhabitants of the area to inherit the land. Besides, Aehrenthal suspected that the four protecting Powers of

14 F.O. 371/654, Russell to Grey, No. 200, 16 December 1909.

Crete were only encouraging Turkey in her bloody deeds to divert her attention from the affairs of Greece and Crete. In June, therefore, he gave some stern advice to Constantinople: Turkey would do well to preserve the Albanian race, which might one day prove an invaluable source of help against Greeks and Slavs. For Austria-Hungary had finally withdrawn from the Sanjak and would be neither willing nor able to come to Turkey's assistance. Whether as a result of this advice or not, the Turks suddenly gave way and pacified the rebels with a commission of enquiry.

Aehrenthal was well pleased. All that needed to be done, he told Kiderlen in August, was to stand by Turkey and resist the attempts of Britain and Russia to revive the policy of intervention. In the same month, he had a very cordial interview with the new grand vizier, Hakki Pasha, at Marienbad. All in all, he was content to regard the Young Turkish regime, for all its faults, as a useful 'lid on the pot that keeps the stuff inside from boiling over'.[15] Not that the pot was anywhere near boiling in the autumn of 1910. Indeed, the Balkans were unusually calm. And this was due in no small measure to the efforts of Aehrenthal, who, ever since the Bosnian crisis had carefully abstained from anything that might excite the Balkan states either against Turkey or against each other. In the summer of 1909 he had sternly reminded the Serbs, when they sounded him about the future of the Sanjak, that this was Turkish property and could not form the subject of any discussion. And early in 1910 he poured cold water on suggestions from Bucharest that the Monarchy might help Roumania to secure compensation from Bulgaria in the event of a Balkan conflagration, observing that the Monarchy's policy was one of strict non-intervention.

Certainly, there was no urgent reason for intervention. The threat of a Russian-organized Balkan league was showing no signs of materializing. Serbia and Bulgaria seemed quite unable to agree on an equitable partition of Macedonia; the old dynastic quarrel between Serbia and Montenegro revived after plotters from Belgrade tried to assassinate Nikita in the spring of 1910; and although Sazonov, who in the autumn replaced the rancorous Izvolsky at St Petersburg was as keen as his predecessor to organize a league to frustrate 'the ambitious designs of Austria-Hungary' – and even warned the Greeks that unless they looked to

[15] Grey MSS., Vol. 2, Cartwright to Grey, 28 September 1910.

their defences they would see the Austrians at Salonica – he was equally unsuccessful. Negotiations between Greece and Bulgaria soon foundered on the Macedonian rock. Above all, the Austrians could take cheer from the fact that Russia was no longer finding the Western Powers so ready to support her efforts as they had been during and immediately after the Bosnian crisis. In this respect at least, Aehrenthal's policy of non-intervention and the *status quo* was paying good dividends.

The Italians, for example, had for some months after the end of the Bosnian crisis continued extremely anxious about the possibility of further surprises from Vienna. They encouraged Russia in her efforts to found a Balkan League, and in October 1909 gave a very cordial welcome at Racconigi to Izvolsky and the tsar, who had travelled from Odessa by an extraordinarily circuitous route through North Germany, demonstratively avoiding setting foot on Austro-Hungarian territory. Izvolsky and Tittoni agreed to co-operate to maintain the *status quo*, and to make no Balkan agreements with a third party (i.e. Austria-Hungary) without informing each other: there were to be no more Buchlaus. Indeed, Tittoni felt that Austria-Hungary could not be too carefully watched, and would have liked to secure similar pledges from all the other Powers. But the British felt that this would be too insulting to the Monarchy, and he had to desist. In fact, the Racconigi agreement gave no offence at Vienna. After all, it only endorsed principles which Aehrenthal himself professed; and he was in any case anxious to do something to improve Austro-Italian relations. In December 1909 a similar Austro-Italian agreement endorsed the *status quo*, and further confirmed the Monarchy's retreat from the Sanjak by bringing an eventual re-occupation of the territory within the purview of Article VII of the Triple Alliance (Document 34). Much of the tension now went out of relations between Vienna and Rome; and within a year Aehrenthal was speaking of them in the Delegations in glowing terms.

The Monarchy's relations with Britain also made a gradual but almost complete recovery. True, in the summer of 1909 there was still enough mutual mistrust to prevent a visit by Edward VII to Franz Joseph; and Edward VII refused to congratulate Aehrenthal when Franz Joseph recognized his services with the title of Count, in August. But as time went on, the British began to weary of Izvolsky's obsessive concern about alleged Austrian plots in the Balkans. When he came with the tsar to Cowes in August, he 'could harp on little else';[16] and the tsar's route to Racconigi was noted in London as yet another 'rather mean example' of how Izvolsky was 'always trying to score off Aehrenthal'.[17] Thanks to Cartwright's able dispatches, the British gradually reached the conclusion that Aehrenthal was in fact sincerely anxious both to maintain the *status quo* and to resist dictation from Berlin. After the autumn of 1909 they began to look askance at Izvolsky's Balkan league projects: these, by provoking Aehrenthal unnecessarily, seemed more likely to cause than to prevent trouble in the Balkans. By the spring of 1910 London and Vienna were agreed that normal relations had been restored. Another royal visit was agreed in principle, and only prevented by the death of Edward VII in May.

Only with Russia was there no improvement. The intense personal animosity prevailing between Izvolsky and Aehrenthal (the two foreign ministers now referred to each other in such terms as *'ce sale juif'* and *'ce crapaud'*) was hardly conducive to cordial relations between the two governments. And the two men added fuel to the flames in the autumn by reviving the whole Buchlau controversy in an acrimonious exchange of inspired articles in the *Fortnightly Review*. The real obstacle to a reconciliation was, however, Izvolsky's ineradicable conviction that Aehrenthal could never again be trusted, and Aehrenthal's determination not to take any first step that might be interpreted as contrition or truckling to St Petersburg.

By the end of 1909 the two governments were beginning to see the advantages of restoring something like normal relations. Aehrenthal was temporarily worried about Turkey, where the new grand vizier, Hakki Pasha, was as yet an unknown quantity; and the Russians were anxious about the activities of the United States and Japan in the Far East. But when negotiations started, on the basis of the conservative principles of 1897, the two governments were soon at cross purposes. Whereas Izvolsky was seeking to bind Aehrenthal over to keep the peace, by an elaborate document which could then be presented to the other Powers for safe keeping, Aehrenthal insisted that it was simply a matter of

[16] Cartwright MSS., Hardinge to Cartwright, 9 August 1909.
[17] Ibid., 11 January 1910.

restoring normal relations, and that this was the concern of no other Power, not even of Germany. (This attitude was resented by the Germans, ever suspicious of attempts to regulate Austro-Russian relations without Germany's brokerage; and it was at this time that the German embassy at Vienna fired the first shots in what was to become a sustained campaign against Aehrenthal in the Viennese press.) By March normal relations had been restored with St Petersburg; but Izvolsky's proceeding to circulate copies of the recent Austro-Russian exchanges to the other Powers without Aehrenthal's permission showed that what passed for normality in Austro-Russian relations still left much to be desired.

Not that the Monarchy's relations even with the Western Powers were entirely unclouded. Confronted with the steady growth of the Italian navy, the Austro-Hungarian government in the summer of 1909 began to consider building four dreadnoughts to restore the balance in the Adriatic. This was seen in turn by the British as a concealed addition to the German fleet: Vienna's payment to Berlin for services rendered in the Bosnian crisis – a far-fetched interpretation which, as Aehrenthal bitterly remarked to the British ambassador, betrayed an unbalanced outlook and could only make him laugh. In any case, the dreadnoughts could not be built for some time. The Monarchy was desperately short of money, and the Delegations did not meet to vote any until the autumn of 1910. Franz Ferdinand, an ardent supporter of naval expansion, managed to raise a certain amount, but in the meantime, all that could be done was to arrange for two dreadnoughts to be built as a speculative venture by the *Stabilmento Tecnico* of Trieste on the chance that the government would eventually be able to buy them. This was by no means certain. Aehrenthal and Admiral Montecuccoli were confronted in the council of ministers by Austrian and Hungarian prime ministers who talked of the Monarchy's being actually bankrupt. They were also faced with absurdities such as the Hungarian demand that half the ships be built in Hungary, although there were as yet no suitable dockyards in that kingdom. The basic difficulty was financial. It was not only the old problem that the Monarchy was in any case ill equipped to compete in an arms race with the more advanced Western Powers; she now found her difficulties augmented by Great Power alignments beyond her control. In the summer of 1910 the Hungarian government failed to secure a loan at Paris, and in London the foreign office intervened to prevent its conclusion on the grounds that it might be spent on armaments. In the end, recourse was reluctantly had to the German Rothschilds, forging yet another link, as the British consul-general at Budapest sadly observed, 'in the chain which binds the Dual Monarchy *nolens volens* to Germany'.[18]

Aehrenthal was to some extent making a virtue out of necessity, therefore, when in the winter of 1910–11 he began to plead in the council of ministers for a slower pace with regard to armaments. But this also made good political sense: greater activity on the part of Austria-Hungary could only spur on her opponents to yet greater efforts. And Aehrenthal was still above all anxious to improve relations with Italy. Thus, in a conference in March 1911 he lent his assistance to the Austrian and Hungarian prime ministers in frustrating Conrad's demands for more armaments. As he saw it, if Austria-Hungary could establish tolerable relations with her open or potential opponents, she could be more independent of Germany. This was always a major theme in Aehrenthal's policy, especially when, as after 1910, his relations with Berlin deteriorated again. In Berlin, his independent attitude was greatly resented – as was in Vienna William II's visit of September 1910 with its flamboyant and highly inopportune emphasis on Austro-German solidarity in the 'shining armour' speech. When William II proceeded to receive the tsar and Sazonov at Potsdam in November, and the German chancellor, Bethmann-Hollweg, assured the Russians that Germany would not support any aggressive designs of Austria-Hungary in the Balkans, Franz Joseph was deeply hurt. Aehrenthal was less upset: he had no aggressive designs anyway; and the Potsdam meeting, portending a Russo-German agreement about Persia and the Baghdad railway, seemed far more likely to cause a rift in the Anglo-Russian *entente* than in the Dual Alliance. Besides, any confirmation of the fact that the Monarchy would have to stand on its own feet was quite welcome to him. After all, if Austria-Hungary received little help from her friends and allies, she would be under equally little obligation to trim her sails to suit them, and could defend her own interests as she saw fit. In the Albanian and Moroccan crises of the summer of 1911, Austria-Hungary pursued a policy of a 'free hand'.

[18] F.O. 371/825, Howard to Grey, No. 67, 17 October 1910.

By the spring of 1911 Aehrenthal was fast losing faith in the Young Turks. They had persisted in their brutal Ottomanization policies in Albania, despite his advice; and they were doing nothing to facilitate the repatriation of a large body of Albanian refugees who had been imposing a heavy burden on the impecunious Montenegrin government ever since the revolt of 1910. By March 1911 some 5,000 Albanian tribesmen were again in revolt; and the refugee issue was threatening to develop into a Turco-Montenegrin war. The same religious and political considerations now prompted Aehrenthal to help the Albanians as in 1910; and much the same political considerations made him anxious to protect Montenegro, both as a potential counter to an over-ambitious Serbia, and as a buffer state between the Monarchy and the deepening chaos of Turkey-in-Europe.

For two months Vienna did nothing. Aehrenthal, his strength sapped by advancing leukaemia, had retired in March to seek recuperation at Abbazia, leaving the Ballhausplatz in the care of Pallavicini, a single-minded Turcophile. But after his return to Vienna on 23 May he lost no time in speaking sternly to the Turkish ambassador; and on 8 June the semi-official *Fremdenblatt* carried a summons to the Young Turks to put their house in order. Constantinople only expressed its pained surprise, and continued in its repressive policies. At this Aehrenthal began to lose patience. He did not conceal his 'great annoyance'[19] at the unhelpful attitude of Germany, who on 25 June proclaimed her wholehearted support for Turkey. True, he was not much enamoured of Grey's suggestion that Austria-Hungary, Russia, and Italy, as the three most interested Powers, pacify the rebels by guaranteeing the execution of Turkey's vague promises of reform: this sounded all too ominously like a return to the international intervention of unhappy memory. But in the end he embarked on some desultory discussions with Rome and St Petersburg with a view to mediating between Turkey and Montenegro. That he found the Russians so anxious to keep in touch was no sign of an impending *rapprochement*: they were afraid that the Austrians, if left to themselves, might assume the role of sole protectors of Montenegro, or even exploit the crisis to invade and annex Albania. Before anything came of these discussions, however, the Turks suddenly accepted all the rebels' demands (1

---

[19] F.O. 120/883, Cartwright to Grey, Tel. 49, 28 May 1911.

August) and the crisis ended at once. This was fortunate for Aehrenthal, whom the Turco-Albanian quarrel had presented with an
insoluble dilemma. His policy of steering a middle course and
attempting to reconcile the two sides perhaps accorded best with
any rational assessment of the Monarchy's interests; but the
application of a rational policy to the ferocious and irrational
Turco-Albanian dispute had served only to arouse the resentment
and suspicion of the Turks without yet satisfying the Albanians.

In so far as Germany's clumsy meddling in Balkan affairs infuriated the Austrians, the Moroccan crisis of 1911, which served
as a timely distraction for Berlin, was welcome to Vienna. In the
early stages it was particularly fortunate for the French that the
Ballhausplatz was in the care of Pallavicini, who was simply concerned to tide things over without complications until Aehrenthal
returned, and who never tired of expressing his 'total ignorance'
of Moroccan affairs.[20] He raised no objections to the French
occupation of Fez in April, and allowed Paris considerable latitude
in interpreting the Act of Algeciras. But it soon became apparent
that the Monarchy had an axe to grind, even if only a small one:
the Hungarian government was again seeking to place a loan in
Paris. It was perhaps in this connexion that on 15 May the *Sonn-
und Montagszeitung* carried an article – allegedly inspired by Aehrenthal from Abbazia – warning Germany not to make trouble in
Morocco. The German ambassador made a fearful scene; but he
could not persuade the Austrians to give Germany anything like
positive support. Indeed, Aehrenthal, on his return stoutly defended the Hungarian prime minister's announcement to parliament that the Moroccan question lay outside the scope of the
Triple Alliance. For why should he support Germany? – after all,
she had given him no advance warning whatever of the *Panther*'s
expedition to Agadir; and he felt that her troubles were really of
her own making: it was Germany's flirting with Russia at Potsdam that had provoked France to assert herself in Morocco. He
was frankly at a loss to understand Germany's Moroccan policy,
which seemed to him 'just Krupp and Mannesmann'.[21] As for
the Monarchy: 'What more can I do? We can pursue no
Weltpolitik.'[22] Austria-Hungary would loyally stand guard for

[20] F.O. 120/883, Cartwright to Grey, No. 69, 27 April 1911.
[21] F. Fellner (ed.), *Das politische Tagebuch Joseph Redlichs*, 20 July 1911.
[22] Ibid., 7 August 1911.

Germany in the Near East; but she could not follow her to Agadir.[23]

Nevertheless, the charge made in Pan-German circles that in the second Moroccan crisis Aehrenthal simply 'remained as dumb as a fish'[24] is perhaps unfair. In fact, as the crisis dragged on into August, and Aehrenthal began to fear – as in the Bosnian crisis – that Britain was seeking to bring about a general war to settle accounts with Germany, he tried to put in a word for the Germans at Paris; and in November he urged the British to help Spain in her negotiations with France for the sake of monarchical interests. (This was the last appearance of Kálnoky's doctrine – somewhat threadbare since the fiasco of the Spanish-American war and the fall of the Portuguese monarchy in 1910 – of supporting the Iberian monarchies.) But neither in London nor in Paris was his voice much heeded. Not that this was his fault: the Monarchy was only remotely concerned in the affair; and in Paris was in the position of a beggar. The fate of the Hungarian loan was still in the balance. It was becoming increasingly unlikely that any member of the Triple Alliance would succeed in securing loans from France, where, in the wake of the Moroccan crisis a chauvinist wave was welling up that was to last until 1914. Still, Aehrenthal made an effort, and readily accepted the Franco-German Moroccan agreement in November. But the cumbersome Austrian and Hungarian governments took such a long time about giving their approval that a nationalist deputy in the French chamber denounced the Monarchy for trying to extract the loan by blackmail. For the French press and public opinion this was the last straw. No more was heard of the loan.

The resurgence of nationalism in France during the second Moroccan crisis was only one symptom of a general worsening of the international situation after 1911. Indeed, in a sense, the Moroccan crisis itself was only the first link in a chain of crises which was to sweep through Turkish North Africa into European Turkey and the Balkan states to engulf, after an uneasy nine months' truce, the Dual Monarchy and the other Great Powers. Diplomacy seemed to be helpless in the face of a spreading fashion for violent solutions to international problems – problems which in themselves were more than usually serious, complicated, and inter-connected. By January 1912 the British permanent

[23] Ibid.   [24] H. Kanner, p. 75.

under-secretary, Sir Arthur Nicolson, had 'never seen the world in such a disturbed condition'.[25] In this situation, those very diplomatic ties and alignments that were supposed to provide security only made it all the more difficult for the Great Powers to cope with the situation in a bold and imaginative way. Prisoners of past commitments and future fears, the Powers lurched from one desperate shift to another, barely escaping from one dilemma before the next presented itself.

Even before France had finally established her protectorate over Morocco, it was clear that Italy would not be long in seizing her compensatory pound of flesh in Libya. Yet, as Italo-Turkish relations inexorably deteriorated in the summer of 1911, no Great Power dared to intervene. After all, they had all recognized Italy's ultimate claims to the province. Aehrenthal was certainly put out by Italy's choosing to enter into her Turkish inheritance at this moment and by violent means: a war might bring about the total collapse of the Ottoman Empire. Yet Italy was an ally after all; and she had just been astute enough to hint at a possible early renewal of the Triple Alliance. This counted for much with one so anxious to improve Austro-Italian relations as Aehrenthal. Although hardly convinced by Italy's sudden discovery that Italian nationals in Libya were the objects of appalling persecution, he coldly advised the Turks, when they appealed to him on 28 September, to put their North African house in order.

When, on the following day, Italy declared war on Turkey and invaded Libya, Aehrenthal at once declared Austria-Hungary's neutrality. He was concerned not so much to stop the war as to confine it to North Africa, and above all to prevent its spreading to the Balkans. True, the Balkan states obliged with solemn promises of good behaviour; but he still thought it important to warn Italy against undertaking any operations in the Adriatic. This he told Rome, would entitle the Monarchy to compensation under the terms of Article VII of the Triple Alliance (an interpretation which was to cause the Monarchy some embarrassment when it came to undertake military operations of its own in the Balkans in 1914–15). As regards mediation to stop the war, the Great Powers were all concerned primarily, and usually solely, not with the merits or feasibility of a particular mediation proposal, but with its possible effects on their relations with each other and

[25] F.O. 800/185, Lowther MSS., Nicolson to Lowther, 15 January 1912.

with the belligerents – who were, after all, the two most delicately balanced members of the European Concert. Aehrenthal had originally inclined to the idea of joint mediation by all the Powers; but when it seemed for a brief spell that mediation might be successful, he agreed with Berlin that the Central Powers might do well to act alone and secure all the credit for themselves. He soon abandoned this idea. In the first place, he heard that the Germans were putting the plan to Rome as their own idea, and casting Austria-Hungary in the role of humble retainer; in the second, Italy's formal announcement of the outright annexation of Libya (5 November), before she had even conquered the country, convinced him that the mediator's task at Constantinople would be both thankless and futile. He consequently reverted to the idea of a general mediation, whereby all the Powers might share the odium or humiliation; and finding Grey in agreement, he was pleased to tell himself that he had 'restored the Concert of Europe as a makeshift' (*notdürftig*).[26] Such manoeuvrings, on the part of all the Powers, were typical of the futile diplomacy of the Tripoli War.

Far from futile, by contrast, were Aehrenthal's efforts to improve Austro-Italian relations. November saw his final triumph over Conrad von Hoetzendorf, who since the start of the Tripoli War had been declaiming against his policy and demanding that the Monarchy seize the opportunity of Italy's involvement in North Africa to deal her such a blow as would eliminate her as a potential opponent once and for all. Aehrenthal had the support of the emperor, who made his views clear to Conrad in a stormy interview on 15 November: 'These incessant attacks on Aehrenthal, these pinpricks, I forbid them . . . The ever-recurring reproaches regarding Italy and the Balkans are directed at Me. Policy – it is I who make it! . . . My policy is a policy of peace . . . It is possible, even probable, that such a war may come about; but it will not be waged until Italy attacks us.'[27] Conrad prepared himself to argue back in another interview on 30 November; but Franz Joseph forestalled him with the news of his dismissal from the post of chief of staff. It was in line with this that Aehrenthal emphasized to a conference of ministers on 6 December[28] that,

[26] Redlich, *Tagebuch*, ed. F. Fellner, 19 November 1911.
[27] Conrad v. Hoetzendorf, Vol. 2, p. 282.
[28] P.A. XL/310, Ministerratsprotokoll, 6 December 1911.

particularly in view of the prevailing Anglo-German tension, which he felt would probably lead within two or three years to the 'now virtually inevitable (*kaum noch vermeidbaren*) European war',[29] the Monarchy must be careful to cultivate its relations with Italy. Hence there must be no big armaments programme which would give offence at Rome. The parsimonious governments of Austria and Hungary were of course delighted; but the government at Rome was not unappreciative either. All in all, the Tripoli War was tending to bring Italy back into the bosom of the Alliance. For she was finding her allies on the whole more congenial, or at least less embarrassing, company than her late friends in the Triple *Entente*: France, who was heavily committed financially to the Ottoman Empire; Britain, who was allegedly permitting the transport of Turkish troops through Egypt to Libya, and who ungraciously ordered Italy to give up one of her few conquests (the fortress of Sollum on the Egyptian-Libyan frontier); and, worst of all, Russia, who by the autumn of 1911 seemed about to offer Turkey an alliance.

Indeed, by October 1911 the Russian ambassador at Constantinople, Charykov, was attempting to cajole and bully the Turks into accepting an arrangement whereby Russia would promise to defend the Dardanelles against an Italian attack, while Turkey would not only join a Balkan league, but grant Russia sole rights of passage through the Straits. This so-called Charykov Kite was anathema to Vienna. Aehrenthal decided that Russia must be aiming at nothing less than a protectorate over the whole of Turkey; and if she were ever in a position to transfer her entire naval forces to the Black Sea, she would dominate the entire Balkan peninsula as well. Although – like the British in 1908 – he was prepared to see the Straits open to all the Powers on an equal basis, he insisted (and this was a measure of the fundamental change that had come over Austro-Russian relations since 1908) that if the Black Sea were to become a Russian *mare clausum*, the Mediterranean interests of the Monarchy would be endangered. He decided, therefore, that as the Buchlau agreement could no longer be considered valid – in view of the attitude adopted by St Petersburg towards the annexation of Bosnia – he would have to think about Russia's proposals. Meanwhile, he advised the Turks to beware of them.

[29] Redlich, *Tagebuch*, ed. F. Fellner, 5 December 1911.

He found little support elsewhere. The supineness of the Germans, who blandly asserted that the task of opposing Russia could well be left to the British, drive him into a fury. Ever since Potsdam, he told himself bitterly, the Germans had done nothing but truckle to Russia – and all because of their ridiculous obsession about Britain. To the British he now himself appealed in desperation on 7 December (just two days before Sazonov's public disavowal of Charykov put an end to the whole affair) and asked them to restrain Russia from pursuing the matter. But the British did not respond. Like Goluchowski in 1903 and 1904, they rated an *entente* with Russia more highly than a few strategic advantages in the eastern Mediterranean. Not that they liked Charykov's scheme, nor in the least resented Aehrenthal's appeal. On the contrary, they were much impressed by Vienna's steady devotion to the *status quo* over the last few years. In January 1912 they even made a wistful suggestion that an Austro-Russian *entente* would be highly conducive to Balkan peace. But the French sharply reminded them of their *entente* commitments, adding the warning – always effective in London – that an Austro-Russian *entente* would herald the return of the dreaded Three Emperors' Alliance.

Of this, there was no sign. The Russians remained as suspicious as ever of Austria-Hungary, and as untiring as ever in their efforts to construct a Balkan league – this time, in view of the failure of the Charykov Kite, without Turkey. And since the late summer of 1911, when Serbia, Bulgaria, and Greece, encouraged by Turkey's embarrassments, had begun to draw together Russia's hopes appeared brighter. Not that this worried Aehrenthal. Until the day of his death he always regarded a Balkan league as an idle chimera (and if events proved him right in the long run, he nevertheless disastrously misjudged the chances of a short-term combination). Hence, he was never worried about the possibility that his own conservative and pacific policy might be playing into the hands of a Russia who seemed to have more to offer. He was not interested in contriving counter-alliances against what he believed to be a shadow. In January 1912 he again turned a deaf ear to Turkey who, convinced by the reactions of the Powers to the Charykov Kite that Austria-Hungary was her only friend, offered a military convention as the basis for an Austro-Turco-Roumanian league. (Turkey was in any case too unstable a Power to be underwritten with an alliance.) At the same time, Aehrenthal's anxiety to do nothing to weaken Turkey, and the calming advice he gave to the visiting King Ferdinand in December, only disappointed the Bulgarians and made them more ready to listen to Russian and Serbian advice. Lastly, he made a serious miscalculation in refusing to deny certain rumours that circulated among the Balkan states from time to time, to the effect that the Monarchy was only waiting to exploit any disturbances that might occur in the Balkans as a pretext to embark on the march to Salonica. He hoped by maintaining a sphinx-like attitude to frighten the Balkan states into keeping the peace. But the effect in the Balkan states was not terrified paralysis, but feverish activity to create a defensive bloc against the evil day. When Aehrenthal died, on 17 February 1912, the Balkan league was in fact well on the way to formation.

This ominous development seemed to set the seal on the deterioration of the international position of the Monarchy since 1906. Not that the picture was completely black. The clearing up of the ambiguous status of Bosnia and the Herzegovina – a problem that had worried successive foreign ministers since at least 1882 – was undoubtedly a notable achievement. And the deterioration of the Monarchy's relations with Russia and the Western Powers was by no means solely Aehrenthal's fault. Certainly, Russian and Serbian hatred had been fired to white heat by the annexation; but, as the reactions of Russia and Serbia to Aehrenthal's conservative and pacific policy after 1909 amply demonstrated, this hatred was one which fed itself, and burned ever fiercer by a process of nationalist internal combustion. Although the closer links between the Western Powers and Russia had been to a great extent forged in the heat of the annexation crisis, and now ensured that, even if France and Britain no longer bore a grudge, the Monarchy definitely could not count on their active co-operation in the Near East, it must be admitted that Britain and France had good reasons of their own for preferring Russia to Austria-Hungary. And after all, the deterioration in relations with Russia had been to some extent offset by an undoubted improvement in relations with Italy. That was Aehrenthal's great achievement: the Russo-Italian pincer he had discerned on the horizon in 1901 had been broken up. Even the Dual Alliance had for once proved of some use in a diplomatic crisis; although friction over Aehrenthal's determination to pursue an independent policy, and over Berlin's pro-Russian proclivities, had all too soon re-created the familiar situation in which an alliance designed for use in war proved to be of little use in day-to-day diplomacy.

The decline in the Monarchy's position was to some extent concealed by the undoubtedly great personal prestige of Aehrenthal, whom even old opponents in London now mourned as 'not only the doyen, but the most important of the continental foreign ministers'.[30] Even in St Petersburg he was respected, if not much liked. Inside the Monarchy, the vigorous policy of his early years had been very favourably compared to the indolence of 'Goluschlafski', and had established his reputation as the Austrian Bismarck. In fact, the analogy would not be inappropriate to his whole term of office. Like Bismarck, Aehrenthal was essentially an extreme conservative; like the Treaty of Frankfort, the annexation of Bosnia marked a final advance (if advance it may be called, marking as it did a retreat from the Sanjak and from all intervention in the internal affairs of Turkey); like Bismarck, Aehrenthal was the object of growing criticism at home in his later years – from Conrad and the military, from Archduke Franz Ferdinand (who resented his surrender to, or recognition of, the power of the Magyars) and the clericals; and just as there were people in Austria who were seriously concerned, until well into the 'seventies, with fending off Bismarck's alleged designs on the German provinces of Austria, so it was hardly surprising that, a mere three years after the annexation, there were people in Russia and the Balkan states who credited Aehrenthal with plans of expansion as far as Salonica. Had he lived, he might have been able in time to dispel these fears. As it was, his death added yet another element of instability to an uncertain situation.

In London, for example, there was little confidence that the new foreign minister, Leopold Count Berchtold, whom Nicolson remembered from St Petersburg as 'a most charming man but not of much strength of character'[31] would hold out so manfully as Aehrenthal had done against the Italophobes surrounding Franz Ferdinand, or against German influences. Yet Berchtold was no mere cipher. Entering the foreign service in 1893, he had spent

[30] P.A. VIII/147, Mensdorff to Berchtold, private, 20 February 1912.
[31] F.O. 800/183, Lowther MSS., Nicolson to Lowther, 19 February 1912.

three years in London before Aehrenthal spotted him and acquired him as counsellor of embassy at St Petersburg in 1902. Intelligent, hardworking, possessed of a great personal charm and a sardonic sense of humour, but conscientious to a fault and somewhat diffident, Berchtold was not an ambitious man. Indeed, in 1905, finding that the cold, damp, climate of St Petersburg was ruining his health, he had left the diplomatic service, altogether; and it had taken a good deal of persuasion before Aehrenthal could get him to return to St Petersburg as ambassador in 1906 – and then only on condition that the appointment was limited to two years. He served, in the event, for a very wearing four and a half, retiring again into private life in April 1911. Even as minister for foreign affairs, he served chiefly from a sense of duty to his sovereign, and, as his diary reveals, was plagued constantly by the desire to resign and retire from the irksome tasks of office. An aristocrat with great estates in Hungary and Bohemia, his views on domestic affairs were simple, unimaginative, and faintly pessimistic – those of a conventional conservative supporter of the dualist system. He penned no long memoranda on the restructuring of the Monarchy such as Aehrenthal had done. Nor was it simply that he had learned from the failure of Aehrenthal's grand designs in the face of Magyar opposition. He had himself, as a Hungarian magnate, on occasion supported this opposition – for example, in resisting Aehrenthal's plans to conciliate Serbia at the expense of Hungarian agriculturalists.

In foreign affairs, the new appointment did not herald any radical changes. Berchtold was no expansionist but, like Aehrenthal, a firm believer in the Monarchy's role as a conservative *status quo* Power. There were differences of tone and emphasis, however, and these stemmed not from Berchtold's alleged pliability, but, on the contrary, from firm convictions he had acquired during the course of his diplomatic career. He had developed a certain amount of trust and respect for the British, even as opponents; and having observed at close quarters the differences underlying the Anglo-Russian *entente*, he had hopes of making something more positive out of the Anglo-Austrian *détente* bequeathed to him by Aehrenthal. It was partly with this in mind that he was generally ready to work with Grey to solve international problems by Concert diplomacy. But his faith in the Concert stemmed essentially from his nerve-racking experiences at St Petersburg during the Sanjak railway and Bosnian crises, when Aehrenthal, to Berchtold's sincere dismay, had stubbornly insisted on defending Austria-Hungary's interests by single-handed action, paying no regard to the susceptibilities of other Powers less directly concerned. Compared with these experiences, the frustrations inherent in Concert diplomacy, even in dealing with issues of such labyrinthine complexity as Macedonia, seemed to Berchtold mild. His experiences at St Petersburg had made him a devotee of the Concert of Europe – albeit without any real experience of the deficiencies of the Concert in a major crisis. And just as he was ready to put his faith in co-operative action abroad, so at home he was inclined to ask, and often accept, the advice of others in the making of policy. Whereas Aehrenthal had spoken with a clear, firm voice, under Berchtold, many voices were heard in the Ballhausplatz – and not only those of the emperor, the Hungarian prime minister, and the military. Archduke Franz Ferdinand now looked forward to a voice in foreign affairs, and showered advice on the new foreign minister who he was sure would be very different from his 'frightful predecessors, Goluchowski and Aehrenthal'.[32] This, as Berchtold, although hardly an Italophobe, was not one to run after Italy, boded ill for the continuance of the Austro-Italian *rapprochement* so carefully tended by Aehrenthal.

Not that the behaviour of Italy herself was conducive to its continuance. Unable to defeat the Turks in Libya, she brought the war perilously near to the heart of the Ottoman empire, even undertaking operations near the Dardanelles in the spring. The Turks countered this simply by closing the Straits to all traffic, whereupon the Powers called Italy to order. But by May Italy's annexation of a whole series of islands in the Aegean was coming to be regarded at Vienna as a dangerous disturbance of the Near Eastern balance of power. And Austrian exasperation was only increased by Germany's ostentatiously friendly attitude towards the wayward ally: a flamboyant visit by William II to Venice at this time was particularly galling. Berchtold, who in March had already asked Mensdorff to keep an eye open for a chance to establish closer relations with Britain now sent another dispatch – approved by Franz Joseph as 'excellent'[33] – to London. The Germans, he

[32] Berchtold MSS., Franz Ferdinand to Berchtold, 16 January 1913.
[33] W. Wagner, p. 260.

explained, with their truckling to Russia since Potsdam, and their notorious designs on Turkey's Asian possessions, could no longer be regarded as a bulwark of the *status quo* in the Near East; nor, of course, could Italy. Austria-Hungary would do well, therefore – without, of course, abandoning her allies – to keep in touch with Britain. But the only result was a friendly conversation between Mensdorff and Grey. The British would never be in two minds between the Anglo-Russian *entente* and a revival of the Mediterranean agreements in such a vague and truncated form as Berchtold seemed to be hinting at. In fact, in the summer of 1912 the Monarchy seemed to be in some danger of falling between two stools: a marked deterioration in its relations with its allies had not been made good by closer relations with Britain. In July a cordial meeting between William II and the tsar at Baltisch Port was a further indication that Austria-Hungary, despite her alliances, was for practical purposes of day-to-day diplomacy, painfully isolated. Indeed, dangerously so, given that at any moment a serious Near Eastern crisis might blow up which would require her to speak with authority in defence of her vital interests.

The first signs of possible trouble had gone unnoticed in Vienna. In the first place, the Austrians had little evidence that there was anything afoot at all among the Balkan states. It was not until late May that they learned from Berlin and Bucharest of the secret Serbo-Bulgarian treaty of 12 March (and the Austro-Hungarian minister at Sofia continued to deny its existence as late as October). Nor did the news that the impossible had happened cause any serious alarm at Vienna. Like their informants, the Austrians were unaware of the contents of the treaty – of its defensive clauses aimed against Austria-Hungary, and offensive secret annex providing for the partition of Macedonia. Indeed, Berchtold accepted Kiderlen's view that in so far as Russia herself professed her concern to restrain the Balkan states, the treaty concluded under her patronage would serve only to reinforce the *status quo*. The Greco-Bulgarian treaty of 29 May, which was known to be unpopular in St Petersburg, alarmed Vienna even less. The Common War Minister, Auffenberg, could secure no money for an armaments increase; and Berchtold was content to assume that recent developments merely indicated that the Balkan states had determined to act together, and not against each other, when the crash eventually came in Turkey.

By the summer, the crash was clearly impending. As if the territorial problems of the Ottoman Empire – which by June had not only the Italian war, but another Albanian revolt and a frontier dispute with Montenegro to contend with – were not enough to tempt the Balkan states to action, a major political and military crisis soon gripped the government at Constantinople itself. There, the Young Turks had at last been driven from power; but they remained strong enough in the army, and even in the government, and had enough backing from chauvinist elements, to make any Turkish government think twice about making concessions to the enemies of Ottomanism. When the government, in a desperate effort to settle the Albanian crisis, granted virtual autonomy to the rebels in August, this only further embittered the strife at Constantinople. The crisis began to assume dangerous proportions. Not only did the Balkan states take great alarm at the concessions granted to the Albanians – clearly there was no time to lose if Macedonia were to be saved for Greek and Slav – but the Turkish government chose this critical moment to draw the teeth of the Young Turks, instituting a major purge of the army. The resultant disorganization of the military forces of the Empire provided yet a further incitement to the Balkan states to concert their plans with all possible speed.

Similarly, the efforts of the Great Powers to arrest the crisis only precipitated events. On 13 August Berchtold proposed that the Powers urge the Turks to extend their commendable decentralization policy from Albania to the whole of Macedonia; and at the same time urge the Balkan states to give Turkey time to put her house in order. This proposal was ill received. In the first place, it represented an attempt by Berchtold not only to demonstrate Austria-Hungary's devotion to peace and the territorial *status quo*, but also to seize the lead in the Concert, and to demonstrate the independence of Vienna from Berlin. Yet even if the Germans had not been so put out by Berchtold's failure to consult them beforehand, and even if France and Russia had not been so obsessed about *entente* solidarity, the proposal could hardly have solved the crisis. The hard-pressed Turkish government simply could not consider further concessions, if only for fear of provoking a chauvinist outburst that would bring the Young Turks back to power. (It was for this reason that Britain was reluctant to support any proposals involving pressure on Constantinople.) At the same time, the very fact that a Great Power had made a serious proposal, feasible or not, with a view to preserving the Ottoman empire, was to the Balkan states only a further incentive to act before it was too late. By mid-September, they were determined on war. Sazonov's efforts to calm the situation came to grief for the same reasons as Berchtold's – the difficult situation at Constantinople and the determination of the Balkan states. At the eleventh hour, France and Germany persuaded Russia and Austria-Hungary to act as spokesmen for the Powers, informing Constantinople that the Powers would 'take reforms in hand', and warning the Balkan states to keep the peace, for the Powers would permit no changes in the territorial *status quo*. But this belated appeal to the ghost of Mürzsteg made no impression at Constantinople; nor could it prevail against Balkan nationalism in full flood. Indeed, the whole exercise had been planned not so much in the hope of preventing war as of localizing it by constraining Russia and Austria-Hungary in a strait-jacket inside the Concert.

This was perhaps unnecessary. The Monarchy was not in fact planning to embark on an active policy. Had not Berchtold confessed to the Bulgarians on 10 August that Austria-Hungary had no intention of interposing 'her own body' to arrest the natural course of events if Turkey's last hour should strike? Thereby he declared his allegiance to the same policy of non-intervention that Goluchowski had announced to the Russians in 1897 and Aehrenthal to the Italians in 1907 and 1909. Moreover, not only Berchtold, but Franz Joseph, Franz Ferdinand, and the Common War Minister, Auffenberg, were all united against any military action; and so was the conference of ministers of 14 September, when Auffenberg explained that the army was by no means prepared for war. (The chief of staff, Schemua, was of a different opinion: but he was not invited to the conference and his views were disregarded.) Not only this, the international situation, with Germany and Italy, in Berchtold's opinion, only doubtfully loyal, and France and Russia probably hostile, was hardly encouraging. Besides, intervention would only serve to unite the Balkan League, when it was in the Monarchy's interests to see its disruption. Not that a policy of non-intervention implied an attitude of complete passivity. After all, vital interests of the Monarchy were at stake; and like Goluchowski and Aehrenthal before him, Berchtold always insisted that the Monarchy would have to have a voice in the final settlement. But for the time being, he was in no hurry to commit himself to a public definition of the Monarchy's vital interests. A sphinx-like attitude towards the Balkan states might well serve to restrain them; and in any case, the Austrians had not yet themselves decided which interests were vital and which were not. And how much they would need to say at all depended on the course of the war. This, they expected to be a long drawn out affair.

In the event, the main results of the war were clear by the end of October, by which time the Turkish armies, disorganized and unadvisedly switching to an offensive strategy for which they were ill prepared, had been driven back to the Chataldja lines, a mere thirty miles from Constantinople. By December, their Macedonian and Albanian possessions were reduced to the fortresses of Adrianople, Scutari and Janina and the Turks were suing for peace. Whatever the Great Powers might have said in October, the territorial *status quo* was now clearly lost beyond recall.

Austria-Hungary was the first Great Power officially to recognize this fact. A series of conferences in the Ballhausplatz in October had decided for a policy broadly in line with the non-interventionist traditions of the past fifteen years: the Monarchy had no interest in territorial acquisitions in the Balkans, nor in reoccupying the Sanjak. Its positive aims and the general principles which would determine its attitude towards a final settlement, Berchtold announced at the end of October. In the first place, any territorial gains for Serbia must be accompanied by guarantees of her future good behaviour, perhaps in the form of close economic co-operation with the Monarchy (in which case the latter was prepared to be generous). Even so, in no circumstances must Serbia extend her frontiers to the Adriatic. Basically this principle expressed the fear that a Serbian port might some day become a Russian port (or, as Franz Ferdinand feared, an Italian port); the well-founded apprehensions of Vienna as to the effect on the south Slavs of the Monarchy of too great an increase in Serbia's prestige; and the desire to restrict Serbia's economic independence by forcing her to channel her drive to the sea through Austro-Hungarian territory (as Aehrenthal had tried to do in 1909). But the principle of 'the Balkans for the Balkan peoples', which Berchtold also fell back on in this connexion, was not mere hypocrisy. Any port that Serbia acquired would of necessity lie in Albanian territory; and the creation of a viable Albania was another cardinal point in Berchtold's declaration of principles. The Monarchy would also seek compensation for Roumania, according to the principle of maintaining the Balkan balance of power; and the safeguarding of its own trading interests in areas formerly Turkish, particularly at Salonica.

Although in most quarters Berchtold's statement was considered surprisingly moderate, it provoked a serious crisis in Austro-Serbian relations. The Serbs were absolutely determined to acquire an Adriatic port. Already their armies were fighting their way through to the coast and crushing the resistance of Austria-Hungary's Catholic Albanian protégés with a savagery that equalled anything the Turks had done in the past. True, some voices were raised in the Monarchy – notably in Slav circles – and at the Austro-Hungarian embassy at St Petersburg in favour of yielding to Serbia's demands for a port so as to win her over into the Austro-Hungarian camp. And Pasić was even willing to come to Vienna to discuss a closer commercial alignment of Serbia with the Monarchy. But this was only to become operative after the expiry of Serbia's existing commercial treaties in 1917; and Berchtold was unwilling to abandon such a time-honoured tenet of Austro-Hungarian policy as the exclusion of Serbia from the Adriatic. In any case, he was no longer a free agent, for Italy – fearful lest a Serbian port might some day become an Austro-Hungarian port – was equally adamant on this point. Not that all this deterred the Serbs, who continued their bloody advance towards the Adriatic undaunted by the frowns of the Triple Alliance; and even boasted in Berlin of Russia's support. In mid-November tension rose higher between Vienna and Belgrade, as disputes between Serbian military and Austro-Hungarian consular officials in Macedonia led to the intercepting by the Serbs of Austro-Hungarian consular mail, the cutting of communications between the Austro-Hungarian government and several of its consulates, and even the abduction by Serbian troops of the Austro-Hungarian consul at Uesküb.

The Austro-Serbian crisis was all the more serious in that it coincided with and exacerbated a deterioration in Austro-Russian relations. Russia seemed determined during these weeks to support Serbia's pretensions; and her military posture had been somewhat threatening from the very start of the Balkan crisis, at which time she had happened to carry out a trial mobilization. At the end of

October the Austrians had been moved to take some counter-measures, and decided to retain with the colours a portion of the third-year levy of troops due to be dismissed when the new recruits were called in. Already in the spring the government had at last managed – albeit at the price of police intervention in the riotous Hungarian parliament – to raise the size of the contingents recruited by the Common Army beyond the level fixed in 1889. As a result 181,000 new recruits enlisted in October 1912 – some 42,000 more than in 1911. In November the forces facing the Russians in Galicia were stepped up; and on 12 December Conrad von Hoetzendorf resumed the post of chief of staff.

If these military measures were not enough, the Monarchy managed to put on an imposing diplomatic front. Germany, Italy, and Austria-Hungary, notoriously united on the question of a Serbian port, emphasized their solidarity by formally renewing the Triple Alliance on 5 December. Already in November a demonstrative visit by Franz Ferdinand and Schemua to Berlin had given food for thought in the *Entente* capitals. The Austrian visitors had been well satisfied to find Berlin neither hectoring nor nagging, but resolutely behind them in defence of the position Berchtold had taken up. Admittedly Franz Joseph still had doubts about Germany's steadfastness of purpose, even after Bethmann-Hollweg, in a speech to the Reichstag on 2 December, had pledged Germany to come to the aid of the Dual Monarchy should it be attacked by a third Power while making good its Balkan interests. Similarly, although a visit by Conrad to Bucharest at this time convinced the Austrians of Roumania's reliability, and although the alliance was renewed without any trouble in January 1913, Russian diplomats were known to be busy at Bucharest – some of them actually offering the bait of Transylvania – and the Austrians proved unable to bring about a *rapprochement* between Roumania and Bulgaria as a first step to breaking up the Balkan league. Even so, despite these weaknesses, the Monarchy's position was still imposing enough to impress Russia, particularly as the latter was having great difficulty in rousing much enthusiasm for Serbia in Paris and London. By 22 November Russia had abandoned hope of securing an Adriatic port for her protégé. Serbia herself gave up hope a month later. And although Russian and Austro-Hungarian military preparations continued to cause concern, the settlement of the Austro-Serbian consular dispute (with a formal apology from Serbia) in mid-December marked a definite lessening of the tension.

Meanwhile, although the peace negotiations soon to start in London between Turkey and the Balkan states could hardly be relied on to produce a solution in accordance with the vital interests of the Great Powers, a notable step towards preventing a major conflagration had been taken early in December, when the Great Powers accepted a proposal of Grey's for an informal conference of ambassadors to settle the contentious issues, at least in broad outline. Berchtold liked the idea of this kind of academic discussion, which offered the chance of positive results while yet avoiding the dangers involved in a formal conference (the failure of which might prove too great a strain on the international nerves). Moreover, he trusted in Grey as an impartial statesman, and readily agreed that the matter should be left to the ambassadors at London – rather than at Paris, where the rancorous Izvolsky might make trouble. The first meeting of the ambassadors seemed to justify his hopes. The vexed issue of a Serbian port finally disappeared when it was agreed that the frontiers of Albania should extend from Montenegro in the north to Greece in the south; and the decision to entrust Austria-Hungary and Italy with the task of devising a scheme of autonomous government for Albania seemed a further recognition of Austria-Hungary's interest in the area.

Not that Vienna's wishes were entirely fulfilled. The decision to allow Serbia free access to a commercial port in Albania seriously compromised Berchtold's hopes of drawing her into the Bosnian-Austro-Hungarian commercial system. And there was still plenty of room for dispute about the future frontiers of Albania, particularly in Macedonia. The Austrians wished to make the new state, a potential ally in any war against the Balkan Slavs, as big as possible; and they had a useful argument to hand in that the frontiers they were demanding were in fact very much in accordance with the ethnic character of the area. The other Great Powers, however, were all unanimous in declaring that ethnic considerations could not be the sole criterion, and that some account must be taken of Serbia's and Montenegro's claims by right of conquest. The crucial issue in the debate was Scutari, which the Austrians, in view of its continuing and surprising resistance to Montenegrin besieging forces, now decided must go to Albania (although Berchtold had not dared hope for this in October). Scutari was, after all, an Albanian town – indeed, the focal point of several north Albanian tribes. Russia, of course, was equally insistent in defence of Montenegro. Even Grey now argued that as St Petersburg had given way on the question of a Serbian port, it was up to Vienna to give way over Scutari; and Mensdorff received practically no support from his German and Italian colleagues in opposing this horse-trading and demanding a settlement according to the merits of the case. By mid-December, there was a complete deadlock. An attempt to find a way out by direct Austro-Russian negotiations got nowhere; and tension between Vienna and St Petersburg began to mount again as the Austrians, in an effort to strengthen their bargaining position, put their forces in Bosnia, Herzegovina and Dalmatia on a war footing.

Not that they were anxious for war. On the contrary, as the Common Finance Minister observed on 4 January 1913, war might well mean the total economic collapse of the Monarchy. The emperor, Franz Ferdinand, and Berchtold shared his pacific views. Nor was there any enthusiasm among the allies for a war-like policy. True, Berchtold thought that Bethmann-Hollweg was going too far when he urged Vienna to accept a peaceful compromise solution of the Albanian question for the sake of Anglo-German relations: this showed an 'impertinent' disregard for Austria-Hungary's vital interests.[34] But he agreed with Franz Joseph who, early in February, rejected yet another plea from Conrad for an attack on Serbia. Russia would intervene, the emperor felt, and Germany was not ready for war. It was his duty, therefore, to keep the peace. To this end, he sent Prince Gottfried Hohenlohe as his special envoy to Nicholas II, to tell the tsar personally that although Austria-Hungary had certain Balkan interests which she must at all costs guard, she bore no hostility towards Russia. But such vague assurances, however sincere, could do little to improve Austro-Russian relations, let alone solve the deadlock. The Russians continued to insist on mutual disarmament as a precondition of negotiations, whereas the Austrians refused to reduce their forces until they were assured of a satisfactory frontier for Albania.

In the end, the deadlock was resolved by the diplomatic retreat

[34] H. Hantsch, *Berchtold*, Vol. 1, p. 388.

of Austria-Hungary. Scutari was saved for Albania; but to secure this, Berchtold had to make sweeping concessions in favour of Serbia and Montenegro on the north-eastern frontier of Albania, giving up not only all the areas which he had originally listed as possible bargaining counters, but the important market towns of Dibra and Djakova, which were notoriously purely Albanian in character. He had only steeled himself to these concessions after a lot of heart-searching. But German and Italian support had been practically non-existent, and the emperor himself had advised surrender. Above all, time was running out: if the Montenegrins were allowed to capture Scutari, the problem of evicting them from that inaccessible mountain fastness would complicate matters to a fearsome degree. Yet although the settlement of the Scutari issue by the end of March had produced a temporary *détente* which even enabled Russia and Austria-Hungary to start reducing their opposing military forces, plenty of ill will remained. In St Petersburg, the crisis had finally dissipated any faith Nicholas II personally still had in the Austrians: in Vienna, there was both deep disillusionment about the high price paid in terms of Albanian (and thereby Austro-Hungarian) interests for the solution eventually devised by the Concert, and a fanatical determination that, having paid that price, the Monarchy must insist on the fulfilment of the bargain on the part of the Concert.

The futile efforts of the Powers in the next six weeks to bring Montenegro to accept their decision on Scutari provided Berchtold with yet a second disillusioning lesson in Concert diplomacy. It needed a threat of separate coercive action by Austria-Hungary before the Powers would agree to a naval demonstration to persuade the Montenegrins to desist from the siege; and even then, the French dragged their feet, and the Russian government, mindful of public opinion, refused to participate at all. In this situation, the naval demonstration was completely ineffective: the Montenegrins simply laughed at the Powers, and continued the siege until Essad Pasha surrendered the city on 23 April. Another week followed in which the Powers proved incapable of action. As Grey insisted to Mensdorff, the only guarantee of peace was the Concert; but the Concert could only function on a basis of unanimity. And Russia refused to act.

By 29 April the patience of Vienna was exhausted. After consulting Rome, Berchtold discussed with the Austrian and

Hungarian governments the possibility of some separate Austro-Hungarian or Austro-Italian action. This might have involved a serious risk of war: an Austro-Hungarian action against Montenegro would almost certainly bring Serbian forces into the fray; and Russia had let it be known that she would not tolerate an Austro-Hungarian attack on Serbia. Nevertheless, the conference of ministers of 2 May was undaunted, and the forces in Bosnia, Herzegovina and Dalmatia were put on a complete war footing. 'Mobilization was in full swing, even if it was not so labelled.'[35] These measures proved infinitely more effective than the notes and demonstrations of the Concert. News of them caused utter panic at Cetinje, and the Montenegrins lost no time in promising to withdraw from Scutari. That was enough for Berchtold. A council of ministers of 3 May would have liked to humiliate Montenegro further, by sending her an ultimatum with a formal request to withdraw; and they went so far as to overrule Berchtold, who was obliged reluctantly to transmit their wishes to the emperor. But Franz Joseph was taking no unnecessary risks. Only a warning telegram was sent to Cetinje. On 5 May the Montenegrins marched out of Scutari, tension relaxed, Austria-Hungary's latest military measures were countermanded, and Conrad lamented that yet another opportunity for war had been lost.

The main crisis was now over, and the London conference proceeded to settle the remaining points of detail. On 30 May the Balkan states and Turkey signed the Treaty of London, leaving to the decision of the Great Powers the settlement of such contentious issues as the final frontier of Albania, and the ultimate disposition of the Aegean Islands (many of which had remained in Italian occupation since the Tripoli war). As regards Albania, the Austro-Italian draft proposals for the constitutional ordering of the new state were by and large accepted, despite some French opposition; and the choice of the German Prince, William of Wied, a nephew of the queen of Roumania, to be the first head of state was another feather in the cap of the Triple Alliance. But the Austrians were by no means completely satisfied. Berchtold's disillusionment with Concert diplomacy as a means of safeguarding the vital interests of the Monarchy is discernible in the letter he wrote on 18 June congratulating Mensdorff on having achieved so much from such a difficult position 'between hostile Triple

[35] E. Helmreich, p. 322.

Entente colleagues and feeble Triple Alliance colleagues'.[36] Indeed, as the conference discussions on the southern frontier of
Albania dragged on into July, with the French ardently champion-
ing the claims of Athens, and with the credibility of Austro-
Italian support for Albania constantly undermined by William
II's notorious Grecophile sympathies, Mensdorff thought he
could detect signs of growing bad temper in the 'peremptory'
instructions he now began to receive from Vienna.[37] Still, Berchtold's tough resistance was rewarded: although the final details
were left to a boundary commission which was to start work on
the spot in the autumn, the southern frontier of Albania was
broadly in accordance with Austro-Italian wishes. His obstinacy
may have owed something to a desire to pay Russia back in her
own coin – at least that was Mensdorff's opinion. Certainly,
Austro-Russian relations had in no sense improved.

Indeed, a new struggle had already opened between the two
Powers in May, when a quarrel broke out between Serbia and
Bulgaria which portended the disruption of the Balkan league.
The Serbs, thwarted in their Albanian ambitions, were demanding
compensation from Bulgaria – not only the whole of the zone
which the Serbo-Bulgarian treaty of March 1912 had earmarked
for arbitration by the tsar, but areas of Macedonia which the
treaty had indisputably assigned to Bulgaria. And by the end
of May a secret treaty assured them of Greek support. The
Bulgarians, for their part, demanded the enforcement of the
treaty.

In all this, Berchtold, ever anxious to reduce Serbia's prestige,
and to lessen her attractive power over the increasingly discontented south Slavs of the Monarchy, saw a chance that Bulgaria
might pull Austria-Hungary's chestnuts out of the fire. Bulgaria
was thought to be easily capable of defeating both Serbia and
Greece if it came to a war. The trouble was that she would not be
able to cope with Roumania as well. Berchtold, therefore, urged
Sofia to make sure of Roumania's neutrality by granting her some
territorial concessions. He was setting himself no easy task in
seeking to bring about a sincere *rapprochement* between Roumania
and Bulgaria: the St Petersburg Protocol of 17 April, by which
the Great Powers had assigned to Roumania the Bulgarian town

[36] Mensdorff MSS., Karton 9, Berchtold to Mensdorff, 18 June 1913.
[37] Mensdorff MSS., Karton 4, Tagebuch, 6 July 1913.

of Silistria as compensation for Bulgaria's recent gains, had left both parties bitterly discontented. But he did not despair. After all, a Bulgarian-Roumanian *rapprochement* under the auspices of the Triple Alliance would be, even in general political terms, a valuable prize indeed; and especially valuable for the Monarchy, now resigned to accepting Serbia's 'open hostility' as ineradicable.[38] So convinced was Berchtold of this that on 24 June he went so far as to offer the Bulgarians both 'sympathy and active support' in resisting any further expansion of Serbia – but again, only on condition that they first squared Roumania.[39]

His grand design came to grief for two reasons. First, he found himself crossed at every turn by the Balkan diplomacy of Berlin. The Germans were not in the least interested in his projected Bulgarian-Roumanian alignment. Indeed, since the death in December 1912 of Kiderlen (who had encouraged Berchtold's hopes of disrupting the Balkan league by winning over Bulgaria) German policy had become positively hostile to Bulgaria – largely a reflection of William II's personal dislike of King Ferdinand. In April 1913 the Germans had sided with the Triple *Entente* Powers at the St Petersburg conference to thwart Berchtold's hopes of sugaring the Silistrian pill for Bulgaria by awarding Salonica to her in return. Salonica, the Germans declared, must go to Greece (where on 18 March William II's brother-in-law, Constantine, had ascended the throne). In fact, the Germans had a grand design of their own for the Balkans: a combination of Roumania, Greece, and Serbia. For this, of course, the Austrians had no use at all; and they pointed out that Germany was playing into the hands of the Triple *Entente* Powers, who were striving to build up just such a combination for their own purposes. Serbia was now, in Berchtold's opinion, hopelessly hostile; and distant Greece, with her ingrained aversion to Bulgaria and Albania, could never be of much use to Austria-Hungary. Even Goluchowski's old idea of a Greco-Roumanian combination had few attractions for Berchtold: it was bound to have anti-Slav overtones, and could therefore hardly be acceptable to Austria-Hungary as a semi-Slav Power – or, so at any rate, despite his solicitude for Albania, he told Berlin. But the Germans were impervious to his arguments. They refused to lift a finger to bring Bulgaria and Roumania to terms, or even to lend Vienna any

[38] O-U.A., Vol. 6, 7486.   [39] Ibid.

serious support in dissuading the Roumanians from listening to Serbian overtures.

Yet although the vagaries of German diplomacy – which certainly undermined the credibility of Austro-Hungarian policy at Bucharest and Sofia – were exasperating, it was the domestic situation in Bulgaria that was really fatal to Berchtold's designs. His advice was never taken seriously by either Gueshev or by his successor as prime minister, Danev. Neither made a serious effort to come to terms with Bucharest: both put their trust implicitly in Russia to restrain Roumania – and also to protect Bulgaria's interests in Macedonia. Indeed, it was in consequence of Danev's boundless faith in Russia – and not, as was believed in *Entente* circles, as a result of Austro-Hungarian prompting – that the Bulgarians decided at the end of June to seize from the occupying Greek and Serbian forces some of the positions in Macedonia to which they believed themselves entitled by treaty. They seem to have been hoping to strengthen their bargaining position and to force the Russians to settle the wearisome dispute speedily by arbitration. Greece and Serbia, however, delighted to see that Bulgaria had put herself in the wrong, responded with declarations of war. The Second Balkan War had begun.

As in October 1912, fears of Austro-Hungarian intervention spread apace. They were equally groundless. In the first place, the domestic situation, just calming down after six months of alarms, was anything but favourable to an active policy. Commercial circles were aghast at the prospect of further upheavals. The Balkan wars had severely disrupted Austria-Hungary's Near Eastern trade: goods had been held up at the frontiers, or even sent back; and the Balkan states had imposed moratoria on all payments. The mobilization measures in May had caused a panic in Galicia and a general crisis of credit; there was a shortage of money in circulation since people had taken to hoarding; and the sum result was depression and a disturbing growth in unemployment. At the same time, the protectionist policy of Budapest kept food prices high throughout the Monarchy. The cost of living had risen by one third between 1900 and 1910. The Lord Mayor of London, on an official visit to Prague in September 1911 was subjected to a demonstration against high food prices – but he was ignorant of Czech and, according to the German consul, mistook the shouts of the crowd for applause, his waving handkerchief only serving to increase their exasperation.[40] September 1912 had witnessed serious street demonstrations and broken windows in Vienna. And if the agitated domestic situation did not give the government food for thought, it was accompanied by wide-spread apathy, even pacifism, among the public on questions of foreign affairs. The anti-war movement propagated by the Social Democrats, although heavily defeated in the 1912 election (fought on the slogan 'For Dreadnoughts, against Social Democracy') seemed at last to be gaining a hold over the working classes.[41] Demands were raised on all sides for the demobilization of the few troops still remaining on a war footing in the southern provinces. And pacific feelings were by no means confined to the street. The emperor himself and Archduke Franz Ferdinand – admittedly motivated more by considerations of high policy – were also strongly for peace (Document 35). 'Sit back calmly and watch', the archduke exhorted Berchtold, 'while this rabble, these unreliable, useless gentlemen break each other's heads.'[42]

The external political situation, too, was hardly such as to encourage intervention, even when Serbia and Greece, aided by Roumania, proceeded to crush Bulgaria. The Bulgarians continued to look to St Petersburg for assistance, until even Berchtold despaired of them and determined, under pressure from the emperor and Franz Ferdinand, to concentrate on wooing Roumania. Roumania's intervention in the war had in fact been decisive, sealing the fate both of Bulgaria and of Berchtold's schemes, admittedly now rather threadbare. For it meant that the Monarchy could not help Bulgaria, or even restrain Serbia, without dealing a mortal blow at the Austro-Roumanian alliance. Berlin was particularly anxious that nothing be done to offend Roumania, for the Triple *Entente* Powers were known to be assiduous at Bucharest; and there was not the slightest chance that the emperor or Franz Ferdinand would sanction a policy hostile to Roumania. In this situation, there really was no need for Berlin and Rome to 'restrain' Vienna; and San Giuliano's famous remark about holding Austria-Hungary back 'by the coat tails' was the

[40] German Foreign Ministry microfilms, Foreign Office Library, London, 10/189, Gebsattel to Bethmann-Hollweg, No. 145, 19 September 1911.

[41] K. B. Winogradow and J. A. Pissarew, 'Die internationale Lage der österreichisch-ungarischen Monarchie 1900–1918', in F. Klein (ed.), p. 9.

[42] Berchtold MSS., Franz Ferdinand to Berchtold, 4 July 1913.

result of a misunderstanding of her intentions.[43] Berchtold could only try to salvage what he could by diplomacy: he announced that Austria-Hungary's interests would have to be taken into account in the final settlement, which he reserved the right to approve.

At first, this did not seem too much to hope for. In mid-July, when Russia proved unable to stop the war, the Bulgarians in desperation appointed an Austrophile cabinet under Radoslavov and appealed to Franz Joseph for advice. Even a faint hope of a Bulgarian-Roumanian *rapprochement* appeared when Franz Joseph advised Ferdinand to appeal direct to King Carol, and when Austro-Hungarian pressure on Bucharest brought Roumania, herself not keen to see the Balkan balance swing too far in favour of Serbia and Greece, to summon those two states to cease their advance and negotiate. Consequently, Berchtold was only too willing to lend his effective support to Roumania's suggestion that the peace conference be held not at St Petersburg but at Bucharest; all the more so as the Roumanians promised to speak up in defence of Austria-Hungary's interests. Moreover, it seemed certain, as the conference got under way, and as deadlock arose over Greece's claim to retain the port of Kavalla, that the Great Powers would have to intervene directly. At least, Russia and Austria-Hungary were for once in agreement in insisting on their right to revise the final settlement. Berchtold was hoping both to reduce Serbia's gains, and to secure Kavalla for Bulgaria. On this latter point Sazonov, anxious for Russia's position at Sofia, supported him, or at least rivalled him in enthusiasm. Indeed, it was only on the understanding that the settlement would be revised by the Powers that Bulgaria signed the Treaty of Bucharest on 10 August, conceding most of northern Macedonia to Serbia, and Kavalla to Greece.

In the end, however, Berchtold's hopes of revising the peace treaty ended as ignominiously as his efforts to reconcile Roumania and Bulgaria before the war. And again it seemed that the chief architect of Austria-Hungary's disgrace was her German ally. Germany, struggling with France for influence at Athens, was resolutely opposed to the revision of the treaty; and when the French persuaded Sazonov to give way on the point of Kavalla, Russia too lost all interest in revision. William II's lavish

[43] O-U.A., Vol. 6, 7748.

distribution of congratulatory telegrams and decorations to victorious Greek and Roumanian notables proclaimed to the world that Germany regarded the Treaty of Bucharest as final and definitive. This, together with the fact that nobody else, not even the Italians, was interested in revision, ensured the final collapse of Berchtold's policy.

Great was the wrath in Vienna. It was only with difficulty that Franz Joseph and Berchtold dissuaded Conrad from boycotting the forthcoming German manoeuvres. And even Franz Joseph, according to Czernin, felt that 'the Treaty of Bucharest is untenable and we are moving towards another war. May God grant that it is confined to the Balkans!'[44] Berchtold was bitterly disappointed. The Treaty of Bucharest, confirming the triumph of expansionist Serbia, and of Albania's other enemy, Greece, and disastrously reducing in size and military potential the only Balkan state which had no conflict of interests with Austria-Hungary, was without any doubt a great disaster for the Monarchy. And it was all the more galling to Berchtold that Germany had persisted in her blindness despite his repeated attempts to enlighten her. For example, on 1 August he had drawn up a long memorandum[45] for the better information of Berlin: Austro-Serbian hostility was irremediable (*unüberbrückbar*) and would soon end in war. It was essential, therefore, to win over Bulgaria by giving her some timely assistance – without, of course, losing Roumania. It was high time that Germany gave up her independent Balkan policy. But his warnings of impending dangers, and his fears that the next Balkan league would be directed against Austria-Hungary, made no impression in Berlin.

All in all, the Austrians were highly dissatisfied. Indeed, the events of the past year had dealt a death-blow to Berchtold's faith in Concert diplomacy. The lessons he had drawn from his experiences in 1908 had borne bitter fruit in 1913. Had Austria-Hungary no interests of her own to guard? he exasperatedly asked the Germans. Must she always submit to the common interest of Europe? It is true that many of the Monarchy's recent embarrassments were attributable simply to the force of events; but Concert diplomacy, in so far as it tied Austria-Hungary's hands, had certainly contributed to her humiliation. Not that Berchtold had any

[44] O. Czernin, *Im Weltkrieg*, Berlin, 1919.
[45] O-U.A., Vol. 7, 8157.

immediate plans to take the initiative, or much idea at all as to possible remedies. When Mensdorff visited Vienna in September he was depressed by the 'indecision and helplessness (*Unselbst-ständigkeit*) of our excellent Leopold'.[46] But if the Monarchy were further provoked, if another crisis were forced on it from out-side, then perhaps independent action – as in the Scutari crisis – might appear to offer the best hope of safeguarding its vital interests.

Just such a crisis was provoked by Serbia who, in defiance of repeated admonitions from the Powers, continued in occupation of territory allotted by the London conference to Albania. She pleaded the necessity of suppressing disorders fomented, allegedly, by Austria-Hungary, Bulgaria and Turkey; but in fact she was aiming to secure more territory, or at least to embarrass, and possibly to overthrow, the new Albanian government. Given Russia's declared sympathy for Serbia's attitude the Concert was hardly likely to provide a speedy solution. So early in October a council of ministers at Vienna decided that it was for Austria-Hungary to prevent – by means of an ultimatum if necessary – any further expansion of Serbia at Albania's expense. Berchtold asked the Serbs to explain themselves, and informed Berlin and Rome that the Monarchy was determined to see the decisions of the London conference enforced.

The German reply was an enthusiastic promise of support, while the Italian reply was more reserved, but still positive. But already Berchtold, with the full support of the emperor, had de-cided on firm action, for the Serbs had sent an evasive answer and had advanced still further into Albania. On 17 October an Austro-Hungarian ultimatum gave the Serbs eight days' notice to quit Albania. Of this, the allies were informed only after the event. And Rome was somewhat piqued. The Triple *Entente* Powers were even more ruffled by Berchtold's 'too precipitate' action.[47] In France, particularly, the press raged, and the government closed the market to Austro-Hungarian loans until the Monarchy mended its ways. But there had in fact been little risk of war, for the Monarchy had, after all, only been acting to enforce an inter-nationally agreed decision. Even Hartwig, the fiery Russian minister at Belgrade, urged the Serbs to climb down, and Rou-

[46] Mensdorff MSS., Karton 4, Tagebuch, 29 September 1913.
[47] B.D., Vol. 10/1, No. 47.

mania warned Serbia that she could not support her on this issue. Consequently, the Serbs made haste to comply with the ultimatum. Independent action seemed after all to be the most effective means of defending the Monarchy's interests.

For Berchtold, one of the most heartening aspects of the affair had been the attitude of the Germans, who were both glad to receive proof of the strength and vitality of their ally and eager to seize the opportunity to efface recent differences within the Dual Alliance. William II had even hoped that Serbia would reject the ultimatum and give Austria-Hungary a chance to chastise her; and at the unveiling of the memorial commemorating the hundredth anniversary of the battle of Leipzig on 18 October, his language to Conrad betrayed a new and surprising hostility to Serbia. His zeal had not abated when he talked to Berchtold during a visit to Vienna a week later. After expatiating at some length on the Panslav menace, and observing that after all 'the Slavs were born not to rule but to serve',[48] he advised Berchtold to bind Serbia, perhaps by economic ties, in the service of the Monarchy. Berchtold replied that this would hardly be possible. The emperor then recommended stronger measures of compulsion: 'When His Majesty Emperor Franz Joseph demands something the Serbian government must give way, and if it does not then Belgrade will be bombarded and occupied until the will of His Majesty is fulfilled. And of this you can be certain, that I stand beside you and am ready to draw the sabre whenever your action makes it necessary.'[49] The assurance that the Monarchy could 'fully and completely count on him' ran through the emperor's remarks, Berchtold was pleased to note, 'like a red thread'.[50] It seemed that after eighteen disastrous months of dissension, the Dual Alliance had suddenly become stronger and more serviceable than ever.

Yet Berchtold was to discover, like Kálnoky, Goluchowski, and Aehrenthal before him, that William II's brave words did not always amount to much in terms of practical politics. For the Austrians, the eternal problem of the Dual Alliance remained: how effectively could an alliance designed to cope with the contingency of war serve the Monarchy's interests in the day-to-day diplomacy of peace? In this latter respect, it soon became clear that the interests of Germany and Austria-Hungary had by no

[48] O-U.A., Vol. 7, 8934.   [49] Ibid.   [50] Ibid.

means been brought into line. In fact, the last nine months of peace saw the Dual Alliance descend to a new nadir as far as diplomatic achievements were concerned. The old conflicts of interest reappeared, now exacerbated by the fact that Germany, increasingly anxious for her own direct imperialist interests in Turkey – and who could tell whether Turkey-in-Asia and the Baghdad railway would not soon follow Macedonia into the diplomatic market? – was no longer content to rely on the Austrians to stand guard over her Balkan interests. Germany was now set on building her own causeway to Constantinople, even if this meant shouldering her ally out of the way. Not that the Austrians, increasingly anxious for their own position after the recent disastrous events, felt either willing or able to serve as catspaws for the Germans. Nor were they anxious to involve themselves in quarrels where they considered only German interests to be involved. The fiasco of Germany's attempt to strengthen her influence in Turkey by the abortive mission of General Liman von Sanders met with little sympathy in Vienna, where the whole affair was condemned as a most unfortunate and unnecessary provocation of Russia. Similarly, when the Austrians in the spring of 1914 were talking of intervening by force to prevent the realization of a new Serbian plan to reach the Adriatic (by means of a union with Montenegro) William II declared that a war for such a purpose would leave Berlin 'completely cold': Vienna was 'crazy' to consider it.[51] Far from standing by their promises of October 1913, the Germans seemed to have retreated beyond the position of December 1912 (Document 36).

Meanwhile the two allies floundered about in a morass of Balkan diplomacy with policies hardly less conflicting than those of the summer of 1913. The Monarchy's plans still revolved round Bulgaria, Germany's round Greece. True, the Monarchy scored some successes. When the Powers came to define the Southern Albanian frontier in the winter of 1913–14 Austria-Hungary and Italy managed with British help to win several points for Albania despite the Greek proclivities of Berlin. But when the two Adriatic Powers on 30 October – less than a fortnight after Berchtold's ultimatum to Belgrade – suddenly presented Greece with a summons to evacuate Southern Albania by the end of the year, a further severe blow was dealt to the Concert of Europe; and, as

[51] G.P., Vol. 38, 15539.

not even Germany had been informed beforehand, to the unity of the Triple Alliance Powers. True, the latter managed at the turn of the year to stand together to thwart a British proposal to bribe Greece out of Southern Albania by awarding her most of the Aegean Islands. But further attempts by the two Adriatic Powers to call Greece peremptorily to order in the spring of 1914 caused almost as much exasperation in Berlin as in the *Entente* capitals, and cast a lurid light not only on the death throes of the Concert of 1912–13 but also on the state of relations within the Triple Alliance. Germany, for her part, lent her allies practically no support in their vain struggle to resist the demands of the Triple *Entente* Powers for a measure of international control over the finances of the new Albanian state; or in their efforts to establish the Prince of Wied firmly on his ramshackle throne.

Perhaps even more serious, from Berchtold's point of view, was Germany's outright opposition to his attempts to ward off the threat of a new Balkan League by drawing at least Bulgaria and Turkey together under the auspices of the Triple Alliance. By December 1913 these two states, both of which had revisionist claims against the *de jure* – or in Turkey's case the *de facto* – *status quo*, had actually drafted a military convention with Austria-Hungary's blessing. But the negotiations came to nothing. The new military government in Constantinople was unstable and timid; and Bulgaria in the end shrank from involvement in Turkey's continuing quarrel with Greece over the fate of the Aegean Islands.

Not that Berchtold had received any assistance or encouragement from Berlin. Despite the fact that the Triple *Entente* Powers were pressing the Bulgarians to accept a French loan and to install a Russophile government, it was not until June 1914 that he could persuade the Germans to grant a loan to Bulgaria. The Germans showed not the slightest interest in a Turco-Bulgarian *entente*: this would probably be anti-Greek; and William II was never in two minds between his brother-in-law in Athens and the hated Ferdinand. True, the German ambassador at Constantinople recognized that Berchtold's plan was the only feasible one; but the Kaiser persisted, as late as May 1914, in his vain efforts to reconcile Turkey and Greece, perpetually on the brink of war as neither would accept the compromise decision of the Powers on the fate of the Aegean Islands. Nor was Berchtold able to remove a further obstacle to a *rapprochement* between Bulgaria and the Triple Alliance – the continuing bad relations between Bulgaria and Roumania, resulting from their divergent attitudes towards the Treaty of Bucharest.

The possible defection of Roumania at least presented the Central Powers with a common cause for concern. The Germans strove manfully and with some success – King Carol was, after all, a Hohenzollern – to preserve the alliance; and although Berchtold's wooing of revisionist Bulgaria certainly annoyed the Roumanians, the blame for the growing estrangement cannot be laid entirely at the door of the Ballhausplatz. That same Treaty of Bucharest which had made Roumania, to Berchtold's chagrin, a pillar of the *status quo* in the Balkans, had given a tremendous boost to her self-confidence and to Roumanian irredentism, concentrated on Transylvania. The allied Monarchy was coming to be regarded in Roumania as a source, less of support than of booty. By the autumn of 1913 the Austrians were very worried indeed. Count Ottokar Czernin, a protégé of that great hater of Magyars, Franz Ferdinand, was sent as minister to Bucharest in an effort to cultivate goodwill. Even the Magyars seemed to be making an effort. In January 1914 Tisza announced an 'era of unity and well-being' and opened talks with the committee of the Roumanian nationalist party in Transylvania. But there could be no compromise between Roumanian nationalism and the iron principles of Magyar supremacy on which the Hungarian state was based. By mid-February, things were back to normal in Hungary, and the nationalities law of 1868 remained a dead letter. Meanwhile, in Roumania, the Russophile Liberal party under Bratianu had secured a resounding victory in the elections of January 1914; and all the time the diplomats of the Triple *Entente* were busy. In June Tsar Nicholas and his family paid a state visit to King Carol at Constantsa; talk of a marriage between Prince Carol and one of the tsar's daughters seemed to threaten even the dynastic foothold of the Central Powers in Roumania; and Tisza was enraged to hear that during the visit Sazonov and Bratianu had made a motor-car excursion across the frontier into Transylvanian territory. At the same time, threatening though developments in Roumania might be, the existence of even a formal alliance meant that the Monarchy could hardly undertake extensive frontier fortifications against Roumania to make Transylvania absolutely secure. In this respect, as well as in regard to Berchtold's Bulgarian plans, the Roumanian alliance was becoming something of a liability.

If Austria-Hungary, despite German support, was losing her grip in Roumania by the summer of 1914, it was not surprising that she fared even worse in areas where her allies failed to support, or even actively opposed, her. At every turn she seemed to come up against the economic imperialism of Germany. At the end of 1913 Berchtold opened negotiations with Paris with a view to creating two international companies to run those sections of the Orient Railway recently incorporated into Serbia and Greece. As the controlling interest in both would be French and Austro-Hungarian, the plan offered a measure of economic influence in Serbia as well as some security for the bond-holders of the Orient Railway Company. And the negotiations at first went well – Berchtold almost managed to secure the re-opening of the French market to Austro-Hungarian loans. But in the end, the Austrians had to sell the line to Serbia direct (and the Serbs drove a hard bargain). For the Paris negotiations came to nothing in the face of opposition from Serbia and the other Powers, to which Germany did not fail to add her strident voice. Indeed, in Conrad's view, Germany was aiming at nothing less than the complete annihilation of Austro-Hungarian commercial influence not only in Serbia but throughout the Balkans.[52]

Equally damaging to Austro-Hungarian prestige and to alliance solidarity was the stubborn opposition of both Germany and Italy to the Monarchy's attempts to secure a foothold in Asia Minor, where the Great Powers were engaged in marking out spheres of interest against the day of partition.[53] True, Berchtold was unable to arouse much enthusiasm for his project in commercial circles and his hopes that it might serve as a distraction from the eternal wranglings of the nationalities at home (*Nationalitätenherd*) were certainly over-optimistic. But he was chiefly motivated by the desire to do something for the Monarchy's ailing

[52] F. Klein, 'Probleme des Bündnisses zwischen Oesterreich-Ungarn und Deutschland am Vorabend des ersten Weltkrieges', in F. Klein (ed.), pp. 159–60.

[53] F. R. Bridge, '*Tarde venientibus ossa:* Austro-Hungarian colonial aspirations in Asia Minor, 1913–14', *Middle Eastern Studies*, October 1970, pp. 319–30.

prestige; or at least to prevent yet a further loss of prestige – it would never do if the Monarchy were the only Power to receive nothing at all in the general scramble. Germany and Italy were unmoved, however, and refused to make room for their ally within their own spheres of interest – the Germans talked of co-operating with France and Britain, even of ending the alliance, if Austria-Hungary continued to pester them. Berchtold persisted nevertheless. But by June 1914 he had made no progress at all.

In Albania the prospects were equally depressing, although here it was the Italian ally rather than the German who was the chief worry. Even here, Germany's Greek proclivities were anything but helpful at a time when Greek troops remained in illegal occupation of large areas of southern Albania long after the collapse of the Greek puppet state of 'Northern Epirus'. But far more serious was the attempt of the Albanian minister of the interior, Essad Pasha (who owed his rise partly to Serbian support and was now notoriously in Italian pay) to carve out a principality for himself in Central Albania. At one stage, the Prince of Wied was driven to take refuge in a boat off the coast. Indeed, that very Albanian state which, so long as it had been a mere project of the future, had been a source of unity and co-operation between Vienna and Rome, had proved on its realization a veritable apple of discord. Even an Austro-Italian gentlemen's agreement on spheres of influence in the new state (April 1914) provided, when it came to be applied in practice, yet another source of wrangling between Vienna and Rome.

The Italians in turn were greatly worried by rumours of an Austro-Hungarian plan to purchase Mount Lovćen – an important strategic point dominating the bay of Cattaro – from Montenegro. Indeed, they talked of going to war rather than permit this. Nor was irredentism dead. In August 1913 the hysterical reaction in Italy to the decree of the *Statthalter* of Trieste removing Italian nationals from the city council had shown that large numbers of Italians still took a sweeping view of what was their concern. True, some military men in Italy, notably the chief of staff, General Pollio, were still loyal to the alliance; and in the summer of 1913 an Austro-Italian naval agreement provided for wartime co-operation against the French in the Mediterranean, under an Austro-Hungarian supreme command. But the Italian military attaché left Conrad in no doubt as to the realities of the situation;

and Conrad rightly regarded Austro-Italian military conversations as no more than window-dressing. As he told Franz Joseph in March 1914, one thing was certain: Italy would not fulfil any of her alliance commitments – in this, respect, at least, she was a reliable ally.[54]

The Triple Alliance being in such disarray, it was little wonder that the purposeful diplomacy of the Triple *Entente* Powers was achieving success after success; and that, in so far as these successes served also to whet the appetite of Serbia, a situation of some menace to the Monarchy was developing (Document 36). Not that there was any imminent danger of war. Although Pašić had been convinced since the end of the Second Balkan War that Serbia, having dealt with Turkey, must prepare for 'the second round against Austria',[55] and although during his visit to St Petersburg in February 1914 he received from the tsar himself the promise that Russia would some day come to the rescue of Serbia's kinsmen held in bondage across the Save, he was certainly not interested in war at this stage. Indeed, in June he expressly warned Athens not to let the Aegean Islands dispute develop to the point of war, for Serbia was not yet in any condition to fight. The government in Belgrade was for the present fully occupied with Serbia's recuperation after the exertions of 1912–13; and most of its new subjects in Macedonia had yet to be bludgeoned into submission.

Of course, even if Serbia was not planning to go to war, her behaviour still seemed obnoxious enough to Vienna. Not only had the Serbian government, in flagrant violation of its promise of 1909 to live on good neighbourly terms with Austria-Hungary, continued to tolerate on its territory propaganda organizations, and even terrorist groups, who operated in the south Slav areas of the Monarchy. (The most spectacular action of these people so far had been an abortive attempt to assassinate the Ban of Croatia in 1912.) Equally objectionable in political if not in legal terms, was the Serbian government's alleged official support for a Serbo-Montenegrin union, or, even worse, for a new Balkan league. Whether this last was envisaged as defensive or not, the Austro-Hungarian press was in no doubt whatever as to its ultimate purpose, and was in fact almost obsessively sensitive on the point.

[54] N. Stone, 'Moltke-Conrad . . .', p. 214.
[55] M. Bogitschewitsch, *Causes of the War* (London, 1919), p. 53.

A brief stop in Bucharest by the prime ministers of Serbia and Greece on their way back from St Petersburg in February – in fact, little more than a demonstration of solidarity against Bulgarian revisionism by the victors of the Second Balkan War – threw the *Neue Freie Presse* into great alarm about a new Balkan league which would be 'a dagger in the hand of Russia pointed straight at the heart of Austria'.[56]

Indeed, by the spring of 1914 rumours of the impending formation of a new Balkan league had provoked in the Monarchy a veritable press campaign against Russia. The furore was augmented by an armaments race, the Monarchy countering the steady growth of Russia's forces with another army bill (June 1914), envisaging a gradual increase in the size of the contingents annually recruited to the Common Army to 252,000 by 1918. Even an Austro-Russian irredentist dispute came to light with mutual accusations about Catholic intrigues among Russia's Ruthenian subjects and Russian Orthodox propaganda flooding into the Ruthenian areas of Galicia. Berchtold himself declared in June that the Ruthenian question would be 'decisive' for Austro-Russian relations.[57] But 'the plans which Serbia is weaving in the Balkans under Russian auspices'[58] continued to cause Vienna even more concern. Whatever the cause, Austro-Russian relations went steadily from bad to worse in 1914. The conciliatory Thurn was recalled from the St Petersburg embassy; even Tisza was gradually losing all faith in Russia; and Franz Joseph himself now decided in view of Russia's remorseless arming that she was a hopeless case, and that nothing more could be done about her.[59] Meanwhile, the press continued to use language that would have been more appropriate had Russia and Austria-Hungary been on the verge of actual war.

Berchtold decided to seek his salvation not in war, but in a diplomatic offensive. He was now convinced – and Franz Joseph agreed with him – that something would have to be done to arrest the steady and disastrous deterioration of the diplomatic situation. In June he determined to take the initiative and call the

[56] B.D., Vol. 10/1, No. 346.
[57] Z. A. B. Zeman, *The Break-up of the Habsburg Empire*, London, 1961, p. 12.
[58] Mensdorff MSS., Karton 9, Forgách to Mensdorff, 5 February 1914.
[59] W. Wagner, p. 275.

wayward German allies to order, directing Baron Matscheko (one of his assistants at the Ballhausplatz to draw up a memorandum (Document 37) on Balkan questions for the enlightenment of Berlin.[60] It was essential that Germany should bring her policy into line with Austria-Hungary's if there was to be any hope of frustrating the efforts of the Triple *Entente* Powers to build up a new Balkan league completing the encirclement of the Monarchy from the south. In practical terms, the Roumanian government should be summoned to show its colours and announce the alliance to the public. If it did not dare do this, then Vienna would at least know the worst, and could look to the defence of Transylvania without regard for an alliance that had proved itself a worthless scrap of paper. Roumanian susceptibilities should not be allowed to stand in the way of a serious effort to make an alliance with Bulgaria – and possibly Turkey might be brought in too. Even Serbia might yet be brought to reason by economic concessions and Roumanian advice: but the Matscheko memorandum was not very hopeful about this, and aimed on the whole to convince Berlin that Serbia was probably irreconcilable.

The memorandum contained not the slightest hint of war. Certainly, it marks the end of a long period of drift and indecision in the Ballhausplatz, and an attempt by the Austrians to give a firm lead and to devise a feasible Balkan policy for the Dual Alliance. Nevertheless, this was still a long-term policy, an attempt to solve the problem by patient and persevering diplomacy. The Ballhausplatz was in no great hurry: Matscheko had completed his draft memorandum by 24 June; and four days later it was still lying on Berchtold's writing-table awaiting approval when Archduke Franz Ferdinand and his consort arrived at Sarajevo.

The Sarajevo assassinations radically transformed the situation. Suddenly and dramatically, it seemed to Vienna, that brand of south Slav nationalism which flourished in Serbia and spread its tentacles into the Monarchy appeared as an immediate and mortal threat to the position of the Habsburgs as lords of Bosnia, and by implication, to the very existence of Austria-Hungary as a Great Power. To most people in the Ballhausplatz, the necessity for drastic action now seemed self-evident; and not only against a south Slav terrorist organization, but against that Serbian govern-

[60] M. B. A. Peterson, 'Das österreichisch-ungarische Memorandum an Deutschland vom 5 Juli 1914', *Scandia*, 1964, Vol. 30, pp. 138–90.

ment which had connived at its activities. Serbian promises of good behaviour, such as that by which Serbia had escaped invasion in March 1909, were clearly no answer. Nor, it now seemed, could a secret and laborious diplomatic offensive of the kind envisaged by the Matscheko memorandum save the situation. That would do nothing to counteract the effect on the public mind of the spectacular deeds of nationalist terrorism. On the contrary, as far as the public would be able to see, the Monarchy would appear to be doing nothing – to lack even the will to survive.

As regards the international scene, too, Berchtold decided that a mere continuation, even in a more effective form, of the diplomatic manoeuvres of the last six months would no longer suffice. Tisza was still for patience, arguing that the diplomatic situation might yet improve – for instance, given time, the Monarchy might manage to win over Bulgaria and make sure of Roumania. But Berchtold was adamant: in view of Russia's armaments programme, the general situation could only get worse with time; and as regards the Balkan situation, a failure to take vigorous action on this occasion would be universally regarded as such a clear 'renunciation of our Great Power position'[61] as would in itself deprive any diplomatic offensive of all hope of success. No Balkan government would dream of casting in its lot with such a feeble Power. On the contrary, the disastrous trends of the past six months would only be accelerated: a new Balkan league would soon be on the scene. After Sarajevo the Matscheko memorandum could no longer save the situation. There would have to be vigorous action, either to reduce Serbia to the status of a harmless vassal, or to annihilate her and partition her between Bulgaria, Albania, and Greece (thereby neatly bringing those states too into the Austro-Hungarian orbit) – in any case, as Franz Joseph wrote to William II on 2 July, 'to eliminate Serbia as a political power-factor (*Machtfaktor*) in the Balkans'.[62]

Such a course of action would have grave international implications. The very considerations that made it seem attractive to Vienna had themselves broader implications that made it totally unacceptable to St Petersburg. To Vienna, it was obvious that the downfall of Serbia – and, even more, Russia's inability to prevent it – would serve as such an object-lesson to the Balkan states as to put an end to all talk of Balkan leagues directed from

[61] H. Hantsch, *Berchtold*, Vol. 2, p. 562.   [62] O-U.A., Vol. 8, 9984.

St Petersburg against the Dual Monarchy. More than this: as Berchtold himself admitted, Russian influence in the Balkans would be destroyed for many years.[63] It was this fact that was likely to compel Russia to intervene despite any threats that Germany might utter; and herein lay the danger of a continental war. Even this the Austrians were prepared to contemplate. Although in June 1914 neither Vienna, Belgrade, nor St Petersburg had been thinking in terms of war, the terrorists at Sarajevo had contrived a situation that hardly admitted of a compromise solution by diplomacy. After Sarajevo, there could be no return to that situation of balance in the Balkans which had existed before the Balkan Wars, and which the Matscheko memorandum was seeking in a sense to restore. To the statesmen of Vienna, the choice now seemed clear and stark, and the facts of the situation inescapable. Inaction would mean the total collapse of Austria-Hungary's diplomatic position and of any hopes of saving it by diplomacy: action would equally inevitably entail the total destruction of Russia's diplomatic position – which St Petersburg could hardly accept without a fight. However the chancelleries might manoeuvre, there was no escaping this.

In this situation, the domestic, economic, and military situation in the Monarchy could hardly have any really determining effect on the government's decision either way. True, the view that the Dual Monarchy was by 1914 in a critical state bordering on dissolution, which rendered some foreign action imperative as a diversion or as a solution, is not without a certain plausibility. The problem of south Slav discontent exacerbated by a major quarrel between Budapest and the Croatian Diet had become more serious since 1912, and was in no way alleviated by the government's continuing to treat Bosnia and the Herzegovina essentially as a colony or militarily occupied territory unintegrated into the general political structure of the Monarchy. At the same time, the triumphs of Serbia in the Balkan Wars had increased the attractiveness to some south Slav enthusiasts inside the Monarchy of the self-styled 'Piedmont of the southern Slavs'. And elsewhere, quarrels between Czechs and Germans over language issues had resulted in the suspension by the summer of 1914 of both the Diet in Prague and the Reichsrat in Vienna. Nor did there seem to be any way out by means of domestic reform. The parliamentary

[63] H. Hantsch, *Berchtold*, Vol. 2, pp. 608, 625, 664.

bodies were hardly in a state to undertake it; and as Aehrenthal had realized after 1909, any radical reform would involve the tremendous upheaval of a showdown with the Magyars and perhaps civil war. Military coercion of some kind would almost certainly be necessary before the Magyars would accept anything remotely resembling Trialism – indeed, Franz Ferdinand made his calculations on that assumption. And the Czechs were almost equally fanatical opponents of Trialism, which would entail the disappearance of their south Slav allies from the Reichsrat at Vienna. Finally, the worsening of the international situation in 1913–14 only made it all the more difficult to consider embarking on the hazardous and turbulent sea of a major domestic reform.

Yet observers such as the German ambassador, Tschirschky, who in May 1914 declared that the Monarchy seemed to be 'falling apart at the seams' (*in allen Fugen*)[64] were perhaps unduly alarmist. After all, the Monarchy had survived far more serious crises in the past; and it had not been driven by them to seek its salvation in war. Apart from a brief spell in 1906–8, parliamentary life in Austria had hardly functioned properly for the past twenty years. The domestic situation in 1914 was not nearly so serious as that of 1903–6: then, one of the master races had been in open revolt, and the result had been the virtual paralysis of the Monarchy in foreign affairs. In 1914 the Magyars were undoubtedly loyal. Indeed, demands for action came even more strongly from the opposition in Hungary than from those defenders of the 1867 system on whom Berchtold relied for support. The nationalist wrangles that paralysed parliamentary life in Austria and Bohemia were squabbles within a political élite. The mass of the emperor's subjects in 1914 would have been very surprised to hear that the Monarchy was 'falling apart'.

Even with hindsight, the 'pessimist' view is by no means unassailable. The Dual Monarchy of 1914 was yet to survive another four years of even more serious crisis, during which the Common Army – the sinews of the Monarchy – remained for the great part impeccably loyal. The outbreak of war saw no refusals to enlist, such as had occurred among Czech reservists in Galicia in 1913. The south Slav regiments, as if to wash their hand of all guilt for the Sarajevo murders (which had precipitated serious anti-Serbian riots in Bosnia and Croatia), were particularly

[11] G.P. Vol. 39, 15734.

zealous in demonstrating their loyalty. And on no occasion in the entire war did the government have to order its troops to fire on its subjects, as the British were to do in Ireland. It was hardly the threat of imminent collapse that drove the Monarchy to war in 1914. The threat in 1914 was a foreign one, to the Monarchy's prestige as a Great Power in Europe. And although the Russo-Serbian threat certainly had domestic implications, these were only, in 1914 at least, that the south Slavs would become more difficult, rather than impossible, to govern. In a sense, the very fact that the domestic situation in 1914 was not all that serious made war more likely. The crisis of 1903–6, portending the actual disintegration of the Monarchy, had been so catastrophic as to paralyse it in foreign affairs. The domestic situation in 1914 was infinitely less grave – but still serious enough to engender enough pessimism, or exasperation, to provide an additional incentive to action.

Similarly, the economic situation, although not so bad as to paralyse the government or to leave it with no alternative but a desperate *coup*, was yet gloomy enough to give grounds for hope that something might be gained by action. The effects of the Balkan Wars were still being felt. According to the Russian consul at Vienna, many industries were in a very bad way as late as December 1913, as a result of the falling off of trade and the upheaval of mobilization. On the other hand, 1914 saw some improvement as the Balkans calmed down and the money held up by moratoria began to come in from the Balkan states. Hoarding declined and specie came back into circulation. By March, the government was able to reduce the bank rate from 6 per cent to 4 per cent, and even managed to raise loans for the new armaments programme. But it was a struggle; government credit was not high, and the loans had to be floated at 6 per cent. Internationally, the Monarchy still remained a weak state, financially dependent on others – above all on the Germans, who controlled more than half of the foreign investment in Austria-Hungary and bought some 40 per cent of her produce. Although, economically, the Monarchy had known worse times than 1914, there was still room for improvement – such as might occur if the Monarchy could re-establish its position in the Balkans.

The military situation too was a mixture of good and bad. The army bills of 1912 and 1914 had raised the level of the standing army to 475,000 (and a wartime strength of one and a half millions, compared with the million or so envisaged by the law of 1889, with which the Monarchy had had to manage for the past twenty-four years). This was no doubt a significant improvement; but it was partly offset by the fact that, with the increase coming so late in the day, the Common Army was still in the throes of re-organization in 1914. And even this improvement was unlikely to be more than temporary, given the frantic activity of France and Russia. In May 1914 Moltke admitted to Conrad that the German army was not superior in numbers to the French – which naturally rendered the Schlieffen plan (and any Austro-Hungarian plans based on it) hazardous in the extreme. And the Russian arma-ments programme of December 1913 planned to increase the size of the army by some 500,000 – i.e. by more than the total size of the Austro-Hungarian peacetime forces – to a wartime strength of 2,000,000 within the next five years. The military situation in 1914 was hardly tempting, from an Austro-Hungarian point of view. Conrad was aware of the deficiencies, of the near certainty that Russia would intervene, and the equal certainty that neither Italy nor Roumania would lend the Monarchy any assistance. Nevertheless, he threw his support behind Berchtold and against Tisza in demanding action. For the relatively healthy position of the Austro-Hungarian army, with its recent additions of strength, would be bound to deteriorate year by year in the face of Russian armaments with which the Monarchy could never hope to com-pete. Unless Austria-Hungary was prepared at once to abdicate as a Great Power by abandoning any possibility of defending her interests by force, then delay could only be suicidal. As the unre-pentant Conrad later observed: in 1909 it would have been a game with stacked cards, in 1912 with equal chances, by 1914 it was *va banque*.

Even so, it was by no means certain for a couple of weeks after Sarajevo that the Monarchy would be able to proceed to war. The attitude of the allies had yet to be ascertained. Germany's support would be essential against any Russian intervention; and in view of her recent behaviour Franz Joseph felt there was reason to doubt whether she would lend any help at all. Nor could the Monarchy embark on war against the opposition of Hungary. Tisza had good reasons for opposing war: defeat would mean the annihilation of Great Hungary; whereas victory might, as had been feared in the years after the Austro-Prussian war, strengthen the hand of the dynasty to implement centralist or trialist policies that would be equally disastrous for Magyar supremacy. On 1 July Tisza wrote to the emperor himself to protest against the very idea of war.

Berchtold was not deterred. He proceeded to redraft the Matscheko memorandum, turning it from a programme of long-term diplomatic action into what was virtually a plea for the immediate coercion of Serbia (Document 37). This, he saw would involve a serious risk of a major war. Hence, he eliminated from the Roumanian section of the memorandum the proposal that Roumania be summoned at once to declare herself openly either for or against the alliance. Such a demand would be needlessly risky at a moment when the Monarchy might find itself in desperate need of Roumania's goodwill. At the same time, he expanded the section that dealt with the threat to the Monarchy from Serbia and from a new Balkan league under Russian auspices. On 5 July Count Hoyos took the revised memorandum to Berlin, together with a letter from Franz Joseph to William II asking whether, if Austria-Hungary took a strong line with Serbia, and Russia intervened, Germany would stand by her ally.

The Austrians need not have worried. The Germans had good reasons enough of their own to support, and even encourage, Vienna in taking a strong line. Of recent weeks, they had been coming to view the fiasco of their own Balkan diplomacy with a frustration and despair that rivalled that of the Austrians. The prospect of a Balkan league directed from St Petersburg, a causeway of Russian influence stretching from Roumania to the Adriatic, and sealing off not only Austria-Hungary, but Germany too, with her vast stake in the Ottoman Empire, was not unnaturally a cause of great concern to Berlin. Berchtold's arguments found ready ears.

In more general terms too, the Germans now feared that if, after all the friction of the past six months, they were to thwart their Austro-Hungarian allies yet again, the result might be the total isolation of Germany and the final destruction of her position in the Near East – Austria-Hungary might either lose all patience with Germany, and seek her salvation in an Austro-Russian *entente*; or she might lapse into complete apathy and despair, virtually ceasing to exist as a Great Power. Ironically enough, one of Berchtold's arguments for taking a strong line was that otherwise Germany might despair of Austria-Hungary and abandon her for lost. In the final crisis, the solidarity of the Dual Alliance Powers was more the product of their mutual mistrust than of *deutsche Treue*. The German emperor's flamboyant declarations of support to Hoyos and the Austro-Hungarian ambassador were to some extent merely the elation of a neurotic: the past six months of tiresome and futile diplomatic wrangling could at last be resolved in action and brotherhood in arms.

The Germans, therefore, promised their full support; and emphasized that if Vienna decided to act against Serbia, then there was every reason to act with all possible speed. It was important to make use of the shock effect which the Sarajevo assassinations had produced at Tsarskoe Selo if there was to be any hope of restraining Russia from intervention. Altogether, the international situation seemed to Berlin uniquely favourable to an attempt to restore the Near Eastern position of the Central Powers. If France and Russia would rather fight than tolerate this, so much the better: for later the military situation could only get worse from Germany's point of view. Moreover, the relations of the Central Powers with London being excellent, there seemed a fair chance that Britain would remain neutral – although this situation might not hold for long if the rumoured Anglo-Russian negotiations for a naval convention were given time to mature. Lastly, Berlin could feel more sure of Austria-Hungary's loyalty in a war about a Balkan issue than in one arising from a Franco-German dispute.

Berchtold found the German expressions of support very useful. In the first place, they helped him to convince Budapest of the need for firm action.[65] As late as 7 July Tisza still held out against everybody else in a conference of ministers, and demanded a diplomatic solution to the crisis. True, he was beginning to wonder whether Serbia was not perhaps a hopeless case, especially as the Serbian press had maintained an unrepentant, indeed boastful, attitude ever since the assassinations. But it was probably strong pressure from Berchtold, from the Common Finance Minister, Burián, and, above all, from the German ambassador, that by 14 July brought him to accept the necessity for war. The

[65] N. Stone, 'Hungary and the Crisis of July 1914', *Journal of Contemporary History*, Vol. 1, 1966, pp. 153–70.

lesson of Sadowa, that the independence of Hungary depended in the last resort on the goodwill of Germany, was still valid after Sarajevo.

Not that Germany's pledge of support, essential though it might have been to any plan of action, determined the timing and manner of its implementation. Austro-Hungarian policy was still not made in Berlin. Despite German advice urging the advisability of acting with speed Berchtold was determined not to be hurried. Serbia, it was decided in a conference of ministers of 14 July, was to be presented with a very strong note (Document 38). The charge against her, however, was not one of complicity in the assassinations (which Austro-Hungarian investigations had failed to prove) but the more general one that she had blatantly violated her promise of 31 March 1909 to live on good neighbourly terms with the Dual Monarchy. For some three weeks Austro-Hungarian foreign office officials worked busily on a painstaking collation of Serbian misdeeds since 1909, producing a weighty memorandum which, it was hoped, would impress the Powers and justify the Austro-Hungarian note. This would be difficult. For it was not so much the demands of the note – more or less, that Serbia behave as she had promised to behave in 1909 – that were considered unreasonable, as the means envisaged to secure the observance of those demands – for example, the presence of Austro-Hungarian officials in Serbia to assist in suppressing seditious movements. This would have reduced Serbia to a satellite of the Monarchy. Whether the Austro-Hungarian note was designed to be unacceptable or not, whether Tisza's view that no Serbian territory be annexed to the Monarchy would have prevailed in Vienna or not, whether Serbia submitted herself to her new role as a satellite, or refused to submit and was overwhelmed, was immaterial. The result would be disastrous in all cases from a Russian point of view. The issue was whether Serbia was to be allowed to continue to exist as a Russian outpost, indeed, the kingpin of the Russian position in the Balkans; or whether Austria-Hungary was to liberate herself from the menace, even if this meant destroying Serbia's liberty and Russia's prestige at the same time.

The issue at stake was compelling enough to force the Monarchy, once assured of the vital German support, to go ahead without waiting further to make sure of the problematical support of its other allies. No attempt was made to activate the Triple and Roumanian alliances. In the first place, the state of Vienna's relations with Rome and Bucharest hardly gave grounds for hope that Italy and Roumania would recognize the *casus foederis* in any circumstances, let alone as a result of a war started by Austria-Hungary. Besides, if the Austrians took Rome and Bucharest into their confidence there would be a serious danger of their plans being leaked to St Petersburg before they could be put into operation. It was for similar reasons that Berchtold delayed the presentation of the note to Serbia till 23 July, by which time President Poincaré would have ended his state visit to Russia and be safely on the high seas. During the three weeks in which the indictment against Serbia was being prepared the Ballhausplatz moved with the greatest secrecy. Surprise would greatly increase the chances of a successful *coup*.

Once the Serbs refused to submit to the note – fobbing off the Austrians with a virtual repetition of their promises of 1909 with no guarantees as to their fulfilment – Vienna acted with great speed and determination. On 25 July diplomatic relations with Belgrade were broken off; Austria-Hungary declared war on 28 July; and although the army could not be mobilized for any major operations for a further three weeks, Belgrade was bombarded on 29 July. True, Conrad would have preferred to delay the declaration of war until the army was ready to start operations; but Berchtold insisted that 'the diplomatic situation will not hold that long'.[66] He was anxious for some demonstrative military action that would transfer the crisis immediately and irrevocably from the diplomatic to the military sphere, and forestall any attempt by the Great Powers to intervene with another face-saving but worthless diplomatic solution (Document 39).

There must be no more compromises, of that he was determined – either direct as in 1909, or under the cloak of the Concert as in 1912 and 1913. This being the case, Grey's mediation proposals would hardly have had a chance of success at Vienna even if Berlin had seriously supported them. At first, Berchtold refused to discuss the situation directly with St Petersburg either, arguing that the Russians should be satisfied with his promises not to incorporate any Serbian territory into the Monarchy. On 30 July he relented somewhat and agreed to an exchange of views with St Petersburg, and perhaps even with London. But these discussions were hardly likely to lead to much. Berchtold was interested only

[66] Conrad v. Hoetzendorf, Vol. 4, p. 132.

in discussing the means by which the Powers might bring Serbia to submit to the note of 23 July: the Powers should give their blessing to the reduction of Serbia to an Austro-Hungarian satellite. This was asking far more than Aehrenthal had asked in 1909; and the crisis of 1909 was not repeated. Indeed the discussions hardly progressed at all in the face of Berchtold's refusal to accept Sazonov's preliminary stipulation that the Monarchy first cease all military operations against Serbia. Nevertheless, the Austro-Russian negotiations were still going on, or rather, the deadlock was still being discussed, when Russia's mobilization and Germany's reaction to it announced the outbreak of European war.

This development, although hardly unexpected, was highly unwelcome to Vienna at this juncture. Austro-Hungarian policy was still made with an eye to the Near Eastern balance of power, not to a world balance (which became the issue when Britain joined the war against Germany on 4 August). The Austrians were above all concerned to re-establish their position in the Near East by crushing Serbia and destroying the influence of Russia. And although they were undeterred by the thought that this might well entail a European war, they had few interests of their own in such a war. Austria-Hungary's sense of priorities, therefore, was quite different from Germany's; and the resultant conflict of interests was to render the life of the Dual Alliance in war as turbulent and strife-ridden as it had been in thirty-five wearisome years of peace. Needless to say, the Triple and Roumanian alliances did not operate at all. Not that Austria-Hungary's offensive operations raised the *casus foederis* anyway. King Carol and the aged Carp would have liked to join the Monarchy; but they could not prevail against the rest of the government in Bucharest. Roumania declared her neutrality on 4 August. Italy had already done so on 3 August.[67] It was henceforth a question of what compensation the Monarchy would have to pay to hold her to mere neutrality; and as Rome began to talk at once of compensation from the territory of the Monarchy, Kálnoky's sins of omission of 1887 were now visited on his successors.

The Dual Alliance was hardly in any happier condition. It was

[67] Not that the Western Powers were completely satisfied with Italy's attitude, which a French diplomat characterized with some acerbity: 'l'Italie volera au secours du vainqueur.' L. Villari, *The War on the Italian Front*, London, 1925.

not until 6 August, after a week of hectoring from Berlin, that the Monarchy declared war on Russia. Nor was there any desire in Vienna to force a Mediterranean confrontation with the fleets of the Western Powers. France and Britain, ironically enough, were afraid of the Austro-Hungarian fleet, which with four dreadnoughts was potentially dangerous so long as the French fleet was engaged in ferrying troops to Europe from North Africa. It was only on 12 August that the Western Powers declared war on Austria-Hungary.[68] An even more striking illustration of the divergent interests of Vienna and Berlin was the fact that whereas the Germans wanted an immediate and powerful Austro-Hungarian offensive into Poland to take on the weight of Russia's forces, Conrad in fact implemented 'Plan-B', sending the supplementary *B-Staffel* not to Galicia but to the Balkan front. Despite the fact that Russian intervention had been regarded as virtually inevitable since 27 July, he fobbed the Germans off with the plea that the technical difficulties of mobilization forbade the transfer of *B-Staffel* to the northern front. (In fact, it could have been sent north as late as 1 August.) He persisted in this plan until 5 August. Like Berchtold, he was above all intent on re-establishing the Monarchy's position in the Near East by finally crushing Serbia, and Germany's demands for action in the north were given short shrift. (After all, for Conrad, Germany was as much a threat to Austria-Hungary's Balkan position as Russia was.) In the end, it was only an even more flagrant breach of faith by Germany – who refused to undertake any offensive at all from East Prussia – that forced Conrad to a belated and disastrous implementation of 'Plan-R'. Berchtold's threats to denounce the alliance were at such a moment hardly convincing: there was nothing for it but to try to counteract the vast Russian force in Poland by transferring *B-Staffel* from the Balkan front to Galicia. In September, the long-planned Austro-Hungarian offensive into Poland got under way, but without any German support. The result was the disastrous battle of Lemberg, which destroyed the Austro-Hungarian army as a first-class fighting force. As Norman Stone observes, the Germans had 'won this competition in *deutsche Treue*, and Austria-Hungary bled to death in order to defend Berlin'.[69]

[68] F. R. Bridge, 'The British Declaration of War on Austria-Hungary in 1914', *Slavonic Review*, Vol. 47, 1969, pp. 401–22.
[69] N. Stone, 'Moltke-Conrad . . .', p. 202.

Chapter 8

Conclusion

Austria-Hungary's decision to go to war in 1914 led ultimately, through four years of war and revolution, to such an appalling loss of life that it is hardly surprising that even after fifty years it is still the object of moralizing and indignation. On the one hand, progressive historians denounce the decision of the rulers of the 'anachronistic' Dual Monarchy, 'notoriously unable to adapt their regime to the exigencies of modern times' to deal with 'the most dynamic element in the Balkans'[1] by brute force; on the other, the sentimentalist school in Austria has little time for the foreign historian who, although he 'sees perhaps the symptoms of the disease, but does not feel the pain',[2] presumes to utter so much as a breath of criticism of Berchtold's policy in the July crisis. But the historian is no better (and no worse) equipped than any other man to pronounce on the ultimate rights and wrongs of the matter. He can only point out that whether the explosive south Slav question, with its international ramifications, arose from Austro-Hungarian misrule or from Serbian and Russian intrigues, nevertheless by the standards of the conventional political and international morality of the time, no Great Power would have felt obliged to admit the right of a small neighbour to interfere in, or even officially to express an opinion on, its domestic affairs; and that in an age which did not accept the doctrine of self-determination of peoples as a desirable basis for determining the frontiers of Great Powers, the Monarchy's decision to defend its integrity was morally at least as justifiable as Serbia's striving to undermine it.

As early as January 1913 the British ambassador in Vienna had described 'how exasperated people are getting here at the continual worry which . . . Serbia causes to Austria under encouragement from Russia. It may be compared to a certain extent to the

---

[1] I. Geiss, *July 1914* (London, 1967), pp. 49–51.
[2] H. Hantsch, *Berchtold*, Vol. 2, p. 647.

trouble we had to suffer through the hostile attitude formerly assumed against us by the Transvaal Republic under the guiding hand of Germany.'[3] The simple fact was that in the pre-1914 world a Great Power would not tolerate obstreperous behaviour from a little Power indefinitely – especially when such behaviour seemed to threaten the very existence of the Great Power. Apart from Russia, where Panslav feeling was strong, no other Great Power in 1914 seriously questioned Austria-Hungary's aim (as distinct from her methods) in the July crisis. Sir Edward Grey, a fairly objective observer, told the Austro-Hungarian ambassador[4] that if Austria-Hungary could make war on Serbia and at the same time satisfy Russia, well and good: he could 'take a holiday tomorrow'. But if not, the consequences would be incalculable. No cry of 'gallant little Serbia' was raised in Britain.

As far as his professional competence is concerned, therefore, the historian can only consider the question of why – moral considerations apart – in 1914 the statesmen of the Dual Monarchy, when confronted with a crisis that was after all only another phase of a problem that had faced the Monarchy for half a century, resorted to war – a solution rejected time and again in the previous fifty years. The possibility of armed action against Serbia, Roumania or Russia, had been discussed often enough since 1866. For three decades prior to 1914 the Monarchy's whole alliance system had been designed to meet the contingency of war in the east; and Austro-Serbian relations had been deplorable for a decade already before 1914. But war had been avoided. The question remains: what was peculiar about the situation in 1914?

It would be futile to seek an answer merely in the personalities of the decision-makers of the time. The same emperor ruled who had ruled for the past forty-eight years of continuous peace; and if Conrad von Hoetzendorf had been pressing for war for eight years, Berchtold, who counted for more, had in his first two years of office shown himself to be eminently pacific. The men of 1914 were hardly inferior in ability or intelligence, and no less conscientious than the men who had avoided war in the previous four decades. The uniqueness of the 1914 situation must be sought not in the personalities of the ruling élite, but in the facts of the diplomatic situation – or rather in the narrow selection of facts that

[3] B.D., Vol. 9/2, No. 582.
[4] F. R. Bridge, 'The British Declaration of War on Austria-Hungary in 1914'.

presented itself as 'the situation', to the exclusive circle of decision-makers responsible for Austro-Hungarian policy.

The men of 1914 came from the same social background – the landowning aristocracy and higher bureaucracy – as their predecessors, and shared their military-aristocratic *Weltanschauung*. Their basic ideas were traditional enough, and would have been regarded by their predecessors as eminently sensible. Since 1866, or at least since 1871, it had been axiomatic in the Ballhausplatz that the chief threat to the vital interests of Austria-Hungary was that posed to its territorial integrity by irredentism, whether of a south Slav, Roumanian, or Italian variety. With irredentism there could be no compromise: if nationality ever replaced dynasticism as the principle on which the state was based, the Habsburg Monarchy would cease to exist, its southern provinces lost to the new national states on its borders, and the rest torn asunder by conflicting nationalisms within. It was equally axiomatic that so long as the Imperial and Royal Army, the lynch-pin of the whole Habsburg system, continued supranational and loyal, the Monarchy would be able to cope with the threat from Serbia, Roumania or Italy. Irredentism could only pose a mortal threat to the Monarchy if it gained the support of a Great Power with a military capacity equal or superior to that of the Habsburgs. By 1871 of the three Great Powers – Russia, France and Prussia – who had harassed the Monarchy for a decade after the Crimean War, only Russia still seemed likely to throw in her lot with the Monarchy's irredentist foes. Hence, the unflagging efforts of Austro-Hungarian statesmen to prevent the realization of the fatal combination of irredentist ambition and Russia's quest for security through control of the Balkans and the Straits. The Triple Alliance sought to ensure Italy's neutrality in the event of war with Russia; the alliances with the rulers of Serbia and Roumania to keep them in Austria-Hungary's orbit and to encourage them to impose a restraint on irredentism at home; and the various agreements concluded with Russia herself to dissuade her from taking up the irredentist cause. Basically, these combinations were attempts to prevent Russia's *Drang Nach Westen* from combining with irredentism to form an 'iron ring' encircling the Monarchy from Poland to the Adriatic.

For more than four decades, the Monarchy managed, by one diplomatic means or another, to stave off this threat. But the sudden disappearance in 1912–13 of that bastion of the *status quo*, Turkey-in-Europe, and Russia's subsequent diplomatic successes in the Balkans raised in a most menacing form the spectre of irredentism, backed by a Great Power and advancing under cover of a new Balkan league. Although as late as June 1914 the Austrians were still hoping to launch a diplomatic counter-offensive, the Sarajevo assassinations convinced them that the issue would no longer admit of any but a military solution.

To Vienna the arguments for an alternative, more pacific, course of action seemed unconvincing. Domestic reform to turn the south Slavs of the Monarchy into contented subjects hardly seemed feasible, given the rigid dualistic structure of the Monarchy and the determination of the whole Magyar ruling élite to preserve it. Even if radical reforms could have been carried out with the support of only a minority of the conflicting racial groups in Austria and at the risk of civil war in Hungary, their very success might only have served to precipitate an attack from Serbian and Roumanian irredentists, confident since 1913 that the international situation had turned in their favour – just as the prospect of reform in the Ottoman Empire had only served to precipitate the attack of the Balkan states on Turkey in 1912.

It is true that had the Austrians decided to wait and trust in diplomacy the situation might yet have changed to their advantage. The Triple *Entente* might in time have broken up: it was already undermined by Anglo-Russian disputes over Persia and by growing fears in London that Russia might some day replace Germany as the chief threat to the balance of Power. But this was only a long-term and uncertain possibility. What seemed certain to Vienna in 1914 was that the relative strength of irredentist forces, apparently backed by Russia and France, posed an immediate threat to the Monarchy; and that in the immediate future, this threat would continue to grow. Failure to act after Sarajevo would destroy the Monarchy's prestige as a Great Power and with it any chances of its breaking out from encirclement by a diplomatic campaign. This being the view of the decision-makers in Vienna, their policy of eliminating Serbia without delay was intelligible enough.

Yet, whereas in 1914 the arguments in favour of war seemed to Austrian minds to outweigh those in favour of peace, in the preceding forty-eight years the case was different: the decisions invariably went the other way. The long period of peace after 1866 can no more be explained in terms of personalities than can its sudden end in 1914: the statesmen of 1866–1912, like the men of 1914, simply took their decisions after weighing the arguments for war or peace in the light of the situation as it appeared to them. And the decisions were sometimes fine ones. The Hungarians were tenacious advocates of war in the 1880s, and many of the higher military after 1906, when Conrad succeeded the pacific, conservative, Beck. But the emperor and his foreign minister had always prevailed against warmongers in Budapest or in the General Staff. In 1914, however, the emperor and the minister for foreign affairs joined with the military in opting for war, and only the Hungarian prime minister was for peace. On all other occasions between 1866 and 1914, the threats to the vital interests of the Monarchy never seemed, in the eyes of the narrow circle of decision-makers, so serious or direct as to override the weighty general arguments against resorting to war that formed the bases of Habsburg foreign policy.

These arguments were numerous and various, and generally held good throughout the period under review. In the first place, once the Monarchy had ceased to weep for its lost position in Italy and Germany it had nothing to gain from war. Any increase of territory could only bring in more south Slavs and upset the internal balance of nationalities to the detriment of the 'master races', Magyars, Germans and Poles. Since the 1880s any armed action that was contemplated against Serbia was always to be in the nature of a punitive expedition to reduce the Serbs to a proper obedience. War against Russia it was generally recognized could bring no positive gains to compensate for the immense destruction and loss of life it would entail. It could only be justified if it were a question of breaking what seemed to be a Russian stranglehold in the south which would at best leave Austria-Hungary with no sphere in which she could exert herself as a Great Power either commercially or politically, and at worst threaten the territorial integrity of the Monarchy itself.

The second basis of Habsburg foreign policy was a profound belief in the importance of monarchical solidarity in defence of the internal *status quo* against an international revolutionary movement. Although the defeat of the Revolution in 1849 had given continental governments everywhere a new confidence to pursue their interests even to the point of war, the Paris Commune and the Second International served as a painful reminder of the connexion between war and revolution and inaugurated a period of peace reminiscent of the age of the neo-Holy Alliance. The opportunist Beust may have had little time for monarchical solidarity; but it was certainly an important element in the Three Emperors' League of the 1870s and even more so in the Three Emperors' Alliance. And in the 1880s Vienna made alliances with Serbia, Italy, and Roumania, all consciously designed to bolster up dynasties whose loyalty was the chief mainstay of Austria-Hungary's position in those states. The Monarchy's links with Spain through the Mediterranean agreements of 1887 lasted for a decade and the interest which Kálnoky and his successor continued to take in the well-being of the Italian and Iberian monarchies bore witness to what was for Vienna a serious concern – the need to resist the supposed plans of the *Umsturzpartei* to create a federation of Latin republics as a prelude to an attack on the great Slav and German monarchies. In the *entente* of 1897 the idea of monarchical solidarity was perhaps less marked – Goluchowski, as a Pole, had little love for the House of Romanov, and indeed, by 1906 seemed to have given the tsardom up for lost. But once Aehrenthal was in office monarchical solidarity against the proletarian and parliamentary threat was again the order of the day until the rift with Russia in 1908. Even in 1914 Berchtold was hoping that the tsar might think twice about coming to the defence of Serbian regicides. But outside the Monarchy hardly anyone on the continent attached much importance to the principle of monarchical solidarity: to William II it was 'not worth a rap' ('*ganz schnuppe*'),[5] where the struggle was one between Slav and German; and since 1913 Nicholas II had been looking forward with composure to the impending dissolution of the Habsburg Monarchy.[6] Perhaps William I and Nicholas I had been better judges of their dynasties' interests – witness the collapse of all three empires in the World War. For all three Eastern monarchies, the principle of monarchical solidarity that loomed so large in Habsburg foreign policy throughout this period, was basically sound.

General theoretical considerations were reinforced by arguments of a more practical nature – the domestic situation in the

[5] O-U.A., Vol. 7, No. 8934.   [6] B.D., Vol. 9/2, No. 849.

Habsburg Monarchy, its economic weakness and its cumbersome political structure, all of which were reflected, especially after the middle 'nineties, in the comparative weakness of the Common Army and the inadequacy of the Monarchy's strategic railways and frontier defences. These were serious deficiencies at a time when, owing to the deterioration of relations with Serbia and Italy after the turn of the century, the Monarchy might find itself faced with war on three fronts. Altogether, therefore, the arguments in favour of defending the Monarchy's vital interests by diplomatic means if at all possible were overwhelming.

This task was no easy one. Austria-Hungary was only one Power among six, and a weak Power at that. Franz Joseph could not issue commands to Europe as Napoleon I had done; he would have to try, rather, like Metternich, to persuade the other Powers that Austria-Hungary's interests were their own. If he failed, the Monarchy would be isolated and its interests ignored – as even Metternich had found in the 1820s. The statesmen of Vienna, therefore, had always to be prepared to tack, and adjust their policies to the facts of a diplomatic situation which was often beyond their control, making use of such bargaining power as the Monarchy possessed to persuade others to follow them if the opportunity arose. The rivalries of the other Powers provided a certain amount of scope for this; but all the same it would have been fatal for a statesman of a Power so weak as Austria-Hungary to ignore Lord Salisbury's dictum: 'the commonest error in politics is sticking to the carcasses of dead policies.'[7]

Of the foreign ministers of the Dual Monarchy in the period between Sadowa and Sarajevo, all seven were confronted with the problem of an intractable diplomatic situation, and all seven showed themselves versatile enough to overcome it. Although all took office with a blueprint for a policy which proved impractical, owing to the intractability of the international situation, all managed without sacrificing any vital interests of the Monarchy to adjust their policies to reality. Beust, who spent most of his years at the Ballhausplatz working for an alignment with France against Russia and Prussia over the Eastern question ended by accepting Prussia's domination of Germany, and laid the foundations of the Austro-German alliance. Andrássy, faced

[7] Lady Gwendolen Cecil, *Life of Robert, Marquis of Salisbury*, Vol. 2, London, 1921, p. 145.

with British and German hesitations, soon had to abandon his ideal of a grand alliance against Russia; and for most of the 'seventies worked in uneasy partnership with that Power in the Three Emperors' League. Even when in 1879 he secured the alliance with Germany, he had by no means realized his ideal. Haymerle, who shared his views, was forced by the attitudes of Britain and Germany along the path of reconciliation with Russia. And Kálnoky, who took office with the intention of strengthening cordial relations with Russia, spent most of his time in building up two imposing blocs against her – reinforcing the Dual Alliance with military agreements and Italian and Roumanian alliances, and creating the Mediterranean *entente*. Goluchowski, at first hopeful of developing the Mediterranean *entente* into something approaching an alliance, regretfully decided after two years to abandon it altogether and to seek some accommodation with Russia. Aehrenthal, the greatest partisan of the Austro-Russian *entente*, presided over its collapse; and after spending three years on schemes and blueprints as bold as any of Andrássy's embarked on three years of the strictest conservatism. Finally, Berchtold, who on taking office placed his hopes in Concert diplomacy and co-operation with Britain, was within two years convinced that the best defence of the Monarchy's interests lay in single-handed action.

However versatile and open-minded the statesmen of the Monarchy may have been as regards the means they adopted to defend the continuing interests of the Monarchy, nevertheless, versatility and open-mindedness were no sure guarantee of success. The international situation changed so often and so radically in the half-century after 1866 that it was hardly surprising that the makers of Austro-Hungarian foreign policy were often in difficulties. Even so, the crisis of 1914 was in nearly fifty years the only one that seemed to Vienna to demand a military solution. For the rest, diplomatic compromises were considered acceptable.

For most of that time, there seemed to be no threat to the Monarchy's vital interests urgent enough to raise the prospect of war – simply because Russia, weak or preoccupied elsewhere, was disposed for a time to respect those interests. This situation, the most desirable from the point of view of the security of the Monarchy, was also the most common and prevailed for more than half of the period under review – the years of the Three Emperors'

League, the Three Emperors' Alliance, and the Austro-Russian *entente*.

On certain occasions the threat posed by Russia and by Balkan irredentism seemed indeed acute, but was effectively parried. The menace of the Treaty of San Stefano was dispelled by the Congress of Berlin and the Dual Alliance; the Mediterranean *entente* of 1887 and Germany's support for that combination after 1890 put an end to any risk that Russia might establish a military presence in Bulgaria; and in 1909 the Austro-German alliance overcame the opposition of Serbia and the Triple *Entente* Powers to the annexation of Bosnia. On these occasions diplomatic means sufficed to bring the Monarchy great victories.

In other crisis situations, however, Austria-Hungary, although not pushed to the point of war, suffered signal diplomatic defeats. Sometimes, she was isolated and facing overwhelming odds: Beust's ambitious policy of opposing the combination of Russia and Prussia was bound to fail when France offered assistance only on terms that would drive the rest of Germany into Prussia's arms. Sometimes Austria-Hungary had friends and allies enough but they failed her: this was the case in the middle 'nineties when Goluchowski, finding little sympathy in Berlin and only problematical support in London, was forced to come to terms with St Petersburg; in the years of the Austro-Russian *entente* (which undoubtedly drew much of its vitality from the lamentable relations prevailing between the members of the Triple Alliance); and in the years between the Bosnian crisis and the eve of war, when the Dual Alliance served more to draw an increasingly threadbare veil over the mutual suspicions of Vienna and Berlin than to display their solidarity to the world.

Indeed, the very *ententes* and alliances which seemed to strengthen Austria-Hungary's diplomatic position sometimes served, rather, to weaken it; or at least to deter the Monarchy from taking effective action to protect those interests which the *entente* or alliance was itself designed to safeguard. It is not only the crisis emanating from Budapest but the respect felt in Vienna for the Austro-Russian *entente* that explain the Monarchy's failure to intervene in Serbia after the revolution of 1903, or to take advantage of Russia's involvement in the Far East to make Austro-Hungarian influence predominant in the Balkans. The alliances with Serbia, with Italy, and, particularly in the last years of peace, the alliance with Roumania, had a similar restrictive effect. Certainly the solution, or palliative, they offered was cheaper than war; and if it were effective, on all counts to be preferred. But possibly the Monarchy missed chances to attempt a military solution with a hope of success. And for some ten years before 1914 the Dual Alliance concealed what was virtually a commercial war between the allies in the Near East – a war that gravely damaged the interests of Austria-Hungary.

Nevertheless, in the half-century between Sadowa and Sarajevo the Monarchy suffered no reverses comparable to those of 1859 and 1866. Diplomacy provided an adequate defence for Austria-Hungary's vital interests, and even brought some brilliant successes and the acquisition of two provinces. True, these years saw a gradual and fairly steady decline in the Great Power status of the Monarchy, unable to compete in economic terms with the advanced states of north-west Europe, or in terms of population with Russia – on which factors the military potential of a state, and hence its Great Power status ultimately depended. But the situation did not become really grave until 1912. And it was not until July 1914 that Vienna decided that all hope of salvation by diplomacy was lost. Only after Sarajevo did the statesmen in the Ballhausplatz, weighing much the same arguments for war and peace as their predecessors ever since Sadowa, decide that the balance had changed for the first time; and that the risks of peace were now greater than the risks of war.

Documents

1. *Beust to Metternich, confidential, 27 April 1867* (Kab. 17)
[Beust describes his conversation with the French ambassador about Napoleon III's proposal for an offensive and defensive alliance against Prussia. He doubts whether it will find favour with German-Austrian, Slav or Hungarian opinion.]

Certainly I am not insensible to the advantages that a French alliance could offer to Austria. There are eventualities – in the Eastern question for example – where I should desire such an alliance with all my heart, and should not shrink before any of its possible consequences, not even before an aggrandizement of France in Germany – provided that this could be presented not as the principal and immediate aim of the war but as an accessory consequence, so to speak, of a struggle which started elsewhere over other interests. The terrain on which the French government is placing itself today is evidently the most unfavourable for the conclusion of this alliance with us, for the alliance is proposed on terms which are too offensive (*qui froissent trop*) to the ideas and innermost convictions of one of the nationalities, perhaps the most important one, in the whole Empire: all the national feelings of Germany would be stirred as soon as war breaks out over a question in which the interests of France and Germany are directly opposed, and the German populations of Austria would not be able to remain aloof from such a movement.

'Finally there is', I added, 'another consideration, which makes us hesitate to accept your offers. I admit that morality must not direct the conduct of governments in politics in the same way that it should govern the actions of men in private life. Nevertheless, morality has certain laws which one cannot entirely trample underfoot. Now, would it not be a direct violation of all moral law if Austria sought to aggrandize herself at the expense of the states of Germany who, although their attitude left something to be desired, were nevertheless our allies during the last war?'

2. *Beust, report to Franz Joseph, 1867* (Kab. 17)
[Beust advises caution in the forthcoming Salzburg meeting with Napoleon III, 'in view of the indubitable fact that Austria has an absolute need of peace for a long time'. But Austria should maintain a friendly attitude towards France, who is after all watching over Austrian interests in Germany.]

As regards the South German question, it is obvious that Austria has a decided interest in preventing the extension of the North German Confederation to South Germany. For if this happens, and the Prussian ring is by this means extended from Oderburg to Salzburg and Bregenz, the Imperial Government's position in the German provinces will be exposed to continual disturbance (*Beunruhigung*). Austria cannot have an interest, therefore, in supporting the Prussian advance and in weakening French resistance to it by assuming a passive attitude. Indeed, Austria would not be able to escape the necessity of acting in some mediatory sense which would leave both Prussia and the South German states in no doubt that she will keep her complete freedom of action in the event of war.

But such a friendly attitude towards France depends very much on France's assuming an attitude, not only of benevolence but of active support, over matters which affect the Austrian Monarchy much more closely and deeply. The most imminent danger to Austria threatens from Russia, and agreement about the Balkan (*orientalische*) question or rather, about the whole Eastern question is more important than anything else. France must either stand up firmly against Russia's policy towards Turkey and Austria, or must offer us, by means of a common agreement with Russia, some guarantees against Russian expansion. If we cannot bring France radically to change her attitude in the Cretan question and to help in destroying Russia's prestige among the Christian peoples of Turkey; and decidedly to oppose a Russian occupation of the Danubian principalities and support an eventual Austrian intervention, then we shall have to think about seeking a *rapprochement* with Prussia.

3. *Beust memorandum, 25 September 1868, 'concerning the organiza-
tional plans of the insurrectionary committees in Turkey, the Danubian
Principalities, and Greece'* (Kab. 17)

[The ambassador at Constantinople accepts Beust's documentary
evidence and believes that the Bucharest revolutionary committee
is controlled by Bratianu who, like Prince Carol, is in turn controlled by Bismarck.]

Now it seems only natural that Bismarck is hoping for (*herbei-
wünscht*) conditions which will enable him to put his further
designs against Austria into operation before our internal position
is settled and consolidated. [The ambassador thinks that Bismarck
is not yet ready to unleash the 'rabble' against Turkey, but] it
seems to us clear beyond all doubt from all the reports and facts
(*Umstände*) that the attack on Turkey, undertaken with Count
Bismarck's approval, is only a means, whereas the ultimate aim of
M. Bratianu, who calls himself the Roumanian Cavour, is the
attack on Austria.

4. *The Schönbrunn Convention, 6 June 1873* (translated from G.P.
Vol. 1, pp. 206–7)

His Majesty the Emperor of Austria and King of Hungary
and His Majesty the Emperor of All the Russias:
Wishing to give a practical form to the sentiments that inspire
Their close understanding (*entente*),
With a view to consolidating the state of peace that now exists in
Europe, having at heart the elimination of the risks of war that
might disturb it,
Convinced that this aim cannot be better achieved than by a direct
personal understanding between the sovereigns independent of
changes that may occur in their administrations, have agreed on
the following points:

1. Their Majesties promise each other, in the event of the interests
of Their countries appearing to diverge over particular (*spéciales*)
questions, to concert together to ensure that these divergences do
not prevail over the considerations of a higher order that are
Their chief concern.
Their Majesties are determined to prevent anyone from dividing
Them as in respect of the principles which They consider Themselves solely able to safeguard, and, if necessary, to enforce the

maintenance of European peace against all disturbances from any quarter whatever.

2. In the event of a threat to the peace arising from the aggression of a third Power, Their Majesties promise each other to reach an understanding with each other first of all and, without seeking or contracting new alliances, to agree on a line of action to be pursued in common.

3. If in consequence of this understanding military action should become necessary it shall be regulated (*réglée*) by a special convention to be concluded between Their Majesties.

4. If one of the High Contracting Parties should wish to denounce this present agreement to recover his freedom of action, he must give two years' notice of his intention so as to allow the other Party time to make such arrangements as he finds convenient.

Schönbrunn, 25 May/6 June 1873.   Franz Joseph. Alexander.

His Majesty the Emperor of Germany, having taken note of the above agreement, drawn up and signed at Schönbrunn by Their Majesties the Emperor of Austria and King of Hungary and the Emperor of All the Russias, and finding its content in conformity with the sentiments embodied in the agreement signed at St Petersburg between Their Majesties the Emperor William and the Emperor Alexander, acceded to its stipulations in every respect.

Their Majesties the Emperor and King William and the Emperor and King Franz Joseph in approving and signing this act of accession will bring it to the knowledge of the Emperor Alexander.

Schönbrunn, 22 October 1873.

William.   Franz Joseph.

5. *Andrássy to Franz Joseph, 27 August 1875* (Kab. 18)

Baron Rodich [Governor of Dalmatia] proposes that we negotiate immediately with Serbia and Montenegro and buy them off (especially Montenegro) with offers of territory; and that although we did not march in at the beginning of the rebellion (which would have meant ending the Three Emperors' League and disturbing the peace of Europe), we should do so if the Turks stay in Bosnia.

Rodich's assumptions are quite false. The obstacles to an occupation he sees in Serbia and Montenegro, not where they really are, in Russia and the rest of Europe. He hears only the appeals of Herzegovina . . . like a mouse that sees the cheese but not the trap.

This is especially strange as it is becoming increasingly clear that if we once square Russia and Europe, then Serbia and Montenegro will *have to* accept any conditions we lay down; whereas if we are not in the clear with Russia and Europe, Serbia and Montenegro would demand very stiff terms – and would certainly not stand by them.

The result of Rodich's policy would be, therefore:

1. we should create an Eastern Piedmont out of Montenegro, to our own cost and peril;
2. we should very probably destroy the Three Emperors' Alliance;
3. we should assume the mantle of conquerors, but not on our own behalf;
4. we should create a situation whereby we should have against us existing treaties, Turkey, very probably Russia, and – except for a south Slav party – public opinion at home and in Europe. Our only allies would be Serbia and Montenegro, who could always hope for as much from Russia as from us. At best, we should march in, carry out a brief and costly occupation, and then march out under pressure from Europe. Perhaps we might have sufficient military forces ready. But the diplomatic and political situation must be the prime consideration; otherwise no army could help matters.

6. *Andrássy to Franz Joseph, telegram, Berlin, 12 May 1876, 2.36 p.m.* (Kab. 18)

The Emperor Alexander received me . . . [yesterday] in an extraordinarily gracious and friendly manner. First, he pointed to his breast, where he was wearing Austrian and German decorations, and said, 'Here is my programme.' Then he emphasized his desire for a conference of the six Powers. While I was with him he received several dispatches from Ignatiev, all implying that Turkey was in the process of collapsing. The Emperor Alexander remarked in this respect: 'Turkey could easily surprise us with her collapse', whereupon I emphasized that it was all the more necessary for the three Empires to hold together, adding that I was sure that we should be able to agree, as an intimate group, even about this question. He took this idea up very warmly and said, 'yes, above all, the two of us'.

So far all was well. From the emperor I went to Prince Gorchakov who read me a memorandum he had already drawn up, and told me of the project of assembling here the representatives of the six Powers with the exception of Turkey, and of communicating the memorandum to them in our names. The contents of the document are absolutely unacceptable. Alongside unintelligible phrases it contains the idea of an occupation; coercive measures against Turkey, to be decided in a congress; a panegyric on the insurrection, etc. In the evening, Prince Gorchakov, Bismarck and I discussed it. I stated that I could not accept these proposals on any terms. I pleaded my lack of instructions, whereat Gorchakov objected that there was no time to wait for them now, and that I enjoyed the confidence of my master. He gave me permission to make changes in the memorandum, but I must work out a formal counter-proposal, which we are to discuss this evening.

I am sure that the project was as much of a surprise to people here as it was for me. I am counting on the support of the Emperor Alexander and of Prince Bismarck. Whether I shall succeed, I cannot say; but my sense of responsibility will not permit me to agree at any price to the communication of the present memorandum to the representatives of the six Powers.

7. *Andrássy to Franz Joseph, telegram, Berlin, 12 May 1876, 10.35 p.m.* (Kab. 18)

Situation totally changed. Prince Gorchakov soft as butter, has given way completely on all points that displeased us. Now I hope that the *Entente* and our interests will come out of this meeting unharmed. Tomorrow Gorchakov will read my proposal, which he has accepted, to the representatives of the six Powers in his own name. Proposal contains two points:

1. a two months' cease-fire for the carrying out of reforms and pacification,
2. an agreement on sending warships.

Congress and all other projects (*Eventualitäten*) precluded. Agreement about Montenegro left for later. I talked to Prince

Gorchakov about future plans and got him to declare that he has
no objection to an annexation of Turkish Croatia. Enough for a
start.

8. *Treaty of Alliance between Austria-Hungary and Germany, 7 October,
1879* (printed in A. F. Pribram, *Secret Treaties*, Vol. 1, pp.
25–31)

Inasmuch as Their Majesties the Emperor of Austria, King of
Hungary, and the German Emperor, King of Prussia, must consider it Their imperative duty as Monarchs to provide for the
security of Their Empires and the peace of Their subjects, under
all circumstances;

inasmuch as the two Sovereigns, as was the case under the
former existing relations of alliance, will be enabled by the close
union of the two Empires to fulfil this duty more easily and more
efficaciously;

inasmuch as, finally, an intimate co-operation of Germany and
Austria-Hungary can menace no one, but is rather calculated to
consolidate the peace of Europe as established by the stipulations
of Berlin;

Their Majesties the Emperor of Austria, King of Hungary, and
the Emperor of Germany, while solemnly promising each other
never to allow Their purely defensive Agreement to develop an
aggressive tendency in any direction, have determined to conclude an Alliance of peace and mutual defence.

For this purpose Their Most Exalted Majesties have designated
as Their Plenipotentiaries:

His Most Exalted Majesty the Emperor of Austria, King of
Hungary, His Actual Privy Councillor, Minister of the Imperial
Household and of Foreign Affairs, Lieutenant-Field-Marshal
Count Julius Andrássy of Czik-Szent-Király and Kraszna-Horka,
etc., etc.,

His most Exalted Majesty the German Emperor, His Ambassador Extraordinary and Plenipotentiary, Lieutenant-General
Prince Henry VII of Reuss, etc., etc.,

who have met this day at Vienna, and, after the exchange of
their full powers, found in good and due form, have agreed upon
the following Articles:

ARTICLE I

Should, contrary to their hope, and against the loyal desire of the two High Contracting Parties, one of the two Empires be attacked by Russia, the High Contracting Parties are bound to come to the assistance one of the other with the whole war strength of their Empires, and accordingly only to conclude peace together and upon mutual agreement.

ARTICLE II

Should one of the High Contracting Parties be attacked by another Power, the other High Contracting Party binds itself hereby, not only not to support the aggressor against its high Ally, but to observe at least a benevolent neutral attitude towards its fellow Contracting Party.

Should, however, the attacking party in such a case be supported by Russia, either by an active co-operation or by military measures which constitute a menace to the Party attacked, then the obligation stipulated in Article I of this Treaty, for reciprocal assistance with the whole fighting force, becomes equally operative, and the conduct of the war by the two High Contracting Parties shall in this case also be in common until the conclusion of a common peace.

ARTICLE III

The duration of this Treaty shall be provisionally fixed at five years from the day of ratification. One year before the expiration of this period the two High Contracting Parties shall consult together concerning the question whether the conditions serving as the basis of the Treaty still prevail, and reach an agreement in regard to the further continuance or possible modification of certain details. If in the course of the first months of the last year of the Treaty no invitation has been received from either side to open these negotiations, the Treaty shall be considered as renewed for a further period of three years.

ARTICLE IV

This Treaty shall, in conformity with its peaceful character, and to avoid any misinterpretation, be kept secret by the two High Contracting Parties, and only communicated to a third Power upon a joint understanding between the two Parties, and according to the terms of a special Agreement.

The two High Contracting Parties venture to hope, after the sentiments expressed by the Emperor Alexander at the meeting at Alexandrovo, that the armaments of Russia will not in reality prove to be menacing to them, and have on that account no reason for making a communication at present; should, however, this hope, contrary to their expectations, prove to be erroneous, the two High Contracting Parties would consider it their loyal obligation to let the Emperor Alexander know, at least confidentially, that they must consider an attack on either of them as directed against both.

ARTICLE V

This Treaty shall derive its validity from the approbation of the two Exalted Sovereigns and shall be ratified within fourteen days after this approbation has been granted by Their Most Exalted Majesties.

In witness whereof the Plenipotentiaries have signed this Treaty with their own hands and affixed their arms.

Done at Vienna, October 7, 1879.

Andrássy.   H. VII v. Reuss.
L.S.   L.S.

9. *Kálnoky to Haymerle, 18 February 1881* (P.A. I/469, Aehrenthal memorandum)

Your Excellency knows my conviction that our relationship with Russia, which has so far been without any real basis, and neither good nor bad, cannot be maintained in the long run. We just cannot change the fact that we have this colossal empire on our frontiers, and we are faced with the alternative either of co-existing with Russia, or of hurling her back into Asia. The latter, every conscientious statesman must admit, is an impossibility for Austria-Hungary, either now or in the distant future. We *must*, therefore, co-exist. And once that is admitted, then there can be no doubt that the most vital interests of the Monarchy demand a measure of stability in our relations with the great Slav empire, just *because* our interests clash in the Near East, precisely *because* Russia's political, national, and religious tentacles (*Wurzelfäden*) reach across our frontiers. We have an absolute need of tranquillity and peace, and if, as I hope, Your Excellency can bring about an agreement with Russia which will generally safeguard our interests in the East and which will limit the chances of a war, as far as human foresight can do, Your Excellency will have rendered the state a great service. In any agreement with Russia the danger for us lies in the fact that in working it we do not have such great and various means at our disposal, nor such powerful weapons, as the Russians are wont to use. Because of this disparity an *entente à deux* between us and Russia is impossible. On the other hand, the situation is now unusually favourable for a sincere attempt at an agreement, because our close alliance with Germany gives us the necessary backing.

10. *The Three Emperors' Alliance, 1881* (printed in A. F. Pribram, *Secret Treaties*, Vol. 1, pp. 37–47)

  (*a*) Convention between Austria-Hungary, the German Empire, and Russia.

Berlin, June 18, 1881

The Courts of Austria-Hungary, of Germany, and of Russia, animated by an equal desire to consolidate the general peace by an understanding intended to assure the defensive position of their respective States, have come into agreement on certain questions which more especially concern their reciprocal interests.

With this purpose the three Courts have appointed: . . .

ARTICLE I

In case one of the High Contracting Parties should find itself at war with a fourth Great Power, the two others shall maintain towards it a benevolent neutrality and shall devote their efforts to the localization of the conflict.

This stipulation shall apply likewise to a war between one of the three Powers and Turkey, but only in the case where a previous agreement shall have been reached between the three Courts as to the results of this war.

In the special case where one of them should obtain a more positive support from one of its two Allies, the obligatory value of the present Article shall remain in all its force for the third.

ARTICLE II

Russia, in agreement with Germany, declares her firm resolution to respect the interests arising from the new position assured to Austria-Hungary by the Treaty of Berlin.

The three Courts, desirous of avoiding all discord between them, engage to take account of their respective interests in the Balkan Peninsula. They further promise one another that any new modifications in the territorial *status quo* of Turkey in Europe can be accomplished only in virtue of a common agreement between them.

In order to facilitate the agreement contemplated by the present Article, an agreement of which it is impossible to foresee all the conditions, the three Courts from the present moment record in the Protocol annexed to this Treaty the points on which an understanding has already been established in principle.

ARTICLE III

The three Courts recognize the European and mutually obligatory character of the principle of the closing of the Straits of the Bosphorus and of the Dardanelles, founded on international law, confirmed by treaties, and summed up in the declaration of the second Plenipotentiary of Russia at the session of July 12 of the Congress of Berlin (Protocol 19).

They will take care in common that Turkey shall make no exception to this rule in favour of the interests of any Government whatsoever, by lending to warlike operations of a belligerent Power the portion of its Empire constituted by the Straits.

In case of infringement, or to prevent it if such infringement should be in prospect, the three Courts will inform Turkey that they would regard her, in that event, as putting herself in a state of war towards the injured Party, and as having deprived herself thenceforth of the benefits of the security assured to her territorial *status quo* by the Treaty of Berlin.

[ARTICLES IV – VII relating to duration, secrecy, and ratification of the Treaty]
   (*b*) Separate Protocol on the same date to the Convention
of Berlin, June 18, 1881

The undersigned Plenipotentiaries . . .
having recorded in accordance with Article II of the secret Treaty concluded today the points affecting the interests of the

three Courts of Austria-Hungary, Germany, and Russia in the Balkan Peninsula upon which an understanding has already been reached among them, have agreed to the following Protocol:

I. BOSNIA AND HERZEGOVINA

Austria-Hungary reserves the right to annex these provinces at whatever moment she shall deem opportune.

2. SANJAK OF NOVIBAZAR

The Declaration exchanged between the Austro-Hungarian Plenipotentiaries and the Russian Plenipotentiaries at the Congress of Berlin under date of July 13/1, 1878, remains in force.

3. EASTERN RUMELIA

The three Powers agree in regarding the eventuality of an occupation either of Eastern Rumelia or of the Balkans as full of perils for the general peace. In case this should occur, they will employ their efforts to dissuade the Porte from such an enterprise, it being well understood that Bulgaria and Eastern Rumelia on their part are to abstain from provoking the Porte by attacks emanating from their territories against the other provinces of the Ottoman Empire.

4. BULGARIA

The three Powers will not oppose the eventual reunion of Bulgaria and Eastern Rumelia within the territorial limits assigned to them by the Treaty of Berlin, if this question should come up by the force of circumstances. They agree to dissuade the Bulgarians from all aggression against the neighbouring provinces, particularly Macedonia; and to inform them that in such a case they would be acting at their own risk and peril.

5. ATTITUDE OF AGENTS IN THE EAST

In order to avoid collisions of interests in the local questions which may arise, the three Courts will furnish their representatives and agents in the Orient with a general instruction, directing them to endeavour to smooth out their divergences by friendly explanations between themselves in each special case; and, in the cases where they do not succeed in doing so, to refer the matters to their Governments.

6

The present Protocol forms an integral part of the secret Treaty signed on this day at Berlin, and shall have the same force and validity.

In witness whereof the respective Plenipotentiaries have signed it and have affixed thereto the seal of their arms.

Done at Berlin, June 18, 1881

L.S.   Széchenyi
L.S.   v. Bismarck

L.S.   Sabouroff.

11. *Treaty of Alliance between Austria-Hungary and Serbia, Belgrade, 16/28 June, 1881* (printed in A. F. Pribram, *Secret Treaties*, Vol. 1, pp. 53—61)

His Majesty the Emperor of Austria, King of Bohemia, etc., and Apostolic King of Hungary, and

His Highness the Prince of Serbia, animated by the desire to maintain peace in the Orient and to guarantee against all eventualities the relations of perfect friendship which exist between Their Governments, have resolved to conclude to this end a Treaty and have appointed as Their Plenipotentiaries . . .

ARTICLE I

There shall be stable peace and friendship between Austria-Hungary and Serbia. The two Governments engage to follow mutually a friendly policy.

ARTICLE II

Serbia will not tolerate political, religious, or other intrigues, which, taking her territory as a point of departure, might be directed against the Austro-Hungarian Monarchy, including therein Bosnia, Herzegovina, and the Sanjak of Novibazar.

Austria-Hungary assumes the same obligation with regard to Serbia and her dynasty, the maintenance and strengthening of which she will support with all her influence.

ARTICLE III

If the Prince of Serbia should deem it necessary, in the interest of

His dynasty and of His country, to take on behalf of Himself and of His descendants the title of King, Austria-Hungary will recognize this title as soon as its proclamation shall have been made in legal form, and will use her influence to secure recognition for it on the part of the other Powers.

ARTICLE IV

Austria-Hungary will use her influence with the other European Cabinets to second the interests of Serbia.

Without a previous understanding with Austria-Hungary, Serbia will neither negotiate nor conclude any political treaty with another Government, and will not admit to her territory a foreign armed force, regular or irregular, even as volunteers.

ARTICLE V

If Austria-Hungary should be threatened with war or find herself at war with one or more other Powers, Serbia will observe a friendly neutrality towards the Austro-Hungarian Monarchy, including therein Bosnia, Herzegovina and the Sanjak of Novibazar, and will accord to it all possible facilities, in conformity with their close friendship and the spirit of this Treaty.

Austria-Hungary assumes the same obligation towards Serbia, in case the latter should be threatened with war or find herself at war.

ARTICLE VI

In any case where military co-operation is considered necessary by the two Contracting Parties, the questions touching this co-operation, especially those of the superior command and of the contingent passage of troops through the respective territories, shall be regulated by a military convention.

ARTICLE VII

If, as a result of a combination of circumstances whose development is not to be foreseen at present, Serbia were in a position to make territorial acquisitions in the direction of her southern frontiers (with the exception of the Sanjak of Novibazar), Austria-Hungary will not oppose herself thereto, and will use her influence with the other Powers for the purpose of winning them over to an attitude favourable to Serbia.

[ARTICLES VIII – X relating to duration, secrecy and ratification of the Treaty]

12. *Kálnoky to Kállay, private, St Petersburg, 14 October 1881*
   (P.A. I/467)
[If Haymerle's successor is faced with a difficult inheritance, this is the result, not of difficulties in the field of foreign affairs, but of other factors]: above all, the confused situation resulting from the passionate party conflicts in Cisleithania, and, secondly, the impossible legal position of the minister for foreign affairs. These two factors are of such overriding importance as to be decisive in answering the present pressing question – from what category of men must the future foreign minister be chosen, if he is to be able to carry out his important task with the necessary calm assurance and without perpetually worrying about his position?

   Two years ago, after the eventful and exciting ministry of Count Andrássy, after the fierce parliamentary battles over the occupation [of Bosnia], the quarrelsome elements in the Reichsrat and among the public were so overcome with exhaustion that it was not only possible, but generally felt to be necessary, to summon a proven and completely reliable diplomat to the foreign ministry. All parties and shades of opinion in the Monarchy were well satisfied with H.M. the Emperor's choice of Baron Haymerle and nobody raised any obstacles in his path. How right the choice was, and how proficiently Baron Haymerle guarded the dignity and interests of the Empire can be seen from the unusual unanimity of the numerous expressions of regret, at home and abroad, and from all the courts and governments of Europe, on the occasion of the late statesman's death. But although his conduct of foreign policy is now generally recognized to have been unimpeachable, and although he enjoyed the Emperor's confidence, I doubt very much whether he could have maintained his position for much longer. Sooner or later, one or other of the parties in the Reichsrat or the Hungarian parliament, or all together, would have made his existence impossible – out of pure party passion, or because he kept out of the party struggle and refused to throw his weight on one side or the other. If, in the present state of party warfare a *professional diplomat* should be so bold as to try to

imitate the feat (*Kunststück*) that Baron Haymerle kept up successfully for a few years, and to take up a position outside the party
conflict, his position would certainly be rendered impossible from
the start. He would be driven out (*herausgebissen*) within a year
even if he were a second Kaunitz!

This is so clear to me that I should regard the appointment, in
present circumstances, of another professional diplomat to the
post as a very risky undertaking (*gewagt*). Indeed, I will go further
and say that nobody at all will be able to hold this post honourably
for many years (and that is a factor to be considered, as far as the
continuity of foreign policy is concerned) unless he can count
with certainty on the firm support of at least one of the two parliaments. Mere contacts, or a certain measure of influence over the
two governments, seem to me quite insufficient. Only the firm
support of a parliamentary majority *of which he is in control* can
give the Common Minister for Foreign Affairs that weight he
needs *in his own country* and without which his position at home
must always be uncertain and unsatisfactory, however brilliant
his position may be abroad. In this respect it was very instructive
to see how much more highly and more accurately Haymerle was
rated by foreigners than by his own countrymen, especially those
in Vienna. The foreign minister should not, of course, be a
party politician (*Parteimann*); but he must not be without a
party (*parteilos*) either.

It would take too long, and I should only be repeating what I
have told you before, if I went into the impossible position which
the law assigns to the foreign minister. He has to abstain from
exercising influence over internal affairs and the governments of
the two halves of the empire. Yet both prime ministers have the
right and duty to influence him in respect of foreign affairs and to
control him; so that in effect his position depends on their goodwill and support – unless *he* enjoys by virtue of his personality and
his position in the country an *extra-legal* (*ungesetzliche*) controlling
influence over the governments and parties in the country.

How, in such circumstances, can a professional diplomat, who
has spent his career abroad and has, naturally, no links to speak
of with the parties at home, who has to work with the two
prime ministers backed up by (*getragen von*) parliamentary majori-
ties, and is yet precluded from all direct influence on the parliaments – how can he lead any but a pitiable, or at best an ephemeral,

existence in such an important position as that of minister for foreign affairs?

From the above hasty remarks the conclusion is self-evident: it is impossible for *me* to be, as the newspapers say, a candidate for the succession to Baron Haymerle. About that I am perfectly clear in my own mind. Twenty-eight years ago I left the Ballplatz to start out on my career, and since then I have been circling round the foreign ministry, like the earth round the sun, at a respectful distance. In these accustomed tracks I move surely and unerringly, and in my view my personal abilities do not equip me to move out of this sphere – that would be to nobody's benefit.

13. *First Treaty of Alliance between Austria-Hungary, Germany, and Italy, Vienna, 20 May 1882* (printed in A. F. Pribram, *Secret Treaties*, Vol. 1, pp. 65–73)

Their Majesties the Emperor of Austria, King of Bohemia, etc., and Apostolic King of Hungary, the Emperor of Germany, King of Prussia, and the King of Italy, animated by the desire to increase the guaranties of the general peace, to fortify the monarchical principle and thereby to assure the unimpaired maintenance of the social and political order in Their respective States, have agreed to conclude a Treaty which, by its essentially conservative and defensive nature, pursues only the aim of forestalling the dangers which might threaten the security of Their States and the peace of Europe.

To this end Their Majesties have appointed . . .

ARTICLE I

The High Contracting Parties mutually promise peace and friendship, and will enter into no alliance or engagement directed against any one of their States.

They engage to proceed to an exchange of ideas on political and economic questions of a general nature which may arise, and they further promise one another mutual support within the limits of their own interests.

ARTICLE II

In case Italy, without direct provocation on her part, should be attacked by France for any reason whatsoever, the two other

Contracting Parties shall be bound to lend help and assistance with all their forces to the Party attacked.

This same obligation shall devolve upon Italy in case of any aggression without direct provocation by France against Germany.

ARTICLE III

If one, or two, of the High Contracting Parties, without direct provocation on their part, should chance to be attacked and to be engaged in a war with two or more Great Powers nonsignatory to the present Treaty, the *casus foederis* will arise simultaneously for all the High Contracting Parties.

ARTICLE IV

In case a Great Power nonsignatory to the present Treaty should threaten the security of the states of one of the High Contracting Parties, and the threatened Party should find itself forced on that account to make war against it, the two others bind themselves to observe towards their Ally a benevolent neutrality. Each of them reserves to itself, in this case, the right to take part in the war, if it should see fit, to make common cause with its Ally.

ARTICLE V

If the peace of any of the High Contracting Parties should chance to be threatened under the circumstances foreseen by the preceding Articles, the High Contracting Parties shall take counsel together in ample time as to the military measures to be taken with a view to eventual co-operation.

They engage henceforward, in all cases of common participation in a war, to conclude neither armistice, nor peace, nor treaty, except by common agreement among themselves.

[ARTICLES VI – VIII relating to secrecy, duration, and ratification of the Treaty]

Ministerial Declaration[1]

The Imperial and Royal Government declares that the provisions of the secret Treaty concluded May 20, 1882, between Austria-Hungary, Germany, and Italy, cannot, as has been previously

[1] The Austro-Hungarian version of the so-called Mancini Declaration.

agreed, in any case be regarded as being directed against England.

In witness whereof the present ministerial Declaration, which equally must remain secret, has been drawn up to be exchanged against identic Declarations of the Imperial Government of Germany and of the Royal Government of Italy.

The Imperial and Royal Minister of Foreign Affairs.
Vienna, May 28, 1882

14. *Kálnoky to Mayr, 1 July 1883* (quoted in E.R. v. Rutkowski, 'Oesterreich-Ungarn und Roumanien . . .', pp. 242–3)

[As regards the Jassy banquet affair] such an insolent parading of a hostile national programme – on such a ceremonious occasion before the very eyes of the King and the ministers – can only be regarded by the Imperial and Royal Government as a flagrant provocation likely to injure the dignity of the Monarchy and cause disturbances in our border territories. If the Roumanian government now hesitates to repudiate in the most binding form the shameless utterances of its supporters, if it does not clearly state that it disavows their policy of national ambitions as bound to lead to a disturbance of the peace, and that it repudiates all those tendencies which offend against treaties and against a friendly, good-neighbourly relationship with the Monarchy, then for us the desire to maintain good relations with Roumania will move into the background, and it will become our duty to consider first and foremost such measures as may secure the repose of our border territories. . . It is up to King Carol's ministers to issue a clear public statement to reassure our public opinion, which is irritated with good reason, and to restore our shattered faith in the possibility of lasting good relations.

[Later on the same day Kálnoky sent a second telegram to Mayr.]

We must now insist on a clear public declaration that the government condemns the illicit agitation directed against the repose of our border territories, and, as is its duty, will not tolerate it . . . Proceed with such firmness as is necessary to make it clear to people in Bucharest that we are determined to put an end to this dangerous activity. In this we are completely in the right and will pursue the matter if necessary to the point of war (*bis in den letzten Konsequenzen*).

Documents

15. *Treaty of Alliance between Austria-Hungary and Roumania,
Vienna, 30 October 1883* (printed in A. F. Pribram, *Secret
Treaties*, Vol. 1, pp. 79–83)

His Majesty the Emperor of Austria, King of Bohemia, etc., and
Apostolic King of Hungary, and

His Majesty the King of Roumania, animated by an equal desire
to maintain the general peace, in conformity with the aim pursued
by the Austro-Hungarian and German Alliance, to assure the
political order, and to guarantee against all eventualities the perfect friendship which binds Them together, have determined to
conclude to this end a Treaty which by its essentially conservative
and defensive nature pursues only the aim of forestalling the
dangers which might menace the peace of Their States.

For this purpose Their said Majesties have named as Their
Plenipotentiaries. . . .

ARTICLE I

The High Contracting Parties promise one another peace and
friendship, and will enter into no alliance or engagement directed
against any one of their States. They engage to follow a friendly
policy and to lend one another mutual support within the limits
of their interests.

ARTICLE II

If Roumania, without any provocation on her part, should be
attacked, Austria-Hungary is bound to bring her in ample time
help and assistance against the aggressor. If Austria-Hungary be
attacked under the same circumstances in a portion of her states
bordering on Roumania, the *casus foederis* will immediately arise
for the latter.

ARTICLE III

If one of the High Contracting Parties should find itself threatened
by an aggression under the abovementioned conditions, the
respective Governments shall put themselves in agreement as to
the measures to be taken with a view to co-operation of their
armies. These military questions, especially that of the unity of
operations and of passage through the respective territories, shall
be regulated by a military convention.

ARTICLE IV

If, contrary to their desire and hope, the High Contracting Parties are forced into a common war under the circumstances foreseen by the preceding Articles, they engage neither to negotiate nor to conclude peace separately.

[ARTICLES V – VII relating to duration, secrecy and ratification of the Treaty]

16. *Kálnoky to Wolkenstein, private, 2 December 1885* (P.A. XV/85)
Dear Friend,

The impression that the success of Khevenhüller's mission has made in St Petersburg is easily explained. Given that they feel powerless to intervene effectively in the developments in the Balkans without being untrue to their present policy, the fact that *we* have been able to do this must be infinitely unpleasant for the Russians, because they are afraid that our prestige must thereby grow. The complaints that Giers is making about us really are without foundation. I had spoken to Prince Lobanov about Khevenhüller's mission on the same day it was decided on, and he brought me a telegram from Giers which assented to it if I thought it necessary. I had also informed him of the contents of the instructions I sent to Khevenhüller; I could not do any more than that, as there was danger in delay – and anyway I did not myself know how far Khevenhüller would have to go in his declaration. Giers is therefore not serious when he gives the impression of being offended by Khevenhüller's remarks, even if the latter did in fact go further than his instructions warranted. It is quite obvious that the interpretation coming from Sofia is tendentious. But the second factor in this question is the personal one of M. de Giers. It is infinitely regrettable, that whenever something startling happens the question of the personal position of the minister is immediately raised. Yet we cannot simply for that reason throw away the advantages of the situation, nor, in the present case, allow ourselves to be held back from defending such clear and vital interests of peace, domestic and European. Lobanov, with whom I discussed the matter in all its aspects, shares my view entirely and I hope that his reports to St Petersburg are as moderate as his spoken words. He too, however, laments Giers' regrettable nervousness in the face of public opinion, and says that it is the newspapers and a few people in the Council of the Empire who have bowled Giers over.

17. *Austrian Note to Great Britain proposing a further agreement in the Mediterranean, London, 12 December 1887* (printed in A. F. Pribram, *Secret Treaties*, Vol. 1, pp. 125–7)

His Excellency the Marquess of Salisbury.

London, December 12, 1887

As a result of the understanding reached between the Governments of His Majesty the Emperor of Austria, King of Hungary, and of Their Majesties the Queen of the United Kingdom of Great Britain and Ireland and the King of Italy by the exchange of Notes effected at London in the month of March, 1887, the Government of His Imperial and Royal Apostolic Majesty has come to an agreement with the Government of Italy to propose to the Government of Great Britain the adoption of the following points, intended to confirm the principles established by the aforementioned exchange of Notes and to define the common attitude of the three Powers in prospect of the eventualities which might occur in the Orient.

1. The maintenance of peace and the exclusion of all policy of aggression.

2. The maintenance of the *status quo* in the Orient, based on the treaties, to the exclusion of all policy of compensation.

3. The maintenance of the local autonomies established by these same treaties.

4. The independence of Turkey, as guardian of important European interests (independence of the Caliphate, the freedom of the Straits, etc.), of all foreign preponderating influence.

5. Consequently, Turkey can neither cede nor delegate her suzerain rights over Bulgaria to any other Power, nor intervene in order to establish a foreign administration there, nor tolerate acts of coercion undertaken with this latter object, under the form either of a military occupation or of the despatch of volunteers. Likewise Turkey, constituted by the treaties guardian of the Straits, can neither cede any portion of her sovereign rights, nor delegate her authority to any other Power in Asia Minor.

6. The desire of the three Powers to be associated with Turkey for the common defence of these principles.

7. In case of Turkey resisting any illegal enterprises such as are indicated in Article 5, the three Powers will immediately come to an agreement as to the measures to be taken for causing to be respected the independence of the Ottoman Empire and the integrity of its territory, as secured by previous treaties.

8. Should the conduct of the Porte, however, in the opinion of the three Powers, assume the character of complicity with or connivance at any such illegal enterprise, the three Powers will consider themselves justified by existing treaties in proceeding either jointly or separately, to the provisional occupation by their forces, military or naval, of such points of Ottoman territory as they may agree to consider it necessary to occupy in order to secure the objects determined by previous treaties.

9. The existence and the contents of the present Agreement between the three Powers shall not be revealed, either to Turkey or to any other Powers who have not yet been informed of it, without the previous consent of all and each of the three Powers aforesaid.

The undersigned Ambassador Extraordinary and Minister Plenipotentiary of His Imperial and Royal Apostolic Majesty has been instructed by his Government to sign the present Note and to exchange it against a similar Note of the Government of Her Britannic Majesty.

The undersigned takes this occasion to renew to His Excellency the Marquess of Salisbury, Principal Secretary of State for Foreign Affairs of Her Majesty the Queen, the expression of his highest consideration.

Signed Károlyi.[1]

18. *Kálnoky to Széchenyi, No. 2, secret, 12 January 1888* (P.A. I/464)
In my dispatch of 22 December, suggesting preliminary discussions about the military consequences of the *casus foederis*, I also asked – chiefly because the military urgently wanted to know before determining the measures they would take in the event of war – whether it would not be advisable to examine in good time the conditions under which the *casus foederis* would arise. The answer given to you and Baron Steininger by the Secretary of State, Count Bismarck, and similar communications from Prince

[1] Identical British and Italian notes were dated London, 12 December, and Vienna, 16 December respectively.

Reuss, leave no doubt about it that Prince Bismarck refuses to discuss the subject, pleading the text of the alliance, which neither demands nor permits any further interpretation or extension. The Imperial Chancellor thinks that the alliance is so clear and conclusive about when the *casus foederis* arises that no doubt can exist. If Russia attacks us, then Germany would not hesitate for one moment about fulfilling her alliance obligations. If we, however, in any circumstances whatever, are the attackers, then Germany would stay neutral, according to the treaty, even if the attack had the defensive character of anticipating an enemy attack; and we should have to rely on our own strength and on any support our other allies supplied. It is undeniable that this interpretation is in accordance with the text of our treaty in the strictest sense, and that we cannot object to it. Nor do we intend to pursue this delicate question further at the present moment, when fears of war, so prevalent at the end of last year, have yielded to a new peaceful spirit. But we think it is important to emphasize even now a few points which we think must be considered.

First of all, I exclude completely from the discussion the idea that Austria-Hungary wishes to launch an offensive war against Russia, or wants to provoke any kind of war with that Empire. It is out of the question that Austria-Hungary *alone* should attack Russia, and therefore all combinations based on this case and Germany's treaty right to neutrality in that event can be ignored (*fallen . . . weg*). We are quite aware that it would be madness, both from a military and from a political point of view, to undertake alone an aggressive war against Russia. For if Count Herbert Bismarck alluded to the military support of Italy, England and Turkey, I am sure that he did this only in order to indicate that we could *not* count on these Powers. Not only have we placed ourselves with Italy and England on the basis of excluding any aggressive policy in principle, but Italy, engaged in Massawa and with obligations towards Germany, would hardly be able to commit herself to major military efforts anyway. As regards England, there is no doubt whatever that public opinion there will declare *against* the aggressor, whoever this may be. Finally, Berlin knows as well as we do with what measure of certainty one could count on Turkish military support. I can, therefore, only repeat that Austria-Hungary would in no circumstances commit the folly (*Wahnsinn*) of undertaking an aggressive war against Russia.

It is another matter, and to this we attach the greatest importance, that the highest military authorities unanimously declare that, by awaiting the Russian attack, both Austria-Hungary and Germany would give up the most important military advantages and heavily compromise the whole success of the war. In view of the quite exceptionally unfavourable position and geographical conformation of Galicia and the extremely difficult line of march of our army, the guarantee of success lies only in the immediate attack, combined with a simultaneous thrust on the part of the German army. Obviously this is not a question of an offensive war and a breach of the peace, but a question – in the event of an inevitable (*unausweichlichen und unabwendbaren*) war – of that initiative and that anticipation which history has so often shown to have determined the victorious outcome of a campaign.

If one considers Russia's armaments, military preparations, and threatening plans for troop movements (*Dislokationspläne*) (which we are officially informed will certainly be carried out), one must come to the conclusion that sooner or later war with Russia is increasingly probable – unless one wanted to avoid it at any price. In the event of war with Russia, however, the above-mentioned question of the *casus foederis* is of such decisive importance that in my opinion it should be clarified in a definitive sense as soon as possible; and I have no doubt that further developments will show the necessity of returning to a thorough examination of it. If we know that we should certainly have to forgo the huge military advantages which in certain circumstances would accrue from a bold (*scharf*) advance into enemy territory by our armies, and if we were reduced to letting the enemy into the country and starting such a difficult campaign under such decidedly unfavourable conditions, then it would be our duty to consider again and in good time how and under what circumstances it would be possible and advisable to wage war against Russia, and whether it should be undertaken at all or avoided. These considerations may be premature today, when the issue is in any case not one of war, but of peace; but circumstances could easily make the question we have raised a pressing (*aktuell*) one, and render urgent a definitive clarification of the same. I think a formula could easily be found which would exclude the possibility of a modification of the defensive character of the alliance which the Imperial Chancellor is afraid of and which could still provide the firm basis essential for military planning. The dimensions and consequences of a war with Russia can be so vast that, from a military point of view too, it must only be started under the most favourable conditions possible.

In view of the trust and unity (*vertrauensvolle Uebereinstimmung*) which prevail between our two governments in assessing the political situation generally, and in avoiding war as far as possible, I do not doubt that if circumstances demand it we shall attain a unity of view also about this question of great political and military importance.

Your Excellency will kindly bring these considerations very confidentially to the attention of the Secretary of State, and inform me of the reception they meet with.

19. *Treaty of Alliance between Austria-Hungary, the German Empire, and Italy, Berlin, 6 May 1891* (printed in A. F. Pribram, *Secret Treaties*, Vol. 1, pp. 151–63)

Their Majesties the Emperor of Austria, King of Bohemia, etc., and Apostolic King of Hungary, the Emperor of Germany, King of Prussia, and the King of Italy, firmly resolved to assure to Their States the continuation of the benefits which the maintenance of the Triple Alliance guarantees to them, from the political point of view as well as from the monarchical and social point of view, and wishing with this purpose to prolong the duration of this Alliance, concluded on May 20, 1882, and already renewed a first time by the Treaties of February 20, 1887, whose expiration was fixed for May 30, 1892, have, for this purpose, appointed as Their Plenipotentiaries, . . .

[ARTICLES I – V as ARTICLES I – V of the Treaty of 20 May 1882]

ARTICLE VI

Germany and Italy, having in mind only the maintenance, so far as possible, of the territorial *status quo* in the Orient, engage to use their influence to forestall, on the Ottoman coasts and islands in the Adriatic and the Aegean Seas, any territorial modification which might be injurious to one or the other of the Powers signatory to the present Treaty. To this end, they will communicate to one another all information of a nature to enlighten each other mutually concerning their own dispositions, as well as those of other Powers.

ARTICLE VII[1]

Austria-Hungary and Italy, having in mind only the maintenance, so far as possible, of the territorial *status quo* in the Orient, engage to use their influence to forestall any territorial modification which might be injurious to one or the other of the Powers signatory to the present Treaty. To this end, they shall communicate to one another all information of a nature to enlighten each other mutually concerning their own dispositions, as well as those of other Powers.

However, if, in the course of events, the maintenance of the *status quo* in the regions of the Balkans or of the Ottoman coasts and islands in the Adriatic and in the Aegean Sea should become impossible, and if, whether in consequence of the action of a third Power or otherwise, Austria-Hungary or Italy should find themselves under the necessity of modifying it by a temporary or permanent occupation on their part, this occupation shall take place only after a previous agreement between the two Powers, based upon the principle of a reciprocal compensation for every advantage, territorial or other, which each of them might obtain beyond the present *status quo*, and giving satisfaction to the interests and well-founded claims of the two Parties.

ARTICLE VIII

The stipulations of Articles VI and VII shall apply in no way to the Egyptian question, with regard to which the High Contracting Parties preserve respectively their freedom of action, regard being always paid to the principles upon which the present Treaty rests.

[ARTICLES IX – X, Italo-German clauses concerning North Africa]

[ARTICLES XI – XV, concerning secrecy, duration and ratification of the Treaty]

[1] Identical with Article 1 of the Austro-Hungarian-Italian Separate Treaty of 20 February 1887.

Documents

PROTOCOL

At the moment of proceeding to the signing of the Treaty of this day between Austria-Hungary, Germany, and Italy, the undersigned Plenipotentiaries of these three Powers, thereto duly authorized, mutually declare themselves as follows:

1. Under reserve of parliamentary approval for the executory stipulations proceeding from the present declaration of principle, the High Contracting Parties promise each other, from this moment, in economic matters (finances, customs, railways), in addition to most-favoured-nation treatment, all of the facilities and special advantages which would be compatible with the requirements of each of the three States and with their respective engagements with third Powers.

2. The accession of England being already acquired, in principle, to the stipulations of the Treaty of this day which concern the Orient, properly so-called, to wit, the territories of the Ottoman Empire, the High Contracting Parties shall exert themselves at the opportune moment, and to the extent that circumstances may permit it, to bring about an analogous accession with regard to the North African territories of the central and western part of the Mediterranean, including Morocco. This accession might be realized by an acceptance, on the part of England, of the programme established by Articles IX and X of the Treaty of this day.

In witness whereof the three Plenipotentiaries have signed the present Protocol in triplicate.

Done at Berlin, the sixth day of the month of May, one thousand eight hundred and ninety-one.

Széchenyi
v. Caprivi
Launay.

20. *Kálnoky to Deym, No. 1, secret, 25 January 1894*

[Reports a conversation with the British ambassador, Sir Edward Monson, concerning the Russian threat to the *status quo* at the Straits.]

In all questions concerning the Near East the most important factor, for us, and for everybody, is England. I would go so far as to say that, in view of recent developments, our future attitude in the Eastern question will depend almost exclusively on whether or not England is determined in all circumstances to defend her interests and her prestige in the Mediterranean against France and Russia.

So long as it was chiefly a question of protecting the Danube and the Balkans (*Balkanländer*) against the preponderance of Russia – as has been the case since the Congress of Berlin – Austria-Hungary was in the first line, and coped with this somewhat perilous task successfully. In this, I willingly grant, cooperation with England and the declarations made in 1887 by Lord Salisbury about the English government's Near Eastern policy contributed materially to strengthening our confidence and firmness.

Now, however, it seems . . . that the Russian government has changed the direction, even if not the ultimate aims, of its Near Eastern aspirations. Today the Russian government, and even the Russian press, is only marginally interested in Bulgaria and the Balkans, and it is becoming increasingly clear that they have been pushed into the background by Mediterranean questions. I need not refer again to the way in which the announcement that Russia wishes to keep a squadron permanently in the Mediterranean, coming together with the Toulon visit, suddenly revealed to the political world the direction in which the Franco-Russian bloc (*Vereinigung*) will assert itself in the immediate future. Lord Rosebery is aware of the various attempts made by the Russian government in recent years to challenge (*anzurütteln*) indirectly the closure of the Straits to ships of war. The question of coaling stations that has now arisen furnishes further proof of St Petersburg's determination to create the necessary conditions of existence for a Russian naval force in the Mediterranean.

It seems to me, therefore, all the more timely to raise the matter very confidentially for discussion in London, in that I believe the English government has not yet gone into it, and even Lord Rosebery is not clear in his mind about it. Sir E. Monson is making a full report to London about our latest conversations, and I should be pleased if Lord Rosebery already knew my main arguments before Your Excellency discusses the contents of this dispatch with him.

The reason why I am raising this question is clear enough. For us, it is a matter of undertaking a revision of our political inventory, so as to secure for our own policy a firm basis against all possible contingencies. All the Powers of Europe are in a state of complete readiness for war. In such a dangerous situation any error of political judgment or any miscalculation could precipitate a catastrophe. It is, therefore, my bounden duty to ascertain which factors we can count on. From . . . my private letter of 25 October 1887 to Baron Biegeleben[1] Your Excellency will see that at that time, when it was a question of helping Lord Salisbury to make a clear declaration about his Eastern policy, I defined our position quite frankly, namely, that if England for any reason whatever had to give up her traditional policy in the Straits question, we should not be in a position (*ausser Stande wären*) to defend Constantinople, and it would then become necessary for us to guard and secure just *our* interests in the Balkans, and to leave the distant Straits to their fate and to Russia. At that time the English government, after considering my arguments, decided in favour of holding to England's old Eastern policy. Today Lord Rosebery will not be able to escape the necessity of putting this question to the cabinet again.

It is undeniable that the conditions under which the question is posed today are markedly more unfavourable than in 1887. In the first place, the Russian fleet constitutes a much more significant force today than it did in 1887; moreover, the union (*Vereinigung*) between Russia and France has been completed, which is particularly ominous (*bedenklich*) as regards the Mediterranean question, and points to their common action in all political questions. Nevertheless, the English government still has it within its power to maintain England's historic position if it makes a firm decision for a courageous policy regardless of party difficulties and financial sacrifices. To try to defer this decision until the hour of acute danger arrives would, for England, involve a huge responsibility; to the Austro-Hungarian government, however, an evasive or dilatory handling of this question would be unacceptable, and we should have to insist that England comes down on one side or the other in this matter, which affects the interests both of England and of Europe equally deeply.

First, however, I just wish – without making any political proposals – to move Lord Rosebery to give serious consideration to the Mediterranean issues at hand.

[1] Austro-Hungarian chargé d'affaires at London in October 1887.

21. *Austro-Italian Agreement concerning Albania, 1900* (printed in
    A. F. Pribram, *Secret Treaties*, Vol. 1, pp. 197–207)
    Dispatch[1] from the Austrian Government to the Am-
    bassador in Rome, Vienna, February 9, 1901
Submitted to His Majesty

Draft

of a strictly confidential despatch to Baron Pasetti at Rome.

On his return from Rome, Count Nigra directed my attention
to the reply given by His Excellency the Minister of Foreign
Affairs of the Kingdom of Italy to the interpellation recently
addressed to him in the Chamber of Deputies on the subject of
Albania; and at the same time expressed the hope that I might
find the declarations which it contains in conformity with the
principles upon which we came to an agreement in 1897 at the
time of my interview with Marquis Visconti-Venosta at the Castle
of Monza.

In the strictly confidential exchange of views which took place
in our conversations in respect to that question, we recognized in
effect the necessity

1. Of maintaining the *status quo* as long as circumstances permitted;

2. In case the present state of affairs could not be preserved, or in
case changes should be imperative, of using our efforts to the end
that the modifications relative thereto should be made in the
direction of autonomy, just as we have decided; in general,

3. The disposition on both sides to seek in common, and as often
as there is a reason for it, the most appropriate ways and means to
reconcile and to safeguard our reciprocal interests.

Such being the case, I am pleased to state that the pronounce-
ment of Marquis Visconti-Venosta has been received with lively
satisfaction by the Imperial and Royal Cabinet; and requesting
you, my dear Baron, to inform his Excellency the Minister of
Foreign Affairs of this, I avail myself of this occasion, etc.

22. *Goluchowski to Aehrenthal, private and very confidential, No. 557,
    29 December 1901* (P.A. I/475 Liasse xxxii/g)
Dear Baron,

By to-day's courier Your Excellency will receive a dispatch in

[1] In acknowledgment of a dispatch of the Italian Government of 20
December 1900.

which I have pulled together my ideas about the present position in the Near East and the tactics which I think we should adopt in handling these questions, bearing in mind the desirability of agreement with the Russian government. If I now add these few lines, that is because of your secret letter of 15 November, on the content of which I should like to comment in detail.

First of all, I must say that no one is more convinced than I of the necessity of cultivating as intimate and friendly a relationship with Russia as possible. My efforts to produce the *rapprochement* between the two Empires in 1897 prove this, a *rapprochement* which I prepared for in numerous conversations with Count Kapnist for months before the journey of Our Gracious Master to St Petersburg, and which still would serve today as the basis for a formal and lasting *entente* such as I had in mind at that time.

On this point of principle, therefore, I quite agree with Your Excellency, even if I am not so sure whether the statement on which you base your view – namely, that we have a greater interest in Russia's friendship than Russia has in ours – is necessarily correct. If it is a question of assessing the power of the two parties, then doubtless Russia is stronger than we are in a simple *tête-à-tête*, and under such conditions we are in an unfavourable position *vis-à-vis* Russia. If, however, one takes into account the general interest in preserving peace which is also a Russian interest today and probably for the foreseeable future, then I should like to say that (as far as the Near East is concerned) we are just as important a factor for Russia as she is for us. This one must assume, otherwise all attempts to reach agreement must be doomed to failure from the start; and I cannot see how Russia could be brought to make concessions just for the sake of pleasing us, if she were in a position to impose her ... will and push her demands through unhindered and regardless of our specific interests.

Another point on which I readily agree with Your Excellency is the cultivation of warm and trusting relations between the rulers of both Empires and the necessity of activating these sentiments through more frequent personal contact. I am firmly convinced that His Majesty the Emperor, Our Gracious Master, would welcome a meeting with the Emperor Nicholas any time, and that there will be certainly nothing lacking on His Majesty's part to smooth the way for such a meeting. But that is assuming that the Russians are similarly disposed...

Yet, however much I agree with the basic ideas of Your Excellency's letter, I cannot agree to the same extent with the reflections that accompany them, nor with your critical remarks about either the past or the tactics which we should adopt in the future. Our policy in both the Cretan and Chinese questions was so sound, I think, that if the situation recurred and a similar decision had to be made, I could not with a clear conscience recommend any other course to the Emperor than that which I did. For apart from the fact that the sudden change of policy on the part of the Russian government in the Cretan affair gave us a welcome opportunity to escape from the numerous burdens which staying in the island is today imposing on the other Powers, and which we should not have been able to justify to our parliaments once the danger of serious complications, which had existed at the beginning of the crisis, had disappeared – apart from this there was also the consideration that the service we should then have rendered Russia would hardly have brought us anything more than platonic thanks, but would have given the impression that we would put up with anything just to avoid differences of opinion with the government of St Petersburg. This would have had evil consequences for the future, and it was therefore necessary to make clear right from the start the standpoint that we intended to maintain within the *entente* relationship. Our attitude in the China affair seems to me to have been equally well-founded and justified. To have tried to make capital out of it would have been a great mistake and would have caused serious ill feeling against us in Berlin without moving Russia to render any tangible political reward in return.

When Your Excellency further describes our attitude to Milan's régime in Serbia as a justified Russian grievance, I must sincerely confess that this causes me no little surprise, especially as I must assume that Your Excellency is well enough informed about the events of that time to judge them objectively. We had no part at all in the return of King Milan to Serbia, and were just as passive towards it as towards the change three years later, when it would not have been much trouble for us to persuade King Milan to return to Belgrade to bring his son to reason and to restore a situation more satisfactory to us. On both occasions we held fast to the principle of absolute neutrality because we regarded the Milan question as a purely internal Serbian question which, according to the principles agreed in the so-called St Petersburg *Entente* of 1897, did not admit of any foreign intervention.

Whether, and how far, it is true that King Milan had promised Russia never again to set foot on Serbian soil I do not know; here he has always firmly denied it; but we for our part had no valid motive, a few months after the *rapprochement* had begun, to deny one of its basic principles and to allow ourselves to be led into taking a step which was certainly likely to damage our prestige (*Ansehen*) in the Balkans very seriously. We should have appeared to be the executors of the all-powerful will of Russia, and should have greatly diminished the value of our friendship and support in the eyes of those elements who look to us, and would have given them the impression, logically enough, that only those who fully enjoyed the favour of Russia had any prospect of achieving anything.

No Great Power could freely submit to such a loss of face (*capitis diminutio*) and Russia has the least right of all to demand it – Russia who, as is well known, never lets her friends down, even when their behaviour is temporarily inopportune and unwelcome to her. Whatever one thinks of Milan, it is certain that he has never denied his sympathy for our Monarchy, that despite his political past he enjoyed an undoubted popularity in Serbia and especially in the Serbian army, and that with his undisputed talent (*Begabung*) he was a political factor which one would have had to reckon with under certain circumstances. They knew that very well in St Petersburg – hence the determination with which they always worked to paralyse him and remove him from the political scene. We loyally confined ourselves to doing nothing either for or against him and left it to the Serbs to come to terms with him. If our attitude is misrepresented as something else and tendentiously interpreted there is really nothing *we* can do about it.

All these, however, are retrospective observations only intended to put certain events of the recent past in a proper light. As regards the present and the immediate future I think that however desirable it may be for us to have warm and confidential relations with Russia, these can only be achieved and have any practical meaning if the other side recognizes that we must be treated as equals. . .

A situation in which we were concerned only to avoid clashing anywhere and adopted the role of a passive spectator, while Russia pursued systematically and unhindered her policy of advance, would be quite unacceptable, as it would put us in a decidedly worse position than that which existed before 1897. I am not saying that Russia should be confronted immediately with a stark choice 'either . . . or' and be forced to make binding declarations at once; at the same time, however, no opportunity should be lost to remind her of our point of view and to let her see that much as we are willing to deal with the Eastern question in common, we should in the end have to choose other ways of protecting our specific interests if Russia confines herself to platonic assurances and continues to behave in practice as she has done so far.

I think that altogether more frequent suggestions for common discussion of Balkan affairs would be a good thing; first, because they would accord with the spirit of the 1897 agreement, which is designed not only to stem the competition, so dangerous to peace, between Russia and Austria-Hungary, but also to prepare the settlement, in common accord, of any questions that may arise; second, because they might provide some information for assessing Russia's intentions, which must determine our own attitude; finally, because we should thereby get an opportunity to renew repeatedly the reservations which in view of our specific interests we must uphold, and in respect of which there can be no question of concessions on our part. The formulation of concrete proposals, however, to remedy any evils that come to light, we can leave to Russia, reserving our right to examine them. So on these conditions and as far as it is a question of positive agreements I have no objection to waiting patiently as Your Excellency recommends.

And now to conclude, one more word. Your Excellency stressed the importance of Bulgaria in your letter, remarking that as the principality's desires for territorial expansion clash nowhere with our interests, we can have no grounds to be especially sparing in the warmth we display towards her. I agree generally with this view, but I think that, especially as far as our benevolence is concerned, the Bulgarians certainly have no reason to complain, as we have already given them many proofs of our friendly disposition, and the impending conclusion of a consular convention which is of great political importance to them, is the most eloquent illustration of the interest we take in their country.

But the cultivation of this relationship must be very carefully handled so as not to estrange Roumania, who is politically and strategically at least as important for us.

A lasting *rapprochement* or ending of differences between Bulgaria and Serbia is, I think, highly improbable; neither the improved relations between Roumania and Greece, nor the patronage of Russia even, will bring it about. An agreement between Roumania and Bulgaria with a view to future eventualities seems to me much more likely, and it can only be in our interests to further it as much as possible.

Finally, as regards Serbia, conditions there, from the point of view of the Balkans in general, are serious, of course. But they contain no particular dangers for us. Politically in complete disorder, financially on the verge of bankruptcy, militarily quite insignificant and weak, this country lies so much within our power (*Machtsphäre*) that it will always be dependent on us. There is no room for a Great-Serbia so long as the Monarchy exists; but only by leaning on us can the Serbia of today exist and have any hope of prospering (*halbwegs gedeihen*). King Milan rightly grasped this, and every thinking Serb must gradually come to the same conclusion, despite the temporary aberrations and gestures of defiance (*Entgleisungen und Boutaden*) that happen from time to time in Belgrade which we can, therefore, regard with a degree of composure.

23. *Goluchowski to Szögyény, private, 17 January 1902* (P.A. I/480)
Dear friend,

With today's courier you will receive a dispatch on the question of the renewal of the Triple Alliance, to enable you to explain my view of this question to Prince Bülow. I leave it to you to judge whether the present moment is the right time to take up the matter, or whether it might not be better to wait a while, so as to avoid giving the impression that we have been especially upset by Bülow's latest pronouncements and are, therefore, in a greater hurry to fix and secure our alliance relationships.

In any case the matter must be cleared up, and Italy brought to make a positive statement, before May, as otherwise there could be unpleasant controversies, and we might even be exposed to the surprise that one fine day the Rome government, contrary to what Berlin likes to think, might declare itself no longer bound after the expiry of the present alliance. This danger must be warded off in good time, and it seems to me best that the German Government should propose negotiations to Rome.

How far Lanza is correct in his assumption that Prinetti might be prepared to accept Baron Marschall's interpretation of the duration of the Triple Alliance treaty, I do not know. I am not absolutely convinced, however, after the rather academic conversations I had about this with the Italian ambassador here; and rather got the impression, from Count Nigra's hint that the Consulta would rather like to mix up the renewal of the Alliance Treaty with the negotiations about the Commercial Treaty, that Prinetti's views are by no means so accommodating as Lanza seems to assume, and that the question will need a lot of discussion before we reach a satisfactory conclusion. I immediately expressed to the ambassador my opposition to the idea of dealing with the two questions at once, pointing to my speech in the Delegations of last year, and describing such a procedure as impossible for reasons of timing, and politically dangerous; and I think I convinced Count Nigra of the sincerity of my opinions, especially as he very strongly urged me to let Rome know my view as soon as possible, and also to get in touch with Berlin to move the Germans to make an analogous *démarche*.

Nigra spoke in similar terms to Prince Eulenburg, who recently raised the matter with me. I lost no time in giving him my opinion straight out, and promised at his request to send instructions to you very soon to guide you in talking to Bülow. Doubtless Eulenburg has already reported our conversation to Berlin, so you should find the terrain well prepared.

I find Bülow's last speech extremely clumsy and it has made a bad impression in all quarters here. That a Great Power like Germany does not rely altogether on *one* particular combination may well be true. We too could say the same with equal justification, and I do not even know that we could not bear the dissolution of the Triple Alliance (given the continuing possibility of agreement with Russia and France) even more easily than Germany could. But I am doubtful, to say the least, whether it is sensible and prudent just at this moment to make light of (*bagatelisieren*) an alliance which is under concentrated fire from several quarters seeking to undermine it and which we want to preserve, as Bülow has done by actually honouring in an extempore variation the song of Kramarz about a 'played-out piano'.

The rumbling against the English, too, was quite superfluous, especially as Chamberlain himself had already explained that he never intended to insult the German Army, and a reference to this explanation should have been regarded as quite acceptable satisfaction. Not that Chamberlain was stuck for a reply, and the riposte, which friend Bülow richly deserved, will only serve to start a new quarrel which really would have been better avoided.

Altogether, the ways that German policy has been going of late give indeed great cause for concern. The ever-increasing arrogance, the desire to play the schoolmaster everywhere, the lack of consideration with which Berlin often proceeds, are things which create a highly uncomfortable atmosphere in the field of foreign affairs, and cannot but have harmful repercussions on our own relationship with Germany in the long run.

Let there be no mistake about this – just as one must also not forget that written treaties can only have real value if they meet with warm, sincere support from the public opinion of the countries concerned.

Now not only have the Germans for a long time paid no attention to this last consideration, but rather the policy of our allied neighbouring Empire has moved much more in a direction which is exactly calculated (*gerade dazu angetan*) to make the alliance really unpopular in Austria-Hungary. To justify this view, one needs only to consider the latest tariff, by which the Germans have managed to cause serious disappointment and ill-feeling among large sections of the population, regardless of nationality, both in Austria and in Hungary; the attitude of a series of bodies in Germany towards the '*Los von Rom*' movement, which has had a highly irritating effect on clerical circles here; the eternal agitation of the German newspapers against the Czechs, whom we cannot treat as a *quantité négligeable*, however unpleasant and inconvenient their proceedings may be at times, and in whom such attacks and methods will never inculcate a sensible appreciation of our co-operation with Germany; and finally Prussia's Polish policy, which has now had the effect of upsetting that very element which was, along with Germans and Hungarians, the most solid supporter of the Triple Alliance.

The things that are happening in this last respect are quite unintelligible to me, especially as the experiences of the recent past should have taught the rulers of Prussia that in this field nothing can be achieved by force, that pressure only creates counter-pressure and a resistance all that much firmer, the more people are wounded in their inmost feelings, and that the sharpening of national conflicts must all the more surely produce those conditions through which the Ostmarken really will become an Achilles heel.

And in fact, if I look back to the time of my stay in Berlin at the beginning of the 'seventies, and compare conditions then with those today, this truth is strikingly plain to see. In those days the Prussian Poles were materially well off; in West Prussia and Posen their individuality was respected; in Silesia there was no mention of national conflicts; indeed, I can remember very well from my own observations how well they had come to terms with their lot, and how little they wished to change it. Only with the *Kulturkampf* and the new Polish policy it entailed did the picture change in a flash, and today, when everything is being done to ruin them economically, and to annihilate their nationality, the struggle for existence is raging with a cheerless ferocity (*ungemütlicher Heftigkeit*) even in Silesia, which was neutral until very recently – a struggle which goads the weaker party on according to the degree to which it had nothing to lose, and which will only create a Polish irredenta to the delight of Russia, who alone will profit from it.

For true as it might be that, as you rightly say in one of your last letters, Prince Bismarck owed his later great successes to Prussia's attitude towards the Polish revolt of 1863, it would be very risky, to say the least, to count on the alleged Polish danger still today as a cement (*Kitt*) between Russia and Germany; first, because the same thing very rarely happens twice; but even more because diplomatic alignments in Europe have changed enormously since that time, and Russia today would wish her German rival anything but an increase in power as a result of a favourable turn of events at home. Russia would be more concerned covertly to intensify Germany's difficulties in this field, than to co-operate in removing them.

In my opinion Count Caprivi was the only man amongst the rulers of Prussia who assessed the situation soberly and correctly, and the time will probably soon come when people will regret having departed from the line he laid down. May this realization not come too late! For here it is a question which, even if it is specifically Prussian, has implications (*hinübergreift*) for international affairs, and in this respect I cannot conceal the great concern which it inspires in us for the future.

24. *Memorandum by Legationsrat, Count von Rhemen, on the agreements made between Austria-Hungary and Russia concerning Bosnia and the Herzegovina (1873–1902), secret, January 1903* (P.A. I/475)

Entente of 1897
When . . . Austro-Russian relations improved, the *Entente* of 1897 was concluded. In this, too, there was mention of Bosnia-Herzegovina; and the Russian government again tended to evade a clear recognition of the rights conceded (*zugestanden*) to Austria-Hungary.

In the notes exchanged at the time, the Austro-Hungarian résumé of the Winter Palace discussions said (Dispatch to Liechtenstein):

'Les avantages territoriaux reconnus à l'Autriche-Hongrie par le Traité de Berlin lui sont et demeurent acquis. Par conséquent la possession de la Bosnie, de la Hercégovine et du Sanjak de Novipazar ne pourra faire l'objet d'une discussion quelconque, le gouvernement de Sa Majesté Impériale et Royale Apostolique se réservant la faculté de substituer, le moment venu, au titre actuel d'occupation et droit de garnison celui d'annexion.'

The Russian counter-note reads:

'Le Comte Goluchowski fixe comme base d'une pareille entente les 4 points suivants:
(a) les avantages reconnus a l'Autriche-Hongrie par le Traité de Berlin lui sont et demeurent acquis.
En souscrivant à ce principe nous croyons devoir observer que le Traité de Berlin assure à l'Autriche-Hongrie le droit d'occuper militairement la Bosnie et l'Hercégovine. L'annexion des ces deux provinces soulèverait une question plus étendue qui exigerait un examen spécial en temps et lieux. Quant au Sanjak de Novi Pazar,

il y aurait de plus à en préciser les limites qui, de fait, n'ont jamais été suffisamment définies.'

This obscure and involved reply of Count Mouravieff of 5/17 May 1897 cannot detract at all, however, from the legal position (*Rechtsstandpunkt*) which at the conference of emperors and ministers in the Winter Palace 'not only met with no contradiction but was even most expressly recognized by H.M. the Emperor Nicholas as something self-evident' (Dispatch to Aehrenthal, No. 132, 2 March 1899).

If the Vienna government refrained from questioning this part of the note – and it would have had sufficient reason to question its view of the occupation mandate (a view since admitted by Kapnist to be a mistaken one) – this was because we did not wish to give St Petersburg the impression that we still regarded this as a matter for discussion, and wanted from Russia a new declaration in order to legitimize Austria-Hungary's claim.

As regards the other points of the 1897 *entente*, Mouravieff's note affirmed the principles that the two Powers should try to maintain the *status quo* in the Balkans as long as possible; if this were no longer possible they would make a new agreement; and the two governments would do nothing to impede the survival (*Erhaltung*), consolidation, and development of the existing Balkan states.

Many subsequent developments, however, especially the attitude of Russia's representatives in the Balkans, and the language of the Russian press, were hardly in accordance with the above principles, and His Imperial and Royal Apostolic Majesty had to speak very seriously to Count Mouravieff when he came to Vienna in the autumn of 1898, and to stress four aspects of the St Petersburg discussions:

1. the maintenance of the territorial *status quo* in the Balkans.
2. the independence of the Balkan states – interference in their internal affairs is therefore precluded;
3. absolute respect for Austria-Hungary's rights in Bosnia-Herzegovina
4. the necessity for common opposition to any agitation against these principles and for instructing the representatives of the two countries in this sense.

Unrest in Macedonia

The increasingly threatening ferment in Macedonia of recent years caused us last year to draw St Petersburg's attention to the dangerous situation and the necessity for common action to cure it. The Russian view about this wavered somewhat between optimism and pessimism. But Count Lamsdorff's present journey shows very well that the Russian government now recognizes the seriousness of the situation.

25. *Joint Declaration of Austria-Hungary and Russia in regard to the maintenance of neutrality by either if the other is at war, St Petersburg, 2/15 October 1904*

(printed in A. F. Pribram, *Secret Treaties*, Vol. 1, pp. 237–9)

The undersigned, duly authorized by their August Sovereigns, have met together today at the Imperial Ministry of Foreign Affairs to sign the following Declaration:

Austria-Hungary and Russia, united by identical views as to the conservative policy to be followed in the Balkan countries, and much satisfied with the result obtained so far by their close collaboration, are firmly decided to persevere in this course. Happy to record once more this understanding, the Cabinets of Vienna and of St Petersburg attach great importance to offering each other in due form a mark of friendship and reciprocal confidence.

It is with this purpose that the two Powers have come to an agreement to observe a loyal and absolute neutrality in case one of the two Parties signatory to this Declaration should find itself, alone and without provocation on its part, in a state of war with a third Power which sought to endanger its security or the *status quo*; the maintenance of which constitutes the basis of their understanding, as pacific as it is conservative.

The engagement between Austria-Hungary and Russia stipulated in the above naturally does not apply to the Balkan countries, whose destinies are obviously closely attached to the agreement established between the two neighbouring Empires. The said engagement is understood to remain valid so long as these two great Powers shall pursue their policy of an understanding in the affairs of Turkey; it shall be kept secret, and cannot be communicated to any other Government, except after a previous understanding between the Cabinets of Vienna and of St Petersburg.

Done in duplicate at St. Petersburg, October 2/15, 1904.
L. Aehrenthal.   Count Lamsdorff.

26. *Berchtold to Aehrenthal, No. 21, very confidential, St Petersburg, 15/28 May 1907* (P.A. XII/339)

So much for the Russian government's memorandum [in reply to Aehrenthal's suggestion that the Mürzsteg Powers seek French and German support for their conservative policy in Macedonia.] As it seemed to me to reveal in several places a mistaken understanding of Your Excellency's proposal, I readily took up M. Izvolsky's suggestion that we discuss the memorandum.

With regard to the memorandum's use of the term *'groupe de puissances'*, I emphasized above all that there was no question of any grouping of the Powers, and that Your Excellency was not thinking of this at all.[1] I refused to admit the validity of the minister's excuse, that even if it was not spelt out, this was what it would amount to in practice. I said that at most one could talk of a 'kernel of ambassadors', as it was not any grouping of the Powers that was envisaged but merely a confidential sounding of the German and French ambassadors by our ambassadors. M. Izvolsky did not go further into this, but stressed that those Powers could only be brought in on the basis of a concrete project of reform determined by the two empires; because any general co-operation not closely circumscribed would necessarily extend to an examination of the reform project at present in the process of formulation, and the lead would slip from our hands, which would complicate the work materially. I replied that this was not Your Excellency's intention, and that you held firm, as hitherto, to the principles of the *entente à deux*.

A further matter I felt I ought to raise was that of the difficulties which an attempt at a *rapprochement* might encounter in Paris. I mentioned how well disposed Your Excellency had found Berlin towards talks with France about Morocco. In the absence of such talks, each side looks to its own interests and this gives rise to friction. If there is at present, as the minister claims, some ill-feeling in France about Germany's mining activities, one can assume that talks will remove the differences, or at least alleviate them. But as regards France's inclination to draw closer to

---

[1] At this point in the dispatch Aehrenthal minuted – 'quite right'.

England, I said that it was up to M. Izvolsky to work against this tendency and to try to draw France closer to us by all possible means – that is, if he seriously intended to continue to pursue a conservative policy in the Near East. The minister – somewhat disconcerted, it seemed to me – assured me that he wanted nothing else than to tie (*dienstbar machen*) France to our policy and would certainly do what he could to achieve this. But it seemed to him rather pointless to try to bring France to co-operate with Germany so long as the present ill-feeling persists. It was highly desirable that the unfriendly feelings that lay at the root of this should disappear, 'all the more so as this could result in a continental combination, which would be simply ideal'.

The impression I have so far formed from my talks and correspondence with the minister about Your Excellency's proposal I should like to sum up as follows: after at first welcoming the plan with apparently sincere satisfaction, M. Izvolsky has become rather more reserved after thinking it over, which does not seem to be exactly a favourable sign. Nor is the memorandum's feeble acceptance (*marklose Konstatieren*) of France's pro-English proclivities exactly something which inspires special confidence in Izvolsky's performing glorious deeds (*tatkräftiges Eingreifen*). Nevertheless, I think I can assume after our last talk that something might be done if it comes to the point (*gegebenen Falles*) – provided that the approach to Paris is confined within the limits described above, and that the French government is in a better mood than it is at present.

27. *Fürstenberg*[1] *to Berchtold, private, 14 July 1907* (Berchtold MSS.) I poured out my heart to Aehr[enthal] and tried above all to assuage (*abzudämpfen*) the mistrust of Izvolsky that weighs on *his* heart; I think I succeeded; the atmosphere became noticeably milder; but the end result was still the following exclamation: 'Yes, yes, but obviously (!!) if he doesn't go through thick and thin with us in the Balkans, then I shall be the one who will go FIRST to the English!!' During all this I was subjected to close scrutiny from a distance of two decimeters. I gulped audibly and just took note (*verhielt mich receptiv*).

---

[1] Counsellor of Embassy, St Petersburg.

Documents

28. *Aehrenthal to Pallavicini, private, 30 January 1908* (P.A. XII/339)
With regard to Your Excellency's telegram of the 26th inst., No.
23 . . . there is undoubtedly a lot to be said for the idea that it
might be advisable, immediately following the presentation of the
judicial reform note, to enter into a confidential exchange of
views with the Grand Vizier to let him know (*anzudeuten*) that
under certain circumstances [i.e. if the Porte renewed the man-
dates of the reform bodies operating in Macedonia] the Powers
might be open to negotiation (*mit sich sprechen liessen*) about the
matter of judicial reform. As Your Excellency's relations with
Ferid Pasha are especially close (*vertrauensvoll*), it would also seem
reasonable that, after the St Petersburg government has been
consulted, it should be Your Excellency who puts the suggestion
to the Grand Vizier.

But I can see that the handling of this matter would require the
utmost caution. For as Your Excellency will see from the en-
closed documents, brought by today's courier from St Petersburg
. . . people there are somewhat startled by the fact that we have
raised the matter of the Uvać-Mitrovitsa railway link at Constantinople at the present moment. People on the Neva will
probably be inclined to assume that our attitude towards Turkey
in the matter of reform might now be influenced by concern for
our railway project. In these circumstances it could easily happen
that, if we suggested that Your Excellency might hold out to
Turkey the prospect of a certain amount of flexibility in the
judicial reform question, it might be misinterpreted in the above
sense.

I also see from your telegram of 28 January, No. 25, that the
idea of confidentially sounding the Porte immediately *after the
presentation of the judicial reform note* is no longer so urgent (*aktuell*),
as it seems very doubtful whether there will not have to be some
delay in presenting the note in view of the attitude of Baron
Marschall as you describe it.

I am making use of the last-mentioned telegram to discuss with
St Petersburg whether it would not be advisable for us, even
before the next meeting of the ambassadors about the judicial
reform question, to undertake a *démarche à deux* at Berlin to
bring the German government to put appropriate pressure on
Baron Marschall.

29. *Pallavicini to Aehrenthal, No. 12B, confidential, 19 February, 1908* (P.A. XII/339)

[None of the six governments was prepared to use coercion to secure the judicial reform. Pallavicini explains that as the British and Russian ambassadors were both for caution, he was reluctant to take the lead in demanding extreme measures. Besides, all the Powers are pursuing their own interests in Turkey. Pallavicini had to make every effort (*Alles daranzusetzen*) to secure the railway concession.]

We must not deceive ourselves, however; and must admit that the judicial reform affair has suffered as a result of our successful petition (*durch die Anbringung und Durchführung unseres Wunsches*) in the matter of the Sanjak Railway. [The British ambassador said] 'It has never happened before that anybody has secured such an *iradé* from the Sultan in such a short time.' . . . But the chief point was that we took advantage of the situation; obviously without holding out to the Turks any kind of hope that we should be more amenable in the judicial reform question.

30. *Aehrenthal to Pallavicini, No. 228, confidential, 27 February 1908* (P.A. XII/339)

I am especially pleased to note that Your Excellency established no connexion whatever between your attitude in the matter of judicial reform and your *démarches* to secure the imperial *iradé*, and that you carefully avoided holding out to the *Porte* any kind of hope that out of regard for our railway petition we might prove more amenable in the matter of judicial reform. . . .

31. *Szögyény to Aehrenthal, 15 October 1908* (Aehrenthal MSS., Karton 4)

Csoor p. Székesfehérvar,
15 October 1908

On my arrival in Berlin on the 4th inst. I found the Wilhelmstrasse in a mood of great irritation. Under-Secretary of State, Stemrich, and his chief *aide*, Baron Griesinger (who would rather like to play the role of a Holstein reincarnate but has much less skill and knowledge, of course), had very little information about the important events of the last few weeks. Our action regarding the annexation was in the air; but as Schoen's reports of his interview with you, and your detailed letter to the Imperial Chancellor, did not come to the Secretary of State's knowledge until the 5th, the Wilhelmstrasse had no exact information about the whole affair until then. The newspaper reports of the handing over of the Emperor's letter to President Fallières had the effect of a bomb and . . . the Emperor William was in a very bad temper about this news, which he too had got from the newspapers. By the way, I might add that my alleged interview with the correspondent of the *Zeit*, to which you were so good as to draw my attention, did not take place at all. All the Berlin newspapers have busied themselves with the premature presentation of the Imperial letter to President Fallières, and so it was not difficult for the correspondent in question to put something together about it. In my many years of experience in dealings with journalists I have always been extremely careful; but the warning example of my friend and colleague, Rudi Khevenhüller, made me doubly careful in this particular case!

I sent the Imperial letter to the Emperor William through the Foreign Office, so that it would be in His Majesty's hands before the 7th, at any rate. Herr Stemrich thought it very important that your letter to Prince Bülow and the Imperial Chancellor's report about it should be in the Emperor's hands before my audience; he wanted to persuade me that, once the Imperial letter had been sent off, an audience was actually superfluous; but I insisted on one and received . . . an immediate telegraphic reply, that the Emperor William would deign to receive me on the morning of the 7th in the hunting lodge at Rominten. The journey . . . was long and fatiguing. After a fourteen-hour train journey I had to spend the night at Gumbinnen, whence I proceeded first thing the next day by local train to Nosswede. There, a splendid imperial motor car was awaiting me. But after a journey of only a few minutes this magnificent vehicle overturned; we escaped, fortunately, with just a fright, and had to finish our journey in the uncomfortable baggage coach that was following. In Rominten H.M. the Empress was awaiting us at the entry to the park, and greeted us with enchantingly gracious kindness. Her Majesty and the Emperor William, who returned a little later from the morning's shooting, were both quite inconsolable about our accident.

I have already reported to you by telegram about the long conversation I had with His Majesty, and my discussions with Herr v.

Schoen and Prince Bülow. Their content is completely consistent and is, as you will see, satisfactory in every respect. The language of the German official and semi-official press is admittedly not quite in line with the declarations of loyalty to the alliance of the emperor and his advisers, but this is because, as Herr v. Schoen assured me, these journalistic pronouncements are intended *ad usum delphini*, i.e. for the consumption of public opinion, both German and Turkish. Germany has, in fact, done so much brilliant commercial business at the Golden Horn in the last decade that it is understandable if the Germans make the greatest efforts to dispel the ill-feeling there, which is also directed at Germany.

Nevertheless, it seems to me that the German government must work on the German press to get it to stop its attacks, even the veiled ones, on our action. The Imperial Chancellor and the Secretary of State promised me that they would act decisively. That the Emperor William and the Imperial Chancellor will stand loyally by us, even in the event of most serious complications, is beyond all doubt, in view of their precise declarations. A congress or a conference Prince Bülow would like to avoid at any price, because he fears, I think quite rightly, that that would produce a grouping of the Powers in which we – Austria-Hungary and Germany – would be in a minority. Bülow has no faith at all in Italy, and thinks that she will not be independent and energetic enough to expose herself to the risk of a conflict with England, even if Tittoni stays in power.

The forthcoming talks between Bülow and Izvolsky will probably not be all that pleasant. In talking to Count Wolff-Metternich, the Russian foreign minister has attacked our action with great vehemence.

32. *Khevenhüller to Aehrenthal, Paris, 17 October 1908* (Aehrenthal MSS., Karton 3)

That I am by nature impulsive, I know only too well, but at my age it is difficult to change a basic characteristic. Anyway, the era of interviews is now closed.

[Khevenhüller explains why he presented Franz Joseph's letter to President Fallières – who was going away for the weekend – prematurely on 3 October.]

And now, I take the liberty of speaking quite frankly. After what you said to me, I was bound to think that the agreement with Russia and Italy was perfect (*einwandfrei*). Had I known that Izvolsky had such strong reservations about your policy, I should not have mentioned his consent here. Anyway, my assertion has had some good results here. Izvolsky's insincerity has been exposed. His latest *coup*, with the publication of the nine points [of the conference programme] has done him a lot of harm in Paris.

What a liar Izvolsky is, is clear from his remark to Mensdorff concerning my language about Bulgaria. . . . In moments of acute crisis I have always preferred, ever since I have been in the service, to act on my own initiative (*mich selbst zu exponieren*), for if it doesn't suit, then I can be disavowed, and that would be the lesser evil.

33. Note verbale *of the Serbian legation, 31 March 1909* (O-U.A., Vol. 2, No. 1425)

With reference to the previous note[1] from the Serbian Government to the Austro-Hungarian government, and with a view to removing any misunderstandings that might result from it, the Serbian Minister has received the order to furnish the following explanations to the Imperial and Royal Minister for Foreign Affairs: Serbia recognizes that her rights have not been injured (*qu'elle n'a pas été atteinte dans ses droits*) by the *fait accompli* created in Bosnia-Herzegovina, and that she will therefore conform to whatever decision the Powers make regarding Article XXV of the Treaty of Berlin. Deferring (*se rendant*) to the advice of the Great Powers, Serbia pledges herself, as from now, to abandon the attitude of protest and opposition which she has maintained towards the annexation since last autumn, and further pledges herself to change the course of her present policy towards Austria-Hungary, so as to live henceforth on a good-neighbourly footing (*sur le pied d'un bon voisinage*) with the latter. In conformity with these declarations, and trusting in the pacific intentions of Austria-Hungary, Serbia will reduce her army to the position of the spring of 1908 as regards its organization, disposition, and effective strength. She will disarm and dismiss her volunteers and bands, and will prevent the formation of new irregular units on her territory.

[1] 15 March, see p. 317.

34. *Agreement between Austria-Hungary and Italy, explaining and
    supplementing Article VII of the Treaty of the Triple Alliance
    of 1887, secret, Vienna, November 30 [Rome, December 15]
    1909* (printed in A. F. Pribram, *Secret Treaties*, Vol. 1, pp.
    241–3)

In the conferences which I [you] have lately had with Duke
Avarna [Count Aehrenthal] with a view to defining and perfecting
Article VII of the Treaty of the Triple Alliance, we [you] have
agreed, to begin with, that, Austria-Hungary having renounced
the rights which the Treaty of Berlin had conferred upon her in
respect to the Sanjak of Novibazar, the provisions of the aforesaid
Article of the Triple Alliance apply to the Sanjak as well as to the
other parts of the Ottoman Empire. If, then, in consequence of
the impossibility of maintaining the *status quo* in the Balkans,
Austria-Hungary should be compelled by the force of circumstances to proceed to a temporary or permanent occupation of
the Sanjak of Novibazar, that occupation shall be effected only
after a previous agreement with Italy, based on the principle of
compensation.

Faithful to the spirit which has inspired the Treaty of the Triple
Alliance, and with a view to defining exactly and by mutual agreement the procedure which the two Allied Cabinets intend to adopt
in certain eventualities, we, Duke Avarna and I [you, with Count
Aehrenthal,] have also agreed upon the following:

Each of the two Cabinets binds itself not to conclude with a
third Power any agreement whatsoever concerning Balkan questions without the participation of the other Cabinet on a footing
of absolute equality; likewise, the two Cabinets bind themselves
to communicate to each other every proposition which may be
made to the one or to the other by a third Power, running contrary to the principle of non-intervention and tending to a modification of the *status quo* in the regions of the Balkans or of the
Ottoman coasts and islands in the Adriatic and of the Aegean
Sea.

It goes without saying that Article VII of the Treaty of the
Triple Alliance, which the above provisions only render more
specific and complete, remains in force in its entirety.

As to the duration of the engagement which the two Cabinets
assume in virtue of the above, it is understood that it shall coincide
with that of the Treaty of the Triple Alliance . . .

35. *Franz Ferdinand to Berchtold, 4 July 1913* (Berchtold MSS.)
As I am preparing to leave for Blankenberghe I received several
reports this morning about the latest events in the Balkans and I
must write a few lines to Your Excellency in all haste to ask you
again to stand by the policy which we have so often discussed
together in *perfect harmony*, and not to let yourself be influenced by
Conrad. For naturally, Conrad will again be for all kinds of wars
and a great Hurrah-Policy, to conquer the Serbs and God knows
what. He will be still more wild as a result of the frightful affair
(Redl) and seek in war a remedy for a lot of abuses for which he –
strictly between you and me – is also partly to blame.

Sorry as I am, and sincerely as I regret the keeping of the
reservists under arms, I quite see that they cannot be demobilized
at present.

But for the rest, keep a cool head, indeed do *nothing* at all, do
not play the role of a *Balkan State;* and, as I have explained from
the beginning was the basis of my policy . . . *watch calmly from the
wings* (in der Loge) *while this rabble, these unreliable useless people break
each other's heads!!!* Only for God's sake do not, for the sake of this
Bulgarian who is leading the whole world by the nose, do not
attack the Serbs or do anything of that kind, which is all that
Conrad wants. For then we should have the business with Russia
again, and to quarrel (*anzubändeln*) with Russia *now* would be *sheer
unforgivable madness*, because the Roumanian divisions are *not
available* and Germany would *certainly* leave us in the lurch indirectly and only send a very few reserves.

It is indeed immensely fortunate that *all* these Balkan dogs
should break loose all at once. So, just don't interfere, and watch
calmly from the wings.

This is my well-considered view of both the political and the
military situation, and I ask your Excellency to trust in me more
than in my subordinate, the good Conrad, who is often a very
rash daredevil who sees his whole salvation in a war, which
would be a disaster for the Monarchy.

Dixi et salvavi animam meam! I wanted to tell your Excellency
this in old friendship, and I ask that you keep me up to date in
Blankenberghe and above all that no important decisions are
taken without my knowledge.

And in conclusion, once again, do not set too much store by the
advice of Conrad, who will now harass you frightfully. I have

known him well, as he has served under me for six years. He is very good under a *very* energetic hand for war and for manoeuvres; as a politician and in peacetime he is liable to bolt (*Durchgeher ganz sprunghaft*) and is *not* to be used as an adviser; moreover, he is *always exceeding his powers* and one must constantly pull on the reins. I only accepted him last year when the time was so critical.

So, once again, Your Excellency, please remain in the wings and watch, and trust me as you have done in the past. I cannot tell you enough how I appreciate it and how happy it makes me, and, if we are in such harmony as heretofore, we shall best be serving our Emperor and our country.

My thoughts and best wishes are with you, and if you need me urgently I can come from Blankenberghe, but in any case we can keep in constant touch.

36. *Berchtold to Szögyény, No. 2176, very confidential, 16 May 1914*
    (O-U.A., Vol. 8, 9674)

I see time and again from your reports that Your Excellency has pointed out clearly and objectively to leading German statesmen the difficulties which must make us doubt whether attempts to put relations between the Monarchy and Serbia on a better footing can succeed. Nevertheless, people in Berlin do not seem to have been able to free themselves, even yet, from the idea of a political *rapprochement* between Austria-Hungary and Serbia – an idea which must be regarded as hopeless (*aussichtslos*) in view of the animosity towards Austria-Hungary deep-rooted in the Serbian national consciousness, and the hopes – cherished everywhere in Serbia and brazenly paraded – of incorporating component parts of the Monarchy.

We have to hand particularly, as Your Excellency is aware, remarks of His Majesty the Emperor William – very recent ones too – which show that misapprehensions persist in this respect (*die eine radikale Aufklärung . . . nach dieser Richtung nicht erkennen lassen*), at least on His Majesty's part. I need hardly repeat here that despite the tendencies prevailing in Serbia which I have mentioned – and which, I can indeed say, are generally known elsewhere – the Imperial and Royal Government is steadfastly following the path it has marked out for itself, of establishing as friendly a relationship as possible with the Kingdom on the Save.

This is also proved by the negotiations, which are still going on, about the Orient Railway.

But so long as people in Germany have no clear picture of Serbian feelings and future plans they will hardly appreciate the importance we attach to this question in the formulation of our foreign policy. The Imperial and Royal military attaché at Belgrade . . . has described the 'Easter spirit' of the Serbian press, giving a very apposite picture of the mood of the Serbian people. The phrase about the resurrection of the whole Serbian race is not just an indication of a passing symptom, but sums up the whole content (*das Um und Auf*) of a political idea which dominates an entire people. I urge Your Excellency to show this remarkable report from Belgrade to the leading statesmen in Berlin; and it might be of advantage if His Majesty the Emperor William also had the opportunity of seeing it.

Enclosure: *Report from the military attaché at Belgrade to the Chief of the General Staff, Res. No. 69, 20 April 1914. Copy.*

Pan-Serbian Easter Greetings. Just as the church and the clergy in Serbia serve chiefly political and national ends, so also the most important religious festivals here are used to express national feeling and the desires and hopes it gives rise to. This was shown in drastic fashion in the Easter greetings of the Serbian press this year. First and foremost, *Politika*, the most highly regarded Serbian newspaper, summed up in its leading article, 'Our resurrection', the satisfaction of the Pan-Serbs with developments since last Easter and their aspirations as to the future . . . *Straža* compares the ultimate liberation of the Serbs with the passion of Christ: 'The year 1908 likewise signifies for us a Good Friday, which was followed in 1912–13 by the Resurrection. The Serbia of Dušan has celebrated its resurrection, and the Easter festival of the whole Serbian people too, the day of national unification, which will gather into one state all who speak Serbian, is no longer far off . . . There, across the Save and the Danube, on the banks of the foaming Narenta and on the Adriatic, languish Slavs who look out on today's great Christian festival in sorrow, seeking to discern the gleam of Serbian bayonets, for these form their only hope of a final resurrection. Let us therefore stand closer together and hasten to the assistance of those who cannot yet feel with us the joy of this year's feast of resurrection.' Most of the other daily papers express themselves in a similar sense. The burning desire for union with our south Slavs expressed in all these leading articles is nothing new, even in this unvarnished form. But now associated with it is the increasingly prominent firm conviction that our Serbs, Croats, and Slovenes have no other political concern but to look longingly across the Serbian frontier in the hope that the Serbian 'liberators' will come. This view, which is general here, and widespread even in educated circles, must be regarded as a factor that could easily lead Serbia into an adventurous policy towards the Monarchy.

37. *Memorandum by Sektionsrat Franz Baron von Matscheko, secret, undated (before 24 June 1914)* (O-U.A., Vol. 8, 9918)

Conditions in the Balkans are now clear enough after the great upheavals of the last two years to permit one to assess the results of the crisis and to decide whether and how far the interests of the Triple Alliance Powers, especially the two Central Powers, have been affected by these events, and what conclusions follow for the European and Balkan policy of these Powers.

If the present situation is compared objectively with that before the great crisis one must admit that the total result, from the point of view both of Austria-Hungary and the Triple Alliance, can by no means be said to be favourable.

Of course the balance sheet shows a few positive features. It has been possible to create, as a barrier to Serbia's advance, an independent Albanian state which after a few years, when its internal organization has been completed, will yet be able to be counted as another military factor in the calculations of the Triple Alliance. The relations of the Triple Alliance to the strengthened and enlarged Greek kingdom have generally developed in such a way that Greece, despite her alliance with Serbia, is not necessarily to be regarded as an opponent. Above all, Bulgaria, as a result of the events leading up to the Second Balkan War, has awakened from the hypnosis of Russia and can no longer be regarded today as an exponent of Russian policy. On the contrary, the Bulgarian government is seeking to establish closer relations with the Triple Alliance.

Set against these favourable factors, however, are unfavourable ones, which weigh heavier in the balance. Turkey, who had a natural community of interests with the Triple Alliance, and who was a strong counter-weight against Russia and the Balkan states, has been pushed out of Europe almost completely, and her Great Power position has suffered a real loss.

Serbia, whose policy has for years been motivated by tendencies hostile to Austria-Hungary, and who is entirely under Russian influence, has achieved an increase of territory and population which far exceeds her own expectations; the possibility of her further enlargement by means of a union with Montenegro has moved markedly nearer realization as a result of her territorial proximity to Montenegro and the general strengthening of the pan-Serbian idea. Finally, Roumania has been forced by events into co-operation with Serbia, and a durable Roumanian-Serbian solidarity still persists – even if it is restricted to certain questions. This, and the simultaneous shift of Roumanian public opinion in favour of Russia make it seem at least doubtful whether Roumania will not at a given moment come out as an enemy of the Triple Alliance instead of as a friend. This extremely important question will be examined more thoroughly below.

Whereas the Balkan crisis thus had results that were in themselves unfavourable enough for the Triple Alliance, and which bore within them the seed of a future development that Austria-Hungary, particularly, could not wish for, we see on the other hand that French and Russian diplomacy has inaugurated a coherent planned action to develop the advantages already gained, and to change the few remaining unfavourable factors.

A brief survey of the European situation shows clearly why the Triple *Entente* – rather, the Dual Alliance of Russia and France, as England has . . . assumed a reserved attitude, since the Balkan crisis – cannot by any means rest content with the favourable displacement of power in the Balkans so far achieved.

Whereas the policy of the two Empires and to a certain degree, of Italy too, is a conservative policy of peace, the policy of Russia, like that of France, is pursuing aims that are in the last resort aggressive and directed against the *status quo*; and the Franco-Russian alliance, as a product of these parallel tendencies, is decidedly of an offensive nature.

That the policy of the Triple Alliance has so far prevailed, and that European peace has been preserved from disturbance by Russia and France is attributable to the military superiority which the armies of the Triple Alliance, chiefly Austria-Hungary's and

Germany's, undoubtedly possessed over those of Russia and France – in which superiority the alliance of Roumania with the Empires was a valuable element.

The idea of freeing the Christian peoples of the Balkans from the Turkish yoke so as to use them as a weapon against Central Europe has been for ages the practical political (*realpolitische*) basis of Russia's traditional interest in these peoples. Recently there developed from this the idea of uniting the Balkan States in a Balkan League, as a means of putting an end to the military superiority of the Triple Alliance. The first pre-condition of the realization of this plan was that Turkey should be driven out of the territories inhabited by the Christian peoples of the Balkans, so as to strengthen these states and free them for action in the West. This precondition was on the whole fulfilled by the last war. On the other hand, after the crisis ended there appeared a division of the Balkan States into two groups almost equal in strength – Turkey and Bulgaria on the one side, the two Serbian states, Greece and Roumania on the other. The result of this has been that the two groups tie each other down and cannot for the present be used by the *Entente* Powers to displace the European balance of power.

In the light of this, it seems to us fully understandable that for months now Russia and France . . . have been developing an intensive diplomatic activity at the Bosphorus and in all the Balkan capitals to end the division of the Balkan states and to unite them all, or a decisive majority of them, in a new Balkan League directed against the West.

Conditions already favoured the activity of the Dual Alliance Powers, in so far as an alliance already existed between Serbia and Greece, and Roumania not only declares her solidarity with these two Powers as regards the results of the Treaty of Bucharest, but is also turning her sympathies away from the Monarchy – which has had a noticeable effect on Roumania's official policy. For the Dual Alliance Powers, therefore, it was really a question of smoothing over Bulgaria's deep differences with Greece, and above all with Serbia, in the Macedonian question; further, of finding a basis on which Roumania would be prepared to come right over into the Dual Alliance camp, and even to enter into a political combination with the Bulgaria she mistrusts; and finally to bring about a peaceful solution of the Islands question, if possible, so as to prepare the way for Turkey's joining the Balkan States.

There can be no doubt about the basis on which Russian and French diplomacy envisages the smoothing out of all these differences and rivalries and the founding of the new Balkan League. In present-day conditions, where a common action against Turkey can no longer be considered, an alliance of the Balkan states can only be directed against one opponent – namely Austria-Hungary; and such an alliance can only be brought about on the basis of a programme that, in the last resort, offers to all participants expansion at the expense of the territorial integrity of the Monarchy, by means of a step-like (*staffelweise*) shifting of frontiers from east to west. One can hardly imagine a union of Balkan States on any other basis; but on this basis it is certainly not impossible; indeed, without any effective counter-action, it is even probable.

There is no doubt that Serbia, under Russian pressure, would agree to pay a fair price in Macedonia for Bulgaria's entry into an alliance directed against Austria-Hungary and aiming at the acquisition of Bosnia.

The difficulties in Sofia are greater . . .

* * *

[France and Russia are trying to force Bulgaria into line by isolating her; and to win over Turkey and Roumania.] Austria-Hungary's relations with Roumania are at present characterized by the fact that the Monarchy stands firmly by the Alliance . . . whereas Roumania unilaterally declares herself free of her alliance obligations and only holds out to the Monarchy the prospect of a neutral attitude. And even the mere neutrality of Roumania is assured to the Monarchy only by a personal pledge of King Carol's . . . the fulfilment of which depends on the king's always keeping the direction of foreign policy entirely in his own hands. That this task, in a time when the whole country is excited, could be beyond the strength of the foreign-born king, is all the more likely in that already today King Carol points to public opinion to justify Roumania's inability entirely to fulfil her treaty obligations.

* * *

The continuance of an unclear relationship with Roumania would mean that the value of the Roumanian alliance to the Monarchy would remain illusory, indeed, negative, while the Monarchy for its part would be prevented – out of consideration for the alliance relationship still formally existing – from taking in good time political measures, such as drawing in other states, or military measures, such as the fortification of the Transylvanian frontier, to remove or at least mitigate the ill effects of the neutrality and possible hostility of the neighbouring kingdom.

* * *

It would, therefore, be irresponsibly negligent and would put important imperial defence interests at risk, if those who determine the Monarchy's foreign policy remained more or less passive in the face of present developments in Roumania and failed to press most energetically for a clarification of the situation.

[In the third draft, of 1 July 1914, as amended by Berchtold – O-U.A., 9984 – the two paragraphs quoted immediately above are replaced by others reflecting the changed situation after Sarajevo: If the Monarchy confronted Roumania with 'a categorical "either . . . or" ' this 'could lead to an open breach', and was hardly desirable. 'It would be not only pointless, but in view of Roumania's political and military importance, irresponsibly negligent and would put important imperial defence interests at risk if the Monarchy remained more or less passive in the face of present developments in Roumania, and failed to undertake without delay the necessary military preparations and political measures to remove or at least to mitigate the effects of Roumania's neutrality and possible hostility'.]

* * *

[If Roumania refuses to show her colours, the Monarchy should seek an alignment with Bulgaria and Turkey, and look to the defence of the Transylvanian frontier. Germany, too, is threatened by Russia's activities.]

Russia's manifest design to encircle (*Einkreisungstendenzen*) the Monarchy, which has no world-wide ambitions (*die keine Weltpolitik treibt*), is directed in the last resort towards making it impossible for Germany to resist Russia's ultimate aims or her political and commercial supremacy. Therefore, one can only describe as shortsighted that view, on the basis of which the policy of the German Empire has recently been criticized in

Germany itself, that Germany is, out of loyalty to the Alliance, standing up for specifically Austro-Hungarian interests that lie far from Germany's sphere of interests.

And for these reasons, those who direct the foreign policy of Austria-Hungary are also convinced that it is a common interest of Austria-Hungary, no less than of Germany, in the present stage of the Balkan crisis to oppose in good time, and energetically, a development which is being striven for and furthered by Russia according to plan, and which later will perhaps be irreversible.

[The draft of 1 July continues:

The above memorandum had just been completed when the frightful events occurred at Sarajevo. The momentous consequences of the wicked (*ruchlos*) murder can hardly be overlooked today. But in any case it provides irrefutable evidence, if any had still been lacking, of the unbridgeable nature of the opposition between the Monarchy and Serbia, and of the dangerous character and intensity of pan-Serbian aspirations, which stop at nothing.

Austria-Hungary has not been lacking in goodwill and conciliation in her efforts to establish a tolerable relationship with Serbia. But it has again been shown that these efforts were quite vain, and that the Monarchy will also have to reckon in future with the tenacious, irreconcilable, aggressive hostility of Serbia.

For the Monarchy, the necessity imposes itself all the more imperatively to tear apart with a firm hand the threads which its opponents are seeking to form into a net above its head.]

38. *Berchtold to Mérey, private, 21 July 1914* (O-U.A., Vol. 8, 10459)

I see from your last letter to Forgách that on the whole you approve of the firm attitude we are planning to adopt towards Serbia . . . I only wish to say that we were determined by both domestic and foreign political motives. It was increasingly certain that the subversive activity pursued on Bosnian-Herzegovinian soil to a frightful degree, and with ramifications in Dalmatia, Croatia, Slavonia and Hungary could be checked only by energetic action at Belgrade, where the threads run together; and that a new grouping of Powers is coming into being in the Balkans with the connivance of Roumania and Russia, with the destruction of the Monarchy as its ultimate aim. I am well aware of my grave responsibility, given our exposed position, the unreliability and jealousy of our Italian ally, the hostility of Roumanian public opinion, and the weight Slavophile advice carries at the court of the tsar. But the responsibility for doing nothing and letting things drift on until the waves meet over our heads would seem to me even more serious – even if for the moment an easier one – than that of facing up to the danger and taking the consequences.

In drafting the note to Serbia it seemed to us essential, not only to document before the whole world our good right to put certain demands to Serbia for the preservation of our internal tranquillity; but to formulate these demands in such a way as would oblige Serbia to take up a clear position against propaganda hostile to the Monarchy, as regards the past and in the future, and as would give us a chance of making our voice heard in the matter in future.

For us, it was not a question of humiliating Serbia, but of bringing about a clear situation regarding Serbia's relations with the Monarchy as a neighbour, and, as a practical result, either, in the event of our demands being accepted, a thorough clearing up of the situation in Serbia with our co-operation (*Mitwirkung*); or, in the event of their being refused, settling the matter by force of arms and paralysing Serbia as much as possible.

As you can imagine, it was not all that easy to reach agreement over the drafting of the note in the council of ministers. A certain difference appeared especially between me and Stürgkh on the one hand, and Tisza on the other, over our assessment of the situation, in that Tisza regards even a mere diplomatic success as securing our position in the Balkans, and wanted to avoid a breach as much as possible (*tunlichst vermieden haben will*) whereas I am *extremely* sceptical about a new peaceful triumph, in view of the diplomatic successes achieved in 1909 and 1912, which have not helped us and have only embittered (*verschärft*) our relations with Serbia. On this, Stürgkh shares my view entirely. By gradual compromises from both sides, we managed in the end to reach an agreement – also about the ultimate aim of any war, in respect of which Tisza wanted to insist absolutely on a declaration that there was no question of any annexation of Serbian territory by the Monarchy. In the end we finally consented to this, with the proviso that we should demand strategic frontier rectifications and guarantees of Serbia's future behaviour (military convention, etc.) as well as cessions of territory to other Balkan states.

Yours will now be the task, certainly no easy one, of keeping the Italian government on our side.

39. *Extract from Conrad von Hoetzendorf's Diary, 26 July 1914*
(Conrad, *Aus meiner Dienstzeit*, Vol. 4, pp. 131–2)

I then spoke with Count Berchtold alone; he said:

'We should like to present the declaration of war on Serbia as soon as possible, so that various influences may cease [to operate]. When do you want the declaration of war?'

I: 'Only when we have progressed far enough for operations to begin – about 12 August.'

Count Berchtold: 'The diplomatic situation will not hold that long. Nor do we know that there won't be fighting on the frontier.'

I said that in this case matters would take their own course, and suggested he postpone a declaration of war for the present, but send for me if for diplomatic reasons delay should no longer seem advisable. We could surely wait for a few days – it was not all that urgent. I advised him (*legte nahe*) to hold back Montenegro as long as possible, and not to 'stir up' Bulgaria against Roumania, as we had to humour (*schonen*) Roumania. But the most important thing was to find out definitely about Russia's attitude. It would be desirable to have done this by 4, or at the latest 5 August.

Count Berchtold: 'That won't be possible!' (*Das wird nicht gehen!*)

Summing up, I said that the fact was that if it was clear by this date that Russia was 'going for' us (*gegen uns 'los gehe'*), we should proceed against Russia from the start (*von Haus aus*), but otherwise against Serbia; if Russia moved against us later, however, we should at first be weaker in the northern theatre of operations.

Bibliography

The most comprehensive recent bibliographies are to be found in C. A. Macartney, *The Habsburg Monarchy, 1790–1918* (London, 1968), and F. R. Bridge, *The Habsburg Monarchy 1804–1918. Books and pamphlets published in the United Kingdom between 1818 and 1967. A critical bibliography* (School of Slavonic and East European Studies, University of London, 1967).

Archive sources

(*a*) *Private papers*

Aehrenthal MSS.	Haus-, Hof-, und Staatsarchiv, Vienna
Berchtold MSS.	Haus-, Hof-, und Staatsarchiv, Vienna
Cartwright MSS.	Delapre Abbey, Northamptonshire
Grey MSS.	Public Record Office, London
Hardinge MSS.	University Library, Cambridge
Kállay MSS.	Haus-, Hof-, und Staatsarchiv, Vienna
Mensdorff MSS.	Haus-, Hof-, und Staatsarchiv, Vienna
Mérey MSS.	Haus-, Hof-, und Staatsarchiv, Vienna

(*b*) *Official papers*

Foreign Office correspondence in the Public Record Office, London

Series F.O. 7, Austria

F.O. 120, Vienna embassy and consular archives

F.O. 368, commercial

F.O. 371, political

German Foreign Ministry microfilms in the Public Record Office, London

Politisches Archiv, in the Haus-, Hof-, und Staatsarchiv, Vienna

Series P.A. I Allgemeines

P.A. III Preussen

P.A. VIII England

Bibliography

P.A.   IX   Frankreich
P.A.   X   Russland
P.A.   XII   Türkei
P.A.   XV   Bulgarien
P.A.   XXXII   Marokko
P.A.   XL   Interna
Kabinettsarchiv
Administrative Registratur

Official publications of documents

Les origines diplomatiques de la guerre de 1870–1871 (29 vols), Ministère des affaires étrangères, Paris, 1910–32.

Documents diplomatiques français, 1871–1914, Ministère des affaires étrangères, Paris, 1929–55.

Documenti diplomatici italiani, 1861–1914, Ministero degli affari esteri, Rome, 1952– .

Die grosse Politik der europäischen Kabinette, 1871–1914 (40 vols), eds Lepsius, J., Mendelssohn-Bartholdy, A., and Thimme, F., 1922–7.

British Documents on the Origins of the War, 1898–1914, eds Gooch, G.P., and Temperley, H. W. V. (11 vols), London 1926–38.

Die auswärtige Politik Serbiens, 1903–1914, ed. Bogitschewitsch, M. (3 vols), Berlin, 1928–31.

Oesterreich-Ungarns Aussenpolitik, 1908–1914, eds Bittner, L., and Uebersberger, H. (8 vols), Vienna, 1930.

Secondary sources

ANDERSON, M. S., *The Eastern Question, 1774–1923*, London, 1966.

ANDRÁSSY, J., *Bismarck, Andrássy, and Their Successors*, London, 1927.

BAERNREITHER, J. M., *Fragmente eines politischen Tagebuchs* (ed. J. Redlich), Berlin, 1928.

BENEDIKT, H., *Die wirtschaftliche Entwicklung in der Franz-Joseph-Zeit*, Vienna, 1958.

BESTUZHEV, I. V. (ed.), 'Borba v pravyaschikh krugakh Rossii po voprosam vneshnei politiki vo vremya Bosniiskogo krizisa', *Istoricheskii Arkhiv*, 5, 1962.

Bibliography

BISMARCK, O. VON, *Die gesammelten Werke* (19 vols), Berlin, 1924–32.

BLAAS, R., 'Il problema veneto e la diplomazia austriaca', in *Conferenze e note accademiche nel I centenario dell'unione del Veneto all'Italia*, Padua, 1967.

BOGITSCHEWITSCH, M., *Causes of the War*, London, 1919.

BOURNE, K., 'Great Britain and the Cretan Revolt, 1868–9', *Slavonic and East European Review*, 35, 1956.

BRIDGE, F. R., *Great Britain and Austria-Hungary 1906–1914. A Diplomatic History*, London, 1972.

BRIDGE, F. R., '*Tarde venientibus ossa*: Austro-Hungarian colonial aspirations in Asia Minor, 1913–14', *Middle Eastern Studies*, October 1970.

BRIDGE, F. R., 'The British declaration of war on Austria-Hungary in 1914', *Slavonic and East European Review*, 47, 1969.

BUCKLE, G. E., *Life of Benjamin Disraeli, Earl of Beaconsfield*, Vol. 6, London, 1920.

CARLGREN, W. M., *Iswolsky und Aehrenthal vor der bosnischen Annexionskrise*, Uppsala, 1955.

CARLGREN, W. M., 'Informationsstykken från Abdul Hamids senare regeringsår', *Historisk Tidskrift*, 1952.

CECIL, LADY GWENDOLEN, *Life of Robert, Marquis of Salisbury* (4 vols), London, 1922–32.

CRAMPTON, R. J., 'The diplomatic relations between Great Britain and Germany in the Balkans and the Eastern Mediterranean from the Agadir Crisis to the murder at Sarajevo', London Ph.D. thesis, 1971.

CZERNIN, O., *Im Weltkrieg*, Berlin, 1919.

DAKIN, D., *The Greek Struggle in Macedonia*, Salonica, 1969.

DEDIJER, V., *The Road to Sarajevo*, London, 1967.

DRAGE, G., *Austria-Hungary*, London, 1909.

ENGEL-JANOSI, F., *Geschichte auf dem Ballhausplatz*, Vienna, 1963.

FELLNER, F., *Der Dreibund*, Vienna, 1960.

FELLNER, F., 'Die Haltung Oesterreich-Ungarns während der Konferenz von Algeciras, 1906', *Mitteilungen des Instituts für österreichische Geschichtsforschung*, 71, 1963.

FELLNER, F. (ed.), *Das politische Tagebuch Josef Redlichs*, Kommission für neuere Geschichte Oesterreichs, No. 39, 1953.

FISCHER, F., 'Weltpolitik, Weltmachtstreben und deutsche Kriegsziele', *Historische Zeitschrift*, 1964.

Bibliography

GEISS, I., *July 1914*, London, 1967.

GLADSTONE, W. E., *Political speeches in Scotland, November and December 1879 (March and April 1880 . . .)*, Edinburgh, 1880.

GLAISE-HORSTENAU, E. VON, *Franz Josephs Weggefährte. Das Leben des Generalstabschefs Grafen Beck*, Vienna, 1930.

GOOCH, G. P., *Before the War: Studies in diplomacy* (2 vols), London, 1938.

GRENVILLE, J. A. S., 'Goluchowski, Salisbury, and the Mediterranean Agreements, 1895–97', *Slavonic and East European Review*, 36, 1958.

HANTSCH, H., *Leopold, Graf Berchtold* (2 vols), Graz, 1963.

HEGEDÜS, R., 'The foreign policy of Count Julius Andrássy', *The Hungarian Quarterly*, Vol. 3, No. 3, 1937.

HELMREICH, E. C., *The Diplomacy of the Balkan Wars, 1912–1913*, Cambridge, Mass., 1938.

HOETZENDORF, CONRAD VON F., *Aus meiner Dienstzeit*, Vols. 1–4, Vienna, 1921.

HOHENBALKEN, P. (ed.), *Heinrich, Graf Lützow. Im diplomatischen Dienst der k.u.k. Monarchie*, Vienna, 1971.

JEFFERSON, MARGARET M., 'The place of Constantinople and the Straits in British Foreign Policy 1890–1902', M.A. thesis, London, 1959.

JEFFERSON, MARGARET M., 'Lord Salisbury and the Eastern Question 1890–1898', *Slavonic and East European Review*, 39, 1960.

JELAVICH, C., *Tsarist Russia and Balkan nationalism*, UCLA, 1962.

KANNER, H., *Kaiserliche Katastrophenpolitik*, Vienna, 1922.

KISZLING, R., 'Heer und Kriegsmarine in den letzten Jahrzehnten vor Ausbruch des ersten Weltkrieges', *Oesterreich in Geschichte und Literatur*, VII, 1963.

KLEIN, F. (ed.), *Oesterreich-Ungarn in der Weltpolitik 1900–1914*, Akademie-Verlag, Berlin, 1965.

LANGER, W. L., *European Alliances and Alignments, 1871–90*, New York, 1950.

LANGER, W. L., *The Diplomacy of Imperialism, 1890–1902*, New York, 1956.

LOWE, C. J., *Salisbury and the Mediterranean, 1886–96*, London, 1965.

MACARTNEY, C. A., *The Habsburg Monarchy, 1790–1918*, London, 1968.

MACARTNEY, C. A., *Problems of the Danube Basin*, Cambridge, 1942.

Bibliography

MARGUTTI, A., *The Emperor Francis Joseph and his Times*, London, 1921.

MAY, A. J., 'The Novibazar Railroad Project', *Journal of Modern History*, 10/4, 1938.

MAY, A. J., *The Hapsburg Monarchy, 1867–1914*, Harvard, 1965.

MEDLICOTT, W. N., *The Congress of Berlin and After*, London, 1963.

MEDLICOTT, W. N., 'British Foreign Policy in the Near East, from the Congress of Berlin to the accession of Ferdinand of Coburg', M.A. thesis, London, 1926.

MEDLICOTT, W. N., *Bismarck, Gladstone, and the Concert of Europe*, London, 1956.

MEDLICOTT, W. N., 'The Mediterranean Agreements of 1887', *Slavonic and East European Review*, 5, 1926–7.

MEDLICOTT, W. N., 'Bismarck und Haymerle: ein Gespräch über Russland', *Berliner Monatshefte*, November, 1940.

MUSULIN, A. VON, *Das Haus am Ballplatz*, Munich, 1924.

NOVOTNY, A., *Quellen und Studien zur Geschichte des Berliner Kongresses, 1878*, (2 vols) Graz, 1957.

PAUPIÉ, K., *Handbuch der österreichischen Pressegeschichte*, Vol. 2, Vienna, 1966.

PETERSON, M. B. A., 'Das österreichisch-ungarische Memorandum an Deutschland vom 5 Juli 1914', *Scandia*, 30, 1964.

POTTHOFF, H., *Die deutsche Politik Beusts*, Bonn, 1968.

PRIBRAM, A. F., *The Secret Treaties of Austria-Hungary* (2 vols.), Cambridge, Mass., 1921.

PRIBRAM, A. F., *Austria-Hungary and Great Britain 1908–1914*, Oxford, 1951.

PRIBRAM, A. F., 'Milan IV von Serbien und die Geheimverträge Oesterreich-Ungarns mit Serbien 1881–1889', *Historische Blätter*, 1921.

PRZIBRAM, L. RITTER VON, *Erinnerungen eines alten Oesterreichers* (2 vols), Stuttgart, 1912.

RAMM, AGATHA, 'European Alliances and Ententes 1879–1885, a study of contemporary British information', M.A. thesis, London.

REDLICH, J., *Emperor Francis Joseph of Austria: a Biography*, London, 1929.

RITTER, G., 'Die Zusammenarbeit der Generalstäbe Deutschlands und Oesterreich-Ungarns vor dem ersten Weltkrieg' in *Zur Geschichte und Problematik der Demokratie*, Berlin, 1958.

Bibliography

RUTKOWSKI, E. R. VON, 'Gustav, Graf Kálnoky von Köröspatak, Oesterreich-Ungarns Aussenpolitik von 1881–1885', Doctoral Dissertation, Vienna, 1952.

RUTKOWSKI, E. R. VON, 'Osterreich-Ungarn und Rumänien 1880–83, die Proklamierung des Königreiches und die rumänischen Irredenta', *Südost-Forschungen*, 25, 1966.

RUTKOWSKI, E. R. VON, 'General Skobelev, die Krise des Jahres 1882 und die Anfänge der militärischen Vereinbarungen zwischen Oesterreich-Ungarn und Deutschland', *Ostdeutsche Wissenschaft*, 10, 1963.

SALVATORELLI, L., *La triplice alleanza, storia diplomatica*, Milan, 1939.

SANDONÀ, A., *L'irredentismo nelle lotte politische a nelle contese diplomatiche italo-austriache* (3 vols), Bologna, 1932.

SCHOENHALS, K. P., *The Russian Policy of Count Friedrich Ferdinand von Beust, 1866–71*, University Microfilm Inc., Ann Arbor, 1964.

SCHMITT, B., *The Annexation of Bosnia*, London, 1937.

SCHWARZENBERG, A., *Prince Felix zu Schwarzenberg*, New York, 1946.

SETON-WATSON, R. W., 'The role of Bosnia in international politics, 1875–1914', *Proceedings of the British Academy*, 1931.

SETON-WATSON, R. W., 'William II's Balkan policy', *Slavonic and East European Review*, 7, 1928.

SOSNOSKY, T. VON, *Die Balkanpolitik Oesterreich-Ungarns seit 1866* (2 vols), Stuttgart, 1913–14.

SRBIK, H. RITTER VON, *Aus Oesterreichs Vergangenheit*, Salzburg, 1949.

STONE, N., 'Army and Society in the Habsburg Monarchy, 1900–1914', *Past and Present*, 33, 1966.

STONE, N., 'Constitutional crises in Hungary, 1903–1908', *Slavonic and East European Review*, 45, 1967.

STONE, N., 'Mottke-Conrad: Relations between the Austro-Hungarian and German General Staffs 1909–1914', *Historical Journal*, 1966.

STONE, N., 'Hungary and the crisis of July 1914', *Journal of Contemporary History*, 1, 1966.

TAYLOR, A. J. P., *The Habsburg Monarchy*, London, 1949.

TAYLOR, A. J. P., *The Struggle for Mastery in Europe*, Oxford, 1954.

TEMPERLEY, H. W. V., and PENSON, LILLIAN M., *Foundations of British Foreign Policy 1792–1902*, London, 1938.

Bibliography

THADEN, E. C., *Russia and the Balkan Alliance of 1912*, Pennsylvania State University, 1965.

VILLARI, L., *The War on the Italian Front*, London, 1925.

WAGNER, W., 'Kaiser Franz Joseph und das deutsche Reich', Doctoral Dissertation, Vienna, 1951.

WALTERS, E., 'Unpublished Documents. Lord Salisbury's refusal to revise and renew the Mediterranean Agreements', *Slavonic and East European Review*, 29, 1950.

WALTERS, E., 'Unpublished Documents. Austro-Russian relations under Goluchowski' 1895–1906 [I–III]', *Slavonic and East European Review*, 31, 32, 1953, 1954.

WALTERS, E., 'Franco-Russian discussions on the partition of Austria-Hungary, 1899', *Slavonic and East European Review*, 28, 1949.

WALTERS, E., 'Unpublished Documents. Aehrenthal's attempt in 1907 to re-group the European Powers', *Slavonic and East European Review*, 30, 1951.

WANK, S., 'Aehrenthal's programme for the constitutional transformation of the Habsburg Monarchy: three secret *Mémoires*', *Slavonic and East European Review*, 41, 1963.

WANK, S., 'Aehrenthal and the Sanjak of Novibazar railway project: a re-appraisal', *Slavonic and East European Review*, 42, 1964.

WEDEL, O. H., *Austro-German diplomatic relations 1908–1914*, Stanford, 1932.

WERTHEIMER, E. VON, *Graf Julius Andrássy, sein Leben und seine Zeit* (3 vols), Stuttgart, 1910.

WINDELBAND, W., *Bismarck und die europäischen Grossmächte 1879–1885*, Essen, 1942.

WITTICH, A. VON, 'Die Rüstungen Oesterreich-Ungarns von 1866 bis 1914', *Berliner Monatshefte*, 1932.

WORMS, H. DE, *The Austro-Hungarian Empire and the policy of Count Beust*, London, 1877.

ZEMAN, Z. A. B., *The Break-up of the Habsburg Empire*, London, 1961.

Index of Names

459

Index of Names

Alphonso XII (1857–85), King of Spain 1874–85: 65

Alphonso XIII (1886–1941), King of Spain 1902–31 (Regency 1885–1902, *see* Maria Cristina): 293

Andrássy von Csik-Szent-Király u. Kraszna-Horka, Julius Count (1823–90), Hungarian minister-president 1867–71, I. and R. foreign minister 1871–9: character and personal, 16, 21, 60–1, 63, 72, 74–6, 87, 90, 101, 125–6, 162, 201, 209, 404; and Germany, 55, 59, 62–8, 75, 79–80, 83–4, 88, 90–1, 101–2, 152, 386–7; and Austro-German Alliance, 104–7, 387; and Russia, 50–2, 62–8, 72–84, 86–8, 94, 97–8, 101–2, 105, 124, 142, 152, 157, 162, 386–7, 393–5; and Three Emperors' League, 67, 76–7, 84, 88–9, 101–2, 107, 387, 393–5; and Italy, 62, 65, 130, 152; and Great Britain, 62–3, 77, 80–1, 84, 87–8, 90, 97–8, 101–2, 105–7, 112, 152, 386–7; and France, 62, 65–6, 81, 105–7; and Ottoman Empire, 63, 69–70, 72, 74, 77, 83, 90–5, 97–8, 127, 394–6; and Eastern question, 52, 61–2, 67, 72–5, 77, 79, 81–2, 87, 93, 124, 142, 201, 227, 393–5; and Congress of Berlin, 90–4, 142; and Albania, 77; and Bosnia, 19, 67–8, 70, 72, 75, 77, 81–2, 89, 90–2, 94–7, 102, 393–4, 396; and Sanjak of Novibazar, 77, 82, 89, 93, 96–7; and Bulgaria, 77, 81, 89–90, 96, 98, 121, 146, 155, 157; and Greece, 77, 143; and Montenegro, 70, 72–3, 77, 93, 97, 227, 393–4, 396; and Roumania, 62, 68–9, 81, 83, 93, 111; and Serbia, 46, 62, 69, 72–3, 77, 93, 97, 121, 227, 393–4; and commercial policy, 82, 94; and military questions, 81, 86–8, 95; and domestic politics, 19, 61–2, 78, 83, 87, 89, 91–2, 98–101, 404; as Hungarian minister-president, 31, 46, 49, 53, 59; and the press, 100; and the Church, 65–6, 125; and monarchical principle, 65, 67, 106, 130

Auersperg, Adolf Prince (1821–85), Austrian minister-president 1871–9: 89

Auersperg, Karl-Wilhelm, Prince (1814–90), Austrian minister-president 1867–1868: 31

Auffenberg von Komaróv, Moritz

Baron (1852–1928), I. and R. War Minister 1911–12: 343, 345

Avarna dei duchi di Gualtieri, Giuseppe, Duke of (1843–1916), Italian minister at Belgrade 1894–6, at Athens 1896–1902, at Berne 1902–4, ambassador at Vienna 1904–15: 439

Avellan, Fedor Karlovich, Admiral (1839–1916), Russian admiral, minister of marine 1903–5: 195

Avezzana, General Guiseppe, president of the *Italia Irredenta*: 130

Baernreither, Joseph Maria (1845–1925), Austrian writer and politician, minister of commerce 1898: 253–4

Banffy zu Losoncz, Desiderius Baron von (1843–1911), Hungarian minister-president 1895–9: 208

Beck, Max Vladimir Baron (1854–1943), Austrian minister-president 1906–8: 288

Beck-Rzikowski, Friedrich (1906 Count) (1830–1920), Head of Emperor's Military Chancellery 1867–81, Chief of I.R. (1889 I. and R.) General Staff 1881–1906: 32–3, 50, 71–2, 80, 83, 86–87, 101, 112, 117, 124–5, 130, 139, 143–4, 179, 202–3, 213–14, 219, 222, 227–8, 231–2, 255, 257, 267, 270, 276, 384; and Austro-German military plans, 134–5, 172, 180–2, 193–5, 202–203, 217, 227–8, 257

Benedikt, Moriz (1849–1920), chief editor of *Neue Freie Presse*: 27

Berchtold von u. zu Ungarschitz, Fratting u. Pullitz, Leopold Count (1863–1942), served in I. and R. embassies at Paris 1894–9, at London 1899–1903, at St Petersburg 1903–5, ambassador at St Petersburg 1906–11, minister for foreign affairs 1912–15: character and personal, 13, 16, 20–2, 290, 303, 310, 340–2, 359, 381, 385; and Germany, 294, 344–5, 348, 350, 354, 358–60, 362, 364, 368, 375–6, 441–2; and Austro-German Alliance, 360, 379; and Russia, 294, 310, 314, 342–3, 345, 359, 367, 369–70, 377–8, 385, 433, 448–50; and Italy, 342, 345, 347, 351–2, 358–9, 377, 449–50; and Great Britain, 341–3, 349, 359; and France, 345, 359, 364, 377; and Ottoman Empire, 344, 362,

Index of Names

Bratianu, Ion, the younger (1864–1927), Roumanian minister-president 1909, 1910–11, 1914–18: 363, 392

Bülow, Bernhard (1899 Count, 1905 Prince) von (1849–1929), German minister at Bucharest 1888–93, ambassador at Rome 1893–7, secretary of state at the Wilhelmstrasse 1897–1900, chancellor 1900–9: 249–50, 252, 425–7, 436–7

Bülow, Bernhard Ernst von (1815–79), secretary of state at the Wilhelmstrasse 1873–9: 77

Burián von Rajecz, Stephen Baron (1851–1922), I. and R. consul-general at Sofia 1887–95, minister at Stuttgart 1896–7, at Athens 1897–1903, Common Finance Minister 1903–12, minister for foreign affairs 1915–16, Common Finance Minister 1916–18, minister for foreign affairs 1918: 21, 375

Calice, Heinrich Baron (1906 Count) (1831–1913), I. and R. ambassador at Constantinople 1880–1906: 128, 170–1, 195, 197, 215, 219, 225, 227

Campbell-Bannerman, Sir Henry (1836–1908), British prime minister 1905–8: 284, 293

Canning, George (1770–1827), British foreign secretary 1822–7, prime minister 1827: 4

Caprivi, Georg Leo Count (1831–99), German chancellor 1890–4: 189–90, 193, 197, 203, 417, 428–9

Carol I (Charles of Hohenzollern-Sigmaringen) (1839–1914), Prince of Moldo-Wallachia 1866–72, of Roumania 1872–81, King of Roumania 1881–1914: 9, 40–1, 47, 62, 68, 110, 137–40, 168, 184–5, 214, 219, 222, 242, 357, 363, 378, 392, 408–9, 446

Carp, Petru (1837–1919), Roumanian minister-president 1900–1, 1911–12: 378

Cartwright, Sir Fairfax (1857–1928), British minister at Munich 1906–8, ambassador at Vienna 1908–13: 18, 24, 290, 317–18, 329–30, 380–1

Catherine II (1729–96), Empress of Russia 1762–96: 2, 202

Cavour, Count Camillo (1810–61), prime minister of Piedmont 1852–9, 1860–1, of Italy 1861: 9

Charles V (1500–58), King of Spain 1516–56, Holy Roman Emperor 1519–1556: 1

Charykov, Nicholas Vassilievich (1855–1930), Russian minister at Belgrade 1900–5, assistant to foreign minister 1908–9, ambassador at Constantinople 1909–12: 240, 337–8

Chotek von Chotkowa u. Wognin, Bohuslav Count (1829–96), I. and R. minister at St Petersburg 1869–71, at Madrid 1871–2, at Brussels 1872–88, at Dresden 1888–95: 50

Conrad von Hoetzendorf, Franz Baron (1852–1925), Chief of I. and R. General Staff 1906–11, 1912–17: 10, 212, 217, 288, 291, 312, 314–16, 331, 336, 340, 348, 352, 358, 360, 364–6, 373, 377, 379, 381, 384, 440–1, 450

Constantine I (1868–1923), King of the Hellenes 1913–17, 1920–2: 354, 362

Crispi, Francesco (1819–1901), Italian prime minister and minister for foreign affairs 1887–91, 1893–6: 171, 176–8, 182, 187, 198–9

Currie, Sir Philip (1834–1906), British ambassador at Constantinople 1894–8, at Rome 1898–1903: 197

Czernin von u. zu Chudenitz, Ottokar Count (1872–1932), I. and R. minister at Bucharest 1913–16, minister for foreign affairs 1916–18: 358, 363

Danev, Stojan (b. 1858), Bulgarian prime minister 1902–3, 1913: 355

Deák von Kehida, Francis (1803–76), Hungarian minister of justice 1848: 61

Deym von Stritez, Franz Count (1835–1903), I. and R. ambassador at London 1888–1903: 196–7, 218, 228, 248

Disraeli, Benjamin (1876 1st earl of Beaconsfield) (1804–81), British prime minister 1868, 1874–80: 63, 98, 108, 121

Doczy von Nemet-Keresztur, Ludwig Baron (1845–1919), head of Literary Office at the Ballhausplatz 1895–1902: 21, 244

Draga Masin (1863–1903), Queen of Serbia 1900–3: 239, 262

Index of Names

Dreyfus, Alfred (1859–1935): 321

Dumba, Konstantin Theodor Count (1856–1947), I. and R. minister at Belgrade 1903–5, in the Ballhausplatz 1905–9, at Stockholm 1909–13, at Washington 1913–16: 263, 268–9

Edward VII (1841–1910), King of Great Britain and Ireland 1901–10: 21, 293, 295, 299–300, 328–9

Ehrenroth, General Johann Casimir (1883–1913): 169–70

Elena of Montenegro (1873–1953), Queen of Italy 1900–46: 251

Elizabeth of Bavaria (1837–98), Empress of Austria 1854–98: 13, 96

Elizabeth of Wied (1843–1916), Princess of Moldo-Wallachia 1869–72, of Roumania 1872–81, Queen of Roumania 1881–1914: 138, 352

Essad Pasha (1863–1920), Albanian minister of the interior and war minister 1914, president 1914–16: 351, 365

Eugénie de Montijo (1826–1920), Empress of the French 1853–70: 270

Eulenburg und Hertefeld, Philipp Count (1900 Prince) (1847–1921), German ambassador at Vienna 1894–1902: 203, 220, 321, 426

Fadeyev, General Ratislav Andreyevich (1824–84): 47

Fallières, Armand (1841–1931), French president 1906–13: 305, 436–7

Ferdinand of Saxe-Coburg-Koháry (1861–1948), Prince of Bulgaria 1887–1908, King of Bulgaria 1908–18: 169–170, 180, 186–7, 219, 241, 304, 339, 354, 362, 440

Fergusson, Sir James (1832–1907), British parliamentary under-secretary for foreign affairs 1886–91: 187–8

Forgách von Ghymes u. Gács, Johann Count (1870–1935), I. and R. minister at Belgrade 1907–11, at Dresden 1911–13, Sektionschef in the Ballhausplatz 1913–17: 448

Francis I (1768–1835), Holy Roman Emperor (Francis II) 1792–1806, Emperor of Austria 1804–35: 1

Franz Ferdinand, Archduke (1863–1914), heir apparent 1894–1914: 13, 27, 192, 246, 250, 288, 291, 321, 326, 330, 340, 342, 345–6, 348, 350, 356, 363, 368, 371, 440–1

Franz Joseph I (1830–1916), Emperor of Austria 1848–1916: character and personal, 10–11, 13, 30, 33, 58, 71, 87, 101, 118, 124, 133, 159, 211–12, 245, 249, 270, 328, 381; influence over foreign policy, 10–12, 14–16, 18, 33, 49, 51–2, 56, 64–5, 70, 72, 78, 87, 91, 99–101, 105, 115, 125–6, 148, 154–5, 169–70, 211, 221, 243–5, 249, 264, 281, 283, 311, 336, 342, 350–2, 356, 367, 374, 386, 404, 430; and Prussia, 6–8, 33–4, 36, 38, 54–5; and Germany, 56–57, 63–5, 88, 91, 105–8, 124, 146–7, 170–1, 178–81, 198, 203, 221, 250, 264, 281, 311, 316, 331, 348, 358, 360, 373, 393, 436–7; and Austro-German Alliance, 102–3, 108, 117, 175–6, 181, 216, 257, 300, 374, 396–8; and Russia, 5, 7, 65, 67, 79, 83–5, 112–13, 118, 145–7, 151, 170–2, 179, 181, 192, 216, 224, 231–2, 235, 242, 244, 264–5, 271, 284–5, 350, 367, 392–3, 421, 430–1; and Three Emperors' Alliance, 124, 151; and Great Britain, 67, 84, 113, 188, 221, 230, 247, 295, 300, 328, 342, 411–12; and France, 7, 37–8, 43–4, 51, 66–7, 281, 311; and Italian question, 7, 12; and Italy, 133–4, 165, 252, 283, 412; and Triple Alliance, 165, 224, 257, 283, 366, 406–8, 415–16; and Ottoman Empire, 43, 79, 85, 95; and Eastern question, 52, 85, 96, 179, 230, 232, 264, 358, 367; and Bosnia, 12, 70–73, 91, 94, 96, 165, 301; and Bulgaria, 169–70, 186, 219, 232, 241, 304, 357; and Montenegro, 18, 237, 352; and Roumania, 117, 139, 154–5, 219, 222, 232, 242, 356–7, 409–10; and Serbia, 140, 145, 148, 154–5, 159, 184, 262–3, 316, 359, 369, 402–3; and domestic policy, 11, 15–16, 99, 270, 287; and 'Austrian' governments, 10, 31, 57, 61, 79, 99–100, 125, 179, 193, 287–8; and Hungarians, 5, 6, 10–11, 16, 31, 79, 148, 219, 270, 287–8, 374; and the Germans, 37, 54, 61, 79, 100; and the Slavs, 11, 57, 100; and the Church, 12, 65, 71, 131–2, 266; and the military, 10, 12, 41, 50, 64, 80, 87, 95, 124–5, 134, 172–6, 255–6, 270, 314, 316, 336,

Index of Names

Index of Names

Mehemet Ali (1769–1849), Pasha of Egypt 1805–49: 3

Menelek II (1844–1911), Emperor of Ethiopia 1889–1911: 206

Mensdorff-Pouilly-Dietrichstein, Albert Count (1861–1945), I. and R. chargé d'affaires at London 1903–4, ambassador 1904–14: 21, 290 304, 342–3, 350–3, 359, 381, 438

Mensdorff-Pouilly-Dietrichstein zu Nikolsburg, Alexander Count (1813–1871), Austrian foreign minister 1864–1866: 9

Mérey von Kapos-Mére, Kajetan Count (1861–1931), Sektionsrat in the Ballhausplatz 1895–1901, 2nd Sektionschef 1901–7, 1st Sektionschef 1907–1910, I. and R. ambassador at Rome 1910–15: 263, 448–50

Metternich-Winneburg, Clemens Wenzel Lothar Count (1813 Prince) (1773–1859), Austrian ambassador at Paris 1806–9, minister for foreign affairs 1809–21, chancellor 1821–48: 3–5, 19, 21, 29, 31, 72, 386

Metternich-Winneburg, Richard Prince (1829–95), Austrian (1867 I. and R.) ambassador at Paris 1859–71: 49, 390

Michael Obrenović (1823–68), Prince of Serbia 1839–42 and 1860–8: 9, 45, 123

Mijatović, Chedomil, Serbian foreign minister: 158

Milan IV, Obrenović (1854–1901), Prince of Serbia 1868–82, King of Serbia 1882–9: 62, 70, 73, 76, 110, 121–123, 128, 140–2, 149–50, 154–6, 158–9, 167, 183–4, 235, 238–40, 402–3, 422–3, 425

Mingrelia, Nicholas Dadian Prince of (1847–1903): 162

Mingrelia, Marie, Princess of (1849–1926): 162

Mollinary von Monte Pastello, Anton Baron (1820–1904), commander in Dalmatia: 72

Moltke, Helmut Count von, the elder (1800–91), chief of the Prussian general staff 1858–88: 134–5, 172, 175, 182

Moltke, Helmut Count von, the younger (1848–1916), chief of the Prussian general staff 1906–14: 314–16, 373

Monson, Sir Edmund John (1834–1909), British minister at Brussels 1892–3,

ambassador at Vienna 1893–6, at Paris 1896–1905: 417–18

Montecuccoli degli Erri, Rudolf Count (1843–1922), Admiral, head of the naval section of the I. and R. Common War Ministry 1904–14: 270, 330

Mouraviev, Count Michael Alexandrovich (1845–1900), Russian foreign minister 1896–1900: 235, 430

Napoleon I (1769–1821), Emperor of the French 1804–14: 2, 80, 386

Napoleon III (1808–73), Emperor of the French 1852–70: 5, 7, 8, 33–4, 36–8, 41–4, 59, 67, 390–1

Natalie Keško (b. 1859), Princess of Serbia 1875–82, Queen of Serbia 1882–9, Regent 1889–93: 149, 159, 167, 183–4

Nicholas I (1796–1855), Emperor of Russia 1825–55: 4, 5, 67, 385

Nicholas II (1868–1918), Emperor of Russia 1894–1917: 200, 202, 204, 224, 232, 234–5, 237, 247, 264–5, 271, 284–285, 292, 299, 305, 313, 328–9, 331, 343, 350–1, 353, 363, 366, 385, 421, 430–1, 449

Nicolson, Sir Arthur (1849–1928) British permanent under-secretary of state for foreign affairs 1910–16: 334–5, 340

Nigra, Constantino (1882 Count) (1828–1907), Italian ambassador at St Petersburg 1878–82, at London 1882–5, at Vienna 1885–1904: 420, 426

Nikita Petrović (1841–1921), Prince of Montenegro 1860–1910, King of Montenegro 1910–18: 45, 73, 159, 235, 237–8, 251, 262, 327

Novikoff, Eugene Petrovich (1826–1903), Russian ambassador at Vienna 1870–80: 47

Oberdank, Wilhelm (Guglielmo Oberdan) (1858–82), Austrian deserter, Italian patriot: 133, 178

O'Conor, Sir Nicholas (1843–1908), British ambassador at St Petersburg 1895–8, at Constantinople 1898–1908: 296, 298, 435

Paget, Sir Augustus (1823–96), British minister at Florence 1867–71, at Rome 1871–6, ambassador at Rome 1876–83, at Vienna 1884–93: 166

Index of Names

Palacky, František (1798–1876), Czech historian and politician: 3

Pallavicini, Johann Margrave (1848–1941), I. and R. minister at Bucharest 1899–1906, ambassador at Constantinople 1906–18, acting minister for foreign affairs March–May 1911: 293, 296, 298, 332–3, 434–5

Palmerston, 3rd Viscount (1784–1865), British foreign secretary 1830–4, 1835–41, 1846–51, prime minister 1855–8, 1859–65: 5, 125

Parnell, Charles Stewart (1846–91), Irish politician: 321

Pasetti-Angeli von Friedenburg, Marius Freiherr von (1841–1913), I. and R. ambassador at Rome 1895–1904: 420

Pašić, Nikola (1846–1926), Serbian prime minister 1906–8, 1909–11, prime minister and foreign minister 1912–18: 347, 366

Petar Karageorgević (1844–1921), King of Serbia 1903–18, of the Serbs, Croats and Slovenes 1918–21: 240, 262–3

Pius IX (1792–1878), Pope 1846–78: 42, 56, 65, 125

Pius X (1835–1914), Pope 1903–14: 266

Plehve, Viatscheslav Constantinovich (1846–1904), Russian minister of the interior 1902–4: 259

Poincaré, Raymond (1860–1934) French prime minister and minister for foreign affairs 1912–13, president 1913–20: 377

Prinetti di Merate, Giulio (1903 marchese) (1851–1908), Italian foreign minister 1901–3: 266, 420, 426

Radetzky von Radetz, Joseph Count (1836 Field Marshal) (1766–1858), military and civil governor of the Lombardo-Venetian Kingdom 1849–1857: 6, 71

Radoslavov, Vasil (1854–1929), Bulgarian prime minister 1886–7, 1894, minister of the interior 1899–1900, prime minister 1913–18: 357

Rampolla, Cardinal Mariano, marchese del Tindaro (1843–1913), cardinal secretary of state of Leo XIII 1887–1903: 221, 266

Reuss, Heinrich VII Prince (1825–1906), German ambassador at Vienna 1878–94: 124, 132, 199, 396, 398

Rhemen zu Barensfeld, Hugo Freiherr von (b. 1861), counsellor in the Ballhausplatz 1897–1903, 1908–18: 429–31

Ristić, Jovan (1831–99), Serbian prime minister 1867, 1875, 1877–81, 1887–8, regent, 1889–93: 110, 121, 167, 184

Rodich, Gabriel Baron von (1812–90), governor of Dalmatia: 73, 83, 393–4

Rosebery, 5th Earl of (1847–1929), British foreign secretary 1885–6, 1892–4, prime minister 1894–5: 154, 189, 196–7, 418–19

Rouvier, Maurice (1842–1911), French prime minister 1887, 1905–6: 277

Rudini, Antonio Starabba marchese di (1839–1908), Italian prime minister 1891–2, 1896–8: 187–8, 232

Rudolph of Habsburg-Lorraine (1858–1889), crown prince of Austria: 13, 88, 178

Saburov, Peter Alexandrovich, Russian ambassador at Berlin 1880–4: 115, 168, 399–402

Salisbury, 3rd Marquess of (1830–1903), British foreign secretary 1878–1880, 1885–6, 1887–92, 1895–1900, prime minister 1885–6, 1886–92, 1895–1920: 80, 91–2, 107, 152, 161, 166, 172, 188–9, 214–15, 217–18, 222, 228–30, 232, 386, 411–12, 418–19

San Giuliano, Antonio marchese di (1852–1914), Italian foreign minister 1905–6, ambassador at London 1906–1910, at Paris 1910, foreign minister 1910–14: 356

Sazonov, Sergei Dmitrievich (1860–1927), Russian minister at the Vatican 1906–9, assistant to the foreign minister 1909–10, foreign minister 1910–16: 327–8, 331, 345, 357, 363, 378

Schäffle, Albert (1831–1903), Austrian minister of commerce 1870: 57

Schemua, Blasius (1856–1920), I. and R. chief of the general staff 1911–12: 345, 348

Schlieffen, Alfred Count von (1833–1913), chief of the Prussian general staff 1891–1905: 182, 193–5, 198, 217

Index of Names

Schoen, Wilhelm von (1909 Baron) (1851–1933), German ambassador at St Petersburg 1905–7, foreign minister 1907–10, ambassador at Paris 1910–14: 303, 305, 436–7

Schönaich, Franz Freiherr von (1844–1916), I. and R. war minister 1906–11: 288, 316

Schönburg-Hartenstein, Johann Prince (1864–1937), I. and R. secretary of embassy at London 1904–6, minister at Bucharest 1906–11: 21

Schwarzenberg, Felix Prince zu (1800–52), Austrian minister-president minister for foreign affairs 1848–52: 7, 31

Skobelev, General Michael Dmitrievich (1843–82): 129–30, 132, 209

Stamboulov, Stefan Nikolov (1854–95), Bulgarian prime minister and minister of the interior 1887–94: 185–6, 191, 213

Stanley, Edward Henry (1869 15th Earl of Derby), British foreign secretary 1866–8, 1874–8: 125

Steininger, Baron, I. and R. military attaché at Berlin: 412

Stemrich, Wilhelm von, under-secretary of state in the Wilhelmstrasse 1907–11: 435–6

Stoilov, Constantine (1852–1901), Bulgarian prime minister 1887, 1894–9: 241

Stolypin, Peter Arkadievich (1862–1911), Russian minister-president 1906–11: 313

Stourdza, Demeter (1833–1914), Roumanian foreign minister 1883–8, prime minister 1895–6, 1897–9, 1901–1906, 1907–9: 138–9, 168, 222

Stürgkh, Karl Count (1859–1916), Austrian minister-president 1911–16: 449

Széchenyi von Sárvar u. Felsö-Videk, Emmerich Count (1825–98), I. and R. ambassador at Berlin 1878–92: 164–6, 174–5, 399–402, 412–15, 417

Szécsen von Temerin, Nicholas Count (1857–1926), 2nd Sektionschef in the Ballhausplatz 1895–1900, 1st Sektionschef 1900–1, I. and R. ambassador at the Vatican 1901–11, at Paris 1911–14: 256

Szögyény-Marich von Magyar-Szögyen u. Szolgaegyháza, Ladislas Count

(1841–1916), I. and R. ambassador at Berlin 1892–1914: 196, 204, 206, 243–4, 259, 268, 425–9, 435–7, 441–2

Taaffe, Eduard Count (1833–95), Austrian minister-president 1879–93: 100, 103, 125–6, 137, 149–50, 178–9, 192–3, 287

Talleyrand-Périgord, Charles Maurice 1st Duc de (1754–1838): 4

Tauffkirchen zu Guttemberg, Maximilian Count von (1815–71), Bavarian diplomat: 36

Tegetthof, Wilhelm von (1866 Vice-Admiral) (1827–71), head of the naval division of the I. and R. war ministry 1868–71: 71

Thun und Hohenstein, Franz Count (1911 Prince) (1847–1916), governor of Bohemia 1889–96, Austrian minister-president and minister of the interior 1898–9, governor of Bohemia 1911–15: 248–9

Thurn und Valsássina, Duglas Count, I. and R. diplomatic agent (1909 minister) at Sofia 1905–9, ambassador at St Petersburg 1911–14: 367

Tisza von Borosjenö u. Szeged, Koloman von (1830–1902), Hungarian minister-president 1875–90: 61, 78, 83, 89, 94, 99, 147–8, 161, 174, 179

Tisza von Borosjenö u. Szeged, Stephen (1897 Count) (1861–1918), Hungarian minister-president 1903–5, 1913–17: 14, 19, 270, 363, 367, 369, 373–6, 449

Tittoni, Tommaso (1855–1931), Italian foreign minister 1903–5, ambassador at London 1906, foreign minister 1906–9, ambassador at Paris 1910–16: 266–7, 276, 291, 303, 305, 312, 328

Tschirschky u. Bögendorff, Heinrich von (1858–1916), German foreign minister 1906–7, ambassador at Vienna 1907–16: 333, 371, 375

Vasić, Vladimir, confidant of the I. and R. legation at Belgrade: 320

Verdy du Vernois, Julius von (1832–1910), Prussian war minister 1889–90: 180–1

Victor Emmanuel II (1820–78), King of Piedmont-Sardinia 1849–61, King of Italy 1861–78: 9

General Index

African questions, 131, 147, 150, 165, 187–8, 196–9, 203–4, 206–7, 220–1, 413, 417; *see also* Egypt, Morocco

ALLIANCES AND ENTENTES

Anglo-Russian *Entente*, 229, 295, 298, 300, 331, 338–9, 341, 343, 383

Austro-German Alliance, 1879–1918: text, 396–8; projects, 7–8, 24, 55–7, 59, 62–3, 65, 88, 91, 101–2, 104; diplomatic aspects, 104–8, 111–12, 117–19, 135–6, 146–7, 152, 163, 173, 176, 181–2, 198–200, 209–10, 216, 225, 227–8, 245, 248–50, 259, 268, 276–7, 286, 290–1, 300–1, 314, 318–19, 323, 331, 339–40, 343, 345, 357, 360–1, 364, 373–5, 378–9, 386–8, 399, 437, 440, 448; commercial aspects, 136–7, 164, 189–90, 249, 254–5, 268–9, 361, 364, 379, 389; military and strategic aspects, 117, 135–6, 163–4, 172–6, 179–82, 193–5, 202–3, 217, 227, 257, 314–16, 373, 379, 387, 412–14; and public opinion, 17, 164, 177–9, 248–9, 268–9, 294, 427–9

Austro-Roumanian Alliance, 1883–1916: text, 409–10; political, 28, 139–141, 144, 152, 159–60, 168, 184–5, 207, 209–10, 219, 222, 242–3, 322, 348, 356, 363–4, 367, 369, 374, 376–8, 382, 385, 387, 389, 440, 444–7, 450; commercial, 28, 148–9, 160, 168, 185, 190; and Germany, 140, 177, 185, 222, 363; and Italy, 176–7

Austro-Russian *Entente*, 1897–1908: text, 429–30; proposals for, 24, 26, 214, 217, 219, 224, 231–2; diplomatic aspects, 232–46, 250, 257–62, 264, 473–4, 290, 297–8, 301, 306–9, 323, 385, 387–388, 420–6; public opinion and, 235; revival suggested, 338, 374; Mürzsteg *entente*, 267, 274, 276, 293, 295–9, 308, 345, 431–4

Austro-Serbian Alliance, 1881–95: text, 402–3; political, 122–3, 140–1, 149, 152, 156, 158–9, 167, 183–4, 210, 382, 385, 388; commercial, 121–2, 148, 190, 219

Balkan League projects, 45, 123, 151, 278, 313, 323–4, 327–8, 337–9, 362, 367–70, 374, 383, 445–6, 448–9; Balkan League of 1912–13, 343, 345–6, 348, 352–4, 383

Franco-Russian Alliance, 1894–1917: 250, 285, 339, 418–19, 444–5

Holy Alliance, 4, 36, 287

Mediterranean *Entente*, 1887–97: text, 411–12; diplomatic, 166–7, 170–2, 186–9, 195–7, 200, 205–6, 210, 214–23, 228–30, 233, 236, 246, 259–60, 295, 343, 387, 413, 417–19; and Spain, 167, 205–6, 217, 220–2, 385

Three Emperors' Alliance, 1881–7: text, 399–402; political, 20, 25, 115–21, 123–31, 141–2, 144, 146–7, 150–3, 155–63, 168–9, 209, 236, 259, 306, 323, 385, 388, 398–9; possible revival of, 13, 221, 250, 259, 272–3, 284–7, 292, 338

Three Emperors' League, 1873–8: text, 392–3; political, 67–8, 76–7, 84, 88–9, 101–2, 259, 306, 385, 387–8, 393; possible revival of, 90, 107–8, 112

Triple Alliance, 1882–1915: text, 406–8, 415–17; Article VII, 328, 335, 416, 439; diplomatic aspects, 130–3, 145, 147, 150, 152, 159, 164–6, 182–3, 187–8, 196–7, 206–7, 209–10, 220–1, 224, 236, 245, 248, 250–2, 267–8, 282–283, 285, 290, 312, 328, 333–5, 337, 342–3, 345, 347–8, 350–2, 354, 362, 364–6, 376–8, 382, 385, 387–8, 413, 425–6, 443–5, 449–50; commercial aspects, 190, 251, 267, 417; military and strategic aspects, 133, 166, 176, 183, 187, 202–3, 225, 257, 267–8; and

472

General Index